NORTHWEST
BEST PLACES

NORTHWEST BEST PLACES

Restaurants, Lodgings, and Touring
in Oregon, Washington, and British Columbia

Stephanie Irving
David Brewster

SASQUATCH BOOKS
SEATTLE

Printed in the United States of America.
Distributed in Canada by Raincoast Books Ltd.

Eleventh edition. Second Printing 1996.

Library of Congress Catalog Card Number LC88-655110

Contributors: Molly Dee Anderson, Michael Boxall, Barbara Brennan, Kim
Carlson, Andrea Charles, Corbet Clark, Leslie Cole, Roger Downey, Sheri Doyle,
Susan English, Richard Fencsak, Carrie Floyd, Jim Goldsmith, Joan Gregory,
Helen Gould, Diane Griggs, Jan Halliday, Kitty Harmon, John Hughes, Pippa
Kiraly, Scott Maben, Kerry McPhedran, Lane Morgan, Susan Myers, Cynthia
Nims, Tim Pawsey, Dave Preston, Kathryn Robinson, David Sarasohn, Eric
Scigliano, Nina Shapiro, Marilyn and Fred Tausend, Sarah Thomas, Cleve
Twitchell, Kasey Wilson, Kathy Witkowsky.

Associate editor: Nancy Leson
Copy editor: Carolyn Smith
Proofreader: Don Roberts
Factchecker: Amy Egert
Interior design and composition: Lynne Faulk
Cover design and maps: Karen Schober

The *Best Places* guidebooks have been published continuously since 1975.
Readers are advised that places listed in previous editions may have closed
or changed management or may no longer be recommended by this series.
The reviews in this edition are based on information available at press time
and are subject to change.

All *Best Places* guides are available at bulk discounts for corporate gifts,
conventions, and fund-raising sales for clubs and organizations.

Sasquatch Books
1008 Western Avenue
Seattle, Washington 98104
(206) 467-4300; (800) 775-0817

CONTENTS

Introduction

Let me tell you a little story. I recently dropped into a marvelous Bellingham bookstore and introduced myself to the proprietor. Presently, he introduced me to a couple browsing the shelves—operators of a nearby bed and breakfast. The innkeepers wanted to thank me for listing them in our guides. "We opened in time for Vancouver's Expo '86," one of them said, "so we made a lot of money that year. Then the bottom dropped out. It's only because of your books that we were able to survive. And now here we are today, doing just fine."

Naturally, I love to hear stories like that. This book, the first serious guidebook to the Northwest, has made a huge difference in encouraging tourism and in helping dedicated operators. As the Expo story makes clear, the travel business is treacherously cyclical—even more so in a region that has a relatively short fair-weather season. To make it in the service industry, and to hew to quality, you have to have a steady flow of return visitors—both from the region and from the hometown. To raise and sustain high standards, you need discriminating visitors who demand excellence in service, are willing to pay for it, and are happy to spread the good word. (Tourist ghettoes, by contrast, don't worry about repeat business; they just fleece 'em once.)

In 1975, when we first started the research for the initial volume in this enterprise, the Northwest was quite uncharted, supposedly a culinary backwater. No one thought of it, as we do today, as prime country for the gourmet, marvelous land for country inns, a region appropriate and accessible for the discerning traveler. People pretty much laughed when I sat down to play this piano. "I suppose you're going to find a good place to eat in *Centralia!*" they cackled. (To my delight, we did.) It was a hunch, a dare.

And it turned out that there were about 300 "best places." I remember the great pleasure I got as friends or people I met at book signings would say (in astonished voices, as if I had performed some sort of magic stunt) that they had enjoyed terrific meals in Wenatchee, or Penticton, or McMinnville, thanks to this book. All these good places *were* out there, labors of love created by the kinds of folks who opened that B&B in Bellingham. They were the treasured secrets of knowledgeable locals (whom we used to help track these places down), but they were known to few travelers.

The list is much longer now, 20-odd years after those first scouting expeditions. Northwest restaurants have a deserved national reputation. We are creating a new, nature-cherishing form of eco-tourism that beautifully suits the landscape. Arts festivals and urban-style amenities now grace remote villages. It's been an astonishing transformation, helped by readers like you and the hundreds of inspectors and scouts who have made these books as good as they are. It's agreeable to think that we, rather than a passing surge from an Expo '86, have done the most to bring about this enhancement of Northwest travel.

—David Brewster

ABOUT *BEST PLACES* GUIDEBOOKS

The *Best Places* series is unique in that the guidebooks are written by and for locals—which makes them coveted by travelers. *Northwest Best Places* is written for people who live in the Northwest and who enjoy exploring its bounty. It's written for those who like out-of-the-way places of high character and individualism, and who take the time to seek out such places. Paradoxically, those very characteristics make *Northwest Best Places* ideal for tourists, too. The best places in the region are the ones that denizens favor: independently owned establishments of good value, touched with local history, run by lively individuals, and graced with natural beauty. Here is a guide that will lead you not only to salmon in champagne sauce in Vancouver, British Columbia, but also to plate-size omelets with spuds in Troutdale, Oregon, to a glorious retreat in the Gulf Islands, or to a quiet lodge on the Olympic Peninsula.

The *Best Places* guides are completely independent: no advertisers, no sponsors, no favors. Our reviewers know the territory, work incognito, and seek out the very best the Northwest has to offer. We both re-evaluate old favorites and seek out new discoveries. Because we accept no free meals, accommodations, or other complimentary services, we are free to provide tough, candid reports about places that have rested too long on their laurels and to delight in new places whose efforts have paid off. We describe the true strengths, foibles, and unique characteristics of each establishment listed. With this latest edition of *Northwest Best Places*, the grandfather of all regional guides, travelers will find the information they need: where to go and when, what to order, which rooms to request (and which to avoid). We're so sure you'll be satisfied with our guide, we guarantee it.

HOW TO USE THIS BOOK

This book is arranged by regions within Oregon, Washington, and British Columbia. All evaluations are based on numerous reports from local and traveling inspectors. *Best Places* reporters do not identify themselves when they review an establishment, and they accept no free meals, accommodations, or any other services. Final judgments are made by the editors. Every place featured in this book is recommended.

Stars   Restaurants and hotels are rated on a scale of zero to four stars, based on uniqueness, loyalty of local clientele, performance measured against goals, excellence of cooking, value, and professionalism of service. Reviews are listed alphabetically within each star rating.

> ★★★★   The very best in the region
>
> ★★★   Distinguished; many outstanding features
>
> ★★   Excellent; some wonderful qualities
>
> ★   A good place
>
> (no stars)   Worth knowing about, if nearby
>
> *[unrated]*   New or undergoing major changes

This symbol congratulates those establishments that were in David Brewster's original edition of *Northwest Best Places*.

    ♿ Appears after listings that have wheelchair-accessible facilities.

Price Range   Prices are based on high-season rates. Prices throughout the British Columbia section are in Canadian dollars.

    $$$ Expensive (more than $80 for dinner for two; more than $90 for lodgings for two)

    $$ Moderate (between expensive and inexpensive)

    $ Inexpensive (less than $30 for dinner for two; less than $60 for lodgings for two)

Checks and Credit Cards   Most establishments that accept checks also require a major credit card for identification. Credit cards are abbreviated in this book as follows: American Express (AE); Diners Club (DC); MasterCard (MC); Visa (V). In British Columbia there are two more cards that are often used: Enroute (E) and a Japanese credit card (JCB).

Maps and Directions   Each section in this book begins with a regional map that shows the towns being covered. Throughout the book are town maps, and basic directions are provided with each entry. Whenever possible, call ahead to confirm hours and location.

Bed and Breakfasts   Many B&Bs have a two-night minimum-stay requirement during the peak season, and a number of them do not welcome children. Ask about a bed and breakfast's policies before you make your reservation.

Smoking   Assume a no-smoking (or outdoors only) policy except where noted otherwise, but call ahead to confirm.

Pets   Assume that no pets are allowed, unless otherwise specified in the review.

Index   All restaurants, lodgings, town names, and major tourist attractions are listed alphabetically at the back of the book.

Reader Reports   At the end of the book is a report form. We receive hundreds of reports from readers suggesting new places or agreeing or disagreeing with our assessments. They greatly help in our evaluations. We encourage you to respond.

Money-Back Guarantee   Yes, this is true. See the back page for details.

OREGON

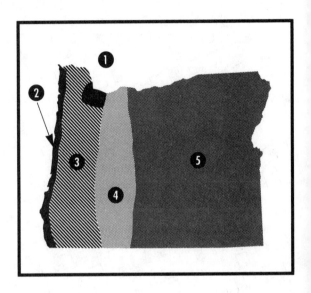

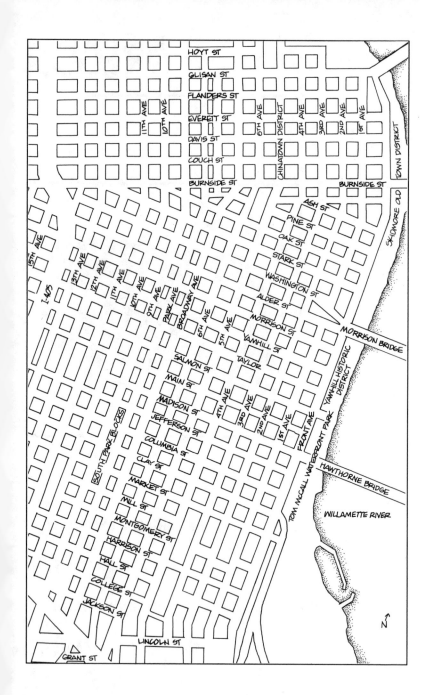

Portland and Environs

Including outlying areas: Forest Grove, Beaverton, Hillsboro, and Tigard to the west, Lake Oswego and West Linn to the south, Milwaukie to the southeast, Gresham to the east.

PORTLAND

For decades, Portlanders worked hard to make the Rose City a great place to live, and by almost every measure they've succeeded. With its plethora of parks, its charming downtown core, its splendid westside riverfront, and its proximity to so many of Oregon's finest diversions, Portland is a gem. Now the secret's out, and Portlanders are bracing for dramatic population growth. Still, there's every reason to think that this city can hold on to those ideals that have made it great.

It's easy to see what makes Portland such a sought-after place. During the past few years, it has acquired a nationally noted light-rail service, which goes to Gresham and soon to Beaverton; a small jewel of a downtown performing arts center and an art museum within a few blocks of one another; a downtown shopping complex starring Saks Fifth Avenue; a major convention center; and stunning digs for its science museum, Oregon Museum of Science and Industry. The development on the southwest side of the downtown riverfront continues apace, with new housing and office buildings spreading southward.

Portlanders insist that their city must not become a place only for networking or catching planes to other places, but must remain a city for living. What they prize about their town is not its per capita income but its rivers, its neighborhoods, its waterfront festivals, its microbreweries, and, most of the time, its Trailblazers. Like any city, Portland has its flaws, but better than most, it's able to meet them head-on.

Below is a glimpse of Portland (followed by reviews of its top restaurants and lodgings); for a more comprehensive city guide, see our series companion, *Portland Best Places*.

THE ARTS

Music. Nothing has ever done so much for this city's aural offerings as the Arlene Schnitzer Concert Hall. Portlanders pack the place 52 weeks a year. Besides the essential house "given"—the Oregon Symphony Orchestra, under conductor James DePreist—the "Schnitz" has expanded Portland's musical agenda significantly; (503)228-1353. Chamber Music Northwest presents a five-week-long summer festival spanning four centuries of music; (503)223-3202.

Theater. Neighboring the Schnitz is the Center for Performing Arts, which contains two performance spaces. Its full-time resident company, Portland Center Stage, (503)274-6588, began as an offshoot of the acclaimed Shakespeare festival in Ashland, but is now wholly independent. PCS offers excellent production values, whatever the play (light comedies seem to play best). You can always be assured of work by Shakespeare with productions by Tygres Heart, (503)222-9220, housed in the same facility. The Portland Repertory Theater, (503)224-4491, puts on dependable productions in a theater just off Front Street. Musicals of any caliber land at the Portland Civic (home of the Portland Opera).

Visual Arts. Gallery walks once a month (on "First Thursdays") have encouraged the expansion of the Portland art community: The Portland Art Museum, Augen, Blue Sky, Quartersaw, Blackfish, Elizabeth Leach, Pulliam Deffenbaugh Nugent, and Laura Russo are among the hot showcases of both local and national work. The city is popping with public art, too; just start watching for it. Pioneer Courthouse Square is a good place to begin your search.

Dance. The Oregon Ballet Theater enlists youth and daring to serve the needs of Portland's ballet fans; (503)227-6867. Perhaps the most creative productions are performed by Oslund and Company, (503)236-3265.

Literature. Besides Powell's, the superpower of bookstores, Portland has a flock of other strong bookstores, including Looking Glass Books, one of the loveliest bookstores in town; A Children's Place, with a huge selection of reading material for the young set; the handsomely refurbished Annie Bloom's Books; and Murder by the Book, which is to mysteries what Powell's is to everything else. Many of these, as well as local churches and colleges, present readings by local or visiting writers. Literary Arts produces a series of lectures by nationally known literary figures—the Portland Arts and Lectures Series—and although tickets are scarce, you might get lucky; (503)227-2583.

Architecture. Portland's downtown skyline has become dramatically sophisticated in recent years. Zimmer Gunsul Frasca's (ZGF) Convention Center, with its distinctive illuminated twin towers, won the American Institute of Architecture's most prestigious National Honor Award. Other outstanding buildings include Pietro Belluschi's glass-box Equitable Building, Michael Graves's controversial postmodern Portland Building, Will Martin's swank, complexly designed Pioneer Courthouse Square, A.E. Doyle's spectacularly ornate Old U.S. Bank Building, ZGF's KOIN Center and its blue-reflective One Financial Center, and the city's most recent architectural entry, Broome, Oringdulth, O'Toole, Rudolf, Boles and Associates' 1000 Broadway, distinguished by its copper-colored glass and white illuminated dome.

OTHER THINGS TO DO

Nightlife. Check local newspapers' calendar listings for what's happening in the jazz world (*Willamette Week* is out each Wednesday; the *Oregonian*'s entertainment section is in Friday's paper). One gig you can depend on is at The Portland Art Museum; its After Hours programs on Wednesday evenings draw a crowd. Rock fans get their best licks at LaLuna or the Roseland, while folkies hang at the Aladdin. Music on or past the edge—and followers of the same—can be found at Satyricon, in Old Town.

Sports. The town's only big-league action is the Portland Trailblazers basketball team. While they usually manage to make the playoffs, the Blazers have a penchant for fizzling in the finals; (503)231-8000. The Winter Hawks, member of the Western Hockey League, hit the ice 72 times a season in Memorial Coliseum; (503)238-6366. Individual sports thrive in the region: runners have access to over 50 manicured miles of trail in the 5,000-acre Forest Park complex; rowers are guaranteed miles of flat water on the Willamette; and bicyclists use more than 100 miles of off-street paved bike paths in the greater Portland area.

Parks and Gardens. Besides the sprawling and primitive Forest Park, there are nearly 150 other parks in the city. The Hoyt Arboretum, close to the Washington Park Zoo, has the most impressive collection of native and exotic flora, as well as the best-kept trails. More formalized grounds are the International Rose Test Garden, the Japanese Gardens, and the Crystal Springs Rhododendron Gardens. The World Forestry Center Building, also next to the zoo, has ongoing displays worth checking. And the largest memorial of its kind in the nation, the Vietnam Veterans' Living Memorial, is an inspiring outdoor cathedral commemorating the Oregon victims of that conflict; call Washington Park for more information, (503) 796-5274.

Shopping. Crafts and renaissance-style goods can be found weekends at Saturday Market under the Burnside Bridge; upscale specialty shops and eateries are found at Pioneer Place, the Water Tower at John's Landing, and Lloyd Center—or at suburban malls Clackamas Town Center and Washington Square. Northwest Portland's 23rd Avenue and SE Hawthorne Boulevard between 35th and 45th feature great neighborhood merchants; NE Broadway and Multnomah (in Southwest Portland) are up-and-comers in the neighborhood shopping scene. Antiques are found in Sellwood, in the city's southeast corner.

Transportation. The city's public transportation system, Tri-Met, runs throughout the metropolitan area and is free in the downtown core area. The light-rail system, MAX, is a speedy conduit to the east side, going as far as Gresham now, but soon heading west to Beaverton as well. Amtrak heads north, south, and east from the handsome Union Station. The airport (PDX) is a $20 cab ride (or pay less than half that for airport shuttle buses from major downtown hotels). Parking meters must be fed even on Saturdays in Portland.

RESTAURANTS

20 YEARS **Genoa** ★★★★ Genoa has been one of the city's defining restaurants for a quarter of a century. The remarkable part is that the extravagant meals and the three hours still pass leaving one seduced—not overwhelmed. The famously dark dining room has lightened a bit, and strictly Northern Italian seven-course meals are about to give way to a four-course option on weekdays. On the minimal-choice menu you might find a risotto flavored with radicchio and shrimp, a Tuscan tomato and bread soup, a luscious ravioli, entrees including a Paduan mixed grill and a stuffed pheasant, and the drop-dead dessert tray. Not every course will be spectacular, but a couple will certainly be, and the rest will be very good. Knowledgeable staff carefully describe the food and know the wine list. Weekend theatergoers should choose the abridged version of dinner served at 5:30pm and 6pm and then again at 10pm and 10:30pm. Genoa was awarded two chef's hats in Italy's _Veronelli Guide to the United States_, the highest rating of any Northwest restaurant. No argument here. ■ _NE 29th and Belmont; (503) 238-1464; 2832 SE Belmont St, Portland; $$$; beer and wine and aperitifs; AE, DC, MC, V; checks OK; dinner Mon–Sat._ &

The Heathman Restaurant and Bar ★★★★ When chef Greg Higgins departed to set up his own eponymous place, the Heathman responded boldly—and, it turns out, brilliantly. The

hotel brought in Philippe Boulot, from The Mark hotel in New York (via Paris). Boulot doesn't exactly merge classic French cuisine with Pacific Northwest trends; rather, he expands the classics to absorb local ingredients, producing, maybe, a pasta tossed with Pacific prawns and buttery nuggets of foie gras or a stunning salmon in a pesto crust with a shard of crisp salmon skin planted on top, as though Boulot were staking a claim. He's also trying to increase the Heathman's use of local game and involvement in the local wine scene—building on what was already Portland's largest Oregon wine list. His wife, Susan, Portlander and pâtissier, does dazzling things with local fruits and fabulous chocolate. Boulot has, of course, an excellent foundation. The Heathman remains Portland's premier power breakfast and lunch location—the king salmon hash endures at breakfast—and even offers what you might call a power tea.
■ *Salmon and SW Broadway; (503)241-4100; 1009 SW Broadway, Portland; $$$; full bar; AE, DC, MC, V; checks OK; breakfast, lunch, dinner every day.* &

Zefiro ★★★★ High profile, yet solidly down-to-earth. Of course, you can't sit down here without having the feeling there might be someone rather famous at the next table, but what you'll really be thinking about is the food: innovative, highly consistent cooking that's always beautifully presented. That—coupled with flattering lighting that makes everyone look fabulous and the most polished service in town—adds up to a dining experience that really shouldn't be missed. The menu spans from Spain to Thailand with an emphasis on the Mediterranean. After a sabbatical in Southeast Asia, chef Christopher Israel adds new touches such as a warm Vietnamese quail salad in a fruity, gingery vinaigrette or grilled Alaskan halibut with a Thai tamarind sauce. Signature dishes include a creamy, inviting risotto with ingredients nodding to the season and the chef's whim, and a crisp, perfect caesar salad for two. Desserts never disappoint. Zefiro's bar area (a good bet if you arrive without a reservation) is *the* place to sip from an ever-changing drink list. ■ *Corner of NW 21st and Glisan; (503)226-3394; 500 NW 21st, Portland; $$$; full bar; AE, DC, MC, V; local checks only; lunch Mon–Fri, dinner Mon–Sat.* &

Atwater's ★★★ Following chef Mark Gould's deft menu redesign at this 30th-story aerie, the management responded with a physical overhaul. It's still hard for anything to compete with the view of two rivers, two states, and one city, but Gould's skill and dedication to local fare with a particular flair for combining local seafood and Asian inspirations have enlivened this restaurant. Desserts are consistently impressive. Meanwhile, interior innovations continue. The bar's transformation is the most dramatic (now a warm bistro rather than an afterthought) with jazz on weekends. The sommelier, Steve Sells, recently of

Seattle's Four Seasons, mans the huge, etched-glass wine cellar in the middle of the dining room. A few feet away, there's a Chef's Table for six, where a multicourse meal is presented by the chef himself. ■ *Off W Burnside on 5th; (503) 275-3600; 111 SW 5th Ave, Portland; $$$; full bar; AE, DC, MC, V; no checks; dinner every day.* ⅋

Briggs and Crampton's Table for Two ★★★ What began as a testing ground for Nancy Briggs's catering business has grown to a restaurant with an identity perhaps unmatched the world over. Every week one of the talented B&C cooks writes a new menu, and each lunch consists of an appetizer, intermezzo, and an entree—perhaps fresh seafood with an elaborate sauce or roasted rack of lamb in a saffron-tomato demiglace—and then a blow-your-socks-off dessert. The intricate presentation of each course dazzles, as does the pretty china and intimate setting. Most linger here long into the afternoon. Catch is, it's a one-table restaurant that's open for lunch only, weekdays only. You can snag *the* table if at 8:30am sharp on the first business day of the next quarter you call. Be patient; even the price, soaring to $75 for two (before wine or tip), hasn't slowed the phones. ■ *Montgomery Park between Thurman and Vaughn; (503) 223-8690; 1902 NW 24th Ave, Portland; $$$; beer and wine; MC, V; checks OK; lunch Tues–Fri (by appointment only).*

Cafe des Amis ★★★ Choices, choices, choices. There are a tremendous amount of them here, but you'll still have trouble deciding between a luscious duck in blackberry sauce, a moist salmon, and a buttery, 2-inch-thick filet of beef in a port and garlic sauce—but all of them are sensational. Of course, you might just skip the entree and make a light, satisfying meal of soup and salad and the wild mushroom ravioli appetizer. Dennis Baker shows a deft hand with soups—from cream of mussel to carrot with a hint of lemon grass and wasabe—and the green salad is dressed with walnut oil and accessorized with toasted walnuts and grated Jarlsberg. In his cozy, intimate cafe tucked onto a northwest Portland residential street, Baker is sticking with what works—and there's no reason in the world why he shouldn't. ■ *Corner of 20th and NW Kearney; (503) 295-6487; 1987 NW Kearney St, Portland; $$; full bar; AE, MC, V; checks OK; dinner Mon–Sat.* ⅋

Esparza's Tex-Mex Cafe ★★★ When the Texas-sized expansion is complete, Esparza's will have all the ingredients (and finally enough seating) of a blue-ribbon restaurant: loads of atmosphere, from the King on the jukebox to the marionettes dancing over the bar; a varied menu that covers a surprising stretch of ground as it moves from nopalitos—the best cactus appetizer around—to some of Portland's freshest-tasting tacos to good ol' mashed potatoes; and service that's both prompt and well-informed about the myriad options. Once you sit down you're in for a treat—especially if smoky beef brisket wrapped in fresh tortillas and served with all the jalapeños you can manage is your idea of a hot time. Joe, from his perch at the bar, keeps as watchful an eye on the food as he does on the proceedings. ■ *1 block south of E Burnside on the corner of SE 28th and Ankeny; (503)234-7909; 2725 SE Ankeny, Portland; $$; full bar; AE, MC, V; no checks; lunch, dinner Tues–Sat.*

Higgins ★★★ After a decade at the Heathman Hotel, building its reputation as the local landmark of Pacific Northwest cuisine, chef Greg Higgins opened his own place. Higgins offers imaginative and elaborate dishes that occasionally confuse but often dazzle, with a vivid sense of the season's offerings. The most seductive dishes will be found among the seafood offerings, perhaps a roasted salmon coated in a mustard crumb crust. (Higgins has a particular allure for people who like their fish cooked gently.) Indulge in an electric finish of fresh peach fritters in marionberry sauce. Thinner wallets will appreciate Higgins's bar next door, which serves bistro fare after 2pm every day. This may be the only fine restaurant in the city that goes out of its way to welcome young children. ■ *Corner of SW Jefferson and Broadway; (503)222-9070; 1239 SW Broadway, Portland; $$$; full bar; AE, DC, MC, V; checks OK; lunch Mon–Fri, dinner every day.* ♿

 Indigine ★★★ Beloved by many, Indigine is low-key in the best sense of the expression—but don't walk in without a reservation. Owner/chef Millie Howe has an innovative touch when it comes to blending Northwest ingredients with Eastern spices. Saturdays are reserved for the blowout East Indian feast, an extravaganza that might start with something like tandoori chicken wings and apricot chutney, followed by a fresh seafood salad. Weeknight suppers have Latin American, European, or Pacific Northwest overtones: roast chicken stuffed beneath the skin with garlicky pesto, or seafood enchiladas with hot chiles and cream. A choice of desserts—saffron-laced yogurt or boccone dolce—will send you away purring. When the weather allows, dinner on the back deck is delightful. ■ *A few blocks east of Nature's on SE Division; (503)238-1470; 3725 SE Division St, Portland; $$; beer and wine; MC, V; checks OK; dinner Tues–Sat.* ♿

L'Auberge ★★★ After 25 years as a powerhouse Portland restaurant with its three-hour, six-course prix-fixe meals, L'Auberge surrendered to the Puritan and parsimonious '90s. The menu is now à la carte, and the intriguing lower-cost bar meals have surfaced in the dining room as "bistro entrees." (This comes as no surprise to some Portlanders who preferred the more energetic bar menu.) Now you might start with the Dungeness crab cake with saffron beurre blanc, then cut to the robust cassoulet. Whatever pattern you follow, someone at the table should have the scallops in thyme cream or the rack of lamb in port garlic sauce. Traditionalists, rest assured: fixed-price menus are still available—but now they're only three or four courses, and about $10 less than before.

Up a few steps from the relaxed, restrained elegance of the dining room, the bar is a softly lit den of upscale hipness with a well-stoked hearth in winter, a homey outdoor dining deck in summer, and, in all seasons, a witty, personable staff. Sunday night, this relaxing retreat offers its own classic movies, terrific ribs, and what can only be called haute cuisine cheeseburgers. ■ *26th and Vaughn; (503)223-3302; 2601 NW Vaughn St, Portland; $$$; full bar; AE, DC, MC, V; local checks only; dinner every day; Sunday, bar only.* &

Lemongrass ★★★ A dozen years ago, Srichan Miller set off serious Thai cooking in Portland by opening Bangkok Kitchen at this address. Now, daughter Shelley Siripatrapa has opened up her own place here, and turns out the best Thai food in town. Lines stretch out the door for the few tables, and service at times seems glacial and befuddled. But the real magic of this place happens behind the stove, where Siripatrapa makes a handful of chicken and seafood dishes that snap with freshness and are a perfect harmony of sharp, sweet, and hot. Heat ranges from toasty to volcanic, and people are coming from all over town to sample the green curry. ■ *Take the 58th Ave exit off the Banfield (I-84); (503)231-5780; 5832 NE Glisan St, Portland; $$; beer and wine; no credit cards; checks OK; lunch Mon–Fri (except Wed), dinner every day.*

L'Etoile ★★★ In just a few years, John Zweben has created something remarkable—an impressive classic French restaurant that's slowly becoming a local favorite, at a time when the food fashion runs in other directions. Zweben never stints on richness. He fans foie gras across a pool of sweet wine and orange, and spreads a roasted beet glaze over seared sea scallops, calling the results "Coquilles St. Jacques Assassin." If you see either veal with morels or salmon with a honey-bacon glaze, order quickly. Leave room for elaborately arrayed desserts, from a jewel-like cookie plate under a cloud of caramel spun sugar to a classic tarte Tatin to a ginger-sauced poached pear with pear sorbet. Zweben has added to his operation outside garden seating and a bar with a bistro menu. ■ *NE Fremont and 46th; (503)281-4869; 4627 NE Fremont St, Portland; $$$; full bar; AE, MC, V; local checks only; dinner Tues–Sat.* &

McCormick & Schmick's Seafood Restaurant ★★★ Under the bold, imaginative new direction of Ken Hays, M&S has maintained its excitement edge over its corporate elder brother, Jake's, and other Portland seafood restaurants. The choices can extend from simple grilled sturgeon to a seafood mu-shu. Grilled smoked salmon and seafood stew are permanent favorites, but the fresh dragnet extends from Alaska to Florida to Chile, and the fish caught in it can end up in roasted garlic vinaigrette, tandoori glaze, or fresh raspberry beurre rouge. The place is frequently jammed, offering a lively bar scene, complete with a pianist and an extraordinary selection of single-malt Scotches. One popular new development: monthly Cigar Nights. ■ *Oak St and 1st Ave; (503) 224-7522; 235 SW 1st Ave, Portland; $$; full bar; AE, DC, MC, V; checks OK; lunch Mon–Fri, dinner every day.* &

Murata ★★★ Murata often seems directly aimed at visiting Japanese businessmen: the specials are listed in Japanese without translation, and it is perhaps the only serious restaurant not open for Saturday dinner. That said, Murata may just be the best Japanese restaurant in Portland. Once someone has translated the specials, they're often worth the culinary gamble—crisp grilled sardines, or tender salmon cheeks. If there's kasu cod, by all means order it, and if you've got some friends along, try one of the nabe—huge bowls of stewlike soups, thick with seafood. Those with time, money, and nerve should order (in advance) an elaborate Japanese multicourse banquet, kaiseki, starting at $35 per person and running as high as your wallet allows. ■ *Downtown on SW Market between 2nd and 3rd; (503) 227-0080; 200 SW Market, Portland; $$; beer and wine; AE, MC, V; no checks; lunch, dinner Mon–Fri.*

Papa Haydn ★★★ In northwest Portland, a part of town where good restaurants are more common than espresso joints, Papa Haydn continues to satisfy with its salads and sandwiches—and to wow with its bountiful dessert selection. Once, one would not have expected this restaurant to offer a veal chop at $23.50, but the place has come a long way since the days when it served up lunchy items so people wouldn't feel guilty about just eating dessert. That said, the best-known aspect of Papa Haydn is still the display of towering, intense finishes, led by the Autumn Meringue—layers of chocolate mousse and baked meringue festooned with chocolate leaves—and the boccone dolce, a mountain of whipped cream, meringue, chocolate, and fresh berries. The southeast location (on Milwaukie Avenue) is more low-key, but both have lines stretching out the door. ■ *Irving and NW 23rd; (503) 228-7317; 701 NW 23rd Ave, Portland; full bar.* ■ *In Sellwood district; (503) 232-9440; 5829 SE Milwaukie Ave, Portland; $$; beer and wine; AE, MC, V; local checks only; lunch, dinner Tues–Sat, brunch Sun.* &

Pazzo Ristorante ★★★ What's impressive about Pazzo, now established as one of Portland's most beloved restaurants, is not only chef David Machado's consistently creative cuisine, but Pazzo's dining room options: the brick dining room with heavenly scents from its wood-fired grill, the bar where garlic hangs overhead, or the glass-enclosed private rooms. On Friday and Saturday nights, there's reserved seating in the romantic downstairs wine cellar. Machado shows off his ability to blend Italian with Northwest in a menu mainstay of smoked salmon ravioli in a light lemon cream. But he can impress with a dish as familiar as a veal scalloppine with capers—richly cast over a bed of spinach. Highlights include fish grilled over wood fires, interesting pastas, and the day's specials, recited tableside, in reverent detail. Listen closely to the entire description; your entree choice may hang on whether the accompaniment is silken garlic mashed potatoes or an aggressive Tuscan bread salad. ■ *Corner of SW Broadway and Washington; (503) 228-1515; 627 SW Washington St, Portland; $$; full bar; AE, DC, MC, V; checks OK; breakfast, lunch, dinner every day.* ᕫ

3 Doors Down ★★★ The only problem with this notable addition to the Hawthorne scene is that it doesn't take reservations—but when you taste dishes such as the bountiful seafood Fra Diavolo, that hardly seems like a problem at all. The kitchen brings together Northwest seafood with Italian instincts. The small, spare storefront, three doors down from Hawthorne Boulevard—hence the name—has a warm atmosphere and a way with the fruits of the sea, shown in gently cooked sea scallops, Parmesan-laced steamed clams, and pasta studded with Copper River salmon. There are occasional slips, but the odds are in your favor, especially if you start with the outsized antipasto of tender marinated eggplant and finish with an intense chocolate torte or the dauntingly rich cheesecake. Pace yourself—you can always come back, and you probably will. ■ *North of Hawthorne on SE 37th; (503) 236-6886; 1429 SE 37th Ave, Portland; $$; beer and wine; AE, MC, V; checks OK; dinner Tues–Sat, open Sun Apr–Aug.* ᕫ

Wildwood ★★★ Cory Schreiber, who found fame as a chef in San Francisco, returned to his hometown in 1994 to open Wildwood (named after a trail in Forest Park). The applause has yet to die down. Wildwood is somewhat San Francisco in feel; that is, it's open, it's boisterous, and there's always a notable designer pizza on the daily-changing menu. But it's Oregon in flavor (lots of local ingredients). From the skillet-roasted mussel starters to the luscious green apple sorbet at the end, everything's superb. A huge, wood-fired brick oven roasts chicken wings to a spicy juiciness and salmon to a gentle perfection. If there's a salad on the menu that features fried oysters and pancetta on an herbed crêpe, make it your starter. Free parking in the lot next to the building. ■ *Corner of NW 21st Ave and Overton; (503) 248-9663; 1221 NW 21st Ave,*

Portland; $$$; full bar; AE, DC, MC, V; checks OK; lunch, dinner every day, Sun brunch. &

Al-Amir ★★ As the scene in this corner of downtown heats up ever so subtly, Al-Amir, inside the elaborately crenellated Bishop's House, is showing a bit more flash itself. But the core of the place is still a solid, consistent Middle Eastern kitchen. The shish kabob, lamb vibrant with spices and juices, highlights a menu that stretches to kharouf muammar, a huge pile of moist, faintly sweet lamb chunks; and dujaj musahab, a charcoal-grilled chicken breast in lemon and olive oil. Holding everything together are pools of creamy hummus and baba ghanouj. A little Lebanese beer makes the light through the stained-glass windows shine even more brightly. ■ *Between 2nd and 3rd, downtown; (503)274-0010; 223 SW Stark St, Portland; $$; full bar; AE, MC, V; local checks only; lunch Mon–Fri, dinner every day.* &

Alexis ★★ The party begins with a shout of "Opa!" as flaming saganaki (Greek cheese ignited with ouzo) arrives. From the first course of chewy squid to the last of melt-in-your-mouth baklava, the food here is authentic and memorable. Plump grape leaf packets are available meatless or with lamb; the little pillows of filo and feta known as tiropitas are worth the 15-minute wait. In fact, regulars often order these and other appetizers and call it dinner. Baskets of warm house bread come with the meal—and if you like what you taste, take heart: Alexis sells it by the loaf. The Alexis Bakourous family and their loyal staff attentively patrol the premises, and on weekends they're joined by Aurelia, the region's hottest Middle Eastern dancer. ■ *Between 2nd and 3rd on W Burnside; (503)224-8577; 215 W Burnside, Portland; $$; full bar; AE, DC, MC, V; local checks only; lunch Mon–Fri, dinner every day.* &

Avalon Grill ★★ It might seem more buzz than brilliance, but Avalon has certainly been one of the more striking openings in Portland, with its dramatic, angular design by Lee Winn, its riverside location, and its immediate identity as a place to be seen (but barely heard). Some fish dishes are admirable, but several entrees seem unsettlingly sweet: lamb chops with maple syrup? Still, the excitement is unquestionably here, and the place can surprise with unexpected approaches. Where else can you find grits in a veal reduction—in a high-tech, postmodern setting? ■ *Macadam Ave, near Johns Landing; (503)227-4630; 4630 SW Macadam, Portland; $$; full bar; AE, MC, V; checks OK; lunch, Mon–Fri, dinner every day, Sun brunch.* &

B. Moloch/The Heathman Bakery and Pub ★★ Portlanders crowd into this place, with its walls of windows, high ceilings hung with artful banners, and intriguing menu. Some new-comers find the order-at-the-cashier concept unsettling, but usually they leave any misgivings behind when the food arrives. Heathman Hotel chef Philippe Boulot has brushed up the Pub's menu: order the smoked salmon hash, grana ravioli, or pan-seared halibut, but steer clear of dishes that take time, like risotto, as it may arrive undercooked, well after your dinner companion has finished a plate-sized pizza from the 25-ton wood-fired oven. B. Moloch still serves one of the city's better breakfasts, with such dishes as an open-faced smoked salmon and crème fraîche omelet. Salmon, peppered ham, and sun-dried tomatoes are cured in a cold-smoker in back of the massive baking furnace, and the smell mingles with the pungent aromas from the Widmer microbrew pub that sits beyond the restaurant. ▪ *At the north end of the South Park Blocks; (503)227-5700; 901 SW Salmon St, Portland; $$; beer and wine; AE, DC, MC, V; checks OK; breakfast, lunch, dinner every day.* ♿

Bangkok Kitchen ★★ Portland's first Thai restaurant is still dependable for the unadorned basics of Southeast Asian cooking: hot and sour soups, curries, salads of fresh shrimp and lime, and noodles. The funky, informal atmosphere—with waiters in jeans and T-shirts and a no-frills decor—has attracted a faithful following of neighborhood locals and cross-river pilgrims who come for the family feeling and the famous whole crispy sea bass in chile sauce. Kids are more than welcome—the staff members wear their sense of humor like name tags. ▪ *On SE Belmont St at 25th Ave; (503)236-7349; 2534 SE Belmont St, Portland; $; beer and wine; no credit cards; checks OK; lunch Tues–Fri, dinner Tues–Sat.* ♿

Basta's ★★ As the march of restaurants continues apace up and down NW 21st Avenue, Basta's (a Restaurant Row tenant since 1991) continues doing what it has done well since its opening: serving well-priced and mostly reliable Italian fare in a Tuscan-fun atmosphere (a former fast-food hangout nicely modified into an art-filled trattoria). Although the diners on the patio might be casually attired, there's a well-dressed caesar salad on the menu and a handsome grilled shrimp in a wrap of house-cured pancetta. The kitchen has a way with lamb—especially the slow-cooked lamb shank in an herby tomato-pancetta sauce. The breads are irresistible. ▪ *Near Glisan on NW 21st; (503)274-1572; 410 NW 21st Ave, Portland; $$; full bar; MC, V; checks OK; lunch Mon–Fri, dinner every day.* ♿

Berbati ★★ This Greek restaurant has long been a favorite of ours, but a recent expansion into nightlife (billiards, a game room, and more space for live music) has taken away some of the intimacy. Still, the kitchen seems to have kept its focus on the rustic, hearty fare for which it's known. Order a tableful of appetizers and expect to be perfectly satisfied. The chicken souvlaki is served alongside a wedge of buttery, mustard-kissed potato. The tiropita—a hot, cheese-filled pastry—is so smooth it cries out for an accompanying glass of pine-scented retsina. And the calamari is simply the best fried squid in town. If anything, Berbati has just become more of a hangout—but we've been hanging out here all along. ■ *1 block south of W Burnside on 2nd; (503)226-2122; 19 SW 2nd Ave, Portland; $$; full bar; MC, V; local checks only; lunch Tues–Fri, dinner Tues–Sun.* &

BJ's Brazilian Restaurant ★★ There's a new owner at Portland's only Brazilian restaurant, and the place is lighter and more open. But you'll still find reasonably good versions of specialties such as Brazil's national dish of feijoada, a stew of black beans and pork. Chicken dishes, including one baked in dark beer and red palm oil, are also admirable, as are the small, deep-fried meat pies called pastels. Everything comes with rice, a grain dish called farofa, and a mixture of chopped cilantro and red pepper that should be spooned on everything in sight. A dark Brazilian beer called Xingu is served up in huge bottles, or try the potent cacha, a sugar cane liquor. ■ *A half block off Bybee on Milwaukie; (503)236-9629; 7019 SE Milwaukie Ave, Portland; $$; beer and wine; MC, V; checks OK; lunch Mon–Fri, dinner Mon–Sat.* &

Brasserie Montmartre ★★ The Brasserie has recently bolstered its presence in Portland's downtown scene with a major outside facelift, a burst of glass and wood at least as flashy as the restaurant's black-and-white checked floor. The Bra offers perhaps the widest variety of late-night dishes available in Portland (until 2am weekdays, 3am weekends). Whatever the hour, it's surprising how consistent the fare can be. The major ingredient may be the scene—Doc Martens and suits, hot local jazz with no cover, and dancing—but the food deserves notice too, especially the linguine with pesto and scallops or the salmon with lingonberry sauce. Unfortunately, the artsy setting does have a bad influence on the predictability of the service. ■ *Between Alder and Morrison; (503)224-5552; 626 SW Park Ave, Portland; $$; full bar; AE, DC, MC, V; checks OK; lunch Mon–Fri, dinner every day, brunch Sat–Sun.* &

Bread and Ink Cafe ★★ A lofty, well-lit bistro in the heart of the Hawthorne district—a Portland favorite. The menu is eclectic, with Mexican, American, and Mediterranean leanings: chicken enchiladas with a tomatillo salsa, broiled salmon with juniper berries and orange zest, and roasted Cornish game hen with Algerian spices. The black bean chili is tried and true, the wild green salad is wonderful, and the hamburger might just be the best in town, with homemade condiments that do it justice. Desserts here have nurtured a clientele of addicts. Breakfast means omelets served with delicious home-fries and, on Sundays, a three-course Jewish-style brunch. ■ *Corner of SE 36th and Hawthorne; (503)239-4756; 3610 SE Hawthorne Blvd, Portland; $$; beer and wine; AE, MC, V; checks OK; breakfast, lunch, dinner Mon–Sat, brunch Sun.* &

Bush Garden ★★ There are several strategies to ordering at this longtime downtown sushi bar: quickly rattle off words like uni, ama ebi, and toro; point and look hopeful; or just ask the chef to surprise you. Chefs here turn out versions of sushi and sashimi not found elsewhere—Alaskan roll with crab and smoked salmon, fiery spicy tuna maki, pungent pickled plums. They also like to show off; ask for a translation of the day's specials. Or just leave it to the chef's inspiration, and end up with something like a deliciously crunchy, sweet soft-shell spider crab roll. The regular Japanese fare, offered in tatami rooms, is rarely exciting; better to belly up to the sushi bar. ■ *9th and Morrison near Nordstrom; (503)226-7181; 900 SW Morrison St, Portland; $$; full bar; AE, DC, MC, V; no checks; lunch Mon–Fri, dinner every day.* &

Campbell's Barbecue ★★ The setting in a little house along Powell Boulevard is quaint, the servers cheerful and efficient, and side dishes—especially the potato salad and cornbread—are darn good. But the real reason the place is usually packed is the BBQ. Pork ribs are messy and satisfying, slathered with the smoky brown sugar sauce, but there are plenty of other options: smoked turkey, chicken, beef, or sausages. A space is available for parties, but some people claim any meal here is a party. The party's never over until they've run out of peach cobbler. ■ *Powell St exit off I-205, corner SE 85th and Powell; (503)777-9795; 8701 SE Powell, Portland; $; no alcohol; MC, V; checks OK; lunch Tues–Fri, dinner Tues–Sat.* &

Chen's Dynasty/Chen's Dynasty West ★★ The menu is huge with excursions into each region of China, and now that it's run by the Chen family there are more steamed, boiled, and vegetarian dishes. But it shouldn't dissuade you from the Heavenly Sliced Duck, or the minced squab in bamboo cup, or the four-color scallops, or even—if you're in the right kind of mood—peppered crunchy pig's ears. Leave time for eating here: you may need longer than you think to order from the lengthy menu, but you'll also want to pay attention to the food. Chen's Dynasty West is a roomier spot with an ocean-sized selection of seafood entrees. ■ *Between SW Broadway and 6th; (503)248-9491; 622 SW Washington St, Portland; $$; full bar; AE, MC, V; no checks; lunch, dinner every day.* & ■ *Near Scholl's Ferry Rd; (503)292-4898; 6750 SW Beaverton-Hillsdale Hwy, Beaverton; $$; full bar; AE, DC, MC, V; no checks; lunch, dinner every day.*

Delfina's ★★ Restaurants don't often succeed with an identity change, but Delfina's (ahem, "Delphina's" until a year or so ago) seems to have pulled it off; what was a popular pizza and pasta place has followed the trend toward greater Italian authenticity. Its menu is now smaller and oft-changing and the results are pleasing. The bruschetta with marinated seafood, Dungeness crab and pasta in a lemon cream sauce, and braised rabbit are striking additions; meanwhile the pastas are considerably less predictable than they once were and, well, a lot more interesting. Delfina's is building its own popular ambience with low lighting, fresh-baked rustic breads that require manual disassembly, and Italian language lessons broadcast in the restaurant. ■ *On the corner of NW 21st and Kearney; 503 221-1195; 2112 NW Kearney St, Portland; $$; full bar; AE, DC, MC, V; local checks only; lunch Mon–Fri, dinner every day.* ঙ

Earl Restaurant ★★ Portland can always use another serious seafood restaurant, especially one with a pedigree like this one has. Owner David Hearing started the landmark Bay House in Lincoln City, and has brought some of his seaside secrets with him. Hearing is a man who knows how to grill a salmon, sauté a plate of oysters (Wednesday nights are Oyster Nights), and create a vividly flavored paella. He celebrated his first year in Portland by adding a Sunday brunch. ■ *Corner of SE 12th and Morrison; (503) 232-3275; 1205 SE Morrison St, Portland; $$; beer and wine; MC, V; checks OK; dinner Tues–Sat, Sun brunch.*

Esplanade at RiverPlace (RiverPlace Hotel) ★★ Esplanade has so many advantages and attractions—we're sure the food will catch up with them someday. It's not that it's bad—but it could be better. Esplanade is a visually stunning place with picture windows that front the RiverPlace marina. Executive chef John Zenger is deep into yet another food format, which might be described as Northwest nouvelle with continental input. There are some imaginative efforts like Dungeness crab and bay shrimp cakes, and lunchers can light into a Northwest salmon club sandwich on herbed sourdough toast. Enduring on the menu are a few specialties that have survived all menu formats, such as the deeply rich lobster bisque (but the chef often has more fun with the soup du jour) and artfully constructed salads (spinach with smoked salmon and bay shrimp wontons). The admirable and elaborate sit-down brunch probably won't be washed away either. ■ *Harbor Way off SW Front; (503) 295-6166; 1510 SW Harbor Way, Portland; $$$; full bar; AE, DC, MC, V; checks OK; breakfast, lunch, dinner Mon–Fri, brunch Sun.* ঙ

Fong Chong ★★ This is where Portland's dim sum devotees put the cart before each course. The much larger House of

Louie, under the same ownership, is across the street. But whether it's the Chinese grocery next door, or because the place is crowded and loud, or because watching the carts maneuver through the tables is like watching the Super Mario Brothers, we like Fong Chong better. It's fun, inexpensive, and impressively tasty. Don't leave without sampling the sticky rice wrapped in a lotus leaf. At night, Fong Chong is transformed into a quiet Cantonese eatery, with average preparations and a few surprises. ■ *Everett and NW 4th; (503)220-0235; 301 NW 4th Ave, Portland; $; full bar; MC, V; checks OK; lunch, dinner every day.*

Fuji ★★ While other Japanese restaurants may be decorated with delicate Hokusai prints, this one gets right to the point, with elaborate depictions of sushi. Fujio Handa regularly departs from old-school rules of sushi-making to whip up creative concoctions (incorporating Western ingredients) that would make natives of Tokyo ask for more. Ignore the so-so Japanese standards, this is a sushi shack for sashimi addicts. ■ *South of Powell on SE 28th; (503)233-0577; 2878 SE Gladstone St, Portland; $; beer and wine; MC, V; no checks; dinner Tues–Sun.* &

Il Piatto ★★ Il Piatto is a neighborhood cafe that draws enthusiastic diners from far beyond the neighborhood. They come for the good cheer and good food, all in a romantic setting. Even waiting for a table is a sensual experience: you get comfortable in one of the well-worn red-velvet couches, while someone brings you warm bread and maybe a bottle of reasonably priced wine from the mostly Italian list. Steamed mussels in a broth of saffron and white wine and Torta al Formaggio de Capra (layered potatoes and herb goat cheese) are a good start for a meal of appetizers. The rest of the menu is weighted with pastas—the most simple preparations are best. A cinnamon gelato makes an outrageous finale. ■ *Corner of SE 24th and Ankeny; (503) 236-4997; 2348 SE Ankeny, Portland; $$; beer and wine; MC, V; checks OK; lunch Tues–Fri, dinner every day.*

Jake's Famous Crawfish ★★ Quintessential Portland: this restaurant may be 100 years old, but the menu gets reinvented every day. The combination of old tradition and new ideas about very fresh seafood could keep Jake's going for another century. Those without reservations might wait an hour, knowing their patience will be rewarded with some of the better seafood in the city and some of the best service anywhere. The fresh list will include some surprises, but what happens to the seafood may be more surprising—ahi tuna in a kung pao or grilled with pear ketchup—and the seafood's quality is matched only by the chef's imagination. Even less exotic inspirations, such as the bouillabaisse, or any variation on the theme of sturgeon or Copper River king salmon, prove that when Jake's is hot, it's really hot. The ultrarich truffle cake leads the desserts, but the three-berry cobbler is coming to rival it. ■ *Stark and SW 12th; (503)226-1419; 401 SW 12th Ave, Portland; $$; full bar; AE, DC, MC, V; checks OK; lunch Mon–Fri, dinner every day.* ♿

Jarra's Ethiopian Restaurant ★★ Several new Ethiopian restaurants have appeared in Portland recently, but Jarra's is still the place to get into an explosive, sweat-inducing Abyssinian stew. This is the restaurant to teach you what's wat: made with chicken, lamb, or beef, the wat (stews) are deep red, oily, and packed with peppery after-kicks. Full dinners come with assorted stewed meats and vegetables, all permeated with vibrant spices and mounded on injera—the spongy Ethiopian bread that doubles as plate and fork. Stashed into the bottom of an old Portland home, this is the neighborhood's unequaled heat champ. ■ *SE 14th and Hawthorne; (503)230-8990; 1435 SE Hawthorne Blvd, Portland; $; beer and wine; MC, V; local checks only; lunch Tues–Fri, dinner Tues–Sat.* ♿

Jo Bar and Rotisserie ★★ The broiler brother of next-door Papa Haydn has emerged as a big player in the Northwest 23rd restaurant stakes; loyal customers have made this young restaurant a busy place. Two huge wood-burning ovens blaze along the back wall, roasting succulent chicken, duck, pork loin, and leg of lamb. Burgers and breads also go through the fire. Salads, such as smoked salmon and caviar on wild greens, are inventive and inviting. Service and desserts can be uneven, but the restaurant bloodlines here are terrific. And any place that makes Paul Thomas Cabernet Merlot its house wine must know what it's doing. ■ *NW 23rd and Irving; (503)222-0048; 715 NW 23rd Ave, Portland; $$; full bar; AE, MC, V; checks OK; lunch Tues–Fri, dinner Tues–Sun, Sun brunch.* ♿

La Catalana ★★ In a storefront on SE Stark, charming La Catalana remains the city's only Catalonian restaurant, but its popularity might just start a food trend. The cuisine of Northeast Spain, based largely on equal parts seafood and garlic, is a big hit in Portland. The menu includes tapas such as pa amb tomaquet (grilled bread rubbed with tomato and garlic), escalavada (roasted eggplant with red pepper) and xato (fresh tuna served with a pungent romesco sauce). On a table bedecked with green olives and crusty peasant bread, diners enjoy, among other garlic-heavy entrees, mar i muntanya, chicken and seafood cooked with olive oil and white wine, and the stew sarsuela, made with fish and shellfish. Make a reservation—the place is small. ■ *SE Stark and 28th Ave; (503)232-0948; 2821 SE Stark St, Portland; $$; beer and wine; AE, DC, MC, V; checks OK; dinner Tues–Sun.* ♿

▼

Portland

Restaurants

▲

Le Bistro Montage ★★ Le Bistro Montage is one of the more vigorous dining scenes in Portland. Crowds flock to the high-ceilinged, low-lit dining room filled with long tables for such Cajun specialties as Spicy Mac (glorified macaroni with Cajun gravy, jalapeños, tomatoes, and Parmesan), blackened snapper, or jambalaya topped with crab, rabbit sausage, or alligator meat. Round out your meal with a slice of pecan pie. The loud hum of conversation and music (is that Eddy Arnold?) is punctuated with waiters' shouts to the open kitchen announcing an order of an oyster shooter single. Lots of wines by the glass, promptly refilled with a nod in the right direction. There's often a wait, whether you arrive early or *very* early (it closes at 4am). The top-notch waiters manage to look as if they're having as good a time as most of the guests. ■ *Underneath the Morrison St. Bridge; (503) 234-1324; 301 SE Morrison St, Portland; $; beer and wine; no credit cards; checks OK; dinner every day.* &

Le Canelet ★★ What Hawthorne—or any Portland neighborhood for that matter—really needed was a small, friendly bistro, with entrees under $15 and space for those seeking nothing more than a glass of wine and a nibble. Le Canelet delivered. The food is fine, ranging from an impressive veal medallion in Madeira to a flame chicken liver tart. The duck confit with ra~~spberry~~ tru~~lly~~, but never too sweet—is a specialty. The bi~~stro~~ attitude is enhanced by friendly service and by a nightly, $16 three-course special. ■ *On Hawthorne at 19th; (503) 232-0667; 1925 SE Hawthorne Blvd, Portland; $$; beer and wine; MC, V; local checks only; dinner Mon–Sat.* &

London Grill (Benson Hotel) ★★ In the hearts of many Portlanders and power lunchers, the London Grill occupies a permanent position. While Trader Vic's, its fellow Benson restaurant, remodels and reformats, the London Grill remains steady. The tableside cooking carts still glide across the room, the ingredients are still of highest quality, and the strains of the harpist still wash over the deep, comfortable armchairs at each table. Waiters, practiced in the art of tableside service, produce endearing versions of steak Diane and crêpes Suzette, and the crab cakes are thick with crabmeat. But in many cases, both innovation and flavoring seem to be restrained (okay, subtle menu changes reflect an interest in heart-healthy cuisine). The wine list is the longest in town, especially strong on French bottlings. ■ *SW Broadway at Oak St; (503) 295-4110; 309 SW Broadway, Portland; $$$; full bar; AE, DC, MC, V; checks OK; breakfast, lunch, dinner every day, brunch Sun.* &

Marco's Cafe and Espresso Bar ★★ In recent years Marco's, with its high ceilings, sunny dining rooms, and intriguing prints on the walls, has become something of a hangout in Multnomah. There's a rack of reading material by the front door, and you could easily lose yourself over a cappuccino and a newspaper until you remember the egg bread stuffed with apples and cinnamon and drenched with apple-flavored syrup. Evenings, Marco's turns into an imaginative and accomplished dinner operation with paella and pork medallions, for example, and inspirations ranging from Italy to Thailand. The desserts are Marco's own. Children fit right in. ▪ *Multnomah Blvd and 35th Ave; (503)245-0199; 7910 SW 35th Ave, Portland; $–$$; beer and wine; DC, MC, V; local checks only; breakfast, lunch, dinner every day.* &

Opus Too ★★ Opus Too's new chef has loosened things up considerably; where once the great slabs of mesquite-grilled meat or fresh seafood appeared only in cream or butter sauces, diners now may encounter weekly specials such as halibut in a spicy peanut sauce or pork chops sauced with figs, garlic, and Marsala. But fear not: the béarnaise and beurre rouge are still available, along with the shrewd hand at the grill that has always made the place work. The decor is urban cool—tile floor, dark-wood booths, and a long swivel-chair bar overlooking the open kitchen and grills. A terrific sourdough bread is part of the deal, as is the live jazz that floats in from Jazz de Opus next door. A respectable wine list, fine desserts, and piles of fettuccine. ▪ *NW Couch and 2nd, Old Town district; (503)222-6077; 33 NW 2nd Ave, Portland; $$; full bar; AE, DC, MC, V; local checks only; lunch Mon–Sat, dinner every day.* &

The Original Pancake House ★★ On Saturday morning the parking lot is jammed, and you can expect a 20-minute wait—*if* you get there early. This landmark restaurant hums from the time it opens at 7am practically until it closes in mid-afternoon. The sourdough flapjacks—from wine-spiked cherry to wheat germ to a behemoth apple pancake with a sticky cinnamon glaze—are made from scratch. A good bet is the egg-rich Dutch baby, which arrives looking like a huge, sunken birthday cake, dusted with powdered sugar and served with fresh lemon. Omelets big enough for two (made from a half-dozen eggs) arrive with a short stack. The service is cheerful and efficient; the coffee is the only disappointment. ▪ *Barbur Blvd exit of I-5 south; SW 24th and Barbur; (503)246-9007; 8600 SW Barbur Blvd, Portland; $; no alcohol; no credit cards; checks OK; breakfast, lunch Wed–Sun.* &

Portofino ★★ Proprietor and floor show, owner Carlo Rostagni swoops through the storefront dining room with style and Sambuca, welcoming arrivals and warmly commenting on the food and anything else. The place has gotten a bit fancier, and the menu expanded to include more seafood, but the most exciting dishes are the ones Rostagni whips up tableside, such as the zabaglione, an eggy, liqueur-drenched custard; gamberi al Sambuca, huge prawns sautéed in garlic and shallots and perched on toast points; or steak Diane. Rostagni has opened a new bistro in Lake Oswego. Fans worry that might limit Rostagni's presence here. We hope not, but if so, we'll just have to go to Lake Oswego for our entertainment. ■ *On SE 13th near Tacoma; (503)234-8259; 8075 SE 13th Ave, Portland; $$; beer and wine; MC, V; no checks; dinner Tues–Sat.* ⅋

The Ringside ★★ In 1994, the Ringside turned 50, and it celebrated by doing something wild—adding lamb chops to the menu. But a few changes around the edges aren't fooling anybody: people come here for beef and that's what they get—in large, juicy slabs. In this territory these steaks are hard to beat; for texture, color, flavor, and character, they're everything you could want from a hunk of steer. Still, it's the plump, light, slightly salty onion rings, made with Walla Walla sweets, that single-handedly made the Ringside famous—an order is essential. The greatest triumph of the 50th anniversary is the considerable improvement in the dessert offerings. The dignified black-jacketed and bow-tied waiters are eminently professional. ■ *2 blocks west of Civic Stadium; (503)223-1513; 2165 W Burnside, Portland; $$; full bar; AE, DC, MC, V; checks OK; dinner every day.* ⅋

Ron Paul Catering and Charcuterie ★★ The outposts on Broadway and Macadam have indisputably lifted Ron Paul from quaint takeout to thriving bistro, but we still like it best for a quick bite after a movie. A range of distinctive dishes keeps the menu interesting: barbecued chicken, spinach-mushroom lasagne, pan-fried oysters, lively salads, and some of the best specialty breads in town (try the rich, dark walnut wheat). Desserts, from the rhubarb pie with filo crust to the ultrarich Black Angus Cookies to the carrot cake with ricotta and raisins, rank high. Quality control here is an obvious priority: the kitchen cures the salmon, smokes the sausages, and mixes the pâtés. The service can be brusque, but you can always take your treats to go. ■ *NW corner of NE Broadway and 15th; (503)284-5347; 1441 NE Broadway, Portland.* ■ *SW Macadam at Carolina; (503)977-0313; 6141 SW Macadam Ave, Portland; $$; beer and wine; AE, MC, V; checks OK; continental breakfast Mon–Fri, lunch every day, dinner Mon–Sat, brunch Sat–Sun.* ⅋

Shakers ★★ Although there's a new owner, Portlanders still love this little throwback to the '50s with all its novelty salt and pepper shakers. In the past the breakfast menu always drew the largest crowd, and that hasn't changed much: Scottish oats served with a pitcher of milk, thick challah bread French toast, breakfast chilaquiles, and blue-corn pancakes. Lunch brings in those hungry for a bowl of mean Texas chili, hamburgers, and a frosty chocolate or vanilla shake. New owner Raf Nazario has revved up the dinner menu a bit with lots of pasta and a little Tex-Mex—racy grilled vegetable tacos. So now Pearl District neighbors stick around for dinner, too. ▪ *Pearl District; (503) 221-0011; 1212 NW Glisan, Portland; $; wine and beer; no credit cards; checks OK; breakfast, lunch Mon–Sat, dinner Tues–Sat.*

Thai Orchid ★★ Owners Na and Penny Saenguraiporn have a flair for the authentic, from their Evil Jungle Noodles to the piped-in Thai pop music. In their cheery storefront they consistently produce reasonably priced and more than reasonably spiced Thai food. The place looks so mild, you may be surprised with both the size and range of the menu and its powers of heat generation—a fact not lost on faithful take-out customers. Entrees tend to be more interesting than appetizers, especially seafood in chili sauce and deep-fried whole fish. Beef salad is pungent and mouth-clearing. ▪ *On W Burnside at NW 22nd Ave; (503) 226-4542; 2231 W Burnside St, Portland; $; beer and wine; MC, V; checks OK; lunch Mon–Fri, dinner every day.* &

Westmoreland Bistro and Wines ★★ Noted Northwest chefs Caprial and John Pence quietly grace this neighborhood with their inventions. Appetizers might include pan-fried ravioli with a roasted tomato sauce or mussels in curry broth with apples and Chinese sausage. Strong flavors carry through to the entrees as well: seared tuna with a black bean and smoked mushroom sauce, osso bucco with a dried cherry reduction, or bouillabaisse. Most dishes are successful, though a few run the risk of too many flavors packed onto one plate. Peruse the sizable retail wine supply; a $2 corkage fee gets any bottle from the shelf to your table. ▪ *Across from U.S. Bank; (503) 236-6457; 7015 SE Milwaukie Ave, Portland; $$; beer and wine; MC, V; checks OK; lunch, dinner Tues–Sat.*

Vat & Tonsure ★★ In a world that's continually redefining itself, people appreciate the Vat for staying the same. Few things ever change here—not the waiters, not the menu, not the background of rapturous classical and opera music. Owner/chef Rose-Marie Barbeau turns out perfectly seasoned game hens, rosemary-basted lamb chops, and buttery sautéed prawns. The lunch list doubles as the late-night menu, and such mainstays as bockwurst with sauerkraut, artichokes with caper mayonnaise, and cheese and bread go nicely with a pint of Bridgeport or a bottle of wine. Only one dessert—but one bite of the Vat's custard and you'll understand the beauty of simplicity. ▪ *1 block west of Broadway between Yamhill and Taylor; (503) 227-1845; 822 SW Park Ave, Portland; $$; beer and wine; no credit cards; checks OK; lunch, dinner Mon–Sat.* &

Zell's: An American Cafe ★★ Expect a warm welcome here, even on chilly weekend mornings when you may be forced to wait outside for a table: the awning is outfitted with heating elements, and with a hot cup of coffee to warm your hands, you may not notice the cold. Breakfast is the meal, and you'll begin it with a plate of house-baked scones; if there are children in your party they'll be cheerfully outfitted with toys and books and a snack of their own. Omelets might be filled with chanterelle mushrooms, pancakes with huckleberries, and the Portland Potatoes with enough flavor to keep your taste buds awake until dinner. This establishment boasts one of the few original soda fountains around—not a campy imitation. ■ *13 blocks east of the Morrison Bridge; (503) 239-0196; 1300 SE Morrison St, Portland; $; beer and wine; AE, MC, V; checks OK; breakfast, lunch every day.* ♿

Doris' Cafe ★ Doris' has become a meeting place in inner northeast Portland, and it carries a role wider than a kitchen; it's one of the few places around where black and white Portlanders regularly run into each other, and a pile of rib tips isn't the worst accompaniment for it. Unlike the tired little house that Doris' once called home, this location is a cool, attractive space with wood floors and high ceilings. Fortunately, nobody's updated the food—the smoky barbecue with the sauce more sweet than angry, the fried chicken that's lovely, fresh, and gently complex. Desserts vary, but the buttery pound cake and the mousselike sweet potato pie should not be missed. To its new space, Doris' has now added a bar; there's a destiny to matching beer and barbecue. ■ *Near Kirby exit off I-5 northbound; (503) 287-9249; 325 NE Russell, Portland; $; beer and wine; AE, MC, V; local checks only; lunch, dinner Mon–Sat.* ♿

Hunan ★ The specialties here have been on the menu from the beginning—and there must be a reason for that. After 15 years and several expansions, Hunan still produces some of Portland's most consistently good Chinese cooking—at a more reasonable cost than many of Portland's Peking palaces. The changes, for the most part, are more architectural than culinary; favorites, such as Lake T'ung T'ing Shrimp, dumplings in hot oil, and beef with orange flavor still grace the menu. One new offering—crispy shrimp in a creamy sauce—may delight you. The restaurant's versions of the spicy standards—General Tso's chicken, twice-cooked pork, chicken in tangy sauce—are pungent and massively popular. ■ *Between Washington and Alder on SW Broadway; (503) 224-8063; 515 SW Broadway, Portland; $$; full bar; MC, V; no checks; lunch, dinner every day.*

Jake's Grill ★ The Mick & Schmick folks (heretofore known for their way with seafood) now run the Governor Hotel dining room, and it seems a good match. The high-ceilinged room is done in the image of their other restaurants, but the emphasis here is on steak rather than salmon, and there's a big glass wall that lets you watch the chef meet your beef. If you waiver from the beef—not necessarily a good idea—the comfort food section on the menu offers chicken potpie and macaroni and cheese. Seafood dishes seem less reliable than at the organization's other operations, but the appetizers and desserts are reassuringly familiar. Maybe they just need a little more time. ■ *SW 10th St and Alder; (503)241-2100; 611 SW 10th St, Portland; $$; full bar; AE, DC, MC, V; checks OK; breakfast, lunch, dinner every day.* &

Kornblatt's ★ Big on bagels, Kornblatt's offers the best version of the holey bread around—and in dizzying varieties. The smoked fish does not dishonor the bagels, and here's where you'll find Portland's closest approximation of a *real* corned beef on rye—with a pickle bowl on the table providing support and atmosphere. Kornblatt's still hasn't figured out how to manage dinner entrees—which now include just a few hot gravied sandwiches and a deli omelet—though the cabbage borscht could easily turn a pastrami sandwich into dinner. ■ *NW 23rd near Glisan; (503)242-0055; 628 NW 23rd Ave, Portland; $; beer and wine; MC, V; checks OK; breakfast, lunch, dinner every day.* &

Marrakesh ★ Marrakesh has moved down a few blocks to join others on restaurant row (NW 21st Avenue). The new surroundings are every bit as exotic as the previous ones: low lights reveal tapestried walls and yards of fabric draped tentlike from the ceiling. Unfortunately, the food falls short of fabulous, but you'll probably be so occupied with the scene that you may not notice. Get comfortable on a cushion at one of the knee-high dining tables: you're here for a five-course royal feast. The meal begins with the customary finger-washing ceremony and ends with the sprinkling of orange water over your hands. In between, you eat without the benefit of utensils (cumin-and-coriander lentil soup, eggplant salad to start). The sweetened bastela royale (chicken pie) paves the way for your entree—maybe the lamb with eggplant or the braised hare in a rich cumin and paprika sauce. ■ *NW 21st and Northrup; (503) 248-9442; 1201 NW 21st Ave, Portland; $$; beer and wine; MC, V; checks OK; dinner every day.* &

Plainfield's Mayur ★ Portland's oldest Indian restaurant is also its fanciest and most expensive—more in the style of the subcontinent's swank, postcolonial eateries than its more indigenous and democratic diners and curry houses. The china, crystal, chandeliers, and white linen tablecloths announce an extensive (and nationally noted) wine list heavy with California chardonnays and cabernets, but beer or champagne might better complement the Mogul cuisine. The tandoori dishes, roasted in authentic style in a huge oven, are highlights. The biryanis, fragrant rice concoctions, are served with an intriguingly edible silver foil, which has been hammered thin, the management says, by Indian monks in the Himalayan foothills.

■ *1 block west of Civic Stadium; (503) 223-2995; 852 SW 21st Ave, Portland; $$; full bar; AE, DC, MC, V; checks OK; dinner every day.* &

Thien Hong ★ An erstwhile fast-food joint on outer Sandy Boulevard is now a popular hub for pho, the steaming bowls of Vietnamese noodle soup that keep the Formica tables crowded here late into the night. The place bustles with fans from Hollywood's Southeast Asian community and others who come to satisfy cravings for salad rolls and crunchy bites of pepper-salted squid. The large menu occasionally strays into Chinese territory, and steamed ginger chicken rarely misses. ■ *Sandy Blvd at NE 67th Ave; (503) 281-1247; 6749 NE Sandy Blvd, Portland; $; beer and wine; MC, V; no checks; lunch, dinner every day.*

LODGINGS

The Heathman Hotel ★★★★ The intimate, elegant Heathman has been long hailed as the best place to stay in Portland. While its appeal is broad—there are excellent business services, a central downtown location, fine artistic details—guests especially appreciate the meticulously courteous staff. This landmark hotel provides exceptional but low-key service from checkin to checkout. The common rooms are handsomely appointed with Burmese teak paneling, and the elegant lobby lounge is a great place to enjoy afternoon tea or evening jazz performances. Depending on your interests, you might be impressed by the video collection, the library (with author-signed volumes), or the fitness suite (personal trainer available). A strong supporter of the arts, the hotel itself features a stunning display of original artwork. Eighty guest rooms have an exclusive view of a fanciful Henk Pander mural on the east wall of the Arlene Schnitzer Concert Hall. And finally, you're just steps (or room service) away from one of the Northwest's few four-star restaurants (see review). ■ *SW Broadway at Salmon; (503) 241-4100 or (800) 551-0011; 1001 SW Broadway, Portland, OR 97205; $$$; AE, DC, MC, V; checks OK.* &

Hotel Vintage Plaza ★★★★ This refined, smart, newer hotel in the heart of the city is run by the Kimpton Group, and like many of the other Kimpton hotels, it is elegant but not opulent. We like the intimate scale of the Vintage Plaza (107 rooms), the inviting lobby, and the graciousness of the staff. Among the niceties that are standard at the Vintage Plaza are attentive bellhops who don't let you lift a thing, the crackling fire regularly stoked by the doorman, and the complimentary Oregon wines and classical piano in the early evening. Attention shows in details, like hidden televisions, plush towels, and the fact that there are lots of convenient places to stow your belongings. Best rooms are the stunning bi-level suites or the starlight rooms with greenhouse-style windows (ask for one of the larger corner rooms). All rooms come with complimentary shoe shine, nightly turn-down service, morning coffee and baked goods in the lobby, and the newspaper delivered to your door. Pazzo Ristorante on the main floor serves excellent Northern Italian cuisine in a variety of settings (see review). ■ *SW Broadway at Washington; (503)228-1212 or (800)243-0555; 422 SW Broadway, Portland, OR 97205; $$$; AE, DC, MC, V; checks OK.* &

 The Benson ★★★ Still the first choice for politicos and film stars, the Benson was for many years the only classy lodging in town. A $17 million restoration almost 80 years after lumber tycoon Simon Benson built the original hotel was a gallant attempt to return it to its original stature. The marbled elegance of the palatial lobby has returned (stamped-tin ceiling, mammoth chandeliers, stately columns, and panels of carved Circassian walnut imported from Russia). Now owned by WestCoast Hotels, the 287-room Benson distinguishes itself with stunning architecture and an opulent interior. Characterized by service that's completely competent, if somewhat impersonal, the Benson is, literally and figuratively, really quite corporate. A brusqueness that may go unnoticed by the hurried businessman can leave a more leisurely traveler feeling chilled. ■ *SW Broadway at Washington; (503) 228-2000 or (800)426-0670; 309 SW Broadway, Portland OR 97205; $$$; AE, DC, MC, V; checks OK.* &

Governor Hotel ★★★ If the Heathman Hotel celebrates art and the Hotel Vintage Plaza celebrates wine, this hotel—the newest of Portland's luxury lodgings—celebrates history. Nowhere is that more apparent than in the hotel's clubby lobby, which features a long and dramatic mural depicting scenes from the Lewis and Clark journey, Arts and Crafts–style furniture, and yards of mahogany. Welcome to Wild West grandeur. The rooms are a departure from the lobby: done in cool Northwest earth tones, they feature standard but not altogether unattractive hotel furnishings (although there is an irritating lack of places to set things). Some rooms have a whirlpool tub; suites feature fireplaces, wet bars, and balconies. Almost all the rooms have big windows, but don't expect much from the view; the hotel's location is more convenient than scenic. The list of amenities is long; among them is access to the Princeton Athletic Club and the business center, and 24-hour maid service. Even the restaurant, Jake's Grill, has history: Jake's Famous Crawfish, a centenarian down the block,

is its parent. ■ *SW 10th and Alder; (503)224-3400 or (800)
554-3456; 611 SW 10th Ave, Portland, OR 97205; $$$; AE,
DC, MC, V; checks OK.*

Heron Haus B&B ★★★ Set in the exclusive hills overlooking
the city, Heron Haus is just blocks away from Portland's trendi-
est restaurants and hippest boutiques. The common areas in
this luxurious 7,500-square-foot English Tudor home include
a bright, cushy-sofaed living room, a mahogany-paneled li-
brary, and a wicker-furnished sunroom that overlooks the out-
door swimming pool. Five guest rooms (one has a bath with a
seven-nozzle shower) are comfortably furnished with sitting ar-
eas, telephones, and TVs. The extraordinary bath in the Kulia
Room features an elevated spa with a city view and all the
deluxe bathing accoutrements one could want—from his-and-
her robes to a rubber ducky. Don't expect a lot of gushy fuss-
ing-over by the innkeeper during your stay—guests are kindly
left to their own devices. And don't get your heart set on a par-
ticular room. Continental breakfasts are served. ■ *NW 25th
and Johnson; (503)274-1846; 2545 NW Westover Rd, Port-
land, OR 97210; $$$; MC, V; checks OK.*

The Lion and the Rose ★★★ One of Portland's newer B&Bs,
housed in a 1906 Queen Anne mansion in the Irvington district, the Lion and the Rose is truly elegant. The three hosts
let few details go unchecked—from the candles in the baths
to beverages in the refrigerator to the extra blankets upon request. Magazines are current, cookies are fresh, the fire crack-
les. Depending on your particular room, the interior might
seem rather masculine (the Starina, with its high-back bed and
linens of rust and gold, exemplifies the Ralph Lauren look) or
particularly feminine (the lavender-and-white Lavonna room,
with window seats in the cupola, evokes Laura Ashley), but
it all feels indisputably *decorated*. Breakfast is lavish and a
lovely tea is offered from 4 until 6pm. ■ *1 block north of NE
Broadway on 15th Ave; (503)287-9245 or (800)955-1647;
1810 NE 15th Ave, Portland, OR 97212; $$$; AE, MC, V;
checks OK.*

RiverPlace Hotel ★★★ If you're looking for a room with a
view, look no further than RiverPlace. The only downtown lux-
ury hotel that fronts the busy Willamette River—and the boat
show that comes with it—the pink-hued RiverPlace (run by
WestCoast Hotels) is lovely to look at and glorious to look out
from. The better among the 84 rooms—doubles, suites, and
condominiums—face the water or look north across park
lawns to the downtown cityscape. Inside are plush furnishings,
TVs concealed in armoires, generously sized bathrooms, and
a lively night scene from which you can watch the roller
bladers whiz by. Complimentary continental breakfast can be
brought to your room, along with *The New York Times*. Use of

the adjacent RiverPlace Athletic Club is extra, but there's also plenty of opportunity for exercise right outside: wide, paved paths lead from the hotel through the fountains and monuments of Tom McCall Waterfront Park. No doubt, the Esplanade Restaurant is a stunning location for a meal (see review). ■ *Harbor Way off Front Ave; (503)228-3233 or (800)227-1333; 1510 SW Harbor Way, Portland, OR 97201; $$$; AE, DC, MC, V; checks OK.* &

Portland Guest House ★★ Owner Susan Gisvold has created an urban retreat just off NE Broadway. White carpets and antique linens lend the classiness of an intimate hotel. Gisvold doesn't live here, but she's usually around long enough to advise you on Portland doings and make sure the flowers in the window boxes are watered. In the morning, she'll drop in to serve a fine breakfast of fresh fruit, scones, and an omelet. Each of the seven rooms has its own phone and clock (items not standard in many B&Bs). When the weather's warm, the garden brick patio is the spot to be; when it's not, relax in the simple parlor. ■ *NE Broadway and 15th; (503)282-1402; 1720 NE 15th Ave, Portland, OR 97212; $$; AE, DC, MC, V; checks OK.*

Portland's White House ★★ This place looks a bit like its Washington, D.C., namesake, complete with fountains, carriage house, and circular driveway. It was built of solid Honduras mahogany by a local timber baron, Robert F. Lytle; the Japanese maples flanking Greek columns at the entrance enhance the mansion's imposing stature. Inside are six exquisite guest rooms, each with its own bath. The Canopy Room is especially inviting, with its large canopied bed and bright bath. The Garden Room's private terrace is nice in summertime. Tea is served late afternoon; evenings, wander down to the formal parlor for a glass of sherry or a game of chess. ■ *Coliseum exit from I-5, head east to NE 22nd; (503)287-7131; 1914 NE 22nd Ave, Portland, OR 97212; $$$; MC, V; checks OK.*

Sheraton Airport Hotel ★★ For the traveling businessperson, the airport's Sheraton tops the list. For one thing, it's located—literally—on the airport grounds (FedEx planes load up next door, and arrival and departure times are broadcast at the hotel's main entrance). Inside, amenities abound: everything from meeting rooms and a complete, complimentary business center (IBMs, printers, fax machine, and secretarial services) to an indoor swimming pool, sauna, and workout room. The executive suites consider the personal needs of the businessperson, providing two phones, sitting areas, jacks for computer hookup, and pullout makeup mirrors in the bathrooms. Mount Hood stands tall to the east, but you'd never know it from the airport-facing rooms. ■ *On Airport Way just before the terminal; (503)281-2500 or (800)325-3535; 8235*

NE Airport Way, Portland, OR 97220; $$$; AE, DC, MC, V; checks OK. &

Mallory Motor Hotel ★ Located just out of the downtown core, but only a 15-minute stroll to Nordstrom, the beloved Mallory remains the favorite lodging of many regular visitors to the City of Roses—and has been since they were kids. It's an older establishment in every sense—from the massive hunks of ornate wooden lobby furniture to the senior staff. It's also one of the best bargains in town, starting at $60 for a double and topping out at $100 for a suite—so it's a good idea to reserve a room far in advance. The Mallory sits in a quiet area where parking is easy and mostly meter-free. Have breakfast in the restaurant, dinner downtown. Simple, charming touches and almost motherly service. ■ *Corner of SW 15th and Yamhill; (503)223-6311 or (800)228-8657; 729 SW 15th Ave, Portland, OR 97205; $; AE, DC, MC, V; checks OK.* &

Marriott Residence Inn/Lloyd Center ★ This hotel near the Lloyd Center Cinema has 168 rooms that you might mistake, from the outside at least, for apartments. It's geared toward longer stays (4–7 days): each room has a full kitchen and most have wood-burning fireplaces. Extras include a continental breakfast served in the lobby and a grocery-shopping service. There isn't much of a view and there's no restaurant, but the rooms are more spacious than usual. A couple of Jacuzzis and a heated outdoor pool are provided for guest use. An extra $4 gains you access to the Lloyd Center Athletic Club seven blocks away. ■ *2 blocks east of Lloyd Center on Multnomah; (503)288-1400; 176 NE Multnomah, Portland, OR 97232; $$$; AE, DC, MC, V; checks OK.* &

Red Lion at Lloyd Center ★ Its daunting size (a map in the lobby directs you to the three restaurants) and proximity to the Lloyd Center, Memorial Coliseum, and the Convention Center make this corporate hotel a good choice for eastside conventions or seminars. With 476 guest rooms, it's Oregon's second-largest hotel (the Portland Marriott is slightly bigger), outfitted with a number of well-organized meeting rooms, an outdoor pool, a workout room, and a courtesy airport van. Reserve an east-facing room above the fifth floor for a view of Mount Hood. The hotel's revamped restaurant, Maxi's, has been winning praise recently, turning out better-than-average Northwest cuisine. ■ *Lloyd Center/Weidler exit from I-5; (503)281-6111 or (800)547-8010; 1000 NE Multnomah St, Portland, OR 97232; $$$; AE, DC, MC, V; checks OK.* &

FOREST GROVE

Pacific University is probably why most people come here, and the towering firs on the small campus do justice to the town's name. But there's also quite a collection of local wineries now, making the area worth exploring, perhaps on your way to the ocean. South of town on Highway 47 is the huge new **Montinore Vineyards**, (503)359-5012, which has a fancy tasting room and wines that are improving with each vintage. In nearby Gaston, **Elk Cove Vineyards**, (503)985-7760, has a spectacular site for a tasting room perched on a forested ridge, and **Kramer Vineyards**, (503)662-4545, is a tiny place in the woods with tasty pinot noir and excellent raspberry wine. West of Forest Grove on Highway 8, on the site of a historic Oregon winery, **Laurel Ridge Winery**, (503)359-5436, specializes in sparkling wines and also makes good sauvignon blanc. **Shafer Vineyards**, (503)357-6604, has produced some fine, ageable chardonnays, and **Tualatin Vineyards**, (503)357-5005, produces exquisite chardonnay, as well as a tasty Müller Thurgau. Finally, just outside of town you can sample sake from **Momokawe Sake**, (503)357-7056, a Japanese producer building a new Oregon brewery.

RESTAURANTS

El Torero ★ You may have a tough time getting past the terrific, light, crisp chips, but if you do, you'll probably end up devouring all your excellent homemade-tasting refritos. For the main course, stick with the specialty beef items—the massive serving of carnitas de res is super. The decor is college hangout, but the service is very friendly and the English (authentically) limited. ■ *Just off Hwy 8 on Main; (503)359-8471; 2009 Main, Forest Grove; $; full bar; MC, V; checks OK; lunch, dinner every day.* ᴦ

BEAVERTON

RESTAURANTS

Ikenohana ★★ The suburban strip mall storefront opens into a modest space (with a tiny sushi bar in one corner) where Japanese paper screens and lanterns give a private and charming feel, and even when it's busy it's not noisy. The menu allows a wide range of options, from sushi and sashimi to tempura, katsu dishes, teriyaki and noodles. You can't go wrong here: the sashimi is elegantly presented and very fresh and firm. A plentiful plate of sushi includes wonderful mackerel and eel. Even the simple yakisoba noodles are spicy and cooked just right. If you look like you don't know how to mix the mustard sauce for the sushi, the waitress will show you. ■ *Shopping center at Murray and Allen; (503)646-1267; 14308 SW Allen Blvd, Beaverton; $; beer and wine; MC, V; no checks; lunch Tues–Fri, dinner Tues–Sun.* ᴦ

McCormick's Fish House and Bar ★★ Chef Jon Wirtis has maintained the suburban outpost of the M&S empire as a solid seafood house, with few nonmaritime options. With the same fresh list—and the same knowing, professional service—as the other links in the chain, McCormick's Fish House produces solid, skillful food that sometimes surprises. And every Thursday night, Wirtis busts out with a Jewish menu, offering the brisket or gefilte fish of his roots. The mood and the feeling are more casual than downtown, but don't take that as a sign that you can confidently walk in without a reservation on weekends, on Thursday nights, or for Sunday brunch. ■ *About a mile east on Hwy 10 from Hwy 217; (503) 643-1322; 9945 SW Beaverton-Hillsdale Hwy, Beaverton; $$; full bar; AE, DC, MC, V; checks OK; lunch Mon–Fri, dinner every day, Sun brunch.* ⑤

Swagat ★★ This little suburban ranch house bursts with wonderful aromas and noisy, happy crowds. It's the spicy food of southern India that packs them in, and the flavors will dazzle (and sometimes scorch) your palate. Start your meal with crispy deep-fried pakoras and move on to tender roasted meats from the tandoori oven or subtle, saffron-flavored rice biryanis. Sample the cuisine with the thali dinner (the heat factor ranges from cool cucumber salad to spicy lentils to raging hot vegetables). The range of textures and flavors is amazing—and the lunch buffet, a true feast. Be prepared for service that is neither speedy nor especially warm. The exotic foods, however, are worth savoring. ■ *Off Beaverton-Hillsdale Hwy on SW 109th; (503) 626-3000; 4325 SW 109th Ave, Beaverton; $; beer and wine; AE, DC, MC, V; local checks only; lunch, dinner every day.*

Hall Street Bar & Grill ★ With high, vaulted ceilings and oak floors, Hall Street looks like a typical fern bar. But the kitchen—even after recent simplifications—offers some skillful surprises. Burning under the grill are local vineyard cuttings, giving salmon and seafood specials an inviting, tangy undertone. Off the grill, fish meets ingredients like lime, ginger, basil, hazelnuts, and avocado salsa. The rock salt–roasted prime rib is a permanent menu fixture—a favorite that has been known to sell out quickly—and the grilled steaks are terrific. A superb burnt cream with a hard sugar crust leads the strong list of desserts; the wine list emphasizes California and Northwest wines. ■ *Take Cedar Hills Blvd exit off Hwy 26, turn left at Hall, 1 block; (503) 641-6161; 3775 SW Hall Blvd, Beaverton; $$; full bar; AE, DC, MC, V; checks OK; lunch Mon–Fri, dinner every day.* ⑤

LODGINGS

Greenwood Inn ★ Billed as a city hotel with resort-style comfort, the 253-room complex delivers, for the most part, on its promises (especially since it's now under the wing of the

Heathman Management Group). True, the primary draw for businessmen is the hotel's location—just off Highway 217, a few exits away from the high-tech offices of the Silicon Forest. There are two outdoor swimming pools in the verdant courtyard and a few of the suites have Jacuzzis and kitchens. There's been an attempt to sharpen the Pavilion Restaurant with a new chef and a revamped menu. The overhaul may take a little while to get completed—and consistent—but the potential is there (especially with the Heathman in the background). Let's keep an eye on it. ■ *Hwy 217 and Allen Blvd; (503) 643-7444 or (800) 289-1300; 10700 SW Allen Blvd, Beaverton, OR 97005; $$; full bar; AE, DC, MC, V; checks OK; breakfast, lunch, dinner every day, Sun brunch.* &

LAKE OSWEGO

RESTAURANTS

Thai Villa ★★ The hot thermometer ranges from "calm" to "volcano" (with little in between). A popular Lake Oswego restaurant, Thai Villa specializes in pungent soups served swirling in a moat around a pillar of flame, and a wide range of seafood dishes. The chef is handy with basil, garlic, and subtle hints of sweetness, and the prices are reasonable, especially on a cost-per-tingle basis. It's a good thing this place sits near the Lake Oswego fire department because someday someone is going to take an innocent bite of volcano gang galee (chicken curry with potatoes) and self-combust. ■ *Downtown Lake Oswego; (503) 635-6164; 340 N 1st St, Lake Oswego; $; beer and wine; MC, V; no checks; lunch Mon–Fri, dinner every day.*

Riccardo's Restaurant & Espresso Bar ★ Owner/chef Richard Spaccarelli is a serious oenophile, as the over 300 bottles of Italian-only wine (and Riccardo's own wine shop across the way) attest. That list benefits from some of the most knowledgeable wine discussion around. The kitchen produces some intriguing pastas and an impressively meaty veal chop, although dishes can sometimes be a bit uneven and the service less than perfect. This is one of the few places around where you can chase your pasta with a glass of grappa—or a selection of them. The outside dining area blossoms in nice weather. ■ *Lake Grove; (503) 636-4104; 16035 SW Boones Ferry Rd, Lake Oswego; $$; full bar; AE, DC, MC, V; checks OK; lunch Mon–Fri, dinner Mon–Sat.* &

Wu's Open Kitchen ★ The flames leaping high behind the windows in the back of the restaurant are firing the large woks in the kitchen, and you can watch the cooks deftly preparing dishes while you wait for dinner. Chef Jimmy Wu's extended family helps run this place, serving a variety of spicy and not-so-spicy dishes from all over China (but the cooks reckon on the American palate—the hot dishes won't wilt too many taste buds). Seafood is fresh, vegetables are crisp, sauces are light, service is speedy and attentive. Kids will feel right at home, and parents will appreciate the modest prices. Prepare for a wait on weekends—it has been discovered by locals. At press time a second restaurant opened its doors in Tigard. ▪ *Shopping center off Boone's Ferry Rd, just east of I-5; (503)636-8899; 17773 SW Boone's Ferry Rd, Lake Oswego;* ▪ *12180 SW Scholls Ferry Rd, Tigard; (503)579-8899; $; full bar; MC, V; checks OK; lunch, dinner every day.* ⅁

MILWAUKIE

RESTAURANTS

Thai Restaurant ★★ If you look quickly, you might think it's still a fast-food restaurant. But when you connect with Emerald Pork and its spinach and peanut sauce; with Panang Nuea, beef in a blast of fiery red curry; or with a sizzling salad of grilled shrimp with chile and lemon grass, you may be transported, culinarily speaking, from this location in an old fast-food joint on a street populated largely with *new* fast-food joints. ▪ *Milwaukie/Gladstone; (503)786-0410; 14211 SE McLoughlin Blvd, Milwaukie; $; beer and wine; MC, V; no checks; lunch, dinner Tues–Sun.*

Buster's Smokehouse Texas-Style Bar-Be-Que ★ Take a deep whiff. The wood-smoke ovens leave their mark on both the meat and the atmosphere. Brisket, links, chicken, beef, and pork ribs all pass through the cooker and come out estimably smoky and juicy. The barbecue sauces have a sweet brown-sugar base and come in three temps. Have a beer with the hottest. Accompaniments are simple: fries, slaw, beans, and stuffed jalapeño peppers—for devils only. Equal emphasis on barbecue essentials at both the original Milwaukie location and at the Gresham branch (1355 E Burnside, Gresham; (503)667-4811). The newer Buster's in Tigard (11419 SW Pacific Hwy, Tigard; (503)452-8384) features a mesquite broiler, for those of fainter disposition. ▪ *2 miles north of I-205, take Oregon City exit; (503)652-1076; 17883 SE McLoughlin Blvd, Milwaukie; $; beer and wine; MC, V; local checks only; lunch, dinner every day.* ⅁

Mediterranean Grill ★ Joe Wisher spent years traveling the Mediterranean and returned to open a restaurant overlooking a 7-Eleven in Milwaukie. The results? A tangy orange-cured salmon fillet or a chick-pea pancake in a veal stock sauce, and you might get as far from the Mediterranean as a pork Normande. With luck, the baked apple with caramel and mascarpone will be available at the finish. And despite the Slurpees down the hill, this is a very comfortable restaurant with the feel of a seaside villa enhanced by the stucco walls and an extensive display of Mediterranean artwork. Apparently, Wisher didn't just pick up recipes. ■ *Park Ave in Milwaukie, between McLoughlin and Oatfield; (503)654-7039; 2818 SE Park Ave, Milwaukie; $$; full bar; AE, MC, V; local checks only; lunch and dinner Tues–Sun, Sun brunch.* ⅃

GRESHAM

RESTAURANTS

Roland's ★★ The best reason to go to Gresham since MAX. Roland Blasi's traditional continental cuisine—sizable portions and strong flavors, gathered from his cooking odyssey through four continents—has taken root in Gresham. Roland's is a very personal restaurant in feel and menu; Blasi draws ideas from the full range of European cooking, and comes up with some of his own. So you're offered not only a pungent gypsy chicken, but also a heartwarming pasta Angelo made with Italian sausage, and a deep, fragrant onion soup. ■ *Right off Powell (Hwy 26); 2 blocks from downtown Gresham; (503)665-7215; 155 SE Vista, Gresham; $$; beer and wine; MC, V; local checks only; dinner Tues–Sat.* ⅃

WEST LINN

RESTAURANTS

Bugatti's Ristorante ★★ Lydia Bugatti and John Cress's endearing Italian neighborhood restaurant features seasonal foods and a menu that changes every few weeks. Anytime, keep watch for rigatoni carbonara and spaghetti frutti di mare. There's a nice olive oil spiked with garlic for bread-dipping, but save room for dazzling desserts like the cloudlike tiramisu. The place has picked up a strong endorsement from Trailblazer coach and New Jersey Italian food aficionado P.J. Carlesimo, who hangs out here frequently. ■ *South of Lake Oswego on Hwy 43, ½ mile past Marylhurst College; (503)636-9555; 18740 Willamette Dr, West Linn; $$; beer and wine; MC, V; local checks only; dinner every day.*

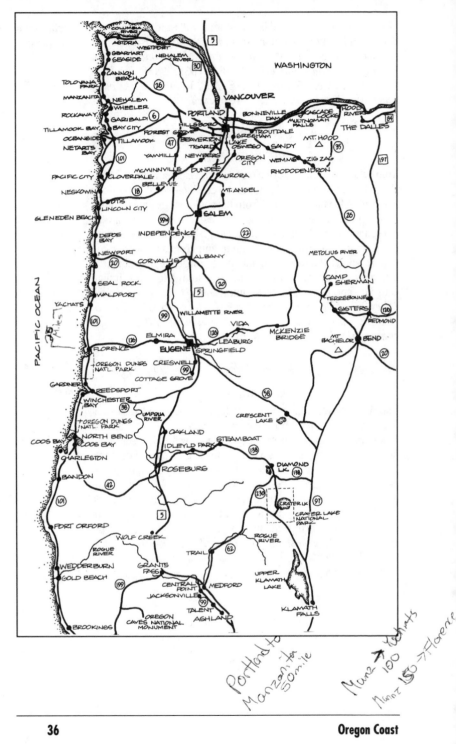

Oregon Coast

Oregon Coast

*From Astoria (at the mouth of the Columbia River),
a southward route down the coast.*

ASTORIA

Founded in 1811 by John Jacob Astor's fur traders, Astoria lays
claim to being the oldest permanent American settlement west
of the Rockies. Today this town at the mouth of the Columbia
River is like a museum without walls. Well-maintained Victorian homes line the hillside at Franklin, Grand, and Irving avenues—testimony to the town's heyday as a salmon-canning
and shipping center. The bustling waterfront—once the locale
of canneries and river steamers—is now an active port for
oceangoing vessels and fishing boats.

Astoria likes to tout its history (and not only with its architecture). The **Columbia River Maritime Museum** (1792
Marine Drive, (503)325-2323) is the finest of its kind in the
Northwest. Restored small craft are displayed in the Great Hall,
and seven thematic galleries depict different aspects of the region's maritime history. The lightship *Columbia*, the last of its
kind on the Pacific Coast, is moored outside (there's a self-
guided tour). Named for a prominent 19th-century businessman and Columbia River bar pilot, the **Captain George Flavel
House** (8th and Duane streets, (503)325-2563) is the city's best
example of ornate Queen Anne architecture. Both it and the restored **Heritage Museum** (8 blocks away at 1618 Exchange
Street, (503)325-2203) feature local history. Six miles southwest of Astoria, off Highway 101, Lewis and Clark's 1805–06
winter encampment is re-created at the **Fort Clatsop National
Memorial**, (503)861-2471. Besides audiovisuals and exhibits in

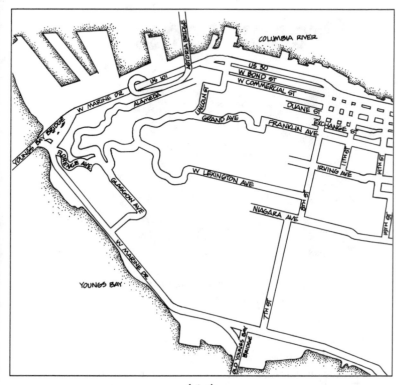

Astoria

the visitors center, there are living history demonstrations (musket firing, candle-making) during the summer.

For a breathtaking panorama of the Columbia River estuary, the Pacific Ocean, and more, climb the 160 steps of the **Astoria Column**, which sits atop the city's highest point, Coxcomb Hill. To get there, drive to the top of 16th Street and follow the signs.

Josephson's Smokehouse (106 Marine Drive, (503)325-2190) prepares superb alder-smoked salmon, tuna, and sturgeon, and serves cups of clam chowder. Astoria Coffee Co. (1154 Commercial Street, (503)325-7173) is the place for local chit-chat. Astoria's intelligentsia frequent Ricciardi Gallery (108 10th Street, (503)325-5450), which offers pleasing local and regional art. Parnassus Books (234 10th Street, (503)325-1363) is a good browse.

Fort Stevens State Park, 20 minutes northwest of Astoria off Highway 101, (503)861-1671, is a 3,500-acre outdoor wonderland of paved bike paths, forest trails, a freshwater lake, and uncrowded beaches—including the permanent resting spot of the hulk of the *Peter Iredale*, wrecked in 1906. The 604 campsites make Fort Stevens Oregon's largest publicly owned campground. Within the park, the South Jetty lookout tower, perched at Oregon's northwesternmost point, is a supreme storm-watching spot. It also marks the start of the Oregon Coast Trail, which traverses sandy beaches and forested headlands all the way to the California border.

Approximately 48 eagles feed and roost at **Twilight Eagle Sanctuary**, 8 miles east of Astoria (off Highway 30 on Burnside Road). The **Jewell elk refuge** is an area of rolling meadows, at times populated by hundreds of elk; 26 miles east of town on Highway 202, (503)755-2264. Salmon- and bottom-fishing trips leave from the West End mooring basin, just west of the interstate bridge.

RESTAURANTS

Columbian Cafe ★★ The more publicity the Columbian gets (and it gets plenty), the more crowded it becomes. But this small, vegetarian-oriented cafe continues to be Astoria's best bet for good grub. Be prepared for long waits, cramped quarters, erratic hours, uneven service, an eccentric chef, and great food—perhaps the finest seafood and pasta dishes on the Oregon Coast. If you're feeling frisky, order the Chef's Mercy, an eclectic combination of the day's best (and freshest) ingredients. ■ *11th St and Marine Dr, next to the movie theater; (503)325-2233; 1114 Marine Dr, Astoria; $; beer and wine; no credit cards; checks OK; breakfast, lunch Mon–Sat, dinner Wed–Sat.* ♿

▼

Astoria

Restaurants

▲

Cafe Uniontown ★ A new chef *can* make a difference. Just ask owners Jim and Regina Wilkins, who watched their cafe slip into mediocrity until Ira Mittelman came on the scene. And now—well, this place is a culinary adventure. Enjoy a gravlox appetizer, and then a 10-greens salad laced with feta, walnuts, and sundried-tomato vinaigrette, served with bread and a red-pepper pesto. Select one of the stunning entrees, such as the salmon lasagne with pine-nut cream sauce, or the snapper with an avocado purée. Rich wood paneling decorates the two dining rooms; the lounge is a visual delight. The cafe is also getting a reputation as a live-music hotspot. ■ *Underneath the interstate bridge on Marine Dr; (503)325-8708; 218 W Marine Dr, Astoria; $$; full bar; AE, MC, V; local checks only; lunch, dinner Tues–Sat (dinner Sun in summer).* ♿

Rio Cafe ★ The Mexican-food pipeline has finally reached Astoria, but instead of the usual Tex-Mex fare, this gaily decorated cantina offers inspired south-of-the-border cuisine. Salads feature assorted fruits and veggies, tiny shrimp, and a zingy jalapeño dressing. Three snappy salsas are a perfect match for the huge, handcrafted, crispy chips called totopos. And the Pescado Rojo—fresh sole or cod—is lightly breaded and grilled with a hot-and-sassy red chile and garlic sauce. If you're hankering for more, check out the Mexican specialty foods sold next door. ▪ *On 9th, a block from the Columbia River; (503)325-2409; 125 9th St, Astoria; $; beer and wine; MC, V; checks OK; lunch, Mon–Sat, dinner Thurs–Sat.* &

Victoria Dahl's ★ Situated in a seedy section of town, Victoria Dahl's (named after the owner's grandmother) is a beautifully restored restaurant with a gorgeous interior. The mostly Italian menu emphasizes fresh seafood and pasta. The prawns a caponata features succulent sautéed shrimp served over fettuccine with a luscious eggplant relish. Seafood fettucine showcases correctly cooked bay shrimp, clams, and oysters, with olive oil, garlic overtones, and a light alfredo sauce. Willapa oysters are sautéed, then topped with pesto and Parmesan. A gem in the rough. ▪ *On the main drag, on the east side of town; (503)325-7109; 2921 Marine Dr, Astoria; $$; beer and wine; DC, MC, V; checks OK; lunch Tues–Sun, dinner Tues–Sat (call for winter hours).* &

The Ship Inn An Astoria waterfront institution, this congenial and crowded eatery, operated by English expatriates Jill and Fenton Stokeld, is home to some great fish 'n' chips. The fish is double-dipped in a delicately seasoned batter and never overcooked. The chips are made from large potato slices. Somehow, neither is greasy, and both go down easily with a pint of Watney's (on tap). Ask for a window table, where you can watch bar and river pilots get on and off oceangoing vessels in the river channel just a hundred yards away. No reservations are accepted, but a hospitable bar affords a cozy (but smoky) waiting area. ▪ *Just off the main drag, on the waterfront at the foot of 2nd St; (503)325-0033; 1 2nd St, Astoria; $$; full bar; MC, V; checks OK; lunch, dinner every day.* &

LODGINGS

Rosebriar Hotel ★★ At the turn of the century, the Rosebriar was a private residence. Next it became a convent and then a halfway house for the mentally disabled. Now in its finest reincarnation, the place is a rambling, 11-room inn. Guest rooms, though generally small, are beautifully furnished and have private baths. A full breakfast is included in the reasonable rates (beginning at $49). The common rooms are spacious and homey, and the outside grounds afford a gardenlike setting and a view of the Columbia River. All within easy walking distance of downtown. ▪ *Franklin and 14th; (503)325-7427 or (800)487-0224; 636 14th St, Astoria, OR 97103; $; MC, V; checks OK.*

Crest Motel ★ With 40 rooms sited on a forested bluff overlooking the Columbia River, the Crest offers the best motel view in town. It's at the east edge of Astoria, back from the highway and therefore quiet—except, of course, for the sound of foghorns, which on winter evenings bellow up the hillside from the ship traffic below. In the large backyard, you can recline in lawn chairs and enjoy a bird's-eye view of the in- and outgoing tankers and freighters, or unwind in a gazebo-enclosed whirlpool. Pets welcome; so is smoking in one section.

▪ *2 miles east of downtown; (503) 325-3141; 5366 Leif Erikson Dr, Astoria, OR 97103; $$; AE, DC, MC, V; no checks.*

Franklin Street Station ★ The location, two blocks from downtown on a rather ordinary street lacking greenery, could be better (especially in a town known for its trees). But the house itself has style and elegance. A local shipbuilder constructed the home at the turn of the century; lavish woodwork attests to his fondness for local forest products. The interior is exquisitely appointed with Victorian furnishings, while frilly drapes frame the windows. There are six guest rooms. Two rooms look out to the river and have their own decks. An attic room, the Captain's Quarters, has the best view and its own living room. Unfortunately, the owners do not live on-site, and therefore are not always available. ▪ *Between 11th and 12th on Franklin; (503) 325-4314 or (800) 448-1098; 1140 Franklin St, Astoria, OR 97103; $$; AE, MC, V; checks OK.*

▼

GEARHART

Surely Gearhart, with its assortment of beachfront, weathered-wood homes in shades of gray and white, is the town with the most (and the best) examples of Oregon Coast architecture. Fashionable Portlanders put their summer cottages here—some of which are substantial dwellings—when the coast was first "discovered." Unlike other coastal towns, Gearhart is mostly residential. Razor-clam digging is popular, and many gas stations (located along Highway 101) rent shovels. The wide beach is backed by lovely dunes. Gearhart Golf Course, which opened in 1892, is the second-oldest course in the West—a 6,089-yard layout with sandy soil that dries quickly; open to the public, (503) 738-3538.

RESTAURANTS

Pacific Way Bakery and Cafe ★ This airy cafe, with hardwood floors, lots of windows, hip service, cool sounds, and plenty of espresso, is the only restaurant in downtown (such as it is) Gearhart. It continues to thrive on a mix of suspender-and-clam-shovel locals and out-of-town "gearheads"—the BMW-and-summer-beachfront-home crowd who come to hang out, hobnob, and sample the best pastries and breads on the northern Oregon coast. Lunch fare is also fine, including the Greek sandwich, a lusty affair with gobs of salami, olives, and cheese; and the curried chicken salad featuring poached chicken breast, fruits, nuts, greens, and a tangy curry dressing. ▪ *Downtown*

Gearhart, corner of Cottage and Pacific Way; (503) 738-0245; 601 Pacific Way, Gearhart; $; beer and wine; MC, V; checks OK; continental breakfast, lunch, dinner Wed–Sun. ♿

SEASIDE

One hundred years ago, affluent Portland beach-goers rode Columbia River steamers to Astoria, then hopped a stagecoach to Seaside, the Oregon Coast's first resort town. The place has become more crowded ever since (knotty summer traffic is second only to Lincoln City). The hordes mill along Broadway, eyeing the entertainment parlors, taffy concession, and bumper cars, and then emerge at **the Prom**, the 2-mile-long cement "boardwalk" that's ideal for strolling.

Before you head for the Prom, browse the shelves at Charlie's Turnaround Books (111 Broadway, (503)738-3211). The Little New Yorker on Broadway (604 Broadway, (503)738-5992) doles out two-fisted meatball sandwiches, Italian specialties, and the best cheesecake around.

Activities. Surf fishing is popular, particularly at the south end of town in the cove area. Steelhead and salmon can be taken (in season) from the Necanicum River, which flows through town. Occasional minus tides provide good razor clamming along the wide, flat beach. Sunset Empire Park and Recreation District, headquartered at Sunset Pool, 1140 E Broadway, (503)738-3311, offers $2.25 lap swims and information about activities from biathlons to seasonal outdoor concerts. Quatat Marine Park, downtown on the Necanicum River, is a relaxing picnic spot and the setting for free summer concerts. Surfers head for "the Point" at the south edge of town to catch the finest left-handed waves north of Santa Barbara.

South of Seaside, a 7-mile trail (that begins at the end of Sunset Boulevard) winds over **Tillamook Head**, high above the water—part of Ecola State Park (primitive camping facilities only)—and ends at Indian Beach and (farther still) Ecola Point and Cannon Beach.

▼
Gearhart

Restaurants

▲

RESTAURANTS

Miguel's ★ This tiny Mexican eatery is scrunched midblock on bustling Broadway; inside, the ambience is south-of-the-border cozy. The tortilla chips are baked daily and served oven-warm with handcrafted salsa. Main-course winners include the seafood tacos, stuffed to the brim with sautéed shrimp and cod. The chiles rellenos, a dish rarely done right in these parts, are perfect. Hungry overachievers can opt for Huevos Miguel's, a massive corn tortilla loaded with ground beef and topped with a snappy green chili sauce, two eggs, and cheese. ▪ *On Broadway, across from Dooger's; (503) 738-0171; 412 Broadway, Seaside; $; beer and wine; MC, V; local checks only; lunch* and dinner *Thurs–Sun (in winter: lunch Fri–Sun, dinner Wed–Sun, closed Mon–Tues).* &

Dooger's As the line outside on weekends (and sometimes during the week) will attest, this place is popular. Inside, it's a clean, smokeless, unkitschy, family place with friendly service. Stick with the simpler offerings, like chowder and the local catch, which you can have prepared a number of ways. The Dooger's empire is growing: there's a larger version in Cannon Beach at 1371 S Hemlock, (503)436-2225; and another on 900 S Pacific in Long Beach, Washington, (360)642-4224. ■ *Broadway and Franklin; (503)738-3773; 505 Broadway, Seaside; $$; beer and wine; MC, V; local checks only; lunch, dinner every day.* &

Vista Sea Cafe It may be frenzied outside at Seaside's busiest intersection, but inside Vista Sea Cafe you'll find a pleasant respite from the crowds. There are five wooden booths, a couple of tables, lots of plants, and some pretty fair pizzas. Choose from dozens of toppings, including some unorthodox cheeses (Montrachet, Oregon blue), to create your own mouthwatering pie built on a hefty, chewy crust. Salads, such as the Greek pasta, are excellent alternatives. ■ *On the corner of Broadway and Columbia; (503)738-8108; 150 Broadway, Seaside; $; beer and wine; MC, V; local checks only; lunch, dinner every day (closed Wed–Thurs in winter).* &

LODGINGS

Anderson's Boarding House (formerly The Boarding House)
★ Fir tongue-and-groove walls, beamed ceilings, and wood paneling recall traditional boardinghouse decor at this turn-of-the-century Victorian. The house fronts Seaside's busy Holladay Drive, but the backyard slopes gently to the Necanicum River—convenient and close to the beach. All six guest rooms have private baths and a wicker-and-wood beachy feeling. There's also a miniature cottage that sleeps up to six people. Full breakfasts included. ■ *N Holladay and 3rd; (503)738-9055; 208 N Holladay Dr, Seaside; PO Box 573, Seaside, OR 97138; $$; MC, V; checks OK.*

Beachwood Bed and Breakfast Beachwood, just a block east of the beach, is nicely ensconced in a quiet residential neighborhood, nestled in among coastal pines, and an easy walk from downtown. The 1900 Craftsman-style lodging offers four guest rooms with private baths. The Astor Room is outfitted with an unusual sleigh-shaped bed and a comfy window seat with a peek of the Pacific. The first-floor Holladay Suite has a frilly canopy bed, a gas fireplace, and Jacuzzi. No children or pets. ■ *Beach Dr and Ave G; (503)738-9585; 671 Beach Dr, Seaside, OR 97138; $$; MC, V; checks OK (closed mid-Nov to mid-Feb).*

Shilo Inn We're wary of glitzy establishments that hog the shoreline, but this one has a good reputation. The setting, of course, is superb; the lobby is stylish and mirrored; and the prices are stratospheric. But all of the amenities expected in a resort hotel are here: indoor pool, steam room, sauna, workout room, and therapy pool. The choicest rooms face the ocean and are further graced with fireplaces, kitchens, and private patios. The Shilo frequently hosts conventions, so it's not the place to get away from the hubbub of urban life. The restaurant is spendy and not your best choice in town, but the adjacent piano bar has a gorgeous view. ■ *N Prom and Broadway at Seaside's turnaround; (503) 738-9571 or (800) 222-2244; 30 N Prom, Seaside, OR 97138; $$$; AE, DC, MC, V; checks OK.* ⅗

CANNON BEACH

Cannon Beach is the Carmel of the Northwest, an artsy community with a hip ambience and strict building codes that ensure only aesthetically pleasing structures are built, usually of cedar and weathered wood. Still, the town is tourist-oriented, and during the summer (and most winter weekends as well), it explodes with visitors who come to browse the galleries and crafts shops or rub shoulders with coastal intelligentsia on crowded Hemlock Street.

The main draw continues to be the wide-open, white-sand beach, dominated by **Haystack Rock**, one of the world's largest coastal monoliths. At low tide you can observe rich marine life in the tidal pools. Less crowded stretches of sand are located at Chapman Point, at the north end of town (although parking is limited), and at Tolovana Park Wayside, at the south end. The Cannon Beach Energy-Conservation Project operates a natural gas–powered, free shuttle in the Cannon Beach–Tolovana Park area year-round.

Arts. Galleries abound, most clustered on Hemlock Street, the main drag. Three especially good ones are the White Bird (251 N Hemlock, (503) 436-2681), which has a variety of arts and crafts; the Haystack Gallery (183 N Hemlock, (503) 436-2547), with a wide range of prints and photography; and Jeffrey Hull Watercolors, Sandpiper Square (178 N Hemlock, (503) 436-2600), a collection of delicately brushed seascapes.

Haystack Program in the Arts, offered through Portland State University, conducts music, art, writing, and gardening workshops throughout the summer; (503) 725-8500. Coaster Theater (108 N Hemlock, (503) 436-1242) hosts good summer plays and year-round entertainment.

Shops. Brady's Cannon Beach Bakery (144 N Hemlock, (503) 436-2592) has one of the few remaining brick oil-fired hearth ovens on the West Coast. Visit Osburn's Ice Creamery

& Deli (240 N Hemlock, (503)436-2234) for picnic fixings. Bill's Tavern (188 N Hemlock, (503)436-2202) is the town's hot spot for music and gab, while Pizza 'a Fetta (231 N Hemlock, (503)436-0333) offers handcrafted pizza by the slice. Hane's Bakerie (1064 S Hemlock, (503)436-0120) features the town's best breads, muffins, and croissants.

Discover a surprisingly extensive selection of books at Cannon Beach Book Company (132 N Hemlock, (503)436-1301). El Mundo for Women (215 N Hemlock, (503)436-1572) and El Mundo for Men (231 N Hemlock, (503)436-1002) both specialize in natural-fiber clothing in youthful styles.

Hiking. Ecola State Park (on the town's north end) has fabulous views, quiet picnic areas, and fantastic hiking trails. Head up the trail from Indian Beach and catch a glimpse of the former Tillamook Rock Light Station, a lighthouse built off-shore more than 100 years ago and abandoned in 1957. Today it's a columbarium (where cremated remains are stored) named Eternity at Sea. Camping is permitted at primitive camp-sites atop Tillamook Head.

RESTAURANTS

Cafe de la Mer ★★★ This post-'60s coffeehouse, which became Cannon Beach's first fine-dining establishment 15 or so years ago, has won a considerable following. The location, on crowded Hemlock, isn't ideal. But the atmosphere inside is warm, and the food continues to shine. Seafood, simply and perfectly prepared, is this cafe's raison d'être, manifest in appetizers such as Dungeness crab legs Dijon, scallop ceviche redolent of lime and cilantro, or the choicest steamed clams and mussels in town. Entrees can be as unorthodox as scallops and shrimp sautéed with filberts or as traditional as a lusty bouillabaisse. Salmon, oysters tarragon, and (in a gesture to carnivores) rack of lamb—it's all good, and at times outstanding. Prices are high and portions are small. ▪ *Hemlock and Dawes; (503)436-1179; 1287 S Hemlock St, Cannon Beach; $$$; beer and wine; AE, MC, V; checks OK; dinner every day (call for winter hours).*

The Bistro ★★ Located in an alley off Hemlock Street, the Bistro is hard to find. But once inside, you'll appreciate its intimate (and nonsmoking) interior, with the hanging plants, open-beamed ceiling, and spackled, whitewashed walls. Owners Matt and Anita Dueber know where to procure the finest local ingredients (from their greenhouse next door, for instance) and every four-course dinner is substantial, tasty, and reasonably priced. You may start with an antipasto plate, then move on to soup (Greek lemon, perhaps, or a robust black bean), and a simple salad. You can't go wrong with the salmon, which may be wrapped in leeks and baked in foil, or coated with herbs and baked in a sun-dried tomato sauce. The service is polished, though on the slow side of casual. ■ *Opposite Spruce in downtown Cannon Beach; (503) 436-2661; 263 N Hemlock, Cannon Beach; $$; full bar; MC, V; local checks only; dinner every day (closed Wed in winter).*

Midtown Cafe ★★ Cannon Beachers don't like the fact that the secret's out about their favorite hangout. There are just not enough stools for everyone. Grab a fresh bagel when they're available, then hunker down for some frittatas, nitrate-free bacon, or the tofeta—a scramble of tofu, feta cheese, onions, and spices. Midday at the Midtown features almost legendary burritos, as well as scrumptious soups and sands. Don't miss the lip-smackin'-good fruit smoothies, and be on the lookout for the incredibly luscious Jamaican stew. ■ *8 blocks south of downtown, on Hemlock, the main drag; (503) 436-1016; 1235 S Hemlock, Cannon Beach; $; beer and wine; no credit cards; local checks only; breakfast, lunch Wed–Sat, brunch only Sun (closed Jan).* 失

Knoodlz ★ It figures that the bento craze (Japanese-style fast food in a box) would take hold in trendy Cannon Beach. Knoodlz features, naturally, noodles, with an East Asian theme and served up in white cardboard containers. The myriad choices vary from angel hair thin to fettuccine-thick, and range from Chinese wheat noodles (in a ginger-soy sauce with vegetables) to Vietnamese rice noodles (in a zesty peanut sauce with lemon grass, vegetables, peanuts, and cilantro). The portions are hearty, and the bevy of sensational handmade sauces vary on the heat scale from mild to wild. Delicious and nutritious fruit drinks and smoothies are made to order. Seating is limited to a few counter stools. ■ *On Sunset Blvd, halfway between Hemlock and Hwy 101; (503) 436-0123; 171 Sunset Blvd, Cannon Beach; $; no alcohol; AE, MC, V; local checks only; lunch, dinner every day.* 失

Lazy Susan Cafe ★ Very Oregon. Definitely Cannon Beach. Everyone in town seems to gather at this airy, sunny, double-deck restaurant in a courtyard opposite the Coaster Theater. The interior is bright with natural wood, plants hanging from the balcony, and local art on the walls. Breakfast is the best time here, when you can order omelets, oatmeal, waffles topped with fresh fruit and yogurt, and excellent coffee to prolong your stay. Eggs—sided with home-fries—are correctly cooked. Lunch includes quiche and some interesting sandwiches. Expect long waits on sunny weekends. ■ *Coaster Square; (503) 436-2816; 126 N Hemlock, Cannon Beach; $; beer and wine; no credit cards; checks OK; breakfast, lunch Wed–Mon, brunch only Sun.*

LODGINGS

The Argonauta Inn ★ In downtown Cannon Beach, between bustling Hemlock Street and the beach, there are a confusing number of lodging options. The Argonauta, not really an inn but rather a cluster of five well-situated residences, is the best of the bunch. All units come equipped with comfy beds, pleasant furnishings, fireplaces, and color TVs. All but one have a complete kitchen. The Lower Lighthouse, a cozy retreat for two, is the best deal. The Beach House, while expensive, is more like a miniature lodge (with a river-rock fireplace, a spacious living room, two sun porches, three bedrooms, and two baths). Two suites within the Beach House, perfect for couples, are available at select times during the year. ▪ *Corner of 2nd and Larch; (503)436-2601; 188 W 2nd, Cannon Beach, OR 97110; $$; MC, V; checks OK.*

Cannon Beach Hotel Lodgings ★ Originally a boardinghouse, the Cannon Beach Hotel is a tidy, nine-room operation with a decidedly European flavor. The rooms are reasonably priced (especially compared to the pricey motels nearby), and vary from a nicely decorated, one-bed arrangement to a one-bedroom suite with a gas fireplace, spa, and ocean view. All rooms include a light breakfast. Pets are not allowed, and neither is smoking. J.P.'s (1116 S Hemlock, (503)436-0908), the restaurant adjacent to the hotel, is worth a visit regardless of where you're staying. It sports a hip attitude, with an open kitchen that features a theatrical chef (who manhandles fry pans awash with sherry), and serves up a nice selection of tantalizing preparations, including super salads and first-rate halibut and pastas. At press time, a sister hotel called the Courtyard Inn opened just a half block from the beach. Sounds like it might even be a notch fussier. ▪ *Corner of Gower and S Hemlock; (503)436-1392; 1116 S Hemlock, Cannon Beach, OR 97110; $$; beer and wine; MC, V; checks OK; lunch, dinner, every day (restaurant closed Sun in winter except holidays).*

TOLOVANA PARK

Nestled on Cannon Beach's south side, Tolovana Park is laid back and less crowded, with a more residential character. Leave your vehicle at the Tolovana Park Wayside (with parking and restrooms) and stroll a quiet beach, especially in the off season. At low tide you can walk all the way to Arch Cape, some 5 miles south, where you can pick up the Oregon Coast Trail. (But be careful, the incoming tide might block your return.)

LODGINGS

Stephanie Inn ★★ Gorgeous and (relatively) new, this oceanfront lodging radiates the elegance of a New England country inn. Situated amid other motels and residences, it's not isolated but feels exclusive. Inside, the emphasis is on pampered and purposeful service. All of the 46 rooms include gas fireplaces, Jacuzzis, VCRs, and stunning furnishings; the deck rooms on the third floor are best. A full complimentary breakfast is served in the dining room. Come evening, Northwest wines are profiled in the library. Watch the ocean, play the piano, or cozy up to the fireplace in the hotel's Chart Room. Prix-fixe dinners are available to guests on a daily basis. ■ *On the beach, at Mantanuska and Pacific; (503)436-2221 or (800)633-3466; 2740 S Pacific, Tolovana Park, OR 97145; $$$; AE, DC, MC, V; checks OK.* &

Sea Sprite Motel This cute, always popular ocean-front motel is a good getaway choice for couples or the family (but no pets). Each of the six small but homey units includes a kitchen and color TV. Most have woodstoves. There's a washer and dryer on the premises, and firewood, beach towels, and blankets provided. If the Sea Sprite is full, ask about the Hearthstone Inn (nonsmoking), located up the road in Cannon Beach and under the same ownership. ■ *At Nebesna and Oceanfront; (503)436-2266; PO Box 66, Tolovana Park, OR 97145; $$; MC, V; checks OK.*

MANZANITA

Resting mostly on a sandy peninsula with undulating dunes covered in beach grass, shore pine, and Scotch broom, Manzanita is a lazy but growing community gaining popularity as a coastal getaway for in-the-know urbanites. The adjacent beach and nearby Nehalem Bay have become windsurfing hot spots. **Nehalem Bay State Park**, just south of town, offers hiking and biking trails as well as miles of little-used beaches. There's beachcombing galore on either the ocean or the Nehalem Bay side of Manzanita Peninsula. Overlooking it all is nearby **Neahkahnie Mountain**, with a steep, switchbacked trail leading to its 1,600-foot summit—the best viewpoint on the northern Oregon Coast.

Just north of town, **Oswald West State Park** has one of the finest campgrounds on any coast in the world. You walk a half-mile from the parking lot (where wheelbarrows are available to carry your gear) to tent sites among old-growth trees; the ocean, with a massive cove and tidepools, is just beyond. Surfing and kayaking are favorite year-round activities. No reservations, and even though the walk cuts down on the crowds, the place can be packed in summer. Be sure to secure all of your valuables out of sight in your car, or take them with you. Call (503)731-3411 for advance word on availability.

RESTAURANTS

Jarboe's ★★★ Jarboe's is set in a snug (eight tables), remodeled cottage, where the mood is mellow and the food sublime. The place is modestly decorated, with unobtrusive lighting and simple furnishings. Danish-born owner/chef Klaus Monberg is responsible for the imaginative and frequently changing menu. Soups are unusual creations, such as a velvety-smooth, nectarlike crawfish bisque with bay scallops. Simple salads containing radishes, endive, filberts, and sun-dried tomatoes are works of art. Entrees run to mesquite-broiled meat, fowl, and seafood; with Monberg in charge, simple, fresh ingredients (snapper, perhaps, or skewers of scallops and oysters) take on new textures and flavors. Sauces are ethereal and full of flavor, and desserts (a poached pear with crème Anglaise or an almond-crusted chocolate cake) are tantalizingly understated. ■ *Laneda and Carmel; (503)368-5113; 137 Laneda Ave, Manzanita; $$$; beer and wine; MC, V; local checks only; dinner Thurs–Mon (Thurs–Sun in winter).*

Blue Sky Cafe ★★ Comfortable but not too casual. Elegant but untraditional (as you'll know right away by the salt and pepper shakers). Seasonal offerings here include such culture-crossing appetizers as delicate sushi served with potted Montrachet and entrees such as a spicy Sichuan chicken and roasted stuffed poblano chiles—a delight of colors and tastes. The extensive wine list has an all-Oregon reserve pinot noir section. ■ *Laneda and 2nd; (503)368-5712; 154 Laneda Ave, Manzanita; $$; full bar; no credit cards; checks OK; dinner Wed–Sun.* &

▼

▲

Cassandra's ★★ Under the direction of transplanted New Yorker Fawn de Turk, Cassandra's has evolved from a cool place to catch some hot pizza to an overall outstanding eatery (and the finest pizzeria on the coast). Fawn chooses organic produce for her salads and toppings, and only meats and flour without preservatives for her pizzas. The new, larger location, just a block off the Manzanita ocean front, is a shrine to ocean-play, decorated with vintage surfboards, saltwater paraphernalia, and imprints of water creatures. Pizzas range from traditional to way-different; the primavera pizza is outstanding. ■ *A block off the beach on Laneda; (503)368-5593; 60 Laneda Ave, Manzanita; $; beer and wine; no credit cards; checks OK; dinner every day.* &

LODGINGS

The Inn at Manzanita ★★ One block off the beach, occupying a multilevel, woodsy setting similar to a Japanese garden, the Inn at Manzanita is a quiet, tranquil retreat. Inside, each of the 10 spacious units is finished in pine or cedar, with panels of stained glass here and there. All rooms have a gas fireplace, a good-sized spa, a TV with VCR, down comforters on the queen-size beds, and (with the exception of the Hummingbird unit) tree-top ocean views. The Cottage (a newer addition) features a full kitchen and a separate bedroom. Extra touches include daily fresh flowers, terrycloth robes, and the morning

I

paper at your door: _neda;_ _(503)368-6754; 6_ _$$$;_ _MC, V; checks OK._

Ocean Inn ★ You'd   any closer than this to t   re- modeled and attractiv   om units, with knotty-pin   (with mi- crowaves), wood stov   places, fold-out futons, and of course, ocean views. Unit 1 is the nicest, with a living room and a sheltered deck facing the waves and towering Neahkahnie Mountain. Pets (and smoking) are permitted in two of the units. One-week minimum stay, July and August. ▪ _On the beach at Laneda; (503)368-6797 or (800)579-9801; 20 Laneda, Manzanita, OR 97130; $$; MC, V; checks OK._

GARIBALDI/BAY CITY

Tillamook Bay is one of the homes for the summer salmon-fishing fleet, and these two burgs on Highway 101 are good places to find fresh seafood. In Garibaldi, stop by Miller Seafood (on Highway 101, (503)322-0355) or Smith's Pacific Shrimp Co. (608 Commercial Drive, (503)322-3316), and ask what's fresh.

If you'd rather catch your own, head for Siggi-G Ocean Charters in Garibaldi (611 Commercial Drive, (503)322-3285). Or try your luck in the bay or nearby rivers. Anglers routinely haul in 30-plus-pound chinooks from the Ghost's Hole section of Tillamook Bay, and the Kilchis, Wilson, Tillamook, and Trask rivers are superb salmon and steelhead streams.

RESTAURANTS

Downie's Cafe A neighborhood eatery patronized almost entirely by locals, Downie's is right off the set of "Mayberry R.F.D." That might be the town's police chief in the booth behind you, so watch your manners. Clean, tidy, unpretentious, and small, Downie's offers down-home service and food. Clam chowder is good—a rich, creamy potion of potatoes, celery, and thick chunks of clam. Although the hand-hewn chips are greasy, the fish fried in a light batter is not. Pies are yummy too. ▪ _5th and C streets; (503)377-2220; 9320 5th St, Bay City; $; no alcohol; no credit cards; checks OK; breakfast, lunch every day, dinner Tues–Sat._ ৬

TILLAMOOK

A broad, flat expanse of bottomland created by the confluence of three rivers (Tillamook, Trask, and Wilson), Tillamook is best known as dairy country. On the north end of town along Highway 101 sits the home of Tillamook cheese, the

▼

Manzanita

Lodgings

▲

Tillamook County Creamery Association plant and visitors center (4175 Highway 101 N, (503)842-4481). The tour is self-guided and, frankly, there's not that much to see, but there are free cheese samples and Tillamook ice cream to buy afterward.

A better choice for browsing is the **Blue Heron Cheese Company**, about one mile south on 101 (2001 Blue Heron Drive, (503)842-8281). Less kitschy and better stocked than the Tillamook Creamery, Blue Heron offers a variety of cheeses and other made-in-Oregon munchies, and has a wine-tasting room for Northwest wines.

Bear Creek Artichokes (in Hemlock, 11½ miles south of Tillamook; (503)398-5411) features a first-class selection of fruits, veggies, and herbs.

good town

OCEANSIDE

A tiny seaside resort that defines "quaint," Oceanside lies 8 miles west of Tillamook along the 22-mile **Three Capes Scenic Drive**. Tracing one of Oregon's most beautiful stretches of coastline, the narrow, winding Three Capes road skirts the outline of Tillamook Bay, climbs over Cape Meares (where you can walk up to, and inside, the Cape Meares light-house), then traverses the shores of Netarts Bay before reaching **Cape Lookout State Park**, (503)842-3182, another jewel in Oregon's park system. The park offers 250 campsites, along with headland-hugging trails and a huge stretch of little-used beach. The scenic drive scales Cape Lookout, the western-most headland on the northern Oregon Coast. Back at sea level lies a desertlike landscape of thousands of acres of sandy dunes, a favorite area for off-road recreational vehicles (which are required to stay in designated areas). The road to Pacific City and the route's third cape, Kiwanda, runs through lush, green dairy country.

RESTAURANTS

Roseanna's Oceanside Cafe ★ The sole restaurant in pretty, pint-size Oceanside (well, except for the tavern across the street), Roseanna's feels like a funky fern bar—lots of plants, a piano, an overdone pink-and-mauve motif with a ubiquitous signature parrot, all packed into an old, converted grocery store with wooden floors. Try a bowl of tasty clam chowder, a wedge of quiche, or a plate of grilled oysters. Desserts score high points, especially an oven-warmed Toll House pie topped with Tillamook ice cream. Dining room views of the ocean and nearby Three Arch Rocks make meals more memorable. ■ *On Oceanside's main drag; (503)842-7351; 1490 Pacific St, Oceanside; $$; full bar; MC, V; checks OK; lunch, dinner every day, breakfast Thurs–Tues.* ♿

LODGINGS

House on the Hill Bring your binoculars. The setting, on a bluff overlooking Three Arch Rocks (a bird, seal, and sea lion sanctuary) and the blue Pacific, is unbeatable. The "house" is actually four buildings, with 16 remodeled units and a honeymoon suite. Nothing fancy (and the trapezoidal architecture is a bit odd), but the views are tops. Choose a unit with a kitchen and stock up on groceries in Tillamook. The Rock Room, with telescopes to spy on the wildlife and scan the horizon for whales, is open to all guests. Kids are fine. ■ *Maxwell Mountain Rd at Maxwell Point; (503) 842-6030; 1816 Maxwell Mountain Rd, Oceanside, OR 97134; $$; MC, V; no checks.*

CLOVERDALE

This is lush, green Tillamook County dairy country. The town of Cloverdale, with its high-arched bridge, raised wooden sidewalks, and stately church steeples, bills itself as "Oregon's Best Kept Secret," and that it must be because we still haven't discovered anything but cows.

LODGINGS

Hudson House Bed & Breakfast ★★ Perched on a bluff in the middle of nowhere, the picturesque Hudson House, built in 1906 and on the Historic Register, evokes memories of a country weekend at Grandma's. The entire restored Victorian farmhouse is dedicated to the guests; your hosts, Richard and Judy Shinton, reside next door. The four guest rooms are decorated in an early-century country style and look out on forested hillsides surrounding the pastoral Nestucca River valley. Breakfasts are exceptional, including unusual treats such as cheese casseroles, puff pancakes filled with apples, and homemade Wholly Cow cereal. ■ *2½ miles south of Cloverdale and east of Pacific City; (503) 392-3533; 37700 Hwy 101 S, Cloverdale, OR 97112; $$; AE, MC, V; checks OK.*

PACIFIC CITY

Pacific City is the home of the dory fleet, Oregon's classic fishing boats. The boats enter the ocean in the south lee of Cape Kiwanda, sometimes competing with surfers and kayakers for water space. Up above, hang gliders swoop off the slopes of the cape and land on the sandy expanses below. The region's second Haystack Rock (Cannon Beach has the other) sits a half mile offshore.

Robert Straub State Park is situated at the south end of town and occupies most of the Nestucca beach sandspit. Fishing enthusiasts flock to the Pacific City area—the

Nestucca and Little Nestucca rivers are known as two of the finest salmon and steelhead streams in the state.

RESTAURANTS

Grateful Bread Bakery ★ Transplanted New Yorkers Laura and Gary Seide tempt you with robust breads, muffins, and a scrumptious array of sweets—carrot cake and gargantuan cinnamon rolls, to name a few—in a cheerful, beachy setting. There are extensive breakfast and lunch menus, listing some very cheesy New York–style pizza, veggie lasagne, and a few hearty soups. An array of imaginative sandwiches includes a spicy Creole egg salad with a side of roasted red potatoes. Enjoy your coffee and cake out on the deck, and take a loaf of bread or a baguette with you when you leave. ▪ *On the Pacific City loop road; (503)965-7337; 34805 Brooten Rd, Pacific City; $; no alcohol; MC, V; checks OK; breakfast, lunch every day (closed Jan).* &

Riverhouse Restaurant You might see a great blue heron perched on a log on the Nestucca River, which flows idly to the sea right outside the window. The Riverhouse is a calming stop, 3 miles off Highway 101, and far removed from the typical tourist trappings. It's small—10 or so tables—with hanging plants and a piano in the corner for local musicians who perform on weekends. Everything's homemade. Don't miss the apple pie. ▪ *¼ mile north of the stoplight on Brooten Rd; (503)965-6722; 34450 Brooten Rd, Pacific City; $$; full bar; MC, V; checks OK; lunch, dinner every day (days vary in winter).* &

NESKOWIN

A diminutive, mostly residential community lying in the lee of Cascade Head—a steeply sloped and forested promontory—Neskowin is the final port of refuge before the touristy "20 Miracle Miles" (as the stretch from Lincoln City to Newport used to be called). The beach here is narrower but less crowded than other locales. Proposal Rock, an offshore island, can be reached at very low tides.

Cascade Head has miles of little-used hiking trails that traverse rain forests and meadows, then skirt rocky cliffs. The trails begin at a marked trailhead about 2 miles south (visible from Highway 101). The old Neskowin Road, a narrow route that winds through horse farms and old-growth forests, is an enchanting side trip.

The **Sitka Center for Art and Ecology** operates on the south side of Cascade Head and offers seasonal classes on many subjects, plus numerous talks and exhibits; (503)994-5485. The Hawk Creek Cafe (4505 Salem, (503)392-3838) is a good bet to enjoy a beer or a snack from an outdoor view deck.

LODGINGS

The Chelan ★ This attractive white-and-blue adobe structure encompasses nine condominium units, all with lovely ocean views. Private homes are nearby, but this place feels like a get-away retreat. There's a manicured front lawn, lush gardens, and a secluded atmosphere. All of the condos have a well-equipped kitchen, a large living room with a picture window, and a brick fireplace. Most have two bedrooms. Ground-floor units have a private entrance to a small backyard, with the ocean just beyond. Upstairs accommodations (off-limits to children) enjoy private balconies. ■ *On Breakers Blvd, just off Salem Blvd; (503)392-3270; 48750 Breakers Blvd, Neskowin, OR 97149; $$$; MC, V; checks OK.*

Pacific Sands A stone's throw from breaking waves, this well-maintained resort condo-motel with an average, bland exterior, enjoys a spectacular setting. Only 10 of the condos are for rent; each has a fireplace, kitchen, and more than enough room to stretch out and get comfortable. Opt for a beachfront unit (if available), and step out to miles of untrampled sand and primitive Cascade Head a short distance to the south. ■ *Breakers Blvd and Amity; (503)392-3101; 48250 Breakers Blvd, Neskowin, OR 97149; $$; MC, V; checks OK.* &

▼

Neskowin

Lodgings

▲

OTIS

RESTAURANTS

Otis Cafe ★ The Otis Cafe is simply *thriving*. It does all those things small-town eateries all over America used to do—serve honest, no-frills food at old-fashioned prices. Everyone appreciates this basic ethic, and on summer weekends they line up for it. Inside, contented diners nosh on beefy burgers, thick 'n' chunky soups, filling breakfasts (including plate-sized portions of hashbrowns, onions, peppers, and melted cheese), and huge malts and milk shakes. Dinner offerings include fish, pork chops, and chicken-fried steak. The buttery black bread is sold to go, in case you can't get enough of it while you're there; other baked items, especially the pies, are delish. At press time a second Otis Cafe was scheduled to open in Lincoln City. ■ *Otis Junction; (503)994-2813; Hwy 18, Otis; $; beer and wine; AE, MC, V; checks OK; breakfast, lunch every day, dinner Fri–Sun.*

LINCOLN CITY

There is no off season here. Every weekend is crowded, and traffic can be the pits. A slew of factory outlets (more than 50 at last count) located halfway through town has created even more gridlock. Whether you come for summer sun or winter storms, be prepared to move slowly through these parts. The good news is that the restaurant, lodging, and activity choices have never been so favorable. You can seek some solitude on the 7 miles of continuous sandy beach that begin at Roads End (at the north end of town) and continue all the way to Siletz Bay.

Barnacle Bill's seafood store (2174 NE Hwy 101, (503) 994-3022) is well known (and open daily) for fresh and smoked fish: salmon, sturgeon, albacore tuna, black cod, crab, and shrimp. On the north end of town, **Lighthouse Brewpub** (4157 N Highway 101, (503)994-7238) handcrafts some alluring ales (and offers 25 beers on tap). Right in the midst of all the hubbub.

Catch the Wind Kite Shop (266 SE Highway 101, (503) 994-9500) is the headquarters for a successful kite manufacturing company, with eight outlets along the coast from Seaside to Florence. **Mossy Creek Pottery** in Kernville, just south of Lincoln City, ½ mile up Immonen Road, (503)996-2415, sells some of the area's best locally made, high-fired stoneware and porcelain.

RESTAURANTS

Bay House ★★★ Shoreside restaurants with spectacular views can often get away with serving overpriced, mediocre food. Happily, this is not the case at the Bay House, located on the banks of Siletz Bay, just out of reach of the glitzy Lincoln City tourist trade. The ambience is traditional—crisp tablecloths and lots of richly finished wood and brass. The seasonal menu features mostly seafood, sometimes in imaginative preparations such as a grilled catch-of-the-day with shiitake and oyster mushrooms in a Bordeaux sauce, along with a bluecheese potato pancake. Halibut might be brushed with Parmesan, baked, and served on a lily white béchamel sauce. Oysters, scallops, crab legs (served with angel hair pasta)—they're all afforded reverential treatment at the hands of chef Greg Meixner. So, too, is rack of lamb roasted in an herb crust with port demiglace, or roasted chicken marinated in curried yogurt. Desserts (lemon cheesecake, for instance) are ethereal. Time your reservations with sunset and experience the solace of Siletz Bay. ■ *On Hwy 101, at the south edge of town; (503)996-3222; 5911 SW Hwy 101, Lincoln City; $$$; full bar; AE, MC, V; checks OK; dinner every day (Wed–Sun only in winter).* &

Chameleon Cafe ★ This small storefront cafe packs one heck of a culinary punch, with plenty of variety. Reggae or Caribbean tunes emanate from the sound system, and the interior is sparsely decorated with outrageous art and patrolled by hip, "with-it" waitresses. The intriguing menu features dishes such as salmon cakes in a yogurt and garlic sauce, and spicy fish tacos with black beans, rice, and a scintillating salsa. Greek and

Middle Eastern specialties are also in evidence. Then there's the ghnoki—plump cheese-filled dumplings served over a bed of garlic-laced spinach fettuccine. The wine selection is substantial. ■ *On the west side of Hwy 101; (503)994-8422; 2145 NW Hwy 101, Lincoln City; $; beer and wine; MC, V; checks OK; lunch, dinner Mon–Sat.* &

Salmon River Cafe ★ Part deli, part bistro, this is the place for picnic fixings and quality fast food. A large glass case displays unusual salads, meats, pastas, and pastries, including buttermilk scones and some mighty fine cinnamon rolls. Sit-down diners will appreciate the cheerful service and the tempting aromas wafting from the open kitchen, presided over by Barbara Lowry (who formerly headed the kitchen at the Bay House). Breakfast features smoked salmon and scrambled eggs served with rosemary-and-garlic-kissed potatoes; lunch offerings include Italian-inspired sandwiches and Lincoln City's finest cheeseburgers; dinner will make you want to return the next morning. ■ *On the north end of town, next to Safeway; (503)996-3663; 4079B NW Logan Rd, Lincoln City; $; beer and wine; no credit cards; checks OK; breakfast, lunch every day, dinner Wed–Sun.* &

Dory Cove Appreciative crowds continue to flock to this place rain or shine, especially since the menu has expanded. Hearty Americana, Oregon Coast–style, is the theme here: lots of seafood, steak, tasty chowder, and 20-plus kinds of burgers (including a half-pound monster). Dessert centers around homemade pie à la mode. Road's End Wayside, a small state park (good clamming), is right next door. ■ *Next to state park; (503)994-5180; 5819 Logan Rd, Lincoln City; $; beer and wine; AE, MC, V; checks OK; lunch, dinner every day.* &

LODGINGS

Palmer House ★ Palmer House is a perfect alternative to Lincoln City's glitzy beachfront lodgings. It's still close to the beach (less than ¼ mile away), but situated in a woodsy setting. The house, originally John Gray's (the developer of the Salishan, a few miles to the south), is built in the Northwest regional style with three bright, airy guest rooms (all with private bath). The Azalea Room has an ocean view and fireplace; the Agate features a large skylight over the bed. A memorable three-course breakfast may offer omelets, crêpes, handmade sausage, breads, scones, marmalade, and lots of fresh fruit. ■ *On Inlet, ¼ mile north of the D River Wayside; (503)994-7932; 646 NW Inlet, Lincoln City, OR 97367; $$$; AE, MC, V; checks OK.*

GLENEDEN BEACH

Across the highway from Salishan, a cluster of shops includes the Gallery at Salishan (800-764-2318), which exhibits superlative paintings, sculpture, and pottery. Farther south along Highway 101, stop at the Lincoln Beach Bagel Company (3930 Highway 101, (503) 764-3882) for a snack.

RESTAURANTS

Chez Jeannette ★★★ Windows with flower boxes, whitewashed brick walls, and an intimate woodsy setting (as well as two fireplaces, usually blazing away in winter) give this establishment the appearance of a French country inn. The food is French—traditionally so: butter and cream are used in abundance and most entrees are carefully sauced. And, bucking the seafood tradition seen up and down the coast, veal, rack of lamb, duckling (recently served in a hazelnut demiglace sauce and garnished with poached pears), and filet mignon make appearances on the menu. But Chez Jeannette is by no means a slouch when it comes to seafood: witness the Umpqua oysters, local mussels in sumptuous cream sauce, and salmon poached in Triple Sec and served with a rhubarb compote. ■ *¼ mile south of Salishan Lodge; (503) 764-3434; 7150 Old Hwy 101, Gleneden Beach; $$$; full bar; AE, MC, V; checks OK; dinner every day (Tues–Sat only in winter).* &

LODGINGS

Salishan Lodge ★★ Salishan, the first and perhaps the biggest resort on the Oregon Coast, can seem stuffy (and there's certainly a sense of exclusivity), but the place *is* special. Sprawled over 14 acres, Salishan includes 205 guest rooms, arranged in eight-plex units nicely dispersed over the lush, green landscape. There's an 18-hole (par 72) golf course, plus driving range, pro shop, and resident PGA professional. You can swim in an indoor pool, work out in the sizable fitness center, sweat in a sauna, or jog on the trails winding through the 750-acre forest. Kids have their own game room and play area. The focal point is a huge lodge with restaurants, a nightclub, a library, meeting rooms, and a gift shop. The guest units are spacious and tastefully furnished but not extravagant, with brick fireplaces, view balconies, splashes of regional art, and individual covered carports. Distances within Salishan are considerable, so specify where you'd like to stay depending on what you want to be near (for example: Spruce, Fairway, Chieftain House South, and Sunset Suite overlook the links; Tennis House is near the courts; and the Blue Heron and Tide units have the best views of Siletz Bay and the ocean). The beach is a good half mile away. In the main dining room, pricey entrees sound special but execution is notoriously inconsistent. The voluminous wine list represents a cellar stocked with 20,000 bottles, perhaps the foremost selection in the Northwest. ■ *Hwy 101 in Gleneden Beach; (503) 764-3600 or (800) 452-2300; PO Box 118, Gleneden Beach, OR 97388; $$$; AE, DC, MC, V; checks OK; breakfast, lunch, dinner every day.* &

DEPOE BAY

Once a charming coastal community, Depoe Bay is today mostly an extension of Lincoln City's strip development. Fortunately, some of the original town, including its picturesque and tiny (surely one of the smallest anywhere) harbor, remains intact. Depoe Bay bills itself as a whale-watching mecca, and during the gray whale migratory season (December through April), the leviathans may cruise within hailing distance of headlands. **Deep Sea Trollers** is one of several operations offering whale-watching cruises; (503) 765-2248.

The Channel Bookstore (Hwy 101, one block south of the bridge, (503) 765-2352) is a used-book paradise. The O'Connell Gallery (42 N Hwy 101, (503) 765-3331) features environmental art and a great water-level view.

LODGINGS

Channel House ★ Intimate seaside inns (generally larger than B&Bs) with great settings and gracious service are the latest news in the Northwest, and the Channel House was among the first. Spectacularly situated on a cliff overlooking the ocean and Depoe Bay Channel (literally right above the water, since there's no beach below), this place has 12 rooms, all with private baths and ocean views. They're truly special accommodations (starting at $120), each outfitted with private deck, gas fireplace, spa, and in the morning, a breakfast that's aimed to satisfy anyone's hunger. Be sure to bring your binoculars, especially during whale-watching season. ■ *At the end of Ellingson St, above the ocean; (503) 765-2140 or (800) 447-2140; 35 Ellingson St, Depoe Bay, OR 97341; $$$; MC, V; checks OK.*

Inn at Otter Crest ★ This rambling destination resort perched on 100 acres at Cape Foulweather is lushly landscaped with evergreens, coastal shrubs, and every color of rhododendron imaginable. Breathtaking views abound, and an isolated low-tide beach awaits at sea level, 50 or so feet below. However, it's not exactly paradise. For starters, Cape Foulweather is aptly named, as fog often enshrouds the headland, though sunny skies may prevail just north and south. The resort hosts many conventions, which can be intrusive. And it's so large (more than 280 rooms and suites) that a personal touch can sometimes be lacking (so large, in fact, that you leave your car a short distance away and hop a shuttle van to your room). Still, most of the rooms open onto marvelous views, and many have fireplaces and full kitchens. All in all, a nice but expensive alternative to beachfront motel life. ■ *Otter Crest Loop, 2 miles south of Depoe Bay; (503) 765-2111 or (800) 452-2101; 301*

▼
Depoe Bay
▲

NEWPORT

The most popular tourist destination on the Oregon Coast, Newport blends tasteful development (the Performing Arts Center, for example) with unending shopping center sprawl. To discover all that Newport has to offer, steer away from Highway 101's commercial chaos. The bay front is a working harbor going full tilt, where fishing boats of all types—trollers, trawlers, shrimpers, and crabbers—berth year-round. A number of **charter boats** operate from here. They'll provide bait and tackle, clean and fillet your catch, and even smoke or can it for you. Many charter operators have initiated whale-watching excursions, in addition to their half- and full-day fishing trips. Sea Gull Charters (343 SW Bay Boulevard, (503)265-7441) and Newport Sport Fishing (1000 SE Bay Boulevard, (503)265-7558 or (800)828-8777) are two popular operators. Also check out Marine Discovery Tours (345 SW Bay Boulevard, (503)265-6200 or (800)903-2628) for unusual saltwater adventures. Rent clam shovels and crabbing gear, as well as boats and bicycles, at the Embarcadero Dock (1000 SE Bay Boulevard, (503)265-5435). Afterward, quaff a native beer at the **Bayfront Brewery** (748 SW Bay Boulevard (503)265-3188), home to the local microbrew, Rogue Ale.

Newport

Oceanic Arts Center (444 SW Bay Boulevard, (503)265-5963) and the **Wood Gallery** (818 SW Bay Boulevard, (503)265-6843), both on the bay front, are galleries worth visiting. The former offers mostly jewelry, paintings, pottery, and sculpture; the latter, functional sculpture, woodwork, pottery, and weaving.

The Nye Beach area, on the ocean side of the highway, has fewer tourists and more of an arts-community feel, housing a potpourri of neo-professionals, tourists, writers, artists, and fishermen. The **Newport Performing Arts Center** (777 S Olive, (503)265-ARTS) is an attractive wooden structure that hosts music, theater, and other events, some of national caliber. The **Visual Arts Center** at 839 NW Beach, (503)265-5133, offers an ocean-front setting for exhibits and classes. For a bird's-eye perspective of boats, bay, and ocean, take a drive through Yaquina Bay State Park, which wraps around the south end of town.

On the southeast side of the Yaquina Bay Bridge, Oregon State University's **Hatfield Marine Science Center** (2030 S Marine Science Drive, (503)867-0100) offers displays, a facsimile tidepool, and a full range of free nature walks, field trips (including whale-watching excursions, which have an admission charge), and films, especially during the summer

Seatauqua program. Nearby, the pride of Newport, the **Oregon Coast Aquarium** (2820 SE Ferry Slip Road, (503)867-3474), features furry, finny, and feathery creatures cavorting in re-created tidepools, cliffs, and caves. The exhibits are first-class. A drive out the South Jetty Road affords sea-level views of harbor ship traffic. A couple of miles farther south is the area's best, and most extensive, camping site, **South Beach State Park**; (503)867-4715.

North of town, above Agate Beach, **Yaquina Head Outstanding Natural Area** features the restored Yaquina Lighthouse (circa 1873 and open to the public), hiking trails, and fantastic cliff-front panoramas. There is a new showcase intertidal area for viewing marine birds, fish, and mammals; it's handicap-accessible and safe for kids.

RESTAURANTS

Canyon Way Restaurant and Bookstore ★★ Canyon Way is as much an emporium as an eatery, with a bookstore, gift shop, deli, and a restaurant on the premises. You could easily get sidetracked on the way to your table, or decide to forgo a sit-down meal in favor of the many take-out munchies available. If you stay, you'll find a pleasingly diverse menu loaded with seafood and fresh pasta plates. A Cajun turkey sandwich, grilled lingcod 'n' chips, and Dungeness crab cakes with angel-hair onion rings, along with a variety of salads, are good noon-time options. For dinner, there's a different baked oyster preparation daily, and choices as diverse as chicken curry and prawns Provençal. On sunny days, request an outdoor table overlooking the bay. ■ *Between Herbert St and Bay Blvd; (503)265-8319; 1216 SW Canyon Way, Newport; $$; full bar; AE, MC, V; checks OK; lunch Mon–Sat, dinner Tues–Sat; bookstore and deli open every day.* &

▼
Newport
▲

The Whale's Tale ★★ In tourist-oriented Newport, where mediocre restaurants come and go, the Whale's Tale has been serving up some of the best food in town inside the bay front's hippest setting for many a year. Customers are a zesty mix of fishermen, aging hippies, Newport yuppies, and adventuresome tourists who've forsaken Mo's (just down the block). Breakfasts are outstanding, with fresh jalapeño omelets, scrumptious poppyseed pancakes, and home-fried potatoes with onions and green chiles smothered in cheese. Lunches include good-sized sandwiches, sumptuous, well-seasoned soups, and a lusty cioppino. A plate of grilled Yaquina oysters is a dinnertime favorite, along with lasagne, German sausage and sauerkraut, and excellent black bread. Save room for the signature mousse-in-a-bag dessert. ■ *At SW Bay and Fall; (503)265-8660; 452 SW Bay Blvd, Newport; $$; beer and wine; AE, DC, MC, V; checks OK; breakfast, lunch, dinner every day (closed Wed in winter).*

Sylvia Beach Hotel ★★ Owners Goody Cable and Sally Ford have dedicated their pleasantly funky bluff-top hotel to bookworms and their literary heroes and heroines. They gave several like-minded friends the task of decorating each of the 20 rooms, and the results are rich in whimsy and fresh, distinct personality—a true beach place, endearingly worn. Best way to do this place is to book (well in advance) one of the three "classics." The Agatha Christie suite, for instance, is decorated in a lush green English chintz, with a tiled fireplace, a large deck facing out over the sea cliff below, and—best of all—clues from the writer's many murders. The "bestsellers" (views) and the "novels" (non-views) are quite small, not as impressive, but they are equally imaginative. Books and comfortable chairs abound in the library, where hot wine is served nightly at 10pm. Prepare for a stay sans phones, radios, TVs, and stress. Breakfast is included in the price of the room. Dinners in the hotel's Tables of Content restaurant are prix-fixe, reservation-only affairs. The main attraction is the company; the food (although it's noteworthy) gets secondary billing. ■ *West on NW 3rd off Hwy 101, 6 blocks to NW Cliff; (503)265-5428; 267 NW Cliff, Newport, OR 97365; $$; AE, MC, V; checks OK; breakfast, dinner every day.* ઙ

Ocean House ★ If you haven't been here in a while, you'll be surprised. It's bigger, and perhaps not quite as cozy, but host Bob Garrard is still the epitome of congeniality and the setting remains picture-perfect—overlooking the surf at Agate Beach, with Yaquina Head and its lighthouse towering nearby. The four guest rooms are comfortable—neither elegant nor luxurious. There's a small library with cushy chairs and a roaring fireplace in the winter. Outside, you can relax and sunbathe protected from the summer northwest wind (but not from the neighbors) in the sheltered backyard and garden. A short trail leads to the beach below. ■ *Just off Hwy 101 N in Agate Beach (1 block south of Yaquina Head Light House Rd); (503)265-6158 or (800)56BANDB; 4920 NW Woody Way, Newport, OR 97365; $$; MC, V; checks OK.*

▼
Seal Rock
▲

SEAL ROCK

Artists and others seeking elbow room have moved here recently from crowded Newport. It's still not much more than a patch of strip development along Highway 101, but within that patch are a few keepers. Some interesting chainsaw art is being created at **Seal Rock Woodworks** (along Highway 101, (503)563-2452). Also along the highway, a tiny storefront with a sign proclaiming "Fudge" sells a variety of light and dark fudge and some tasty ice cream; (503)563-2766. Farther south, **Art on the Rocks** (5667 NW Pacific Coast Highway, 2 miles north of the Alsea Bay Bridge, (503)563-3920) has paintings, carvings, crafts, and jewelry. **Ona Beach State Park** (a mile north of town) provides fishing, swimming, and bird-watching possibilities.

RESTAURANTS

Yuzen ★ You may think you're hallucinating. A Japanese restaurant residing in a Bavarian-styled building, located in Seal Rock, a blink of a town with a wild West motif? No, Yuzen is for real—the home of the coast's finest Japanese cuisine. Even if raw fish isn't your idea of a delectable morsel, you'll enjoy the mildly flavored tuna, salmon, and prawn served in the sushi sampler appetizer. Sukiyaki is splendid, as are the tempura dishes. Dinners include a decent miso soup and a small salad. There's even a wafu steak, a traditional Japanese grilled New York steak with veggies. Service can be painfully slow. ■ *8 miles south of Newport on Hwy 101; (503)563-4766; PO Box 411, Seal Rock; $$; beer and wine; MC, V; checks OK; lunch, dinner Tues–Sun.*

WALDPORT

▼

Seal Rock

▲

Waldport is a town in coastal limbo, overshadowed by its larger, better-known neighbors—Newport to the north and Yachats to the south. Not to worry—Waldport has much to recommend it, including the lovely Alsea River estuary, untrampled beaches at either end of town, and a city center unspoiled by tourism. At the south end of the Alsea Bay Bridge (beautifully rebuilt in 1991) is an interpretive center with historic transportation displays. There's good clamming and crabbing in the bay, and equipment (including boats) can be rented at the Dock of the Bay Marina (1245 Mill, (503)563-2003) in the Old Town section, on the water just east of the highway.

The remote, pocket-sized **Drift Creek Wilderness** is tucked into the Coast Range halfway between Seal Rock and Waldport. Contact the Waldport Ranger District office, (503) 563-3211, for maps and information.

LODGINGS

Cliff House Bed and Breakfast ★★ We're happy to report that after a few ups and downs the magic has returned at this B&B perched on a cliff atop what must surely be one of the Oregon Coast's most prized vistas. Seals and salmon-hungry sea lions frequent the mouth of the Alsea River, just below, and migrating whales pass across the watery Pacific panorama. Sunsets are memorable. Four ultra-posh rooms are available, and all include antique furnishings, chandeliers, color TVs, water views, and balcony overlooks. The Bridal Suite (mucho spendy at $225) houses a tufted velvet sleigh bed with canopy, an ocean-front mirrored bath with Jacuzzi, and a shower for two. Out back, there's an ocean-view deck with an oversize spa, as well as a sauna and steam room, croquet course, and a hammock for two. ■ *1 block west of Hwy 101 on Adahi Rd; (503)563-2506; 1450 Adahi Rd, Waldport, OR 97394; $$$; MC, V; checks OK.*

Cape Cod Cottages ★ Between Waldport and Yachats, the beach becomes narrower and less used. Cape Cod Cottages, sitting on a low-lying bank just off Highway 101, occupies 300 feet of this ocean frontage. There are 10 cozy one- and two-bedroom units—spic-and-span, and complete with fully equipped kitchens, fireplaces (with wood provided), decks, and picture windows overlooking the ocean. Some even have garages. All in all, a nice, out-of-the-way place where children are welcome. ■ *2½ miles south of Waldport, on Hwy 101; (503)563-2106; 4150 SW Pacific Coast Hwy, Waldport, OR 97394; $$; AE, MC, V; checks OK.*

Edgewater Cottages ★ Lots of honeymooners land here, and the place is usually booked from the beginning of the tourist season. The seven units are varied and rustic-looking, with lots of wood paneling and a beachy feel throughout. The cute, pint-size Wheel House (a steal at $45) and Crow's Nest are strictly two-person affairs, while the Beachcomber can accommodate as many as 15 guests. Every cottage has an ocean view, a fireplace (firewood provided), a kitchen, and a sun deck. There's only one phone on the premises, but other necessities, such as corkscrews, popcorn poppers, and food processors, are plentiful. Kids and well-behaved dogs are fine (but pets cost extra). There are minimum stay requirements. ■ *2½ miles south of Waldport, on Hwy 101; (503)563-2240; 3978 SW Pacific Coast Hwy, Waldport, OR 97394; $$; no credit cards; checks OK.*

Yachats

YACHATS

Yachats (pronounced ya-hots) means "at the foot of the mountain." Tidepools teeming with marine life dot the rocky shoreline; beyond them loom spectacular headlands that afford excellent ocean and whale-watching vistas. The Yachats River intersects downtown and empties into the Pacific, providing a playground for seabirds, seals, and sea lions. Between April and October, sea-run smelt (savory, sardine-like fish) are harvested in the coast's sandy coves. The town has a hip, arts-community flavor, with an interesting mix of aging counterculturalists, yups, and tourists. Good local galleries include the Earthworks Gallery (2222 N Highway 101, (503)547-4300) and the Backporch Gallery (Fourth & Highway 101, (503)547-4500). Yachats is also home to the Oregon

Coast's oldest kite festival; call (503)547-3530 for information.

Yachats is situated at the threshold of the spectacular 2,700-acre **Cape Perpetua Scenic Area**. Hiking trails lead to isolated coves and rocky ledges constantly bombarded by ocean waves. Other paths head deep into bona fide rain forest. Driving along Highway 101 provides an exhilarating journey, packed with panoramas of rugged cliffs abutting the ever-charging Pacific. The Cape Perpetua Visitors Center (2400 Highway 101 S, (503)547-3289) offers films, displays, maps, and a logical starting point.

RESTAURANTS

La Serre ★ La Serre ("the greenhouse") is one of the better restaurants in the culinary poverty zone between Newport and Coos Bay. The dining area has an airy, open-beamed ceiling with skylights overhead and the largest collection of plants this side of Cape Perpetua's rain forest. The aroma of garlic and saffron drifts down from the open kitchen. Seafood, as befits a seaside town, is a good bet, be it catch-of-the-day Pacific whitefish, Umpqua oysters, or zesty cioppino. ■ *2nd and Beach, downtown Yachats; (503)547-3420; 160 W 2nd, Yachats; $$; full bar; AE, MC, V; local checks only; dinner every day, breakfast Sun (closed Jan, closed Tues Oct to June).*

New Morning Coffeehouse ★ A cross-section of Yachats society frequents the New Morning: tourists, hip locals in Gore-Tex and faded jeans, Eugene weekenders, and out-of-area tourists. Muffins, Danish, pies, and coffee cakes are superb. Savory soups and black bean chili are typical luncheon fare. Lately, darn good pasta dinners have been available Thursday, Friday, and Saturday. Enjoy it all by the homey wood stove— just what a soul needs on a stormy day at the coast. ■ *At Hwy 101 and 4th St; (503)547-3848; 373 Hwy 101 N, Yachats; $; beer and wine; no credit cards; checks OK; breakfast, lunch every day, dinner Thurs–Sat (closed Mon–Tues).*

LODGINGS

Sea Quest Bed & Breakfast ★★ Few B&Bs on the Oregon Coast are better situated than this (well, the Ziggurat next door, perhaps). At Sea Quest you spend the night in a luxurious, estatelike structure located on a sandy, beach-grassed bluff right above the ocean and nearby Ten Mile Creek. Four out of the five guest rooms have a spa in their baths, plush queen-size beds, private entrances, and an ocean view. Miles of Pacific vistas are yours to enjoy from the living room. ■ *6½ miles south of Yachats on west side of Hwy 101 (between mile markers 171 and 172); (503)547-3782; 95354 Hwy 101, Yachats, OR 97498; $$$; MC, V; checks OK.*

Ziggurat ★★ This stunning glass-and-wood four-story structure takes its name from the Sumerian word for "terraced

pyramid.' [...........] ows keep most
guests oc [...........] vever, there are
also plen [...........] 000-square-foot
living roc [...........] le the west suite
has a round, glass-block shower and a magnificent view. Upstairs, at the apex of the pyramid, is a guest room with open-
air decks. ■ *6½ miles south of Yachats on west side of Hwy
101; (503) 547-3925; 95330 Hwy 101, Yachats; PO Box 757,
Yachats, OR 97498; $$$; no credit cards; checks OK.*

The Adobe Resort ★ Ensconced in a private, parklike
setting, the Adobe fans out around the edge of a basalt-
bumpy shore. At high tide, waves crash onto the rocks
below while their thunder echoes into the rooms. The original
rooms—with beamed ceilings, fireplaces, and ocean views—
are quite popular; the two newer wings have more amenities
(refrigerators and coffee-makers), but only some have fire-
places and face the ocean. There's a six-person Jacuzzi and a
sauna for all. Children are welcome, as are some pets. The
spectacularly situated restaurant, as ocean-front as you can get,
rates a notch above the usual mediocre beachtown fare. ■ *In
downtown Yachats, just off Hwy 101; (503) 547-3141; 1555
Hwy 101, Yachats; PO Box 219, Yachats, OR 97498; $$; full
bar; AE, DC, MC, V; checks OK; breakfast, lunch Mon–Sat,
dinner every day, brunch Sun.* &

Burd's Nest Inn Bed and Breakfast ★ This is one distinctive
roost, perched halfway up a hillside and enjoying a big birds-
eye view of the Pacific. The half-century-old home has a cluttered but comfortable look, especially inside, where antiques,
unusual toys, and knickknacks compete for wall and table
space. Proprietors Big Burd and Joni Bicksler, escapees from
Southern California, lend an animated, friendly ambience and
specialize in big Mexican breakfasts. ■ *East side of Hwy 101,
just before the bridge; (503) 547-3683; 664 Yachats River Rd,
Yachats, OR 97498; $$; MC, V; no checks.*

Oregon House You can't see Oregon House from the highway,
and therein lies the charm of this interesting five-building com-
plex set in the woods above the ocean. It's definitely private,
out of the wind, and away from the hustle and bustle. There's
a cliffside trail down to an uncrowded beach. Some of the units
have fireplaces, but none have phones or TVs; in some you'll
step out on the balcony to enjoy the ocean breeze, in others
you'll relax in a wicker rocking chair or a big brass bed. All
have kitchen facilities and most have ocean views. Kids are
fine. ■ *8 miles south of Yachats on the west side of Hwy 101;
(503) 547-3329; 94288 Hwy 101, Yachats, OR 97498; $$;
MC, V; checks OK.* &

Yachats

Lodgings

Florence is intersected by the deep, green Siuslaw River and surrounded by the beauty of the Oregon Dunes National Recreation Area, several large freshwater lakes, and in May, bright pink and red rhododendron flowers. The geography here, and for 50 miles south, is devoid of the trademark rugged Oregon Coast headlands. Instead, expansive sand dunes, some of them hundreds of feet high, dominate the landscape.

Florence has transformed itself from a sleepy fishing village to a tourist mecca. The revitalized **Old Town**, a continually upgraded few blocks of shops, restaurants, and some of the town's oldest structures, has become visitor-oriented without selling out to schlock. At the **Old Town Coffee Company**, 1269 Bay Street, (503)997-7300, you can scope out the scene and pick up local chit-chat.

The **Oregon Dunes National Recreation Area** (see Reedsport for headquarters info) extends for more than 50 miles from Heceta Beach to Coos Bay—32,000 acres of mountainous sand dunes. Orient yourself to this intriguing ecosystem by exploring the South Jetty Road just south of Florence, or the Oregon Dunes Overlook, another 11 miles south on Highway 101. The dunes, which reach 600 feet high, hide lakes with excellent swimming potential and mysterious tree islands.

▼

Florence

▲

Five miles north of Florence is **Darlingtonia Botanical Wayside**, a bog featuring insect-eating plants called cobra lilies. Their unusual burgundy flowers bloom in May. Another 6 miles farther brings you to the famous (or infamous) **Sea Lion Caves**, 91560 Highway 101, (503)547-3111 (much less kitschy than the advance hype might suggest). You descend 21 stories to a peephole in a natural, surf-swept cavern, where hundreds of sea lions frolic or doze on the rocks.

Also north of town is **Heceta Head Lighthouse**, the Oregon Coast's most powerful beacon and, perhaps, the most photographed lighthouse on the West Coast. Situated just off Highway 101, the lighthouse itself isn't open to the public, although the former lightkeeper's quarters are. This (supposedly) haunted but truly lovely house can be reserved for weddings or other gatherings; (503)997-8444.

RESTAURANTS

Blue Hen Cafe ★ Just try to suppress a cackle when you notice the glass, ceramic, and plastic chickens—blue, naturally—everywhere. What's important, though, is that the place is friendly, the prices are reasonable, the food is tasty, and there's lots of it. As you might expect, chicken (mostly fried) dominates the menu. You'd be hard-pressed to finish off an entire "four-clack" special. ■ *On Hwy 101 in the north part of town; (503)997-3907; 1675 Hwy 101 N, Florence; $; beer and wine;*

International C-Food Market ★ Cook it fresh and keep it simple. It's a big, sprawling seafood operation right on the Siuslaw River pier at the edge of Old Town. The fish-receiving station and the fishing fleet are just outside the restaurant. It's fun when you can eat on the deck and watch the boats offload. Fresh fish, crab, oysters, and clams are served any way you like 'em. Or cook it yourself—there's an attached seafood market if you want to take home your catch. ▪ *Bay St and the Siuslaw River, next to Mo's; (503) 997-9646; 1498 Bay St, Florence; $$; full bar; MC, V; checks OK; lunch, dinner every day.* ♧

LODGINGS

Johnson House Bed & Breakfast ★★ We can't recommend *any* hotels in Florence, so we're thankful for the wit, curiosity, and lofty aesthetic standards Jayne and Ron Fraese bring to their perennially popular B&B. Reflecting the Fraeses' interests (he's a political science prof, she's an English teacher), the library is strong on local history, natural history, politics, and collections of essays, letters, cartoons, and poetry. There are six guest rooms, one of which is a cute garden cottage. Breakfasts, which include fresh garden fruit and produce (grown out back) and home-baked bread, are among the best on the coast. Two additional cabins are 10 miles north—calling their location breathtaking would be an understatement. ▪ *One block north of the river at 216 Maple St; (503) 997-8000 or (800) 768-9488; 216 Maple St, Florence; PO Box 1892, Florence, OR 97439; $$ (cabins $$$); MC, V; checks OK.* ♧

▼

**Reedsport
and
Winchester
Bay**

▲

Edwin K Bed & Breakfast ★ Built in 1914 by one of Florence's founders, the Edwin K is set in a quiet residential neighborhood beyond the bustle of Old Town. Inside, the place looks formal but feels warm and homey. Ivory wall-to-wall carpeting contrasts nicely with aged and swarthy Douglas fir woodwork. All six spacious guest rooms are fitted with private baths and adorned with antiques. Breakfast is served in the exquisitely appointed dining room, another shrine to the woodcrafter's art. Out back, there's a private courtyard with a waterfall. ▪ *On the west edge of Old Town, across the street from the river; (503) 997-8360 or (800) 8EDWINK; 1155 Bay St, Florence, OR 97439; $$; MC, V; checks OK.*

REEDSPORT AND WINCHESTER BAY

Reedsport is a port town on the Umpqua River a few miles inland, while Winchester Bay is at the river's mouth. The real draw along this section of the coast is the 53-mile-long **Oregon Dunes National Recreation Area**. Because you can catch only glimpses of this sandy wilderness from the highway, plan to stop and explore on foot. Headquarters are located in Reedsport at the intersection of Highway 101 and Route 38; 855 Highway Avenue, (503)271-3611.

The numerous lakes in the Oregon Dunes make refreshing, warm-water (in season) swimming holes; the larger lakes such as Siltcoos, Tahkenitch, and Tenmile provide freshwater angling and boating. Large portions of the dunes are open to off-road recreational vehicles. Check a map to find out who's allowed where.

The former Antarctic research vessel *Hero* is moored on the Reedsport riverfront and is open to the public. Adjacent is the **Umpqua Discovery Center Museum**, which features a weather station and exhibits on marine life, ocean beaches, and logging; 409 Riverfront Way, (503)271-4816. The **Dean Creek Elk Reserve**, where you can observe wild elk grazing on protected land, is 4 miles east of town on Route 38.

The **Umpqua Lighthouse** (not open to the public) and Coastal Visitor Center are perched atop a headland overlooking Winchester Bay and the river mouth. Follow the signs to Umpqua Lighthouse State Park.

NORTH BEND

North of town, just before the bay bridge, is the turnoff to Horsfall Beach and the southernmost access to the **Oregon Dunes Recreation Area**. On the other side of Highway 101, **Clausen Oysters**, 811 N Bay Drive, on Haynes Inlet, (503)756-3600, is the place to buy oysters.

COOS BAY

The south bay's port city and formerly the world's foremost wood-products exporter, Coos Bay has been undercut by a sagging timber industry and the political struggle to control the Northwest's forests. But it's still the Oregon Coast's largest city and the largest natural harbor between San Francisco and Seattle. And it's currently making the painfully slow transition from an economy based on natural resources to one that's more service-based (but still a bit rough around the edges).

The **Coos Art Museum**, 235 Anderson, (503)267-3901, offers many exhibits of big-city quality. **Southwestern Oregon Community College**, 1988 Newmark, (503)888-2525, schedules art shows and musical performances. The **Oregon Coast Music Festival** happens every summer, (503)267-0938.

RESTAURANTS

Blue Heron Bistro ★★★ *Voilà*, a real bistro with European flair in the heart of Coos Bay—airy atmosphere, outdoor sidewalk

tables, and a reasonably priced innovative menu. Owner
Wim De Vriend keeps people coming back at all times of day.
For waffles, breakfast parfaits (yogurt, fruit, and muesli),
and good strong jolts of joe in the morning. For an array of
salads and sandwiches (such as blackened snapper on a
toasted onion roll with green chiles) or a German sausage plate
(without nitrates, and served with red cabbage, potatoes,
and hot mustard) at lunch. For handcrafted pasta or conti-
nent-hopping cuisine for dinner. Salmon, no matter how it's
prepared (grilled with fresh salsa and served with rice, black
beans, and corn relish), is always a winner here. So are
the more than 40 varieties of bottled beer and desserts that
include the coast's finest apple pie. ■ *Hwy 101 and Commer-
cial; (503)267-3933; 100 W Commercial, Coos Bay; $$; beer
and wine; MC, V; local checks only; breakfast, lunch, dinner
every day.* ᕲ

Kum-Yon's ★ Kum-Yon has transformed a nondescript eatery
into a showcase of South Korean cuisine. Some Japanese
(sushi, sashimi) and Chinese (eggflower soup, fried rice, chow
mein) dishes are offered, but to discover what really makes this
place special, you'll have to venture into the unknown. Try spicy
hot chap-chae (transparent noodles pan-fried with veggies and
beef) or bulgoki (thinly sliced sirloin marinated in honey and
spices). Get there early on weekends. ■ *On the south end of
the main drag; (503)269-2662; 835 S Broadway, Coos Bay;
$; beer and wine; AE, MC, V; local checks only; lunch, dinner
every day.* ᕲ

LODGINGS

Coos Bay Manor Bed & Breakfast Inn ★ Head up the hill away
from the commercial glitz of Highway 101 and you'll discover
beautifully restored homes among deciduous and coniferous
trees and flowering shrubs. The Coos Bay Manor, a grand Colo-
nial-style structure, is such a place, located on a quiet residen-
tial street with a waterfront panorama. The view is even more
stunning from the upstairs balcony patio where Patricia
Williams serves breakfast on mellow summer mornings. The
five guest rooms are all distinctively decorated (the cattle
baron's room is decked out with bear and coyote rugs; the Vic-
torian features lots of lace and ruffles). Mannerly children and
dogs (who tolerate cats) are welcome. ■ *On S 5th, 4 blocks
above the waterfront; (503)269-1224 or (800)269-1224; 955
S 5th St, Coos Bay, OR 97420; $$; MC, V; checks OK.*

CHARLESTON

Charleston's docks moor the bay's commercial fishing fleet.
Fresh fish is inexpensive, the pace is slow, and there's lots
to do.

Oregon Institute of Marine Biology is the University of Oregon's respected research station; (503)888-2581. Visit Chuck's Seafood, 5055 Boat Basin Drive, (503)888-5525, for fish and **Qualman Oyster Farms**, 4898 Crown Point Road, (503)888-3145, for oysters. Hikers, canoeists, and kayakers (no motor boaters) like to explore the **South Slough National Estuarine Research Center Reserve**, 4 miles south of Charleston, (503)888-5558, headquartered at an interpretive center—a good source for information and free maps.

Sunset Bay State Park, with year-round camping, has a bowl-shaped cove with 50-foot-high cliffs on either side, a good spot to take a swim as the water in the protected cove is perpetually calm; (503)888-4902. Just down the road at **Shore Acres State Park**, a colorful botanical gardens complex contains a restored caretaker's house and an impeccably maintained display of native and exotic plants and flowers; (503) 888-3732. At the park, there's also an enclosed shelter to view winter storms and watch for whales. Farther south, **Cape Arago State Park** overlooks the Oregon Islands National Wildlife Refuge, home to birds, seals, and sea lions. The **Oregon Coast Trail** winds through all three parks.

RESTAURANTS

Portside ★ It's dark and cavernous inside, so you'll notice the lighted glass tanks containing live crabs and lobsters—a good sign that the kitchen is concerned with fresh ingredients. From your table, you can watch fishing gear being repaired and vessels coming and going in the Charleston Boat Basin. Naturally, fresh seafood, simply prepared, is the house specialty. Fridays there's a sumptuous Chinese seafood buffet that includes everything but the anchor. ■ *Just over the Charleston bridge, in the midst of the boat basin; (503)888-5544; 8001 Kingfisher Rd, Charleston; $$; full bar; AE, DC, MC, V; local checks only; lunch, dinner every day.*

BANDON

The town of Bandon looks—and feels—newly painted, freshly scrubbed, and friendly. Some locals believe Bandon sits on a "ley line," an underground crystalline structure that is reputed to be the focus of powerful cosmic energies. Certainly there's magic here.

Bandon's cranberry bogs make it one of the nation's largest producers. Call (503)347-9616 or (503)347-3230 for a tour (May through November). There are a number of galleries, including the **Second Street Gallery** (210 Second, (503)347-4133); and the **Clock Tower Gallery** (198 Second, (503)347-4721).

The best beach access is from the south jetty or **Face**

Rock Viewpoint on Beach Loop Road. This route parallels the ocean in view of weather-sculpted rock formations and is a good alternative to Highway 101 (especially if you're on a bike). Just north of Bandon, **Bullards Beach State Park** occupies an expansive area crosscut with hiking and biking trails leading to uncrowded, driftwood-and-kelp-cluttered beaches. The 1896 Coquille River Lighthouse (open to the public) is located at the end of the park's main road. Good windsurfing beaches abound on the river and ocean side of the park; (503)347-2209.

Buy fish 'n' chips at Bandon Fisheries (250 1st SW, Bandon; (503)347-4282) and nosh at the public pier. Sample the famous cheddar cheeses (especially the squeaky cheese curds) at **Bandon Cheese** at 680 Second, (503)347-2456. For another treat, try the *New York Times*–touted handmade candies (fudge, creams, and taffy) at **Cranberry Sweets**, First and Chicago, (503)347-9475 (generous with free samples). Six miles south of Bandon, the **West Coast Game Park Safari** is a special "petting" park where you can view lions, tigers, and elk, among others; (503)347-3106.

RESTAURANTS

Andrea's ★★ A piano player at breakfast? It can happen at Andrea's, an Old Town landmark with New Age artwork, lots of greenery, massive (and comfy) wooden booths. Breakfast here is first-rate (just ask the ivory tickler). Omelets and steaming bowls of oatmeal topped with raisins and bananas are right up there with the best pastries in town. Lunch includes substantial sandwiches on homemade, wholegrain breads, sumptuous soups (excellent clam chowder), and pizza by the slice. For dinner, Andrea's draws on many traditions, from Cajun to Russian, but seafood cooked any of six different ways (from blackened to fat-free) takes center stage. The seafood hash and the apple cranberry blintzes say Oregon Coast in one bite—but don't stop there. ■ *1 block east of the ocean; (503)347-3022; 160 Baltimore, Bandon; $$; beer and wine; no credit cards; checks OK; breakfast, lunch Mon–Sat, dinner every day, brunch Sun (dinner Fri–Sat only during winter).*

Harp's ★★ Don't look for unusual background music. The name is derived from the presence of affable chef/owner Michael Harpster. Do look for some wonderful halibut with hot pistachio sauce. Ditto for the grilled snapper, pasta with prawns and a hot pepper and lemon sauce, and the charbroiled filet mignon marinated in garlic and teriyaki. Salads, a simple enticing mix of homegrown greens, come with a tantalizing garlicky balsamic house dressing. Harpster also does a good job with his sweet onion soup made with beef broth and cognac. The intimate interior, decorated in various shades of

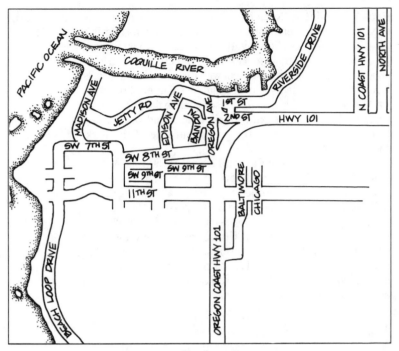

Bandon

green and brown with rough-cut wood paneling, has a floor that tilts to port and starboard, making this place feel like a shipboard cabin. ■ *Half a block east of the harbor; (503) 347-9057; 130 Chicago St, Bandon; $$; beer and wine; AE, MC, V; checks OK; dinner every day (Tues–Sat in winter).*

Sea Star Bistro and Guest House ★★ If Bandon encapsulates the coast—dramatic seascapes, quaint atmosphere, unspoiled beaches, good eats and sleeps, even a free daily morning news sheet—the Sea Star encapsulates Bandon. The Sea Star began years ago as a friendly hostel. In time, it grew to include more private accommodations and a small bistro, which is now one of Bandon's better restaurants. Banana-nut pancakes are a breakfast favorite, and dinners please with such dishes as a tasty chicken in pineapple sauce, and hearty rigatoni with Italian sausage. The place is small with an open kitchen, way-friendly waitstaff, and well-pawed magazines on a rack.

The Guest House, with natural wood interior, skylights, and harbor-view deck, offers a comparatively lavish alternative to the informal hostel connected by a courtyard. Nice sun decks. ■ *Take 2nd St off Hwy 101 into Old Town; (503) 347-9632; 375 2nd St, Bandon, OR 97411; $$; beer and wine; MC, V; local checks only; breakfast, lunch, dinner every day (Bistro closed Jan).*

Lighthouse Bed & Breakfast ★★ Spacious and appealing (although the groundskeeping leaves something to be desired), this contemporary home has windows opening toward the Coquille River, its lighthouse, and the ocean, which is a short walk away. Guests can watch fishing boats, seals, and seabirds. Of the four rooms, the expansive Greenhouse Room—with king-size bed, fireplace, whirlpool tub, and TV—is the true stunner. At least ask for a room that views the ocean. Breakfasts are top-notch. ▪ *1st St at Jetty Rd; (503) 347-9316; 650 Jetty Rd, Bandon; PO Box 24, Bandon, OR 97411; $$; MC, V; checks OK.*

Inn at Face Rock Choose simple one-bedroom units or opt for two-bedroom, two-bath suites with kitchens, fireplaces, and balconies. Many rooms have views (the inn is across the street from the beach), and prices vary as dramatically as the weather, with bargains available year-round. The outdoor, but secluded, Jacuzzi is exclusive to guests; the nine-hole golf course (fraught with irritating winds), restaurant, and bar are not. With the addition of chef Christophe Baudry, formerly of the Sixes River Hotel, the food has improved; now it's time to give the rest of the place an overhaul. ▪ *On Beach Loop Rd, 2 miles south of downtown Bandon; (503) 347-9441 or (800) 638-3092; 3225 Beach Loop Rd, Bandon, OR 97411; $$; AE, DC, MC, V; checks OK.* ⅄

▼

Port Orford

PORT ORFORD

▲

Oregon's oldest coastal town, Port Orford is a premier whale-watching location (occasionally an individual or small groups of whales spend all year in the quiet kelp-protected coves found here). It's a town far removed from big-city nuances—sheep ranching, fishing, sea-urchin harvesting, and cranberries dominate town life. Yet it's hip in its own way, especially considering the seasonal proliferation of surfers and board sailors, who head for **Battle Rock** and **Hubbard's Creek** beaches and the windy waters of Floras Lake. Fishing fanatics should visit the **Elk and Sixes rivers** for the salmon and steelhead runs. And—bonus of bonuses—Port Orford marks the beginning of Oregon's coastal "banana belt," which stretches to the California border and means warmer winter temperatures, an earlier spring, and more sunshine than other coastal areas.

One warning: From here south, poison oak grows close to the ocean. Watch out for it at Battle Rock.

Cape Blanco Lighthouse, situated in Cape Blanco State Park (six miles west of Highway 101, (503) 332-6774), is the most westerly lighthouse in the lower 48 states. The lighthouse, closed to the public, is approached via a windy, narrow, and potholed road. On the west side of the light station, a path through the grass leads to the end of the cape—the edge of the continent. Blanco is the windiest station on the coast, so if the view doesn't claim your breath, the wind will.

Boice-Cope County Park is the site of the large, freshwater Floras Lake, popular with boaters, anglers, and board sailors; take Floras Lake Road off Highway 101, near Langlois. This area has the coast's best (and little-used) trail system, perfect for hiking, running, horseback riding, and mountain biking.

RESTAURANTS

Sixes River Hotel This hundred-year-old farmhouse, once part of a sheep ranch and the last remaining structure from the original town of Sixes, is now a beautifully restored hotel and restaurant. Hand-hewn cedar beams and tongue-and-groove floors and ceilings are cut from old-growth Douglas fir. Chef Baudry is no longer here, but the restaurant is still holding up—and the lamb is still our recommendation. Many vegetables and herbs are grown out back, and vegetarian meals are available on request. The dining room seats only 25 people, so reservations are a must. ▪ *Turn east off Hwy 101 onto Sixes River Rd at Sixes and watch for driveway ⅛ mile on right; (503)332-3900 or (800)828-5161; 93316 Sixes River Rd, Sixes, OR 97476; $$; full bar; MC, V; checks OK; dinner Wed–Sun, brunch Sun.*

Truculent Oyster Restaurant and Peg Leg Saloon Enter the dark nautical interior of the Truculent Oyster through the Peg Leg Saloon. The fresh oyster shooters, homemade soups (clam chowder, split pea with ham), weekend prime rib, and mild Mexican entrees are the strong points on an eclectic menu. The slow-broiled chinook salmon (seasonal) can be outstanding. Portions are sizable and service is prompt. ▪ *At the south end of town; (503)332-9461; 236 6th St, Port Orford; $$; full bar; AE, MC, V; checks OK; lunch Thurs–Sun, dinner every day.* &

LODGINGS

Floras Lake House Bed & Breakfast ★ If the hot summer sun beckons you to cool swims in a freshwater lake, choose Floras. This modern two-story house offers four spacious rooms, each with a bath and deck access; two enjoy fireplaces. Most elegant are the North and South rooms. You can see Floras Lake and the ocean beyond from all rooms. Hiking and biking trails abound in this isolated area, and Floras Lake is great for windsurfers (and you might just have the beach to yourself). ▪ *From Hwy 101, turn west on Floras Lake Loop, 9 mi north of Port Orford, and follow signs to Boice Cope Park; (503)348-2573; 92870 Boice Cope Rd, Langlois, OR 97450; $$$; MC, V; checks OK.*

Home by the Sea Bed & Breakfast ★ The ocean view is one
of southern Oregon's best, and you can see it from both guest
rooms in this modest, homey B&B that sits atop a bluff near
Battle Rock. There's easy beach access, and guests have the
run of a large dining/living room area, also with ocean view.
Quiche, waffles, omelets, and fresh strawberries are the morning mainstays. You can surf the Internet with Alan Mitchell, a
friendly whirlwind of information and a "Mac" enthusiast. ■ *1
block west of Hwy 101 on Jackson St; (503)332-2855; 444
Jackson St, Port Orford; PO Box 606-B, Port Orford, OR
97465; $$; MC, V; checks OK.*

Castaway by the Sea This bluff-top, 14-unit, two-story motel
literally sits on history: ancient Indian artifacts, plus the former
sites of both Fort Orford, the oldest military installation on the
Oregon Coast, and the Castaway Lodge, once frequented by
Jack London. The two three-bedroom units have kitchenettes
and glassed-in sun decks with harbor and ocean views. Avoid
the dank older section under the office, except in a pinch. It's
an easy stroll to the beach, harbor, or shops. ■ *Between Ocean
and Harbor drives on W 5th; (503)332-4502; 545 W 5th, Port
Orford; PO Box 844, Port Orford, OR 97465; $$; MC, V; local checks only.*

▼

GOLD BEACH

Gold Beach is famous as the town at the ocean end of the
Rogue River, one of only a dozen Wild and Scenic Rivers in the
country. It's also a supply town for hikers heading up the Rogue
into the remote Kalmiopsis Wilderness Area.

Fishing. The river is famous for steelhead and salmon.
You might want to visit some of the lodges favored by fisher-
folk to pick up tips, or rent clam shovels and fishing gear at the
Rogue Outdoor Store, 560 N Ellensburg, (503)247-7142.

Jet boat trips. Guides will discuss the area's natural history and stop to observe wildlife on these thrilling trips from 64
to 104 miles up the Rogue River. You'll even get a hearty lunch
or dinner, usually with local sweet corn and tomatoes, at one
of the inns along the way (extra charge). One caution: Prepare
for sun exposure, as most of these boats are open. Call **Jerry's
Rogue Jets**, Port of Gold Beach, PO Box 1011, Gold Beach,
OR 97444, (503)247-7601, for information or (800)451-3645 for
reservations; **Mail Boat Hydro-Jets**, PO Box 1165-G, Gold
Beach, OR 97444, (503)247-7033 for information or (800)458-
3511 for reservations. Better yet, call **Rogue River Reservations**, (503)247-6504 or (800)525-2161, for information and
bookings on just about any Rogue River outing, jet boat trip, or
overnight stay in the wilderness.

Whitewater trips. Traffic on the all-too-popular Wild and

Scenic part of the Rogue is controlled. People interested in un-supervised trips must sign up for a lottery—the first six weeks in the new year—with the U.S. Forest Service; (503)479-3735.

Hiking. Trails cut deep into the Kalmiopsis Wilderness or the Siskiyou National Forest, or follow the Rogue River up-stream. A jet boat can drop you off to explore part or all of the 40-mile-long Rogue River Trail along the river's north bank. Spring is the best time for a trek, before 90-degree heat makes the rock-face trail intolerable.

Stay at any or all of seven remote lodges, where—for prices ranging from $55 to $180 per night—you end your day with a shower and dinner, and begin with breakfast and sack lunch for the next day. (Reservations are a must.) In the Ag-ness area the lodges are Cougar Lane Lodge, 04219 Agness Road, Agness, OR 97406, (503)247-7233; Lucas Pioneer Ranch, 03904 Cougar Lane (PO Box 37), Agness, OR 97406, (503)247-7443; and Singing Springs Resort, 34501 Agness-Illahee Road (PO Box 68), Agness, OR 97406, (503)247-6162.

In the Rogue River Wilderness, contact **Rogue River Reservations** (PO Box 456, Gold Beach, OR 97444, (503)247-6504 or (800)525-2161) for accommodations at Clay Hill Lodge, Wild River Lodge, or the crown jewel, the Paradise Bar Lodge. Or reserve a room at Half Moon Bar Lodge (PO Box 10, Ag-ness, OR 97406, (503)247-6968). For information about trails, contact the Gold Beach Ranger District, 1225 S Ellensburg, Gold Beach, OR 97444, (503)247-6651.

Gold Beach Vacation Rentals can put you in someone's private three- or four-bedroom home while the family is on va-cation, for $50 to $150 a night, less in winter. There's usually a minimum stay of three nights. Contact the Gold Beach Cham-ber of Commerce, (800)525-2334.

RESTAURANTS

The Captain's Table ★ This is Gold Beach's old favorite. Noth-ing is breaded and deep-fried, so a broiled salmon or halibut is a good choice (doneness is not always consistent). The corn-fed beef from Kansas City is meat you can't often get this far west. And, as in the Midwest, you can help yourself to as much salad as you want. The dining area is moderately small, fur-nished with antiques, and can get smoky from the popular bar. The staff is courteous, enthusiastic, and speedy. Nice ocean views. ■ *On Hwy 101, south end of town; (503)247-6308; 1295 S Ellensburg Ave, Gold Beach; $$; full bar; MC, V; lo-cal checks only; dinner every day.*

Nor'Wester ★ From the windows of the Nor'Wester you may watch fishermen delivering your meal: local sole, snapper, hal-ibut, lingcod, and salmon. Most seafood is correctly cooked (broiled or sautéed), and served garnished with almonds or some other simple topping. Forgo the more complicated, saucy preparations (such as the snapper Florentine). You can also find a decent steak, or chicken with Dijon or orange glaze. Dinners feature both soup and salad, served simultaneously. ■ *On the waterfront; (503)247-2333; Port of Gold Beach, Gold Beach; $$; full bar; AE, MC, V; checks OK; dinner every day.*

LODGINGS

Tu Tu'Tun Lodge ★★★ The lodge is one of the loveliest on the coast, though you are 7 miles inland from the ocean. Tall, mist-cloudy trees line the north shore of the Rogue River. The building is handsomely designed, with such niceties as private porches overlooking the river, racks to hold fishing gear, and stylish, rustic decor throughout. There are 16 units in the two-story main building and two larger, noisier kitchen suites in the lodge. In the apple orchard is a lovely garden house (sleeps six) with an old stone fireplace. You can swim in the heated lap pool, use the four-hole pitch-and-putt course, play horseshoes, relax around the mammoth rock fireplace, hike, or fish.

Three meals a day are served. The prix-fixe dinner begins with hors d'oeuvres in the bar. Your own fish might be the entree, or perhaps chicken breasts with a champagne sauce, or prime rib. Only the two river suites and garden house are available in winter. ■ *Follow the Rogue River from the bridge up the north bank for 7 miles; (503)247-6664; 96550 North Bank Rogue, Gold Beach, OR 97444; $$$; full bar; MC, V; checks OK; restaurant open May through Oct only.*

Inn at Nesika Beach ★★ The south coast's favorite romantic getaway. This three-story neo-Victorian, built in 1992, is a jewel of a structure right on a bluff overlooking the ocean. The expansive interior is grandly decorated. Wine and nibbles are offered each evening in the parlor and living room. An ocean-front breakfast may include crêpes, scones, fresh asparagus, and homemade muffins. All four spacious bedrooms have feather beds, private baths with whirlpool tubs, and fabulous ocean views. There are fireplaces in all but one room. ■ *West off Hwy 101 on Nesika Rd 5 miles north of Gold Beach; (503)247-6434; 33026 Nesika Rd, Gold Beach, OR 97444; $$; no credit cards; checks OK.*

Jot's Resort ★ The manicured grounds of this lovely resort spread out on the north bank of the Rogue River near the historic Rogue River Bridge, just across the river from the lights (and the traffic) of Gold Beach. The 140 rooms are spacious, tastefully decorated, and many have refrigerators. If you just want a standard room ($80), ask for one of the newer ones. For twice the price a two-bedroom condo accommodates six. There's an indoor pool, spa, and weight room. Rent a bike (or a boat) to explore the riverfront. Rogue River jet boats and guided fishing trips leave right from the resort's docks. And of course, the lodge rents all the necessary angling gear. ▪ *At the Rogue River Bridge on Wedderburn Loop; (503) 247-6676 or (800) 367-5687; 94360 Wedderburn Loop, Gold Beach; PO Box J, Gold Beach, OR 97444; $$; AE, DC, MC, V; checks OK.* ♿

Gold Beach Resort If you're looking for oceanfront accommodations, this sprawling complex is your best bet. All rooms have private decks and ocean views. There's an indoor pool and spa, and it's just a short walk over the dunes to the ocean. During the summer season the 39 units range from $89 for a standard room to $125 and up for a condo with fireplace and kitchen. Most are quite spacious. ▪ *Hwy 101, near south end of town; (503) 247-7066 or (800) 541-0947; 1300 S Ellensburg, Gold Beach, OR 97444; $$; AE, DC, MC, V; no checks.* ♿

BROOKINGS

Brookings sits in Oregon's "banana belt," just 6 miles north of the California line, and it enjoys the state's mildest winter temperatures. In addition, the town is bookended by breathtaking beauty. To the northwest are the **Samuel H. Boardman** and **Harris Beach** state parks. To the east are the verdant Siskiyou Mountains, deeply cut by the Chetco and Winchuck rivers. Brookings also boasts the safest harbor on the Oregon Coast—and therefore a busy port.

Azalea State Park is just east of Highway 101. Fragrant Western azaleas bloom in May, alongside wild strawberries, fruit trees, and violets; you can picnic amid all this splendor on hand-hewn myrtlewood tables. Myrtlewood (which grows only on the southern Oregon Coast and in Palestine) can be seen in groves in Loeb Park, 8 miles east of town on North Bank Chetco River Road.

Fishing is usually good here: the fleet operates from the south end of town. Stop in at Sporthaven Marina (16372 Lower Harbor Road, (503) 469-3301) for supplies and info; and nearby Tidewind Charters (16368 Lower Harbor Road, (503) 469-0337) for oceangoing fishing adventures. Soak up this Chetco Harbor ambience, and scarf an order of halibut 'n' chips at Pelican Bay Seafoods (16403 Lower Harbor Road, (503) 469-7971).

Old-growth. The Redwood Nature Trail in the Siskiyou National Forest winds through one of the few remaining groves of old-growth coastal redwoods in Oregon.

RESTAURANTS

Hog Wild Cafe ★ This boutiquey restaurant has gone a bit wild on the pig theme, what with pig dolls, pig cups, and a sign that reads, "Please don't hog the bathroom." But the food is worth a pig-out. You'll find jambalaya, veggie lasagne, and

Cajun meat loaf on the regular menu, plus a good many blackboard items, such as a vegetable frittata or prime rib sandwich. Wednesdays are barbecue nights. ▪ *West side of Hwy 101, 1 mile south of Brookings-Harbor bridge; (503) 469-8869; 16158 Hwy 101 S, Harbor; $; beer and wine; AE, MC, V; local checks only; breakfast, lunch every day, dinner Wed, Fri–Sat.* &

Rubio's ★ The salsa is outstanding; you can buy bottles of it here and elsewhere in Brookings. But the restaurant itself is the only place you can get Rubio's incredible chiles rellenos and chile verde. And—wow—the Seafood à la Rubio combines fresh lingcod, scallops, and prawns in a butter, garlic, wine, and jalapeño sauce. Avoid the greasy entomatada. There's also a drive-thru for take-out orders, when there's not enough room to squeeze one more customer into the restaurant. ▪ *At the north end of town; (503) 469-4919; 1136 Chetco Ave, Brookings; $$; beer and wine; AE, MC, V; local checks only; lunch, dinner Tues–Sun.* &

LODGINGS

Chetco River Inn ★★ Expect a culture shock: this fishing retreat sits on 35 acres of a peninsula wrapped by the turquoise Chetco River, 17 miles east of Brookings (pavement ends after 14 miles) and 6 miles from a phone. There's a radiophone operator, so forget private conversations. The lovely deep green marble floors are a purposefully practical choice for muddy fishermen's boots. The place is not so remote that you can't read by safety propane lights and watch TV via satellite (there's even a VCR). The large, open main floor offers views of the river, myrtlewood groves, and wildlife. Innkeeper Sandra Brugger will provide early-riser breakfast service, pack a deluxe sack lunch, or serve an exemplary five-course dinner on request. All told, this is getting away from it all in fishing style. ▪ *Follow North Bank Rd 16 miles, left after South Fork Bridge, take second guest driveway on left; (503) 469-8128 (radiophone) or (800) 327-2688 (Pelican Bay Travel); 21202 High Prarie Rd, Brookings, OR 97415; $$; MC, V; checks OK.*

Holmes Sea Cove Bed & Breakfast ★ Jack and Lorene Holmes offer two guest rooms on the lower level of their cozy ocean-view home north of town (as well as a private guest cottage with a living room nook, refrigerator, and private deck). The home sits on a waterfront bluff, with a trail that winds its way down to the ocean and to a private park with picnic tables. Lorene brings a continental breakfast to your room. ▪ *Take Hwy 101 north to Dawson Rd, left to Holmes Dr; (503) 469-3025; 17350 Holmes Dr, Brookings, OR 97415; $$; MC, V; checks OK.*

Oregon Coast

Beachfront Inn Sure, it's only a Best Western, but if you want an ocean-front motel room in Brookings, this is the closest you can get. Nothing special besides the view and the beach. Some units have kitchens, one has a two-person Jacuzzi. ■ *On Lower Harbor Rd, south of the Port of Brookings; (503) 469-7779 or (800) 468-4081; 16008 Boat Basin Rd, Brookings Harbor; PO Box 2729, Brookings Harbor, OR 97415; $$; AE, DC, MC, V; checks OK.* &

Willamette Valley and Southern Oregon

North to south roughly along the I-5 corridor from Yamhill and Washington counties in the north to the Rogue River Valley in southern Oregon.

AURORA

In 1856, Dr. William Keil brought a group of Pennsylvania Germans to establish a communal settlement. Called the Harmonites, the commune faded away after the death of its founder, but the town remains a well-preserved, turn-of-the-century village on the National Register of Historic Places. Most people come to comb through the myriad antique stores that now occupy the many clapboard and Victorian houses along the highway. The **Old Aurora Colony Museum** offers tours that recount the communal history of the town; (503)678-5754.

History-minded visitors will also enjoy **Champoeg State Park**, site of one of the first settlements in the Willamette Valley and now a fine place to picnic, hike, or bike along the river, with a small campground available as well. And rose lovers will want to wander a few miles farther up the river (west on Champoeg Road and across Highway 219) to **Heirloom Old Garden Roses**, (503)538-1576, one of the premier commercial growers of old garden roses in the country.

WILLAMETTE VALLEY WINERIES

The Oregon wine country now stretches from Portland all the way south (more or less along the I-5 corridor) to the California border. But the greatest concentration of wineries is in Yamhill County, mostly between Newberg and McMinnville. Here, among rolling oak-covered hills, are increasing numbers of vineyards and enough wineries to keep the touring wine lover tipsy for a week.

The good news is that this is not yet Napa Valley. Although summer weekends can be quite busy, many wineries are small family operations well off the beaten track, and visitors are still rare enough that they receive hearty welcomes. The downside is that some wineries have limited hours, and a few are not open to visitors at all. The best advice is to arm yourself with a map (it's easy to get lost on the backroads) and the winery guide from the **Oregon Winegrowers Association**, 1200 NW Front Avenue, Suite 400, Portland OR 97209, (503)228-0713, or any member winery. In fine weather take along a picnic lunch: many wineries have tables outside, some sell chilled wine and picnic supplies.

Driving south on Highway 99W, you will first hit **Veritas Vineyards**, (503)538-1470, makers of excellent chardonnay; and **Rex Hill Vineyards**, (503)538-0666, a decidedly upscale winery with a splendid tasting room and outstanding (if pricey) pinot noir. In the hills west of Newberg is **Autumn Wind Vineyard**, (503)538-6931, a small place beginning to turn out fine pinot noir.

Just outside Dundee, **Duck Pond Cellars**, (503)538-3199, makes a pleasant stop and has a number of good value wines. In Dundee, you can't miss the tasting room of **Argyle**, (503)538-8520, which is producing some of the best sparkling wines in the region. Behind Dundee are **Cameron Winery**, (503)538-0336 (open only by appointment), with its lovely view and stylish wines; and **Lange Winery**, (503)538-6476, where you can try an interesting pinot gris, the hot new white wine in Oregon. Nearby are two much larger wineries: **Knudsen Erath Winery**, (503)538-3318, one of the oldest and largest in the state (nearby Crabtree Park makes a nice midday stop), with a full lineup of wines in a variety of price and quality categories (one of the best values in pinot noir); and **Sokol Blosser Winery**, (503)864-2282, another large and high-quality producer with a most handsome tasting room. Just south, outside Lafayette (home of a Trappist monastery, Our Lady of Guadeloupe), **Chateau Benoit**, (503)864-3666, sits right on the crest of a ridge, with spacious visitor facilities. They specialize in Müller Thurgau (a great picnic wine).

Driving south of McMinnville on Highway 18 to the ocean you will pass **Yamhill Valley Vineyards**, (503)843-3100, a lovely winery that makes sturdy pinot noir and is set among old oaks, which provide good shade for lunch on a hot day. Just a bit farther along is the **Oregon Wine Tasting Room**, (503) 843-3787, which stocks a huge variety of wines for sale and always has an interesting assortment to taste. You'll find wines from places such as top-notch producer **Eyrie Vineyards**, which are not open to the public on a regular basis. If you take 99W out of town, you will drive past the Eola Hills, home to another half-dozen or so wineries, including **Amity Vineyards**, (503) 835-2362, a rustic winery that consistently produces excellent pinot noir, gewürztraminer, and dry riesling. Continuing south you will see signs for **Bethel Heights Vineyard**, (503) 581-2262, another winery high on a hill (one of the oldest vineyard sites in the area) that makes tasty chenin blanc and fine pinot noir in several price ranges. **Eola Hills Winery**, (503) 623-2405, in Rickreall, makes good cabernet sauvignon, a rarity for the Willamette Valley.

Farther south in a small valley near Highway 99W are two neighboring wineries, both very small and off the beaten track. **Airlie Winery**, (503) 838-6013, makes excellent Müller Thurgau and has well-priced wines (take some extra time and visit the birds at their pond). **Serendipity Cellars**, (503) 838-4284, makes some unusual wines, including Marechal Foch, a very good (and rare) red. **Tyee Wine Cellars**, (503) 753-8754, south of Corvallis, makes excellent pinot gris and gewürztraminer. Right in Monroe is **Broadley Vineyards**, (503) 847-5934, a storefront winery that's not much to look at but has some powerful pinots. In the hills to the west is picturesque **Alpine Vineyards**, (503) 424-5851, about the only winery in the Willamette Valley to make good cabernet consistently (as well as a fine riesling).

Don't overlook the wineries in the **Tualatin Valley** that lie in the suburbs just west of Portland. Beaverton's **Ponzi Vineyards**, (503) 628-1227, is an excellent close-in destination that produces powerful pinot noir, elegant chardonnay, and fine pinot gris and dry riesling (an outstanding lineup). **Cooper Mountain Vineyards**, (503) 649-0027, has a beautiful hilltop site and makes tasty pinot gris and promising pinot noir. South of Hillsboro, **Oak Knoll Winery**, (503) 648-8198, in an old dairy barn, maintains an Oregon tradition of fruit wines (these are very good), but also produces fine, fruity pinot noir and a variety of other wines at good prices.

▼

NEWBERG

RESTAURANTS

Ixtapa ★ After the long string of fast-food places along 99W, this little restaurant right in town is a refreshing change. You'll be given a hearty welcome as you're ushered into this narrow but colorful and lively place. The service really hustles: you won't get much time to peruse the long menu. Some will like their Mexican food a little spicier, but most will appreciate the freshness and lightness of the dishes. Grilled chicken is very tasty and the beans, the real test of a Mexican place, are just right. ■ *On Hwy 99W northbound, in town; (503) 538-5956; 307 E 1st St, Newberg; $; full bar; MC, V; checks OK; lunch, dinner every day.* &

LODGINGS

Springbrook Hazelnut Farm ★★ Informal Oregonians will be surprised to step into the colorful elegance of this landmark farmhouse. Owner Ellen McClure is an artist, and it shows. The large, paneled dining room with elegant table and chairs will make you feel as if you're in some Italian palazzo. The B&B guest wing upstairs is spacious, with two shared bathrooms furnished in green wicker. Two downstairs guest rooms offer half-baths, and there's a library and a TV room devoted to guests. The carriage house out back beyond the pond has a perfect little apartment with a well-stocked kitchen (even fixings for breakfast). Guests explore the 60-acre filbert orchard, take a swim in the pool, or play tennis on the private court. ■ *Just off Hwy 99W, north of Newberg; (503) 538-4606; 30295 N Hwy 99W, Newberg, OR 97132; $$$; no credit cards; checks OK.*

The Partridge Farm ★ Yes, they do raise partridges and other exotic and not-so-exotic birds, and the eggs you have for breakfast will be fresh. In fact, many of the ingredients for breakfast—fruit, vegetables, and herbs—are likely to be right out of the garden. The farmhouse is just off the highway, but the broad lawn and garden in back will help you feel way out in the country. The three rooms are furnished in dark antiques and have in-room sinks. The east bedroom is a little larger. A separate parlor downstairs has a TV. The inn is owned by the folks at Rex Hill Vineyards (about a mile away); romantics can arrange a soar in the winery's hot-air balloon. ■ *Just off Hwy 99W, north of Newberg; (503) 538-2050; 4300 E Portland Rd, Newberg, OR 97132; $$; MC, V; checks OK.*

Spring Creek Llama Ranch ★ When they began taking their new baby on backpacking trips, Dave and Melinda Van Bossuyt discovered that llamas make great pack animals. The Van Bossuyts have been aficionados ever since. Their llamas are gentle and eager for visitors (especially at mealtime) and provide fine diversion for children 3 years and up. This large, airy, modern house has two guest rooms (the upstairs room can accommodate a family—there's an adjoining room with twin beds that may be rented as a suite). The openness of the ranch is best for those who like to be social, but its proximity to the trails in the woods, Newberg, and Highway 99W is a plus. ■ *2 miles east of Newberg, please call ahead for specific directions; (503)538-5717; 14700 NE Spring Creek Lane, Newberg, OR 97132; $$; no credit cards; checks OK.*

DUNDEE

RESTAURANTS

Red Hills Provincial Dining ★★★ In a well-preserved older house at the edge of town, with the living room converted to a dining area, jovial co-owner Alice Halstead provides a warm welcome and chefs Nancy and Richard Gehrts preside in the kitchen. The simple dinner menu of a half-dozen items changes weekly, and the choices are all intriguing. Penne with olives, capers, and Montrachet cheese is perfectly balanced, beef tenderloin is thick and succulent, pork medallions on white beans are simple but flavorful. You get the idea: the best of European country cooking. And all the details are just right, whether it's bread dusted with fresh rosemary or a crisp salad of greens or lightly cooked vegetables. Desserts are interesting, too, like a rich, chewy fennel cake or raspberry-filled chocolate cake. Add to this an outstanding wine list, with a huge selection from all over the world, and you have a meal you'll want to linger over. ■ *On Hwy 99W, at north edge of town; (503)538-8224; 276 Hwy 99W, Dundee; $$; beer and wine; MC, V; checks OK; lunch Wed–Fri, dinner Wed–Sun.*

Tina's ★★ Owners Tina Landfried and husband, David Bergen, work their magic in a small, squat building by the side of the road: a vest-pocket herb-and-salad garden outside, plain white walls inside. As for the food, there's a spirit of innovation and creativity. The half-dozen entree choices are on the chalkboard: try rabbit risotto or grilled pork tenderloin in port-garlic sauce. Soup might be a flavorful cream of cucumber with dill and cilantro, and the green salad is simple and absolutely fresh. Wines by the glass offer a good selection of local picks, all reasonably priced. Our one caveat is erratic service, sometimes painfully slow. ■ *On Hwy 99W; (503)538-8880; 760 Hwy 99W, Dundee; $$; beer and wine; AE, MC, V; checks OK; lunch Tues–Fri, dinner Tues–Sun.* ქ

LODGINGS

Wine Country Farm ★ Drive up through the Red Hills of Dundee (the soil really is red), just past the unmarked entrance to Domaine Drouhin, makers of the Northwest's finest pinot noir and France's outpost in Oregon wine country (no visitors). Vineyards all around will remind you that you're in the very heart of wine country. From the hilltop watch clouds (or Oregon's trademark rain squalls) drift across the valley below. Three of the five eclectically furnished bedrooms have spectacular views, and a new two-room suite has been added over the tasting room. Owner Joan Davenport raises Arabian horses and can take you on a buggy ride. Guests take breakfast (home-baked goodies with her own pinot noir jelly) in warm weather on the deck of this restored 1910 white stucco house. At press time, a new restaurant, The Hill at Wine Country Farm, serving dinners featuring regional cuisine, opened to both guests and the public. ■ *From Hwy 99W southbound, turn right onto McDougall just past Sokol Blosser Winery, then right again to Breyman Orchard Rd; (503) 864-3446; 6855 Breyman Orchards Rd, Dayton OR 97114; $$; beer and wine; no credit cards; checks OK; dinner Wed–Sun by reservation only.*

YAMHILL

LODGINGS

Flying M Ranch ★★ This place hasn't completely lost its funkiness, but has gotten a bit upscale. The lodge has a Western-style lounge (with a bar made from 6-ton logs) and a restaurant that serves the standards, but is also experimenting with more exotic fare. The terrific setting is what draws people: literally at the end of the road in the Coast Range—there's nothing around but mountains and forest. Ponds for swimming and fishing, and miles of trails (you can actually follow trails all the way to the coast) should keep anyone busy. The motel rooms are pretty ordinary; savvy visitors rent one of the cabins (one of which has 10 beds)—they have their own kitchens and are plenty rustic, with no phones or TVs ($75–$200). And for a really large group (up to 20), you might check out the small lodge on Trask Mountain (highest peak in the Coast Range) or set up camp (considerably cheaper, of course) along the little creek. You can even fly in—there's an airstrip. For a fee, local cowboys can take you trail riding on one of the Flying M's horses and maybe even grill you a steak on the way. ■ *10 miles west of Yamhill: follow the little red flying M's; (503) 662-3222; 23029 NW Flying M Rd, Yamhill, OR 97148; $$; AE, DC, MC, V; checks OK.*

Dundee

Lodgings

MCMINNVILLE

Prototypical small-town Oregon, where teenagers still cruise bumper-to-bumper down the main drag on Friday night. But the growing wine industry has enlivened things a bit: the central location and a surprising number of tourist facilities make it a good headquarters for wine touring. Serious wine lovers can OD on great wine and food while hobnobbing with wine celebrities (including some of France's hot young winemakers) at the three-day **International Pinot Noir Celebration** in late July on the grounds of gracious old Linfield College; call (503) 472-8964 for information.

RESTAURANTS

Nick's Italian Cafe ★★★ Nick's has settled into its role as local institution and winemakers' culinary headquarters. Owner Nick Peirano is not given to food fads, and what this place does it does better than any other place in the valley. The fixed-price five-course meal includes a second-course tureen of Nick's grandmother's heavenly, rich, garlicky minestrone, followed by a simply dressed green salad and chewy French bread. Seasonal antipasto might include shellfish in winter or prosciutto and melon in summer. The fourth course is always pasta, homemade, and delicious. Entrees might include a perfectly grilled shark or sirloin steak with capers. Nick's mama will insist you try one of her Italian specialties for dessert. Service can be inconsistent, and the setting, a former luncheonette, is far from fancy. But the food and a fabulous, well-priced wine list (with many local treasures unavailable elsewhere) keeps packing them in. ■ *Off Hwy 99W, across from the movie theater; (503)434-4471; 521 E 3rd St, McMinnville; $$; beer and wine; no credit cards; checks OK; dinner Tues–Sun.*

Golden Valley Brewpub and Restaurant ★ This recycled bottling plant is a happening place in McMinnville. The warehouse space is now fitted out with high beams, lots of potted trees, and a huge wooden bar. Half is pub and half is restaurant, though you can eat anywhere. The menu is extensive, from pizza to burgers to a few attempts at fussier dishes. Stick with the basics: burgers are huge and come with interesting toppings, the sausage sandwich bites back. A good selection of their own brews *and* wines. A killer root beer is made on the premises, too. ■ *At intersection of E 3rd and N Johnson; (503)472-2739; 980 E 4th St, McMinnville; $; beer and wine; AE, MC, V; checks OK; lunch, dinner every day.* Ꮨ

Kame ★ McMinnvilleites aren't used to getting their change counted out in Japanese, but for food this good and this inexpensive, they don't seem to mind one bit. A tiny storefront place with white walls, plain wooden tables and chairs, a few artfully placed decorations, and simple Japanese food served graciously. Owner Mieko Nordin learned to cook family style from her mother. A basic (and satisfying) meal might include tasty miso soup, a small salad of pickled cabbage, and chicken or pork with vegetables on a bed of steaming rice. Tempura and teriyaki for dinner, too. ■ *At Evans and 3rd; (503)434-4326; 228 N Evans, McMinnville; $; beer and wine; MC, V; local checks only; lunch Tues–Fri, dinner Tues–Sat.*

LODGINGS

Mattey House ★★ New owners Denise and Jack Seed, world wanderers originally from England, have restored this B&B to its accustomed elegance after it sat vacant for a couple of years.

McMinnville

Lodgings

The new look retains the glories of this 1890s Victorian farm-house, but with a lighter, less formal look: lace curtains, flow-ered wallpaper, comfortable armchairs, lots of flowers. Rooms are (authentically) small, but there are nice touches like a cou-ple of claw-footed bathtubs (only one room has private bath), a cozy fireplace in the living room, and lots of board games. Af-ter a breakfast that might include compote, frittata, or Dutch pancakes, you can wander through the small vineyard and pick your own grapes. ▪ *Just south of Lafayette on Hwy 99W;
(503)434-5058; 10221 NE Mattey Lane, McMinnville, OR
97128; $$; MC, V; checks OK.*

Steiger Haus ★★ Decks wrap the chalet-style house at a cou-ple of levels, offering plenty of opportunities to sip coffee out-side and enjoy the large woodsy backyard. Though you're right in town (and close to Linfield College), it's a peaceful oasis. Five rooms (three downstairs, two up) all have private baths, and a conference room is available. The house has a comfortable, Northwest feel, with lots of light. Owner Doris Steiger is a weaver who sells woolen goods in a small guest shop. Full breakfasts include homemade granola as well as a variety of hot dishes. Children over 10 are welcome. ▪ *From Hwy 99W
turn east on Cowls at the hospital; (503)472-0821; 360 Wil-son St, McMinnville, OR 97128; $$; MC, V; checks OK.*

Safari Motor Inn ★ Just off Highway 99W as it enters McMinnville, this unassuming motor lodge doesn't offer any-thing fancy, but it's ideally located for visitors who shy away from the B&B scene, and the prices can't be beat. The rooms are quiet and beds comfortable. The former motel pool is now pushing up daisies, but if you want to cool off on a hot after-noon, head a quarter mile south on 99W to McMinnville's mod-ern Aquatic Center. For a couple of bucks, you can frolic in a large pool. A small exercise facility with Jacuzzi is available. ▪
*19th St and Hwy 99W; (503)472-5187; 345 N Hwy 99W,
McMinnville, OR 97128; $; AE, DC, MC, V; no checks.* ⴲ

BELLEVUE/SHERIDAN

Bellevue, a tiny crossroads, is the site of three fine establish-ments, all under one roof. The **Oregon Wine Tasting Room**,
(503)843-3787, offers tastes of the best bottlings from two dozen Oregon wineries. **The Lawrence Gallery**, (503)843-3633, is an excellent showcase of fine regional talent in all me-dia. Upstairs is **Augustine's**, one of the region's better restaurants.

RESTAURANTS

Augustine's ★★ An ideal place to take a break and refresh yourself along the road to the beach. The informal, open space has scenic views out both sides: farmland on one side and down into the Lawrence Gallery on the other. You could start your meal with a smoked seafood platter (salmon, mussels, halibut, and cream cheese) or some of the excellent creamy clam chowder. Soup or green salad (veggies and greens come from a local organic farm) is included with the entree. For the main course, zero in on the seasonal seafood (a poached salmon fillet, a tender, fresh sturgeon)—the real focus of owner/chef Jeff Quatraro. The legendary hazelnut cheesecake is rich, light, and not too sweet; citrus tart (orange, lemon, and grapefruit curd) is tangy and refreshing. A good selection of Oregon wines by the bottle and the glass. ■ *Hwy 18, 7 miles west of McMinnville; (503)843-3225; 19706 Hwy 18, Bellevue; $$; full bar; MC, V; checks OK; lunch Wed–Sat, dinner Wed–Sun, brunch Sun.*

LODGINGS

Sheridan Country Inn There's not much in Sheridan (besides the state prison), but you're not far from either the wine country or the ocean. This old house is now an inn with 12 rooms, 8 in the funky but spacious mansion and 4 in outside duplexes. The rooms are large and comfortable and look out on the surrounding acre of grounds. Some rooms come with microwaves, private baths, and TVs; all have refrigerators. Room 7 is a huge suite with a private Jacuzzi. The inn is a friendly place and kids are welcome. ■ *1 mile west of Bridge St on Hwy 18 (business loop); (503)843-3151; 1330 W Main, Sheridan, OR 97378; $$; AE, DC, MC, V; local checks only.* &

Salem

MOUNT ANGEL

Perhaps most famous for its Oktoberfest, the town is home to **Mount Angel Abbey**, a hundred-year-old Benedictine seminary. Visit the abbey on a foggy morning, when its beautiful setting atop a butte sacred to the Indians will make it seem as if it's floating in the clouds. And don't miss the library, a gem by the internationally celebrated Finnish architect Alvar Aalto. For hours, call (503)845-3030. Music lovers descend on the place in July for the Bach Festival.

SALEM

Except for the state capitol and office buildings, it has the look and feel of a small town. The 1938 capitol has an art deco–cum–grandiose-classical look and is worth a visit. Attractive parks flank the building, and just behind is **Willamette University**, the oldest university in the West. The campus is a happy blend of old and new brick buildings, with a small stream, Mill Creek, nicely incorporated into the landscape. A pleasant place to stroll, and plant lovers should visit the small but well-tended botanical gardens on the east side of the campus.

Across the road from Willamette University is **Historic Mission Mill Village**, 1313 Mill Street SE, (503)585-7012. The impressive 42-acre cluster of restored buildings from the 1800s includes a woolen mill, a parsonage, a Presbyterian church, and several homes. The mill, which drew its power from Mill Creek, now houses a museum that literally makes the sounds of the factory come alive. The **Jason Lee House**, dating from 1841, is the oldest remaining frame house in the Northwest; regular tours of the premises run from 10am to 4:30pm, Tuesday–Saturday. Picnic along the stream and feed the ducks, if you like. The **Salem Visitor Information Center** is part of the complex, as are several shops selling handcrafted clothing, gifts, and antiques.

Bush House, 600 Mission Street SE, (503)363-4714, is a Victorian home built in 1877 by pioneer newspaper publisher Asahel Bush. It sits in a large park complete with conservatory, rose gardens, hiking paths, and barn turned art gallery. Tours available.

Gilbert House Children's Museum, (503)371-3631, on the downtown riverfront between the bridges, has a variety of hands-on learning activities for young children. Children will also appreciate **Enchanted Forest**, (503)371-4242, a nicely wooded storybook park with space for picnicking, just off I-5 south of town.

▼

Salem

▲

Salem is off the beaten winery track, but **Willamette Valley Vineyards**, (503)588-9463, a big investor-owned winery offering a broad range of wines, is just off I-5 south of town and commands a spectacular view of the countryside. Just to the north of the city off Highway 221 is **Redhawk Vineyard**, (503) 362-1596, with a variety of good red wines and humorous labels.

Old-fashioned ferries, operated by cable, still cross the Willamette River in a few places and offer a fun alternative to bridges, if you've got some extra time. Two run in the Salem area: the Wheatland ferry, just north of town in Keizer (follow Highway 219 north from downtown and turn off on Wheatland Road), and the Buena Vista (from I-5 take exit 243 and follow Talbot Road west). They run every day (except during storms or high water) and cost very little.

If you're in the area during the 10 days of the **Oregon State Fair** (around Labor Day), don't miss it—it's the biggest in the Northwest and there's enough room so you don't feel jammed in.

RESTAURANTS

Alessandro's Park Plaza ★★ Easily the most elegant place to eat in Salem, this lovely urban oasis overlooks Mill Creek Park just next to the downtown business district. Owner Alessandro Fasani calls it Roman; most diners would call it upscale Italian, with quiet, professional service and a menu that emphasizes elegant pasta and seafood dishes. Nothing particularly original, but the classics are done with flair: perfectly cooked veal piccata, rich meat-stuffed tortellini in light cream sauce. In addition to the regular menu, a multicourse dinner is offered daily; the staff asks only if there's a particular dish you don't like, and they surprise you with the rest. A delight, indeed. ▪ *Trade and High sts; (503)370-9951; 325 High St SE, Salem; $$; full bar; AE, MC, V; local checks only; lunch Mon–Fri, dinner Mon–Sat.* &

DaVinci's ★ A very ambitious, very popular, pizza place. Individual pizzas come with an interesting assortment of toppings, and there are different homemade whole-wheat pastas each day. An appetizer of thin, light bread covered with garlic and herbs is simple and flavorful. The ravioli might be cheese and artichoke covered with a sauce of scallops and tomatoes and herbs—rich and flavorful, but too many disjointed flavors. Eggplant on top of polenta, covered with a tangy tomato sauce, is simpler and more successful. Wine by the glass comes dear: you're better off making a selection of one of the well-priced bottles. The brick-and-dark-wood building opens into two stories inside—avoid sitting near the bustling staircase. ▪ *On High St near Ferry; (503)399-1413; 180 High St, Salem; $$; full bar; AE, MC, V; checks OK; lunch Mon–Fri, dinner every day.* &

La Margarita ★ Definitely one of the livelier spots downtown. The unassuming front opens to a colorfully decorated, two-storied interior, with lots of mirrors to make it look bigger than it is and music to keep it hopping. The staff hops, too—this place is busy. The menu has all the usuals, but the specialty is mesquite grilling, especially the tender and lightly cooked beef and chicken. Sauces are subtle, with the emphasis on eating healthy. The mammoth margaritas blow all those good intentions out the door. ▪ *Near corner of High and Church sts; (503)362-8861; 545 Ferry St SE, Salem; $; full bar; AE, DC, MC, V; checks OK; lunch Mon–Sat, dinner every day.* &

McGrath's Publick Fish House ★ This sharp-looking restaurant might be just a knockoff of more famous Seattle and Portland fish houses, but in restaurant-poor Salem it has a fresh feel. Good prices and special attention to children should keep families happy. Crowds pack this glass-fronted, multitiered building. The menu's diverse, but you should order the seafood off the daily fresh sheet. The blackened oyster appetizer is almost a meal in itself—plump oysters, plenty spicy. Mesquite-broiled salmon and the trout are cooked perfectly, though sauces tend to be uninteresting. No complaints on the chubby marionberry cobbler. The young service lacks real expertise, but is cheerful and eager. ▪ *Chemeketa and Liberty*

Sts; (503)362-0736; 350 Chemeketa, Salem; $$; full bar; AE,
DC, MC, V; checks OK; breakfast, lunch, dinner every day. &

Morton's Bistro Northwest ★ Clever design puts the diner *below* roadway level, looking out on an attractive courtyard backed by an ivy-covered wall. The interior is intimate, with dark wood beams and soft lighting. The menu is probably one of the most ambitious in Salem—predominantly Northwest cuisine with hints of international influences, featuring fresh seafood, veal, and a short list of pasta dishes. The service is expert and pleasant, and there's a very good selection of reasonably priced Northwest wines. ■ *Across the Marion St bridge from downtown; (503)585-1113; 1128 Edgewater, West Salem; $$; full bar; MC, V; checks OK; dinner Tues–Sat.* &

LODGINGS

Marquee House Bed and Breakfast ★ You're a half-dozen blocks from the capitol, but because the house sits away from the street with a broad yard sloping down to Mill Creek, it feels like the country. Owner Rickie Hart, a veteran of Long Beach's Shelburne Inn, has developed a movies theme in this Colonial-style B&B: you might stay in the "Topper" room, with a collection of old hats, or among old Western prints and memorabilia in the "Blazing Saddles" room. Evenings, settle back for movies and popcorn in the living room. Request a room with a view of the creek and a fireplace. Watch for beaver, or spawning salmon in the fall. Breakfast will probably include local fresh fruits and a plentiful supply of egg or pancake dishes, potatoes, pastries, and fresh breads. ■ *Off Center St, just west of intersection with 17th; (503)391-0837; 333 Wyatt Ct NE, Salem, OR 97301; $$; MC, V; checks OK*

Phoenix Inn ★ A new motel geared for the business traveler. Spacious rooms in muted colors all have small refrigerators, microwaves, and coffeepots; some have Jacuzzis. Conference rooms, fax and copy services are available; there's a small pool, Jacuzzi, and fitness room to relax in; and you can load up on the complimentary buffet breakfast in the morning. Staff is friendly and helpful, rates are reasonable, and kids stay free. ■ *From I-5, exit 252, west on Kuebler to Commercial; (503) 588-9220 or (800)445-4498; 4370 Commercial St SE, Salem, OR 97302; $$; AE, DC, MC, V; checks OK.* &

INDEPENDENCE

As long as anyone can remember, **Taylor's Fountain and Gift**, on the corner of Main and Monmouth, has been serving up old-fashioned sodas, burgers, and breakfasts. Marge Taylor, her daughter, and two granddaughters run the place and haven't changed it much in its 50-odd years.

RESTAURANTS

Amador's Alley ★ Here's an unexpected find that produces some of the most honest Mexican fare around. Brothers Manuel and Antonio Amador do the cooking while their families (down to the youngest children) wait on the customers. Nothing elaborate in the way of decor: a whitewashed space, a few Mexican fans, paper flowers. But you know it's going to be good as soon as the first basket of chips arrives (thick, crunchy, homemade) along with a fresh salsa; you can taste the corn and tomatoes. Nothing fancy or unusual, but everything from tacos to enchiladas is exquisitely fresh, piping hot, and lavishly garnished with sour cream, avocado, fresh tomatoes, and green onions. A second Amador's is in Lincoln City; 828 NE Hwy 101, (503)996-4223. ■ *Hoffman Rd and Main St; (503)838-0170; 870 N Main St, Independence; $; full bar; MC, V; checks OK; lunch, dinner Mon–Sat.* ઙ

ALBANY

Once you get off the freeway and past the smell of the pulp mill, you'll discover a fine representative of the small-town Oregon of an earlier era, with broad, quiet streets, neat houses, and a slow pace. Once an important transportation hub in the Willamette Valley, the town has an unequaled selection of historic homes and buildings in a wide variety of styles, many of them lovingly restored.

Historic buildings. A self-guided tour displays 13 distinct architectural styles in the 50-block, 368-building Monteith Historic District alone. Then there are the Hackleman District (28 blocks, 210 buildings) and downtown (9½ blocks, 80 buildings). Many of the buildings are open for inspection on annual tours—the last Saturday in July and the Sunday evening before Christmas Eve. A handy guide is available free of charge from the Albany Chamber of Commerce, 435 W First Avenue, (503)926-1517, or the Albany Convention and Visitors Center at 300 SW Second, (503)928-0911 or (800)526-2256.

You can also take a pleasant stroll on the path along-side the tree-lined Willamette to **Monteith Park** and **Bryant Park**.

Covered bridges. The covered bridges that were so characteristic of this area are disappearing. From 450 their number has dwindled to less than 50, but that's still more than in any state west of the Mississippi. Most of the remaining ones are in the Willamette Valley counties of Lane, Linn, and Lincoln. Local preservationists are fighting to save the remaining bridges. Best starting points for easy-to-follow circuits of the bridges are Albany, Eugene, and Cottage Grove; in addition, many handsome bridges dot the woods of the Oregon Coast

Range. Six of these bridges lie within an 8-mile radius of Scio, northeast of Albany; for a map, contact the Visitors Center. For other tours, send SASE with two first-class stamps to the Covered Bridge Society of Oregon, PO Box 1804, Newport, OR 97365, or call (503)265-2934.

RESTAURANTS

Novak's Hungarian Paprikas ★★ Don't be put off by the strip-mall setting—you'll get a warm welcome from Joseph and Matilda Novak, Hungarian refugees who run this quaintly decorated place with help from their family (so your waitress will help you pronounce the Hungarian dishes). The housemade sausages are mild and delicately spiced, the stuffed cabbage is oozing with flavor, and the sides of tangy spiced cabbage are to kill for (though surprisingly the signature chicken paprika is bland). Huge servings come with lots of vegetables and potatoes, and small prices. Don't forget dessert: the pastry chef is full-time and the dessert menu is longer than the main one. ■ *Take exit 233 toward town; (503)967-9488; 2835 Santiam Hwy SE, Albany; $; no alcohol; MC, V; checks OK; lunch Sun–Fri, dinner every day.* &

▼

Albany

▲

CORVALLIS

The town is dominated by **Oregon State University**, which gives it a more cosmopolitan flavor than most towns of its size. The campus is typical of other Northwest megaversities, with a gracious core of old buildings in several styles, magnificent giant trees, and lots of open space, surrounded by a maze of modern boxlike classroom and residential buildings of little character. Sports are big here, especially basketball and gymnastics, but the basement of Gill Coliseum also houses the **Horner Museum**, which has a wonderfully eclectic, rather dilapidated collection that relates the history of Oregon's development, from Native Americans to the Oregon Trail to economic growth. A grand place for kids, with lots of nooks and crannies and large artifacts from yesteryear. Unfortunately, only open weekends; (503)737-2951. **Corvallis Art Center**, 700 SW Madison, (503)754-1551, located in a renovated 1889 Episcopal church off Central Park, displays local crafts and hosts weekly lunchtime concerts. A well-preserved old downtown district runs along the river: you can poke around in interesting shops and stop in for an outrageously big pastry and a cup of coffee at **New Morning Bakery**, 219 SW Second, (503)754-0181, where you can also get a light lunch or dinner.

Corvallis is ideal for biking and running; most streets include a wide bike lane, and routes follow both the Willamette and Mary's rivers. Avery Park, 15th Street and US 20, offers a maze of wooded trails as well as prime picnic sites and a rose garden. Tree lovers may also enjoy OSU's 40-acre **Peavy Arboretum**, 8 miles north of town on Highway 99W—it has hiking trails and picnic facilities.

RESTAURANTS

The Gables ★★ With all the funky eateries around the university, this is still the place in town for fine, formal dining. The cooking is always consistent. A homey atmosphere—dark wood furnishings, low beams, fireplace—and a courteous staff combine to make this a very comfortable place. The menu features tried-and-true American fare: prime rib, lamb chops, and seafood. Dinners are huge and come with all the expected trimmings: sourdough bread, relish tray, salad or chicken bisque, veggies, rice or potato. The prime rib has the reputation as the best in town. Reserve a table in the wine cellar for special group occasions. ■ *Follow Harrison to 9th; (503) 752-3364; 1121 NW 9th St, Corvallis; $$; full bar; AE, DC, MC, V; checks OK; dinner every day.* &

Bombs Away Cafe ★ A tacqueria with an attitude. You'll find all your Tex-Mex favorites, but with a wholesome twist. So, heaps of herb-flavored brown rice and black beans and hardly any fat in sight. Check this out: a chimichanga stuffed with duck confit and covered with tomatoes and tomatillos. Or how about a goat cheese and black bean quesadilla? Lots of vegetarian choices. In the front room you order at the counter, and the ambience is your basic college-town cafeteria, but the help is friendly and service is speedy. In back there's a full-service room that's quieter, with a slightly fancier menu, where you can also order from an impressive variety of tequilas. ■ *On Monroe at 25th; (503) 757-7221; 2527 NW Monroe, Corvallis; $; full bar; MC, V; checks OK; lunch Mon–Fri, dinner Mon–Sun.* &

Corvallis

Lodgings

▲

Nearly Normal's ★ There's nothing normal about Nearly Normal's (they've dubbed the flamingo their official bird). The aging hippies who run the place advertise their food as "gonzo cuisine": vegetarian food, organically grown, but prepared with originality and panache. There's lots of Mexican on the menu, plus a few Middle Eastern items and excellent veggie burgers. Try the falafel, a hearty mix of spicy garbanzo patties packed into pita with fresh veggies and a cool yogurt sauce, or the Acapulco sunburger, with avocado and salsa. The fresh fruit drinks are great. This place can get crowded, and you bus your own dishes. ■ *Near the corner of Monroe and 15th; (503) 753-0791; 109 NW 15th St, Corvallis; $; beer and wine; no credit cards; checks OK; breakfast, lunch, dinner Mon–Sat.*

LODGINGS

Hanson Country Inn ★★ The inn is just a few minutes from town, but you'll feel you're in the country as you drive up to this wood-and-brick 1928 farmhouse. Formerly a prosperous poultry-breeding ranch, it's now, thanks to an extensive renovation by former San Franciscan Patricia Covey, a registered historic home. The gleaming living room (with piano and fireplace), sun room, and library are often used for weddings. Step outside into a formal lawn and garden. Upstairs are four guest rooms, luxuriously wallpapered and linened. The best suite has a four-poster bed, private bath, and a study. After breakfasting on crêpes with blackberries or a fresh frittata, explore the grounds and original egg house. Bring the kids; a new two-bedroom cottage behind the main house has a fully equipped kitchen, private bath, and living area perfect for families. ■ *5 minutes west of town off West Hills at 35th; (503) 752-2919; 795 SW Hanson St, Corvallis, OR 97333; $$; AE, DC, MC, V; checks OK.*

ELMIRA

LODGINGS

McGillivray's Log Home Bed and Breakfast ★ This spacious log home on 5 wooded acres makes a lovely, pastoral retreat for urbanites and a fine introduction to the beauties of Western Oregon for out-of-staters. The two large guest rooms (one with a king-size bed and two twins—perfect for families) both have private baths. A hearty breakfast is prepared on the wood cookstove with antique griddle, and there are fresh Northwest berries in season. ■ *14 miles west of Eugene off Hwy 126; (503) 935-3564; 88680 Evers Rd, Elmira, OR 97437; $$; MC, V; checks OK.* ♿

EUGENE

Although it's the state's second-largest city, Eugene is still very much Portland's sleepy sister to the south. There's no skyline here—unless you count the grain elevator (well, okay, there's a 12-story Hilton, too). A Eugenean's idea of a traffic jam is when it takes more than five minutes to traverse downtown. There's always parking; people smile at you on the street and, even in its urban heart, Eugene is more treed than paved.

Still, this overgrown town has a sophisticated indigenous culture, from its own symphony (conducted by the justifiably celebrated Marin Alsop), to homegrown ballet, opera, and theater companies. There are more speakers and events (courtesy of the University of Oregon, the state's flagship institution) than one could possibly ever attend. There are good bookstores (don't miss **Smith Family Bookstore**), the requisite number of coffeehouses (including the newest entry into the world of caffeine, **Java Joe's**, out Willamette Street), trendy brew pubs (try **Steelhead** in Station Square), two serious chocolatiers (**Euphoria** and **Fenton & Lee**), and enough local color—from persevering hippies to backcountry loggers—to make life interesting.

Whatever else you do in Eugene, here are the musts: a hike up **Spencer's Butte**, just south of town, for a spectacular view of the town, valley, and its two rivers; a morning at Saturday Market, the state's oldest outdoor crafts fair; an afternoon shopping and eating your way through the Fifth Street Public Market; an evening at the Hult Center for the Performing Arts. If you're in town in early July, don't miss the area's oldest and wildest countercultural celebration, the **Oregon Country Fair**.

Hult Center for the Performing Arts is the city's world-class concert facility, with two architecturally striking halls. The 24-hour concert line is (503)342-5746.

University of Oregon features a lovely art museum with a permanent collection of Orientalia, a new natural history museum, several historic landmark buildings, and a wide variety of speakers and events.

Wistec, a small but nicely conceived hands-on science and technology museum (with accompanying laser light-show planetarium), is the place to take kids on rainy afternoons; open Wednesday through Sunday, noon-5pm, 2300 Centennial Boulevard, (503)484-9027.

Saturday Market, a thriving open-air crafts and food fair, is the ultimate Eugene experience. Unique crafts sold by the artisans themselves, continental noshing, eclectic music, and inspired people-watching; open April through December on High Street at Broadway.

Fifth Street Public Market has undergone a facelift, with an airier, more spacious (and more upscale) crafts area. But the rest of this lovely place, with its three levels of shops surrounding a pretty brick courtyard, remains the same. The Market houses the city's best bakery, Metropol.

Outdoors. The two rivers that run through town, the Willamette and the McKenzie, provide opportunities for canoeists and rafters, both first-timers and whitewater enthusiasts. Hikers will find miles of forest trails just outside the city limits. Runners will love the city's several groomed, packed running trails.

Parks. Run along the banks of the Willamette through Alton Baker Park on the 6.3-kilometer groomed Prefontaine Trail. Women will feel safer on the sloughside 1.6-kilometer circuit that borders Amazon Park, site of spirited outdoor concerts in the summer. Hendricks Park, the city's oldest, features an outstanding 10-acre rhododendron garden (best blooms in May and early June). Skinner's Butte Park, which skirts the Willamette, includes a lovely rose garden, several playgrounds, picnic areas, and a 12-mile bike/running path. Spencer's Butte,

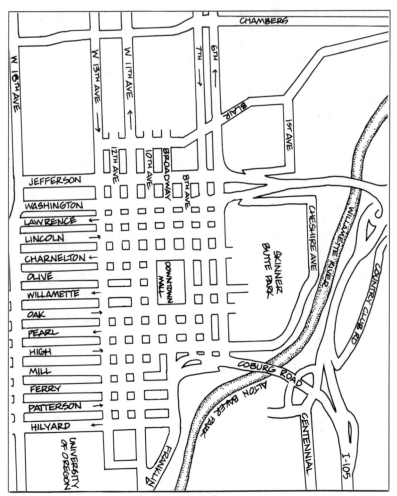

Eugene

just south of town, offers sweeping urban and pastoral views to those who hike up the two relatively easy trails to the top.

RESTAURANTS

Chanterelle ★★★ Understated, sophisticated, and unfailingly wonderful, chef Ralf Schmidt's intimate restaurant offers the very freshest of every season, cooked with respect and restrained imagination. The small menu with its delicate basil scallops and richly sauced tournedos of beef is supplemented by a wide selection of chef's specials. In the spring, there's chinook salmon and local lamb. In the winter, Schmidt's deeply satisfying onion soup will warm the inner you—whatever is fresh and appeals to the chef's sense of adventure. Schmidt does it all alone in a kitchen the size of a walk-in closet—and comes out smiling at the end of the evening to greet his loyal patrons. A respectable wine list; extraordinary desserts. ■ *Across the street from 5th St Public Market; (503)484-4065; 207 E 5th, Eugene; $$; full bar; AE, DC, MC, V; checks OK; dinner Tues–Sat.* &

Excelsior Cafe ★★ Maurizio Paparo stepped into big shoes when he took over Stephanie Pearl's Eugene institution. (Pearl single-handedly brought culinary culture to Eugene.) The menu is moving ever so slightly away from French cuisine in favor of more international selections, but all the "Ex's" standbys are here, from the exquisite pear, butterleaf lettuce, blue cheese, and hazelnut salad, through the perfectly grilled swordfish, and on to the Frangelico cheesecake. Fortunately, Paparo is just as committed to quality and freshness as was the Pearl. The elegant but informal restaurant and its small, bustling bar are favorites with the university crowd. ■ *Across from Sacred Heart Hospital; (503)342-6963; 754 E 13th, Eugene; $$; full bar; AE, MC, V; checks OK; lunch Mon–Sat, dinner every night, brunch Sun.*

Zenon Cafe ★★ Urbane, noisy, crowded—and always interesting—this is the place upscale locals go when they want to pretend they don't live in Eugene, Oregon. Zenon's formidable, ever-changing international menu ranges from blackened catfish to Thai green curried beef, from Greek lamb meatballs to fettuccine with morel, shiitake, and agaricus mushrooms. A good selection of regional wines by the glass is available. And do leave room for dessert (not difficult, since entree portions are small), for Zenon's sweets are among the city's very best. The outdoor seating in mild weather is delightful. ■ *Corner of E Broadway and Pearl; (503)343-3005; 898 Pearl St, Eugene; $$; beer and wine; MC, V; checks OK; breakfast, lunch, dinner every day.* &

Ambrosia ★ The pizza is wonderful here: small, crisp pies topped with rich plum tomato sauce and your choice of trendy ingredients (sun-dried tomatoes, artichoke hearts, roasted eggplant) and baked in a huge, wood-burning oven. But Ambrosia is much more than a designer pizzeria; take, for example, the angel hair noodles topped with grilled, marinated vegetables or the zucchini and fennel lasagne. Fresh fish specials might include a grilled halibut in tomato caper butter or Chilean sea bass finished in dry wine and topped with Dungeness crab and toasted almonds. Gelato cools the evening. ■ *Corner of Broadway and Pearl; (503)342-4141; 174 E Broadway, Eugene; $; full bar; MC, V; checks OK; lunch Mon–Sat, dinner every day.* &

Baja Cafe ★ With its zany decor—watermelon piñatas, spinning globes, a 7-foot mounted swordfish, and lots of turquoise, this informal eatery is a downtown favorite. If you're looking for real Mexican food, don't come here. But if homemade chips with blue-cheese dip, red snapper tacos, and black beans with a sprinkling of Parmesan sound good, Baja is your kind of place. With its fast counter service, flexible kids' menu, and naturally exuberant atmosphere, this is a great place for families. ▪ *Pearl between Broadway and 8th; (503) 683-8606; 860 Pearl, Eugene; $; beer and wine; MC, V; checks OK; lunch, dinner Mon–Sat.* ᕦ

Cafe Navarro ★ Like the world beat music that plays on the sound system, Jorge Navarro's restaurant is a rich cross-cultural experience, with dishes ranging from Africa and Spain to Cuba and the Caribbean. Navarro freely combines cuisines, often arriving at extraordinary results such as his south-of-the-border interpretation of Caribbean cioppino, made here with cilantro, chiles, and roasted tomatoes. There are no bad choices. For lunch, Navarro's version of arroz con pollo, with seared chicken chunks, red peppers, capers, and cilantro, is a good bet. For breakfast, the hands-down favorite is chilaquilas—eggs scrambled with corn tortillas, chipolte salsa and Monterey Jack cheese. ▪ *At the foot of Willamette St; (503) 344-0943; 454 Willamette St, Eugene; $; beer and wine; MC, V; checks OK; lunch Tues–Fri, dinner Tues–Sat, brunch Sat–Sun.* ᕦ

Mekala's ★ A pretty Thai restaurant with its light-filled dining area overlooking the Fifth Street Public Market courtyard (outside seating, weather permitting), Mekala's features a six-page menu with more than a dozen fiery curries and two dozen vegetarian dishes. Chef/owner Payung Van Slyke is an inventive cook who shows sensitivity to a wide range of palates: magnificent angel wings (deboned chicken wings stuffed with ground pork, glass noodles, and bean sprouts), a flavor-packed homoke souffle (shrimp, scallops, and fish in a curry and coconut sauce with fresh lime leaves, green pepper, and cabbage). End the meal with a dish of velvety homemade coconut ice cream. ▪ *In the 5th St Public Market Building; (503) 342-4872; 296 E 5th St, Eugene; $; beer and wine; MC, V; checks OK; lunch, dinner every day.* ᕦ

Napoli ★ Although all of the pasta (and the designer pizza) is good here, possibly the best item on the menu is the simplest: insalata mista, a huge bowl of fresh seasonal greens, artichoke hearts, and roasted bell peppers tossed with Chianti vinaigrette. If you feast on the salad, you could allow yourself a slice of the sinful tiramisu for dessert, a chocolate sponge cake soaked in rum, layered with Italian cream cheese, and topped with shaved bittersweet chocolate. ▪ *Across from Sacred Heart Hospital; (503) 485-4552; 686 E 13th, Eugene; $; beer and wine; MC, V; checks OK; breakfast, lunch, dinner Mon–Sat.* ᕦ

Oregon Electric Station ★ The Electric Station narrows the culinary generation gap between the prime rib–and–baked potato folks and the yellowfin-tuna-in-roasted-pepper-butter crowd. While there is nothing spectacular about the diverse menu— no great risks taken—there are also few failures. The seafood is never overcooked; the steak is invariably juicy. You eat in converted railroad cars parked behind the lovely brick station that gives the restaurant its name. The historical station building with its 30-foot ceilings and arched windows houses the city's prettiest bar. Live jazz on weekends. ■ *2 blocks north of the Hult Center; (503)485-4444; 27 E 5th, Eugene; $; full bar; MC, V; local checks OK; dinner Mon–Sun, brunch Sun.* ዼ

Hilda's Latin American Restaurant Housed in a middling 1930s bungalow and tucked away in a downwardly mobile westside neighborhood, Hilda's, with its exotic menu of Latin American dishes, comes as a lovely surprise. Here you'll find the cuisines of Brazil, Peru, Argentina, Chile, Guatemala, and Venezuela represented by a pleasing diversity of meat, seafood, and vegetarian offerings. ■ *Take W 6th to Blair; (503)343-4322; 400 Blair Blvd, Eugene; $; beer and wine; MC, V; checks OK; lunch Mon–Fri, dinner Mon–Sat.*

Jamie's Take the kids to Jamie's, where they (and you) can eat terrific burgers (14 varieties), inspired onion rings, the best grilled chicken sandwich in town and real—yes, real—milk shakes. Kids can play on the red Vespa and sidecar while you listen to tunes from the '50s jukebox and await your order. There's a second Jamie's in Eugene at 1810 Chambers Street, (503)343-0485, a third in Corvallis, and a fourth in Portland. ■ *Near Hilyard and 24th; (503)342-2206; 2445 Hilyard St, Eugene; $; beer and wine; AE, MC, V; checks OK; lunch, dinner every day.* ዼ

West Brothers Bar-B-Que It's not Texas, but the dry-rubbed baby back ribs give a good imitation. The North Carolina pork shoulder, Louisiana links, and Oregon chicken come tender and tasty with three sauces—hot, sweet, and regular. Black beans, smoked barbecue beans, and a good poppyseeded coleslaw are the sides of choice. On the back of the menu, you'll find unusual choices that serve as a reminder that one of the West brothers used to be a chef at Zenon: jalapeño noodles with mussels, clams, and shrimp; critter potpie; and smoked hominy and black-eyed peas. Eugene City Brewery's fine microbrews are made right on the premises. ■ *Northwest corner of the downtown mall; (503)345-8489; 844 Olive St, Eugene; $; beer and wine; AE, MC, V; checks OK; lunch, dinner every day.* ዼ

▼
Eugene

Lodgings

▲

LODGINGS

Campus Cottage ★★ Eugene's premier bed and breakfast is classy, cozy, comfortable, and convenient. The four guest rooms, all with private baths, are beautifully furnished with antiques. One of the rooms is very private, with its own entrance and bay windows overlooking a pretty garden and deck. Innkeeper Ursula Bates, the doyenne of the Eugene B&B scene, does everything right, from the crisp linen on the beds to the crock full of warm-from-the-oven chocolate chip cookies (cold milk in the guest fridge, of course). Her full breakfasts are both delicious and elegantly served. ■ *1 blk south of the U of O on E 19th; (503) 342-5346; 1136 E 19th Ave, Eugene, OR 97403; $$$; no credit cards; checks OK.*

Maryellen's Guest House ★★ This airy Northwest contemporary tucked into a wooded hillside is just three minutes from the University of Oregon campus. Quiet and unharried, Maryellen's has only two rooms, each of them tastefully decorated (one bath has a double shower and Roman soaking tub). The main house's deck is the real drawing card, with its lovely pool and all-weather hot tub screened by dense greenery and a natural cedar fence. Innkeeper Maryellen Larson is the perfect hostess: friendly, accommodating, knowledgable, and respectful of your privacy. Oh, yes—she's a terrific breakfast chef too, known for her old-fashioned bread pudding with warm berry sauce. ■ *East side of Hendricks Park; (503) 342-7375; 1583 Fircrest, Eugene, OR 97403; $$; AE, MC, V; checks OK.*

Valley River Inn ★★ The Inn's neighbor is a regional shopping mall with acres of parking lots, but the Inn looks to the Willamette River, which it hugs, for its ambience. With pretty inner courtyards, lovely plantings, and an inviting pool area, this sprawling complex effectively creates a world of its own. The rooms are oversize and well decorated, with the best ones facing the river. The outdoor dining area hard by the river is a wonderful place to skip dinner and enjoy drinks and hors d'oeuvres. ■ *Exit 194B off I-5 to 105 (west) to exit 3; (503) 687-0123; 1000 Valley River Way, Eugene, OR 97401; $$$; AE, DC, MC, V; checks OK.* ⅄

Eugene Hilton ★ For convenience to downtown, the Hilton fits the bill. It's across a brick courtyard from the Hult Center for the Performing Arts, a block from the downtown mall, two blocks from the thriving Market district, and within easy strolling distance to a half-dozen good restaurants. The rooms are comfortable and predictable, with nice city views from south-facing rooms and quieter butte views from the north. Amenities include a (very small) indoor pool along with a sauna, Jacuzzi, and fitness room. Don't plan to eat at either of the hotel's two lackluster restaurants. ■ *Exit 194B off I-5, then exit 1 to city center; (503) 342-2000; 66 E 6th Ave, Eugene, OR 97401; $$$; AE, DC, MC, V; checks OK.* ⅄

New Oregon Motel The free sports center and this Best Western's location just across from the University of Oregon elevate this place from mere strip motel status. The 128 rooms are a cut above motel standards. The sports facility includes an indoor pool, Jacuzzi, two saunas, two racquetball courts, and an exercise room. ■ *Across from the university; (503) 683-3669; 1655 Franklin Blvd, Eugene, OR 97403; $$; AE, DC, MC, V; checks OK.* ⅃

SPRINGFIELD

RESTAURANTS

Kuraya's ★ Although its location is off the beaten path, Kuraya's remains a popular spot with local Thai-food lovers. The casual atmosphere, friendly service, and large, inventive menu keep people coming back. So do the seafood basket—shrimp and scallops in a hot, coconutty sauce—and the Bangkok prawns, charcoal-broiled and served with a crabmeat-and-peanut dipping sauce. ■ *Market and Mohawk; (503) 746-2951; 1410 Mohawk Blvd, Springfield; $; beer and wine; MC, V; checks OK; lunch Mon–Sat, dinner every day.* ⅃

Spring Garden ★ This resolutely uncharming spot on Springfield's decaying Main Street serves some of the best Chinese food south of Portland. Although you dine with a panoramic view of a Goodwill Industries outlet, you can feast on truly inspired sizzling rice soup, egg rolls that are simultaneously crunchy and eggy, and a variety of fresh, flavorful entrees. Seafood lovers should make a beeline for the stuffed garlic prawns or the pan-fried shrimp, two of the best items on the menu. Ignore those around you who order the combination plates and deep-fried items. ■ *Downtown Springfield; (503) 747-0338; 215 Main St, Springfield; $; full bar; AE, MC, V; local checks only; lunch, dinner every day.*

LEABURG

LODGINGS

Marjon Bed and Breakfast ★ Thirty minutes east of Eugene, just off the road that threads its way through the Oregon Cascades, sits Margie Haas's immaculate contemporary home on 2 private acres by the banks of the pristine McKenzie, dotted with 2,000 azaleas and 7,000 rhododendrons. The junior room ($95 a night) is a nice-size bedroom with bath (including fishbowl shower) across the hall. The master suite ($125) has a 7-by-12-foot bed, an adjoining bath with sunken tub, and a view of the Japanese garden. Breakfasts are five-course affairs served with seasonal flair. ■ *3 miles east of Leaburg on McKenzie Hwy, turn at Leaburg Dam Rd (milepost 24),* *ignore the dead-end signs; (503)896-3145; 44975 Leaburg Dam Rd, Leaburg, OR 97489; $$$; no credit cards; checks OK.*

OAKLAND

RESTAURANTS

Tolly's ★ Oakland is one of Oregon's older towns, dating back to 1851. Tolly's, a special-occasion place for locals, is a bit of an oddity. Downstairs there's an old-fashioned ice cream parlor, candy counter, and antique gift shop. Upstairs the Tollefsons get a bit more serious. One elegant room, with high wing-back chairs and candlelight, is reserved for couples only and is non-smoking. Chefs change often, but the execution of the grilled swordfish and classic bacon-wrapped tournedos is respectably consistent. The wine list is the region's longest, with close to 100 labels. ■ *Exit 138 off I-5 to center of town; (503)459-3796; 115 Locust St, Oakland; $$; full bar; AE, MC, V; checks OK; lunch, dinner every day.*

STEAMBOAT

LODGINGS

Steamboat Inn ★ On the banks of a fly-only fishing stream is the plain-seeming lodge run for many years by Jim and Sharon Van Loan. Linked by a long verandah paralleling the North Umpqua River are eight small guest cabins with knotty-pine walls and just enough space. In the woods are five secluded cottages with living rooms and kitchens. Latest additions are two riverside suites. Remarkably good family-style dinners are served in the main building each night a half hour after dark, by reservation only ($30 per person, including premium Oregon wines). That's just enough time to prepare your fishing stories. ■ *38 miles east of Roseburg on Hwy 138; (503)498-2411; 42705 N Umpqua Hwy, Steamboat, OR 97447-9703; $$; MC, V; checks OK; breakfast, lunch, and dinner every day; (closed Jan–Feb; Nov–Dec, Mar–Apr open weekends only).*

ROSEBURG

The Roseburg area now has seven wineries, five of which are open for tours and tastings most of the year: **Callahan Ridge**, 340 Busenbark Lane, (503)673-7901; **Girardet Wine Cellars**, 895 Reston Road, (503)679-7252; **Henry Winery**, 687 Hubbard Creek Road, Umpqua, (503)459-5120; **HillCrest Vineyards**, 240 Vineyard Lane, (503)673-3709; and **La Garza**, 491 Winery Lane, (503)679-9654. La Garza also has a tasting-room restaurant, first in the region, serving lunch Wednesday through Sunday and dinner by reservation.

Wildlife Safari allows you to drive through rolling

country to see a quasi-natural wildlife preserve, with predators discreetly fenced from their prey, and to watch baby animals up close. Daily 9am–8pm, shorter hours in winter; Route 99, 4 miles west of I-5, exit 119, (503)679-6761.

Douglas County Museum imaginatively displays logging, fur-trapping, and pioneer items in one of the handsomest contemporary structures you'll find. It's free and open Tuesday through Sunday; off I-5 at the fairgrounds, exit 123, (503)440-4507.

K&R's Drive Inn dishes out huge scoops of Umpqua ice cream. One scoop is really two; two scoops are actually four. Located 20 miles north of Roseburg, at the Rice Hill exit off I-5; the parking lot is full from before noon till after dark, year-round.

RESTAURANTS

Cafe Espresso It's a smart, sunny cafe with black-and-white tiled floor, red-and-white-checked tablecloths, and Roseburg's best espresso bar. They have good coffee and croissants at breakfast, and Italian sodas, soups, salads, and daily specials ranging from beef stroganoff to lasagne. Weekday-only hours confirm our hunch that the locals want to keep this place all to themselves. ▪ *Corner of Douglas and Jackson; (503)672-1859; 368 SE Jackson St, Roseburg; $; no alcohol; no credit cards; checks OK; breakfast, lunch Mon–Fri.*

▼

Grants Pass

▲

WOLF CREEK

LODGINGS

Wolf Creek Tavern An old 1850s stagecoach stop, this eight-room inn was purchased by the state and restored in 1979. There's an attractive parlor and a dining room open to the public for all meals, including Sunday brunch. The fare, while standard, is usually hearty and inexpensive. Rooms are priced fairly too. Children are welcome; certain pets are allowed (with a $10 nonrefundable deposit). ▪ *Exit 76 off I-5; (503)866-2474; 100 Front St, Wolf Creek; PO Box 97, Wolf Creek, OR 97497; $; MC, V; no checks.* &

GRANTS PASS

The Rogue is one of Oregon's most beautiful rivers, chiseled into the coastal mountains from here to Gold Beach, protected by the million-acre Siskiyou National Forest, flecked with abandoned gold-mining sites, and inhabited by splendid steelhead and roaming Californians. Two companies offer jet boat tours. **Hellgate Excursions**, (503)479-7204, departs from the Riverside Inn in Grants Pass. **Jet Boat River Excursions**, (503)582-0800, leaves from the city of Rogue River, 8 miles upstream. One guide service that conducts wild and daring whitewater trips is **Orange Torpedo Trips**, (503)479-5061. Or you can hike the Rogue, a very hot trip in the summer; see Gold Beach listing.

RESTAURANTS

Hamilton House ★ Chef/owner Doug Hamilton grew up in this house, hidden in the trees east of town. Now it is sandwiched between Fred Meyer and Wal-Mart, where it survives as a handsome dinner house. Count on the salmon being moist and exquisite, and the creamy Jamaican jerk chicken over angel hair pasta quite rich. A daily fresh sheet is often likely to feature lingcod, snapper, and halibut, plus all the usual steaks. Grants Pass is noted for inexpensive dining, and Hamilton House fits the mold. Two can get by for $25 in many cases (except when Hamilton House offers dinner theater productions). ▪ *South Grants Pass exit off I-5, 2 blocks to Terry Lane, left 1 block; (503)479-3938; 344 NE Terry Lane, Grants Pass; $; full bar; AE, MC, V; local checks only; dinner every day.* ᕦ

Legrands ★ The fare is surprisingly good and inexpensive at this French/European restaurant in a converted residence near downtown Grants Pass. The two-course veal piccata dinner soars in at less than $11. Other local favorites include medallions of pork with ginger sauce and sauté of squid with shrimp eggplant. That is, if you haven't filled up on their fresh-baked breads: baguettes, onion bread, or a sun-dried tomato and jalapeño variation. ▪ *Corner of E St and 9th; (503)471-1554; 323 NE E St, Grants Pass; $$; full bar; MC, V; local checks only; breakfast Fri–Sun; lunch, dinner every day.* ᕦ

LODGINGS

Paradise Ranch Inn ★ Paradise, once a working dude ranch, is now a full-service resort, right in the heart of the verdant Rogue River Valley. Activities abound: swimming in a heated pool, boating on a 3-acre lake, playing tennis on two lighted courts, golfing on a nine-hole course, riding bicycles or hiking along miles of trails, relaxing in a hot tub. With all this planned action, you might expect a sprawling modern resort, but Paradise Ranch Inn defies that image: there are only 17 large Early American–style guest rooms. Best are those that overlook one of the three ponds. The emphasis is on peace and quiet: no TVs or phones in rooms (but good message-takers in the office). The four-bedroom Sunset House on the back 40 is a good choice for a couple of families or small groups. A continental breakfast is served to overnight guests. As for dinner, the food quality in the restaurant isn't all that it used to be; but all in all, this is still a pleasant getaway. ▪ *Hugo or Merlin exit off I-5, west to Monument Dr; (503)479-4333; 7000 Monument Dr, Grants Pass, OR 97526; $$; MC, V; checks OK;*

dinner every day in summer; Fri–Sat only in off season (closed in Feb).

Pine Meadow Inn ★ Maloy and Nancy Murdock built this elegant two-story, 2,600-square-foot country home in 1991 and styled it after a Midwestern farmhouse. The house sits in the middle of a 9-acre estate surrounded by gardens, a fishpond, graveled paths, and park benches. Three upstairs guest rooms feature turn-of-the-century antiques. The Willow Room is the largest, complete with sitting area, loveseat, and a double vanity bathroom. In the morning the Murdocks are likely to whip up a fresh veggie frittata and strawberry frappé. ▪ *Merlin exit off I-5, 5 miles west, right on Crow Rd; (503)471-6277 or (800)554-0806; 1000 Crow Rd, Merlin, OR 97532; $$; no credit cards; checks OK.*

JACKSONVILLE

The town started with a boom when gold was discovered in Rich Gulch in 1851. Then the railroad bypassed it, and the tidy little city struggled to avoid becoming a ghost town. Much of the 19th-century city has been restored; Jacksonville now boasts 85 historic homes and buildings open to the public. The strip of authentic Gold Rush–era shops, hotels, and saloons along California Street has become a popular stage set for films, including *The Great Northfield, Minnesota Raid* and the TV movie *Inherit the Wind.* Jacksonville is renowned for antique shops.

Britt Festival, an outdoor music and arts series, runs from late June through September on the hillside field where Peter Britt, a famous local photographer and horticulturist, used to have his home. Listeners gather on benches or flop onto blankets on the grass to enjoy open-stage performances of jazz, bluegrass, folk, country, classical music, musical theater, and dance. Quality of performances varies, but the series includes big-name artists, and listening to the music under a twinkling night sky makes for a memorable evening. Begun in 1963, the festival now draws some 50,000 viewers through the summer. For tickets and information, call the Britt Festival office, (503)773-6077 or (800)882-7488.

Jacksonville Museum, housed in the stately 1883 courthouse, follows the history of the railroad in the Rogue Valley with plenty of photos and artifacts. Another section displays works of Peter Britt. The adjacent children's museum lets kids walk through various miniaturized pioneer settings (jail, tepee, schoolhouse) and features a collection of the cartoons and memorabilia of Pinto Colvig, the Jacksonville kid who became Bozo the Clown and the voice of Disney's Pluto, Goofy, and three of the Seven Dwarfs; (503)773-6536.

Valley View Winery, the area's oldest, is at Ruch, 5 miles west of here; (503) 899-8468. The winery maintains a second tasting room in town, at the rear of the Village Gallery, 130 W California Street, (503) 899-1001.

RESTAURANTS

Jacksonville Inn ★★★ Ask a native to name the area's best, and the answer will be the Jacksonville Inn. The staff is considerate, and the antique-furnished dining room, in the original 1863 inn, is elegant and intimate. Executive chef Diane Menzie expertly creates the full realm of continental cuisine: steak, seafood, pasta, plus health-minded low-cholesterol and vegetarian fare. Dinners can be ordered as a leisurely seven-course feast or à la carte (or save money by ordering from the bistro menu in the lounge). À la carte is substantial enough. The petrale sole is a favorite, as are the veal piccata and baked polenta with tomatoes, garlic, cheese, and pesto. Desserts are lovely European creations. Jerry Evans exhibits one of the best-stocked wine cellars in Oregon, with more than 600 domestic and imported labels on hand.

Upstairs, eight refurbished rooms are decorated with 19th-century details: antique four-poster beds, patchwork quilts, and original brickwork on the walls. Modern amenities include private bathrooms and air conditioning (a boon in the 100-degree summer swelter). The rooms, especially the sought-after corner room, are a bit noisy—street sounds easily penetrate the walls. Guests enjoy a full breakfast. Reserve rooms in advance, especially during the Britt Festival. ▪ *On California St, the town's main thoroughfare; (503) 899-1900; 175 E California St, Jacksonville, OR 97530; $$; full bar; AE, DC, MC, V; checks OK; breakfast and dinner every day, lunch Tues–Sat, brunch Sun.*

▼ Jacksonville

▲

McCully House Inn ★★ Chef William Prahl grew up in the Medford area, left to fine-tune his culinary talents, and then came back. Under his supervision the McCully House has become a respected restaurant as well as a popular B&B. Typical of his menu are interesting combinations such as herb-crusted swordfish with caramelized onions, tomato-basil sauce over sweet-pepper fettuccine, and delicate squash and goat cheese ravioli with wilted greens, cranberry beans, and sherry-almond vinaigrette. Or how about cider-spiked pork loin with fennel, leeks, and purple potato crisps? Some of it's just flowery language, but in general the fare has flavor as well as flair.

One of the first six homes in the city, McCully House was built in 1861 for Jacksonville's first doctor, and later housed the first girls' school. It's elegant inside, with hardwood floors, lace curtains, and lovely antiques. Of the three guest rooms, the best flaunts a fireplace, a claw-footed pedestal tub, and the original black-walnut furnishings that traveled 'round the Horn with J.W. McCully. ▪ *Follow the signs from I-5 to 5th and E California; (503) 899-1942; 240 E California St, Jacksonville, OR 97530; $$; full bar; AE, MC, V; checks OK; dinner Wed–Sun, brunch Sun.* &

Bella Union ★ This restaurant, in the original century-old Bella Union Saloon (half of which was constructed when *The Great Northfield, Minnesota Raid* was filmed in Jacksonville in 1969), has everything from pizza and pasta to elegant dinners to picnic baskets for the summertime Britt Music Festival. There's usually a good fresh sheet with choices such as Cajun-style swordfish with black bean sauce and salsa, petrale sole with pesto, lingcod, flounder, and steamed mussels, as well as oyster-mushroom fettuccine. The garden out back is pleasant in warm weather. Proprietor Jerry Hayes is a wine fancier and pours 35 labels by the glass as well as by the bottle. ▪ *On California St; (503) 899-1770; 170 W California St, Jacksonville; $$; full bar; AE, MC, V; local checks only; lunch, dinner every day, brunch Sun.* &

LODGINGS

Old Stage Inn ★★★ This is Jacksonville's classiest B&B: a century-old farmhouse renovated by Hugh and Carla Jones and opened in 1990. There's an extensive library, a parlor, and a formal sitting room with a rare 1865 Hallett & Comston square parlor-grand piano. The two rooms with king-size beds (one of them wheelchair-accessible) have their own baths, while two rooms with queen-size beds share a magnificent bath. In her kitchen, the size of a living room in most normal homes, Carla creates breakfasts of homemade breads, poached pears with raspberry purée, and entrees such as croissants stuffed with mushrooms, cheese, and fresh herbs. She also provides afternoon refreshments. ▪ *Take Oregon St just beyond Livingston Rd to Old Stage Rd; (503) 899-1776 or (800) US-STAGE; 883 Old Stage Rd, Jacksonville; PO Box 579, Jacksonville, OR 97530; $$$; MC, V; checks OK.* &

TouVelle House ★ Frank TouVelle and his new bride built this stately mansion in 1916 after moving to Oregon from Ohio. They lived there for years as Frank became a noted orchardist and politician, the same man for whom TouVelle State Park (on the Rogue River) is named. Today it's a Jacksonville landmark, which Carolee and Dennis Casey run as a six-room B&B. The three-story Craftsman features 5,400 square feet of floor space, extensive wood paneling, and broad square-beamed ceilings. One room's a suite that can accommodate up to four. There's a swimming pool and spa out back. In the morning Carolee will not only feast you, she'll also bring you up to date on town gossip and last night's TV fare. ▪ *On Oregon Street, 2 blocks north*

of California (the main street); (503) 899-8938 or (800) 846-8422; 455 N Oregon St, Jacksonville, OR 97530; $$; AE, DC, MC, V; checks OK.

SHADY COVE/TRAIL

The Upper Rogue area, between Medford and Crater Lake, offers some of the region's most invigorating scenery—rugged mountains, timbered hillsides, and whitewater rapids.

RESTAURANTS

Bel Di's ★★ Ray and Joan Novosad's riverside country dinner house is a lovely place, with a dining room that boasts a grand view of the Rogue River. The full dinner is served with elegance, but you're out in the boonies and don't need to dress up. The overall ambience, the attentive service, and the fine soups and salad dressings are more special than many of the entrees, but try the scampi or the Louisiana stuffed prawns. ■ *North side of Shady Cove's bridge, first driveway after BP station; (503) 878-2010; 21900 Hwy 62, Shady Cove; $$; full bar; MC, V; checks OK; dinner Tues–Sun.* ᕕ

Rogue River Lodge ★ The oldest dinner house in Jackson County has been owned by ex-Navy man Ken Meirstin for two decades now. The walls are decorated with his collection of ship paintings. Dory, his wife, supervises the cooking and maintains a high standard of consistent quality with a somewhat predictable menu: steaks, scampi, teriyaki chicken, and prime rib (on weekends). The view of the Rogue isn't as good as at Bel Di's down the road, but the locals like the ambience, food, and piano bar. ■ *25 miles from Medford on Hwy 62; (503) 878-2555; 24904 Hwy 62, Trail; $$; full bar; MC, V; checks OK; dinner every day (closed Tues in winter).*

MEDFORD

Southern Oregon's largest city may not win any contests with nearby towns for prettiness, but it is the center of things in this part of the world. The city is well known across the nation, due to the marketing efforts of Harry and David's, the mail-order giant known for its pears, other fruit, and condiments.

Harry and David's Original Country Store, Highway 99 south of town, offers "seconds" from gift packs and numerous other items, as well as tours of the complex, which is also the home of **Jackson & Perkins**, the world's largest rose growers. The firm ships from Medford, although most of the flowers are grown in California, (503) 776-2277.

The Grub Street Grill, the Rogue Valley's best pub, serves up Irish stout as well as Northwest microbrews, 35 N Central Avenue, (503) 779-2635. Around the corner is **CK**

Tiffin's, a lunchtime cafeteria that's a mecca for fanciers of vegetarian and low-fat cuisine, 226 E Main Street, (503)779-0480. Locals also like the lunches and dinners at **Samovar**, a nearby Russian cafe, 101 E Main Street, (503)779-4967.

River rafting on a nearby stretch of the Rogue, between Gold Hill and the city of Rogue River, is safe for beginners. You can rent a raft at River Trips in Gold Hill, (503)855-7238, or try one of the shop's Rogue Drifters, a large sack filled with Styrofoam balls.

The Oregon Vortex at the House of Mystery, between Medford and Grants Pass, is a "whirlpool of force" that causes some people to experience strange phenomena such as an inability to stand erect and apparent changes in the laws of perspective; 18 miles northwest of Medford on Sardine Creek Road, Gold Hill, (503)855-1543. Closed in winter.

RESTAURANTS

Genessee Place ★ In a town not noted for its food, Genessee is an oasis. At first chef/owner Michael Isaacson began with lunch and the lure of quiche, potpies, and cheese bread. Now Isaacson's dinners are catching on with the locals: homemade cannelloni with ground chicken and cheese in a Pernod-infused tomato sauce, tournedos with red pepper herb butter, and fresh seafood and veal specialties. The baguette comes with "holy oil" for dipping—olive oil in which Italian spices have been marinated for three weeks. ■ *2 blocks east of I-5, between Main and Jackson sts; (503) 772-5581; 203 Genessee St, Medford; $$; full bar; MC, V; local checks only; lunch, dinner Mon–Sat.* ⑅

Medford

Lodgings

▲

Hungry Woodsman ★ Bob LaFontaine, owner of a Medford hardware store, tired of the rowdy nightclub next door, bought it, tore it down, and erected the Hungry Woodsman. The building is a testimonial to the forest products industry. Old saws, photos, and other logging memorabilia adorn the walls. The menu is pretty basic: steak, prime rib, shrimp, crab, lobster. You're probably best off with a steak or an English cut of prime rib; crab tends to be too pricey here. Locals like the Woodsman, as they call it. Few patrons dress up; even the waiters wear jeans. ■ *Just down from the Rogue Valley Mall; (503) 772-2050; 2001 N Pacific Hwy, Medford; $$; full bar; AE, MC, V; local checks only; lunch Mon–Fri, dinner every day.*

LODGINGS

Under the Greenwood Tree ★★ Innkeeper Renate Ellam—a Cordon Bleu chef and former interior designer—will have you relaxing in the lap of luxury amid green lawns, 300-year-old trees, and her 10-acre farm with an orchard, riding ring, beautiful rose gardens, gazebo, and antique farm buildings. The 1862 home has four guest rooms, each with private bath,

Persian rugs, elegant linens, and nightly turn-down service—a gracious touch. Guests who arrive by 4:30pm receive British-style afternoon tea, and her elaborate three-course breakfasts may include dishes such as vanilla-poached pears with Chantilly cream. ■ *Exit 27 (Barnett Rd) off I-5 to Stewart, left on Hull, right on Bellinger; (503)776-0000; 3045 Bellinger Lane, Medford, OR 97501; $$$; checks OK.*

TALENT

RESTAURANTS

Arbor House ★★ The exterior, enhanced by a Japanese garden, is still modest enough to fool you. Aging granola types consider this place a find, as it remains surprisingly congenial—one of the most comfortable restaurants in the Rogue Valley, with both indoor and outdoor dining. The menu ranges the world—vegetarian plates, curries, sauerbraten, jambalaya, enchiladas, eggplant Parmigiana, fresh seafoods, and good old American steak. Try the chicken with curry and a wealth of vegetables. The menu lists no prices, but don't worry, they won't shock. ■ *Hwy 99 to W Valley View Rd, left on Talent Ave, right on Wagner; (503)535-6817; 103 W Wagner St, Talent; $$; beer and wine; no credit cards; checks OK; dinner Tues–Sat in summer, Wed–Sat in winter.* ♿

New Sammy's Cowboy Bistro ★★ Proprietors Vernon and Charlene Rollins do no advertising, rely entirely on word of mouth (and now a *Best Places* mention). There's no sign other than a flashing light at night. And the outside looks barely a cut above a shack. Inside, though, is as charming a dinner house as you're likely to find in southern Oregon. There are just six tables; reservations are a must, and you may have to wait a couple of weeks to get in. The French-inspired menu usually lists just a handful of entrees—salmon, veal stew, a beef dish (the New York steak was perfectly cooked). The wine list is extensive: 40 choices from Oregon, California, and France. ■ *Halfway between Talent and Ashland on Hwy 99 (Pacific Hwy); (503)535-2779; 2210 S Pacific Hwy, Talent; $$; beer and wine; no credit cards; checks OK; dinner Thurs–Sun.* ♿

ASHLAND

The remarkable success of the Oregon Shakespeare Festival, now over 50 years old, has transformed this sleepy town into one with, per capita, the best tourist amenities in the region. The Festival now draws a total audience of some 350,000 through the nine-month season, filling its theaters to an extraordinary 97 percent capacity. Visitors pour into this town of 17,000, spawning fine shops, restaurants, and bed-and-breakfast places as they do. Amazingly, the town still has its soul: for the most part, it seems a happy little college town, set amid lovely ranch country, that just happens to house one of the largest theater companies in the land. And people still walk downtown at night.

The **Festival** mounts plays in three theaters. In the outdoor Elizabethan Theater, which seats 1,200, appear the famous and authentic nighttime productions of Shakespeare (three different plays) each summer. The outdoor theater has recently been remodeled to improve acoustics. Stretching from February to October, the season for the two indoor theaters includes comedies, contemporary fare, and some experimental works. Visit the Exhibit Center, where you can clown around in costumes from plays past. There are also lectures and concerts at noon, excellent backstage tours each morning, Renaissance music and dance nightly in the courtyard—plus all the nearby daytime attractions of river rafting, picnicking, and historical touring. The best way to get information and tickets (last-minute tickets in the summer are rare) is through a comprehensive agency: Southern Oregon Reservation Center, (503)488-1011, (800)547-8052; PO Box 477, Ashland, OR 97520. Festival box office is (503)482-4331.

Ashland is home to a growing number of smaller theater groups, whose productions are often called **Off Shakespeare** or **Off Bardway**. They are worth checking into. Festival actors frequently join in these small companies, giving audiences a chance to see Shakespearean actors having a bit of fun and going out on a theatrical limb. Oregon Cabaret Theater presents musicals and comedies through much of the year, with dinners, hors d'oeuvres, and desserts for theater patrons; First and Hargadine streets, (503)488-2902. Others include Actors' Theater, now in nearby Talent, (503)482-9659; and Ashland Community Theater, (503)482-7532, in the town hall building at 300 N Pioneer Street, Ashland.

Touring. The Rogue River Recreation Area has fine swimming for the sizzling summer days, as does the lovely Applegate River. Twenty-two scenic miles up Dead Indian Memorial Road is Howard Prairie Lake Resort, where you can camp, park your trailer, shower, rent a boat, and fish all day; (503)482-1979.

Mount Ashland Ski Area, (503)482-2897, 18 miles south of town, offers 22 runs for all classes of skiers, Thanksgiving to April. It's going strong since a 1992 fund drive raised $1.7 million to buy it from an out-of-town owner who had threatened permanent closure.

Lithia Park. Designed by the creator of San Francisco's Golden Gate Park, Ashland's central park runs for 100 acres behind the outdoor theater, providing a lovely mix of duck ponds, Japanese gardens, grassy lawns, playgrounds, groomed or dirt trails for hikes and jogging, and the pungent mineral water that gave the park its name. Great for picnicking, especially after stocking up at nearby Greenleaf Deli, 49 N Main, (503)482-2808.

Mark Antony Hotel. This downtown landmark is of some historic interest. The hotel fell on hard economic times during the 1970s and 1980s, with several changes of ownership. But ownership has stabilized and food service has improved notably; 212 E Main Street, (503)482-1721.

Weisinger Ashland Winery, Ashland Vineyards, and **Rogue Brewery & Public House** offer opportunities to sample Ashland products. The Weisinger winery is snuggled in a Bavarian-style building; the gift shop offers jams, jellies, sauces, and, of course, their wines for sale; Highway 99 just outside Ashland, (503)488-5989. Ashland Vineyards is near the Highway 66 exit from I-5. Turn north onto E Main Street and follow signs; (503)488-0088. Wash down a sandwich or a pizza with a Golden Ale at the Rogue Brewery, located at 31-B Water Street—a good place to unwind after a day of theater; (503) 488-5061.

RESTAURANTS

20 YEARS **Chateaulin** ★★★ Less than a block from the theaters, you'll find a romantic cafe reminiscent of New York's upper West Side; the dark wood-and-brick dining rooms are accented with copper kettles hung from the ceiling and displays of vintage wine bottles. During the Shakespeare season, the place bustles with before- and after-theater crowds gathered for the fine French cuisine or for drinks at the bar. House specialties are pâtés and veal dishes, but seafood is also impressive: the delicate butterflied shrimp in a subtle sauce of sherry, cream, tomato, and brandy were delicious. Chef David Taub and co-owner Michael Donovan change the menu seasonally, and several daily specials feature entrees prepared with classic French flair. The cafe menu is a favorite of the after-show crowd: baked goat cheese marinated in olive oil on featherweight squares of toast, an outrageous onion soup. Service is polished and smooth even during the rush of theater crowds. ■ *Down the walkway from Angus Bowmer Theater; (503)482-2264; 50 E Main, Ashland; $$; full bar; AE, MC, V; local checks only; dinner every day.* &

Monet ★★ The waiters in berets and the reproductions of guess-who on the walls might seem a bit pretentious in this town, but Pierre and Dale Verger have created a French restaurant that has become the talk of Ashland (and even a mention in Portland). Before opening this gentrified French restaurant, Pierre Verger had restaurants in Montreal, New York state, and the San Francisco Bay Area. Favorite dishes include spirales de sole aux ciboulettes, fillet of sole wrapped around salmon and served in a sauce of chives, spinach, and chervil, accompanied by zucchini, puff potatoes, purée of carrots, and fresh herbs. Verger goes out of his way to make interesting vegetarian choices, such as sautéed artichoke hearts with sun-dried tomatoes, olives, mushrooms, garlic, shallots, feta, and Parmesan, or eggplant bathed in tomato, herbs, and Swiss on a bed of creamy spaetzle. The wine list goes on and on. Try for outdoor dining in summer. ■ *Half a block from Main St; (503) 482-1339; 36 S 2nd St, Ashland; $$; full bar; MC, V; checks OK; lunch, dinner every day (closed Sun–Tues in winter).*

Primavera ★★ Even if you find the bold red, blue, and orange decor a bit much, wait for the appetizers—they're among the best in southern Oregon. Pasta with capers, raisins, and shrimp along with tomatoes and browned onions is a meal in itself. Spring rolls filled with duck, served with a raspberry ketchup, will forever alter your feelings about both duck and ketchup. None of the entrees approaches the inspiration or execution of the appetizers, but they are still very good and—like the halibut with mustard and fennel with a tomato coulis—capture intense, clean flavors. Desserts, like everything else, are made on the premises. A thoughtfully selected wine list complements

Ashland

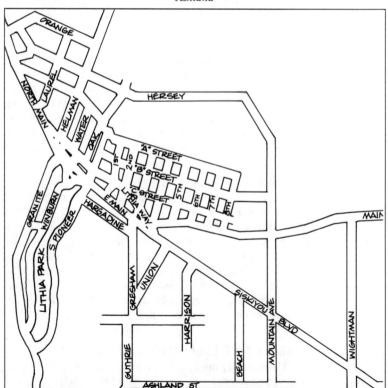

the food. The garden is a gorgeous place for a midsummer's night dinner. ■ *Below Oregon Cabaret Theater; (503)488-1994; 241 Hargadine, Ashland; $$; full bar; MC, V; checks OK; dinner Tues–Sun (Thurs-Sun in winter).* &

The Winchester Country Inn ★★ Pay a visit to the Winchester when you feel like being pampered. You sit amid crisp country furnishings on the slightly sunken ground floor of this century-old Queen Anne–style home and look out on tiers of neatly snipped garden outside. The staff attends to your every need. The menu stretches from Vietnamese marinated and broiled *teng dah* beef to lamb or salmon, as well as a less expensive bistro section with smoked salmon ravioli and polenta aubergine. Owners Michael and Laurie Gibbs are locally famous for the Dickens Feasts they present each December.

In addition to being one of Ashland's finer restaurants, the Winchester provides seven antique-furnished guest rooms upstairs. Guests are treated to full breakfasts. ■ *Half a block from Main St; (503)488-1113; 35 S 2nd St, Ashland, OR 97529; $$; full bar; MC, V; checks OK; dinner every day, brunch Sun.*

Green Springs Inn ★ Here's an escape from the tourist crowds of Ashland—a cozy, rustic spot dishing up Italian specialties in the midst of the splendid hills. The restaurant doubles as a neighborhood convenience store. The 25-minute drive through the red-soil hills, jutting cliffs, and thick evergreens is worth the trip in itself, especially if you want to hike or cross-country ski along the Pacific Crest Trail that runs a quarter mile from the restaurant. The delicious and garlicky black bean soup (lapped up with a subtly sweet black bread) makes a perfect lunch. But if you need a little more substance, try the mushroom fettuccine. ■ *17½ miles east of Ashland; (503)482-0614; 11470 Hwy 66, Ashland; $$; beer and wine; AE, MC, V; checks OK; breakfast, lunch, dinner every day.* &

Il Giardino ★ Order the risotto when you place your reservation—it's as close to Italy as you'll get without a plane ticket. It's not on the menu and it's time-consuming to make, but Franco Minniti and Jennifer and staff love to cook and are anxious to please. Even some dishes which might sound a bit odd—ravioli stuffed with ground veal and topped with a carrot sauce—result in a delightful meal. The place is intimate and can seem crowded. ■ *1½ blocks from Shakespeare Festival; (503)488-0816; #5 Granite St, Ashland; $$; full bar; MC, V; local checks only; dinner every day.*

LODGINGS

Chanticleer Bed & Breakfast Inn ★★★ One of Ashland's original B&Bs is still a preferred destination. The home has an uncluttered country charm, with an open-hearth fireplace in the spacious sitting room and carefully chosen antiques throughout, plus the plush extras of fresh-cut flowers, imported soaps and lotions in the rooms, and scripts of all the plays running at the Shakespeare Festival. In the morning, owner Peggy Kuan serves up a lavish breakfast, with tempting dishes like orange eggs Benedict and artichoke-cheese puffs. It's a setting that promises to rejuvenate your soul and your romance. Chanticleer is four blocks from the theaters, but surprisingly quiet. ■ *2 blocks from the library off Main St; (503) 482-1919 or (800) 898-1950; 120 Gresham St, Ashland, OR 97520; $$$; MC, V; checks OK.*

Mount Ashland Inn ★★★ Wind your way up Mount Ashland Road and you discover a huge, custom-made two-story log cabin. This is the dream home of Jerry and Elaine Shanafelt, who designed and built it using some 275 cedar trees cut from their 160-acre property in the Siskiyous. The magnificent inn is more posh inside than you'd expect from a log house: aromatic golden cedar logs, high-beamed ceilings, large windows, and a huge stone fireplace. Examples of Jerry's handiwork are seen throughout the house: stained-glass windows, a spiral cedar staircase with madrona railing. Guests sleep in handcrafted beds covered with elaborate patchwork quilts. Try for the newer Sky Lakes suite with a two-person whirlpool bathtub, king-size bed, wet bar, private entrance, and a sitting room, plus a view of Mount McLoughlin. Be prepared for snow (November to April). ■ *Follow signs to Mt Ashland Ski Area; (503) 482-8707; 550 Mt Ashland Rd, Ashland, OR 97520; $$$; AE, MC, V; checks OK.*

Romeo Inn ★★★ This imposing Cape Cod home has four plush guest rooms and two suites decorated in contemporary and antique furnishings. The spacious rooms all have king-size beds—covered with hand-stitched Amish quilts—phones, and private baths. The Stratford Suite, a separate structure with its own bedroom, bath, and kitchen, features a vaulted ceiling with skylight, a marble-tiled fireplace, and a raised whirlpool bathtub for two. Owners Bruce and Margaret Halverson give up their own quarters (in summer only) to create a second suite, the Cambridge, with fireplace, patio, and private entrance. There's a baby grand piano off the living room, and the heated pool and hot tub on the large back deck are open year-round. The generous breakfast of baked fruit, specialty main course such as eggs rarebit, and fresh baked goods reportedly satisfies through dinnertime. The Halversons keep a computerized record of what they served you last time, so regular clientele never get the same meal twice. Clever. ■ *Idaho and Holly; (503) 488-0884; 295 Idaho St, Ashland, OR 97520; $$$; MC, V; checks OK.* ♿

Country Willows ★★ Set on 5 acres of farmland 7 minutes

from downtown Ashland, this rebuilt 1896 country home offers peace and quiet and a lovely view of the hills. Dan Durant and David Newton offer five rooms, two suites, and a separate cottage. There's a hot tub on the large back deck for warming up, and a swimming pool for cooling off. Believe it or not, our favorite room is in the barn: it has a two-person soaking tub, fireplace, and private deck. Breakfast is presented on a pretty sun porch. The grounds outside offer running and hiking trails; and the owners keep a small flock of ducks, a gaggle of geese, and even a couple of goats on the property. ■ *4 blocks south on Clay St from Siskiyou Blvd; (503) 488-1590; 1313 Clay St, Ashland, OR 97520; $$$; MC, V; checks OK.* &

Fox House Inn ★★ Jim and Jacqueline Sims remodeled an early Victorian home to create this two-bedroom inn that offers guests the utmost privacy, perfect for families or two couples traveling together. The rooms are furnished with brass beds with half-canopies and private baths with claw-footed tubs; each has a large, private outdoor hot tub. Annabel's Suite is well-suited for a romantic getaway: guests have the entire second story, with private sitting room and dressing room, and a lavish satin-and-lace bedroom. And there's breakfast, of course. ■ *2nd and B off Main; (503) 488-1055; 269 B St, Ashland, OR 97520; $$$; no credit cards; checks OK.*

Peerless Hotel ★★ Originally a hotel built in Ashland's now-historic railroad district in 1900, the building fell into disrepair. Crissy Barnett saved the place, merged old hotel rooms into six new B&B units, two of them suites, and filled them with antiques collected from places as disparate as New Orleans and Hawaii. High ceilings and oversized bathrooms are trademarks. One suite (No. 3) features a bath with his-and-her claw-footed tubs and a glassed-in shower. Several have Jacuzzis. In the morning Barnett serves a buffet. You can walk to the Shakespeare theaters from here. ■ *On 4th St between A and B Sts; (503) 488-1082; 243 4th St, Ashland, OR 97520; $$$; AE, MC, V; checks OK.* &

Arden Forest Inn ★ Walking distance from Shakespeare, this remodeled farmhouse is a refreshing change of pace from the antique motif that abounds in bed and breakfasts. The light and airy living room and each of the four guest rooms are decorated with lovely examples of host/artist Audrey Sochor's vividly hued paintings. Host/Shakespeare teacher Arthur Sochor's extensive theater library is available for guests' perusal, and the longtime theater buff welcomes chats with his show-bound guests. The two carriage-house rooms offer optimum privacy. Children are welcome. ■ *On Hersey at Laurel; (503) 488-1496; 261 W Hersey St, Ashland, OR 97520; $$; AE, MC, V; checks OK.* &

Cowslip's Belle ★ Unintentionally named after a song in *A Midsummer Night's Dream*, the home has a cheery charm, with its swing chair on the front porch, vintage furniture, and fresh flowers inside. There are two lovely bedrooms in the main house, a 1913 Craftsman bungalow, two more in a romantic carriage house in the back, with extra privacy, one of them a suite. A main attraction here is proximity to the theaters, downtown, and Lithia Park, three to four blocks away. ■ *3 blocks north of the theaters on Main; (503) 488-2901 or (800) 888-6819; 159 N Main St, Ashland, OR 97520; $$; MC, V; checks OK.* ♿

Pinehurst Inn at Jenny Creek ★ Rumor has it the old roadhouse, built in the 1920s, was a bordello in earlier days. Today's lodgings mix rustic with elegant. Hosts Mike and Mary Jo Moloney run a country inn with six bed-and-breakfast rooms, two of them suites, and a full-service restaurant open to non-guests. Each room has a great view of trees and mountains. The inn is 23 miles east of Ashland, many of which require negotiating a winding, narrow highway up the Greensprings grade once endured by travelers in covered wagons on the Applegate Trail. It's a 30- to 40-minute drive, but worth it if you want peace and quiet, mountain air and some pretty good food. ■ *On right, between mileposts 23 and 24 on Hwy 66 east of Ashland; (503) 488-1002; 17250 Hwy 66, Ashland, OR 97520; $$; MC, V; checks OK; breakfast, lunch, and dinner every day.*

Woods House ★ This 1908 Craftsman, once the home of a doctor, boasts a beautiful setting out back, with a half-acre of terraced English gardens. Out front is the busy boulevard and traffic, so try for one of the Carriage House units in the rear. All six guest rooms have private baths. A big plus is that you can walk the four blocks to the theaters. Lester and Francoise Roddy are gracious hosts and serve a nifty spinach-cheese egg bake, in the garden when weather cooperates. ■ *4 blocks north of theaters on Main; (503) 488-1598 or (800) 435-8260; 333 N Main St, Ashland, OR 97520; $$$; MC, V; checks OK.*

Windmill's Ashland Hills Inn For those who prefer motels to B&Bs, this is the best Ashland has to offer, with 159 rooms, several elegant suites, a pool, and tennis courts. A new non-smoking unit with nearly 60 suites, B&B–style because rates include breakfast, opened in 1995. The banquet area, Ashland's largest, plays host to everything from wine-tastings to formal balls. ■ *Exit 41 off I-5; (503) 482-8310 or (800) 547-4747; 2525 Ashland St, Ashland, OR 97520; $$; AE, DC, MC, V; checks OK.* ♿

▼

Ashland

Lodgings

▲

CAVE JUNCTION

Though the tight quarters can get awfully packed with tourists, the **Oregon Caves National Monument** is a group of intriguing formations of marble and limestone. Tours leave periodically each day year-round. They are a bit strenuous, and the caves are a chilly 41 degrees. Children under 6 are allowed if they meet the height requirement. However, babysitting service is available. Arrive early during summertime, or you may have a long wait; (503)592-3400.

LODGINGS

Oregon Caves Chateau ★ This fine old wooden lodge is set amid tall trees and a deep canyon. Doors don't always close properly, but the place is restful. The sound of falling water from numerous nearby mountain streams will help lull you to sleep. Views are splendid, the public rooms have the requisite massive fireplaces, and the down-home cooking in the dining room is quite good. The wine list features lots of local bottlings. There are 22 rooms in the lodge—nothing fancy, but clean. ■ *Route 46, 20 miles east of Cave Junction, follow signs; (503)592-3400; PO Box 128, Cave Junction, OR 97523; $$; MC, V; checks OK; open June–Sept.*

Oregon Cascades

*The Columbia River Gorge—Troutdale to The Dalles—
followed by two easterly Cascade crossings: Sandy to Mount
Hood in the north, McKenzie Bridge to Bend midstate.
Finally, a southward progression through the heart of the
mountains to Klamath Falls.*

COLUMBIA RIVER GORGE

The wild Columbia has been dammed into near lakehood,
but its fjordlike majesty is part magnificent waterfalls, part dramatic cliffs and rock formations cut by the country's second-
largest river, and part wind tunnel. Watch for the colorful fleet
of board sailors who have made this stretch of the river world-
renowned.

Most of the traffic is on I-84, which leaves the old **Columbia Gorge Scenic Highway** (Route 30) for take-your-time
wanderers. This 22-mile detour traverses the waterfall-riddled
stretch from Troutdale to Ainsworth Park. Popular viewpoints
and attractions are as follows: **Crown Point**, 725 feet above
the river, features an art deco–style vista house. Below, at
Rooster Rock State Park, one of the attractions is a nude
bathing beach. **Larch Mountain**, 14 miles upriver from Crown
Point, is even more spectacular than the more famous overlooks. **Multnomah Falls** ranks second-highest in the country,
at 620 feet (in two big steps). **Multnomah Falls Lodge**, at the
foot of the falls, was designed in 1925 by Albert E. Doyle, of
Benson Hotel fame, in a rustic stone-and-timber style. Now
a National Historic Landmark, the lodge houses a popular nat-
uralists' and visitors' center; (503)695-2376. It also has a large
restaurant that is a good stop for breakfast, but dinners are

unremarkable (better just to go for dessert). **Oneonta Gorge** is a narrow, dramatic cleft through which a slippery half-mile trail winds to secluded Oneonta Falls. **Bonneville Dam**, the first federal dam on the Columbia, offers self-guided tours of the dam, the fish ladders (seen through underwater viewing windows), and the navigational locks; (503)374-8820. You can tour the Bonneville Fish Hatchery (next to the dam) year-round; however, the best time is in September and November when the chinook are spawning; (503)374-8393.

The old highway disappears briefly at Hood River; it picks up again between Mosier and The Dalles, where the forests give way to grasslands and the clouds vanish. Wildflowers abound from February to May.

TROUTDALE

RESTAURANTS

Tad's Chicken 'n' Dumplings A down-home country restaurant, 20 miles east of Portland as you head up the Columbia Gorge, this decades-old Oregon institution is popular with kids, bargain-hungry families, tourists—and fanciers of chicken. Steaks, prime rib, salmon, and halibut are also on the menu. Sit at a window table where you can watch the sunset and top off your meal with ice cream or homemade pie. The place is usually packed, particularly for Sunday dinner. ■ *Exit 18 off I-84; (503)666-5337; 943 SE Crown Point, Troutdale; $; full bar; AE, MC, V; checks OK; dinner every day.* &

LODGINGS

McMenamins Edgefield ★★ Over the last decade, the McMenamin brothers have enlivened Portland-area neighborhoods with 27 Euro-style pubs. Here they've purchased a former county poor farm, where residents once worked and lived together in a self-sufficient community, and transformed the grounds into a brewery, a winery, and a 3-acre pinot gris vineyard; the old power station is now a lively pub and movie theater (with eight spare bed-and-breakfast rooms upstairs). The administrator's house, an old Craftsman-style bungalow, has an additional six bedrooms. The main lodge, in a four-story brick manor, has 91 guest rooms, wide verandahs, a huge ballroom, and the Black Rabbit dining room and bar. All rooms ($65 to $105; one that sleeps six is $180) are outfitted with beer glasses and a canning jar to carry brew back to your room. Guests are loaned terrycloth robes to make the trek to the shared baths on each wing (which isn't as bad as it sounds).

Not surprisingly, the Black Rabbit restaurant tends to serve dishes that go admirably with a pint of home brew, such as potted Dungeness crab. But it can also do impressive things with a skewer of local lamb or a slab of salmon, and its desserts create impressive new identities for the Gorge's berries. ■ *Wood Village exit off I-84, south to Halsey, turn left, drive ½ mile to Edgefield sign; (503)669-8610 or (800)669-8610 or (503)492-3086 (restaurant); 2126 SW Halsey, Troutdale, OR 97060; $$; full bar; AE, MC, V; checks OK; breakfast, lunch, dinner every day.* ♿

CASCADE LOCKS

Before the dams, riverboats often foundered on nasty rapids here. Locks smoothed things out; riverboat remains are reminders of the past and the centerpiece of the town's Marina Park. A fine little museum at the **Bridge of the Gods** explains the legend of the rapids. There are also the Port of Cascade Locks Visitor Center, a sailboard launch, and oodles of picnic spots. The **Sternwheeler** *Columbia Gorge* revives the Columbia's riverboat days; there are three trips daily and extra lunch, brunch, dinner, and dance cruises, mid-June through the end of September, with stops at Bonneville Dam and Stevenson Landing; (503)374-8427.

LODGINGS

Shahala at the Locks The best thing about this ranch-style bed and breakfast is its location: high on a bluff overlooking the Columbia Gorge. When the weather's nice you can sit on the large patio and watch hawks soar over the river—or lounge in the hot tub tucked in a nearby grove with the same view. Overstuffed couches in the living room provide often drier river-viewing out a large picture window. Request one of the two rooms on the main floor; the others are in the basement. ■ *Exit 44 off I-84; the inn is on Forest Lane, north off WaNaPa St; (503)374-8222; 1280 Forest Lane, Cascade Locks; PO Box 39, Cascade Locks, OR 97014; $$; MC, V; checks OK.* ♿

HOOD RIVER

Fruit orchards are everywhere. Hood River is ideally located on the climatic cusp between the wetter west side and the drier east side of the Cascades, alongside the mighty Columbia, so it gets the sun *and* enough moisture (about 31 inches annually) to keep the creeks flowing and the orchards bearing. Thirty miles to the south, 11,245-foot Mount Hood dominates the horizon; however, from the town itself, the views are of Washington's Mount Adams, the Columbia, and its ubiquitous sailboarders. In town, you're as likely to see orchard workers as boardheads, 2-inch steaks as espresso. New restaurants, inns, and shops are constantly opening (and closing) in flux with the high and low seasons.

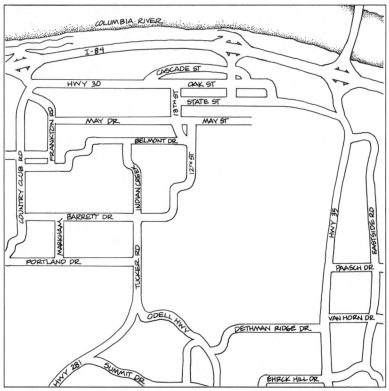

Hood River

Visitors come to hike, fish, climb, and ski on Mount Hood and Mount Adams. In between is the Columbia River. And on it are the boardheads who can't get enough of the famous winds that blow in at that ideal opposite-to-the-current direction. At least 27 local businesses now cater to the sailboard crowd; several offer lessons and rentals, and all will tell you where the winds are on any given day. The **West Jetty** and **Columbia Gorge Sailpark/Marina** are favorites. The latter also features a fitness course, a marina, and a cafe.

As locals strongly attest, there was life in Hood River before board sailors descended. Native American artifacts are on exhibit in the **Hood River County Museum**; (503)386-6772, open 10am–4pm Wednesday through Sunday, April through October, or when flags are flying. The town's Visitor Information Center adjoins, though it is closed on winter weekends; (503)386-2000 or (800)366-3530.

Orchards and vineyards are the valley's other economic mainstays. The wonderful small-town **Blossom Festival** (mid-April) celebrates the flower-to-fruit cycle. From Highway 35 you can catch the vista of the orchards fanning out from the north slopes of Mount Hood. For an old-fashioned trip, take the **Mount Hood Scenic Railroad**; the Fruit Blossom Special departs the quaint Hood River depot mid-April through December. You can buy the fruit bounty at **The Fruit Tree**, 4030 Westcliff Drive, (503)386-6688, near the Columbia Gorge Hotel, or at **River Bend Country Store**, 2363 Tucker Road, (503)386-8766, or (800) 755-7568; the latter specializes in organically grown produce. Or visit the tasting rooms of the **Flerchinger Vineyards**, 4200 Post Canyon Drive, (503)386-2882, or the **Hood River Vineyards**, 4693 Westwood Drive, (503)386-3772, known for its pear and raspberry dessert wines. Beer aficionados will head for the **Full Sail Tasting Room and Pub**, 506 Columbia Street, (503)386-2247, for handcrafted Full Sail ales and appetizers. The outdoor deck provides a fitting place for tired board sailors to unwind while keeping the river in sight.

For a breath-taker, head half a mile south of town on Highway 35 to **Panorama Point**. Or go east on I-84, exit at Mosier, and climb to the **Rowena Crest Viewpoint** on old Highway 30; the grandstand Columbia River view is complemented by a wildflower show in the Tom McCall Preserve, maintained by the Nature Conservancy. **The Coffee Spot**, Oak Street and First, (503)386-1772, is a good spot for picnic sandwiches.

RESTAURANTS

Big City Chicks ★ What began as a concession stand is now a real restaurant. Owner and chef Nan Bain (who collected recipes as she traveled with the film crew for "The Love Boat" TV series) has proven her food works—restaurant or no. The menu incorporates satays from Thailand and curries from India; Mexican moles and Peruvian polentas; Jamaican jerked chicken and Italian pastas. For dessert there are homemade ice creams or key lime pie (lime juice is shipped fresh from Florida). A pretty restaurant furnished in 1930s art deco–style with locally made art lamps. On summer evenings, lineups tend to build after 7:30pm. ■ *13th and B sts; (503)387-3811; 1302 13th St, Hood River; $; full bar; MC, V; local checks only; dinner every day.* ♿

The Mesquitery ★ The mesquite grill takes center stage here. It's housed in a glass-enclosed frame surrounded by booths and small tables. The barbecue is not super-hot, but A-OK. There are baby back ribs, a chicken combo, pollo vaquero (grilled chicken to roll in tortillas with pico de gallo), and fish (maybe a moist halibut in a spicy tomatillo sauce). The apple crisp à la mode is dandy; so are the service and the bill. A good place to bring the kids. ■ *12th and B sts; (503)386-2002; 1219 12th St, Hood River; $; full bar; AE, MC, V; local checks only; lunch Wed–Fri, dinner Mon–Sat (dinner every day in summer months).* ♿

Stonehedge Inn ★ Beyond the funky markers and up a rutted gravel drive to this turn-of-the-century summer estate, owner Jean Harmon makes you instantly at home. She'll get the kids looking through her stereopticon viewer and tell the history behind each decoration as she leads you to a table in the fire-warmed and dark-wood paneled main room, the garden-viewing porch room, the homey library, or the intimate bar. Tender steaks might come buried under whole, fresh chanterelle mushrooms, and the seafood arrives fresh and cooked right—halibut rolled in hazelnuts topped with a blueberry beurre rouge. The famous stuffed potato seemed to be right out of Betty Crocker's kitchen. Sincere service and general high quality keep this on our list. ■ *Exit 62 off I-84; (503) 386-3940; 3405 Cascade Dr, Hood River; $$; full bar; AE, DC, MC, V; checks OK; dinner Wed–Sun.*

Purple Rocks Art Bar and Cafe Despite its name (a self-evident boarder's term), we like this cafe, from the blue-enameled wood stove to the views out paned-glass windows. Art takes the form of sketchbooks filled with patrons' doodles and the kids sit at their own kid-size table. Housed in a cute little cottage on Hood River's main street, this local hangout offers delicious multigrain walnut pancakes and mostly vegetarian fare (sprout and cottage cheese sandwich, lasagne, quiches, and black bean burritos). New owner Denny Thompson has added more meat and seafood to the menu, as well as some pleasant libations. ■ *West on Oak from downtown; (503) 386-6061; 606 Oak St, Hood River; $; beer and wine; MC, V; checks OK; breakfast, lunch every day.*

LODGINGS

Hood River Hotel ★★ A careful 1989 restoration revived this hostelry's past as a turn-of-the-century country hotel. Thirty-two rooms, including nine one-bedroom kitchen suites, come with four-poster, sleigh, and brass beds, pedestal sinks, and plenty of cheerful floral chintz. Since it's in the center of town, there's some noise from the street, the railroad, and I-84.

Pasquale's Ristorante, a small, attractive dining room, serves reasonably priced meals strong on Italian specialties (angel hair pasta with fresh clams and baby sea clams sautéed with garlic in a white wine herb sauce), and local fruit and fish (the seafood salad is packed with the good stuff). Enjoy your espresso or after-dinner drink in front of the lobby fireplace or at an outside table. A casual place with live music on Friday evenings. ■ *Oak and 1st; (503) 386-1900 or (800) 386-1859; 102 Oak St, Hood River, OR 97031; $$; full bar; AE, DC, MC, V; checks OK; breakfast, lunch, dinner every day.* &

Lakecliff Estate ★★ A historic place and everyone's favorite Hood River bed and breakfast. It was built in 1908 by architect

Albert E. Doyle (who also designed Multnomah Falls Lodge and the Benson Hotel in Portland) as a summer estate for a Portland businessman. The manse features five fireplaces of locally quarried stone, a large and inviting living room, a sun-warmed porch, and an elegant dining room where guests often linger over their oatmeal with sautéed nectarines or Dutch babies with fruit sauce while watching windsurfers below. Some rooms have fireplaces and private bathrooms, others have views. You pick your preference. The forest green home is sheltered by woods to create quiet seclusion with an astonishing view of the Columbia River. Fine hospitality in outstanding surroundings. ■ *Exit 62 off I-84, ½ mile west of Hood River; (503)386-7000; 3820 Westcliff Dr, Hood River; PO Box 1220, Hood River, OR 97031; $$; no credit cards; checks OK; (closed Oct to Apr).*

State Street Inn ★★ Mac and Amy Lee fled aerospace careers to live in Hood River. Now Mac works at the Full Sail Brewing Company and Amy runs the B&B. She does it right. The place, an impeccable and well-crafted 1932 English Tudor, is ideally located on a quiet street that's still close to everything. The queen beds are comfy; four rooms share two baths. The Chesapeake-inspired Maryland Room and the bright and colorful California Room are the largest, with views of Mount Adams. Almost everyone gathers around the fire at night and meets again for breakfast (whole-wheat waffles or lemony cream cheese–filled crêpes with fresh fruit) where they sit eye-to-eye with Mount Adams. ■ *Near the corner of State and 10th; (503)386-1899; 1005 State St, Hood River, OR 97031; $$; MC, V; checks OK.*

Columbia Gorge Hotel ★ Lumber baron Simon Benson capped his successful completion of the Columbia Gorge Scenic Highway when he built his luxury hotel in 1921 and brought in his famous chef, Henry Thiele. Instantly the hotel became a favorite of honeymooners and tourists. The old dear (restored a number of times) can't compete with the luxury of 1990 hotels, but it does have some pluses: a stunning structure with a private window on Wah-Gwin-Gwin Falls of the Columbia River; and a colorful past, which included visits by Rudolph Valentino. The public rooms are large and elegant. The guest rooms are rather small (especially for the big price) and we've witnessed cracked sinks and broken fireplace screens. But the price does include turn-down service, a newspaper in the morning, and an insultingly large breakfast. Aim for a gorge-side room; they're quieter and have the best views. The best deals (and the most fun) are packages: whitewater rafting or fly-fishing in the mountains; hiking or horseback riding in the Gorge; skiing on Mount Hood; or golf year-round. ■ *Exit 62 off I-84; (503)386-5566 or (800)345-1921; 4000*

▼

▲

*Westcliff Dr, Hood River, OR 97031; $$$; full bar; AE, DC,
MC, V; checks OK; lunch Mon–Sat, breakfast and dinner every day, Sun brunch.* ♿

Vagabond Lodge ★ The front building is nothing but a nondescript highway-facing unit. The surprise is in back. So ask for a room in the riverfront building. So close to the Columbia Gorge Hotel it could almost be another wing. It's got the identical view as (some say better than) CGH; the rooms are twice the size and a fraction of the price. If there are four of you, get a suite with a fireplace and separate bedroom (it'll cost you less than the smallest room at CGH). ■ *Exit 62 off I-84; (503) 386-2992; 4070 Westcliff Dr, Hood River, OR 97031; $; AE, DC, MC, V; no checks.* ♿

THE DALLES

The Dalles is *the* historical stop along this stretch. For centuries, this area was the meeting place for Native Americans. In the 1840s, it was the official end of the Oregon Trail. Later it served as the only military fort in the Northwest and the county seat of Wasco County, then a 130,000-square-mile vastness that spread from the Cascades to the Rockies. Gold miners loaded up here. Thomas Condon, Oregon's father of geology, got his start amid local basalts.

Signs of all this remain—the Native American **petroglyphs**, the 1850 surgeon's house from the old Fort Dalles (now a museum at 15th and Garrison streets), the east side's "houses of entertainment," and nicely maintained examples of Colonial, gothic revival, Italianate, and American renaissance architecture. Take a tour by car or on foot; maps are available at The Dalles Convention and Visitor Bureau, 404 W Second Street, (503) 296-6616 or (800) 255-3385.

Uphill from downtown are irrigated cherry orchards; Wasco County is the largest producer in the United States and celebrates its **Cherry Festival** in mid-April. Spreading far to the east are the grainfields and grasslands of drier Eastern Oregon. Annual precipitation is no more than 15 inches; trees thin out quickly, and rocks protrude more visibly. Most of the year the ground is golden, except for the wildflowers in spring.

RESTAURANTS

Baldwin Saloon ★ The Baldwin Saloon, built in 1876, has been a steamboat navigational office, a warehouse, coffin storage site, employment office, and saddle shop, and now it's a restaurant and bar. It's nicely done—stripped to the original brick, with fir floors, wooden booths, light streaming in the windows, a mahogany bar, and large turn-of-the-century oil paintings of Northwest nature scenes hanging on the walls. Piano, cello, and violins (on tape) are a nice background—as is the live

▼

Hood River

Lodgings

▲

piano music on weekends. But the food is what impressed us most: fresh oysters on the half shell, smoked salmon mousse, and chicken liver pâté served with homemade bread and fresh vegetables, thick sandwiches, and filet mignon. ■ *At 1st and Court St; (503)296-5666; 1st and Court, The Dalles; $; full bar; MC, V; checks OK; lunch, dinner Mon–Sat.* &

Ole's Supper Club ★ Ole's isn't glamorous. In fact, it's in the industrial west end of The Dalles. But locals like it this way. The consistent quality of the food and the commitment to good wine make Ole's notable—in spite of the fact that it looks like a double-wide mobile home. The house special turns out to be a superb cut of prime rib. Everything is included: delicious homemade soup, a standard salad, a little loaf of hot homemade bread, and the rest. The restaurant has established its reputation on beef, but when fresh razor clams are available, it treats them well. The bar is one of the few in Oregon that doubles as a wine shop; it's known regionally for a wide selection. ■ *Exit 84 off I-84, go west 1 mile; (503)296-6708; 2620 W 2nd St, The Dalles; $$; full bar; AE, MC, V; checks OK; dinner Tues–Sat.*

LODGINGS

Williams House Inn ★★ A manicured 3-acre arboretum surrounds this classic 1899 Queen Anne house. The inn has been in the Williams family for more than 70 years and is on the National Register of Historic Places. Nicaraguan mahogany decorates the walls, and Oriental rugs cover the floor of the large living room that contains a piano, Don Williams's bass fiddle, and a fireplace. Two of the three rooms have their own balcony; all have their own baths. We especially like the downstairs Elizabeth Suite with its separate bedroom, writing desk, hideabed, and private bath with marble-topped washbasin and a 6-foot-long, claw-footed tub. The Williamses serve a fine breakfast of fresh or frozen local fruits, including cherries from their own orchard, home-roasted granola, muffins, fresh-ground coffees, and eggs. Don Williams happily shares his love and encyclopedic knowledge of the area's rich history. ■ *Corner of Trevett and 6th; (503)296-2889; 608 W 6th St, The Dalles, OR 97058; $$; AE, MC, V; checks OK.*

MOUNT HOOD

At 11,245 feet, Hood may not be the highest in the chain of volcanoes in the Cascades, but it *is* one of the best-developed, with five **ski areas** (Mt. Hood Meadows, Summit, Multorpor, Timberline, and Copper Spur) on its base. The Timberline Day Lodge Wy'East, at the 6,000-foot level, has plenty of facilities to equip the mountaineer, hiker, or skier. Chair lifts take you to the Palmer Snowfield, up in the glaciers, where you can ski in the middle of summer. The lower parts are ablaze with rhodo-dendrons (peaking in June) and wildflowers (peaking in July); all are easily reachable from trails that spread out from Timberline Lodge. One of the best trails leads 4½ miles west from Timberline Lodge to flower-studded Paradise Park. Like Rainier, the mountain is girt by a long trail (called Timberline Trail), a 40-mile circuit of the entire peak that traverses snow-fields as well as ancient forests.

Mid-May to mid-July is the prime time for **climbing Mount Hood**, a peak that looks easier than it is, since the last 1,500 feet involve very steep snow climbing. Timberline Mountain Guides, in the Timberline Lodge, equip and conduct climbers to the summit; (503)636-7704.

RESTAURANTS

The Brew Pub at Mount Hood Brewing Company The theme is universal—trout fishing and beer—in this knotty pine brew-pub, where you can watch the brewmasters at work and pon-der what kind of fly the trout over the bar is biting (a bar fly?). Try an oatmeal stout or the popular iceaxe IPA with a pizza you design from toppings that include fontina, feta, Gorgonzola, and smoked cheddar cheeses, Andouille sausage, smoked salmon, pesto, capers, or walnuts. The burgers are excellent choices too. ■ *Take the Government Camp loop off Highway 26; (503)272-3724; 87304 E Government Camp Loop; $; beer and wine; AE, MC, V; checks OK; lunch, dinner every day.* &

LODGINGS

Timberline Lodge ★★ Built in 1937 as a WPA project, Timberline Lodge is a wonderland of American crafts — carved stone, worked metal, massive beams with adze marks plain to see, rugged fireplaces everywhere, and a huge, octagonal lobby that is an inspiring centerpiece for the steep-roofed hotel. Many of the upholsteries, draperies, rugs, and bedspreads in the public and guest rooms have been re-created in their original patterns — in some cases with the help of the original craftspeople. The best rooms are those with fireplaces (but bargain hunters or savvy parents might want to put their kids in the $60 bunk rooms). The resort is known for its year-round skiing, but during the summer, Timberline offers hiking, picnicking, chair-lift rides, and guided nature tours (the staff is a great source for suggestions). There's also a sauna and heated outdoor pool. The lobby's best for lounging (as the rooms are quite small); desk nooks upstairs are the postcard-writing spots.

As for the restaurant, fish is Leif Eric Benson's strong point. The food in the Ram's Head Lounge is not quite as good, but do take time for a drink while looking into the heart of the mountain. Fast food is available in the Wy'East Lodge.

Adventurers might want to sleep over in the newly restored

Silcox Hut, 7,000 feet up the mountain. Built by the same craftsmen who constructed Timberline, Silcox served as the terminus for the Magic Mile chair lift until 1962. It was neglected for 20 years until Friends of Silcox Hut restored it. Now you can rent bunk rooms for $65/person per night (includes dinner, breakfast, and transportation from Timberline). Just bring your sleeping bag. Open to the public 10am–4pm for lunch when the Magic Mile chair lift is running. ■ *60 miles due east of Portland off Hwy 26; (503) 272-3311 or (800) 547-1406; Timberline Ski Area, Timberline Lodge, OR 97028; $$; full bar; AE, MC, V; checks OK; breakfast, lunch, dinner every day.*

Falcon's Crest Inn ★ All in all, this is a fine three-story inn, owned by Bob (B. J.) and Melody Johnson. Heat radiates from the wood stove in the living room and seclusion is yours in any of the three lofty hideaways on the top floor (table games, music, videos, views of SkiBowl). For the most part, the inn is attractively furnished, but you've got to be friendly to teddy bears (there are hundreds) and not mind Christmas ornaments (decorations stick around as long as the snow does, sometimes through March). Rooms are done in themes: lions, tigers, and leopards adorn the Safari; the Cat Ballou has red velvet chairs and an ivory lace comforter; the romantic Master Suite has its own private Jacuzzi deck. B. J. cooks a big breakfast and serves satisfying dinners ($30, open to the public) with 24 hours notice. A variety of wines and beers are available to sip by the fire after a day of mountain-play. ■ *Take the Government Camp Loop off Hwy 26; (503) 272-3403 or (800) 624-7384; 87287 Government Camp Loop Hwy, Government Camp, OR 97028; $$$; beer and wine; AE, MC, V; checks OK; dinner by 24-hour advance reservation.*

Welches

Restaurants

WELCHES

This pretty little town was named after Samuel Welch and his son Billy, who built the Old Welches Inn. For excellent coffee, stop by the little **Mount Hood Coffee Roasters** (64235 E Brightwood Loop, (503) 622-5153), where Serene Elliott-Graber will show you how she roasts coffee beans from around the world.

RESTAURANTS

Chalet Swiss ★★ Open the door and walk into Oregon's version of Switzerland—a world of peasant dresses, cowbells, and hand-carved wooden furniture. New owners Vicki and Greg Guerrero have maintained the Swiss specialties: *Bundner-fleisch* (paper-thin slices of beef salt-cured in alpine air); traditional fondues; raclette (cheese broiled on potatoes and served with pickles and onions); greens dressed with lemon, garlic, and herbs. The Zürcher Geschnetzeltes (veal in cream sauce with mushrooms) is a particular standout. Reservations suggested. ■ *Hwy 26 and E Welches Rd; (503) 622-3600; 24371 E Welches Rd, Welches; $$; full bar; AE, MC, V; checks OK; dinner Wed–Sun.* &

LODGINGS

The Resort at the Mountain ★★ At the right time of the year, you can ski one day and play golf the next. Proximity to Mount Hood and their 27-hole golf course makes the Resort at the Mountain a good choice for the active traveler. The 160 rooms are large and quiet. The key here is to reserve a fireplace room with a gear closet (a necessity here) and a pool- or forest-facing deck (some rooms aim toward the highway). And, as if skiing, golf, and fishing weren't enough, there are six tennis courts, an outdoor heated pool and Jacuzzi, a fitness center, mountain-bike rentals, hikes, horseshoes, golf lessons, volleyball, badminton, croquet, and basketball. Of course, it's also a very popular conference center. ■ *½ mile south of Hwy 26 on E Welches Rd; (503) 622-3101 or (800) 669-7666; 68010 E Fairway Ave, Welches, OR 97067; $$$; full bar; AE, MC, V; checks OK; breakfast, lunch, dinner every day, brunch Sun.* &

Old Welches Inn ★ A hundred years after it opened as the first summer inn on Mount Hood, the Old Welches Inn is still perfectly placed: French windows give views of the Resort at the Mountain's 27-hole golf course, the mountains that ring the valley, and grounds filled with wildflowers that stretch down to the Salmon River. The three upstairs rooms are small, but all are attractive and have big views. Relax by the fire, read in the sun room. Larger groups may prefer to rent the no-frills two-bedroom cabin with fireplace, kitchen, and views. ■ *1 mile south of Hwy 26 on E Welches Rd; (503) 622-3754; 26401 E Welches Rd, Welches, OR 97067; $$; AE, MC, V; checks OK.*

SANDY

A pleasant town on the way to Mount Hood, Sandy (named for the nearby river) offers a white-steepled church, quaint shops, a weekend country market, ski rentals, and big fruit stands purveying the local fruits, vegetables, wines, juices, and filberts. In short—a nice stop en route to the mountains.

The **Oregon Candy Farm** (5½ miles east of Sandy on Highway 26; (503) 668-5066) features Bavarian truffles along with hand-dipped chocolates and caramel. Kids can watch the candymakers in action.

Oral Hull Park is designed for the blind, with splashing water and plants to smell or touch; it is a moving experience even for the sighted; (503) 668-6195.

The Elusive Trout Pub A giant marlin guards the entryway, wagonwheel chandeliers hang over the tables, and an old wooden canoe hanging upside down from the ceiling completes the look. Surprise, surprise, the theme in Sandy's popular pub is fish and fishing; the personal collection of trout flies, fish toys, and other fishy stuff has been gathered and donated by patrons over the years. The menu reflects the slang of one who lived in hip-waders until he spawned the idea for the pub: the Keeper, Bucktail Caddis, Eastern Brookie, Red Sider, and German Brown—all names for better-than-average sandwiches. A large selection of brews is on draft—try the ale sampler, six 5-ounce glasses for $5.75. ■ *At the corner of Hoffman Ave and Proctor Blvd; (503) 668-7884; 39333 Proctor Blvd; $; beer and wine; MC, V; checks OK; lunch, early dinner Tues–Sun.* &

MCKENZIE RIVER

The highway through this river valley is the most beautiful of all the Cascade crossings. Following Highway 126 from Eugene, you pass through farm country alongside the green waters of the McKenzie River. Soon there are lovely campgrounds, waterfalls, and amazingly transparent lakes. At Foley Springs, catch Highway 242 for the pass (opens about July 1 each year). This is volcanic country, with vast 2,000-year-old lava beds.

McKenzie River runs. Long celebrated for trout fishing, the McKenzie has become known for river runs in rafts or the famous McKenzie River boats, rakish dories with upturned bows and sterns. **Dave Helfrich River Outfitter** in Vida is one outfitter who conducts springtime day trips on the river and also arranges for fly-fishing expeditions in drift boats; (503) 896-3786.

Vida

Lodgings

VIDA

LODGINGS

Eagle Rock Lodge ★ A former river-guide dwelling is now a quiet bed and breakfast on the McKenzie River. Laid back but classy, eight-guest-room Eagle Rock is great for a weekend retreat during the river-rafting and fishing season. If you want to avoid river traffic, hit it before April and you may have the run of the place. The Fireside Room is a spacious river-view suite with stone fireplace, comfortable living room, kitchenette with bar, TV, and even a small library, in case you want to read up on Poe, Shakespeare, exotic plants, or whitetail deer. Bring a bottle of wine and stretch out in front of the fire, if the weather's appropriate. Breakfast in hosts Jerry and Susan Motter's attached quarters is filling. A masseur is available by

appointment. ■ *36 miles east of I-5 on Hwy 126 (near Vida);
(503)822-3962; 49198 McKenzie Hwy, Vida, OR 97488; $$;
AE, DC, MC, V; local checks only.*

MCKENZIE BRIDGE

Tokatee Golf Course, 3 miles west of McKenzie Bridge, is
commonly rated one of the five finest in the Northwest: lots of
trees, rolling terrain, and distracting views of the scenery;
(503)822-3220.

RESTAURANTS

Log Cabin Inn The fundamentals of home cooking and clean,
comfortable lodging are enshrined here in eight newly re-
modeled cabins on the water. Dinners are popular and offer a
range as broad as wild boar, buffalo, venison, and quail, as well
as the more traditional prime rib. Folks come from miles
around to top it all off with marionberry cobbler. ■ *50 miles
east of I-5 on Hwy 126; (503)822-3432; 56483 McKenzie
Hwy, McKenzie Bridge; $$; full bar; MC, V; checks OK; lunch,
dinner every day, brunch Sun (winter hours vary).* &

LODGINGS

Vida

Lodgings

Holiday Farm ★ First-time visitors to Holiday Farm wouldn't
know at a glance that the resort encloses 90 acres and a hidden lake or three. They would find a main house (an old stagecoach stop), pleasant dining in the restaurant, and some
amiable riverside cottages with knockout views of the McKenzie. Open year-round, all of the cabins feature decks and bright
windows. Older cabins are green and white (with a rebuilt
porch here and there); others are cedar-sided and more contemporary. Big and Little Rainbow is a large and modern unit
that can be joined for a larger group (two families). The restaurant with its porch over the river makes a very pleasant dining
stop. ■ *3 miles west of McKenzie Bridge on McKenzie River
Dr; (503)822-3715; 54455 McKenzie River Dr, Blue River,
OR 97413; $$$; full bar; AE, MC, V; checks OK; breakfast,
lunch, dinner every day.*

CAMP SHERMAN

LODGINGS

House on the Metolius ★★ This private fly-fishing resort, set
on 200 acres of gorgeous scenery with exclusive access to a
half mile of the majestic Metolius River, usually is open all year.
It's hard to get into and is open only to registered guests. No
stowaways, please. Lodgings are limited to seven cabins, each
with a fully equipped kitchenette, microwave oven, gas barbe-
cue, fireplace, and king-size bed. Units 3 and 4 have ovens.
Reservations needed at least a week in advance. Well-behaved

pets are okay. Don't forget your fly rod. ■ *Forest Service Rd 1420, 2½ miles north of Camp Sherman; (503)595-6620; PO Box 100, Camp Sherman, OR 97730; $$$; MC, V; checks OK.*

Metolius River Resort ★★ Not to be confused with the lower-priced, circa 1923 Metolius River Lodges across the bridge (worn and well-loved like the Velveteen Rabbit, by generations of guests), these 11 lodgettes on the west bank of the Metolius are elegant wood-shake cabins with large decks and river-rock fireplaces. All cabins have river views, master bedrooms and lofts, furnished kitchens—and French doors leading to large river-facing decks. Because the cabins are privately owned, interiors differ; we especially like numbers 2 and 10 with natural ponderosa pine interiors, and number 1, spiffed up in country floral. Don't want to cook? We've heard good reports on the nearby Kokanee Cafe, open May through October. ■ *Camp Sherman, 5 miles north of Highway 20; (503)595-6281 or (800)81-TROUT; 5 Suttle Sherman Rd, Camp Sherman; HCR Box 1210, Camp Sherman, Oregon 97730; $$$; MC, V; checks OK.*

Lake Creek Lodge The resort has been here for over 60 years, popular with families who want a knotty-pine cabin from which to enjoy the fishing, the tiny pond, and the hearty food at the lodge. Best choice is a lodge house, a cheerful, open-ceilinged home with two or three bedrooms, one or two baths, possibly a fireplace, a complete kitchen, living room, and screened porch. Less expensive are the three two-bedroom cottages, which have no kitchens. The cabins are spread around the grassy grounds dotted with pines. Facilities are extensive: an outdoor pool open in summer, tennis (two courts), fishing, hiking, biking, and children's activities. The lodge serves excellent breakfasts and dinners, and if it's not too busy with guests, it is also open for outsiders by reservation. You bring your own wine. ■ *4 miles north of Hwy 20 at Camp Sherman turnoff; (503)595-6331; Star Route, Sisters, OR 97759; $$$; no credit cards; checks OK; breakfast, dinner every day; (restaurant closed in winter).*

▼

Sisters

▲

SISTERS

Named after the three mountain peaks that dominate the horizon (Faith, Hope, and Charity), this little community is becoming a bit of a mecca for tired urban types looking for a taste of cowboy escapism. On a clear day (and there are about 250 of them a year), Sisters is exquisitely beautiful. Surrounded by mountains, trout streams, and pine and cedar forests, this little town capitalizes on the influx of winter skiers and summer camping and fishing enthusiasts.

There's mixed sentiment about the pseudo-Western storefronts that are thematically organizing the town's commerce, but then again, Sisters does host 56,000 visitors for each of four shows during its annual June rodeo. In the early 1970s, Sisters developed the Western theme that by the '90s has grown more sophisticated and even slightly New Age. The town, built on about 30 feet of pumice dust spewed over centuries from the nearby volcanoes, has added numerous mini-mall shopping clusters with courtyards and sidewalks to eliminate blowing dust. There are several large art galleries, a yummy bakery, a knowledgeable mountain supply store and excellent fly-fishing shop, and even a store for freshly roasted coffee beans. Although the population of the town itself is only about 820, more than 7,500 live in the surrounding area on mini-ranches.

RESTAURANTS

Hotel Sisters Restaurant and Bronco Billy's Saloon ★ The social centerpiece of Western-theme Sisters, this bar and eatery serves up Western-style ranch cooking, with good burgers and some Mexican fare served by a friendly and diligent waitstaff. Seafood is fresh, the filet mignon grilled perfectly, the chicken and ribs succulent. For a couple of bucks more, they'll split your single dinner into servings for two. Owners John Keenan, Bill Reed, and John Tehan have succeeded in turning old friendships into a going business consortium, re-creating the look of a first-class hotel, circa 1900. The upstairs hotel rooms are now private dining rooms. A good place for drinks on the deck. ■ *Cascade and Fir sts; (503)549-RIBS; 105 Cascade St, Sisters; $$; full bar; MC, V; checks OK; lunch, dinner every day (lunch Sat–Sun only in winter).* &

Papandrea's Pizza ★ Oregonians love this place. The original link in a small chain of pizzerias, Papandrea's has built a quality reputation on fresh dough, homemade sauce, real cheese, and fresh vegetables. Because of all this freshness, the place does seem to abide by its disclaimer sign—"We will not sacrifice quality for speed, so expect to wait a little longer." Actually, you wait quite a bit longer for the original thick-crust pies, but there's a You-Bake line for take-out. ■ *East end of town; (503)549-6081; E Cascade Hwy, Sisters; $; beer and wine; MC, V; local checks only; lunch, dinner every day.*

LODGINGS

Black Butte Ranch ★★★ With 1,800 acres, this vacation and recreation wonderland remains the darling of Northwest resorts. Rimmed by the Three Sisters mountains, scented by a plain of ponderosa pines, and expertly developed by the Brooks Scanlon Company, these rental condos and private homes draw families year-round to swim, ski, fish, golf, bike, boat, ride horses (summer only), and play tennis. The best way to make a reservation is to state the size of your party and whether or not you want a home (most are quite large and contemporary) or simply a good-sized bed and bath (in the latter case, the lodge condominiums will suffice, although some are dark and dated, with too much orange Formica and brown furniture). The main lodge is a handsome but not overwhelming building that serves as dining headquarters. Tables at the Restaurant at the Lodge are tiered so that everyone can appreciate the meadow panorama beyond.

■ *Hwy 20, 8 miles west of Sisters; (503)595-6211; PO Box 8000, Black Butte Ranch, OR 97759; $$$; full bar; AE, DC, MC, V; checks OK; breakfast, lunch, dinner every day (closed Mon–Tues from Jan to Apr).* ⅃

BEND

Bend was a quiet, undiscovered high-desert paradise until a push in the 1960s to develop recreation and tourism potential tamed Bachelor Butte (later renamed Mount Bachelor) into an alpine playground. Then came the golf courses, the airstrip, the bike trails, the river-rafting companies, the hikers, the tennis players, the rockhounds, and the skiers. Bend's popularity and population (currently 50,000) have been on a steady increase ever since, propelling it into serious destination status. The main thoroughfare, 5 miles of strip development, bypasses the town center, which thrives just to the west between two one-way streets, Wall and Bond. A new, $90 million bypass, the Bend Parkway, is being built to alleviate considerable traffic congestion. Part of the charm of the town comes from the blinding blue sky and the sage-scented air. The other part of its appeal is due to its proximity to the following attractions.

Bend

Mount Bachelor Ski Area (22 miles southwest). Mount Bachelor, the largest ski area in the Pacific Northwest, now has six high-speed lifts for a total of 10 lifts feeding skiers onto 3,100 vertical feet of dry and groomed skiing. **The Skier's Palate** at the midmountain Pine Marten Lodge serves excellent lunches of smoked salmon pasta, lime chicken fettuccine, or a hot sandwich of Dungeness crab and bay shrimp (as well as microbrews and margaritas). The 9,060-foot elevation at the summit makes for late-season skiing (open until July 4th). High-season amenities include ski school, racing, day care, rentals, an entire Nordic program and trails, and better-than-average ski food at three lodges. Call (800)829-2442 or the ski report at (503)382-7888.

The High Desert Museum (59800 S Highway 97, Bend, OR 97702) is an outstanding nonprofit center for natural and cultural history, located 4 miles south of Bend, that includes live-animal educational presentations. Inside, visitors can walk through 100 years of history, featuring excellent dioramas from Native American times through the 1890s. A "Desertarium" exhibits desert animals, including live owls, lizards, and

Lahontan cutthroat trout. Twenty acres of natural trails and out-door exhibits offer replicas of covered wagons, a sheepherder's camp, a settlers' cabin, and an old sawmill; and support three resident river otters, three porcupines, and about a half-dozen raptors (animal presentations daily). A new wing featuring an extensive collection of Columbia River Plateau Indian artifacts is planned as part of a $15 million expansion. Open every day from 9am to 5pm; call (503)382-4754.

Pilot Butte (just east of town). This cinder cone state park with a mile-long road to the top is a good first stop, offering a knockout panorama of the city and the mountains beyond. Be wary of pedestrians on the road.

Newberry National Volcanic Monument (between Bend and La Pine on both sides of Highway 97). This 56,000-acre monument in the Deschutes National Forest is only a few years old, but showcases geologic attractions tens of thousands of years old. Highlights: **Lava Lands Visitor Center** at the base of Lava Butte (12 miles south of Bend) is the interpretive center for miles of lava beds. Be sure to drive or, when cars are barred, take the shuttle up Lava Butte, formed by a volcanic fissure, for a sweeping, dramatic view of the moonlike landscape. Tour **Lava River Cave**, a mile-long lava tube on Highway 97 (13 miles south of Bend). As you descend into the dark and surprisingly eerie depths, you'll need a warm sweater. **Newberry Crater**, 13 miles east of Highway 97 on Forest Road 21, is the heart of the monument. Major attractions include Paulina Peak, the Big Obsidian Flow, Paulina Falls, and East and Paulina lakes, each with a small resort on its shores. Seasons for different Newberry attractions vary, depending on snow, but generally they are open May through October. Call (503)593-2421 or (503)388-5664 for details.

Pine Mountain Observatory, 30 miles southeast of Bend on Highway 20, (503)382-8331, is the University of Oregon's astronomy research facility. One of its three telescopes is the largest in the Northwest.

Deschutes Historical Center (corner of NW Idaho and Wall) features regional history and interesting pioneer paraphernalia, but keeps limited hours (open Tues–Sat, 10am–4:30pm). Call (503)389-1813.

Cascade Lakes Highway/Century Drive. This 100-mile scenic tour needs several hours and a picnic lunch for full appreciation; there are stunning mountain views and a number of lakes along the way. Begin in Bend along the Deschutes River, using the Bend Chamber of Commerce's booklet "Cascade Lakes Discovery Tour."

Smith Rock State Park. Twenty-two miles north of Bend in Terrebonne, some of the finest rock climbers gather to test their skills on the red-rock cliffs. Year-round camping is available. Call (503)548-7501.

The **Crooked River Dinner Train** ambles up the 38-mile Crooked River Valley between Redmond and Prineville with 3-hour scenic excursions and white-tablecloth dinner service. Check the season; special events and theme rides are offered, from murder mystery tours to champagne brunches to Western hoedowns. Reservations required. Call (503)548-8630.

RESTAURANTS

Broken Top Club ★★ The 25,000-square-foot clubhouse of the Broken Top golf course captures an exceptional view of the Cascades with the golf course and lake gracing the foreground. The talents of some of the area's most successful artists are on display everywhere. Make your reservation for a half hour before sunset, and if Mother Nature is accommodating, you'll be treated to a spectacular sunset over the jagged Broken Top and Three Sisters. The food is equally sensational. Chef Gary W. Slattery might start with the shrimp quesadilla with guacamole and tomato, and move to a mixed seafood and spinach lasagne with fresh pesto cream and roasted pine nuts or grilled salmon with wild rice and sweet pepper relish on a tarragon-pecan

Bend

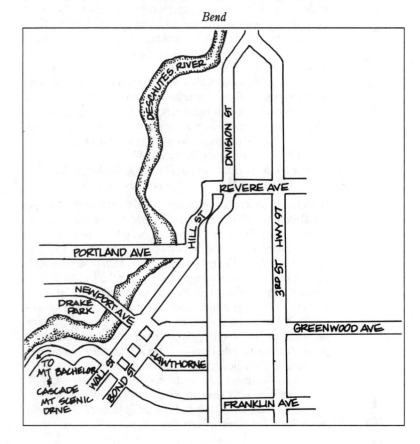

sauce. Elegance in Central Oregon. ■ *Just off Mt Washington Dr (from Century Dr); (503)383-8210; 61999 Broken Top Dr, Bend; $$; full bar; MC, V; local checks only; lunch Tues–Sat, dinner Tues–Sun, brunch Sun.* ♿

Pine Tavern Restaurant ★★ Buttonhole three out of four Bend citizens on the street and tell them you're ready for a fancy night out, with good food, service, atmosphere, and a decent value for your dollar. The recommendation time and again will be the Pine Tavern. This establishment—and 50 years of history make it truly established—has regained its reputation for quality. Request a table by the window (overlooking the placid Mirror Pond) in the main dining room and marvel at the tree growing through the floor. The prime rib petite cut is ample even for a hungry diner, but prime rib is the forte of the restaurant and few can resist the larger cut. Great apple butter for the soft rolls. ■ *Foot of Oregon Ave downtown at Mirror Pond; (503)382-5581; 967 NW Brooks, Bend; $$; full bar; AE, DC, MC, V; checks OK; lunch Mon–Sat, dinner every day.*

Scanlon's ★★ Scanlon's adjoins the Athletic Club of Bend, but aside from an aerobic instructor's distant bark and the slightest whiff of chlorine from the pool, you'd never know it. Once you're ensconced in a cozy white-tablecloth booth, your mind will be on the food—meals start right away with a complimentary caper-loaded caponata and sweet homemade breads (Tuscan and focaccia) with virgin olive oil and balsamic vinegar for dipping. Dinners may be dressed up or dressed down: rock shrimp pizza with roasted red peppers; eggplant piccata with lemon; braised salmon; or oven-roasted rack of lamb. Meats are grilled on cherry wood. The wine list is thoughtful. ■ *Just off Century Dr on the way to Mt Bachelor; (503)382-8769; 61615 Mt Bachelor Dr, Bend; $$; full bar; AE, MC, V; checks OK; lunch Mon–Fri, dinner Tues–Sun.* ♿

Honkers ★ You're bound to see Canada geese flying low over the Deschutes River just outside the 40-table dining area, so reserve a window seat. Honkers, which housed the first Brooks-Scanlon sawmill, pays homage to the town's bygone lumber mill era with cross-cut saws on ponderosa pine walls, exposed rafters, and a stone fireplace near the lounge. Things can be a little overdone here (too many onions in the artichoke and crab dip) and a little underdone there (a bland house salad), but most diners will be satisfied with the charbroiled salmon, pork chops with apple and raisin chutney, or the green-peppercorn steak. Add Honkers' cheesy, signature twice-baked potatoes or their butter rum cake, and you've got yourself a meal worth trumpeting about. ■ *On the east bank of the Deschutes just off Colorado Ave; (503)389-4665; 805 SW Industrial Way, Bend; $$; full bar; MC, V; local checks only; lunch Mon–Fri, dinner every day.* ♿

Le Bistro ★ Don't be put off by the austere old church facade at this French specialty restaurant. Inside, the sidewalk-cafe decor warms things up, as does the superlative waitstaff. Yes, it's expensive and pretentious, but it's tough to fault the food, which you can watch being prepared in the open kitchen. The Seafood Wellington incorporates former owner Axel Hoch's original recipe that extravagantly combines scallops, prawns, Oregon bay shrimp, lobster, and mushrooms sautéed lightly in butter and shallots, flamed with brandy and Madeira, blended with a nantua (lobster) sauce, and carefully stuffed into a fluffy puff pastry shell. For simpler preparations try the broiled rack of lamb or charbroiled venison loin. The lounge downstairs is a good place to take your after-dinner coffee. ■ *1 block off Greenwood on Hwy 97; (503)389-7274; 1203 NE 3rd St, Bend; $$; full bar; AE, DC, MC, V; local checks only; dinner Tues–Sat.*

Pescatore ★ Brad Haun's restaurant is nowhere close to the water, but Pescatore (it means "fisherman") is proud of its Italian renditions of seafood. A lusty penne pescatore is a mixture of clams, mussels, calamari, shrimp, and salmon in a spicy marinara served atop penne; capellini vegetali tangles fresh vegetables in angel hair pasta. Specialty dish Farfalle con Salmone Affumicato offers a unique blend of smoked salmon, dill, crème fraîche and vodka with bowtie pasta. Every entree comes with fresh-baked focaccia bread and extra-virgin olive oil, and a salad or soup (often minestrone). Piano jazz on weekends. Rosy lights, rosy dining room, rosy service. ■ *Minnesota between Wall and Bond; (503)389-6276; 119 NW Minnesota, Bend; $$; full bar; AE, MC, V; checks OK; dinner every day.* &

Deschutes Brewery & Public House It was only a matter of time before this was no longer the only brew pub in town. But it's still the best. The place was designed by Portland city folk, with urbanites in mind: exposed rafters and dark wood wainscoting. The beer is dark, too: a robust Obsidian Stout or a rich Black Butte Porter, and on the lighter side, a hoppy Cascade Golden Ale and the ever-popular Bachelor Bitter. For nondrinkers, a peppery ginger ale is available. The kitchen has created light bar food for midday (French onion soup, black bean chili, and homemade sausages with sauerkraut) and a full dinner menu. But really, most come for the brew. ■ *Near corner of Bond and Greenwood; (503)382-9242; 1044 NW Bond St, Bend; $; beer and wine; MC, V; local checks only; lunch, dinner every day.* &

Westside Bakery and Cafe Once just a bakery in the corner of the building, the ever-popular and somewhat kitschy (toy trains to dinosaur models) Westside has taken over the entire building. You can get good coffee and wholesome baked goods

to go, but most choose to stay for the huevos rancheros, crois-
sant scramble, blueberry pancakes, or homemade granola for
breakfast. Hefty sandwiches on homemade bread fill many
mountain-bound lunch sacks. The staff (and prices) are some
of the friendliest in town. A popular place. Expect to wait up to
20 minutes for a table on weekends. ■ *Past Drake Park to the
other side of the river on Galveston; (503) 382-3426; 1005 NW
Galveston, Bend; $; beer and wine; MC, V; local checks only;
breakfast, lunch, dinner every day.*

LODGINGS

Sunriver Lodge ★★★ More than a resort, Sunriver is
an organized community with its own post office, realty
offices, outdoor mall, grocery store, and 1,000 or so full-
time residents. The unincorporated town now sprawls over
3,300 acres, and its own paved runway for private air commut-
ing does a brisk business. Its specialty is big-time escapist va-
cationing, and this resort has all the facilities to keep families,
couples, or groups of friends busy all week long, year-round.
Summer months offer golf (three 18-hole courses), tennis (25
courts), rafting, canoeing, fishing, swimming (two pools, two
complexes of hot tubs), biking (30 miles of paved trails), and
horseback riding. In winter the resort is home base for skiing
(both Nordic and alpine), ice skating, snowmobiling, and indoor racquetball. For the best bargain, deal through the lodge
reservation service and request one of the large and contemporary homes (these often have luxuries like hot tubs, barbecues, and decks) and split expenses with another family. If you
want access to the pool and hot tub facility, be sure to request
a house that has a pass. Even the bedroom units in the lodge
village have a small deck and fireplace and come with privileges such as discounted recreation, depending on the season.

Lodge dining includes the Meadows, a much-acclaimed
showplace for dinner and Sunday brunch, and the Provision
Company for breakfast and lunch. Off premises, choose from
Chinese to pizza. We like to catch the inexpensive breakfast
down at the Trout House at the Sunriver Marina, too. ■ *Off
Hwy 97, 15 miles south of Bend; (503) 593-1221 or (800) 547-
3922; PO Box 3609, Sunriver, OR 97707; $$$; full bar; AE,
DC, MC, V; checks OK; breakfast, lunch, dinner every day (sea-
sonal hours vary).*

Inn of the Seventh Mountain ★★ The Inn offers the
closest accommodations to Mount Bachelor and is es-
pecially popular with families, no doubt due to the vast
menu of activities built into the multicondominium facility and
the reasonable price tag ($65–$140). It has the biggest (though
not full-size) ice rink around, which converts to a rollerskating
rink in April, a coed sauna large enough for a dozen friends,
three bubbling hot tubs, and two heated swimming pools. In

the summer the pools are the centerpiece of activity—there's a whole layout complete with water slide and wading pool. The Inn does a terrific job of social planning and offers fabulous off-season rates. An activities roster for the week gives the run-down on tennis, horseback riding, biking, skating, rafting, snowmobiling, skiing, aerobics, frisbee, golf—you name it. There is plenty of good eating at the resort. The Poppy Seed Cafe puts on a plentiful and tasty breakfast. Josiah's offers fine dining and fun in the spacious lounge downstairs. ■ *18575 SW Century Dr, 7 miles west of Bend; (503)382-8711 or (800)452-6810; 18575 SW Century Dr, Bend; PO Box 1207, Bend, OR 97702; $$$; full bar; AE, DC, MC, V; checks OK; breakfast, lunch, dinner every day.*

Mount Bachelor Village ★★ You don't want a social chair-man, you can live without an adjacent dining room, and you rarely need a hot-tub soak after 11pm? Then Mount Bachelor Village may be your style. What this development has over some of its more famous neighbor resorts is spacious rooms. Every unit has a completely furnished kitchen, wood-burning fireplace, and private deck. We prefer the newer units, where the color scheme is modern and light and where the sound-proofing helps mute the thud of ski boots. Some units look out to the busy mountain road, but the River Ridge addition looks out over the Deschutes River. There are 125 units to choose from, with prices starting at $97 (a few $68 ones are available without kitchens). Amenities: two outdoor Jacuzzis, seasonal outdoor heated pool, six tennis courts, and a 2.2-mile nature trail. ■ *Toward Mount Bachelor on Century Dr; (503)389-5900 or (800)452-9846; 19717 Mt Bachelor Dr, Bend, OR 97702; $$$; AE, MC, V; checks OK.* ⚬

 Rock Springs Guest Ranch ★★ The emphasis here is very much on family vacations, but only late-June through early September and on major holiday week-ends (the rest of the year it functions as a top-notch conference center). Counselors take care of the kids in special programs all day while adults hit the trail, laze in the pool, play tennis, or meet for hors d'oeuvres every evening on the deck. The cab-ins are quite nice—comfy knotty-pine two- and three-room cot-tages with fireplaces. Only 50 guests stay at the ranch at one time, so it's easy to get to know everyone, particularly since all eat family-style in the lodge. The setting, amid ponderosa pines and junipers alongside a small lake, is secluded and lovely. The main activity here is riding, with nine wranglers and a stable of 65 horses. Summer season is booked by the week only ($1,475 per person—kids for less, children under 2 free), which includes virtually everything with your room. Tennis courts are lit, there's a free-form whirlpool with 15-foot water-fall over volcanic boulders, a sand volleyball court under the tall pines, and fishing in the ranch pond. Note the special financial arrangements for baby-sitters brought for young children. ■ *On Hwy 20, 7 miles from Bend and 20 miles from Sisters; (503)382-1957; 64201 Tyler Rd, Bend, OR 97701; $$; AE, MC, V; checks OK.* &

Entrada Lodge ★ Whether you're a weary traveler or an avid skier just looking for a firm mattress, a dependable shower, a clean room, and decent TV reception, you'll get that and more here. The "more" is a summer pool, a year-round outdoor hot tub, close proximity to the mountain, a spa room, hot chocolate and snacks from 4pm to 6pm by the office fireplace, and free continental breakfast. Friendly owner Brett Evert works hard to personalize this 79-room ranch-style Best Western motel. Pets are allowed with some restrictions—for $5 a night. The price is thrifty, and the proximity to the mountain is a plus. Brett also owns another Best Western in town, the Best Western Inn and Suites of Bend (721 NE Third St, Bend, OR 97701, (503)382-1515). ■ *3 miles from Bend on Century Dr; (503) 382-4080 or (800)528-1234; 19221 Century Dr, Bend, OR 97702; $$; AE, DC, MC, V; no checks.*

Lara House Bed and Breakfast ★ One of Bend's largest and oldest (1910) homes, Lara House is a bright and homey bed and breakfast. The main room is perfect for small-group socializing—with a large stone fireplace and sunny adjacent solarium that looks out over the yard onto the river parkway. A large breakfast is served at small tables on the sun porch as well as at the community oak table. Best of the six rooms is the two-room suite on the third floor. The spa tub on the deck, bicycles, and outdoor games are available for guests. ■ *Louisiana and Congress; (503)388-4064; 640 NW Congress, Bend, OR 97701; $$; AE, MC, V; checks OK.*

The Riverhouse ★ The Riverhouse has become an institution in Bend for comfortable stays at more reasonable rates than the recreation resorts. It's really a glorified motel, and a river runs through it. Amenities are still abundant: indoor and outdoor swimming pools, saunas, three whirlpools, exercise room, and indoor Jacuzzi; 18-hole golf course with driving range; and tennis courts. The Deschutes creates welcome white noise (close to town and Highway 97). Request a room with a view of the river and away from the yahoos in the hot tub. This is where you'll find Mai's Chinese Cuisine, the Poolside Cafe, and the Riverhouse Dining Room, respected for its continental cuisine. The après-ski lounge rocks with contemporary bands six nights a week (country western on Sundays), so avoid nearby rooms unless you plan to dance all night. ■ *On Hwy 97 in Bend; (503)389-3111 or (800)547-3928; 3075 N Hwy 97, Bend, OR 97701; $$; full bar; AE, DC, MC, V; checks OK; breakfast, lunch, dinner every day.* &

ELK LAKE

LODGINGS

Elk Lake Resort ★ Elk Lake is a small mountain lake about 30 miles west of Bend on the edge of the Three Sisters Wilderness Area. This remote fishing lodge—reached by snow-cat or 10 miles of cross-country skiing in the winter—consists of a dozen self-contained cabins, most with fireplace, kitchen, bathroom, and sleeping quarters for two to eight people. It's nothing grand, but the place is much favored by Bend dwellers and the scenery is wonderful. There is a small store and a coffee shop/dining room with standard American grub; reservations required. Getting a reservation can be almost as tough as getting here, since there's only a radiophone (you'll probably have to inquire by mail) and the place is often booked up to a year in advance. ■ *Century Dr, Elk Lake; radiophone YP7 3954; PO Box 789, Bend, OR 97709; $$; MC, V; no checks.*

LA PINE

LODGINGS

Diamond Stone Guest Lodge & Gallery ★ This new bed and breakfast is a diamond in the rough. Innkeepers Doug and Gloria Watt, and Gordon Watt, who run a mortage business, have created a three-room inn along the Little Deschutes River between Sunriver and La Pine. Western art livens up the place (and is for sale). Our favorite is the two-room suite with a view of Bachelor and Quail Run Golf Course. Cable TV and a VCR are included. The living room features a fireplace, vaulted ceiling, and CD player—your choice of tunes. Amenities include outdoor hot tub, sauna, and sun decks. Breakfast keeps even the most active traveler going all day. Help yourself to drinks in the fridge. ■ *8 miles south of Sunriver and 3 miles west of Hwy 97; (503)536-6263 or (800)600-6263; 16696 Sprague Loop, La Pine, OR 97739; $$; AE, MC, V; local checks only.*

▼

Mount Bailey

▲

MOUNT BAILEY

Mount Bailey Alpine Ski Tours offers a true backcountry skiing experience, with snow-cats instead of helicopters to take you to the top of this 8,363-foot ancient volcano, and experienced guides who stress safety. Also in winter: snowmobiling, cross-country skiing, inner-tube and snowboard hills, and ice-skating when the lake permits. Diamond Lake Resort, (503)793-3333, headquarters the guide service. When the snow melts, the operation turns to mountain-bike tours, boating, swimming, and hiking.

WESTFIR

This former logging town flanks the North Fork of the Middle Fork of the Willamette River, excellent for fishing for rainbow trout. The **Aufderheide National Scenic Byway** winds east out of Westfir into the heart of the Cascades, meandering along the river, and is popular with bicyclists, although heavy snowfall closes the route from November until early April.

LODGINGS

Westfir Lodge ★ Westfir Lodge has long anchored the tiny community of Westfir; however, for many years it housed the former lumber company offices. Gerry Chamberlain and Ken Symons converted the two-story building into a very pleasant inn. The no-smoking bedrooms ring the first floor; in the center is a living area, kitchen, and formal dining room where guests are served a full English breakfast (English bangers and fried potatoes, eggs, broiled tomato topped with cheese, and scones). Cottage gardens outside and a plethora of antiques throughout the lodge lend an English country ambience. The longest covered bridge in Oregon—the 180-foot Office Bridge (1944)—is just across the road. ■ *3 miles east of Hwy 58 near Oakridge; (503) 782-3103; 47365 1st St, Westfir, OR, 97492; $$; no credit cards; checks OK.* &

ODELL LAKE

LODGINGS

Odell Lake Lodge and Resort This resort on the shore of Odell Lake is ideal for the fisher, the hiker, and the skier in all of us. The lake's a bit alpine for much swimming; instead cast about for the Mackinaw trout, rainbow, or kokanee. (Most sports equipment, fishing rods to snowshoes, is for rent here.) The small library is the perfect place to sink into an overstuffed chair and read in front of the fireplace. Fresh rainbow trout (of course) is our first choice at the seasonal restaurant. As for accommodations, request a lakeside room. Room 3, specifically. It's a corner suite warmed with knotty pine paneling and views of lake and stream. If you'd rather stay in a cabin, the few additional dollars required to get a lakeside one are well spent. The new well-lit cabin 10 is the best (and the only handicapped-accessible one). Or try cabins 6 or 7. Cabin 12 sleeps a friendly crowd of 16. The second-tier cabins are significantly smaller (no view, too). Pets okay in cabins only; minimum stays during peak season. ■ *From Oakridge, head east on Hwy 58 for 30 miles, take E Odell Lake exit; (503) 433-2540; PO Box 72, Crescent Lake, OR 97425; $$; MC, V; checks OK.* &

CRATER LAKE

Some 6,500 years ago, 15,000-foot Mount Mazama became the Mount St. Helens of its day, blew up, and left behind a deep crater that is now filled with a lake. Plunging to a depth of 1,932 feet, it's the deepest lake in the United States. The area is extraordinary: the impossibly blue lake, eerie volcanic formations, a vast geological wonderland. The visitors center, at the park headquarters, (503)594-2211, offers a theater, an information desk, and a good interpretive exhibit. Visitors can camp at Mazama campground or other designated areas around Crater Lake National Park. You can take the two-hour boat ride from Cleetwood Cove out to Wizard Island and around the lake. There are dozens of trails and climbs to magnificent lookouts. In the winter, when the crowds finally thin out, only the south and west entrance roads are kept open. Cross-country skiing and snowshoe walks are popular activities this time of year.

LODGINGS

Crater Lake Lodge [*unrated*] Originally built in 1909, the historic wood-and-stone building, perched at 7,000 feet on the rim of the caldera, was weakened considerably by decades of heavy snowfall. The four-story lodge has been closed for about six years for a $15 million makeover, and just reopened at press time with a flood of reservations. The renovated summer lodge features 71 rooms; even though only 26 rooms face the lake, all have great views. Best are the eight with claw-footed bathtubs in window alcoves. You won't find TVs or in-room phones. The dining room motif is 1930s lodge decor, conveying the mood of the original and the food of today. ■ *Crater Lake National Park via Hwy 138 or Hwy 62; (503)594-2511; PO Box 128, Crater Lake, OR 97604; $$$; MC, V; checks OK; closed mid–Oct to mid–May.* &

KLAMATH FALLS

This city of 17,000 people, the largest for 70 miles, is so isolated that it once led a movement to secede from Oregon and become the state of Jefferson. Now the residents happily welcome tourists, bird-watchers, and sportspersons from both Oregon and California (just 25 miles south). **Favell Museum of Western Art** is a true Western museum, with arrowheads, Indian artifacts, and the works of more than 200 Western artists; 125 W Main Street, (503)882-9996. The **Klamath County Museum** exhibits the volcanic geology of the region, Indian artifacts from all over Oregon, and relics from the Modoc wars; 1451 Main Street, (503)883-4208.

    Baldwin Hotel Museum, in an old (1906) hotel, retains many fixtures of the era; open June through September, 31

Main Street, (503) 883-4207. **Ross Ragland Theater**, a onetime art deco movie theater, now presents stage plays, concerts, and the like, an impressive 130 nights a year; (503) 884-0651.

Upper Klamath Lake, 143 square miles, is the largest lake in Oregon; it's fine for fishing and serves as the nesting grounds for many birds, including white pelicans. The Williamson River, which flows into the lake, yields plenty of trout.

RESTAURANTS

Chez Nous ★ The name may be French, but Achim and Arlette Bassler serve more of a continental menu in the graceful older home on the south side of town. It's a favorite with locals, who go there for dishes like tournedos gourmet Chez Nous, with artichoke bottoms, scampi, and béarnaise atop the fillets. You get béarnaise with the salmon and halibut, too. The veal Marsala comes on a bed of spinach. And they do chateaubriand or giant lobster for two. Otherwise, it's pretty standard, but nicely done. ▪ *Follow 6th St south, a few blocks past Altamont; (503) 883-8719; 3927 S 6th St, Klamath Falls; $$; full bar; AE, DC, MC, V; local checks only; dinner Tues–Sat; (closed last two weeks of February).* &

Fiorella's ★ Residents of Klamath Falls appreciate the Northern Italian fare at Fiorella and Renato Durighello's restaurant. On a recent visit we had fine scalloppine Marsala and the house special, pastitsio, both of which came with soup, salad (in summer, fresh from their own garden), and garlic bread. The pasta is homemade and delicious. Reservations welcome. ▪ *S 6th St to Simmers; (503) 882-1878; 6139 Simmers Ave, Klamath Falls; $$; full bar; AE, MC, V; local checks only; dinner Tues–Sat.*

Saddle Rock Cafe ★ The Saddle Rock, from the outside, appears a consistent part of the timeworn Klamath Falls: a battered facade that says "old main street cafe" all over it. Inside, though, it's up to the minute: brick walls adorned with local artwork. The bistro fare is equally progressive: fresh pastas with distinctive sauces, polenta, and poultry. Unfortunately, service can be ragged at times. Perhaps that's when they're preoccupied with a catered event. ▪ *Main and 10th sts; (503) 884-1444; 1012 Main St, Klamath Falls; $$; beer and wine; MC, V; checks OK; lunch, dinner Tues–Sat.* &

LODGINGS

Thompson's Bed and Breakfast by the Lake ★ Mary and Bill Pohll offer four bedrooms on a separate level with private entrance. All have private baths. Sunsets over the Cascade Range provide a backdrop to the spectacular view of Upper Klamath Lake. Deer are frequent visitors to the backyard. Bring your binoculars for bird-watching. Bald eagles roost in the backyard.

Mary can cook virtually anything for breakfast, but apple pancakes and French toast are her specialty. This was the first B&B in town, launched when Mary's last name was Thompson. Others have come and gone, but this is still the best. ■ *Call for directions; (503)882-7938; 1420 Wild Plum Court, Klamath Falls, OR 97601; $$; no credit cards; checks OK.* ⓚ

LAKEVIEW

At an elevation of nearly 4,300 feet, Lakeview calls itself "Oregon's Tallest Town." It's better known for its geyser, Old Perpetual—which doesn't exactly rival Yellowstone's Old Faithful, but is Oregon's only geyser. It's located in a pond at **Hunter's Hot Springs**, a 47-acre property dotted by hot-springs pools, on the west side of Highway 395 about 2 miles north of town. The geyser goes off once every 30 seconds or so, shooting 75 feet into the air for 3 to 5 seconds. It's been erupting regularly for some 60 years, apparently unleashed by someone trying to drill a well. **Hunter's Hot Springs** resort, built in the 1920s, now includes an Italian restaurant and a 33-unit motel, with 12 new rooms added in the early 1990s; (503)947-2127.

Abert Lake, 20 miles north of Lakeview, is a stark, shallow body of water over which looms **Abert Rim**, a massive fault scarp. One of the highest exposed geologic faults in North America, the rim towers 2,000 feet above the lake.

BLY

LODGINGS

Aspen Ridge Resort ★ This complex of log homes appears like a mirage in the high meadow of south-central Oregon, reminding one somewhat of an early-day miniature Sunriver. The resort sits on 160 acres, once part of 14,000-acre Fishhole Creek Ranch. The log homes sleep six ($120); the four bedrooms in the main lodge go for less. Most come here to be outside, go mountain biking, or ride horseback...but there is a tennis court for those who prefer to stick around the ranch. If you don't like beef, you don't fit in here. The resort is adjacent to a working cattle and buffalo ranch, which provides a view and influences the restaurant's menu. Best meal bargain is the $26 (for two) steak dinner, barbecued on the back porch. ■ *18 miles SE of Bly on Fishhole Creek Rd; (503)884-8685; Fishhole Creek Rd, Bly; PO Box 2, Bly, OR 97622; $$; full bar; no credit cards; checks OK; breakfast, lunch, dinner every day (closed Mar).*

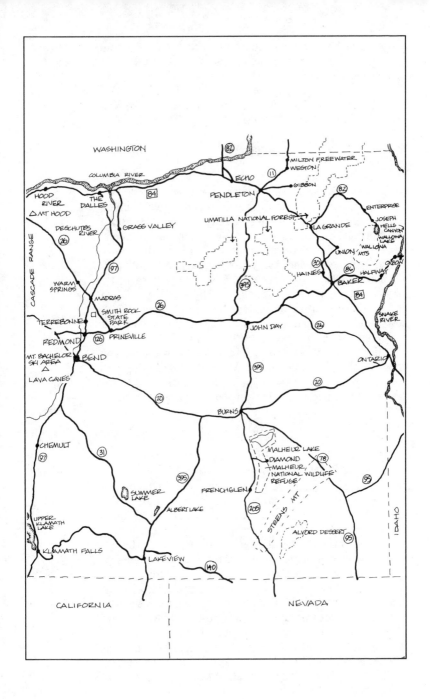

Eastern Oregon

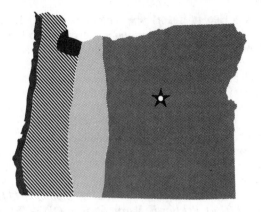

*Two major routes: eastward midstate from Warm Springs
to John Day, and southeastward along I-84 from Pendleton
to the Idaho border (with a diversion into the Wallowas),
turning in-state again to Burns and Frenchglen.*

GRASS VALLEY

RESTAURANTS

Holmestead Wheat and barley farmers, ranchers, and Bend-bound truckers and travelers have one thing in common: an affection for Carol Grout's homemade cinnamon rolls. When Grout sold her cafe last year, the new owners didn't change a thing—the rolls, the malted milk shakes, meaty cheese-burgers, or fresh-cut fries. All road trips deserve a stop like this.
■ *Easy to find; (503)333-2255; Hwy 97, Grass Valley; $; no alcohol; no credit cards; checks OK; breakfast, lunch, dinner every day.*

WARM SPRINGS

For most highway cowboys, Warm Springs is just a small bend in the road at the bottom of a pine-studded rimrock canyon on Highway 26. In 1993, however, **The Museum at Warm Springs**, (503)553-3331, opened on the bank of the Shitike Creek, and what a museum it is. Built by the three Native American tribes (Wasco, Paiute, and Warm Springs) who live on the barren 644,000-acre reservation, the museum houses a permanent collection that includes prized heirlooms, protected by tribal families for generations, on view to the public for the first time. The best of the architecturally magnificent museum is a ceremonial Wasco wedding: tule-mat lodge, wickiup and plankhouse, song chamber, and drumming accompanying rhythmic hoop dancing.

LODGINGS

 Kah-Nee-Ta Resort ★★ The Confederated Tribes of Warm Springs Reservation some years ago built this posh resort, complete with a large, arrowhead-shaped hotel, a vast mineral-springs pool, tepees and cottages for rent, and such amenities as golf, tennis, riding, kayaking, and fancy restaurants. The Indian fry-bread and the bird-in-clay dish are the crowd-pleasers, but the flavors are uninspired. Even so, Kah-Nee-Ta is an unusual experience, with excellent service. You might stay in a roomy tepee (the lodge rooms are usually small) for instance, gathering the family around the fire pit in the evening. During the day, you can ride into the high desert countryside, splash in the pool, or watch Indian dances. ■ *11 miles north of Warm Springs on Hwy 3; (503)553-1112 or (800)831-0100; PO Box K, Warm Springs, OR 97761; $$$; AE, DC, MC, V; checks OK.*

REDMOND

RESTAURANTS

Paradise Grille ★ Inside Eric Laslow's historic 1918 brick bank building is a surprise—Southwestern adobe curved walls, warm colors, and ponderosa pine archways. Curly willow branches arch over the windows. Hungry highway travelers can find a simple meal of mesquite-grilled chicken or steak here, or more complex and delectible fare such as tequila prawns, whiskey fennel sausage, and smoked pork sauté topped with grilled polenta. Eric's signature: five-course wine-and-food-paired dinners. ■ *At Deschutes and 6th; (503)548-0844; 404 SW 6th St, Redmond; $$; full bar; AE, DC, MC, V; checks OK; lunch Mon–Fri, dinner every day.*

LODGINGS

Inn at Eagle's Crest ★★ Sisters has Black Butte, Bend has Sunriver, and Redmond has Eagle's Crest. The private homes at this full resort rim the 18-hole golf course, and visitors choose one of the 75 rooms in the hotel (the best ones have a golf course–facing deck) or a condominium. The condos are the better deal, especially if you come with four to eight people. They've got kitchens and access to the recreation center (not available to those who stay in the main building) with its indoor tennis, squash, and racquetball courts, workout room, masseuse, tanning salon, heated outdoor pool, and tennis courts; miles of biking and jogging trails; an equestrian center; and playfields. The food at the resort's formal Canyon Club is predictable for such a clubby atmosphere, with rancher-size portions. Service can be slow. The three-tiered deck outside provides a good view. ■ *5 miles west of Redmond on Hwy 126, turn south on Cline Falls Rd; (503) 923-2453 or (800) MUCH-SUN; 821 S 6th St, Redmond; PO Box 867, Redmond, OR 97756; $$; full bar; AE, MC, V; checks OK; breakfast, lunch, dinner every day.*

JOHN DAY

You are in the midst of dry cattle country in an area loaded with history: John Day is just off the old Oregon Trail, and the whole region was full of gold (during the height of the Gold Rush in 1862, $26 million in gold was mined in the neighboring town of Canyon City).

Kam Wah Chung Museum, next to the city park, was the stone-walled home of two Chinese herbal doctors at the turn of the century. A tour makes for an interesting glimpse of the Chinese settlement in the West: opium-stained walls, Chinese shrines, and herbal medicines are on display, as well as a small general store. Open May to October.

John Day Fossil Beds National Monument lies 40 to 120 miles west, in three distinct groupings: the banded Painted Hills, extremely ancient fossils, and fascinating geological layers; 420 W Main Street, (503) 575-0721 for maps and brochures.

LODGINGS

The Ponderosa Guest Ranch ★★★ If cowboys are your weakness and cattle country beckons, you can't do better than the Ponderosa, 120,000 acres of rolling rangeland in the splendid Silvies Valley. Here's a dude ranch that isn't a dude ranch. That is to say, it's a bona fide working ranch with up to 4,000 head of cattle and plenty of work to be done. No pokey trail rides here; if you're game, you'll join ranch cowboys in the day-to-day management of the herds. (Of course, you're welcome to disappear by yourself to fly-fish in any of the six streams or just soak in the hot tub near the pond.) April is calving season, when you might help "cut" cows and their offspring into new herds and make sure disoriented calves "mother up." In May you can help round up the calves for branding, and in June move herds to high mountain pastures. For the rest of the summer and into the fall there's continuous culling, sorting, and readying cattle for sale. Ranch manager Garth Johnson is a master at matching one of the ranch's 70 horses to your abilities, and the cowboys offer plenty of encouragement. Don't expect to be shielded from the harsher realities of ranch life, and leave your fancy city-slicker clothes and delicate vegetarian sensibilities at home.

The ranch is a serious and longstanding business, yet the guest lodge, completed in 1993, is not an afterthought. There are eight log guest cabins with three double units each (re-quest Jump Creek with its unobstructed view), and a massive main lodge with a spacious dining room, a bar, and plenty of relaxing areas. Tanya Johnson oversees the lodge and its staff, making sure you are well fed and that your special interests—be they bird-watching on ranch wetlands or a hankering for blueberry buckle for dessert—are accommodated. Hearty ranch fare is served family style, and there's plenty of it, start-ing with eggs and biscuits with sausage gravy and ending with a full steak dinner. In summer you'll share your meals and rides with guests; in winter, there are 35 miles of groomed cross-country trails to explore; and in early spring, you may have the place to yourself. The Johnsons provide a masterful blend of professionalism and casual friendliness that makes this an outstanding experience. And, in case you were wondering, *of course* they have a calf you can name Norman. ■ *On Hwy 395 halfway between Burns and John Day; (503)542-2403 or (800)331-1012; PO Box 190M, Seneca, OR 97873; $$; full bar; AE, MC; meals included. Minimum 2-night stay in winter season (Nov to Apr), minimum 1-week stay in summer season (May to Oct).*

DAYVILLE

LODGINGS

Fish House Inn Mike and Denise Smith escaped San Diego with two young children for considerably smaller Dayville (population 214). They settled into a century-old house built by Dayville's first liquor store owner. Denise has turned the tiny original liquor store into a gift shop; Mike remodeled a small cottage in the back into two private guest rooms. There are three more rooms in the main house as well ($35 to $45), all decorated with stuff gleaned from farm sales (old rakes, ice tongs, and horseshoes), things Piscean (old rods, reels, and creels among them), and baskets Denise wove from river wil-lows. In warm weather a bountiful breakfast (with the best cof-fee in 4,528 mostly empty square miles) is served in the garden. ■ *On Hwy 26 west of John Day at 110 Franklin Ave; (503)987-2124; 110 Franklin Ave, Dayville; PO Box 143, Dayville, OR 97825; $; MC, V; checks OK.*

PENDLETON

In these parts, the name of this town is synonymous with the Wild West. Each September the Pendleton Round-up rolls around—a big event since 1910 that features a dandy rodeo; call (800)524-2984 for tickets and information. **Ham-ley's and Company** has been selling Western clothing, boots, hats, tack items, and custom-made saddles since 1883. It's a kind of shrine, the L.L. Bean of the West; 30 SE Court Street, (503)276-2321.

Pendleton Woolen Mills gives tours Monday through Friday and sells woolen yardage and imperfect blankets at reduced prices; 1307 SE Court Place, (503)276-6911. **Pendleton Underground Tours** provides a 90-minute walk through Pendleton's history—most of it underground—to view the remains of businesses that date back to the turn of the century: bordellos, opium dens, and Chinese jails. Reservations are necessary and should be made at least 24 hours in advance. Price is $10 per adult; 37 SW Emigrant Avenue, (503)276-0730.

RESTAURANTS

Raphael's Restaurant and Lounge ★ In the historic Roy Raley House, across from the landmark Clock Tower, the Hoffmans continue the charming and somewhat eccentric approach to food that they mastered at the former Skyroom. Visit the authentic Native American fine art gallery (Raphael Hoffman is a member of the Nez Percé tribe) while waiting for your table. Her husband Robert, the chef, is not Indian—but some of the dishes show a Native American touch. Emphasis is more on flavor than presentation. Indian salmon wrapped in spinach and smothered with wild huckleberries appears too dark until the pink of the salmon breaks through with the first fork cut; the flavor is incredible. An applewood-smoked prime rib is the most popular beef entree; many of the patrons are crazy about it. Wild game such as alligator, rattlesnake, and elk is featured during the hunters' months of September, October, and November. The wine list features a good selection of moderately priced Northwest wine. Varietal wines are sold by the 8-ounce glass. ■ *Court and Dorion; (503)276-8500; 233 SE 4th, Pendleton; $$; full bar; MC, V; checks OK; lunch Tues–Fri, dinner Tues–Sat.* ⅄

LODGINGS

Swift Station Inn Bed and Breakfast ★ Ken and Lorry Schippers both work full-time for the state of Oregon, but the love of their labor on weekends and evenings has turned one of Pendleton's white elephants into its classiest lodgings. The ground-floor Victorian Room (our favorite) has a private bath. A large hot tub in the backyard melts away the driving fatigue (and you do a lot of it in these parts). Breakfasts are large, and the Schippers are so anxious to please you'll probably leave feeling guilty for not finishing what's on your plate. Well-behaved, courteous children are welcome. Rates are higher during September due to the Round-up. ■ *Exit 210 off I-84, north on State Hwy into town, north on 9th St 3 blocks to Byers; (503)276-3739; 602 SE Byers, Pendleton, OR 97801; $$; MC, V; checks OK.*

Indian Hills Motor Inn A little to the south of Pendleton is the Red Lion's Indian Hills Motor Inn, the most lavish motel in town. Amenities include heated pool, lounge, dining room, and coffee shop. There are outsized, gaudy Western bas-reliefs in the reception areas. The view from your balcony over the low mountains and tilled fields of eastern Oregon can be inspiring—more so than the food, which ranges from indifferent to passable. Sunday morning brunch is the best meal of the week. Well-behaved pets okay. ■ *Exit 210 off I-84 at SE Nye Ave; (503)276-6111; 304 SE Nye Ave, Pendleton; P.O. Box 1556, Pendleton, OR 97801; $$; AE, DC, MC, V; checks OK.* ᕁ

ECHO

RESTAURANTS

The Echo Hotel Restaurant and Lounge ★ The Echo's cedar-shake interior is filled with a bar, a split-level dining area, and three blackjack tables. Co-proprietor Susan Sperr greets every guest. This former rabbit cannery and historic hotel (there are hopes of reopening the upstairs as a bed and breakfast) serves up generous portions of 16-ounce prime rib and ranch-wagon specials. Primarily a whiskey-and-ribs place, the Echo is getting more and more attention for its seafood and Northwest wine by Pendletonites who flock here on weekends. ■ *20 miles west of Pendleton on I-84; (503)376-8354; 110 Main St, Echo; $; full bar; MC, V; local checks only; breakfast, lunch, dinner every day, closed Mon.* ᕁ

WESTON

RESTAURANTS

Tollgate Mountain Chalet Walla Walla folks often drive 50 miles south through the lovely, waving wheat fields to this rustic eating place in the Blue Mountain forest. Locals order the chili, or the prime-rib sandwich on homemade bread, a hamburger, a Reuben sandwich, or a reasonable steak; the pies are homemade and different every day. It makes a particularly good spot for breakfast before a day of hiking or mushroom hunting. ■ *16 miles east of Weston on Tollgate Mtn Hwy; (503)566-2123; Rt 1, Box 80, Weston; $; full bar; MC, V; local checks only; lunch, dinner Tues–Fri; breakfast, lunch, dinner Sat–Sun.* ᕁ

MILTON-FREEWATER

RESTAURANTS

The Oasis This isn't a copy of a 1920s Western roadhouse, it's the real thing—and it hasn't ever changed: linoleum floors and lots of chrome. Eat in the bar and eavesdrop on the cowboys swapping stories. Although not every dish on the menu is a culinary triumph, the steaks are uniformly reliable and gigantic. Prime rib is good. On Sundays, chicken and dumplings is served family style, all you can eat, for about $7 per person—and a fine meal it is. A breakfast platter of biscuits and gravy goes for just over $2. Students from Walla Walla are fascinated with this place. ▪ *Old Milton-Freewater Hwy and State Line Rd; (503)938-4776; $; full bar; MC, V; local checks only; breakfast, lunch, dinner Tues–Sun.* &

LA GRANDE

RESTAURANTS

Golden Harvest Chinese and American Restaurant ★ In 1989, Albert and Monita So (from China and Hong Kong respectively) opened their restaurant in Union. Success in that unlikely place financed the move (and expansion) to La Grande. Now waits for tables in the newly redecorated spacious dining room can be up to 15 minutes, even on weeknights. The sauces lost a little of their authority in the move, but not enough to send us away. The Sichuan dishes are still our favorites. As with most dishes here, order on a heat scale of one to five, but be aware that five almost raises blisters. ▪ *1 block northeast of Adams on Greenwood; (503)963-3288; 214 Greenwood St, La Grande; $; full bar; MC, V; local checks OK; lunch, dinner every day.* &

Mamacita's ★ House specials such as the Full Meal Steal for less than $3 at lunch are usually the best things coming out of the kitchen, typically two chicken soft tacos with beans and rice. Food is not overly spiced and not as fat-laden as Mexican food often is. Local college students provide most of the helpful service. Wine margaritas and an adobe-colored wall adorned with bright splotches of Mexicana complete the experience. ▪ *On Depot near Adams; (503)963-6223; 110 Depot St, La Grande; $; full bar; no credit cards; checks OK; lunch Tues–Fri, dinner Tues–Sun.* &

LODGINGS

Stang Manor Inn ★★★ This restored timber baron's house on the hill behind town returns an elegance to this once-booming town. A sweeping staircase leads up to the four bedrooms. The master suite is, of course, the best—and biggest—accommodation, but even if you opt for the former maid's quarters, you won't have to lift a finger. The owners, Marjorie and Pat McClure, have given personal attention to an already nurturing environment. Cookies—madeleines, perhaps—with tea await you at afternoon check-in. Breakfasts are always served on china and crystal. ▪ *Corner of Spring*

**Eastern
Oregon**

▼

La Grande

Lodgings

▲

157

and Walnut; (503)963-2400; 1612 Walnut St, La Grande, OR 97850; $$; MC, V; checks OK.

JOSEPH

This is the fabled land of the Wallowas, ancestral home of Chief Joseph, from which he fled with a band of Nez Percé warriors to his last stand near the Canadian border. Although Chief Joseph's remains are interred far from his beloved "land of the winding water," he saw to it that his father, Old Chief Joseph, would be buried here, on the north shore of Wallowa Lake. The town itself is becoming something of an art colony. David Manuel, State of Oregon official sculptor for the Oregon Trail Celebration, opened the **Manuel Museum and Studio** on Main Street, (503)432-7235. **Valley Bronze of Oregon** has built a foundry and a showroom in Joseph. Tours are offered on weekdays. Phone (503)432-7551 for information.

Wallowa Lake State Park, on the edge of the Wallowa Whitman National Forest and Eagle Cap Wilderness, is perhaps the only state park in the country where locals still lament the fact that there are "never enough people." An Alpenfest with music, dancing, and Bavarian feasts happens every September, but the peak season is still midsummer, when the pristine lake and its shores are abuzz with go-carts, sailboats, and wind-surfers. In winter the attraction is miles and miles of unpeopled cross-country trails throughout the lovely Wallowa highlands.

Wallowa Lake Tramway at the edge of the park takes you by a steep ascent in a four-passenger gondola to the top of 8,200-foot Mount Howard, with spectacular overlooks and 2 miles of hiking trails. Summer only; (503)432-5331.

Hell's Canyon, 35 miles east of Joseph, is the continent's deepest gorge, an awesome trench cut by the Snake River through sheer lava walls. The best view is from Hat Point near Imnaha, though McGraw Lookout is more accessible if you don't have four-wheel drive. Maps of the region's roads and trails, and information on conditions, are available at the Wallowa Valley Ranger District in Joseph, (503)426-4978.

Hurricane Creek Llamas. You explore the lake-laden Eagle Cap Wilderness with a naturalist, while smiling llamas lug your gear. Hikes vary in length; hearty country meals are included (May to September). Call in advance, (503)432-4455.

Wallowa Alpine Huts. Experienced backcountry ski guides offer 3- to 5-day powder-bound tours for skiers seeking the best of the Wallowa winterland. You stay in spartan tents and dine in a yurt; (208)882-1955.

RESTAURANTS

Vali's Alpine Deli and Restaurant ★ Don't let its "deli" status mislead; a dinner at Vali's usually requires reservations. The

food here is Hungarian-German (and so is the decor) inter-
spersed with a few authentic renditions from other cuisines. Paprika chicken and dumplings is not to be missed when offered.
Wiener schnitzel is also exceptional. At breakfast, Maggie
Vali's homemade doughnuts are local legend, but don't show
up hungry—the morning meal ends there. In the summer,
sausage and cheese are available to take out for picnics. A new
enclosed deck adds a nice touch to the dining experience. ■
*5 miles south of Joseph on Hwy 82 near Wallowa Lake State
Park; (503) 432-5691; 59811 Wallowa Lake Hwy (Hwy 82),
Joseph; $; full bar; no credit cards; checks OK; breakfast, din-
ner Tues–Sun (winters Sat–Sun).*

LODGINGS

Chandlers — Bed, Bread, and Trail Inn ★ Cedar shingles,
multiangled roof lines, and cushiony wall-to-wall carpets make
this bed and breakfast resemble an alpine ski lodge—in the
middle of Joseph. A log staircase climbs from the comfortable
living room to a loft where five simple bedrooms share a sitting
room and workable kitchenette. Three of the five bedrooms
have private baths. The mountains almost climb into room
number 1. The substantial breakfast and knowledgeable hosts
make this a wonderful stopover for area explorers. ■ *700 S
Main St; (503) 432-9765 or (800) 452-3781; 700 S Main St,
Joseph, OR 97846; $; MC, V; checks OK.*

Wallowa Lake Lodge ★ The rooms in this historic lodge are
very small (especially the $50 ones), and you must promise not
to smoke. You'll do best if you reserve one of the originally restored rooms with a lake view. If you plan to stay longer, the
rustic pine cabins on the lake, with a living room, fireplace, and
a kitchen, allow for a bit more flexibility. Even if the rooms *were*
spacious, we'd spend most of the evening in front of the
magnificent stone fireplace in the knotty pine lobby, and the
days on the lake or in the mountains. The deck is a splendid
addition. Winters are painfully slow, especially in the dining
room. ■ *Near Wallowa Lake State Park; (503) 432-9821;
60060 Wallowa Lake Hwy, Joseph, OR 97846; $$; beer and
wine; MC, V; checks OK; breakfast, dinner every day (dinner
Fri–Sat winter).*

HAINES

RESTAURANTS

Haines Steak House ★ There's no mistaking that you're in
cattle country, pilgrim. Most of the vehicles surrounding this
ever-busy spot are of four-wheel-drive breed and many of the
men wear their cowboy hats while eating. Cowbells add to the
ranchlike bedlam about every five minutes to announce a birth-
day or anniversary. We particularly like the log cabin–type

booths and the singletree curtains. Stay with the beef; it's well selected, cut, and cooked. Next to beef, the hashbrowns are the best thing on the menu. ▪ *On old Hwy 30, a short detour from I-84, exit 285 (eastbound) or exit 306 (westbound); (503)856-3639; 910 Front St, Haines, OR 97833; $$; full bar; AE, DC, MC, V; checks OK; dinner Wed–Mon, and lunch starting at 1pm on Sun.* ♿

UNION

LODGINGS

Queen Ann Inn Bed and Breakfast If the immaculately kept grounds at the edge of town and the picture-perfect 1894 Victorian don't draw you in, then the smells from the kitchen and the warmth of your hostess, Blanche Kohler, surely will. It has four oak and ceramic-tiled fireplaces, and fancy moldings and gingerbread trim to spare. Three guest rooms are on the second floor and a fourth takes up the third floor. ▪ *On 5th; (503)562-5566; 782 N 5th St, Union, OR 97883; $$; no credit cards; checks OK.*

BAKER CITY

Baker's restful city park, old-time main street, and mature shade trees may give it a Midwest flavor, but the backdrop is decidedly Northwest. Located in the valley between the Wallowas and the Elkhorns, Baker makes a good base camp for forays into the nearby mountain Gold Rush towns. The **Oregon Trail Interpretive Center**, 4 miles east of I-84 on Hwy 86, is worth the detour. The multimedia walk-through brings the Oregon Trail experience to life. The animals look so real that you might be struck by the lack of normal animal sounds and odors. Open every day except Christmas and New Year's Day. Admission is free; donations accepted.

The Elkhorn Mountains, west of Baker, contain most of the old mining towns, which you can tour on a 100-mile loop from Baker (some on unpaved roads).

Ghost towns. There's a restored narrow-gauge steam train at Sumpter that operates between Memorial Day and Labor Day. The deserted towns of Granite, Bourne, Bonanza, and Whitney are well worth visiting.

Anthony Lakes Ski Area, 20 miles west of North Powder, has good powder snow, a chair lift, and cross-country trails; (503)856-3277.

LODGINGS

À Demain Bed & Breakfast ★ Stuffed French toast is not on the menu every morning, but when it is, you will understand why we would stay here just for the breakfast. The lovely old home is in one of Baker's quiet neighborhoods. The upstairs suite, our favorite, is comprised of two bedrooms that accommodate two couples traveling together (or a small family). And the price is reasonable enough to rent the suite for one. Hostess Kristi Flanagan is fond of down comforters and pillows. ■ *Corner of 4th and Valley sts; (503) 523-2509; 1790 4th St, Baker City, OR 97814; $$; no credit cards; checks OK.*

Best Western Sunridge Inn A sprawling Best Western, it is better than the average motel, with 124 comfortable, spacious, air-conditioned rooms and an attractive pine finish. In the hot summer, you'll appreciate the grassy courtyard/pool area (summers only). Come winter, move indoors to the 18-foot whirlpool. ■ *Off I-84 at City Center exit; (503) 523-6444 or (800) 233-2368; 1 Sunridge Lane, Baker, OR 97814; $; AE, DC, MC, V; checks OK.*

HALFWAY

Once just a midway stop between two bustling mining towns, Halfway is now the quiet centerpiece of Pine Valley—stashed between the fruitful southern slopes of the Wallowa Mountains and the steep cliffs of Hells Canyon.

Hells Canyon, the continent's deepest gorge, begins at Oxbow Dam, 16 miles east of Halfway. For spectacular views of the Snake River, drive from Oxbow to Joseph (take Highway 86 to Forest Road #39; summers only). Maps of the region's roads and trails are available from the Forest Service, just outside Halfway, (503) 742-7511. The folks at **Wallowa Llamas** lead 3- to 8-day trips along the edge of Hells Canyon or into the pristine Eagle Cap Wilderness high in the Wallowas, while their sure-footed beasts lug your gear and plenty of food; for a brochure or information call (503) 742-4930. For those who would rather experience the raging river up close, **Hells Canyon Adventures** in Oxbow arranges jet boat tours or combination excursions leaving from Hells Canyon Dam; call (503) 785-3352.

LODGINGS

Birchleaf Bed and Breakfast Horse pastures, peach trees, and solitude. This pretty home sits on a south-facing slope above Halfway—a little town on the edge of a big outdoors. The rooms are as simple as the town itself. Nothing fancy. If it's summer, the owners will be there to greet you. When the weather cools and business slows, they retreat to Portland and leave the place in the capable hands of friendly local managers. Either way, you'll become part of the family. ■ *4½ miles north of Halfway; (503) 742-2990; Rte 1 Box 91, Halfway, OR 97834; $; no credit cards; checks OK; call ahead for winter openings.*

ONTARIO

RESTAURANTS

Casa Jaramillo This Mexican cantina gives cool respite from the hot eastern Oregon desert. Expanded and remodeled, it has a tropical atmosphere perfect for families. For the past 25 years, John Jaramillo and his family have been turning out authentic Mexican fare. Try the enchiladas rancheros, with fresh crunchy onions and a chile verde sauce that delivers. Great guacamole. ▪ *2 blocks south of Idaho Ave; (503)889-9258; 157 SE 2nd St, Ontario; $; full bar; AE, MC, V; checks OK; lunch, dinner Tues–Sun.*

LODGINGS

Howard Johnson's ★ It keeps changing its affiliation and has been remodeled twice in the past five years, but it continues to be Ontario's finest. All 97 rooms have been completely refurbished. Handicapped and nonsmoking rooms are available. Well-mannered pets are okay. There is a heated outdoor pool for summertime relaxing. No charge for children 18 and under. ▪ *Off I-84 in Ontario; (503)889-8621 or (800)525-5333; 1249 Tapadera Ave, Ontario, OR 97914; $$; AE, DC, MC, V; checks OK.*

BURNS

The town of Burns, once the center of impressive cattle kingdoms ruled by legendary figures Pete French and William Hanley, is a welcome oasis in this desolate high-desert country. The look of the land, formed by 10 million years of volcanic activity, was branded on the American consciousness in a few decades by the thousands of Western movies filmed in the area.

Malheur National Wildlife Refuge, 37 miles south on Route 205, is one of the country's major bird refuges—184,000 acres of verdant marshland and lakes. It is an important stop for migrating waterfowl in spring and fall, and the summer breeding grounds for magnificent sandhill cranes (with wingspans approaching 100 inches), trumpeter swans, and many other birds; (503)493-2612.

RESTAURANTS

Pine Room Cafe ★ The Oltman family now operates this pleasant cafe, and they've kept the same faithful clientele once fed by the Kinders for 30 years. Careful preparations and interesting recipes are the reason: the chicken livers in brandy and wine sauce are different and popular, and the Oltmans still refuse to give out the secret ingredients of their German potato-dumpling soup, a local favorite. They also make their own bread and cut their own steaks in the kitchen. ■ *On Monroe and Egan; (503)573-6631; 543 W Monroe St, Burns, OR 97720; $$; full bar; MC, V; local checks only; dinner Tues-Sat.* &

LODGINGS

Best Western Ponderosa With 52 rooms, this is the preferred place to stay in Burns. It's blessed with a swimming pool to cool you off after a hot day's drive. What more? Pets are okay. ■ *On Hwy 20; (503)573-2047 or (800)528-1234; 577 W Monroe, Burns, OR 97720; $; AE, DC, MC, V; no checks.* &

DIAMOND

LODGINGS

Diamond Hotel Except for the new paint on the Diamond Hotel (and a couple of trucks parked out front) you might mistake Diamond for a ghost town. Its six residents keep the looming ghosts at bay. In 1991, Judy and Jerry Santillie, formerly of the Frenchglen Hotel, remodeled this building and opened it to those exploring Malheur territory. It now quintuples as hotel, general store (with gas), deli, post office, and—late in the afternoon—local watering hole. The five small bedrooms upstairs share two baths and a sitting area on both floors. The Santillies have lived in the area for seven years and are filled with high-desert stories. Judy used to be a ranch cook (there's always meat, potatoes, vegetables, salad, bread). A platter of tenderloin comes with slabs for every taste from well-done to "so rare that a good vet could get it back up on its feet." Desserts (perhaps a marionberry cobbler with ice cream or Judy's Guadalupe River Bottom Cake) are double, no triple, the size you need them to be—and that's okay with us. ■ *12 miles east of Hwy 205; (503)493-1898; Box 10, Diamond, OR 97722; $; beer and wine; MC, V; checks OK; breakfast, dinner every day (hotel guests only).*

▼

Frenchglen

▲

FRENCHGLEN

The flooding around Harney Lake kept tourists away from this beautiful little town (population 15) a few years back, but now, happily, the highway is above water and tourists are once again stopping in while touring Malheur (see Burns introduction) or to spy **Steens Mountain**, Frenchglen's biggest tourist attraction. It rises gently from the west to an elevation of 9,670 feet, then drops sharply to the Alvord Desert in the east. A dirt road goes all the way to the ridge top (summers only), and another skirts this massive escarpment (an adventurous day trip by the vast borax wastelands of the once Alvord Lake, numerous hot springs, and fishing lakes near the northeastern end of the route). Neither route is recommended if there's been much precipitation. Geologically, Steens forms the world's largest block fault, created by volcanic lava flows and glacial action.

LODGINGS

Frenchglen Hotel ★ A small, white frame building that dates back to 1916 has eight small, plain bedrooms upstairs with shared baths, renting for about $45 a night; room 2 is the largest, nicest, and the only one with a view of Steens. Nothing's very square or level here, and that's part of the charm. Downstairs are a large screened-in verandah and the dining room. The current manager, John Ross, will cook up good, simple meals for guests and drop-by visitors. Ranch-style dinner is one seating only (6:30pm sharp) and reservations are a must. But if you miss dinner, John won't let you go hungry (this is ranch country and there's usually leftovers). ■ *60 miles south of Burns; (503) 493-2825; General Delivery, Frenchglen, OR 97736; $; beer and wine; MC, V; checks OK; breakfast, lunch, dinner every day (closed mid–Nov through mid–Mar).*

WASHINGTON

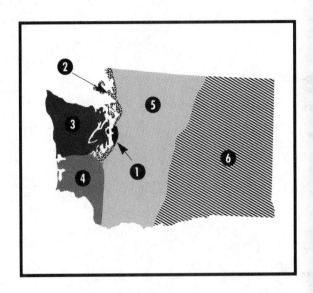

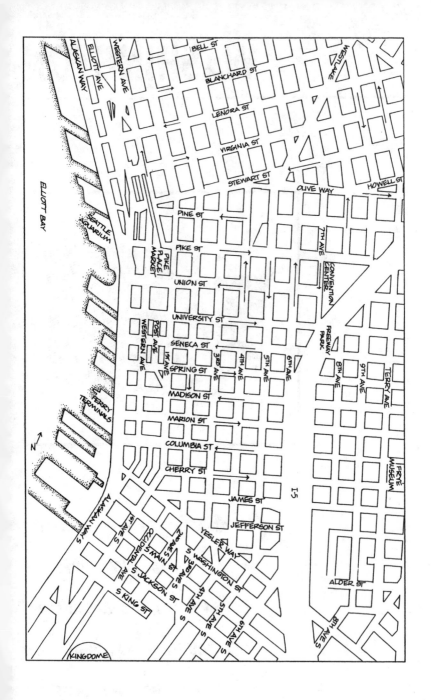

Seattle and Environs

Seattle and Environs

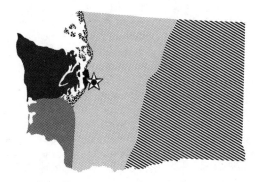

Including Edmonds and Bothell to the north; Woodinville, Redmond, Kirkland, Bellevue, Mercer Island, and Issaquah to the east; Bainbridge Island to the west; and Tukwila, Burien, and Kent to the south.

SEATTLE

Seattle is a charming metropolis grown up in the middle of an evergreen forest. It's a city famous for its enduring relationships with Boeing and Bill Gates, Pearl Jam and Pike Place Market, and coffee, always coffee, available in steaming cups from mobile espresso carts that sprout on street corners like mushrooms after a good rain.

This is a town where cops ride bikes, farmers and fishmongers hawk their wares at open-air markets, gardeners putter be it January or July, and early-morning kayakers paddle in the wake of log booms and container ships that ply the city's busy waterways. Situated between sparkling Puget Sound and Lake Washington, and dotted with lakes, Seattle is nearly surrounded by water, with mountains just about everywhere you look. On clear days, Mount Rainier's distant snow-capped presence has even been known to halt commuter traffic—which has grown worse as the population grows and the city's bedroom communities continue to spread farther afield.

But rapid growth and international sophistication have brought to this city outstanding restaurants, thriving cultural organizations, fine sports, and fabulous citywide festivals.

What follows are a few highlights of Seattle's entertainment; for a detailed city guide, we refer you to our companion book, *Seattle Best Places*.

THE ARTS

Music. Seattle Opera's productions range from creative conceptions (which don't always work) to performances of breathtaking brilliance; (206)389-7699. The **Seattle Symphony**, under conductor Gerard Schwarz, maintains a high level of consistency; its Distinguished Artists series brings in superb recitalists; (206)443-4747. Chamber music has become a local passion, with the International Music Festival of Seattle in June (showcasing many top Russian and European musicians, and including orchestral and vocal performances), and the Seattle Chamber Music Festival in July (at bucolic Lakeside School). The Early Music Guild, Seattle Baroque Orchestra, Northwest Chamber Orchestra, Ladies Musical Club, and the International Chamber Music and President's Piano Series at the University of Washington's Meany Hall, plus many indigenous performances, round out the winter and spring seasons. Choral music is experiencing an upsurge, as evidenced by the Tudor Choir, the Esoterics, Seattle Men's Chorus, and Seattle Choral Company, among others.

Theater. Seattle's big professional theaters used to hire most of their actors from the bounteous local talent pool, and each had its specialty: you went to the Seattle Repertory Theatre ("The Rep") for mainstream comedy and drama, Intiman for the classics, A Contemporary Theatre (ACT) for racier, modern stuff. Now the repertory is more homogenized, and the practice of hiring most actors from out of town has blurred the style boundaries further. Best advice: scan the theater listings and shop by show.

More adventurous theatergoers have a far wider selection: among the dozens of smaller theater companies around town, good work often emerges from the Empty Space (funky, often musical, fun), the Annex (far-out fringe), New City Theater (mainstream avant-garde), the Bathhouse (intimate, emphasis on the classics), the Velvet Elvis Arts Lounge (from campy to just plain crazy), and many more.

Dance. Pacific Northwest Ballet has evolved into a company of national stature; its regular season mixes masterworks with new pieces, and the Christmas highlight is a breathtaking realization of *The Nutcracker* with sets by Maurice Sendak; (206)292-2787. Meany's World Dance series and On the Boards present touring companies.

Visual Arts. The new Seattle Art Museum, designed by Robert Venturi, is by now an established part of the downtown skyline, with Jonathan Borofsky's towering sculpture, *Hammering Man*, at the main entrance. The downtown building on

University Street between First and Second avenues houses the museum's permanent collections, while the new Seattle Asian Art Museum, in the former SAM location in Volunteer Park, offers one of the most extraordinary collections of Asian art in the country. The Henry Art Gallery at UW (closed until early 1997 for renovation) mounts thoughtful and challenging shows. The main art galleries are found predominantly (though not exclusively) in the Pioneer Square area; gallery openings are the first Thursday of every month.

OTHER THINGS TO DO

Nightlife. There are clubs all over town, but Seattle's music scene is neighborhood centered. Pioneer Square offers various acts, from jazz to rock 'n' roll; Ballard brings in the blues, as well as traditional and new folk music; the alternative music scene is found in clubs primarily in the Denny Regrade and Belltown neighborhoods. Dimitriou's Jazz Alley, one of the West Coast's finest jazz clubs, provides an intimate venue and draws an internationally renowned roster of performers. There are good coffeehouses everywhere, but particularly in the University District and on Capitol Hill, which is also the unofficial playground for Seattle's sizable gay and lesbian community.

Exhibits. The Woodland Park Zoo is a world leader in naturalistic displays, particularly the uncannily open African savanna and the exotic Asian elephant forest; (206)684-4800. The Museum of Flight, south of the city, is notable for its sophisticated design and impressive collection. Pacific Science Center, with a planetarium and revolving displays on all sorts of subjects, graces Seattle Center, the legacy of the 1962 World's Fair; there is a decent aquarium on the waterfront; and at the Hiram M. Chittenden Locks in Ballard, where ships are lifted to Lake Washington, you can watch salmon climb the ladders on their way to spawn.

Parks. Seattle's horticultural climate is among the finest in the world—damp and mild all year—so the parks are spectacular and numerous. Washington Park Arboretum, with 5,500 species of plants and gentle pathways amid azaleas, is the loveliest; Discovery Park, with grassy meadows and steep sea cliffs, is the wildest; Green Lake, with its 2.8-mile running-walking-rollerskating track, is by far the most active. Freeway Park, built over I-5 downtown, is the most urban.

Sports. The town is football-mad, which means there are hardly any tickets (test your concierge's powers). The UW Huskies play in one of the land's most beautiful stadiums, with arrival by boat a local custom; the Seahawks lift the roof off the drab Kingdome (when the roof's not falling in, that is). The SuperSonics are playing great basketball in the Coliseum; the UW women's basketball team is very strong; and Seattle's baseball team, the Mariners, are still plodding along in the ill-suited Dome.

Shopping. The downtown area has designer-name stores, plus some excellent full-line department stores and Westlake Center, a glossy mall smack in the middle of the downtown congestion, across from Nordstrom's flagship store. Of the specialty shopping areas, we favor Pike Place Market (for food-stuffs), Capitol Hill (for funky clothes and furnishings), the University District (for books), and Pioneer Square (for fine arts and crafts).

Transportation. The Metro bus is free before 7pm in downtown's commercial core; otherwise the fare is 85 cents within the city ($1.10 during peak hours) and $1.10 if you cross the city line ($1.60 peak); (206)553-3000. Another common commute is on Washington State Ferries, which cross Puget Sound to various destinations frequently. Riding the ferries also happens to be one of the most enjoyable ways to view the city's skyline; (206)464-6400 or (800)843-3779.

RESTAURANTS

Fullers (Seattle Sheraton Hotel and Towers) ★★★★ A hushed elegance complements the stunning display of contemporary Northwest glass and artwork. You sink into a high-backed, almost-private banquette, or into the cushioned comfort of a table next to the calming waterfall of a George Tsutakawa–designed fountain; "Hmmmm," you say. "Nice, in a stuffy, museum-ish way." Prepare for an attitude adjustment. Your taste buds will be spun in all directions by chef Monique Barbeau—third in a line of very young women chef-execs—who has been putting her bold signature on the Fullers menu since 1992. Schooled in the four-star kitchens in New York, Barbeau flouts convention, getting bolder with every local and national award. Bite-size sashimi-grade tuna, flavored with shiso leaf and tossed with wasabi vinaigrette, shows up in an edible potato-parsnip basket; a composed salad of water-melon and feta cheese sports tart red sumac and sage pesto. Some would be better off with a trio of Ellensburg lamb chops in a port demiglace with a luscious potato-goat cheese tart —staid by comparison. We like the casual sophistication of the waitstaff, the fussy press-pot-and-chocolate-straw coffee service, and the chance to prove to ourselves that hotel-restaurant fine dining is *not* a contradiction in terms. ■ *Between Pike and Union on 6th; (206)447-5544; 1400 6th Ave, Seattle; $$$; full bar; AE, MC, V; checks OK; lunch Mon–Fri, dinner Mon–Sat.* ♿

Lampreia ★★★★ Likened to the urbane fine-food haunts of New York and San Francisco, Scott Carsberg's sleek restaurant exudes sophistication. While plate as palette—with splashes of color and unexpected combinations of flavor dazzling the eye and the tongue—has become synonymous with the Seattle food scene, chef Carsberg offers a gentle reprieve: a minimalist approach for maximum effect. In Scott's world, simplicity is key—from what's on the walls (a warm-toned paint and little else) to what's on the table (a heavy fork, a knife, a glass, a linen napkin, a candle), to what's on the plate (food so visually understated that the depth of flavor comes as a complete shock). Zealous use of seasonal, regional, and organic ingredients is akin to religion here. The intermezzo course acts as a preview of things to come, or a light meal in itself: perhaps a thick slice of foie gras atop a bed of spicy-sweet red cabbage, or perfectly sautéed razor clams. A choice of four or five entrees might include a tender veal chop tinged with lemon zest and garnished with giant capers, or a fillet of white king salmon swathed with herbed oil and served essentially unadorned over three fat spikes of asparagus. Indulge in an after-dinner cheese fest; an astounding selection of rare and wonderfully stinky cheeses makes a nice alternative to dessert. The wine list is carefully wrought and reasonably priced. Service is as polished as the silver. ■ *Corner of 1st and Battery; (206) 443-3301; 2400 1st Ave, Seattle; $$$; full bar; AE, MC, V; no checks; dinner Tue–Sat.*

Adriatica ★★★ Climbing the two challenging flights of stairs leading to the Adriatica may be the culinary equivalent of reaching the summit of Mount Rainier: always worth the effort. It's been 15 years since owner Jim Malevitsis opened this handsome tri-level restaurant high above Lake Union where he presides over the comfortably cloistered warren of small dining rooms. Longtime chef Nancy Flume has left her kitchen post in the capable hands of talented young Katherine McKenzie, who continues to turn out Flume's time-tested renderings of herb-kissed grilled meats and other Mediterranean-inspired fare. Start with one of the Greek appetizers; the creamy taramasalata is the best around and the calamari fritti is renowned for the garlic quotient of its skorthallia. If you're inclined to have pasta, the fettucine with smoked duck is a standout. Only a fool would skip dessert here, and the proof is literally in the pudding of a feathery puff pastry layered with lemon custard, and an airy chocolate espresso soufflé. ■ *Corner of Aloha and Dexter; (206) 285-5000; 1107 Dexter Ave N, Seattle; $$$; full bar; AE, DC, MC, V; checks OK; dinner every day.*

Al Boccalino ★★★ The rustic Al Boccalino is equally good for a business get-together, a special celebration, or a meaningful dinner for two. Intoxicating drifts of herbs and garlic wafting from the antipasti table greet you when you enter the old brick building just off Pioneer Square. Its chic mottled mustard-and-raw-brick walls are accented with dark wood and stained glass; a skewed shape to the two rooms creates the desired atmosphere of intimacy and intrigue. The menu features the best of southern Italian cuisine with an expanded focus on Italy's other regions. Split for two, any pasta choice would make a great first course. In these times of restraint, the bistecca alla Fiorentina—a perfectly delicious and perfectly *enormous* aged porterhouse—is not for the faint of heart. It comes simply broiled with olive oil and fresh ground pepper. Seafood shines in this kitchen, where the chefs know a thing or three about timing. Ahi tuna, seared on the outside and pink on the inside, manages to taste at once tart and sweet thanks to a marinade of red wine vinegar and golden raisins flavored with saffron and rosemary. Succulent sea scallops never see the heat longer than necessary and border on divine. The wine list is solidly Italian, as is the noise level when things get busy. Special kudos to the servers who show great patience when the rest of your party is a half-hour late. A great place to do lunch, too. ▪ *At Yesler and Alaskan Way; (206)622-7688; 1 Yesler Way, Seattle; $$$; beer and wine; AE, DC, MC, V; checks OK; lunch Mon–Fri, dinner every day.*

Campagne ▪ Cafe Campagne ★★★ White linen tablecloths, tiny vases of flowers, and wall space dedicated to wine bottles help set the mood for country French in a very urban setting at Campagne. Located in a courtyard of Pike Place Market, the restaurant is inspired by the southern reaches of France. Owner Peter Lewis, one of the city's most gracious hosts, and some of the city's finest servers will ensure that you will dine with gusto. Campagne offers a deliciously rich cassoulet in addition to other nightly specials reflecting the day's catch, the season's offerings, and the soothing inspirations of chef Tamara Murphy (who won the coveted James Beard award for Best Chef in the Northwest in 1995). There are so many successes here, most worth the dear price you will pay. Campagne has a wonderful late-night menu available in the exceptionally romantic (but smoky) bar. Dining at a courtyard table is the next best thing to a trip to France.

Lewis's new **Cafe Campagne**, which opened in 1994 just below its stylish sibling, is already proving too small to accommodate those who throng to this casual bistro-cum-charcuterie. Wherever you sit (at a cherry-wood table or the elegant counter), be sure to utter the most important words spoken here: garlic mashed potatoes. At lunch or dinner, the herby rotisserie chicken or classic steak frites will put you over the edge. Take-out, too. ▪ *Restaurant: At the Inn at the Market, between Stewart and Pine on Post Alley; (206)728-2800; 86 Pine St, Seattle; $$$; full bar; AE, DC, MC, V; no checks; lunch Mon–Sat (summers only), dinner every day (all year). ▪ Cafe: On Post Alley at Pine; (206)728-2233; 1600 Post Alley, Seattle; $; beer and wine; AE, DC, MC, V; local checks only; breakfast, lunch, dinner Mon–Sat, brunch Sun.* ♿

Chez Shea ▪ Shea's Lounge ★★★ Chez Shea really is one of Seattle's gems. You might walk through the Market a hundred times and not know that Sandy Shea's tiny, romantic hideaway is perched just above, looking out over the Sound. Dinner at Chez Shea is a prix-fixe affair, with four courses prepared by adventurous young chef Peter Morrison, reflecting the bounty of the season and ingredients fresh from the market stalls below. A winter meal might begin with a ricotta and Parmesan-rich soufflé set atop a roasted tomato sauce, followed by hubbard squash soup, tangy with diced cabbage and thickened with pearly riso. The main course could be a rack of Ellensburg lamb, roasted with herbes de Provence, or a salt-cured fillet of king salmon, served atop garlic-infused mashed potatoes. Service is always sure and gracious.

In celebration of the restaurant's 10th anniversary, Sandy Shea opened Shea's Lounge, an unpretentious, sexy little bistro that's wed to Chez Shea by way of a common door. The menu offers about a dozen dishes, heavily influenced by the flavors of Spain and Portugal. The perfect place to meet a friend for a little something before or after. ▪ *Across from the clock in Pike Place Market; (206) 467-9990; Corner Market Building, Suite 34, Seattle; $$$ (Chez Shea), $$ (Shea's Lounge); full bar; AE, MC, V; checks OK; dinner Tues–Sun.*

Dahlia Lounge ★★★ The Dahlia Lounge has become, for many locals and out-of-towners, synonymous with the Seattle food scene. Many of us learned about Northwest foods from kitchen maverick Tom Douglas, and grew accustomed to his bold juxtaposition of cultures within a meal, indeed within a plate. With his star ever-rising, Douglas opened Etta's Seafood in 1995 (see review). He now shuttles between the two very different restaurants, yet even in his absence, the extraordinary food at the Dahlia is executed with an artist's eye and an epicure's palate. The Dahlia's scenic appeal lies in a stylish two-level dining landscape of vermilion and gold and brocade (and papier-mâché fish lamps between the booths)—and the intriguing presentations on your plate. Pan-seared calamari in a broth fragrant with chiles, Chinese black beans, and Thai basil is paired with coconut rice cakes. A dish called Persian Ravioli marries Middle Eastern flavorings such as yogurt, mint, and cumin with such Asian ingredients as cilantro and ginger. And you'll not find a better version of the salty-sweet Japanese specialty, kasu cod, than that served here. Finish your meal with an ethereal pear tart or crème caramel. ▪ *4th Ave between Stewart and Virginia; (206) 682-4142; 1904 4th Ave, Seattle; $$; full bar; AE, DC, MC, V; checks OK; lunch Mon–Fri, dinner every day.* ♿

Etta's Seafood ★★★ When Tom Douglas opened his second restaurant, Etta's, in early 1995, it was not immediately clear whether history was being repeated or made. The remodeled, '90s-style seafood house—with one small, conversation-friendly dining room and another larger and much noisier noshery complete with a bar and counter seating—occupies the husk of the late Cafe Sport (where Douglas first made his mark a decade ago before achieving culinary fame at his own Dahlia Lounge—see review). Douglas has the chutzpah to list starter courses like fire-grilled tamales with Jack cheese and ancho chilies ($3 each) alongside beluga caviar ($44 an ounce). His lengthy menu dares you to choose between such wonders as a simple wedge of iceberg lettuce topped with an extraordinary blue cheese dressing or a lively octopus and shiitake salad with a tangy citrus marinade. Choosing from almost as many "sides" to go along with the signature Dungeness crab cakes or a broiled Maine lobster is even more daunting. (Hint: don't miss the red bliss mashed potatoes.) Start with an ass-kicking Bloody Mary, and save room for dessert. ■ *North end of Pike Place Market; (206)443-6000; 2020 Western Ave, Seattle; $$$; AE, DC, MC, V; checks OK; lunch and dinner every day.* ♿

Georgian Room (Four Seasons Olympic Hotel) ★★★ A grand space for those grand occasions, the Georgian Room, with its high ceilings, ornate chandeliers, and all the accoutrements of fine dining, will take you back in time to a place that—believe it or not—still exists. As you sink back into your banquette-built-for-two, the tuxedoed maître d' pours your martini from an elegant shaker, a staff of smiling, professional waiters dressed in full "Love Boat" regalia tend to your every need, and a pianist tinkles the ivories in the center of the room. And you should come prepared to pay a lot for the experience. Chef Kerry Sear prepares a warm salad of winter cabbage speckled with duck cracklings wearing a perfect slice of foie gras. Feather-light nubbins of potato gnocchi stand up to a mushroom broth enriched with sliced cèpes. Entrees appear as objets d'art—a rack of lamb crowns a plate garnished with garlic-stuffed olives and Swiss chard. Four joints of pheasant sauced with caramelized onions beg for a side of Sear's butter-drenched, garlic-whipped yellow Finn potatoes. Private parties can reserve in the Georgette Petite room. ■ *In the Four Seasons Hotel at 4th and University; (206)621-7889; 411 University St, Seattle; $$$; full bar; AE, DC, MC, V; no checks; breakfast every day, dinner Mon–Sat.*

Hunt Club (Sorrento Hotel) ★★★ The Hunt Club, along with Fullers and the Georgian Room, remains in the bold forefront of good, even excellent, hotel dining. The clubby bar and carefully partitioned dining room are warmed with burnished mahogany paneling and deep red brickwork. If the kitchen suffers from a bad case of musical chef-execs, the Powers That Be are quick to ensure that those chefs are worthy of top toque status.

In 1994, chef Eric Lenard, a well-schooled, young upstart from San Francisco, took over where his two talented predecessors left off. Lenard's contribution to the Hunt Club's menu relies on rich reductions and bold flavorings. We've been impressed with the naturally sweet and artfully spiced butternut squash ravioli; a deep, lavender-stoked sauce on a stellar rack of lamb; the roasted smokiness of a fillet of king salmon; and the solicitous-yet-affable service. After dinner, savvy patrons retire to the lobby bar for coffee and dessert—homemade ices or an exceptional crème brûlée. ■ *Madison and Terry; (206) 343-6156; 900 Madison St, Seattle; $$$; full bar; AE, DC, MC, V; checks OK; breakfast, lunch, tea, dinner every day, brunch Sat–Sun.* ♿

Il Bistro ★★★ Through the years, Il Bistro has been a cherished refuge down a narrow cobblestone street in Pike Place Market. The low-ceilinged, intimate rooms, rounded arches, and whitewashed walls are a perfect background for enjoying food, wine, and friends. The lower-level bar is a favorite spot to linger over an aperitif or share a convivial late-night supper. Current owners Tom Martino and Dale Abrams continue to keep the Bistro going strong as they celebrate its 20th anniversary. There are always interesting specials at Il Bistro (say, tiny morel mushrooms playing inspired complement to a tangle of tagliatelle), but this is a place where many patrons know what to order before they leave home. Il Bistro consistently serves one of the best racks of lamb in Seattle—and just the right wines to go along with it (there's a lengthy list of Chiantis). Those who once had a love affair with pasta here may find the offerings hit-or-miss, but the sexy Euro-bistro atmosphere, and the wonderful veal carpaccio and Antipasto Dino, will help you forget the kitchen's occasional flaws. Dessert? The Marquis, a simply deadly piece of chocolate, is divine. ■ *Just below Read All About It in Pike Place Market; (206) 682-3049; 93-A Pike St, Seattle; $$$; full bar; AE, DC, MC, V; no checks; dinner every day.*

Il Terrazzo Carmine ★★★ Be prepared to spend an entire evening at Il Terrazzo, for dining at Carmine Smeraldo's restaurant is an event. Graze through the wonderful antipasti and watch for Seattle's rich and famous, who are likely to be dining beside you in this comfortably airy restaurant or on the outside terrace. Deciding among the pastas is a feat, but it's the sauces on the stunning array of meat entrees here that get the greatest applause. The sweetbreads with prosciutto and peas are lightly smothered in a wonderful wine sauce. And the fork-tender veal piccata, a good test of any Italian restaurant, has an equally good reduction sauce, just slightly zingy from capers. Robust Nebbiolo grapes lend a richness to the Barolo sauce that cloaks the tender filet of beef. The wine list is extensive and includes some prime Tuscan reds found only in tiny hill villages. Prices here are high, but there are tables in the bar where you might share the antipasti and a couple of glasses of wine, and call it dinner. ▪ *1st and King; (206)467-7797; 411 1st Ave S, Seattle; $$$; full bar; AE, DC, MC, V; checks OK; lunch Mon–Fri, dinner Mon–Sat.* ☃

Kaspar's ★★★ Kaspar's by the Bay said goodbye to Belltown and relocated to the elegant, multitiered, remodeled space on lower Queen Anne that once housed the venerable Le Tastevin. We like Kaspar's by the Seattle Center so much better—and so does the pre-theater/opera/ballet crowd who knows where to go for a great opening act. Swiss-born and trained, chef Kaspar Donier imaginatively couples classic international cooking styles with fresh Northwest ingredients, and the best of the results can be astonishing. We've had marvelous muscovy duck breast, garnished with a gingery fruit salsa and escorted by the finest sour cream mashed potatoes imaginable, and perfectly sautéed sea scallops with a spicy bacon sauce over fresh spinach. Desserts consistently reveal the deft hand of a classical pro. Kaspar's wife, Nancy, keeps a watchful eye over a multitude of serving staff, while his brother, Markus, acts as sommelier and catering manager. A lounge area features an affordably priced bar menu. ▪ *1st Ave W and W Harrison; (206)298-0123; 19 W Harrison, Seattle; $$$; full bar; AE, MC, V; no checks; dinner Mon–Sat.* ☃

Le Gourmand ★★★ This unprepossessing, not-quite-Ballard storefront doesn't fit one's image of what a lovely upscale restaurant should be, but lovely it is. Owner Bruce Naftaly has created a calm, intimate dining space with a garden-scene mural, ceiling clouds, and delightful antique mirrors here, there, and everywhere. Seasonal produce and fish arrive daily from Naftaly's carefully chosen list of local suppliers, all to be generously embellished with his forté, sauces, and garnished with edible blossoms from his backyard garden. Dinner here is comprised of appetizer, entree (which carries the price of the meal), and salad. Every dish is carefully considered as to season, taste, and presentation—the entree arrives alone, center stage, on its plate, with vegetables served in a separate dish. Depending on the time of year, you might enjoy an earthy nettle soup at the beginning of your meal, or delicate leek and onion tarts crowned with juniper berries. In the main course, flounder is set off perfectly with tangy parsley butter; tender venison may be complemented by a dark elderberry and pinot noir stock. Finish with a salad of wild greens feathered with calendulas, nasturtiums, and rose petals. ▪ *Corner of Market and 6th; (206)784-3463; 425 NW Market St, Seattle; $$$; beer and wine; AE, MC, V; checks OK; dinner Wed–Sat.*

The Painted Table (Alexis Hotel) ★★★ Chef Tim Kelley honed his craft in NYC at the estimable Vong and Bouley before heading to Seattle. Here in the colorful, contemporary, two-tiered dining room of one of Seattle's finest boutique hotels, Kelley has made his mark offering bold juxtapositions of flavor in clever, artful fashion. His signature appetizer, a layered goat cheese and vegetable "salad," is a textured tower of grilled eggplant, creamy goat cheese, and oven-dried tomatoes with an onion confit and a spray of fresh greens. A stunning rack of baby lamb chops is encrusted with herbs and stacked tall above a glossy reduction sauce; tamarind-basted Long Island duck slices lie on a nest of egg noodles in a Thai-spiced broth. Well-meaning service is often far less polished than the glossy digs might lead you to expect. . ■ *1st and Madison; (206)624-3646; 92 Madison, Seattle; $$$; full bar; AE, DC, MC, V; no checks; breakfast every day, lunch Mon–Fri, dinner every day.*

Pirosmani ★★★ In a city grown jaded to the wildest of world cuisines, Pirosmani—offering the foods of the Republic of Georgia, nestled between the Black and Caspian seas—takes you around the world in the time it takes to navigate Queen Anne Hill. From the polished and refined surroundings—the linen and candlelight, the serene professionalism of the staff, the well-heeled patrons—you might never guess the exotic tastes to come. Then dinner arrives, and you suddenly notice how very red the walls are. Chef Laura Dewell offers a gentle education in the foods of Georgia; her small menu is split between those and dishes from the Mediterranean, which are every bit as alluring. Appetizers with the strangest names yield the loveliest results: khachapuri and spinach pkhali is a spinach pâté tweaked with walnuts, cilantro, and garlic scooped up with a gooey cheese bread. You can gussy up your food still further with a trio of Georgian condiments brought to each table in little pots. Don't hesitate where fish is concerned; a Near Eastern preparation of rare tuna—rubbed with Syrian spices and wrapped in grape leaves—is served over a Turkish sauce of pomegranates, walnuts, and red peppers. Braised duck Satsivi, a classic Georgian creation, comes bone-in, smothered in a thick walnut sauce with the nuances of coriander, cinnamon, cayenne, paprika, and fenugreek. ■ *Queen Anne Ave N, between Boston and McGraw; (206)285-3360; 2220 Queen Anne Ave N, Seattle; $$; beer and wine; AE, DC, MC, V; checks OK; dinner Tues–Sat.*

Place Pigalle ★★★ Long on charm, short on space, this classic Seattle bistro with a Puget Sound view is everything a stylish Northwest restaurant should be, and more. Small wonder, then, that locals find owner Bill Frank's hideaway in Pike Place Market the perfect spot to sip an eau de vie, lunch with a friend, or engage in a romantic dinner à deux. A range of intriguing dishes combine the freshness of Northwest ingredients with recipes that speak of France and Italy here, of New Mexico and New Orleans there, all filtered through the imagination of executive chef Will McNamara and his crew. Ask for a table by the window, and sample something as simple as onion soup gratinée (with its beefy broth, silky onions, and chewy Gruyère), or as sophisticated as roulade of duck confit (a pasta sheet rolled with preserved duck, goat cheese, and butternut squash). On sunny days, a small crowded skyway is used by those anxious to catch every daylight ray, but the inside tables have the advantage of being in the sight line of your waitperson. ■ *Under the clock at Pike Place Market; (206) 624-1756; 81 Pike St, Seattle; $$$; full bar; MC, V; no checks; lunch, dinner Mon–Sat.*

Ponti Seafood Grill ★★★ Ponti, tucked almost under the Fremont Bridge, might inspire dreams of the Mediterranean, with its canalside perch, stucco walls, red-tiled roof, and elegantly understated dining rooms. But its true inspiration is defined by its food, not its mood. Call it pan-Asian, call it fusion cuisine, but give credit where it is due: to chef Alvin Binuya. Borrowing from an array of ethnic flavors (with more than a passing nod to Asia), Binuya performs cross-cultural magic with such signature dishes as black pepper tuna carpaccio (drizzled with soy vinaigrette) and Thai curry penne (with broiled scallops, Dungeness crabmeat, spicy ginger-tomato chutney, and basil chiffonade). Dine outdoors in warm weather, or take advantage of the view during a leisurely Sunday brunch. ■ *Behind the Bleitz Funeral Home; (206) 284-3000; 3014 3rd Ave N, Seattle; $$$; full bar; AE, DC, MC, V; local checks only; lunch, dinner every day, brunch Sun. &*

Queen City Grill ★★★ You slide into a high-backed wooden booth and schmooze with friends. Fashionable people perch at the bar with cigarettes and cocktails. Queen City is a restaurant where the menu is pared down to a short list of dishes done really, really well, offset by a couple of specials—a nice ethic in this era of multiethnic, pan-continental eateries. The disbelieving should sample the melting tuna carpaccio appetizer (tinged with peppercorns and wasabe). Or a genuine caesar salad, done as Cardini envisioned: whole-leaf hearts of romaine, simply dressed in olive oil, lemon, and Worcestershire. The entrees, too, are simply prepared, mostly on the grill—from seared, fresh ahi tuna to a perfect New York steak to Jamaican jerk chicken (spicy and charred on the outside, but fall-off-the-bone tender inside). Service is impeccable, and reservations are recommended. ■ *Corner of Blanchard and 1st; (206) 443-0975; 2201 1st Ave, Seattle; $$$; full bar; AE, DC, MC, V; checks OK; lunch Mon–Fri, dinner every day. &*

Ray's Boathouse ★★★ With its peerless, unabashedly romantic view of Shilshole Bay and the Olympics beyond, Ray's is *the* place for waterfront dining. It's a rare pick—one favored by tourists and locals alike—where the food is superior and the service ever efficient and helpful. Ray's is a good place to educate yourself about seafood—about different kinds of oysters, perhaps—and what wines go well with them. In composing your meal, take advantage of the fresh fish that Ray's is famous for, and pay particular attention to the daily fresh sheet. We've had our socks knocked off by grilled white king salmon smeared with a nutty arugula pesto, and an exceptional steamed smoked black cod fillet. The superb wine list is organized by country and varietal, with a page devoted to splits. If the reservation wait for the dining room proves weeks long (and in summer, it well may), try the moderately priced upstairs cafe, especially popular at happy hour. The view (and the deck seating) helps you forget that the cafe service is less than it should be. ■ *60th NW and Seaview; (206) 789-3770; 6049 Seaview Ave NW, Seattle; $$$; full bar; AE, DC, MC, V; local checks only; lunch, dinner every day.* &

Rover's ★★★ Chef Thierry Rautureau, who began his culinary apprenticeship in the French countryside at age 13, is Seattle's answer to Jacques Pepin—a handsome elf with a warm wit, a world of personality, and an inspired hand in the kitchen. His restaurant, a small house tucked into a garden courtyard in Madison Valley, recently expanded. Best of all, Rover's once-stark, white-walled original dining room has been warmly redecorated. Dinners here are marvelously sauced, classically French-inspired treatments of not strictly Northwest fare. Rautureau's forté is seafood, and he's adept at finding the best-quality ingredients. It may feel a tad fussy and expensive, but portions—with, perhaps, the exception of the precious five-course *menu dégustation*—are served with a generous hand. A whole Maine lobster, out of the shell, steamed and served with a Perigord truffle sauce, is savored with each mouthful. Tender pink slices of venison in a dark green peppercorn sauce taste surprisingly delicate. Expect ever-professional service, and expect sticker shock when perusing the carefully chosen wine list. Dining in the courtyard, weather permitting, is an enchanting experience. ■ *1½ blocks from the Arboretum at 28th and Madison; (206) 325-7442; 2808 E Madison St, Seattle; $$$; beer and wine; AE, DC, MC, V; checks OK; dinner Tues–Sat.*

Saleh al Lago ★★★ Saleh Joudeh is a native of the Middle East who left his heart in central Italy 20-odd years ago. Self-taught and earnest about his restaurant, Joudeh puts out some of the most consistently good central Italian food in Seattle at 13-year-old Saleh al Lago. The two-tiered, pink-hued destination dining place is more popular with Seattle's moneyed mucky-mucks than with the city's youthful trend-seekers (who may find the room too bright, the menu too traditional). But what Saleh al Lago might lack in excitement, it makes up for in execution: the menu is steadfast and true—as is the staff. You're not likely to find a better plate of calamari than this lightly floured version sautéed with lemon, garlic, and parsley. Risotto is done to chewy perfection here, perhaps with a rich red sauce and bits of filet mignon or with chicken, arugula, and gorgonzola. Try the sautéed Provimi veal with its delicate quattro formaggi sauce or the nutmeg-tinged housemade spinach-and-cheese ravioli. Bored with tiramisu? Think again before you pass up Saleh's. ■ *On the east side of Green Lake; (206)524-4044; 6804 E Green Lake Way N, Seattle; $$$; full bar; AE, MC, V; local checks only; lunch Mon–Fri, dinner Mon–Sat.* &

Szmania's ★★★ The pretty neighborhood village of Magnolia may be hard to find, but Szmania's makes it worth the trouble. Ludgar and Julie Szmania (pronounced Smahn-ya) opened their comfortably modern restaurant five years ago; it is now one of the city's most sought-out dining spots. The open kitchen provides a stage set where German-born Ludgar uses Northwest ingredients to create such wide-ranging dishes as Jäegerschnitzel with spaetzle and roasted monkfish with a chanterelle cream sauce. Sit at the bright kitchen counter space and watch him work, or retreat to the far recesses of the dining room. Servings are generous and the Szmanias know it; many entrees are offered in half-portions. Expect strong flavors that work well together—such as a paillard of beef coated with onion and mustard in a rich cabernet sauce—and occasionally some that don't, like an ill-conceived lamb saltimbocca. And take note of the loveliest array of vegetables ever to garnish a plate. For dessert: the signature pots de crème trio. ■ *34th Ave W and McGraw; (206)284-7305; 3321 W McGraw St, Seattle; $$; full bar; AE, DC, MC, V; local checks only; lunch Mon–Sat (March–Dec), dinner Tues–Sun.* &

Tulio (Hotel Vintage Park) ★★★ Tulio's neighborhood Italian charm belies its busy downtown hotel location. The recent addition of an upstairs dining room now allows space for larger parties. Downstairs, where most of the action takes place, tables with red-checkered cloths are packed in tightly, the sweet scent of roasted garlic hangs in the air, and a wood-burning oven and open kitchen make the ever-lively room even livelier. Service is swift, knowledgable, and attentive, and with chef Walter Pisano in charge, your meal is always in good hands. His bruschetta mista (a mix of breads, marinated mushrooms, goat cheese, tapenade, and tomatoes tossed with pine nuts and currants) and the calamari fritti (enough spicy fried squid to feed an army) will start things off right. The artful and very fresh "primi" courses, such as the smoked salmon ravioli tart with a lemon cream sauce, pique the palate. Roasted and grilled cuts of meat and fish round out the dinner menu, while thin-crusted pizzas and cheesy calzones add a casual note to the lunch offerings. Breakfast is a welcome respite from typical hotel fare. ■ *5th and Spring; (206) 624-5500; 1100 5th Ave, Seattle; $$; full bar; AE, DC, MC, V; no checks; breakfast, lunch, dinner every day.*

Union Bay Cafe ★★★ In this softly lit Laurelhurst storefront, folks are as likely to be celebrating a birthday or anniversary as stopping in for a relaxing dinner after a hard day's work. Chef/owner Mark Manley often leaves his open kitchen to welcome guests and discuss dishes. His ever-changing menu is small and trenchant; performance never wavers. Keep a watchful eye for any appetizer made with mushrooms. A starter of Penn Cove mussels, scented with basil and ginger and smoothed with a touch of cream, proves that while his menu leans toward Italian, Manley can do Asian, too. Meats are handled with particular care, as evidenced by slices of venison sauced with chanterelles and huckleberries. Fresh fish and seasonal produce are well respected in this kitchen. You'll find vegetarian options at every meal; a reasonable wine list offers first-rate choices by the glass. For dessert—anything, from the bread pudding to a crisp made with apples and bourbon-soaked cherries. The bill is the final pleasure. ■ *2 blocks east of University Village; (206) 527-8364; 3513 NE 45th St, Seattle; $$; beer and wine; AE, DC, MC, V; checks OK; dinner Tues–Sun.*

Wild Ginger ★★★ The Wild Ginger is wildly popular. Basking in the glow of much national attention are owners Rick and Ann Yoder, whose culinary vision—inspired by much time spent in Southeast Asia—has left a lasting impression on the Seattle restaurant scene. Just as the restaurants and markets of Bangkok, Singapore, Saigon, and Djakarta offer a wide range of multiethnic foods, so does the Wild Ginger, which brings together some of the best dishes from these Southeast Asian cities. At the mahogany satay bar, order from a wide array of sizzling skewered selections: simple seared slices of sweet onion and Chinese eggplant, or tender Bangkok boar basted with coconut milk. Wherever you sit, indulge in the succulent Singapore-style stir-fried crab, fresh from live tanks and redolent with ginger and garlic; mildly hot, slightly sweet beef curry from Thailand; and Laksa, a spicy Malaysian seafood bouillabaisse whose soft, crunchy, slippery textures and hot and salty flavors encompass everything good about Southeast Asian cookery. Great live jazz makes the Ginger the city's most happening scene on Monday nights. ■ *1 block east of the water-*

front on the corner of Western and Union; (206)623-4450; 1400 Western Ave, Seattle; $$; full bar; AE, DC, MC, V; no checks; lunch Mon–Sat, dinner every day. ⅃

Cafe Flora ★★ Cafe Flora's meatless, smokeless, boozeless ethic is rooted in a larger vision: multiculturalism, responsible global stewardship, and a fervid righteousness about health. Political and social agendas aside, this very attractive, very '90s place has become a mecca for vegetarians and carnivores alike. Concessions have been made for the regulars who longed to sip something more potent than rosemary-laced lemonade; you can now enjoy a glass of merlot with your Portobello Wellington (a mushroom-pecan pâté and grilled portobellos wrapped in pastry) or drink a beer with your Oaxaca Tacos (a pair of corn tortillas stuffed with spicy mashed potatoes and cheeses, set off by a flavorful black bean stew and sautéed greens). Soups are always silky and luscious, salads sport interesting (and often organic) ingredients, and those who don't do dairy will always find something cleverly prepared to suit their dietary needs. Never hesitate when the dessert tray makes the rounds. ■ *28th and Madison; (206)325-9100; 2901 E Madison, Seattle; $$; beer and wine; MC, V; checks OK; lunch Tues–Fri, dinner Tues–Sat, brunch Sat–Sun.* ⅃

Cafe Lago ★★ Chefs Jordi Viladas and Carla Leonardi fuel the fires at this rustic Montlake Italian cafe with a flaming brick oven reminiscent of trattorias that dot the hills of Tuscany. The menu is quite small and features a quartet of pasta options that changes nightly. All the ingredients are fresh; even the pasta is handmade. The pizzas are original and some, such as the Pizza Caprino (goat cheese, red onion, garlic, and herbs), win raves. As do the ravioli stuffed with spinach, raisins, and walnuts in a Roquefort/mascarpone sauce, and one of the best antipasti plates in the city. The high ceilings make for a noisy room, but, hey, that's Italian. ■ *On 24th Ave E, 6 blocks south of Hwy 520; (206)329-8005; 2305 24th E, Seattle; $$; beer and wine; MC, V; checks OK; dinner Tues–Sun.* ⅃

El Greco ★★ El Greco is a calm oasis amid the crowded bustle on neon-lit, see-and-be-seen Broadway. Warm wood, linen napkins, fresh flowers, and world-beat music make this Mediterranean-inspired bistro a neighborhood favorite. Hummus and baba ghanouj are to be expected, but such fabulous dishes as creamy, fennel-spiked arborio rice topped with five perfectly cooked prawns and scented with ouzo (we've had risotto half as good at twice the price) and a wild mushroom ragout (an earthy concoction of mushrooms and vegetables served with crisp, smoked-mozzarella potato cakes) are a welcome surprise. Come for a latte served in a big cup and hope for the warm apple and rhubarb crisp served à la mode. ■ *On Broadway between Thomas and John; (206)328-4604;*

*219 Broadway E, Seattle; $; beer and wine; MC, V; checks OK;
breakfast and lunch every day, dinner Mon–Sat.*

I Love Sushi ★★ Chef Tadashi Sato has created a pair of premier Japanese restaurants on either side of Lake Washington.
Both feature bustling, bright, high-energy sushi bars with
exquisitely fresh fish—and a friendly, helpful staff to keep
things running smoothly. At the sushi bar, Sato and his min-
ions—in their traditional hajimaki (headbands)—attract many
Japanese customers who know a good thing when they eat one.
The sushi combinations are a veritable bargain (particularly at
lunch), while such traditional Japanese specialties as sea
urchin, abalone, and fermented bean paste may raise the stakes
somewhat. The hot dishes, including flame-broiled fish cheeks,
the ubiquitous tempura, and chawan mushi—a steamed custard egg soup that is the ultimate in Japanese comfort food—
are excellent. There's not much of a nonsmoking section at the
Lake Union restaurant. In Bellevue, you can sing along nightly
in the karaoke bar. ▪ *On the Yale St Landing off Fairview;
(206) 625-9604; 1001 Fairview Ave N, Seattle; $$; full bar;
AE, MC, V; no checks; lunch Mon–Fri, dinner every day.* ▪
*NE 8th St and 118th Ave NE; (206) 454-5706; 11818 NE 8th
St, Bellevue; $$; full bar; AE, MC, V; no checks; lunch
Mon–Sat, dinner every day.* &

Italia ★★ Lunch is big business at Italia, a pretty, spacious,
brick-lined restaurant that anchors the handsomely restored
National Building. Now that Italia's done away with the cafeteria-style lunch, downtown working stiffs can sit down and be
waited on before forking into generous portions of Italian food,
always very good and always surprisingly inexpensive. We love
the ever-changing recipes for soup and lasagne, the soothingly
creamy polenta with and sauteand roasted vegetables, and the
cracker-thin crusts of the plate-sized pizzas. When night falls,
the linen comes out, the lights dim, and the focus is on more
serious food, with such dishes as bistecca alla griglia (grilled
New York steak) and agnello brasato (roasted rack of lamb).
▪ *Between Madison and Spring on Western; (206) 623-1917;
1010 Western Ave, Seattle; $$; beer and wine; AE, DC, MC,
V; local checks only; lunch Mon–Fri, dinner Mon–Sat.*

Kaizuka Teppanyaki and Sushi Bar ★★ Two years after the
original Nikko restaurant moved to the Westin Hotel, Jeff and
Lisa Kaizuka got their hands on the shabby, vacant space in the
ground floor of a dentist's office and turned it into one of the
city's best-kept secrets: a *quiet*, neighborhood, Mom-and-Pop-
run sushi shop. Kaizuka is now a beautifully and simply deco-
rated Japanese restaurant with six teppanyaki tables, four
private tatami rooms, and a sushi bar that's comfortably small.
Smiling Jeff Kaizuka entertains at the teppanyaki tables, flash-
ing his knives and flash-searing beef, chicken, and seafood.

The generous cuts of maguro, hamachi, and saba folded over lightly seasoned rice are more impressive (and, at $2.50 a pair, much less expensive) than those purveyed elsewhere. Running between the two rooms, Lisa Kaizuka works the floor, tending tables as well as the door, making sure everyone feels at home. On busy nights, service may be a bit slow, but the wait is always worth it. ▪ *At S King and Rainier; (206) 860-1556; 1306 S King St, Seattle; $$; beer and wine; AE, DC, MC, V; no checks; lunch Mon–Fri, dinner Mon–Sat.*

Labuznik ★★ While other chefs have followed fads and experimented with showy Mediterranean, pan-Asian, and nouvelle influences, Peter Cipra has stuck steadfastly by the stolid European-hotel traditions of his native Czechoslovakia. Twenty years since its inception, Labuznik, once *the* standard-bearer by which all Seattle restaurants were measured, appears to be in the throes of a serious slump. Such time-tested specialties as rack of Ellensburg lamb and velvety seasonal mushrooms still have the ability to astound, but the overpriced (and surprisingly ill-prepared) châteaubriand and an overcooked wiener schnitzel were only the start of our complaints on several recent visits. Still, the comfortably cloistered dining room remains minimally decorated and the staff well-drilled. Up front is a small cafe—pleasantest on sunny evenings when the storefront opens onto First Avenue—offering lighter fare at more reasonable prices. ▪ *On 1st between Stewart and Virginia; (206) 441-8899; 1924 1st Ave, Seattle; $$$; full bar; AE, DC, MC, V; no checks; dinner Tues–Sat.*

Manca's ★★ The Manca family has been in the restaurant business for over a century, so if you get the feeling that you're dining among family here, don't be surprised. You are. The handsome young Mancas who run this casual yet elegant Madison Park dining room have a genetic knack for making everyone feel as if they're at a wonderful family gathering. Talented, jovial chef Jodie Benson serves everything from a burger with fries to an enormous rack of meaty barbecued back ribs to a tender filet mignon. Inspired renderings of chicken, seafood, and pastas round it all out, and there's even a listing of spa entrees (no added fats or oils). On weekend mornings, Mark and Mory Manca take over the kitchen and whip up Dutch babies (their secret family recipe for custardy crêpelike pancakes that rise to delectable heights) topped with lemon and powdered sugar. ▪ *Madison and McGilvra; (206) 323-7686; 4000 E Madison, Seattle; $$; full bar; DC, MC, V; checks OK; lunch Tue–Fri, dinner Tue–Sun, brunch Sat–Sun.* &

Maple Leaf Grill ★★ Don't let the pub atmosphere fool you. And whatever you do, don't belittle the culinary artistry of co-owner/chef "Rip" Ripley by calling his food "pub grub." One

▼
Seattle

Restaurants

▲

look down the long, plate-filled bar or into the big, wooden booths proves that "grub" doesn't even come close to describing the food served here. You're just as likely to fork into a grilled breast of rabbit sauced with cumin, garlic, and olives or a Thai-inspired plate of shrimp and basil ravioli as a burger with fries (though they serve plenty of the latter). With the blues on the sound system, and the convivial customers hoisting a brew, waiting for a seat, and trading gibes with co-owner David Albert, you'll get the feeling that you're at a neighborhood house-warming party. ■ *89th and Roosevelt; (206)523-8449; 8909 Roosevelt Way NE, Seattle; $$; beer and wine; MC, V; checks OK; lunch Mon–Fri, dinner every day.* &

Marco's Supperclub ★★ A more appropriate name for the place might be Marco's Success Story. When expat-Chicagoans Marco Rulff and Donna Moodie opened this stylish Belltown bistro, they crossed their fingers in hope that years of tableside experience, an adventurous and capable chef, and a strong staff of friendly yet sophisticated servers would bring business their way. And it was clear from the day the doors opened that the husband-and-wife team had more than luck going for them. Since then, their sexy, noisy, and *busy* restaurant has welcomed hordes of savvy diners who come for the warm, funky atmosphere and the trip-around-the-world menu. Forgo the pastas, but certainly order the fried sage appetizer, pork tenderloin marinated in juniper berries and herbs, subtly spiced Jamaican jerk chicken served up with sautéed greens and mashed sweet potatoes, or cumin- and coriander-spiked Moroccan lamb. A bar running the length of the room is a great perch for those dining alone. In summer, a colorful, plant-filled deck out back practically doubles the seating capacity. ■ *Near 1st and Wall; (206)441-7801; 2510 1st Ave, Seattle; $$; full bar; AE, MC, V; checks OK; dinner every day, brunch Sun.*

Metropolitan Grill ★★ This handsome, money-colored haunt in the heart of the financial district does a booming business among the stockbrokers and Asian tourists. The bovine is divine here at Suit Central, so you'd do well to stick to the steaks. Pastas and appetizers are less well executed, but a list of large, appealing salads, sandwiches, and a daily fish special present good alternatives to beef for the lunch crowd. Waiters are of the no-nonsense school, which suits the table-hopping power brokers just fine. Financiers count on the Met's 30-person private room as a dependable dinner venue. ■ *2nd and Marion; (206)624-3287; 820 2nd Ave, Seattle; full bar; $$$; AE, DC, MC, V; checks Ok; lunch Mon–Fri, dinner every day.* &

Nikko (Westin Hotel) ★★ When the corporate kingpins made Shiro Kashiba an offer he couldn't refuse, Seattle's first (and favorite) sushi chef agreed to sell his restaurant's name and take his show from its inconspicuous International District location to the Westin, where a flashy, highly decorated, $1.5 million remodeled restaurant awaited. (Shiro-san has long since called it quits at Nikko, and at press time has a new sushi bar under construction in Belltown.) Nikko's second incarnation offers one of the few really attractive Japanese dining rooms in the city, and the enormous sushi bar is still a great place to enjoy impeccable raw fish, including the astounding Nikko Roll (seven different pieces of fish rolled with avocado and rice). Perennial non-sushi favorites include black cod marinated in sake lees and then broiled to flaky perfection, or crisp soft-shell crab. One of the most satisfying rainy-day dishes is the much-maligned sukiyaki, a soulful one-pot meal. And you can always enjoy a plate of grilled thises and thats from the robata bar. ■ *In the Westin Hotel at 5th and Westlake; (206)322-4641; 1900 Fifth Ave, Seattle; $$$; full bar; AE, DC, MC, V; local checks only; dinner Mon–Sat.* ♿

Pandasia ★★ We guess the cuddly panda image wasn't enough of an ethnic identifier, so the restaurant formerly known as Panda's has a new name: Pandasia. The sight of steaming pot-stickers, plates of rich orange beef, and sautéed eggplant in a spicy sauce has been known to tempt customers into ordering too much. However, the skillful waitstaff will be happy to suggest the best dishes that night. It's hard to go wrong with the extensive menu, and even harder to find a time when the waiting customers aren't spilling out the door. Somehow Pandasia handles a busy take-out and delivery service as well. The same terrific specialties are at both locations: mu-shu pork with homemade pancakes; perfectly cooked, dry-sautéed green beans with almonds; a standout General Tso's chicken, which quietly explodes inside the mouth with tender meat and vibrant seasoning. There are almost 100 dishes to choose from. ■ *NE 75th and 35th NE; (206)526-5115; 7347 35th Ave NE, Seattle.* ■ *Between 16th W and 17th W; (206)283-9030; 1625 W Dravus, Seattle; $; beer and wine; AE, MC, V; local checks only; lunch Mon–Sat, dinner every day.*

Phoenecia at Alki ★★ Hussein Khazaal's fans (whose devotion verges on the cultish) have followed him from one off-the-track location to another. Finally he and they have a site worthy of his talents. At this, Phoenicia's third incarnation, the ochre-sponged walls seem to glow with the Mediterranean sunshine, even when the sun's not setting over the beach across the street. The standard hummus and baba ghanouj are here, but then it's off on pan-Mediterranean explorations: saffron and pine-nut risotto with shellfish; Moroccan eggplant with penne and tomatoes, excellent inventive thin-crust pizza, several versions of the most fragrant marinated lamb you've ever tasted, and a mariner's ransom of exquisite seafood. To round it all off you may choose, appropriately, between espresso and Turkish coffee, tiramisu and baklava. ■ *Between 59th and 60th; (206)935-6550; 2716 Alki Ave S, Seattle; $$; beer and wine; MC, V; checks OK; lunch Tues–Fri, dinner Tues–Sat.*

The Pink Door ★★ Hidden away in Pike Place Market, this Italian trattoria's low-profile entrance (just a pink door off Post Alley) belies the busy scene within. In the winter, the dining room grows noisy around a burbling fountain, but come warmer weather, everyone vies desperately for a spot on the trellis-covered terrace with its breathtakingly romantic view of the Sound. Owner Jackie Roberts finally did away with her long-standing prix-fixe menu and now serves dinner à la carte, offering hefty plates of pasta and a few fish/meat/poultry dishes. Or you can construct a fine meal from the limited bar menu (the antipasto misto is a Tuscan feast, and the aglio al forno—roasted garlic with a scoop of ricotta-gorgonzola cheese spread—is a most slatherable nosh). The Pink Door overflows with Italian kitsch, which is not lost on the arty, under-30 set that calls the place home. There's often live music at night. ■ *Post Alley between Stewart and Virginia; (206) 443-3241; 1919 Post Alley, Seattle; $$; full bar; AE, MC, V; no checks; lunch, dinner Tues–Sat.*

Reiner's ★★ This handsome, unobtrusive space on Pill Hill offers much in the way of Old World charm: a big, domed ceiling, a sparkling chandelier, European antiques, and equally European servers. It is at the same time elegant and unstuffy, catering to a clientele put off by aggressively trendy restaurants. The food, too, has a rather continental feel: lobster bisque, smoothed with brandy, is stunningly silky; a mixed seafood grill (with some decidedly off-tasting scallops on our last visit) comes sauced with "tarragon and balsamic-infused olive oil"—a béarnaise sauce for the '90s. The roast rack of lamb, four double chops coated with fresh bread crumbs, garlic, Dijon mustard, and rosemary, proved delicious. Wine by the glass is served in miniature pitchers—a lovely touch. Desserts, scrumptious-looking confections all, make up for the lackluster bread that accompanies the meal. ■ *8th and Spring, in the Lowell Apartments building, near Virginia Mason; (206)624-2222; 1106 8th Ave, Seattle; $$; full bar; AE, DC, MC, V; no checks; dinner Tues–Sat.*

Ristorante Buongusto ★★ You've got to hand it to the tireless trio of Varchettas who own and operate Queen Anne Hill's friendly, neighborhood Italian dining room. Roberto (in the kitchen) and his brother and sister-in-law, Salvio and Anna (who run the floor after a busy day at their Pioneer Square cafeteria, Caffe Panini), are a nonstop, homey Italian tour de force. Theirs is a bright, active place with tiled floors and graceful archways that evoke the warmth of an Italian terrazzo. The large remodeled house hums with the voices of a casual crowd that returns again and again for the consistently good southern Italian fare. The menu features some of the most reliable pastas in town—filling rigatoni alla Buongusto, chunks of sausage and eggplant in a perfect ragu sauce; and rotolo di Mamma Flora, medallions of pasta stuffed with bubbling veal, ricotta, and spinach. ■ *Queen Anne Ave and McGraw; (206)284-9040; 2232 Queen Anne Ave N, Seattle; $$; full bar; AE, DC, MC, V; no checks; dinner every day.*

Salvatore ★★ What with so many Italian restaurants going upscale, and every other restaurant in town going Italian, this neighborhood dinner spot continues to impress by getting all the essentials right—the old-fashioned Italian way. Much of the warmth here stems from Salvatore Anania himself, who brings his amore for the southern Italian food of Basilicata to his North End landing. Service is friendly and more than helpful (you might *need* help choosing among the many Italian wines offered). We suggest starting with one of the thin-crusted pizzas but passing on the lackluster salads. Take your waiter's cue when it comes to specials, or order the spicy, satisfying penne puttanesca. Even though they've moved the entranceway and added a few cafe tables, on busy nights Salvatore's no-reservations policy may still leave wannabe diners crowded and waiting in a tight space. ■ *1 block north of Ravenna Blvd on Roosevelt; (206)527-9301; 6100 Roosevelt, Seattle; $$; beer and wine; MC, V; checks OK; dinner Mon–Sat.* &

Sea Garden ★★ The name says it all. This restaurant puts its best efforts into anything that comes from the sea—particularly if it spent its last minutes in the live tank up front. Some of the city's best crab comes kicking to your table at the Sea Garden, where one affirmative nod will find it whisked away to the kitchen, and returned minutes later in a state more suitable for chopsticks. The Sea Garden is nothing fancy, but we've always been enamored of its ability to keep such consistently excellent seafood so reasonably priced. It's subtle Cantonese fare, the tamely spiced stuff we all enjoyed before we developed our culinary crush on fiery Sichuan or Hunan food. Try the excellent braised black cod or the clams with black bean sauce. Larger parties fill the somewhat dreary upstairs room. Open late every day. ■ *Jackson and 7th S; (206)623-2100; 509 7th Ave S, Seattle; $; full bar; AE, MC, V; no checks; lunch, dinner every day.*

Shanghai Garden ★★ Owner/chef Hua Te Su caters to a largely Chinese clientele in this very pink restaurant in the International District. Mr. Su (as he is respectfully known) attracts diners from every Chinese province with regional dishes that change seasonally. The menu is vast and filled with exotica like black moss and bamboo fungus soup, sautéed hog maul, and fish-head casserole. Come prepared to be wowed by anything made with pea vines, or with the chef's special hand-shaven noodles. The vivid tendrils from the sugar-pea plant resemble sautéed spinach, and you'd never imagine that they'd cook up this tender and clean-tasting, never more so than when paired with plump shrimp. The noodles, shaved off a block of dough, are the main ingredient in a dozen different dishes. Try them in what we're sure will be the best chow mein you'll ever eat. This might be the only Chinese restaurant in town where dessert should not be missed. ■ *Corner of 6th Ave S and Weller St; (206) 625-1689; 524 6th Ave S, Seattle; $; beer and wine; MC, V; no checks; lunch, dinner every day.*

Swingside Cafe ★★ Owner/chef Brad Inserra's no longer in the kitchen every night (his cousin John has come on board as a partner), but the Swingside—with its absurdly small kitchen producing a world of big flavors—produces an inventive menu all Inserra's own. There are hearty stews and sautés and pasta dishes of Pittsburgh-Sicilian provenance spiced with unpredictable North African, Creole, and nouvelle-American accents. The brown Moroccan sauce melts in the mouth; tangy seafood dishes sing of the sea. Everything's rich, delicious, and amply portioned; don't overorder or you may have to be carried home. Desserts are a sometime thing, depending on who's supplying. As for atmosphere, you've probably forgotten eating out could be as simple, casual, and friendly as this. ■ *Across from the Buckaroo Tavern at 43rd and Fremont; (206) 633-4057; 4212 Fremont N, Seattle; $$; beer and wine; MC, V; local checks OK; lunch Tues–Fri, dinner Tues–Sat.* &

Toyoda Sushi ★★ Expect to wait in the bright, crowded entrance, and be sure to opt for a seat at the sushi bar where chef/owner Natsuyoshi Toyoda appears to be working with more than one pair of hands while carrying on cheerful conversations with patrons who all swear by this unlikely Lake City find. Sometimes the speed necessary to keep the waiting lines moving comes at a cost: sushi rolls uncurling on the plate, tardy tableside service, or a slightly frozen piece of hamachi. But then comes Toyoda-san's smiling wife, Helen, bearing a spicy cucumber and noodle salad and an array of the freshest seafood: tender amoebi (sweet raw shrimp), lightly smoked salmon, and fatty white albacore tuna, or some of the best gyoza around. When the vibes are this good, who can complain? ■ *125th and Lake City Way; (206) 367-7972; 12543 Lake City Way NE, Seattle; $$; beer and wine; MC, V; local checks only; dinner Wed–Mon.*

Ayutthaya ★ Soft pastel colors and clean, smooth lines create a calming antidote to the fiery food, which is prepared carefully and authentically here on Capitol Hill by the Fuangaromya family (members of which also own Thai Restaurant on lower

Queen Anne). It's good to make reservations; there's little waiting room. The seafood is excellent—a sizzling platter of shrimp spiked with basil, chile, and garlic is a show in itself. With the exception of the fried noodles (too sweet), everything is good. Local businesspeople are catching on to the best lunch deal in town, so arrive early. Service is patient, and the only thing smoking here is the food. ■ *1 block west of Broadway at Harvard and Pike; (206) 324-8833; 727 E Pike St, Seattle; $; beer and wine; AE, MC, V; no checks; lunch Mon–Fri, dinner Mon–Sat.*

El Puerco Lloron ★ This place transports you back to that cafe in Tijuana, the one with the screaming hot pink and aquamarine walls and the bent, scarred "Cerveza Superior" tables. Remember the wailing jukebox and the cut-tin lamps and the woman quietly making corn tortillas by the door? It's all here. Belly up to the cafeteria line, place your order (dishes run a paltry $4–$5), and fight for a table—in warm weather those outdoor ones are as hard to get as parking spots. Try the taquitos plate, three excellent masa corn tortillas rolled around a filling and served with rice, beans, and a scallion. The chiles rellenos, so often bungled by American chefs, are fresh and bright with flavor. At the end of the counter pick up fresh lemonade or a Mexican beer. ■ *On the Pike Place Market Hillclimb; (206) 624-0541; 1501 Western Ave, Seattle; $; beer and wine; AE, MC, V; no checks; lunch, early dinner every day.*

Huong Binh ★ While other less successful eateries come and go, this tidy Vietnamese restaurant, in one of the many strip malls marking the ever-expanding Vietnamese commercial area near the International District, continues to hold its own. We've had feasts here, huge brimming tables-full, for under $20. One such: banh beo (steamed rice cake topped with brilliant orange ground shrimp), cha hue (a pâtélike steamed pork roll), bahn hoi chao tom (grilled shrimp on sugar cane—hint to novices: you eat the shrimp, then suck the cane), and a couple of dishes starring pork and shrimp skewers with rice. Pork is particularly nicely done: tender, pounded thin, and marinated in garlic and lemon grass. Best, these grilled dishes come in traditional Vietnamese fashion with an accompanying fragrant garden of herbs, to allow you to dress your food to your liking.
■ *At S Jackson and 12th; (206) 720-4907; 1207 S Jackson St, Seattle; $; beer and wine; no credit cards; local checks only; lunch, early dinner every day.*

The Kaleenka ★ You'll rarely find food more comforting than that served in this richly decorated Russian cafe whose menu borrows from many regions of the former Soviet Union. Eastern European accents drift from talk at nearby tables as you sit down to a pot of black currant tea served in a graceful Uzbek teapot. Try a filling plate of vareniky (Ukrainian dumplings stuffed with farmer cheese or spicy potato) or some fragrant samsa (pastries filled with cumin-spiced lamb, served with a sour cream–based dill sauce). The garlicky pilmeny (ravioli-like beef dumplings) float in a huge bowl of beef consommé topped with a dollop of sour cream. ■ *Near 1st and Virginia; (206) 728-1278; 1933 1st Ave, Seattle; $$; beer and wine; MC, V; checks OK; lunch, dinner Mon–Sat.*

Mamounia ★ Mamounia is a complete-immersion course in Moroccan cuisine, a long leisurely feast in a desert tent where you sit comfortably on the floor and eat with your hands (right hand preferred). The staff carefully guides you through the strange territory (with a sense of humor when warranted), offering bread from the big basket in the middle of the room, washing your hands for you before and after the meal, and pouring your tea from a standing position into your glass two feet below. Each dinner starts with harira (Moroccan lentil soup), followed by eggplant and tomato salad, and a lovely bastilla—a chicken, egg, and pistachio pastry in flaky dough, topped with cinnamon and sugar—an unusually perfect synthesis of flavors. Then come the entrees, a whole slew of them if you order the chef's special, which we recommend if you're in a group. You'll be tearing into fragrant meats and sauces—couscous with lamb, lemon chicken, lamb in honey sauce, hare with paprika. If there's any room left, you'll nibble on a honey pastry and wash it down with tea. Ramble slowly through your dinner and try not to fill up too fast, since there are no doggie bags here. Not for vegetarians or the terminally uptight. ■ *At E Olive and Denny; (206) 329-3886; 1556 E Olive Way, Seattle; $; beer and wine; MC, V; no checks; dinner Tues–Sun.*

▼

Seattle

Restaurants

▲

(20 YEARS) Maximilien in the Market ★ There is something so undeniably French about this place, something about the mismatched silverware and the broad Elliott Bay view, about the dark wood antiques and the light reflected off the wood-framed mirrors. All you seem to need here is a crusty loaf of bread and a bottle of wine. Luckily, you don't have to stick to bread and wine when a simple lunch can be assembled out of steamed mussels with wine and herbs, a salade Niçoise, or excellent fish 'n' chips. A four-course dinner is available including perhaps a fillet of halibut broiled with a basil beurre blanc, a New York steak with sautéed mushrooms, a bowl of shellfish-rich bouillabaisse, or a simple ham and cheese omelet. Sometimes there are flaws: wine served from a bottle that's been open too long, a salty soupe à l'oignon. But here you simply sigh, slather butter on another round of bread, and nod, *c'est la vie.* ■ *Pike Place Market; (206) 682-7270; 81-A Pike St, Seattle; $$; full bar; AE, DC, MC, V; no checks; breakfast, lunch, dinner Mon–Sat, brunch Sun.* &

McCormick's Fish House and Bar ★ This is certainly the most popular midtown fish house. Lunch is noisy and frenetic, the bar jams up with City Hall types after 5pm, and even dinners feel crowded, particularly during the tourist season. Somehow the waiters remain cheerful amid the bustle. The formula here is simple: the heavy-on-seafood menu offers several types of fish cooked in simple ways. Preparation can be uneven—we've had both tough tuna and near-perfect steelhead—but you can usually rely on decent cooking and generous portions. Oysters are fine, the chowder's good, and the fresh sourdough bread is always a treat. ■ *4th and Columbia; (206) 682-3900; 722 4th Ave, Seattle; $$; full bar; AE, DC, MC, V; local checks only; lunch Mon–Fri, dinner every day.* &

Neelam's Authentic Indian Cuisine ★ Up on the Ave—a strip chock-a-block with ethnic restaurants vying for the dining dollars of starving students—delightfully officious and prettily costumed Neelam Jain is not above rushing to the doorway of her dimly lit East Indian restaurant to convince hesitant passersby to come in and try her bargain-priced dinner specials. And we're not above convincing you. Those specials include, among other offerings, 14 chicken- or lamb-based curries, and for a 10-spot you'll get a hubcap-sized plate with a choice of entree, cooling raita, fragrant dal, cumin-scented basmati rice, feathery-light naan, an appetizer (potato samosas or chicken pakoras), a beverage, *and* dessert. Forget the à la carte stuff. And show restraint when asked how hot you like your curry, or youuuu'll be sorrrrry. ■ *On the Ave (University Way); (206) 523-5275; 4735 University Way NE, Seattle; $; beer and wine; MC, V; checks OK; lunch, dinner every day.*

Piecora's ★ We know people who drive across town just to sit down to one of Piecora's oversized thin-crust pies and dream of New York. You'll know you've come to the right place when you see that damsel of the dispossesed, Lady Liberty, dressed in neon and hoisting a pizza above a crowded storefront. At this busy neighborhood joint decorated with New York subway maps and other Big Apple kitsch, delivery drivers run in and out, the din can reach epic proportions, and pizza tossing is a fine art. Some 20 toppings are available on pizzas sold by the pie, the half pie, and the slice. Pastas, sandwiches, and generous salads, too. Pizza's served until midnight on weekends. ■ *At 14th and Madison; (206) 322-9411; 1401 Madison St, Seattle; $; full bar; MC, V; checks OK; lunch, dinner every day.*

Siam on Broadway ★ Among Seattle's multitude of Thai restaurants, tiny Siam wins the popularity contest, hands down. Working the woks and burners in a tiny open kitchen fronted by counter seating, a quartet of women move with utmost grace, portioning meats and vegetables, dipping into salty potions. They produce, among other flavorful dishes, what might be the city's best tom kah gai—the chicken soup spicy with chiles, sour with lemon grass, and soothed with coconut milk. The menu doesn't stray far from the Bangkok standards, but distinctive dishes are created by the deft hands in the kitchen. Sit at the counter and enjoy the show or wait for one of only 15 tables in the back. You won't have to wait at Siam on Lake Union, a newer, larger outpost. Nor will you have to search for a parking space (they've got a private lot). Though good, the food here doesn't quite live up to its Broadway sibling's. ■ *Broadway E and E Roy; (206)324-0892; 616 Broadway E, Seattle; $; beer and wine; AE, MC, V; checks OK; lunch Mon–Fri, dinner every day.* ■ *On the east side of Lake Union; (206)323-8101; 1880 Fairview Ave E, Seattle; $; full bar; AE, MC, V; checks OK; lunch Mon–Fri, dinner every day.*

Triangle Tavern ★ Hip remodels of skanky old taverns are the thing in Seattle these days. The Triangle (born in the '30s as the Classic Tavern) is one of the most impressively stylish, and the menu's swell. The decor is (naturally) triangular, the service flaky (admittedly hung over), but with the food we have little complaint, nor do any of the legion of fans who stand drinking a brew while waiting for a table. Expansive appetizers include roasted garlic with goat cheese, nicely sided with roasted red peppers, olives, and bread, or a Middle Eastern plate heaped with hummus, baba ghanouj, and tabouli. When dinner arrives (sometimes simultaneously), there's hardly room on the tiny table (or in the stomach) for what may follow: angel hair pasta in a smooth Gorgonzola-spinach sauce, a dependable Creole seafood gumbo, and a spinach lasagne stacked with three cheeses. Sandwiches are fine for dinner as well; a Philadelphia-style cheesesteak sided up with a caesar salad is cheap at twice the price. The small space is noisy and smoky, and the desserts do not inspire; but the food is inventive and well prepared, and there are windows on three sides from which to gaze upon prettified Fremont. ■ *Fremont Pl N and N 35th; (206)632-0880; 3507 Fremont Pl N, Seattle; $; beer and wine; MC, V; local checks only; lunch and dinner every day.*

Two Bells Tavern ★ Belltown's starving artists tried not to tell anyone about the excellent, cheap burgers on sourdough at the funky Two Bells, but word got out, and now the tavern is packed all the time with an eclectic crowd, joining in common worship of the burger. It's big and juicy, smothered in onions and cheese, served on a sourdough roll with your choice of side orders, including a rich, chunky potato salad. Another favorite with the Bells crowd is the hot beer-sausage sandwich. Satisfying isn't the half of it—this food is so full of flavor and freshness and goes so well with the beer that you don't care about getting mustard all over your face. Food is served till 11pm every night, but the tavern stays open till 2am. ■ *4th and Bell; (206) 441-3050; 2313 4th Ave, Seattle; $; beer and wine; MC, V; no checks; lunch, dinner every day, breakfast Sat–Sun.* &

Viet My ★ At lunchtime, this bright, busy spot is standing room only. Owner Chau Tran is a whirlwind of energy: she's either vigorously scraping the grill, doling out menus, or directing the kitchen, which turns out food that is always exact and delicious. Start with the rice-paper rolls, generously stuffed with shrimp, pork, vermicelli, cilantro, and mint. The pho—a fragrant beef broth layered with herbs, scads of noodles, tender beef, and fresh sprouts for dunking—gets better the farther down you go in the bowl, as the herbs infuse and flavors assert themselves. Chau also offers several curries, a half dozen chow meins, and eight or so soups. Even for such generous exotica as beef wrap, you won't pay more than $6, and usually much less. ■ *Just off 4th near Washington; (206) 382-9923; 129 Prefontaine Pl S, Seattle; $; no alcohol; no credit cards; local checks only; lunch, dinner Mon–Fri.*

Seattle Bagel Bakery Seattleites rarely match Manhattanites in their lust for the doughy rings, but this spot next to the Harbor Steps (take a bagel to-go and eat by the fountains) comes close to inspiring the same passion. The only way it differs from what you might find in New York is that it's clean, airy, non-smoking, and full of sunlight. Sometimes warm, always fresh, these little wonders of raisin, cheese, garlic (gotta be a garlic lover, for the cooks are generous), or poppyseed can be eaten alone or split open and heaped with cream cheese and lox or—*Oy!*—turkey and sprouts without smothering the taste of the bagel. ■ *Corner of University and Western; (206) 624-2187; 1302 Western Ave, Seattle; $; no alcohol; no credit cards; local checks only; breakfast, lunch every day.*

LODGINGS

Four Seasons Olympic Hotel ★★★★ Elegance is yours at Seattle's landmark hotel, where grand borders on opulent, and personal around-the-clock service means smiling maids, quick-as-a-wink bellhops, and a team of caring concierges who ensure your every comfort. Luxury extends from the 450 handsome guest rooms and suites tastefully furnished with period reproductions (executive suites feature down-dressed king-size beds separated from an elegant sitting room by French doors) to the venerable Georgian Room (see review), where the talents of chef Kerry Sear, the decorum of liveried waiters, and the strains of a grand piano create a fine-dining experience you won't soon forget. Enjoy afternoon tea in the Garden Court or relax in the solarium spa and pool (where a licensed masseuse is on call). The hotel even goes out of its way for kids, right down to a teddy bear in the crib and a step stool in the bathroom. There are several elegant meeting rooms and fine shops in the retail spaces off the lobby. Prices are steep, especially considering there are few views, but this is Seattle's one venerable world-class contender. ■ *5th and University; (206) 621-1700 or (800) 821-8106; 411 University St, Seattle, WA 98101; $$$; AE, DC, MC, V; checks OK.* ♿

Alexis Hotel ★★★ When the Sultan of Brunei showed up in Seattle on business, this is where he stayed. And if it's good enough for the richest man in the world, you'll probably like it here too. The Alexis is a gem carved out of a lovely turn-of-the-century building in a stylish section of downtown near the waterfront. It's small (54 rooms), full of tasteful touches, and decorated with the suave modernity of Michael Graves's postmodern colors. You'll be pampered here, with Jacuzzis and real-wood fireplaces in some of the suites, a steam room that can be reserved just for you, and nicely insulated walls between rooms to ensure privacy. Request a room that faces the inner courtyard—rooms facing First Avenue can be noisy, especially if you want to open your window. Amenities include complimentary continental breakfasts, a morning newspaper of your choice, shoe shines, and a guest membership in the nearby Seattle Club ($12). There's only one meeting room here, as the Alexis favors well-heeled travelers who prefer quiet poshness. The Painted Table serves innovative Northwest cuisine (see review). Pets are accepted.

For a longer stay, book one of the 43 condos—some have limited water views, all have kitchens—across the street in the jointly managed Arlington Suites. Turndown service, complimentary sherry, and maid and room services are available to condo patrons as well. ■ *1st and Madison; (206) 624-4844 or (800) 426-7033; 1007 1st Ave, Seattle, WA 98104; $$$; AE, DC, MC, V; checks OK.* ♿

Inn at the Market ★★★ The setting—perched just above the fish, flower, and fruit stalls of Pike Place Market with a view of Elliott Bay and adjacent to Seattle's oh-so-special French-inspired restaurant, Campagne (see review)—is unsurpassed. This small hotel (65 rooms) features personalized service that approximates that of a country inn. Despite the downtown location, you won't feel oppressed by conventioneers—conference facilities consist of one meeting room and one outdoor deck. The architecture features oversize rooms, bay windows that let occupants of even some side rooms enjoy big views, and a comfortable, pretty lobby. There is no complimentary breakfast (just coffee), but room service for that meal can be ordered from Bacco in the courtyard; dinner comes from Campagne. ■ *1st and Pine; (206) 443-3600; 86 Pine St, Seattle, WA 98101; $$$; AE, DC, MC, V; checks OK.* ♿

Sorrento Hotel ★★★ Occupying a corner just east of downtown in Seattle's First Hill neighborhood, the Sorrento is an Italianate masterpiece that first opened in 1909, was remodeled to the tune of $4.5 million in 1981, and is now preparing for a floor-by-floor makeover for the millennium. The 76 rooms come decorated in muted good taste with a slight Asian accent. We recommend the 08 series of suites, in the corners. Suites on the top floor make elegant quarters for special meetings or parties—the showstopper being the 3,000-square-foot, $1,000 penthouse, with a grand piano, a patio, a Jacuzzi, a view of the bay, and luxurious multiple rooms. A comfortable, intimate fireside lobby lounge is a civilized place for afternoon tea or sipping Cognac while listening to one of the city's best jazz pianists. Chef Eric Lenard showcases Northwest lamb, among other local culinary treasures, at the manly Hunt Club (see review). Some may find the location—uphill five blocks from the heart of downtown—inconvenient, but we find it quiet and removed. ■ *9th and Madison; (206) 622-6400 or (800) 426-1265; 900 Madison St, Seattle, WA 98104; $$$; AE, DC, MC, V; checks OK.* ＆

Westin Hotel ★★★ Westin's international headquarters is in Seattle, so this flagship hotel has quite a few extras. The twin cylindrical towers may be called corncobs by the natives, but they afford spacious rooms with superb views, particularly above the 20th floor. Convention facilities, spread over several floors of meeting rooms, are quite complete. There is a large pool, along with an exercise room supervised by conditioning experts. On the top floors are some ritzy, glitzy suites. The location, near Westlake Center and the Monorail station, is excellent. For dinner, try superb Japanese food at Nikko (see review) or continental dining at the Palm Court. ■ *Between Stewart and Virginia on 5th; (206) 728-1000 or (800) 228-3000; 1900 5th Ave, Seattle, WA 98101; $$$; AE, DC, MC, V; checks OK.* ＆

The Bacon Mansion/Broadway Guest House ★★ Built by Cecil Bacon in 1909, the three-story Edwardian-style Tudor mansion is fit for a fine bed and breakfast—with some of the original wood and furnishings intact. Nine rooms in the main guest house (seven with private bath) are appointed with antiques and brass fixtures. The top of the line is the Capitol Room, a huge suite on the second floor with a sun room, fireplace, French doors, and a view of the Space Needle. The basement Garden Room has 8-foot ceilings and a kitchenette. The unique Carriage House ($125), a separate, two-story building with hunter green decor, is appropriate for a small family or two couples. An expanded continental breakfast might be served on the spacious patio between main house and carriage house. Proprietor Daryl King is an enthusiastic, friendly host.

■ *Corner of Broadway E and E Prospect Ave on Capitol Hill; (206)329-1864 or (800)240-1864; 959 Broadway E, Seattle, WA 98102; $$; AE, MC, V; checks OK.*

Chambered Nautilus ★★ This blue 1915 Georgian colonial in a woodsy hillside setting in the University District offers six airy guest rooms beautifully furnished with antiques. Four have private baths, and four open onto porches with tree-webbed views of the Cascades. All rooms have robes, desks, flowers, and reading material. This location just across the street from shared student housing units and a few blocks from Fraternity Row can get noisy during rush. Other times, though, it's surprisingly quiet. Innkeepers Bunny and Bill Hagemeyer serve a full breakfast, complimentary afternoon tea, and even homemade lollipops. A spacious public room, meeting facilities, a library of 2,000-plus volumes, and an enclosed porch/reading room with soothing chamber music round out this tasteful inn. Smoking is allowed on the porches and outside. Make prior arrangements for kids under 12. ■ *East on NE 50th St to 21st Ave, and circle left-right-right around the block; (206)522-2536; 5005 22nd Ave NE, Seattle, WA 98105; $$; AE, DC, MC, V; checks OK.*

The Edgewater ★★ Alas, you can't fish from the famous west-facing windows of this waterfront institution anymore. You can, however, still breathe salty air and hear the ferry horns toot. The place has been spiffed up quite a bit, giving the lobby and rooms a rustic tone, with bleached oak and overstuffed chairs, plaid bedspreads, and lots of duck motifs and antler art. It's like a lodge on a busy (and sometimes noisy) Northwest waterfront, but with a reputable restaurant (Ernie's Bar and Grill), a decent bar with a piano, and an uninterrupted view of Elliott Bay, Puget Sound, and the Olympic Mountains. Waterside rooms have the best views, but can get hot on summer afternoons. The cruise ship–style Sunday brunch served here is a veritable extravaganza. The *Victoria Clipper* terminal is just two blocks south. ■ *Pier 67 at Wall St and Alaskan Way; (206)728-7000; Pier 67, 2411 Alaskan Way, Seattle, WA 98121; $$$; AE, DC, MC, V; checks OK.*

Gaslight Inn and Howell Street Suites ★★ Praised by repeat guests and bed-and-breakfast owners alike, the Gaslight is one of the loveliest, most reasonably priced, and friendliest bed and breakfasts in town. Trevor Logan and Steve Bennett have polished this turn-of-the-century mansion into a 10–guest-room jewel, six with private baths, two with fireplaces, each decorated in a distinct style—some contemporary, some antique, some art deco, some mission. Outside are two sun decks and a large heated swimming pool. The Howell Street Suites next door (five full and one studio) are outfitted with kitchens, contemporary furnishings and antiques, a coffeemaker, wineglasses, fruit, and flowers. Targeted at businesspeople, the suites also offer phones, fax availability, off-street parking, maid service, and laundry facilities. There's a hot tub and a garden area between the two houses. No pets or kids, but smoking is okay. ■ *15th and Howell; (206)325-3654; 1727 15th Ave, Seattle, WA 98122; $$; AE, MC, V; checks OK.*

Holiday Inn Crowne Plaza ★★ This hotel bends over backward for the repeat and corporate visitor. The upper-floor rooms are corporate, comfortable, and very clean in striking maroons, mauves, and dark wood. Businesspeople receive a lot of individual attention (for a slightly higher price): free newspapers, a lounge, and their own concierge desk. Lower-floor guests stay in spacious but rather bland rooms. The lobby is elegant and comfortable, the staff attentive and accommodating. In addition to the pleasant City Views Cafe, which features continental fare, the Sax on Seneca lounge offers live music Thursday through Saturday nights. Conference rooms and parking (for a fee) are available. The location is ideal—downtown, near the freeway, and two blocks from the Convention Center. ■ *6th Ave and Seneca St; (206)464-1980 or (800)465-4329; 1113 6th Ave, Seattle, WA 98101; $$$; AE, DC, MC, V; checks OK.* &

Lake Union B&B ★★ Shoes off. If you don't have any socks, they're provided. Then sink into the white cloud of carpet and couches in this modern, three-story house near Gas Works Park, and enjoy a glass of wine by the fireplace. There are three rooms, each with TV, queen-size feather bed, and carefully ironed sheets. Upstairs, two stunning rooms offer Lake Union views. The larger suite also boasts a solarium, fireplace, Jacuzzi, and private bath—and is probably Seattle's finest *affordable* guest room. There's a sauna with piped-in music in the bathroom downstairs. Owner Janice Matthews, a former restaurateur, gladly prepares private dinners on request. The two-night minimum is often waived. ■ *3 blocks north of Gas Works Park; (206)547-9965; 2217 N 36th St, Seattle, WA 98103; $$; MC, V; checks OK.*

Mayflower Park Hotel ★★ Renovations have paid off at this handsome 1927 hotel right in the heart of the downtown shopping district. A coolly elegant lobby opens onto Oliver's (bar and lounge) on one side and Clipper's, one of the prettiest breakfast places in town, on the other. Rooms are small, still bearing charming reminders of the hotel's past: lovely Oriental brass and antique appointments; large, deep tubs; thick walls that trap noise. Modern intrusions are for both better and worse: double-glazed windows in all rooms keep out traffic noise, but there are undistinguished furnishings in many of the rooms. The deluxe rooms are slightly bigger and have corner views; aim for one on a higher floor or you may find yourself facing a brick wall. ▪ *4th and Olive; (206)623-8700; 405 Olive Way, Seattle, WA 98101; $$$; AE, DC, MC, V; checks OK.* ♿

Roberta's ★★ Roberta is the gracious, somewhat loquacious lady of this Capitol Hill house near Volunteer Park and a few blocks from the funky Broadway district. Inside it's lovely: refinished floors throughout, a comfortable blue couch and an old upright piano, books everywhere, and a large oval dining table and country-style chairs. Of the five rooms, the blue-toned Hideaway Suite (the entire third floor), with views of the Cascades from the window seats, skylights, a sitting area with a futon couch and a small desk, and a full bath with a tub, is our favorite. Others prefer the Peach Room with its antique desk, bay window, love seat, and queen-size oak bed. Early risers will enjoy the Madrona Room, with its morning sun and bath. All five rooms have queen-size beds; four have private baths. In the morning, Roberta brings you a wake-up cup of coffee, then later puts out a smashing full breakfast (no meat). No children. No smoking except on the porch. ▪ *16th Ave E north of Prospect; (206)329-3326; 1147 16th Ave E, Seattle, WA 98112; $$; AE, DC, MC, V; checks OK.*

Salisbury House ★★ A welcoming porch wraps around this big, bright Capitol Hill home, an exquisite hostelry neighboring Volunteer Park. Glossy maple floors and lofty beamed ceilings lend a sophisticated air to the guest library (with a chess table and a fireplace) and living room. Up the wide staircase and past the second-level sun porch are four guest rooms (one with a canopy bed, all with queen-size beds and down comforters) with full private baths. Breakfast is taken in the dining room or on the sunny terrace. Classy, dignified, nonsmoking, and devoid of children (under 12) and pets, the Salisbury is a sure bet in one of Seattle's finest neighborhoods. ▪ *E Aloha and 16th Ave E; (206)328-8682; 750 16th Ave E, Seattle, WA 98112; $$; AE, DC, MC, V; checks OK.*

Sheraton Seattle Hotel and Towers ★★ Seattle's Sheraton is an 840-room tower rising as a sleek triangle, the Convention Center in its shadow. It, too, aims at the convention business, so the rooms are smallish and standard, and much emphasis is placed on the meeting rooms and the restaurants. The Pike Street Cafe (formerly Banners) features sandwiches, pastas, and entrees with a Northwest bent (i.e., an overdose of salmon inspirations), plus a 27-foot-long dessert spread; Gooey's is the nightclub. The outstanding four-star restaurant, Fullers, is an oasis of serenity adorned with fine Northwest art (see review). Service is quite efficient. Convention facilities are complete, and the kitchen staff can handle the most complex assignments. Discriminating business travelers can head for the upper four "VIP" floors (31–34), where a hotel-within-a-hotel offers its own lobby, concierge, and considerably more amenities in the rooms (same size as economy). The top floors feature a health club and a private lounge with a knockout city panorama. You pay for parking. ■ *6th and Pike; (206)621-9000 or (800)204-6100; 1400 6th Ave, Seattle, WA 98101; $$$; AE, DC, MC, V; checks OK.* ♿

Stouffer Madison Hotel ★★ This large hotel at the southeast edge of downtown successfully conveys a sense of warmth and intimacy inside. The lobby, dressed in signature greens and peach, is tasteful and uncluttered, and upstairs hallways are softly lit. The rooms sport elegant marble countertops, coffered ceilings, and wood cabinetry. Extras include feather pillows, oversize towels, and morning papers. The pricey "Club Floors" (25 and 26) offer exclusive check-in privileges, concierge services, hors d'oeuvres and continental breakfast at Club Lounge, a library, and the best views (although views from most rooms are quite good). Comfortable conference facilities, parking (for a fee), free in-town transportation, and coffee delivered to your room each morning round out the offerings. Prego, on the 28th floor, offers a fine selection of seafood. ■ *6th and Madison; (206)583-0300; 515 Madison St, Seattle, WA 98104; $$$; AE, DC, MC, V; checks OK.* ♿

Capitol Hill Inn ★ One of the most conveniently located B&Bs in the city—within walking distance of the Convention Center and Broadway shops and restaurants (as long as you don't mind hills). Unfortunately, you give up any charm of a neighborhood for this convenience. The 1903 Queen Anne–style home itself is a lovely place run by pleasant mother/daughter team Katie and Joanne Godmintz, who restored the inn down to its custom-designed wall coverings, period chandeliers, and carved wooden moldings, sleigh and brass beds, and down-filled comforters. There are four rooms upstairs (two with full baths, two with toilets and sinks and a shower down the hall), and two rooms downstairs in the daylight basement (with private bath, fireplace, and Jacuzzi). The Godmintzes live on the third floor. ■ *Belmont and E Olive St; (206)323-1955; 1713 Belmont Ave, Seattle, WA 98122; $$; AE, MC, V; checks OK.*

Marriott Residence Inn—Lake Union ★ Lake Union's first full-scale hotel is not exactly on the lake, but across busy Fairview Avenue. Still, the 234 rooms, most of which boast lake views (request the north-facing rooms on the highest level possible), are decorated with touches of peach, mauve, and teal; the one-bedroom suites are spacious, but the studios feel cozier. All rooms have fully outfitted kitchenettes, and a continental breakfast is presented in the lobby—a light, plant-lined atrium with waterfall—or taken back to your room. There isn't a hotel restaurant, but guests can charge meals to their room at any number of lakeside eateries across the street. Amenities include five quiet meeting rooms, a lap pool, an exercise room, a sauna, and a spa. The nearby docks are a fun place to dream. ■ *Fairview and Boren, at the south end of Lake Union across from the marina; (206) 624-6000; 800 Fairview Ave N, Seattle, WA 98109; $$$; AE, DC, MC, V; checks OK.* ♿

MV Challenger ★ A luxury liner it's not, but if you've got a thing for tugboats, the boat-and-breakfast MV *Challenger*, Captain Jerry Brown's handsomely restored, 96-foot workhorse, is for you. Everything — from the spotless galley to the eight cabins — is shipshape. Lounge topside on a deck chair, or inside around the fireplace, or step out and explore the docks, restaurants, and shops just a stroll away. For utmost quiet and comfort, reserve one of the cabins on the tug's upper deck or consider renting space aboard one of two yachts moored alongside the tug (rates include an exceptional breakfast aboard the *Challenger*). We've all heard tales of notoriously temperamental sea captains, and though *his* boat rarely leaves its Lake Union dock, Captain Brown has been known to exercise that prerogative inappropriately. That said, we've ascertained that the majority of guests will find him a most gracious host. ■ *Yale St Landing; (206) 340-1201; 1001 Fairview Ave N, Seattle, WA 98109; $$; AE, MC, V; checks OK.*

WestCoast Camlin Hotel ★ Like many older hotels in Seattle, this 1926 grande dame has been remodeled and sound-proofed with double-glazed windows. (The elevator and the ventilation system, however, both hark back to an earlier era.) Though its conference facilities are limited, the Camlin appeals to the business traveler, with large rooms that have small sitting/work areas, spacious closets, and spotless bathrooms; those whose numbers end in 10 have windows on three sides. Avoid the cabanas (they're small and dreary and for smokers) and room service, which is quite slow. There's rooftop dining, and a piano bar in the Cloud Room, a retro-chic cocktail lounge favored by locals and out-of-towners. ■ *9th and Olive; (206) 682-0100; 1619 9th Ave, Seattle, WA 98101; $$; AE, DC, MC, V; checks OK.*

WestCoast Roosevelt Hotel ★ Gone is the grand skylit lobby that so distinguished the Roosevelt when it first opened its doors in 1930; the space is now inhabited by Von's Restaurant. The new lobby is low-ceilinged and cramped, but elsewhere the WestCoast installation has somewhat preserved the Roosevelt's art deco sensibilities. The hotel's 20 stories have been redivided for the contemporary traveler, but studios are still almost comically small. The deluxe rooms are a better choice, with adjoining sitting areas; the 13 suites each boast a Jacuzzi and a separate sitting area. Nine floors are nonsmoking. Considering the hotel's proximity to the Convention Center and the shopping district, the Roosevelt's prices—$95 to $170—are decent, but the service could be more polished. ■ *7th and Pine; (206)621-1200; 1531 7th Ave, Seattle, WA 98101; $$$; AE, DC, MC, V; checks OK.* &

The Williams House ★ In its 91-year history, this south-slope Queen Anne residence has been a gentlemen's boardinghouse and an emergency medical clinic for the 1962 Seattle World's Fair. Owners Doug and Sue Williams offer five guest rooms, four with views and two with private baths. The enclosed south sun porch is a nice gathering spot. Brass beds, original fixtures, fireplaces, ornate Italian tiles, and oak floors mirror the home's Edwardian past. A full breakfast is served in the first-floor dining room. Children are welcome by prior arrangement. ■ *Galer and 4th N; (206)285-0810 or (800)880-0810; 1505 4th Ave N, Seattle, WA 98109; $$; AE, DC, MC, V; checks OK.*

The College Inn Guest House With the glorious grounds of the University of Washington practically at your doorstep, you can excuse a little noise (there's a cafe and pub on the premises) and the dormlike quality of the toilet and bathing facilities (separate-sex, rows of showers, down the hall). Housed in the upper three floors of a renovated 1909 Tudor building that's on the National Register of Historic Places, the College Inn is devoid of TV, radio, and in-room phones. Each of the 25 rooms offers a sink, a desk, and a single or double bed. The best of the lot even has window seats. A generous continental breakfast (included in the bargain rates) is served upstairs in the communal living area. ■ *40th and University Way; (206)633-4441; 4000 University Way NE, Seattle, WA 98105; $; MC, V; checks OK.*

GREATER SEATTLE: EDMONDS

The area thought of as Edmonds is just a small village in a much larger area. "Downtown Edmonds" is a throwback to another era with a small movie theater, friendly shopkeepers, wide sidewalks, and waterfront views that encourage evening strolls through town. The ferry departs to Kingston; for information, call (206)464-6400. Edmonds bills itself as the City of Celebrations. Most popular are the **Edmonds Art Festival** (in June) and **A Taste of Edmonds** (third weekend in August).

Brackett's Landing, just north of the ferry terminal, has a jetty and an offshore underwater marine-life park that draws lots of scuba divers. **Edmonds Historic Walk** was prepared by the Centennial Committee and offers a look at old Edmonds. Stop by the Chamber of Commerce, 120 N Fifth Avenue, (206)776-6711, for a free map of the walk.

RESTAURANTS

Chanterelle Specialty Foods ★★ Perhaps better known for breakfast, lunch, and baked goods, casual and kitchen-

confident Chanterelle really shines at dinner, when owner/
chef Denise Linn pulls together a list of nightly specials reflecting an ethnically diverse—and exceptionally well-executed
—range. In addition to a couple of salads and sandwiches and
a killer black-bean burrito, the regular dinner menu features a
half dozen pastas (terrific salads included) in the $10 range.
But locals in the know clamor for the specials—among them
handmade seafood pot-stickers, enormous slabs of sausage-
laden lasagne, and artfully sauced lamb shanks. The mashed
potatoes here are *better* than your mother's. Breakfast,
presided over by Linn's husband, Russ Cluff, is a delightful affair (waffle-lovers should opt for the light, orange-flavored cornmeal waffles). Well-meaning service can prove slow when it's
busy—and it usually is, since this '70s fern-deli-meets-cozy-
bistro is clearly the best restaurant in town. ▪ *Up from ferry
terminal, on Main; (206) 774-0650; 316 Main St, Edmonds;
$; beer and wine; MC, V; checks OK; breakfast, lunch every
day, dinner Tues–Sat.*

Ciao Italia ★★ New owner Patrick Girardi, an earnest young
restaurateur if ever there was one, recently bought this Edmonds favorite from his former employer, Gino Boriello (who
still owns Seattle's Ciao Bella—and just opened Isabella Ris-

torante in Seattle at press time). Ciao Italia's strip-mall location
aside, the pleasant atmosphere—at once candlelit and casual—
works to fine effect. The menu is full of Italian meat and pasta
standards done in better-than-standard fashion. Make sure
someone at the table orders the simple, elegant pizza
margherita, and order pastas off the specials list, which here
always seems to yield the best efforts of the chef. Dinners come
with boring-but-complimentary salads; meat dishes include
outstanding grilled vegetables. ▪ *In the shopping center, south
of 5th and Walnut; (206) 771-7950; 546 5th Ave S, Edmonds;
$; beer and wine; MC, V; local checks OK; dinner Mon–Sat.*

Provinces Asian Restaurant & Bar ★★ Years ago, Asian fare
was either Chinese, Japanese, Cambodian, or Vietnamese. The
thought of a pan-Asian restaurant was too much for monoethnic eaters. Today, such culinary journeys actually work surprisingly so in this suburban, monoethnic town where serene
Edmondites dine in an attractive, dimly lit dining room set in
a quaint shopping mall. We like the friendly, efficient service,
the dish of sweet-and-spicy broccoli stems brought to the table
gratis, and the Bangkok Hot and Sour Soup—served in a clay
pot brimming with large prawns, bay shrimp, fresh scallops,
and straw mushrooms, fragrant with lemon grass, and large
enough to feed four. The Cantonese-style seafood lobster sauce
is dense with shellfish and vegetables and flavored with salty
Chinese black beans. A huge portion of Mongolian ginger beef
(at a diminutive $8.25), is a touch sweet but pleasantly potent

with ginger and garlic. The adjoining cocktail lounge—where the after-work crowd meets to bend an elbow, smoke a cigarette, and make merry—is decidedly more boisterous, though that doesn't seem to affect the green-tea teetotalers in the dining room. ▪ *In upper level of Old Mill Town Mall at 5th and Maple; (206) 744-0288; 201 5th Ave S, Edmonds; $$; full bar; AE, DC, MC, V; local checks only; lunch Mon–Sat, dinner every day.* ⟨

LODGINGS

Edmonds Harbor Inn ★ Strategically located near the Edmonds ferry and train terminals, the inn is an attractive choice for a night in this charming, waterside Seattle suburb. It features 61 large rooms (with views, unfortunately, of the surrounding business park rather than the picturesque Sound), oak furnishings, continental breakfast, and access to an athletic club just next door. If you're traveling with youngsters in tow, the rooms with modern kitchenettes, coupled with the inn's extremely reasonable rates, will be particularly appealing. Get directions—the place is near the harborfront, but is a little difficult to find in the gray sea of new office and shopping developments. ▪ *Dayton and Edmonds Way; (206) 771-5021; 130 W Dayton St, Edmonds, WA 98020; $$; AE, DC, MC, V; checks OK.* ⟨

GREATER SEATTLE: BOTHELL

The town stands at the north end of Lake Washington, on the way into more open country. **Sammamish River Park** is a pleasant spot, and from here you can take a 9.5-mile hike, bike ride, or rollerskating tour along the Sammamish River (often called the Sammamish Slough), stopping part of the way at the Ste. Michelle winery for a picnic; food and wine can be purchased at the winery (see Woodinville).

RESTAURANTS

Gerard's Relais de Lyon ★★★ If you do something special and you do it well, chances are you will endure, and the world will be a better place for having you. If not the world, definitely Bothell. Enter Gerard Parrat, whose outpost and bastion of French cuisine still offers—after twenty years—a last great hope for lovers of fine, formal dining. Choose from the two prix-fixe menus, the découverte (discovery menu, six courses) or dégustation (tasting menu, seven courses), and you're in for a culinary feast lasting two to three hours. The back room of this multiroom converted house is our choice, since cigarette smoke can drift from the middle to the front room. Better even than the warming gas fireplaces is the lovely courtyard out back. Service is friendly and the food consistently superb. A meal might begin with a thin slice of Cognac pâté brought before the first course. From there the meal proceeds through sublime roast garlic soup, a roulade of marinated vegetables, and a sausage-filled ravioli in duck consommé; moves onward to duck in a dark orange sauce and past a palate-freshening salad; and heads finally into a Grand Marnier soufflé. One could faint from sheer delight and volume. Fortunately, you *can* order à la carte if you plan to eat again sometime during the coming week. ■ *Just inside Bothell city limits, north of Seattle; (206) 485-7600; 17121 Bothell Way NE, Bothell; $$$; full bar; AE, DC, MC, V; checks OK; dinner Tues–Sun.* &

GREATER SEATTLE: WOODINVILLE

The suburbs have caught up with this formerly rural outback, paving the dirt roads and lining them with strip malls. Some of the country ambience remains, however, especially to the east where Woodinville fades into the dairy farms of the Snoqualmie Valley. Woodinville's claim to fame is **Chateau Ste. Michelle**, the state's largest winery. The grapes come from Eastern Washington, but experimental vineyards are on-site, and tours of the operation, complete with tastings, run daily every half hour between 10am and 5pm; 14111 NE 145th, (206) 488-1133. Just across the street from Ste. Michelle is **Columbia Winery**, the state's oldest premium-wine company. Columbia offers tours on weekends between 10am and 4pm, and the tasting room is open daily from 10am to 7pm; 14030 NE 145th, (206) 488-2776.

Gardeners from around the region flock to **Molbak's**, the massive nursery and greenhouse at 13625 NE 175th, (206) 483-5000.

Woodinville also carries a leg of the **Sammamish River Trail**, a paved path that runs along the river from Bothell to Marymoor Park in Redmond.

RESTAURANTS

Italianissimo ★★ By now a Seattle legend, Luciano Bardinelli found fame with Settebello in Seattle, impossible rent at Stresa on the Kirkland waterfront, and perhaps the perfect, lasting niche in this unlikely suburban location. Here, he consistently exceeds expectations in a relaxed, casual atmosphere that attracts more families than ultra-discerning foodies. There's a country-kitchen feel here, from the green-and-cream tiled floors to the greeneried patio. The service tends toward casual and the menu looks familiar to those who know Bardinelli—thin-crust pizzas, simple pastas (paglia e fieno, capellini with tomatoes and basil), and meats (a preponderance of veal, which is not a bad thing, considering the delicate preparation of a barely sweet, spicy Marsala and a powerfully rich osso bucco Milanese). The calamari stew is spicy and satisfying.

Antipasti and desserts are temptingly on view as you enter. A second Italianissimo (3701 NE 45th, (206)524-7331) recently opened in Seattle. ■ *At the corner of 140th and 175th; (206)485-6888; 17650 140th NE, Woodinville; $$; beer and wine; AE, DC, MC, V; checks OK; lunch, dinner every day.* &

Armadillo Barbecue ★ Leave refinement in the glove compartment when you enter this West Texas barbecue joint plopped down in the wilds of Woodinville. "Ya just can't use enough disinfectant on these tables," claim owners Bob and Bruce Gill, wielding a garden sprayer. The brothers serve up their own brand of perverse humor as a regular side dish along with tender, lean pork and extra-moist chicken, all thoroughly and powerfully smoked, with a rich hot-sauce tang and sides of molasses-heavy beans and cakey corn bread. It all adds up to a fine Texas feast. Sit at the counter and you can jaw with cooks—all schooled in rapid repartee—sip one of 40 beers, and order a "Snake Plate," which gives you "three bucks worth o' stuff," for $4. Salads won't convert anyone to vegetarianism. The massive oven/smoker, right behind the counter, cannot seem to contain all the smoke it produces, so customers usually go home lightly smoked outside as well as in. ■ *Take Woodinville exit from 522E; (206)481-1417; 13109 NE 175th St, Woodinville; $; beer and wine; AE, MC, V; checks OK; lunch, dinner every day.* &

GREATER SEATTLE: MALTBY

RESTAURANTS

Maltby Cafe ★★ Upstairs, Maltby School gymnasium, a 1937 WPA project, remains as it was. Downstairs, in what used to be the school cafeteria, the Maltby Cafe dishes up outstanding country breakfasts and equally satisfying lunches. Finding the place the first time might be tough, but you'll never forget the way. A Saturday morning repast can fill you for the weekend. Unhurried, bountiful breakfasts feature delicious omelets—the Maltby is a huge affair, stuffed with more than a cup of assorted veggies, ham cubes, even pieces of roast beef—good new potatoes, old-fashioned oatmeal, and thick slices of French toast. If you have to wait for a table (which is usually the case on weekends), order one of the legendary giant cinnamon rolls, then savor it on the steps outside. At lunch, the cafe offers great sandwiches and soups (try a Reuben, made with their own corned beef). ■ *From Hwy 405, go 4½ miles east (toward Monroe) on Hwy 522, turn left at the first light onto Maltby Rd, take a right, and then a left onto 212th St SE; (206)483-3123; 8809 212 St SE, Maltby Rd, Maltby; $; beer and wine; MC, V; checks OK; breakfast, lunch every day.* &

It may be known for its corporate top gun, **Microsoft**, but this city at the north end of Lake Sammamish is also the hub of a lot of local (and national) cycling activity. Every summer at the **Marymoor Velodrome**, the country's best bicyclists gather for the U.S. Track Cycling Championships in **Marymoor Park**. On the north shore of Lake Sammamish, the park is a huge expanse of ball fields and semi-wild grassland that makes for great bird-watching. On weekends, hundreds of dog owners bring their pets to the vast and legally leashless dog run in the fields along the Sammamish River. Less ambitious peddlers enjoy the **Sammamish River Trail**, which runs north along the river.

Redmond's downtown is a traditional suburban amalgamation of strip malls and shopping centers, but Anglophiles should stop for afternoon tea at the **British Pantry**; 8125 161st Avenue NE, (206)883-7511.

RESTAURANTS

Redmond

Restaurants

Il Bacio ★★ The skills of chef Rino Baglio, whose list of credentials runs longer than uncut linguine (he helped prepare the wedding feast for Chuck and Di, and cooked for Princess Caroline of Monaco), deserve a far grander setting and far better seating than this faux-Italian patio in a strip mall. But once you fork into a luscious risotto laden with bits of sausage and porcini mushrooms, or the cappellini all'aragosta (featuring not exactly the advertised lobster tail, but a close crustacean relative, the langoustine) sauced with an intensely flavorful demiglace of lemon, rosemary, and garlic, it won't matter where you are. Baglio's beautifully rendered Italian specialties go a long way toward striking the mood. The creamy tomato-basil soup starts things right, and you'd be foolish not to leave room for dessert, which comes from Baglio's nifty little adjacent Pasticcerie Il Bacio. ■ *Downtown Redmond, on the main eastbound drag; (206)869-8815; 16564 Cleveland St, Redmond; $$; beer and wine; MC, V; local checks only; lunch and dinner Mon–Fri, dinner only Sat.* ᕦ

Kikuya ★★ Though it is tucked away in an unprepossessing strip mall, enough people find their way to this small, informal eatery to make a wait at lunchtime likely. No tatami rooms, no kimonos, just good, straightforward fare prepared well and efficiently served. The excellent sushi bar provides visual entertainment. Watch as the cooks turn out reliable tempura, good gyoza, dependable donburi, spicy yakisoba, and fresh sashimi. Meals come with pickled cucumbers, miso, a small salad, and green tea. ■ *Off Kirkland-Redmond Hwy on 161st NE; (206)881-8771; 8105 161st Ave NE, Redmond; $$; beer and wine; MC, V; no checks; lunch, dinner Tues–Sat.* ᕦ

Big Time Pizza ★ In the face of Big Competition, Big Time maintains its hold on the top spot in byte-land. Even if the pizzas were not so good, built on a rich, flavorful crust from hand-tossed dough with multiethnic toppings, we would go there for the 20-something wines offered by the glass. There are plenty of beers on tap as well. Our faves remain the Pesto Plus (with fontina, sun-dried tomatoes, mushrooms, artichoke hearts, and pesto) and the Greek Pizza (feta, kalamata olives, Roma tomatoes, green peppers, and oregano). Best is Big Time's attention to unusually savory toppings: cappocolla, chorizo, blue cheese, Montrachet, portobello mushrooms. The calzone oozes mozzarella, encased in a deliciously chewy, handmade crust. A few pan-tossed pastas and green salads round out the menu. ■ *Leary Way and W Lake Sammamish; (206)885-6425; 7281 W Lake Sammamish Pkwy NE, Redmond; $; beer and wine; MC, V; checks OK; lunch, dinner every day.*

GREATER SEATTLE: KIRKLAND

This city's comfortable downtown on Lake Washington's Moss Bay is a popular summer strolling ground. Art galleries, restaurants, bookstores, and boutiques line the two-story main street. Several restaurants look out over boats docked at the marina. Grab a muffin and coffee at Triple J's, 101 Central Way, (206)822-7319, a storefront coffee shop, and walk a block to the recently renovated waterfront park, where ducks beg scraps and dodge children on the sandy beach.

On Yarrow Bay at the south end of town lies **Carillon Point,** a glitzy hotel and shopping complex lining a round, red-brick courtyard with views of the lake and the Olympic Mountains in the distance.

To the north, just outside of Kirkland, at **Saint Edward State Park,** spectacular rolling trails amble through old stands of Douglas fir and Western red cedar, eventually winding up on the lakefront.

RESTAURANTS

Cafe Juanita ★★★ This converted creekside house hasn't changed much since Peter Dow opened it in 1979. Inside, it's small and unpretentious, with a few etchings and many, many wine bottles by way of decor. There's no printed menu, just the daily offerings on blackboards (spiedini misti, pollo pistacchi, agnello verdure, anitra con arugula, pasta puttanesca), and servers must rattle off detailed explanations to nodding, short-term–memory-challenged diners — "Now, what were those first three things you said?" Once over that hurdle, it's an easy, consistently pleasurable glide through dinner. The legion of regulars don't even need help deciding among the country-Italian offerings: about half the menu items have been there off-and-on for a decade and more. Dow's presence has kept this ship sailing calm waters over the years, though these days, head chef John Neumark is handling things in the kitchen, putting *his* new mark on Dow's tried-and-true menu. Meanwhile, Dow keeps busy schmoozing diners, dispensing his own wines (Cavatappi sauvignon blanc, cabernet sauvignon, or Maddalena), and only occasionally stepping into the small open kitchen. ■ *116th off I-405, west to 97th; (206) 823-1505; 9702 NE 120th Pl, Kirkland; $$; full bar; MC, V; checks OK; dinner every day.* &

Bistro Provencal ★★ The most dramatic change since Philippe Gayte opened this place in 1973 has been its name. Le Provencal is now Bistro Provencal, and name change or *non*, you won't find a more reliable restaurant on the Eastside. The cozy, country-inn atmo remains, as does the creaky old dessert tray, which could have served napoleons to Napoleon. You're likely to be waited on by one whose native tongue is French and whose service may prove erratic, lacking some attention to detail, but the food has been, is, and probably always will be well worth a minor inconvenience. The menu emphasis is bistro, with a terrific $21.50 four-course prix-fixe meal. Begin with a full and flavorful onion soup, followed by a good crisp salad with a sprinkling of goat cheese. Among the five main-course selections is the Daube Avignonnaise, a very simple, very good Provençal-style beef stew that chef Gayte has been preparing since the day his restaurant opened. Other options might include rabbit stew, steak au poivre, or duck breast with blackberries. You can also choose from more upscale items on the à la carte menu. Or try the deluxe, prix-fixe "menu gastronomie" at $34.50 for five courses. ■ *Downtown Kirkland; (206) 827-3300; 212 Central Wy, Kirkland; $$; full bar; AE, DC, MC, V; local checks OK; dinner every day.* &

Kirkland

Restaurants

Izumi ★★ Tucked into taco-and-burger land in a Kirkland shopping center, Izumi is a favorite among the local Japanese community. Part the dark blue half-curtain inside the front door, and suburbia is left behind; you're in the competent care of servers in traditional sea green kimonos. Things move briskly at lunch, when Japanese families sometimes mingle with the business crowd. (Lunch hours are 11:30am to 1:30pm, and they mean it. If you linger past 2pm, you're likely to realize that the background music has just stopped mid-phase. It's not brusque, just to the point.) Unagi (broiled freshwater eel) and mirugai (geoduck) sushi are outstanding; roe enthusiasts can sample the eggs of four different sea creatures. Tonkatsu, pork cutlet in a light, crisp breading, is juicy, tender, and generously portioned. For those who tread lightly into Japanese cuisine, the tempura crust is exceedingly light and the teriyaki excellent—and not overly sweet. Makunouchi can be had at lunch, or in two sizes at dinner—the larger a feast of sushi, sashimi, tempura, teriyaki, and cooked vegetables presented in a lacquer box. Wash everything down with a big Asahi beer. ▪ *Totem Lake West Shopping Center; (206)821-1959; 12539 116th Ave NE, Kirkland; $$; beer, wine, and sake; AE, MC, V; checks OK; lunch Mon–Fri, dinner every day.* ♿

Ristorante Paradiso ★★ Owner/chef Fabrizio Loi's labor of love, just off Kirkland's main drag, is a surprisingly sophisticated culinary treat in unpretentious digs. Much of the menu remains constant from the 1991 debut. Openers include a beautifully arranged plate of grilled vegetables for two, or a generous bowl of fresh, perfectly cooked mussels and clams in a wine-based broth so good you'll scoop up every drop. There's a range of meat dishes, including a delicate saltimbocca, and a long list of pastas. We like the cannelloni gratinati—lovely pasta crêpes stuffed with a delicate mix of ground veal, chicken, and mozzarella served with two sauces (one red, one white). A great selection of wines, featuring many Italian labels, priced from the mid-teens and up. ▪ *Off Lake Washington St, across from Moss Bay; (206)889-8601; 120 A Park Lane, Kirkland; $$; beer and wine; AE, DC, MC, V; local checks only; lunch Mon–Sat, dinner every day.* ♿

Shamiana ★★ Shamiana stands out among ethnic restaurants on the Eastside, often winning "best-of" polls. Brother-and-sister team Eric and Tracy Larson grew up as foreign service kids in East Pakistan (now Bangladesh), and after their return to the United States found themselves hankering for the food they remembered. Now Eric's in the kitchen, Tracy runs the front of the house, and their mother, Nancy (Memsahib) Larson, oversees the operation. Eastern cooking meets Western chefs here in the happiest of ways: stunning creations include a velvet butter chicken wallowing in cumin-scented butter, tomato, and cream sauce. A Pakistani barbecue turns out flame-broiled meats and some mouth-watering (and mouth-igniting) versions of traditional Indian curries. Vegetarians can select from crisp samosas stuffed with crunchy potatoes or aloo dum Kashmiri, potatoes simmered in spicy yogurt sauce. Instructively, the menu notes which dishes are made without dairy products and gives a heat guide to ordering curries. Dinner may top $20, but lunch is bargain city, with a buffet that changes daily. ▪ *In the Houghton Village at 108th and 68th; (206)827-4902; 10724 NE 68th St, Kirkland; $; beer and wine; AE, DC, MC, V; checks OK; lunch Mon–Fri, dinner every day.* ♿

Yarrow Bay Grill and Beach Cafe ★★ There are two restaurants here, one on top of another, each with a gorgeous Lake Washington view. Originally intended to be an Eastside version of Ray's Boathouse in Shilshole (three of the four Ray's owners started Yarrow Bay), these siblings have evolved over five years into fine, unique dining spots. Chefs have come and gone; quality has dropped and soared. Most recently, with the return of chef Vicki McCaffree, the upstairs grill is better than ever. A piece of fresh Atlantic salmon could not have been more perfectly done, steamed in sake and ginger, and topped with a sesame-kissed shiitake-ginger-butter sauce. Half the entree menu comes from the sea, with such Pacific Rim touches as an appetizer of tea-smoked duck with kim chee, or a Thai-style crab cake. All this is complemented by a deep wine list and plenty of wines by the glass.

Downstairs, the cafe is lively. Knock a few bucks off the upstairs prices and sample a jazzed-up, United Nations menu, with Moroccan chicken, Cajun-fried rock shrimp, or selections from the country-of-the-month. Competition from neighboring Cucina! Cucina! hasn't hurt the "scene" here the least bit. ▪ *In the Carillon Point Plaza, downtown Kirkland; (206)889-9052 (Yarrow Bay Grill) or (206)889-0303 (Beach Cafe); 1270 Carillon Point, Kirkland; $$$; full bar; AE, DC, MC, V; local checks only; lunch, dinner every day.* ♿

Cafe Veloce ★ Amidst decor celebrating the golden age of Italian motorcycle racing, Cafe Veloce delivers intermediate pasta and pizzas for fledgling connoisseurs on spaghetti-and-meatball budgets. For creativity and quality, it beats its bargain-basement pasta-price competitors, like Olive Garden, hands-down. Entrees arrive quickly, thanks to an efficient kitchen, the pastas attractively presented on oversize platters flecked with chopped basil. The Pasta Muffaletta is inspired by the New Orleans sandwich, with a black olive compote and pieces of ham and salami sautéed with penne and olive oil. Pasta Portofino features baby clams and mushrooms, lots of garlic, a little T-sauce, and a couple of fresh basil leaves tossed in for a burst of flavor. Crisp-crusted pizzas include quattro formaggi and clam Victoria. Owner Todd Fell's collection of vintage Italian racing motorcycles are just for looks, not for delivery. ▪ *A block south of the Totem Lake Cinemas on 120th Ave NE; (206)814-2972; 12514 120th Ave NE, Kirkland; $; AE, DC, MC, V; checks OK; lunch, dinner every day, breakfast Sat–Sun.* ♿

Third Floor Fish Cafe ★ For either casual or special–occasion dining, the Third Floor is the place. It's a handsome spot, with varnished dark woods and accents in shades of vermilion, orange, aqua, and yellow. The room is laid out to take advantage of the panoramic view of Lake Washington and Seattle. Too bad the kitchen has long been inconsistent—one minute turning out yummy little crab cakes with a complex corn relish, artfully served on a fish-pattern plate, the next minute slinging a tender piece of mahi with the clumpiest of rice and blandest of veggies. Then the kitchen again soars, executing a superb daily special of mild, sweet monkfish in a flavorful lobster sauce. The best plan is to stick to the basics and trust that the fish will be delicious. The bar is great for grazing, and there's a small banquet room with a bit of a view. ■ *In downtown Kirkland, above the Yacht Club; (206) 822-3553; 205 Lake St, Kirkland; $$$; full bar; AE, DC, MC, V; local checks only; lunch Mon–Fri, dinner Mon–Sat.* ♿

LODGINGS

Woodmark Hotel ★★★ On the eastern shore of Lake Washington, this hotel claims the only lodging actually on the lake. From the outside, it resembles a modern office building, but on the inside one encounters the soft touches of a fine hotel: 100 plush rooms (the best have lake views and sounds of geese honking and ducks quacking) with fully stocked minibars and refrigerators, VCRs (complimentary movies are available at the front desk), terrycloth robes, oversize towels, and service (from laundry to valet) to match. You'll get a complimentary newspaper with the full breakfast. Downstairs on the lake level there's a comfortable living room with a grand piano and well-tended fire. The hotel has its own clubby restaurant, the Carillon Room, with a menu that leans toward escargots and rack of lamb; seafood is the main event next door at the Yarrow Bay Grill and Beach Cafe (see review). Check out the nearby specialty shops or rent a boat from the marina. Business travelers can take advantage of extra amenities such as a pager for off-site calls, a cellular phone, and complimentary use of a laptop computer and printer. Parking access is a bit of a maze. ■ *Kirkland exit off SR 520, north on Lake Washington Blvd NE to Carillon Point; (206) 822-3700; 1200 Carillon Point, Kirkland, WA 98033; $$$; AE, DC, MC, V; checks OK.* ♿

Shumway Mansion ★★ When Richard and Salli Harris heard that developers wanted to demolish this historic 1909 building to make room for condos, they hauled the four-story house to a safe location near Kirkland's Juanita Bay. Now it's a gracious bed and breakfast with an equal emphasis on seminars and receptions. Seven guest rooms are furnished with antiques (an eighth room was being completed at press time), and public rooms overlook the bay (just a short walk away) and the lower parking lots. The ballroom downstairs is often used for weddings or special meetings, opening onto a flowering patio in summer. A full breakfast is served in the dining room on table linens. Guests can use the Columbia Athletic Club a block away for no charge. Children over 12 are welcome. No pets or smoking. ■ *Near NE 116th on 99th Pl NE; (206) 823-2303; 11410 99th Pl NE, Kirkland, WA 98033; $$; AE, MC, V; checks OK.* ♿

This erstwhile hamlet is developing into a sister city of Seattle, boasting its own downtown skyline. Bellevue is the heart of the Eastside—the former suburbs of Seattle, east of Lake Washington—that now stand on their own. As many commuters now leave Seattle in the morning for work on the Eastside as make the traditional suburb-to-Seattle trek.

At the core of downtown Bellevue is **Bellevue Place**, a hotel, restaurant, and shopping complex. Daniel's Broiler on the 21st floor of the Seafirst Office Building offers stunning views of Seattle, Puget Sound, and the Olympics.

Across the street, **Bellevue Square** hosts Nordstrom and hundreds of other stores, but it's also one of the first malls in the country to house a museum—the **Bellevue Art Museum**, specializing in Northwest crafts, (206) 454-6021.

Much of what makes Bellevue such a livable city are the quiet neighborhoods that ring downtown. The neighborhood surrounding **Bridle Trails State Park** on the Kirkland border looks like a condensed version of Virginia equestrian country, with backyards of horses and stables. The park features miles of riding and hiking trails through vast stands of Douglas fir. Day hikers can head east toward Issaquah to explore **Cougar Mountain**, the forested, westernmost hill of an ancient mountain range that stretches from Lake Washington to the younger Cascades.

▼

Bellevue

Restaurants

▲

RESTAURANTS

Azalea's Fountain Court ★★ There is no more romantic dining spot in Bellevue than Azalea's. On weekends, live jazz accompanies dinner; in summer, the courtyard—complete with small fountain—beckons. Any time, the dining room's country/continental ambience provides a warm backdrop for chef Dan Sullivan's seasonal menus. Bites of lamb shank in spring, for instance, zing with the tangy capers, artichokes, and tomatoes. Flaws are few and small—a lunchtime chicken sandwich with shiitakes and havarti offered a strenuous jaw workout, due to overzealously toasted bread. Count on sophisticated service and delicious housemade sorbets and ice creams (try the cinnamon!). ■ *Off Main St on 103rd Ave NE; (206) 451-0426; 22 103rd NE, Bellevue; $$$; full bar; AE, MC, V; checks OK; lunch Tues–Fri, dinner Mon–Sat.* &

Sea Garden of Bellevue ★★ Long a favorite in the International District, known for its subtle Mandarin flavors and consistently excellent seafood, the Sea Garden moved east in 1994 in a big way. Rather than move into used digs, as do many of the Seattle eateries branching into Bellevue and the Eastside, the owners, an extended family, built from the ground up. It's not a grand place, but it is smart and bright. Near the door, live tanks teem with crab, spot prawns, and lobster. Hanging for display in the meat case are, variously, slabs of barbecue beef and pork, ducks, and sometimes even a whole roast pig. The savory barbecue pork surpasses the usual, standard-issue stuff, and heavenly seafood preparations often lift the spirits. Choose lobster or crab and they'll bring it snapping mad in a bucket to your table for inspection. The next time you see that fella, he's going to be perfectly turned out, chopped into tender pieces and served with a consistently finger-lickin' black bean sauce or a refreshing ginger and green onion sauce. Big, succulent sea scallops populate a plate along with honey-glazed walnuts. Naturally sweet spot prawns on wooden skewers burst with flavor. The extensive menu offers plenty of vegetarian options, plus exotics like jellyfish, sea cucumber, or fish maw. Service ranges from adequate to exasperating. ■ *Downtown Bellevue; (206)450-8833; 200 106th Ave NE, Bellevue; $$; full bar; AE, DC, MC, V; no checks; lunch, dinner every day.* &

Mediterranean Kitchen ★ You can practically whiff the garlic in Bel Square, just a couple of blocks up Bellevue Way from the Mediterranean Kitchen. This Eastside version of the lower Queen Anne original serves up Middle Eastern fare powered by the owner's belief in the healthful as well as gustatory properities of this edible bulb. Since the original's 1980 opening, Kamal Aboul Hosn claims to have served over a million of the chicken wings marinated in vinegar and slathered with roasted garlic, just like the ones his grandfather first made in Lebanon. The shawarma (chicken or beef) come balanced by the flavors and textures of grilled onions, green peppers, and tomatoes, served with tahini sauce. Vegetarians can trust the hummus, baba ghanouj, Lebanese Labnie, and tabouli. The food is authentic Middle Eastern, even if the digs aren't much more impressive than when this used to be a one-hour photo shop. ■ *Two blocks south of Bel Square on Bellevue Way; (206)462-9422; 103 Bellevue Way NE, Bellevue; $; beer and wine; AE, DC, MC, V; no checks; lunch Tue–Fri, dinner Tue–Sun.* &

Noble Court ★ During the week, when it's not so crowded, request one of the tables lining the windows looking out on the small creek—and you're less likely to notice the worn interior and slightly uncomfortable seating. The menu ranges from standard kung pao and fried rice to the more exotic shark-fin soup, stewed abalone, and bird's nest with crabmeat soup. Live tanks at the entrance display fish and crustaceans ready for a little black bean sauce. The restaurant is a favorite with the Eastside's growing Chinese population, who show up on weekends for what many consider to be the best dim sum on either side of the Lake Washington bridges. Expect to wait up to an hour. Noble Court now does dim sum during the week as well, though the

**▼
Bellevue**

Restaurants

▲

range of selections is somewhat limited and the ambience can't match those weekend feeding frenzies. ■ *Off Bellevue-Redmond Rd; (206)641-6011; 1644 140th NE, Bellevue; $$; full bar; AE, MC, V; no checks; lunch, dinner every day.* &

Pogacha ★ A pogacha is about the only thing that's escaped from Croatia intact lately. Properly speaking, a pogacha is a chewy Croatian dinner roll baked in a wood-fired oven. Here at this rather stark little eatery, the cooks stretch the dough to make what would look, to the uninitiated, like pizza. They're thin, flavorful, and topped with ingredients that only a few years ago sounded darned exotic (a simple mix of garlic oil, feta, and red onion makes a zingy, zesty pie). Order the Four Seasons for a sampling of four pogachas topped, individually, with artichokes, mushroom and pesto, five cheeses, and tomato and basil (red sauce upon request). There are usually a half dozen pasta dishes, such as the Croatian Cousins, a dish of calamari and shrimp served over cappellini and dressed with a light, garlicky tomato sauce. There's no compelling reason to go beyond basic pasta and pogacha, though a couple of serviceable meat dishes—especially the skewered marinated lamb—aren't bad. ■ *In Bellevue Plaza near 106th NE and Main St; (206)455-5670; 119 106th Ave NE, Bellevue; $; beer and wine; AE, MC, V; no checks; lunch Mon–Fri, dinner Tues–Sat.* &

Seoul Olympic Restaurant ★ Some of the best Korean food in the Seattle area is in a nondescript office complex in Bellevue. There are plenty of choices only a Korean would love, which might explain why they don't even bother to translate some of these on the menu. If you ask, the server might short-circuit your interest, dismissing an entry as "too hot," "not cooked," or simply, "you won't like that one." But if you're the adventuresome type, go for it, and check out a plate of steaming tubular animal innards. Or try the Korean barbecued beef (steeped in a simple marinade of soy sauce, sugar, and wine), or crispy dumplings, or even the salad bar selections, which include a pungent kim chee. ■ *At the corner of NE 12th and 112th NE; (206)455-9305; 1200 112th Ave NE, Bellevue; $$; full bar; AE, MC, V; local checks only; lunch, dinner every day.*

Spazzo ★ The top floor of a glass-and-steel bank building is about as unlikely a place as you'll find for a rustic Mediterranean restaurant. Yet that is the pervasive theme at the oddly named Spazzo (an unfortunate corruption of *spasso*—"fun" in Italian). A showy creation of the Schwartz Brothers dynasty, Spazzo features a menu that supposedly draws from everywhere the olive tree grows, though these days (judging by dinner entrees) it seems to grow mostly in Italy. Other regions are represented mostly in the tapas menu, the restaurant's best feature. You can make a meal of these appetizer-size delights,

▼

Bellevue

Restaurants

▲

everybody ordering two or three, then swapping around. The Med spreads—including baba ghanouj, hummus, whipped feta, taramasalta, and tapenade—are outstanding. Entrees can be adventuresome or just plain tiresome (like the Moroccan lamb couscous—overdone lamb, artichoke hearts warring with cilantro, plus mouthfuls of annoying little unpitted olives). ■ *Downtown Bellevue; (206) 454-8255; 10655 NE 4th, Bellevue; $$; full bar; AE, DC, MC, V; checks OK; lunch Mon–Fri, dinner every day.* &

Tosoni's ★ To its many loyal regulars, it's known as Walter's Place. They know that the humble, strip-mall exterior belies the Old World delights awaiting inside, where chef Walter Walcher and a sous chef work the open kitchen, presiding over a small booth-lined room filled with antique cabinets and armoires. Vegetarians appreciate the porcini risotto and the goat cheese–stuffed morels. Meat eaters have kept the garlic lamb—tender strips sautéed in olive oil, heavily garlicked, and smartly peppered—on the menu for 12 years. While generously portioned main courses are often spectacularly good, side dishes have been known to arrive cool (garlic mashed potatoes) or soggy (beans). ■ *Off 148th Ave NE; (206) 644-1668; 14320 NE 20th N, Bellevue; $$; beer and wine; MC, V; local checks only; dinner Tues–Sat.* &

LODGINGS

The Bellevue Hilton ★★ With every amenity in the book, the Bellevue Hilton is the best bet on the Eastside's Hotel Row. Rooms are tastefully done in warm colors. Amenities include use of a nearby health-and-racquet club, free transportation around Bellevue (within a 5-mile radius), room service until 10pm weekdays and 10:30pm weekends, a Jacuzzi, a sauna, a pool, several free cable channels in every room, and two restaurants. Working stiffs will appreciate the modem hookups and desks in every room; computer, fax machine, and copy machine are also available. Doubles run from $92 to $139; parlor suites, from $179 to $259, have sitting rooms, a wet bar and refrigerator, and dining tables. ■ *Main and 112th NE; (206) 455-3330 or (800) BEL-HILT; 100 112th Ave NE, Bellevue, WA 98004; $$$; AE, DC, MC, V; checks OK.* &

Bellevue Holiday Inn ★★ This understated two-story motel doesn't overload your senses or your budget; many regular visitors to Bellevue won't stay anywhere else. The units are arranged campus-style around a well-manicured lawn and heated pool. The suites are nothing special; the fancy dining room, Jonah's, is better than most. ■ *112th and Main; (206) 455-5240 or (800) 421-8193; 11211 Main St, Bellevue, WA 98004; $$; AE, DC, MC, V; checks OK.* &

Hyatt Regency at Bellevue Place ★★ Hyatt Regency is just one part of Kemper Freeman's splashy, sprawling retail-office-restaurant-hotel-health-club complex called Bellevue Place. The 382-room hotel with 24 stories (the highest in Bellevue) offers many of the extras: pricier "Regency Club" rooms on the top two floors, two big ballrooms, several satellite conference rooms, use of the neighboring Seattle Club (for a $10 fee), and a fine restaurant, Eques. The best rooms are on the south side above the seventh floor. ▪ *NE 8th St and Bellevue Way; (206) 462-1234 or (800) 233-1234; 900 Bellevue Way, Bellevue, WA 98104; $$$; AE, DC, MC, V; checks OK.* ⅌

GREATER SEATTLE: MERCER ISLAND

RESTAURANTS

Caffe Italia ★ Bright yellow walls, a red tile floor, and soft seats make this a fine place to warm up on a cool day with a comforting, best-of-Italy menu. On warm days, it's a place to relax and sip something white and cool and Italian out on the front patio. Waitstaff wears jeans, why shouldn't you? Among the appetizers are the delightful suppli al telefono, the classic Roman street food: fried balls of rice with a gooey mozzarella center, and a little tub of marinara for dipping. Chewy pizzas are piled with robust ingredients (although an overwhelmed palate may wish for a tamer version); pastas, such as the cannelloni with its spicy marinara and ground beef/mozzarella filling, and meats, such as the rosemary chicken, are simple and lovely. Specials may be the classic osso bucco or a subtle ravioli in a creamy sun-dried and fresh tomato sauce. Prices for food and wine are reasonable; when there's a bit of a crowd, service falters. ▪ *Downtown Mercer Island; (206) 232-9009; 2448 76th Ave SE, Mercer Island; $$; beer and wine; AE, MC, V; checks OK; lunch Tues–Fri, dinner Tues–Sun.* ⅌

Pon Proem ★ Sheer, unadulterated capsicum is not the story of Mercer Island's nifty little Thai joint, though it's there in a no-nonsense star scale ("chok dee" next to five stars means "good luck"). Though the red curry chicken lacked a certain oomph, everything else sampled here displayed balance and a deft touch at the wok. Three kinds of soy sauce, plus chili paste, give the chicken dish called gai pahd met ma muang better balance than a gymnastics team. Vegetarian phad Thai is freshened by red cabbage, carrots, and sprouts. Deep-fried dishes consistently please, especially the gai Pon Proem—chewy, mildly spicy chunks of meat for finger-dipping (call it Chicken McNuggets for grownups). Modest digs in a strip-mall setting are warmed by the owner's hand-sewn seat-cushion covers and window treatments. ▪ *On the edge of downtown Mercer*

*Island, next to PayLess; (206) 236-8424; 3039 78th Ave SE,
Mercer Island; $; beer and wine; AE, MC, V; local checks only;
lunch Mon–Fri, dinner every day.* &

GREATER SEATTLE: ISSAQUAH

Fast-food franchises now line I-90, but the center of this old
coal-mining town still resembles small-town America, complete
with a butcher shop and a working dairy. On good days, Mount
Rainier appears between the hills that form the town's southern and eastern borders.

Gilman Village on Gilman Boulevard is a shopping complex with a twist: the developers refurnished old farmhouses,
a barn, and a feed store, then filled them with craft and clothing shops, restaurants, and a woodworking gallery. **Boehm's
Chocolates** on the edge of town still dips its chocolates by
hand and offers tours for groups (reservations are needed);
(206) 392-6652.

The **Issaquah Farmers Market** is open Saturdays
throughout the summer, across from the **Issaquah State
Salmon Hatchery** on Sunset Way, which is open to visitors
daily from 8am to 7:30pm (there aren't any tours, but there are
instructional displays in the lobby).

Lake Sammamish State Park lies between town and
Lake Sammamish, and offers swimming and boat access. **Tiger
Mountain**, the sprawling 13,000-acre state forest that looms to
the east, is a favorite weekend destination for hikers and mountain bikers. Trails wind through alder and evergreen forests
and past old coal-mine shafts.

▼

Issaquah

▲

RESTAURANTS

Mandarin Garden ★ Locals love this place because its unassuming ambience lures mainly those in the know. Truth is, Issaquah's best Chinese food is found amidst a drab decor
beneath off-kilter, ornate lampshades. Chef Andy Wong, a native of Shanghai, handles equally well the delicate flavors of
Mandarin and the heat and spice of Sichuan and Hunan. But
be assured that if you order a starred dish, you're going to get
hot and spicy. A recent lunch, for instance, packed an incen-
diary wallop as well as mess of delectable, deep-fried, then
sautéed chicken. Praiseworthy dishes include melt-in-your-
mouth kung pao chicken, mixed seafood Sichuan, and variations on bean curd. Two private rooms are available for
banquets. Peking duck should be ordered a day in advance. ■
*Exit 17 off I-90 to Sunset Way; (206) 392-9476; 40 E Sunset
Way, Issaquah; $; beer and wine; MC, V; local checks only;
lunch Mon–Sat, dinner every day.*

Nicolino ★ On warm days, the sunny brick courtyard is the
place to be. On cold or rainy days, head for the cheerful little

dining room, pleasantly cluttered with wine bottles and family pictures, maps and mandolins, for a steaming plate of soul-warming pasta. Though they've been known to heavy-hand the prawns and chicken, the pasta (and the low prices) fuel this charmer's reputation and crowd-attracting popularity. You won't find showy dishes, yet a simple pasta can be stunningly executed, while the fork-tender veal shank in the osso bucco Milanese comes atop fettucine so buttery the taste comes right through the tomato sauce and orange zest. Hearty slices of peasant bread are meant to be dredged in herb-, garlic-, and chile-spiked olive oil, and accompanied by a soothing glass of Chianti. ▪ *In Gilman Village; (206)391-8077; 317 NW Gilman Blvd, Issaquah; $$; beer and wine; DC, MC, V; checks OK; lunch, dinner every day.* &

GREATER SEATTLE: BAINBRIDGE ISLAND

Once a major logging port, Bainbridge Island is now a semirural haven for city professionals (who don't mind the half-hour commute via ferry from downtown Seattle), writers, artists, and people seeking simpler lives. It makes a pleasant tour by car or bike, during which you can see small pastoral farms, enviable waterfront homes, and spectacular cityscapes (especially from **Fay Bainbridge State Park** on the northeast corner of the island). The wooded and waterfront trails in **Fort Ward State Park**, on the south end of the island, make for a nice afternoon stroll (good picnic spots, too).

   Bloedel Reserve encompasses 150 acres of lush, tranquil gardens, woods, meadows, and ponds. Plants from all over the world make the grounds interesting any time of the year. Open Wednesday through Sunday; reservations are required and limited; (206)842-7631.

   For a simpler trip, ride over on the ferry, sans car, and walk a few strides up the road to the small, family-owned **Bainbridge Island Winery**, which makes a number of good wines, including a superb strawberry. If it's early in the day, stroll a few blocks through downtown Winslow and have coffee and a pastry at **Pegasus Espresso House**, at the foot of Madison Avenue S, or at Bainbridge Bakers in Winslow Green. In the evening, saunter down to the **Harbour Pub**, overlooking Eagle Harbor, for beer, fish 'n' chips, and local chatter.

RESTAURANTS

Pleasant Beach Grill ★★ Bainbridge Island's only white-linen restaurant is quietly tucked away in a large Tudor house on the island's southwest corner. Islanders have always favored the pine-paneled bar, warmed by a fireplace and with two couches for sinking into with a drink or dessert. Under the direction of chef Hussein Ramadan, the grill has found a pleasant consistency, much appreciated by the locals. His menu includes a sauté of prawns, scallops, and white fish (in a Thai-style sauce of curry, lemon grass, and coconut milk) and an excellent 10-ounce slab of New York pepper steak, with specials inspired by fresh seasonal ingredients. Stick with the simpler grills and seafoods and enjoy the ample portions and skilled service. In warm weather, dine outdoors on the terrace. In winter, reserve a table in the appealing fireside lounge. ■ *Near Lynwood Center, follow signs toward Fort Ward State Park; (206)842-4347; 4738 Lynwood Center NE, Bainbridge Island; $$; full bar; AE, MC, V; no checks; dinner every day.*

Ruby's on Bainbridge ★★ Maura and Aaron Crisp have turned this hobbit-like location next door to the island's only movie theater into a mini-destination restaurant. It's a steamy, garlicky little place—just casual enough for the locals, just sumptuous enough for weekend guests and day-trippers. The menu changes often, but you'll encounter such entrees as fettucine tossed with wild mushrooms, swordfish dressed in soy and ginger, and pork tenderloin with a raspberry reduction. Salads are standouts. ■ *In Lynwood Center; follow signs toward Fort Ward State Park; (206)780-9303; 4569 Lynwood Center Rd, Bainbridge Island; $$; beer and wine; MC, V; checks OK; lunch, dinner Tues–Sun, brunch Sat–Sun.*

Sawatdy Thai Cuisine ★★ Now that islanders have had a couple years of Sawatdy to themselves, perhaps it's time they let Seattle in on their secret: some of the best Thai food in Seattle can be found on Bainbridge Island. Island life is a trade-off, with residents often settling for a mediocre dining experience in exchange for convenience. Not so at this modest mid-island restaurant (no view, and next door to a gas station). Here, Tex Kitnikone runs the place like clockwork, making sure that every fragrant dish is well executed and each customer well cared-for. Reservations are a good idea. ■ *Take Hwy 305, turn west on High School Rd, north on Fletcher Bay Rd to Island Center; (206)780-2429; 8780 Fletcher Bay Rd, Bainbridge Island; $; beer and wine; MC, V; checks OK; lunch Mon–Fri, dinner every day.*

Streamliner Diner ★ The Streamliner Diner (an easy walk from the ferry) is an island institution. This steamy restaurant, here since 1981, built its reputation on satisfying breakfasts and inventive entrees—Mom food with a creative twist. It's a local custom to savor a cup of coffee for as long as you like while visiting friends and trading island gossip. With its kitchen-table decor, the place oozes small-town personality. The omelet list is creative, and the potatoes are chunky and oniony. More than one regular swears by the Potatoes Deluxe, a scramble of spuds, mushrooms, spinach, green onions, tomatoes, and cheddar, with cumin-scented guacamole on top (so good, you can get it to go, weekday mornings, at the Streamliner Express kiosk at the ferry terminal). Good baked items too. Expect a line on weekends. ■ *Winslow Way and Bejune; (206)842-8595; 397 Winslow Way, Bainbridge Island; $; no alcohol; no credit cards; checks OK; breakfast every day, lunch Mon–Sat.*

LODGINGS

The Bombay House ★★ This sprawling turn-of-the-century house with a widow's walk, set in a lavish flower garden with a rough-cedar gazebo overlooking scenic Rich Passage, is just a sweet stroll from Fort Ward State Park. With a hearty dose of island-hideaway atmosphere, the Bombay House has five bedrooms done up in country antiques. Three have private baths, and the vast second-floor Captain's Suite has a wood parlor stove and a claw-footed tub. The living room has a large fireplace. Innkeepers Roger, Bunny, and their daughter, Cameron, are friendly hosts. In the morning, you'll have the good fortune of enjoying one of Bunny's morning feasts with fresh-baked goodies. Children over 6 years are welcome. ■ *4 miles south of the ferry, just off W Blakely Ave; (206)842-3926 or (800)598-3926; 8490 Beck Rd NE, Bainbridge Island, WA 98110; $$; AE, MC, V; checks OK.*

Beach Cottage B&B ★ Right across Eagle Harbor from the ferry-stop town of Winslow is this charming, flower-bedecked four-cottage setup. Each cottage has a queen-size bed, a kitchen (stocked with breakfast fixings), logs for the fireplace, and a stereo. Three are right on the beach, and all four boast decks and a view of Eagle Harbor and its marina. Smoking is allowed (pets and children under 16 are not). ■ *4 miles from the ferry off Eagle Harbor Dr; (206)842-6081; 5831 Ward NE, Bainbridge Island, WA 98110; $$$; no credit cards; checks OK.*

GREATER SEATTLE: SEA-TAC

LODGINGS

Seattle Airport Hilton Hotel ★★ This streamlined four-winged building, camouflaged by trees and plantings, miraculously manages to create a resort atmosphere along an airport strip. The 173 plush, larger-than-standard rooms (at posh prices) feature desks and computer hookups, irons, ironing boards, and coffeemakers, set around a landscaped courtyard with pool and indoor/outdoor Jacuzzi. An exercise room and numerous meeting and party rooms are available. So is a 24-hour business center, complete with fax, copy machine, computer, and laser printer. The Great American Grill serves pastas, seafood, and grilled meats seasoned with fresh herbs from the hotel's garden. ■ *188th St exit off I-5, north 1 mile;*

(206) 244-4800 or (800) HILTONS; 17620 Pacific Hwy S, Seattle, WA 98188; $$$; AE, DC, MC, V; checks OK. &

Seattle Marriott at Sea-Tac ★ Another megamotel, the 451-room Marriott is somewhat concealed by trees, about a block from the airport strip. The lobby's Northwest motif is warm, though somewhat overdone. Rooms are standard, but suites are spacious. A pool and a courtyard area are part of an enormous covered atrium; there are also two Jacuzzis, a sauna, and a well-equipped exercise room. A casual dining room offers all the usual hotel fare—from sandwiches to steaks. ■ *Just east of Pacific Hwy S at S 176th and 32nd Ave S; (206) 241-2000 or (800) 228-9290; 3201 S 176th St, Seattle, WA 98188; $$$; AE, DC, MC, V; checks OK.* &

WestCoast Sea-Tac Hotel ★ This WestCoast outpost has 146 bright rooms (a slightly less upscale WestCoast hotel across the street caters handily to the business traveler; 18415 Pacific Highway S, (206) 248-8200). Terrycloth robes, hair dryers, shoe-shine machines, and a stocked honor bar are available in the 32 limited-edition suites. Meeting facilities accommodate up to 200; an outdoor pool, Jacuzzi, and sauna accommodate everyone. It's the only airport hotel that offers in-house guests free valet parking for seven days. ■ *Across from the airport entrance; (206) 246-5535 or (800) 426-0670; 18220 Pacific Hwy S, Seattle, WA 98188; $$$; AE, DC, MC, V; checks OK.* &

Wyndham Garden Hotel ★ You can't get much closer to the airport than this. Attractive styling inside, warm wood paneling in the lobby lounge, and an inviting library and fireplace make this a bit classier than your standard airport hotel. Accommodations include 180 guest rooms with writing desks, and 24 suites, with in-room coffeemakers, complimentary coffee, and hair dryers. Nonsmoking rooms, room service (early evening only), and meeting space are available. ■ *South of S 176th St; (206) 244-6666; 18118 Pacific Hwy S, Seattle, WA 98188; $$$; AE, DC, MC, V; checks OK.* &

GREATER SEATTLE: BURIEN

RESTAURANTS

Filiberto's ★★ Filiberto's is the most authentic and, on a good day, among the best of the local (and we mean local) Italian restaurants. The look is cheery and trattoria-perfect, with finishing touches of imported tile. Though service can be erratic, the food is consistent, with good attention paid to the basics. The long menu emphasizes Old World Italian preparations of pasta, veal, poultry, and rabbit, right down to a bowl of *real* stracciatella alla Romana. Three special treats: the huge, well-priced selection of Italian wines in a take-your-pick glass case,

Filiberto's pizza oven, and a bocce court out back (if you're lucky, you'll get asked to play). ■ *Off Hwy 518; (206) 248-1944; 14401 Des Moines Memorial Dr S, Burien; $$; full bar; AE, MC, V; checks OK; lunch, dinner Tues–Sat.*

Satsuma ★★ Plain as a box on the outside, this tranquil Burien hideaway has captured the interest of the local Japanese, who come to enjoy the cooking of Tak Suetsugu. The tempura is light as air, the sushi merely creditable. For a twist, try the Washington roll, with smoked salmon, tamagoyaki (similar to an omelet), cucumber, and strips of Washington apple. The black cod kasuzuke, marinated in sake lees and broiled, is a velvety ambrosia. Tatami rooms are available, including one that holds 20—great for a private function. Service is gracious. ■ *Off 148th on Ambaum; (206) 242-1747; 14301 Ambaum Blvd SW, Burien; $; beer and wine; AE, MC, V; no checks; lunch Tues, Wed, Fri, dinner Tues–Sun.*

GREATER SEATTLE: KENT

RESTAURANTS

Caveman Kitchens ★ The late Dick Donley was a tinkerer with both machines and food. He spent years experimenting with methods of smoking ribs, chicken, turkey, sausage, ham, and salmon over alder and (when available) applewood. What he finally achieved was outstanding—especially the moist smoked turkey. Donley's six children carry on after him, and nothing has changed. There is no inside seating, but in warm weather you can eat outside on picnic tables and go across the street to the neighborhood store for beer. Most people take out, loading up on the smoked goods and accompaniments such as beans, potato salad, coleslaw, and a terrific bread pudding with butterscotch whiskey sauce. A second Caveman (11700 Lake City Way, (206) 362-8464) is now open in Seattle. ■ *West Valley Hwy at the James intersection; (206) 854-1210; 807 West Valley Hwy, Kent; $; no alcohol; MC, V; checks OK; lunch, dinner every day.*

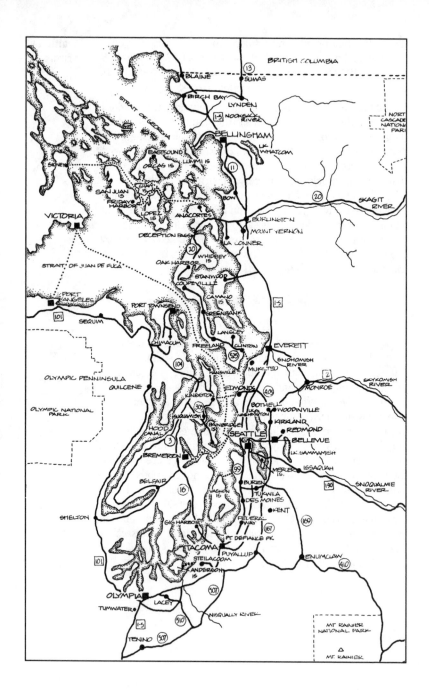

Puget Sound

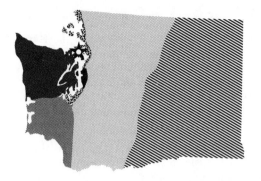

*North to south along the I-5 corridor, including
side trips to the islands.*

BLAINE

LODGINGS

Inn at Semiahmoo ★★ Semiahmoo Spit is a stunning site for
a resort, with beachward views of the sea and the San Juans
from many of the buildings. It sports lots of amenities: a 300-
slip marina convenient to the inn; a house cruise vessel on
which you can book excursions through the San Juans or
scenic fishing trips; a thoroughly outfitted athletic club (an outdoor swimming pool—cold—racquetball, squash, tennis, aerobics, weight lifting, tanning, massage, sauna, and Jacuzzi); an
endless stretch of beach. Three restaurants (Stars, the expensive Northwest gourmet dining room, plus two more casual
spots) provide the necessary range of culinary alternatives. The
golf course, designed by Arnold Palmer, has long, unencum-
bered fairways surrounded by dense woods, excellent use of
water, and lovely sculptural sand traps. The adjacent convention center, where revamped cannery buildings make top-
notch meeting arenas, is really Semiahmoo's greatest strength.
However, lots of little things leave us feeling vaguely as though
Semiahmoo is more glorified motel than luxury resort. Sys-
tems noises have been far too audible through the walls. Views,
splendid from the bayside rooms, are nonexistent in others.
There are frustrating lapses in service, such as an hour-long
wait for a simple continental breakfast from room service, fireplaces bare of wood, and nice touches like coffee pots and hot
water dispensers combined with chipped mugs and no teabags.

Take exit 270 off I-5, travel west, watch for signs; (206) 371-2000; 9565 Semiahmoo Pkwy, Blaine; PO Box 790, Blaine, WA 98230-0790; $$$; AE, DC, MC, V; checks OK; breakfast, lunch, dinner every day. ♿

BIRCH BAY

It's just the place for 1950s teenage nostalgia. The crescent-shaped beach draws throngs of kids—cruising the strip, go-carting, hanging out in the arcade (open Memorial Day through Labor Day). Frankie and Annette would be right at home. There's a state park for camping and lots of sandy beach to wiggle between your toes. Off season can be very off.

LODGINGS

Jacobs Landing Rentals ★★ This is the best of the condo developments, right in the "middle of town," across the main street from the beach. Units are set at angles among the beautifully maintained grounds—affording some of them better water views than others. Suites (one-, two-, and three-bedroom units) are modern and deluxe, with fireplaces, kitchens, and washers and dryers. There are outdoor tennis courts, an indoor heated pool, a Jacuzzi, and racquetball courts to keep everyone busy. ■ *Take exit 270 off I-5, head west for 5 miles, follow signs; (206) 371-7633; 7824 Birch Bay Dr, Birch Bay, WA 98230; $$; AE, MC, V; checks OK.*

LYNDEN

This neat and tidy community with immaculate yards and colorful gardens lining the shady avenue into downtown has adopted a Dutch theme in tribute to a community of early inhabitants. Be sure to visit the charming **Pioneer Museum** full of local memorabilia and antique buggies and motorcars; (206) 354-3675.

RESTAURANTS

Hollandia Riding on the tail of bigger Dutchified establishments is a slightly more tasteful bistro with authentic fare imported from The Netherlands. Chef Dini Mollink works competently on what is, to the American palate, rather heavy cuisine. A safe choice is the Toeristenmenu: Groentesoep (firm, tasty meatballs in a luscious vegetable broth), Schnitzel Hollandia (lightly breaded chicken breast), and dessert (little almond tarts). A less filling selection would be the Koninginnesoep met crackers (the Queen's cream soup, a rich chicken soup served with fresh raisin bread and thin slices of Gouda cheese). A small spice cookie accompanies your after-dinner coffee. ■ *In the Dutch Village at Guide Meridian and Front St; (206) 354-4133; 655 Front St,*

LODGINGS

Dutch Village Inn One might question an inn located in a windmill in a Dutch-theme village. This particular inn, however, provides six tastefully furnished and luxuriously appointed rooms to please all but the most jaded of travelers. Not surprisingly, the rooms are named for the Dutch provinces; Friesland Kamer, the room named for the northernmost province, occupies the top of the windmill. Views are lovely, but interrupted rhythmically as the giant blades of the windmill pass by (turning, fully lit, until 10pm). There are special touches in all the rooms—two have extra beds fitted into curtained alcoves in true Dutch fashion, and two have two-person tubs. Breakfast is on the house. ■ *Front St and Guide Meridian; (206)354-4440; 655 Front St, Lynden, WA 98264; $$; MC, V; checks OK.*

EVERSON

RESTAURANTS

Black Forest Steakhouse Jack Niemann has brought his mesquite-grill technique down from his popular White Rock, BC, eatery to the hamlet of Everson, 30 minutes northeast of Bellingham. Decor is a quirky combination of roughwood rustic and ivy-twined beer garden—just the right mood for the food, which includes the trademark steaks, grilled meats, and outstanding sauerbraten and schnitzels. They don't take reservations and diners tend to linger, so don't be in a rush. ■ *On Everson's main drag (and only commercial street) (360)966-2855; 203 W Main St, Everson; $; full bar; AE, MC, V; checks OK ; lunch Mon–Fri, dinner every day.*

▼

Ferndale

▲

FERNDALE

Hovander Homestead Park. At this county-run working farm, kids can pet the animals or prowl the barn, and families can picnic along the Nooksack River. The centerpiece is the gabled farmhouse and its gardens, built in 1903 by a retired Swedish architect, Holand Hovander; 5299 Nielsen Road, south of Ferndale off Hovander Road, (360)384-3444. Call for hours.

Adjacent to Hovander Park, the **Tenant Lake Interpretive Center and Fragrance Garden** offers boardwalk access to an abundance of birdlife in a wetland setting. The garden was developed with the visually and physically impaired in mind, so many of the raised-bed plantings are identified with braille labels and the garden is wheelchair accessible.

SUMAS

Although Sumas, a small border-crossing town east of Lynden, is not a destination community, it's a good jumping-off point for a trip to Canada. Tuesdays and Wednesdays have the shortest lines at the border.

LODGINGS

Sumas Mountain Village ★ This handsome log lodge—a small-scale replica of the classic Mount Baker Lodge, which was destroyed by fire in 1931—deserves a more rustic setting than Sumas's main drag, steps away from the Canadian border. The nine rustic rooms recapture the aura of the old lodge, with peeled-log beds, wooden floors with braided rugs, and framed black-and-white reproduction photos of Mount Baker Lodge. Six rooms have Jacuzzis; two have river-stone fireplaces. Room 6, Twin Sisters, where the queen-size bed is supplemented with a dandy bunk bed and red tartan curtains, is perfect for families. The downstairs restaurant isn't much for meals, but the chess game set up by the huge (gas) fireplace is a nice touch.
■ *Downtown Sumas; (360) 988-4483; 819 Cherry St, Sumas, WA 98295; $$; AE, MC, V; checks OK.*

▼

Sumas

▲

BELLINGHAM

The mishmash grid of Bellingham's streets is a reminder of its former days as four smaller towns. In recent years the downtown architecture of this city, situated on three rivers flowing into one bay, has been rediscovered: the town is full of fine old houses, award-winning architecture at Western Washington University, stately streets, and lovely parks. An economic boom is bringing change and expansion to Whatcom County, most notably at the handsome port facility that houses the southern terminus of the **Alaska Marine Highway System**; (360) 676-8445 or (800) 642-0066. The **Island Shuttle Express** provides passenger-only ferry service from Bellingham to the San Juan Islands, May through September. Whale watching and overnight cruises are also offered: (360) 671-1137.

Art. The Whatcom Museum of History and Art, 121 Prospect Street, (360) 676-6981, a massive Romanesque building dating from 1892, was used as a city hall until 1940. It has permanent exhibits on historic Bellingham as well as an adventurous art exhibition schedule. Check out the local wildlife and native American culture presentations in the education center down the block, and the Children's Museum Northwest, an associated facility, a few doors farther north. One block from the museum is **R.R. Henderson**, one of the finest used bookstores in the state; 112 Grand Avenue, (360) 734-6855.

Old Homes. Wonderful turn-of-the-century mansions

abound in Bellingham: check out Utter Street, between Madison and Monroe; W Holly Street, from Broadway to C Street; Eldridge Avenue; and N Garden Street, from Myrtle to Champion. In the south end of town, seek out the homes on Knox Avenue from 12th to 17th and on Mill Street near 15th; the 1890 Roland G. Gamwell House at 16th and Douglas; and the Craftsman-style Roeder Home on Sunset Drive, open to the public.

Gardens of Art. The City of Bellingham now owns what was formerly called Big Rock Garden. A vast array of azaleas, rhododendrons, and Japanese maples share this wonderful woodland site with a unique outdoor gallery of garden art. Free live music in the garden on Sunday afternoons, May to August; 2900 Sylvan, near Lake Whatcom; (360) 671-1069.

The **Old Town** around W Holly and Commercial streets

Bellingham

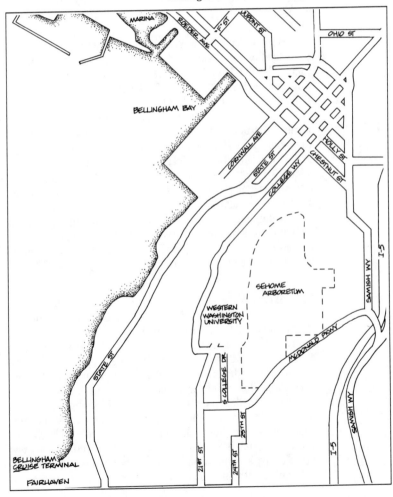

hosts antique and junk shops and some decent eateries. **Fairhaven**, the product of a short-lived railroad boom from 1889 to 1893, is good for exploring. **The Marketplace**, the grand dame and central figure among the attractive old buildings, was restored in 1988 and houses a number of interesting shops and dining options. The district is rich with diversion: crafts galleries, coffeehouses, bookstores, a charming garden/nursery emporium, and a lively evening scene unique to Bellingham.

Western Washington University, on Sehome Hill south of downtown, is a fine expression of the spirit of Northwest architecture: warm materials, formal echoes of European styles, respect for context and the natural backdrop. Also stop at the visitor parking kiosk on the south side of campus for a map of the university's renowned outdoor sculpture collection.

Lake Whatcom Railway—located not on Lake Whatcom, but on Highway 9 at Wickersham—makes scenic runs in July and August using an old Northern Pacific engine; (360) 595-2218.

Mount Baker Vineyards. This attractive, cedar-sided, skylit facility specializes in some of the lesser-known varietals, such as Müller-Thurgau and Madeleine Angevine. Their plum wine, made from local fruit, is delightful; 11 miles east of Bellingham on Mount Baker Highway; (360) 592-2300.

The Ski to Sea Race attracts teams from all over the world to participate in this annual event over Memorial Day weekend (see Calendar).

The Bellingham Music Festival has quickly become an institution, featuring more than two weeks of orchestral, chamber, and jazz performances, beginning the third week of August; (360) 676-5997.

Bellingham Farmers Market features produce (including the county's famed berry harvests), fresh seafood, herbs, flowers, and crafts. Saturdays from April through October, downtown at Railroad Avenue and Magnolia Street; (360) 647-2060.

RESTAURANTS

Cobblestone Cafe ★★ This tiny sidestreet cafe has added what Fairhaven has been missing: an adventurous, top-quality restaurant amid the coffeehouses and pizza joints. Peter Cady always offers local meats and seafood, and at least one vegan selection. Grilled portobello mushrooms are deceptively simple and utterly delicious. A culinary classicist might balk at an occasional dinnertime experiment gone awry, but we've been impressed by delicately flavored lingcod, gently steamed in nori with a hint of wasabe, and a tangy, not sweet, strawberry sauce complementing a chicken breast stuffed with herbed ricotta. The lamb is from a small specialty operation just a few miles away, and the wine list is chosen with equal care. Our only quibble: the bread could be better. ■ *In Fairhaven just* *off Harris Ave; (360)650-0545; 1308B 11th St, Bellingham; $$; beer and wine; MC, V; local checks only; lunch and dinner Tues–Sun, Sunday brunch.*

il fiasco ★★ Under its new owners, Andrew and Kay Moquin, il fiasco (Italian for "the flask") is a bit trendier in decor and slightly less accommodating in wine. However, the Northern Italian cuisine is still excellent, from the squid with artichoke aioli through the penne with chicken and Gorgonzola to the almond flan. Side dishes are particularly satisfactory: crusty, chewy bread with a dip of herb-infused olive oil, perfectly dressed salads, intensely flavorful three-mushroom soup. Occasionally, kitchen experiments go astray, as with a duck ravioli with a too-sweet sauce, but such lapses are rare. Service has lost some polish. ■ *Across from the Parkade at Commercial and Holly; (360)676-9136; 1309 Commercial St, Bellingham; $$; full bar; AE, DC, MC, V; local checks only; lunch Mon–Fri, dinner every day. &*

Pacific Cafe ★★ Tucked into the historic Mount Baker Theater building, the Pacific Cafe has been a leader on Bellingham's gastronomic front since 1985. The ambience is civilized and modern: good abstract watercolors on the walls, quiet jazz on the speakers. The menu reflects a bit of co-owner Robert Fong's Asian influence (he comes to Washington via Hawaii, supplemented with years of travel in Europe, India, China, and Malaysia). The satay sauces are complex, light, and fragrant, and the seafood is noteworthy. Both oysters and squid respond beautifully when matched with shiitakes and Thai chile. Fong is a serious wine collector, and the quality of the vintages presented reflects a fine-tuned palate. Note especially the selection of dessert ports. ■ *Off Holly on Commercial; (360)647-0800; 100 N Commercial, Bellingham; $$; beer and wine; MC, V; local checks only; lunch Mon–Fri, dinner Mon–Sat.*

Bellingham

Restaurants

Pepper Sisters ★★ Cheerful, knowledgeable service, a great location in one of Bellingham's vintage brick commercial buildings, and a wide-awake kitchen have turned Pepper Sisters into an institution. Daily seafood specials are a showcase for the chefs' ability to combine local provender with what the owners call High Desert cuisine: say, oysters in pumpkinseed sauce. The kitchen shows the same verve with plainer fare: roasted potato and garlic enchilada with green chile sauce, or an unctuous, spicy, eggplant tostada. Coffee flan is a standout dessert, and the coffee itself, the local Tony's brand, is brewed with a dusting of cinnamon on the filter. ■ *On State St south of Holly; (360)671-3414; 1055 N State St, Bellingham; $; beer and wine; MC, V; checks OK; dinner Tues–Sun.*

The Bagelry ★ In 1993, the Bagelry doubled its size and diminished the lines somewhat. Everything else is pretty much the same, save the addition of some desserts. The many delectable spreads are sold separately from the deli section: try the Italian version with sun-dried tomato, or the garlic-feta combo. Expat—East Coasters will delight in the dense, crusty New York–style bagels, six or seven kinds of which are offered hot from the ovens throughout the day. Tasty bialys make an addictive base for a smoked Virginia ham sandwich. ▪ *Railroad near Champion; (360) 676-5288; 1319 Railroad Ave, Bellingham; $; no alcohol; no credit cards; local checks only; breakfast, lunch every day.*

Bluewater Bistro ★ The Bluewater provides a cheerful atmosphere, energetic staff, an adventurous attitude in the kitchen, and even a live jazz brunch on Sundays. It's supposed to be fun—and for the most part it is. The delicious garlic burger is served on the Bistro's own brioche bun, with provolone and a tasty marinara dip, while the chicken breast sandwich features mild green chiles. Salads are outstanding, especially the caesar and a Cobb salad with Thai chicken. In keeping with the Bluewater's bistro heritage, wines here tend toward the less patrician, and most are available by the glass. The brews can take you from Kalama, Washington, to Czechoslovakia. ▪ *Holly and Cornwall; (360) 733-6762; 1215½ Cornwall Ave, Bellingham; $; beer and wine; MC, V; checks OK; lunch Mon–Sat, dinner Tues–Sat, brunch Sun.*

Cafe Toulouse ★ Toulouse has dropped its dinner menu and returned to its original claim to fame: huge, well-orchestrated breakfasts and lunches for the local office crowd. This quietly remodeled corner of the old Bon Marché is the best place in town for Sunday brunch. The breakfast and lunch menus offer favorites familiar to Toulouse regulars—Greek and Provençal frittatas, huevos rancheros, hefty sandwiches, soups, and pastas. If there's a weak spot, it's the soups. ▪ *Downtown near Cornwall, next to the Federal Building; (360) 733-8996; 114 W Magnolia St, Bellingham; $; no alcohol; MC, V; checks OK; breakfast, lunch every day.*

Thai House ★ Peggy Rieschl has fashioned a most comfortable spot, located (as many of the great Thai restaurants seem to be) in a strip mall. It's a nice environment in which to savor one's fish cakes or linger over the flavorful hot-and-sour soup chock-full of tender seafood and scented with fresh lemon grass. Tried-and-true favorites include a whole flatfish, deep-fried and smothered in a spicy red sauce, or any one of the curries. But the real finds are likely to be the daily specials posted on the blackboards. Catering, too. ▪ *Across from Bellis Fair Mall; (360) 734-5111; 3630 Meridian Village, Bellingham; $; beer and wine; MC, V; checks OK; lunch Mon–Fri, dinner every day.*

Colophon Cafe Located in the best bookstore in town, Colophon offers table service and an outdoor wine garden on its lower level, booths and sidewalk tables above. The African peanut soup (in vegetarian and nonvegetarian versions) is justly famous—chunky with fresh tomatoes, grainy with peanuts, and pungent with ginger. Real cream pies—rich, light, and wonderful—are another specialty: Key lime, chocolate brandy, and peanut butter. The Colophon encourages patrons to tarry over their espresso. ■ *11th near Harris (in Village Books) in Fairhaven; (360)647-0092; 1208 11th St, Bellingham; $; beer and wine; MC, V; checks OK; breakfast, lunch, dinner every day.* &

Taste of India Tandoori meats and breads and other Punjabi creations are a specialty, but South Indian vegetarian cooking is well represented. The shrimp tandoori is terrific, with sweet, tender-firm shrimp, a perfect masala, and a mint chutney. The vegetarian combination is another triumph of flavor-blending. These are meals for lingering, which allows time to polish off a 22-ounce Taj Mahal beer. The lunch buffet, a bargain, is justly popular with the locals. ■ *Across from Bellis Fair Mall, 2 doors south of Thai Kitchen; (360)647-1589; 3930 Meridian St #J, Bellingham; $; beer and wine; MC, V; local checks only; lunch, dinner every day.*

LODGINGS

▼

Schnauzer Crossing ★★★ Sophisticated and unique, this B&B overlooking Lake Whatcom attracts a surprising range of visitors, from newlyweds to businesspeople to discerning foreign travelers—graciously accommodating them all. Many of Donna and Monty McAllister's guests return again and again to this lovely contemporary home, gardens, and grounds. Three accommodations are available: best is a spacious and elegant suite with fireplace, Jacuzzi, TV/VCR, and a garden view, or the separate luxury cottage overlooking the lake. The McAllisters are sensitive to guests' needs for privacy and have a finely tuned sense of hospitality that's obvious in the small details: extra-thick towels, bathrobes and slippers, and gorgeous flowers year-round. A superior breakfast might include homemade quiche, fresh fruit parfait, and espresso. There's a hot tub in a Japanese garden setting. Reserve several weeks in advance. ■ *Take exit 253 off I-5, go 2½ miles on Lakeway Dr and turn left; (360)734-2808 or (800)562-2808; 4421 Lakeway Dr, Bellingham, WA 98226; $$$; MC, V; checks OK.*

Best Western Heritage Inn ★★ Three tasteful, Wedgwood blue, shuttered and dormered structures nestling amid a small grove of trees and a stream seem incongruous adjacent to I-5 and a conglomeration of malls; however, this Best Western is one of the most professionally run hotels in the area. Rooms are elegantly furnished with exquisite cherry wood four-poster beds, high- and lowboys, wing-backed chairs in rich fabrics, and stylish desks with a comfortable chair. Other thoughtful touches include in-room coffee and tea, hair dryers, guest laundry facility, an attractive outdoor pool (in season) and indoor hot tub. Request a room away from the freeway. Free continental breakfast. ■ *Take I-5 exit 256; (360)647-1912 or (800)528-1234; 151 E McLeod Rd, Bellingham, WA 98226; $$; AE, DC, MC, V; checks OK.* ♿

Anderson Creek Lodge ★ Once a private school, the main house is now an intimate bed and breakfast with five individually designed rooms, three of which have their own fireplaces (there's also a massive stone hearth in the common area). The remainder of the facility has been developed as a conference center, though one can nestle into the lodge without the slightest hint that 70 physicists are conferring just down the lane. Be sure to walk the parklike trail through the woods, and while exploring, seek out resident sculptor James Lapp's studio. Strolling visitors are likely to catch part of a llama-training session. ■ *East of Bellingham, off Mt Baker Hwy; (360)966-2126; 5602 Mission Rd, Bellingham, WA 98226; $$; AE, MC, V; checks OK.*

CLOSED

DeCann House ★ Within this neighborhood of historic homes overlooking Squalicum Harbor Marina, Bellingham Bay, and the San Juan Islands, this unpretentious Victorian bed and breakfast welcomes visitors to a quiet and comfortable haven. Test your skills at the ornate pool table in the front parlor or the interesting collection of wooden mazes in the sitting room. Barbara and Van Hudson maintain an extensive current library of travel-related material and provide a log in which you can pass along your impressions to other travelers. A complete breakfast assures a cheery start to the day. ■ *West on Holly, which turns into Eldridge; (360)734-9172; 2610 Eldridge Ave, Bellingham, WA 98225; $$; no credit cards; checks OK.*

North Garden Inn ★ This Victorian house (on the National Register of Historic Places) boasts over two dozen rooms plus seven baths, the result of additions early in the century. Only 10 are rented as guest rooms; some have lovely views over Bellingham Bay and the islands. All the rooms are attractive, clean, and with a bit more character than usual—due partly to the antique house, partly to the influence of the energetic and talented hosts. Barbara and Frank DeFreytas are both musical—two grand pianos in performance condition are available to guests, and musical or dramatic evenings take place here just as they probably did at the turn of the century. ■ *Maple and N Garden ; (360)671-7828 or (800)922-6414; 1014 N Garden St, Bellingham, WA 98225; $$; MC, V; checks OK.*

Holiday Inn Express of Bellingham The location on the Guide Meridian strip development just north of town is highly unprepossessing, but the hotel itself is a find, especially for

time-pressed business travelers (free shuttle to the airport just
a few miles away). Winner of the chain's Newcomer of the Year
award in 1994, it joins franchise efficiency with some nice
touches. Rooms are spacious and quiet, and a free continental
breakfast is provided at cozy tables with a view of the pool and
Jacuzzi. Great value for your dollar. ■ *Take exit 256 off I-5 and
head north on Guide Meridian; (360)671-4800 or (800)
HOLIDAY; 4160 Guide Meridian, Bellingham, WA 98226; $;
AE, DC, MC, V; checks OK.* &

LUMMI ISLAND

Located just off Gooseberry Point northwest of Bellingham,
Lummi is one of the most overlooked islands of the ferry-accessible San Juans. It echoes the days when the San Juan Islands
were still a hidden treasure, visited only by folks who preferred
bucolic surroundings and deserted beaches to a plethora of
restaurants and gift shops. Private ownership has locked up
most of this pastoral isle, so you won't find state parks or resorts.
A popular path up Mount Lummi was recently closed to the public. To stretch your limbs, head for the peaceful beaches and
country roads. Plan ahead; dining options tend to be seasonal.

Lummi is serviced not by the Washington State ferries but
by the tiny **Whatcom County ferry**, which leaves Gooseberry
Point at 10 minutes past the hour from 7am until midnight
(more frequently on weekdays). It's easy to find (just follow the
signs to Lummi Island from I-5, north of Bellingham), cheap
($4 round-trip for a car and two passengers), and quick (a 6-
minute crossing); call ahead for schedule, (360)676-6730.

Just a few yards from the ferry landing is **The Islander**,
the island's only mercantile, (360)758-2190. Rental bikes are
available at the store next door, if you catch it open. The
Beach Store Cafe offers dinner and brunch; (360)758-7406.
Check out the tiny **Java Hut**, serving baked goods and a light
lunch; (360)758-2509.

LODGINGS

Loganita ★★★ Beautifully situated on the north end of Lummi,
with sweeping views across Georgia and Rosario straits, this elegant 100-year-old lodge invites contemplation and refined relaxation. The spacious downstairs area is furnished with
comfortable leather couches, Oriental rugs, polished tables, and
a fine collection of Northwest art. Huge stone fireplaces stand at
either end, music fills the rooms, and windows on three sides
open to unobstructed views of water, sky, and distant islands.
The Gossage family gives B&B guests exclusive use of the expansive lodge, sprawling decks, award-winning perennial garden, and long stretch of sandy beach. Upstairs, Laura Ashley
bedding and antiques fill the guest rooms. The Sunset Suite's

west-facing bedroom has a fireplace and couch; there's a separate sitting room and a private deck. Groups or families will enjoy the fully equipped, two-bedroom Carriage House out back. Hot tub on the front deck, pool and chess in the main rooms, and endless places to sit and daydream. ■ *From ferry, north on Nugent for 3 miles; (360) 758-2651; 2825 W Shore Dr, Lummi Island, WA 98262; $$$; MC, V; checks OK.*

The Willows ★★★ Run as a resort since the late 1920s, the old Taft family house perches on a knoll 100 feet above the accessible beach, offering sweeping views of the San Juan and Gulf islands. There are four rooms in the main building, a small cottage for two with a kitchen (decor is a bit precious, but the view and privacy are terrific), and a two-bedroom apartment that looks out over the rose garden to the ocean (with a little of the kitchen roof in between). For couples traveling together, the last is our favorite. Arrive in time for complimentary afternoon tea at 3:30pm. Mornings here start at 8am sharp with a knock on your door, as innkeepers Gary and Virginia Flynn deliver a beautiful tray with coffee and a loaf of hot Irish soda bread. A plentiful breakfast is served promptly at 9pm. Many guests feel spoiled by the elaborate atmosphere, but some might find it cloying.

The Willows is one of the few—and definitely the best—places on Lummi for an evening meal. On Fridays, you can order a Parisian-style dinner picnic (bread, cheese, pâté or fruit, and wine) and on Sundays a picnic hamper. But the real event is Saturday night's six-course dinner. Everything about the evening-long meal is sumptuous, from Gary's detailed recitation of the menu to the serving of not one but three wines, each chosen to complement a course. The meal begins in the main room, where a harpist and classical guitarist serenade mingling guests as they partake of sherry and appetizers. Each dish incorporates the freshest ingredients, with many herbs—and edible floral accents—from the Flynns' garden. Not every course works (the medallion of beef with a cherry and port sauce, for instance), but those that do are outstanding. First up might be a fine plate of pâté accompanied by asparagus wrapped in prosciutto, followed by purée of pea and spinach. This feast has become quite popular among locals (who often come from Bellingham just for dinner) and requires reservations often months in advance. ■ *From ferry, north on Nugent for 3½ miles; (360) 758-2620; 2579 W Shore Dr, Lummi Island, WA 98262; $$$; beer and wine; MC, V; checks OK; dinner Fri–Sun.*

CHUCKANUT DRIVE

This famous stretch of road between Bellingham and Bow used to be part of the Pacific Highway; now it is one of the prettiest drives in the state, curving along the Chuckanut Mountains and looking out over Samish Bay and its many islands. Unfortunately, if you're in the driver's seat you'll have to keep your eyes on the road and wait for turnoffs for the view; the road is narrow and winding. Take the Chuckanut Drive exit off I-5 north, or follow 12th Street south in Bellingham.

Teddy Bear Cove is a nudist beach, and a pretty one at that, on a secluded shore along Chuckanut Drive just south of the Bellingham city limits. No signs; watch for the crowd of cars.

Interurban Trail, once the electric rail route from Bellingham to Mount Vernon, is now a 5-mile running, walking, riding, and mountain-biking trail connecting to three parks on Chuckanut Drive: Fairhaven Park to Arroyo Park to Larrabee State Park.

Larrabee State Park, 7 miles south of Bellingham, was Washington's first state park. Beautiful sandstone sculpture along the beaches and cliffs provides a backdrop for exploration of the abundant sea life. Good picnic areas and camping.

BAYVIEW, SAMISH ISLAND, EDISON, BOW

As you wend your way through these bucolic communities of the Skagit Valley, it's hard to imagine I-5 is only minutes away. Removed from traffic and shopping malls you'll discover orchards, oyster beds, slow-moving tractors, and fields of mustard. In Bayview, visit the **Breazeale-Padilla Bay National Estuarine Research Reserve and Interpretive Center**. Learn about **Padilla Bay** estuary through displays, saltwater tanks, a nature trail, and a library. Open Wednesday through Sunday, 10am–5pm; 1043 Bayview-Edison Road, (360)428-1558. Nearby **Bayview State Park** is open year-round with overnight camping and beachfront picnic sites, perfect for winter bird-watching; (360)757-0227.

Permanent and part-time residents inhabit **Samish Island**, as do numerous oyster beds. **Blau Oyster Company** has been selling Samish Bay oysters, clams, and other seafood since 1935. Open Monday through Saturday (call 24 hours in advance and receive a 10 percent discount). Seven miles west of Edison via the Bayview-Edison Road and the Samish Island Road, follow the signs to the shucking sheds; 919 Blue Heron Road, Samish Island, (360)766-6171.

RESTAURANTS

The Oyster Bar ★★ This Samish Bay restaurant with a spectacular view has become an institution on Chuckanut Drive. The award-winning wine list can be a bit intimidating, but a veteran waiter steers you in the right direction. A small but dimensional menu: crab cakes accompanied by a mango-ginger-chutney sauce, a creamy fresh pea soup tanged with apples, a blackened lamb with minted jalapeño jelly, or extra-small Samish Bay oysters touched with Pernod and sautéed in a hazelnut and spinach breading. A light cheese soufflé accompanies each meal. Skip dessert and have an after-dinner drink. No young children. ■ *Exit 250 off I-5; (360) 766-6185; 240 Chuckanut Dr, Bow; $$$; beer and wine; AE, MC, V; local checks only; dinner every day.*

Oyster Creek Inn ★ The windows of this creekside restaurant open onto views of lush, green trees and rippling water. Adjacent to the Samish Bay Shellfish Farm, the Inn has a long history of dedication to seafood. The menu is a bit overwhelming, so keep it simple and start with a glass of house wine, made by manager Doug Charles, and unless you're famished, stay with the small side of the menu (large meals include a spinach timbale and stuffed potato). A pea-cucumber salad in a dill dressing starts the meal a bit slowly, but the mussels in garlic herb sauce served with cold vegetables in a creamy tarragon sauce is a potent entree. You must try the wild blackberry pie. ■ *About ½-hour drive south of Bellingham on Chuckanut Dr; (360) 766-6179; 190 Chuckanut Dr, Bow; $$; beer and wine; AE, MC, V; checks OK; lunch, dinner every day.* ⅙

The Rhododendron Cafe ★ The Rhododendron Cafe is the perfect starting or stopping point for a scenic trek on Chuckanut Drive. It does not have the view other Chuckanut eateries boast, but it serves up some darn good food. Once the site of the Red Crown Service Station in the early nineteen hundreds, the Rhody serves homemade soup (the chowder is excellent), a tasty veggie burger topped with provolone, or lightly breaded and sautéed Samish Bay oysters for lunch. Whatever you do, don't skip the desserts. ■ *At the Bow-Edison junction; (360) 766-6667; 553 Chuckanut Dr, Bow; $$; beer and wine; MC, V; local checks only; lunch Fri–Sat (Wed–Sun spring to fall), dinner Wed–Sun, brunch Sun; (closed late Nov–Dec).* ⅙

LODGINGS

Benson Farmstead Bed & Breakfast As you walk through the back door you may wonder where John Boy is. But this is for real, not fiction. Once part of a working dairy farm, the large 17-room house is packed with antiques and Scandinavian memorabilia. The four upstairs guest rooms are outfitted with iron beds and custom quilts. In the hallways are family photos and artwork by the young Benson brothers. Best are the English Garden Room and Forget-Me-Not Room. In the evening, relax in the hot tub or in the parlor sharing Sharon Benson's desserts and coffee. Jerry Benson cooks a country breakfast. And don't be surprised to hear music in the air—the Bensons are talented pianists and violinists (as are their four sons). Kids will like this place, especially the playroom and the three cats. ■

Exit 231 off I-5 north of Burlington; (360)757-0578; 1009 **Puget Sound**
Avon-Allen Rd, Bow, WA 98232; $$; MC, V; checks OK; (open
weekends only Oct–Mar, except by special arrangement).

ANACORTES

Anacortes, the gateway to the San Juans, is itself on an island—
Fidalgo Island. Though most travelers rush through here on
their way to the ferry, this town adorned with colorful, life-size
cutouts of early pioneers is quietly becoming a place where it's
worth it to slow down. For picnic or ferry food, try **Geppetto's**
(3320 Commercial Avenue, (360)293-5033) for Italian take-out.
Those with a little more time head to **Gere-A-Deli** (502 Com-
mercial Avenue, (360)293-7383), a friendly hangout with good
homemade food in an airy former Bank of Commerce building,
or the new **Anacortes Brewhouse** (320 Commercial Avenue,
(360)293-2444), with their own brews and wood-oven pizzas.
And don't forget the **Calico Cupboard**, offshoot of the well-
known cafe and bakery in La Conner (901 Commercial Street,
(360)293-7315).

If you need reading material for the ferry line, stop by **Wa-
termark Book Company** (612 Commercial, (360)293-4277),
loaded with interesting reads. Seafaring folks should poke
around **Marine Supply and Hardware** (202 Commercial Av-
enue, (360)293-3014). Established in 1913, Marine Supply is
packed to the rafters with basic and hard-to-find specialty ma-
rine items. And for the history of Fidalgo Island, visit **The Ana-
cortes Museum** (1305 Eighth Street, (360)293-1915).

For those who plan to go kayaking in the islands, before
you get to Anacortes, stop by **Eddyline Kayaks** (1344 Ashten
Road, Burlington, (360)757-2300); it is located off SR 20 at the
Port of Skagit County (west of I-5). Test paddle a kayak in their
manmade pond, then rent one for the weekend in the San
Juans. Reservations necessary.

Anacortes

Restaurants

RESTAURANTS

Courtyard Bistro (Majestic Hotel) ★★ It's the most elegant
dining room in Anacortes, where diners are welcomed to a
room filled with white tablecloths and tall-paned windows over-
looking a garden and patio. The bistro has succeeded in com-
bining the harvest of the Pacific Northwest with classic French
cuisine and a Pacific Rim flair. At dinner, begin with Dungeness
crab cake on seasonal greens, served with a spicy remoulade.
Entrees range from a "Pacific Seafood Stock," with shellfish,
calamari, and bean thread noodles in a light broth, to pork loin
with black bean purée and cilantro-lime rice. There's also a
Sunday champagne brunch, and live jazz Friday and Saturday
nights in the pub. ■ *Between 4th and 5th on Commercial;*
(360)299-2923; 419 Commercial Ave, Anacortes; $$; full bar;

AE, MC, V; local checks only; lunch and dinner every day; (closed Tues in winter). &

La Petite ★★ The Hulscher family, longtime owners of this restaurant at the Islands Inn motel, continues to deliver French-inspired food with a touch of Dutch. With only six entrees to choose from, quality is high. Try the lamb marinated in sambal or the popular pork tenderloin served with a mustard sauce. If chateaubriand is on the menu, order it—it's delicious. Soup, salad, and oven-fresh baked bread come with each meal. La Petite has an interesting dessert list, with plenty for chocolate lovers. A fixed-price Dutch breakfast is intended primarily for (but not exclusive to) motel guests. ■ *34th and Commercial; (360)293-4644; 3401 Commercial Ave, Anacortes; $$; full bar; AE, DC, MC, V; local checks only; breakfast every day, dinner Tues–Sun.* &

LODGINGS

Channel House ★★ Just a mile and a half from the ferry dock, Dennis and Pat McIntyre's Channel House is a 1902 Victorian home designed by an Italian count. Each of the four antique-filled rooms has a grand view of Guemes Channel and the San Juan Islands. A cottage contains two suite-style units, complete with fireplaces and private whirlpool baths; the Victorian Rose has its own deck. There is a large hot tub out back, and the McIntyres serve cozy breakfasts (before a roaring fire on chilly days). Freshly baked oatmeal cookies and Irish cream coffee await guests returning from dinner. ■ *At Oakes and Dakota; (360)293-9382 or (800)238-4353; 2902 Oakes Ave, Anacortes, WA 98221; $$; AE, MC, V; checks OK.*

▼

Anacortes

Restaurants

▲

The Majestic Hotel ★★ Truly majestic, this 1889 hotel has been through a number of incarnations, but this is surely the grandest. It belongs on a bluff overlooking the Pacific, but provides a fine night's stay even in the middle of Anacortes. Every one of the 23 rooms is unique, with individualized English antiques; some have oversize tubs with skylights above, some have decks, others have VCRs, and a few have everything. The best rooms are the showy corner suites. On the second floor (the only smoking level) is a small library with a chess table. And up top, a cupola with a 360-degree view of Anacortes, Mount Baker, the Olympics, and the San Juans. There's no better perch in sight for a glass of wine at sunset. ■ *Between 4th and 5th on Commercial; (360)293-3355; 419 Commercial Ave, Anacortes, WA 98221; $$$; AE, MC, V; checks OK.* &

SAN JUAN ISLANDS

There are 743 at low tide and 428 at high tide; 172 have names; 60 are populated; and only 4 have major ferry service. The San Juan Islands are varied, remote, and breathtakingly beautiful.

They are also located in the rain shadow of the Olympics, and most receive half the rainfall of Seattle. The four main islands—Lopez, Shaw, Orcas, and San Juan—have lodgings and eateries and some beautiful parks. Lopez, Orcas, and San Juan are discussed below; Shaw has little on it other than the world's only ferry landing run by nuns (they also have a certified dairy—three cows—and a campground with eight sites).

Getting There. The most obvious and cost-effective way of getting to the San Juans is via the **Washington State ferries** which run year-round from Anacortes, 1½ hours north of Seattle; for schedule and fare information, call (206) 464-6400. However, the sparsely populated islands are rather overrun in the summer months, and getting a ferry out of Anacortes can be a long, dull 3-hours-and-up wait. Bring a good book—or park the car and board with a bike. Money-saving tip: cars only pay westbound. If you plan to visit more than one island, arrange to go to the farthest first (San Juan) and work your way east.

During the summer, there are other options for those who don't need to bring a car. The **Victoria Clipper** makes a once-a-day trip from downtown Seattle to Friday Harbor (with

San Juan Islands

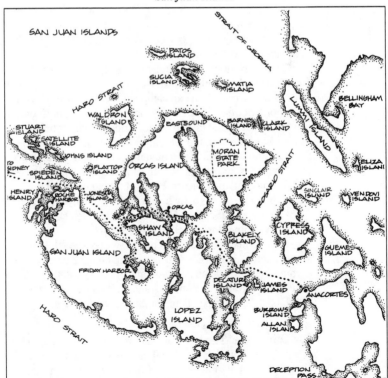

a quick stop in Port Townsend) from mid-May through mid-September. The summer-only ferry departs Pier 69 at 7:30am and arrives in Friday Harbor just before noon; for *Clipper* information, call (206)448-5000 or (800)888-2535. Another summertime option is via Bellingham; the **Island Shuttle Express** provides passenger-only ferry service to the San Juan Islands, May through September. Call for reservations: (206)671-1137.

You can also fly to the islands. **Kenmore Air** schedules four flights a day during peak season. Round-trip flights start at about $99 per person; for more information, call (206)486-8400 or (206)486-1257.

For an active, exciting education about the San Juan Islands ecosystem, immerse yourself (a camp for kids or adults) in a week of marine science activities at the **Island Institute** (PO Box 661, Vashon Island, WA 98070; (206)463-ORCA), based on the privately owned Spieden Island.

SAN JUAN ISLANDS: LOPEZ

**San Juan
Islands**

▲

Lopez Island, flat and shaped like a jigsaw-puzzle piece, is a sleepy, rural place, famous for its friendly locals (drivers always wave) and its cozy coves and full pastures. It has the easiest bicycling in the islands: a 30-mile circuit suitable for the whole family to ride in a day. If you don't care to bring your own bikes, **Cycle San Juans**, (360)468-3251, will deliver rented 21-speed bikes to wherever you're staying. The company also offers full- and half-day bicycle tours.

There are numerous public parks. Two day parks (**Otis Perkins** and **Upright Channel**) are great for exploring, with good beach access. You can camp at **Odlin County Park** (80 acres) or **Spencer Spit State Park** (130 acres), both on the island's north side. Odlin has many nooks and crannies, and grassy sites set among Douglas firs, shrubs, and clover. Spencer Spit has around 30 conventional campsites, and more primitive sites on the hillside. Both parks have water, toilets, and fire pits. **Agate County Park**, at the southwest tip of the island, has a pleasant rocky beach for the tired cyclist. A great place for a sunset. Seals and bald eagles can often be seen from the rocky promontory off **Shark Reef Park**.

Lopez Village is basic, but has a few spots worth knowing about, such as **Holly B's Bakery** in the Lopez Plaza, with celebrated fresh bread and pastries and coffee to wash them down (open June through September), and **Gail's** (Village Center #1, (360)468-2150), for excellent soups and sandwiches.

RESTAURANTS

Bay Cafe ★★★ The Bay Cafe is reason alone to come to this serene isle. Entertaining a full house of both tourists and Lopezians most nights, this storefront restaurant seems only to be increasing in popularity. Specializing in ethnic dishes, owner Bob Wood includes innovative preparations that span many cuisines, from chicken satays with curried noodles (dressed with a Thai-style peanut and lime sauce) to an extraordinarily fresh king salmon with a subtle Creole mustard sauce to a tender beef fillet served with creamy, cheesy risotto cakes, one of the best side dishes we've tasted. Vegetarians can count on at least one option (the tapas are usually excellent). Prices are reasonable, especially considering the inclusion of both soup (perhaps a delicate chanterelle spinach or a wonderfully hot and creamy ginger carrot coconut) and a fresh tossed salad. ■ *Across from the post office in Lopez; (360) 468-3700; Lopez Town, Lopez Island; $$; beer and wine; MC, V; local checks only; dinner every day in summer; (winter days vary).*

LODGINGS

Inn at Swifts Bay ★★★ With their remarkable knack for knowing how to care for guests without ever appearing intrusive, Robert Herrmann and Christopher Brandmeir have turned this former summer home into the most appealing accommodation on Lopez. Choose from two large and comfortable bedrooms or three luxurious suites (with gas log fireplaces). Our favorite, the Red Cabbage Suite, is a very private space with a separate sitting area, afternoon-sun deck, and VCR. There's also a secluded outdoor hot tub that can be scheduled for private sittings (towels, robes, and slippers provided) and a first-class selection of recorded music and movies on tape. Expect to be pampered. Brandmeir is an excellent breakfast chef, and if you're lucky he'll fix you his crab cakes.

You won't get breakfast at the new **Hunter Bay House**—a gorgeously decorated cabin on a bluff overlooking the water—unless you cook it yourself, but you will get a beautiful temporary home for the two of you. Everything you need is here. All you need is a pot of money to enjoy this bit of heaven. Two-night minimum, two-person maximum. ■ *Head 1 mi south of ferry to Port Stanley Rd, left 1 mi; (360) 468-3636; Rt 2, #3402, Lopez Island, WA 98261; $$$; AE, MC, V; checks OK.*

Blue Fjord Cabins ★ Lopez is the most secluded and tranquil of the three ferry-accessible islands, and the Blue Fjord Cabins are the most secluded and tranquil getaway on Lopez. The two log cabins are tucked away up an unmarked dirt road, each concealed from the other by thick woods. They're of modern chalet design, clean and airy, with full kitchens. Three-night minimum in July and August. Doing nothing never had such a congenial setting. ■ *Elliott Rd at Jasper Cove; (360) 468-2749; Rt 1, Box 1450, Lopez Island, WA 98261; $$; no credit cards; checks OK.*

Edenwild Inn ★ There are eight rooms in this Victorian-style bed and breakfast, located in Lopez Village, a very easy stroll from the only restaurants on the island. Each comfortable room has its own bath, a few have fireplaces. All have beautifully stained hardwood floors. The front rooms on the upper floor have the best views: Room 6 features windows overlooking the bay, and has a fireplace and sitting area. Breakfast is served in the dining room at individual tables. The only B&B on the island to accept children. ■ *In Lopez Village; (360)468-3238; PO Box 271, Lopez, WA 98261; $$$; MC, V; checks OK; dinner Wed–Sat.* &

MacKaye Harbor Inn ★ Location, location, location. Bicyclists call it paradise after their sweaty trek from the ferry to this little harbor. The tall powder blue house sits above a sandy, shell-strewn beach, perfect for sunset strolls or pushing off in one of their rented kayaks to explore the scenic waterways. The newly renovated Harbor Suite is our top choice, with its fireplace, private bath, and enclosed sitting area facing the beach. Rent kayaks or mountain bikes, ask the very friendly innkeepers, Brooks and Sharon Broberg, to share their secrets about the island, and you're off to explore. Return in the afternoon for freshly baked cookies. If you do come by bike, be warned: the closest restaurant is 6 miles back in town. Breakfast gets you started before a long morning of paddling out to the otters. ■ *12 miles south of the ferry landing on MacKaye Harbor Rd; (360)468-2253; Rt 1, Box 1940, Lopez Island, WA 98261; $$; MC, V; checks OK.*

SAN JUAN ISLANDS: ORCAS

Named not for the whales (the large cetaceans tend to congregate on the west side of San Juan Island and are rarely spotted here), but for a Spanish explorer, Orcas has a reputation as the most beautiful of the four big San Juan islands. It's also the biggest (geographically) and the hilliest, boasting 2,400-foot **Mount Constitution** as the centerpiece of Moran State Park. Drive, hike, or, if you're feeling up to it, bike to the top, but get there somehow; from the old stone tower you can see Vancouver, Mount Rainier, and everything between. The 4,800-acre **Moran State Park** also has one lake for freshwater swimming, three more for fishing and boating, and nice campsites, but you must write at least two weeks ahead for reservations: Moran, Star Route Box 22, Eastsound, WA 98245, or call (360)376-2326.

The man responsible for the park was shipbuilding tycoon Robert Moran. His old mansion is now the centerpiece of **Rosario Resort**, just west of the park. Unfortunately, the resort doesn't live up to its extravagant billing and prices. But the mansion, decked out in memorabilia and mahogany trim and featuring an enormous pipe organ (still in use; check for concert dates), is certainly worth a sightseeing stop; (360)376-2222.

Although you probably won't see whales around Orcas, there's a plethora of other wildlife, including bald eagles and seals. One good way to get up close: **kayak trips**. Try Shearwater Adventures (360)376-4699, or Island Kayak Guides at Doe Bay Village, (360)376-4755.

Adventure Limo & Taxi Service, (360)376-4994, offers historic tours and trips up Mount Constitution, as well as car rentals for those who prefer to leave behind their vehicles (and the hassle of getting them on the ferry). Or you can rent bicycles by the hour, day, or week from **Dolphin Bay Bicycles**, (360)376-4157, at the Orcas ferry landing and from **Wild Life Cycles**, (360)376-4708, in Eastsound.

Every small, hip town has to lay claim to a small, hip bakery, and Eastsound has **Roses Bakery Cafe**, (360)376-4220. Roses features simple breakfasts and lunches, but locals prefer the outdoor patio for fresh blueberry scones, muffins, savory potpies, and lattes served in enormous bowls.

Orcas Island is the perfect place to relax with a good book in hand, and **Darvill's Book Store**, (360)376-2135, in Eastsound, houses an impressive stock of reading material for any and all interests. Pacific Northwest authors are well-represented here.

RESTAURANTS

Christina's ★★★ Christina's continues to enjoy its long-standing reputation as the premier restaurant in the San Juan Islands. And while Christina Orchid's big-city prices may frighten away the average Islander, her reputation lives up to urban expectations: price, in the end, proves irrelevant. Christina's ever-changing, innovative, neo-Northwest menu incorporates the freshest seasonal ingredients. Singing scallops, gathered off Guemes Island, are gently steamed in their elegant shells with fragrant hints of thyme and garlic. King salmon rests on a salmon-colored, citrus-flavored butter sauce, heralding spring with tender coils of fiddlehead ferns. Even a breast of chicken stuffed with herbed goat cheese—which might strike some as a tiresome recipe—is anything *but* in Christina's interpretation. The decor in this converted 1938 gas station is casually elegant ,with copper-topped tables, silver cutlery, and cloth napkins. The enclosed deck and outdoor patio offer a fantastic view of East Sound. Service, kept running smoothly by Christina's husband, Brooks, is—we're pleased to report—exemplary. ■ *Eastsound at North Beach Rd and Horseshoe Hwy; (360)376-4904; Eastsound; $$$; full bar; AE, DC, MC, V; checks OK; dinner every day June–Sept; (closed Tues during off season).*

Deer Harbor Lodge and Inn ★★ This expansive, rustic dining room with a large view deck is a cozy, soothing place, despite its size. Pam and Craig Carpenter have rescued the inn from its long career as a purveyor of battered chicken and made it home to some very good seafood, with generous portions. About a dozen entrees are outlined on the blackboard at the door and vary according to what's in season. Soups and salads arrive in large serving bowls, and the accompanying bread is homemade. Both the wine list and the beer list are thoughtfully conceived, with novelties like German wheat beer. For lodging, there's a two-story log cabin with eight rooms and two decks; breakfast arrives in a picnic basket outside your door. A new hot tub, too. ■ *From ferry landing, follow signs to Deer Harbor; (360)376-4110; Deer Harbor Rd, Deer Harbor; PO Box 142, Deer Harbor, WA 98243; $$; beer and wine; AE, MC, V; checks OK; dinner every day; (open weekends only off season).* &

Ship Bay Oyster House ★★ Ship Bay has developed a reputation as a great spot for fresh fish and local oysters. Lovers of the briny slimers will be in oyster heaven: baked, stewed, pan-fried, or au naturale (try an oyster shooter, served up in a shot glass with Clamato and sake), there's a 'ster for every palate. The Pacific Coast locale (a comfortable old farmhouse with a view of Ship Bay) belies the Atlantic Coast ambience. The clam chowder—a New Englandy version included with every entree—might be the best in the West, and the kitchen obviously never learned about portion control (just order a *small* slab of spicy-hot barbecue baby back ribs with its exceptional accompaniment of black beans and salsa, and you'll get our drift). ■ *Just east of Eastsound on Horseshoe Hwy; (360)376-5886; Eastsound; $$; full bar; AE, MC, V; checks OK; dinner every day (Tues–Sun off-season); (closed Dec–Feb).*

Bilbo's Festivo ★ Orcas Islanders speak of this cozy little place with reverence. Its decor and setting—mud walls, Mexican tiles, arched windows, big fireplace, handmade wooden benches, spinning fans, in a small house with a flowered courtyard—are charming, and the Navajo and Chimayo weavings on the walls are indeed from New Mexico. The fare includes a combination of Mexican and New Mexican influences, with improvisation on enchiladas, burritos, and chiles rellenos, and mesquite-grilled specials. In summer, lunch is served taqueria-style, grilled to order outdoors, then heaped with the condiments of your choice. ■ *In central Eastsound; (360)376-4728; Northbeach Rd and A St, Eastsound; $; full bar; MC, V; local checks only; dinner every day (lunch May–Oct).*

Cafe Olga ★ You're likely to experience a wait at Cafe Olga, a popular lunch and late-afternoon stop for locals and visitors alike. Luckily, this country kitchen is part of the Orcas Island Artworks, a sprawling cooperative crafts gallery in a picturesque renovated strawberry-packing barn, so you can browse while you work up an appetite. The wholesome international home-style entrees range from a rich Sicilian artichoke pie to a chicken enchilada with black bean sauce to a Greek salad. For dessert, try a massive piece of the blackberry pie. ■ *East of Moran State Park at Olga Junction; (360)376-5098; Olga; $; beer and wine; MC, V; Washington State checks only; lunch every day.*

La Famiglia ★ Here's a mainstream Italian lunch and dinner spot that seems to have achieved the consistency to match its pleasant, sunny decor and reasonable prices (though, of late, we've had a number of reports about less-than-cordial service). The emphasis is on fresh pasta, calzone, and other hearty family fare befitting the name; try the chunks of veal sautéed in butter, wine, and lemon, nestled nicely alongside pasta and vegetables. ■ *Prune Alley and North Beach Rd; (360)376-2335; Prune Alley, Eastsound; $; full bar; AE, MC, V; local checks only; lunch Mon–Sat, dinner every day.* &

LODGINGS

Kangaroo House ★★ The location of this bed and breakfast, next to the Orcas airport, isn't scenic, but the 2-acre grounds are, and it's convenient to Eastsound and North Beach. The beautiful, enormous (6,700 square feet) 1907 Craftsman-style bungalow is done up in period style, with attractive antiques, a fieldstone fireplace in the living room, a rear deck perfect for a late-afternoon cocktail, and a hot tub set jewel-like in the colorful garden. Four guest rooms upstairs have an Amish farmhouse feel. A downstairs suite features a sitting room and private bath. There's a game room with cribbage and Trivial Pursuit for rainy days. Jan and Mike Russillo run their place with a professional blend of warmth and efficiency, and welcome children. ■ *North Beach Rd just north of Eastsound; (360)376-2175; PO Box 334, Eastsound, WA 98245; $$; MC, V; checks OK.*

Spring Bay Inn ★★ Set on 57 heavily wooded acres rife with wildlife and hiking trails, this enormous new waterfront inn adjacent to Obstruction Pass State Park is an outdoor enthusiast's dream-come-true. Sandy Playa and Carl Burger, a youthful pair of retired state park rangers, live a crunchy-granola lifestyle that sets them apart from other upscale B&B owners. Their warm welcome lets you forgive the inn's sometimes overdone wildlife theme and the ill-lit pathways leading up to the house. The high-ceilinged great room offers a stunning view of Spring Bay. Upstairs are four beautiful rooms each with a large bath, Rumford fireplace, and bay view. Come morning, guests are led on a 2-hour kayak tour around Obstruction Island (beginners welcome, kayaks and equipment provided, harbor seal and eagle sightings free of charge), followed by a big, healthy brunch. Evenings, chat by the fire in the sitting room and enjoy a glass of wine and fresh-baked cookies; then sign up for a private soak under the stars in the bayside hot tub. ▪ *Follow Obstruction Pass Rd to Obstruction Pass Park Trailhead, take right fork onto dirt road to Spring Bay gate; (360)376-5531; PO Box 97, Olga, WA 98279; $$$; AE, MC, V; checks OK.*

Turtleback Farm Inn ★★ Located inland amid tall trees, rolling pastures, and private ponds, Turtleback offers seven spotless rooms dressed in simple sophistication. Unfortunately, we've found that the luxury and charm of Turtleback begins and ends with the facility and its scenic location; reports of not-so-gracious hospitality proved true on recent visits. In addition, morning comes earlier than you'd expect on vacation when you're abruptly awakened to the sound of maids cleaning next door. Still, the thought of a pleasant, filling breakfast served outdoors in warm weather, and the pretty-as-a-picture farmhouse with newborn lambs a-prancing below, lets us excuse (this time, at least) the bum's rush atmosphere we've encountered of late. ▪ *10 minutes from the ferry on Crow Valley Rd; (360)376-4914; Rt 1, Box 650, Eastsound, WA 98245; $$$; MC, V; checks OK.*

Beach Haven Resort ★ Regardless of the time of year, this funky family retreat with its long pebble beach, canoes and rowboats, and lack of maid service reminds us of summer camp. No TV. No telephones. No fussy amenities. Expect a seven-day minimum summer stay and consider coming in the off season when rates prove especially affordable (and you'll likely encounter fewer "campers"). Accommodations range through various grades of rustic — the wood stove–heated cabins, shielded by tall trees, are of the genuine log variety — to modern apartments and a "Spectacular Beachcomber" four-bedroom house. ▪ *8½ miles NW of the ferry at President Channel; (360)376-2288; Rt 1, Box 12, Eastsound, WA 98245; $$; MC, V; checks OK.* ♿

North Beach Inn ★ If you like funky, private settings with history and personality, North Beach Inn is the spot. Originally an apple orchard, then converted into a resort in the early '30s, North Beach Inn has remained relatively unchanged ever since. Eleven worn cabins are laid out on a prime stretch of the Gibson family beach. The spiffiest: Columbia, Frazier, and Shamrock (which has a loft that kids adore). Each cabin comes complete with a full kitchen, grill, Adirondack chairs on the beach (bonfires allowed), and a tremendous view. Also likely: duck-print flannel sheets, flimsy floral curtains, or artwork and furniture probably picked up at a local garage sale. Bring Fido if you'd like. One-week minimum stay July and August; two-day minimum rest of the year. ▪ *1½ miles west of the airport at*

North Beach Rd; (360)376-2660; PO Box 80, Eastsound, WA 98245; $$; no credit cards; checks OK; (closed after Thanksgiving through mid-Feb).

Orcas Hotel ★ The 12-room hostelry just above the ferry terminal is a gem, with period pieces (the hotel was first built in 1904), white wicker in the lovely gardens, and a deck overlooking the water (though the gas tanks make for a less-than-perfect view). The best rooms are the two new, larger rooms, which have private balconies and whirlpool tubs. It feels like a small, romantic hotel (breakfast included). The pub with deck is a favorite local watering hole, and the bakery a good place to get bread for an afternoon picnic. The same management rents out a two-bedroom Fox Glove Cottage on the water at Deer Harbor (very pricey privacy). ▪ *Orcas ferry landing; (360)376-4300; PO Box 155, Orcas, WA 98280; $$$; AE, MC, V; checks OK; breakfast, lunch, dinner every day.*

SAN JUAN ISLANDS: SAN JUAN

San Juan Island is the most populated in the archipelago; therefore it supports the biggest town, Friday Harbor, though typically nightlife is scarce even here, especially in the off season. Attractions include the mid-19th-century sites of the **American** and **English Camps**, established when ownership of the island was under dispute. The conflict led to the infamous Pig War of 1859–1860, so called because the sole casualty was a pig. The Americans and British shared joint occupation until 1872, when the dispute was settled in favor of the United States. The English camp, toward the island's north end, is wooded and secluded, while the American camp is open, windy prairie and beach, inhabited now only by thousands of rabbits. Either makes a fine picnic spot. So does **San Juan County Park**, where it's also possible to camp on the dozen often-crowded acres on Smallpox Bay (reservations suggested, (360)378-2992). Another option is **Lakedale Campground** (reservations suggested), 4½ miles from Friday Harbor on Roche Harbor Road, (360)378-2350, which sports 82 acres and three private lakes for swimming and fishing, and is popular with bicyclists. The best diving in the archipelago (some claim it's the best cold-water diving in the world) can be had here; **Emerald Seas Diving Center**, 180 First Street, Friday Harbor, (360)378-2772, rents equipment and runs charter boats. It also rents sea kayaks, a wonderful way to see the island's wildlife up close. If you're lucky (best in late spring), you may even encounter whales that belong to the three native pods of orcas. Or you can join a guided kayak trip; **Shearwater Adventures** runs tours in conjunction with the Whale Museum, 62 First Street, Friday Harbor, (360)378-4710. Several charter boats are also available for whale watching and fishing; try the **Western Prince**, (360)378-5315 or (800)757-ORCA(6722). Those distrustful of their sea legs can visit the nation's first official whale-watching park at **Lime Kiln Point State Park** on the island's west side. Bring binoculars and a lot of patience.

The **San Juan Historical Museum** is located in an old home in Friday Harbor filled with memorabilia from the island's early days. The 90-plus-year-old founder, a third-generation islander, is there two days a week. Admission is free; (360)378-3949. Another bit of history is hidden away at the **Roche Harbor Resort** (see review). Here you'll find a mausoleum, a bizarre monument that may tell more about timber tycoon John McMillin than does all the rest of Roche Harbor. The ashes of family members are contained in a set of stone chairs that surround a concrete dining room table. They're ringed by a set of 30-foot-high columns, symbolic of McMillin's adherence to Masonic beliefs.

Oyster fans will be happy to visit **Westcott Bay Sea Farms** off West Valley Road just north of English Camp, (360)378-2489, where you can help yourself to oysters at bargain prices.

Jazz Festival. Throngs of people infest the streets of Friday Harbor for three days of Dixieland jazz, mid- to late July; for information, call (360)378-5509.

▼

▲

RESTAURANTS

Duck Soup Inn ★★ Richard and Gretchen Allison are committed to continuing the ambitious reach of the kitchen with local seafoods and seasonal ingredients, and they've succeeded admirably. The wood-paneled dining room, with its stone fireplace, wooden booths, and high windows, is a charmer. The menu is limited to house specialties—succulent prawns served in a spicy tomato curry with cucumber dipping sauce, applewood-smoked Westcott Bay oysters, and grilled fresh fish. Housebaked bread served with tangy anchovy paste (and butter), a small bowl of perfectly seasoned soup, and a large green salad accompany the ample portions. No wonder there's little room left for dessert. ■ *4½ miles north of Friday Harbor on Roche Harbor Rd; (360)378-4878; 3090 Roche Harbor Rd, Friday Harbor; $$; beer and wine; DC, MC, V; local checks only; dinner Wed–Sun; (closed in winter).*

Roberto's ★★ Word is, Roberto Carrieri worked in about every restaurant on the island and finally decided to open one himself and do it right. He did. Now everyone's talking about Carrieri and Paul Aiello's tiny Italian restaurant in its little perch above the ferry parking lot. If you want to get in, we suggest the first thing you do upon arriving at Friday Harbor is make reservations (even in the off season). Arrive hungry: portions are huge. And arrive early: the best dishes, such as the ravioli in a sage, Parmesan cheese, and black pepper sauce, disappear early. But even when they do, the rest of the specials are outstanding. Who needs dessert? ■ *Corner of 1st and A sts; (360)378-6333; 205 A St, Friday Harbor; $$$; beer and wine; AE, MC, V; checks OK; dinner every day; (winter hours vary).*

Springtree Cafe ★★ Chef/owner James Boyle garners praise from locals and tourists alike for his consistently excellent Northwest cuisine. Decor is simple—no tablecloths, plain wooden tables graced by a few fresh flowers, some photographs on the walls. But the menu, emphasizing seafood, organics, and local produce, is anything but simple. A recent dinner found us wowed by a spicy Dungeness crab cake and an enormous plate of corkscrew pasta with smoked mussels, prawns, and crabmeat in a basil cream sauce. The best food here is that which is the most adventurous. Vegetarians are well cared for since Boyle eschews meat. Service is folksy and energetic; there's outdoor dining on the small patio, weather permitting. ■ *Under the elm on Spring downtown; (360)378-4848; 310 Spring St, Friday Harbor; $$; full bar; MC, V; local checks only; lunch, dinner every day in summer; (Tues–Sat off-season).*

Katrina's Out of her tiny kitchen in the back of a second-hand store, Kate Stone runs her one-woman culinary show. Except for her signature spinach-cheese pie and green salad with toasted hazelnuts and garlicky blue cheese dressing, you never know what you might find here. Stone's been known to arrive in the morning and ask her first customers if they have any preferences for the day's menu. Odds are, whatever she's serving will be a simple sensation. With three stools inside and a few tippy tables in the ramshackle yard, the food's the real centerpiece here. ■ *2 blocks up from the ferry terminal behind Funk & Junk; (360)378-7290; 65 Nichols St, Friday Harbor; $; no alcohol; no credit cards; checks OK; lunch, early dinners Mon–Fri.* &

LODGINGS

Friday Harbor House ★★★ Some shudder at the exterior architecture of San Juan Island's newest inn, a sister property of the Inn at Langley on Whidbey Island. Others consider this stylish urban hotel in the islands a relief from Victorian B&Bs. Regardless, inside is a bastion of soothing serenity. Each of the 20 rooms is decorated in muted tones, giving them an Oriental ambience, with gas fireplaces, tiny standing-room-only balconies, and Jacuzzis positioned to absorb the warmth from both the fireplace and the harbor view. Just be sure to ask for a room in the main building, as several in a smaller rear building do not have a full waterfront view. Two-night minimum during peak season. Enjoy a continental breakfast of steaming hot scones. We've encountered early praise for chef Greg

Atkinson's beautifully prepared local seafood, game, and meats. ■ *Turn right on 1st and right again on West St; (360) 378-8455; PO Box 1385, 130 West St, Friday Harbor, WA 98250; $$$; full bar; AE, DC, MC, V; checks OK; dinner every day (Thurs–Mon in the winter).* &

Duffy House ★★ This 1920s farmhouse looking out upon Griffin Bay and the Olympics beyond displays an architectural style (Tudor) that's rare in the islands, in a splendid, isolated site. Decorated with antiques and accented with classic mahogany trim, Duffy House offers five comfy guest rooms, all of which now have private baths. The sunken living room sports a large fireplace and a bounty of information about the islands. Even neophyte bird-watchers won't be able to miss the bald eagles here; they nest in the backyard. ■ *Take Argyle Rd south from town to Pear Point Rd; (360) 378-5604 or (800) 972-2089; 760 Pear Point Rd, Friday Harbor, WA 98250; $$; MC, V; checks OK.*

Mariella Inn and Cottages ★★ This 11-room inn, built in 1902, is set on a 9-acre point, an easy stroll from Friday Harbor. The rooms are simple and elegant. Our favorite is the Fleur du Soleil, a large room warmed with sunlight. Others prefer Arequipa, a corner waterside room with its own bath. (Robes are provided.) Prices are high, especially considering the many rooms with shared bath. The better values are to be found in the seven cabins set unobtrusively in the madronas on the waterfront (great for families). The nicest of these are the Maple and Ivy cabins, which have wood stoves, kitchens, and waterfront decks. Guests might spend the day exploring the island (sea kayaks, mountain bikes, daysailers for rent to guests), then return to relax before the parlor fireplace or soak privately in the cedar hot tub. In the morning, guests meet in the dining room for a simple breakfast. Those staying in the cabins get breakfast delivered to their door. A 65-foot classic motor yacht (1927) is available for charter. During the summer, the large lawn is often set for a game of volleyball or a round of croquet. At press time, the inn's restaurant was set to serve dinner in season, although Greg Atkinson, who has moved to Friday Harbor House, will no doubt be missed. ■ *Left on 1st St, follow signs until turns into Turnpoint Rd; (360) 378-6868; 630 Turnpoint Rd, Friday Harbor, WA 98250; $$$; beer and wine; MC, V; checks OK; dinner every day, reservations necessary (winter restaurant hours vary).*

Olympic Lights ★★ As you approach this isolated bed and breakfast, you may recall the movie *Days of Heaven*: the tall Victorian farmhouse sits lonely as a lighthouse in a sea of open meadow. The renovated interior is more modern and elegant: four upstairs rooms, all with queen beds, furnished with antiques, and bathed in sunlight. The downstairs room

San Juan Islands: San Juan

Lodgings

is the only one with a private bath, but you shouldn't let that sway you from choosing this retreat. You must remove your shoes to tread the off-white pile carpet. The panorama of Olympic Mountains and Strait of Juan de Fuca from the south rooms adds to the effect. Breakfast includes fresh eggs from the resident hen; they also have four cats who roam downstairs. ▪ *Take Argyle Ave out of Friday Harbor to Cattle Point Rd; (360)378-3186; 4531-A Cattle Point Rd, Friday Harbor, WA 98250; $$; no credit cards; checks OK.*

Westwinds Bed & Breakfast ★★ Westwinds commands what may easily be the most magnificent view on all of the San Juan Islands. Unfortunately, too few people will enjoy the 6 acres of mountainside abundant with deer and quail. This private glass-and-wood paradise is a two-bedroom facility (guests have the 1,200-square-foot house to themselves). Look from your cathedral-ceilinged bedroom, private bath, patio, living room, or virtually any seat in the house, and you're likely to feel in possession of a large part of the world (or at least the Strait of Juan de Fuca and the Olympic Mountains). Breakfast is almost as majestic. Particularly popular with honeymoon couples (privacy is never an issue), this bed and breakfast is to be enjoyed whatever the occasion, whatever the season. ▪ *2 miles from Lime Kiln Whale Watch Park; (360)378-5283; 4909 H Hannah Highlands, Friday Harbor, WA 98250; $$$; MC, V; checks OK.*

Friday's ★ The former Elite Hotel is living up to its old name. Innkeepers Debbie and Steve Demarest have taken this long-time bunkhouse and given it a completely new life. Nine rooms are decorated in rich colors of wine, water, and wings. The best room in the place is unquestionably the third-floor nest with its own deck (and water view), kitchen, double shower, and Jacuzzi tub. Heated floors in the bathrooms, bowls of candies, and bedtime mints are just some of the thoughtful touches; however, the inn is right in the middle of town and not always the most quiet retreat. Downstairs is a bistro with good pizzas and huge salads. The ambitious Demarests have opened a second inn, five blocks away, called **Panacea**. All four rooms feature private baths, two have Jacuzzis, one has a fireplace. ▪ *2 blocks up from the ferry on 1st St; (360)378-5848 or (800)352-2632; PO Box 2023, Friday Harbor, WA 98250; $$; MC, V; checks OK.*

Hillside House ★ This 4,000-square-foot modern house on the outskirts of Friday Harbor distinguishes itself from other contemporary country-style B&Bs by, among other things, its full-flight aviary. Sleep in one of the rooms adjacent to it and you might find yourself waking up and staring into the face of Bob, an enormous Reeves pheasant. The plushest room is the Eagle's Nest, a third-floor suite with TV, phone, wet bar, a small

▼

San Juan Islands: San Juan

Lodgings

▲

balcony, and a whirlpool tub. Owners Dick and Cathy Robinson keep a fax machine for those who just can't leave it all behind. ■ *On Carter Ave, west of the ferry landing; (360)378-4730 or (800)232-4730; 365 Carter Ave, Friday Harbor, WA 98250; $$; AE, MC, V; checks OK.*

Lonesome Cove Resort ★ Back in 1945, Roy and Neva Durhack sailed their 35-foot yacht here from the Hawaiian Islands. They were getting ready to sail it around the world, but once they saw Lonesome Cove their wanderlust subsided. They're not here anymore but the resort remains a pretty spot. The six immaculate little cabins set among trees at the water's edge, the manicured lawns, and the domesticated deer that wander the 75-acre woods make the place a favorite for lighthearted honeymooners. The sunsets are spectacular, and there's a fine view of nearby Spieden Island. Cabins have a five-night minimum in the summer months (two nights at other times). No pets—too many baby ducks around. ■ *Take Roche Harbor Rd 9 miles north to Lonesome Cove Rd; (360) 378-4477; 5810 Lonesome Cove Rd, Friday Harbor, WA 98250; $$; MC, V; checks OK.* ⅛

Trumpeter Inn ★ Trumpeter Inn is located in splendid isolation in the middle of farmlands about 2 miles outside of Friday Harbor. The pastoral setting is soothing, as are the simply decorated guest rooms with lots of soothing white. All rooms have a king- or queen-size bed with crisp cotton sheets and down comforters, and private baths. We prefer the Bay Laurel room, a second-floor corner room with a great view of the surrounding meadows and the Olympics in the distance. You may even glimpse the trumpeter swans for whom the inn is named if you visit in winter. Leave your car behind; owners will pick up guests from the ferry. ■ *Follow Spring St from Friday Harbor, which runs into San Juan Valley Rd; (360)378-3884 or (800)826-7926; 420 Trumpeter Way, Friday Harbor, WA 98250; $$; MC, V; checks OK.* ⅛

Wharfside Bed & Breakfast ★ If nothing lulls you to sleep like the gentle lap of the waves, the Wharfside's the B&B for you. It's this region's first realization of the European tradition of floating inns. Two guest rooms on the 60-foot sailboat *Jacquelyn* are both very nicely finished with full amenities and that compact precision that only living on a boat can inspire. The fore cabin has a double bed and sleeping berths for kids or extras. When the weather's good, enjoy the huge breakfast on deck and watch the local fishermen gather their nets. ■ *On the K dock in Friday Harbor; (360)378-5661; PO Box 1212, Friday Harbor, WA 98250; $$; V, MC; checks OK.*

Moon & Sixpence Moon & Sixpence is a country B&B with a slightly artsy flourish (witness the nod to W. Somerset

Maugham in the name). Charlie and Evelyn Tuller's sunny farmhouse in the middle of San Juan Island is done up tastefully in a gamut of folk arts. There are four lodging options, but the best spot is the water tower, with exposed post-and-beam construction, a reading loft, bathroom, and pastoral views out of all four sides. The farm pond is a dandy spot for picnics, barbecues, or just counting the clouds. Children welcome (the Island Suite is a good pick for families). ■ *3 miles from the ferry dock on Beaverton Valley Rd; (360)378-4138; 3021 Beaverton Valley Rd, Friday Harbor, WA 98250; $$; no credit cards; checks OK.*

Roche Harbor Resort When you walk out of the stately old ivy-clad Hotel de Haro at Roche Harbor and gaze out at the trellised, cobblestoned waterfront and yacht-dotted bay, you'll forget all about the creaky, uneven floor boards, the somewhat pieced-together wallpaper, the sparse furnishings. The resort evolved from the company town that John McMillin built a century ago for his lime mill, once the largest west of the Mississippi. It has seen some renovation since Teddy Roosevelt visited, but not tons. Still, the 107-year-old resort has a terrific view, a few renovated cottages, and condos. Between strolling the gardens, swimming, tennis, and visiting the mausoleum (really), there's plenty to do at Roche Harbor. Come by boat or plane if you'd like; just make sure you have a way to get into Friday Harbor for dinner. ■ *Roche Harbor; (360)378-2155; PO Box 4001, Roche Harbor, WA 98250; $$$; AE, MC, V; checks OK.*

LA CONNER

La Conner was founded in 1867 by John Conner, a trading-post operator, who named the town after his wife, L(ouisa) A. Conner. Much of what you see today was built before the railroads arrived in the late 1880s, when the fishing and farming communities of Puget Sound traded almost entirely by water. In an age of conformity and efficiency, the town became a literal backwater, and something of a haven for nonconformists (Wobblies, WWII COs, McCarthy-era escapees, beatniks, hippies, and bikers), always with a fair smattering of artists and writers, including Mark Tobey, Morris Graves, Guy Anderson, and Tom Robbins.

This long-standing "live and let live" attitude of the town has allowed the neighboring native American Swinomish community to contribute to the exceptional cultural richness of La Conner. Even the merchants here have created a unique atmosphere, an American bazaar: **Chez la Zoom**, **Cottons**, **Nasty Jack's**, and **Intimate Dwellings**.

Tillinghast Seed Co., at the entrance to town, is the oldest operating retail and mail-order seed store in the Northwest (since 1885); in addition to seeds it has a wonderful nursery, a florist shop, and a general store, (360)466-3329. **Go Outside** is a small but choice garden and garden-accessory store, (360)466-4836. If all this shopping leaves you in need of respite, repair to the **Rose and Thistle** tea room and antique shop for afternoon tea, (360)466-3313.

Gaches Mansion, on Second Street overlooking the main drag, is a wonderful example of American Victorian architecture, with a widow's walk that looks out on the entire Skagit Valley. It is filled with period furnishings, and a small museum of Northwest art occupies the second floor. Open weekends, (360)466-4288.

RESTAURANTS

Palmers Restaurant and Pub ★★ Palmers continues to be La Conner's favorite restaurant. Thomas and Danielle Palmers's place is perched on a knoll just behind town at the far end of the La Conner Country Inn. Locals like the hobbitlike pub with wall murals painted by La Conner artists; but for a more elegant atmosphere, climb the stairs. There are two rooms—one with lace curtains on the west-facing windows that pull in the golden evening sun, another with a wood stove to warm winter evenings. The deck is a pleasant spot too. Dinners are reliable; the massive lamb shank bergère is tender and savory with garlic, tomatoes, mushrooms, and herbs. A special prawn dish, with papaya, kiwi, and cilantro, shows the kitchen can work just as successfully with more exotic flavorings. ■ *2nd and Washington; (360)466-4261; 205 Washington, La Conner; $$; full bar; AE, MC, V; checks OK; lunch, dinner every day.*

▼

La Conner

▲

Calico Cupboard ★ It's awfully cute—Laura Ashley meets Laura Ingalls Wilder—but the bakery is the reason to go, turning out excellent carrot muffins, pecan tarts, shortbread, raspberry bars, currant scones, apple Danish, and much more. Our advice for avoiding the weekend crowds: buy your goodies from the bakery's take-out counter and find a sunny bench by the water. Hearty waffle and omelet breakfasts are offered, but let's face it, most folks come here for the pastries. There's another Calico in Anacortes. ■ *South end of the line on 1st; (360)466-4451; 720 S 1st, La Conner; $; beer and wine; no credit cards; checks OK; breakfast, lunch, every day.*

La Conner Seafood & Prime Rib House ★ Every weekend, those in the know drop in to get their names on the waiting list and pop out again for another 20 minutes of window-shopping. Their reward is excellent seafood (pasta with fresh Dungeness crab or baby Rock Point oysters sautéed with fresh fennel), and the young are happy with fish 'n' chips. In warm weather, diners flee the split-level dining room of channel-view tables for the ample outdoor seating on the deck. ■ *On the waterfront;*

(360)466-4014; 614 1st St, La Conner; $$; full bar; AE, DC, MC, V; checks OK; lunch, dinner every day.

LODGINGS

The Heron in La Conner ★★ The Heron is one of the prettiest hostelries in town, with 12 rooms done in jewel-box fashion. Splurge on room 31, the Bridal Suite with a Jacuzzi and gas fireplace, or room 32, with a fireplace, spacious sitting area, and a wonderful view of the Skagit Valley and Cascades. A redecoration of the rooms was underway at press time; the finished products (so far) were lovely. Downstairs is an elegant living room with wing chairs and a formal breakfast dining room. Out back you may have a barbecue in the stone fire pit or slip into the hot tub. ■ *On the edge of town on Maple St; (360)466-4626; 117 Maple St, La Conner; PO Box 716, La Conner, WA 98257; $$; AE, MC, V; checks OK.*

La Conner Channel Lodge ★★ At the edge of the Swinomish Channel, the Channel Lodge is a fit urban version of its slightly dowdy cousin, The Country Inn, a few blocks inland. It's an appealing place due mainly to its prime waterfront location. Your fireplace (gas) is lit upon arrival and some of the rooms have a Jacuzzi with a channel view. If you're not splurging for a splash, make sure to request a channel-view room away from (or at least not directly underneath) those with potentially noisy waterjets. The decks are nooks—just enough for a chair and fresh air while you watch the tugs work the waterway. Breakfast is rather perfunctory. ■ *On the waterfront at the north end of town; (360)466-1500; 205 N 1st St, La Conner, WA 98257; $$$; AE, DC, MC, V; checks OK.*

La Conner

Lodgings

Rainbow Inn ★★ Set amid acres of Skagit Valley flatlands, this elegant turn-of-the-century farmhouse offers sweeping views of lush pastures, Mount Baker, and the Olympics from eight pretty guest rooms. American country-pine furnishings are in keeping with the farmhouse theme and robes are provided for a dip in the inn's hot tub. Even though one side of the Violet Room faces the road, it's still our favorite with its grand potbelly stove and access to the second-story porch. Downstairs are plenty of lingering zones. Owner Sharon Briggs serves inventive breakfasts (such as black bean pancakes with salsa) on an enchanting French-windowed front porch with tables for two—a plus if you can't handle conversation before coffee. ■ *½ mile east of town; (360)466-4578; 1075 Chilberg Rd, La Conner; PO Box 15, La Conner, WA 98257; $$; MC, V; checks OK.*

White Swan Guest House ★★ Poplars line the driveway, Adirondack chairs are placed throughout the garden grounds, wheat and tulip fields stretch beyond. Peter Goldfarb's house is splashed with warm yellow, salmon, evergreen, and peach, and seems to soak up the sunlight—even in the rain. Pamper yourself with a soak in the large claw-footed tub, or curl up on the pink sofa in front of the wood stove. A charming guest house (one of the few in the valley) out back provides an especially private accommodation; great for families or romantics. Peter serves a breakfast of freshly baked scones or muffins, fruit from his orchard, and coffee. Bring binoculars for bird-watching and bikes for easy touring around the flat farmlands of Fir Island. ▪ *6 miles southeast of La Conner; (360) 445-6805; 1388 Moore Rd, Mt Vernon, WA 98273; $$; MC, V; checks OK.*

The Wild Iris ★ This addition to the La Conner lodging scene gears itself toward romance with its spacious suites, each featuring a gas fireplace, oversize Jacuzzi tub, and panoramic west-facing view. The standard rooms face the parking lot and seem a bit too cramped. If you're here on Friday or Saturday night, do make reservations for dinner (guests only). The dining room has country charm, but the real magic is in the seasonally changing menu, which could include an excellent fresh swordfish with a horseradish crust or a buttery beef tenderloin in a velvety Madeira sauce with shiitake mushrooms. The breakfast buffet is also a treat, offering perhaps a delicious hot, spiced fruit soup or a vegetable quiche. ▪ *On the edge of town on Maple Ave; (360) 466-1400 or (800) 477-1400; 121 Maple Ave, La Conner; PO Box 696, La Conner, WA 98257; $$$; AE, MC, V; checks OK.*

Hotel Planter The most famous (and infamous) characters of La Conner's colorful past once inhabited this end of town. Today, owner Don Hoskins has used his connoisseur's eye and artisan's care to create a style that is a tasteful blend of past (original woodwork staircase and entrance) and present (private baths and armoire-hidden TVs in every room). Six rooms face the waterfront (and the often noisy main street); others overlook a Renaissance garden courtyard (with a reserved hot tub). The staff, well-versed on the Skagit Valley, is exemplary. ▪ *End of the line on the south end of 1st St; (360) 466-4710; 715 S 1st St, La Conner; PO Box 702, La Conner, WA 98257; $$; AE, MC, V; checks OK.* ♿

MOUNT VERNON

Mount Vernon is a rare working town: one in which there are more good restaurants and bookstores than taverns and churches. It is the Big City to residents of surrounding Skagit and Island counties, and a college town to a surprising number of local folk, even though Skagit Valley College is but a blip on the very outskirts of town.

The classy old town center of Mount Vernon heroically

survived the terrible winter floods of 1990, the worst river flooding since the town was founded 101 years before. The Mount Vernon Mall was not so lucky, virtually wiped out that same year by the opening of the Cascade Mall in neighboring Burlington.

To travelers on I-5, it is little more than a blur except during the spring when the lush farmlands are brilliantly swathed in daffodils (mid-March to mid-April), tulips (April through early May), and irises (mid-May to mid-June). The pastoral countryside is flat and ideal for bicyclists, except for the gridlock that occurs on the small farm lanes during the **Tulip Festival** (usually early April). Mount Vernon is really all about fresh food and beautiful flowers, products of surrounding Skagit Valley farms. For information on the many harvest festivals (June is Strawberry Month, September Apple Month, and October Redleaf Month), call the Chamber of Commerce, (360)428-8547.

Little Mountain Park has a terrific picnic spot plus a knockout vista of the valley (look for migratory trumpeter swans in February). On the other end of the spectrum, **The Chuck Wagon Drive Inn** offers 50 different kinds of burgers, electric trains, and the world's largest collection of ceramic whiskey-bottle cowboys.

▼

RESTAURANTS

Wildflowers ★★★ Without doubt, chef David Day and owner Michele Kjosen have created a restaurant worthy of considerable attention. And attention *is* the secret—attention to the smallest detail, in the kitchen, on the plate, in the surrounding ambience. It begins with Kjosen's attention to her guests, which verges on excessive but never crosses the line. Without her help we might have overlooked a marvelous entree: grilled prawns with tamari, ginger, citrus, and herb marinade with a fresh mango-pineapple salsa. Inspirations such as this come on a daily basis. Chef Day has succeeded in nurturing his wildflowers to full bloom year-round. ■ *From I-5, exit at College Way and head east ; (360)424-9724; 2001 E College Way, Mt Vernon; $$$; beer and wine; AE, MC, V; checks OK; dinner Tues–Sat.*

▲

The Longfellow Cafe ★★ Local people fill the Longfellow Cafe because they have come to expect good food. With high volume, high ceilings, and high expectations, chef/co-owner Peter Barnard also has a creative, playful twist or two to lavish on us. The "steamers" with lemon-dill butter were a mélange of butter clams, blue mussels, and pink singing scallops, all locally harvested and wonderfully prepared. Brother-and-sister team Peter and Annye Barnard have worked hard to warm up the cavernous old brick granary, now a showcase of Skagit Valley produce and their solid culinary talents. The adjacent bookstore (Scott's) makes a happy ending. ■ *In the historic*

Granary Building; (360)336-3684; 121 B Freeway Dr, Mt Vernon; $$$; beer and wine; MC, V; local checks only; lunch Mon–Sun, dinner Tues–Sat.

Pacioni's Pizzeria ★ Wafts of fresh bread, fresh herbs, and fresh espresso tug at passersby. Those who give in to temptation congregate at the red-and-white-checkered tables, enjoy a friendly glass of red wine, and savor the pungency of pizza. Young owners Dave and Paula Alberts have thrown their hearts into this restaurant as impressively as Dave throws the pizza dough into the air (remember the mad Italian baker in *Moonstruck*?). Paula (née Pacioni) is the keeper of family secrets, but we'll let you in on our favorite pie, the tri-color pizza (pesto, ricotta, and Roma tomatoes). *Everything* is made to order. ▪ *In old downtown Mt Vernon; (360)336-3314; 606 S 1st St, Mt Vernon; $; beer and wine; no credit cards; checks OK; lunch Tues–Sat, dinner Mon–Sat.*

STANWOOD

Stanwood is a sleepy little farm center with a Scandinavian heritage, a Midwestern air, and one good reason for a few minutes' sightseeing. Years ago, local daughter Martha Anderson started working at *rosemaling*, traditional Norwegian "flower painting," and teaching it to her fellow Stanwoodians. Now they've embellished many everyday businesses with charming rosemaled signs—not for tourist show as in Leavenworth, but out of an authentic impulse to express their heritage and make Main Street pretty.

Mount Vernon

Restaurants

    Pilchuck School. Founded in 1971 by glass artist Dale Chihuly and Seattle art patrons John Hauberg and Anne Gould Hauberg, Pilchuck is an internationally renowned glass art school. Students live and study on this campus, situated in the midst of a country tree farm. An open house twice each summer gives folks a chance to see craftspeople at work; call first for times and directions. Summer: (360)445-3111; winter: (360)621-8422.

CAMANO ISLAND

LODGINGS

Willcox House ★ Out of 60 windows you get fine views of Skagit Bay, and in clear weather you can see Mount Baker from the meadowlike lawn. Four guest rooms in this turretted clapboard house are decorated with antiques and brass and iron beds. All have private baths. The Captain's Room that adjoins the turret is a wonderfully sunny spot to read. The morning's meal might be an omelet of local wild mushrooms, muffins, fruit, juice, and coffee. ▪ *1 mile west of Stanwood;*

(360)629-4746; 1462 Larkspur Lane, Camano Island, WA 98292; $$; MC, V; checks OK.

EVERETT

Timber and fishing were once this county seat's raison d'être, as were the booms and busts that follow the extraction of those natural resources. And while timber still means big business for Everett, the new state-of-the-art U.S. Naval Base will bring even more to the city's growing economy and its ever increasing population (now at 78,000). Everett is experiencing new pride, evident in the revitalization of the downtown core. The redevelopment of the **Hotel Monte Cristo,** a historic landmark boarded up for 20 years, provided a gorgeous new home for the Everett Symphony, the Arts Council, a stunning display of Pilchuck glass, and some fine restaurants.

The **Everett AquaSox** (formerly the Everett Giants, now the single A short-season team for the Seattle Mariners) even draw folks away from Seattle's Kingdome to enjoy baseball the old-fashioned way: outdoors. Call (206)258-3673 for tickets and information.

Boeing's South Everett plant offers free 90-minute tours of the world's largest plant (measured in volume), where you can watch the assembly of the aviation giant's 747s, 767s, and the new 777s (strict height requirements for children, tours fill early); call (206)342-4801.

RESTAURANTS

Passport ★★ Owners/chefs Lil Miller and Nan Wilkinson began an ambitious dream to bring a culinary taste of the world to this mill town. And they have certainly pulled it off. Now in the newly resurrected landmark Hotel Monte Cristo, Passport revels in an even better venue in which to showcase their around-the-world menu. If the food seems unfamiliar, don't be shy: it is all good. Perhaps you'll try a Peruvian pork roast sautéed with apples; an Egyptian asha with grilled and steamed vegetables, lentils, curry, and basmati rice; Thai rice noodles with shrimp, chicken, and vegetables in a minty peanut sauce; or—closer to home in inspiration—crisp salmon cakes and pan-fried oysters. Breads and desserts come from Pavé, Miller and Wilkinson's specialty bakery, a few blocks away on Colby Avenue. ■ *In the Hotel Monte Cristo at Hewitt and Wall; (206)259-5037; 1509 Wall St, Everett; $$; full bar; MC, V; local checks only; lunch Mon–Fri, dinner Mon–Sat.* &

The Sisters This place is as popular as it is funky. Soups such as mulligatawny, gazpacho, or just plain old beef barley can be outstanding. Sandwiches range from average deli stuff to more healthful concoctions, including a vegetarian burger made with chopped cashews and sunflower seeds. Among the morning fare are some delights—the blueberry or pecan hotcakes; granola with yogurt and blueberry sauce; or scrambled eggs with all kinds of extra goodies wrapped in flour tortillas. Fresh-squeezed lemonade and strawberry lemonade will quench your thirst, a big slice of blackberry pie will cure whatever ails you. ■ *8 blocks west of Broadway, in the Everett Public Market; (206)252-0480; 2804 Grand St, Everett; $; no alcohol; MC, V; checks OK; breakfast, lunch Mon–Fri.*

LODGINGS

Marina Village Inn ★★ Waterfront accommodations are a surprising rarity on Puget Sound, making this 27-room inn on Port Gardner Bay all the more attractive. You get many of the perks expected from a big-city hotel without the parking problems and convention crowds—which explains its increasing popularity with corporate executives (so reserve in advance). Rooms are contemporary and stylish, with oak furnishings, tasteful appointments, wet bars, satellite TV, refrigerators, handcrafted ceramic sinks, extension phones in the bathrooms, and trouser presses. Some have notably comfy couches and easy chairs, many have Jacuzzis, and most have telescopes for gazing out over the water. Book a room on the harbor side; sea lions might be lollygagging in the sun on the nearby jetty. ■ *Exit 193 off I-5 onto Pacific Ave, turn right on W Marine View Dr to waterfront; (206)259-4040; 1728 W Marine View Dr, Everett, WA 98201; $$; AE, DC, MC, V; no checks.*

SNOHOMISH

This small community, formerly an active lumber town, now bills itself as the "Antique Capital of the Northwest." It certainly has plenty of antique shops filling the downtown historic district; the **Star Center Mall** is the largest, with 175 antique dealers from all over the area; 829 Second Street, (360)568-2131. When you're through taking in the old, get a new perspective of Snohomish—from the air. Charter a scenic flight at Harvey Field, (360)568-1541; take a trip with Airial Hot Air Balloon Company (360)568-3025; or skydive with the folks at Snohomish Parachute Center, (360)568-5960.

MUKILTEO

Unfortunately, Mukilteo is probably best known for the traffic congestion caused by the **Washington State ferry** to Clinton on Whidbey Island; (360)355-7308. There are, however, a small state park and a historic lighthouse worth seeing. You can also stroll along the waterfront and fish off the docks.

Charles at Smugglers Cove ★★ Chef Claude Faure and his wife, Janet Kingma, took this landmark building, a 1929 speakeasy and distillery set on a bluff above Possession Sound, and turned it into an elegant restaurant. The atmosphere is country French, with dining rooms both upstairs and down, and a small terrace with views of the Sound. Such dishes as mushroom-sauced veal medallions and poulet aux crevettes (breast of chicken with prawns) appear on the classically French (and somewhat outdated) menu—along with the requisite Gruyère-topped onion soup and variations on the escargot theme. Save room for a fancy dessert like crêpes Suzette or Grand Marnier soufflé. ■ *At intersection of Hwys 525 and 526; (206)347-2700; 8340 53rd Ave W, Mukilteo; $$$; full bar; AE, MC, V; local checks only; lunch Tues–Fri, dinner Tues–Sat.*

WHIDBEY ISLAND

Whidbey Island has let just about everyone know that they are officially the longest island in the United States. But they haven't told too many people that Whidbey is only one of eight islands that make up Island County (the others are Camano, Ben Ure, Strawberry, Minor, Baby, Smith, and Deception). Named after Captain Joseph Whidbey, a sailing master for Captain George Vancouver, Whidbey Island was first surveyed and mapped by the two explorers in 1792. More than 200 years later, Whidbey's largest employer is the government (thanks to the Navy base in Oak Harbor). The island boasts pretty towns and communities, historical parks, sandy beaches, and some lovely rolling farmland.

Whidbey Island: Clinton

Although there are no bike lanes, Whidbey's flat, relatively traffic-free roads make it a good warm-weather biking destination, especially if you stay off the main highway.

WHIDBEY ISLAND: CLINTON

You won't find a manicured course or even a clubhouse at **Island Greens** (3890 E French Road, Clinton, (360)321-6042), but the par-3, nine-hole course is challenging, the location is scenic, and fees are amazingly low ($5 per person). This is an "alternative" golf course built by Dave and Karen Anderson on former farmland and maintained with minimal pesticides and fertilizers. **Cultus Bay Nursery** (4000 E Bailey Road, Clinton, (360)579-2329), open four days a week April through September, has a wide array of perennials, herbs, vines, and shrubs in a Victorian setting, and owner Mary Fisher is knowledgeable and helpful. **Jan Smith's Christmas House** (6930 S Cultus Bay Road, Clinton, (360)579-7838), located in a four-room cabin, displays handcrafted items including pottery, baby clothing, kitchen wares, and collectibles from more than 200 Whidbey Island artisans.

WHIDBEY ISLAND: LANGLEY

The nicest town on Whidbey still carries its small-town virtues well, though it may be getting a little too spit-and-polished for some. With the recent addition of Langley Village on Second Street, it has grown into a two-street town.

Shopping. Look for original Northwest art, from paintings and pottery to sculpture and glass at Childers-Proctor Gallery, (360)221-2978, on First Street. Swap stories with Josh Hauser at Moonraker Books, (360)221-6962, then grab a bag of popcorn from the antique- and candy-filled Wayward Son gift shop, (360) 221-3911. For singular shopping, try The Cottage, (360)221-4747, for heirloom lace and linens; Virginia's Antiques, (360) 221-7797, a repository of Asian and American wares; and Boomerang Books, (360)221-5404, with selections in all genres. JB's Ice Creamery and Espresso, (360)221-3888, is the place for both java and ice cream. Head to The Dog House, (360)221-9996, for a pitcher of microbrew (20 on tap, 100 beers total) after a movie or an evening of live theater at The Clyde, (360) 221-5525. The pesto pizza by the slice at Langley Village Bakery, (360)221-3525, is a local favorite. And the Whidbey Island Winery, 5237 S Langley Road, (360)221-2040 (open weekends year round), has a fine tasting room. Try their rhubarb wine.

Public Fishing. The small-boat harbor on Wharf Street has a 160-foot public fishing pier.

RESTAURANTS

Cafe Langley ★★ Owners Shant and Arshavir Gariban have maintained the sparkling consistency that established this downtown storefront cafe as the best bet in town from the moment it opened. Make a reservation (especially on weekends) and prepare for a fine Mediterranean/Greek dining experience. Appetizers range from Indian samosas to crab cakes. Don't overdo on the impossibly delicious hummus served with warm, chewy pita bread. The Greek salad is just the right taste before a feast of Mediterranean seafood stew, a lamb shish kabob, or one of the Land of the Sun–kissed preparations of fresh Northwest salmon or halibut. Split a Russian cream for dessert. ■ *At the south end of town; (360)221-3090; 113 1st St, Langley; $$; beer and wine; AE, MC, V; checks OK; dinner every day, lunch Wed–Mon (closed Tues in winter).*

Star Bistro ★ A steady staple of the Langley bistro scene, the Star (above the Star Store, a steady staple of the Langley shop scene) is a fun and color-splashed place that hops on weekends and after local events. Chef Paul Divina has put together a menu of basic, luscious vacation food—pastry-enclosed French onion soup, creamy oyster stew, spinach and caesar salads, pastas, burgers—along with fancier daily specials, all solid and reliable. There's a kids' menu and a breezy, sun-drenched deck, and you can pull up a stool at the red-topped bar for excellent martinis or margaritas. ■ *Above the Star Store on 1st; (360)221-2627; 201½ 1st St, Langley; $$; full bar; AE, MC, V; checks OK; lunch every day, dinner Tues–Sun.*

LODGINGS

Inn at Langley ★★★ It's difficult to conceive of a more idyllic getaway, or one more evocative of the Pacific Northwest, than Paul and Pam Schell's first private venture, built elegantly into the bluff over the Saratoga Passage. Architect Alan Grainger designed the building in a marriage of three themes: Frank Lloyd Wright's style, Northwest ruggedness, and Pacific Rim tranquility. Inside this rough-hewn, cedar-shingled building are 24 rooms finely decorated with an eye for pleasing detail: simple Asian furnishings, trimmings of three different woods, and a quarry-tiled bathroom with hooks made from alder twigs. Adjacent is a Jacuzzi, from which you can watch the boat traffic on the Passage and the flicker of your fireplace through the translucent shoji-style screen. (Alas, the noises throughout the inn are louder than they should be because of the rumble of the Jacuzzi.) We prefer the upper-level rooms; others are approached by a dark concrete stairwell. The small conference room, equipped with every business necessity, has the expansive view the country dining room lacks. In the morning, guests gather in the dining room for a continental spread.

Chef Steve Nogal is making waves in his country kitchen with five-course prix-fixe weekend dinners (by reservation only). Diners are met at the door with glasses of sherry, which they sip while Nogal delivers his appetite-whetting spiel. It's an evening-long celebration of Northwest foods, a delightful indulgence that can pay off in a fine—if occasionally flawed—meal. A dinner might begin with plump local mussels in a savory reduction of garden herbs and vegetables, followed by a brilliant-orange squash soup (seasonal but much too sweet), and crowned with poached salmon napped in a huckleberry sauce—deservedly one of Nogal's signature dishes. Finally, fresh greens in raspberry vinaigrette. A fresh pear torte draped in thick chocolate completes the meal. ■ *At the edge of town; (360)221-3033; 400 1st St, Langley; PO Box 835, Langley, WA 98260; $$$; beer and wine; AE, MC, V; local checks only; dinner (by reservation only) Fri–Sat (Nov–Apr), Fri–Sun (May–Oct).*

Boatyard Inn ★★ The industrial look of the green siding and corrugated metal roofs of this recently opened inn meshes well with Langley's still colorful working waterfront. The place is so close to the water that the tide rises up against the first floor. Big windows, pine accents, and back-to-basics Eddie Bauer–esque Northwest furnishings characterize the Boatyard's nine huge, breezy suites (the smallest room is 600 square feet), each endowed with a gas fireplace, galley kitchen, queen-size bed topped with cozy flannel coverlets, sofa bed, cable TV, private deck, and water view. Loft units are suitable for families or small groups. ■ *From Cascade Ave, take Wharf St down the hill; (360)221-5120; 200 Wharf St, Langley; PO Box 866, Langley, WA 98260; $$$; AE, DC, MC, V; Washington State checks only.* &

Edgecliff ★★ Money can't buy you love, but in the case of these two retreat homes perched on a bluff overlooking Saratoga Passage, it can buy you a film-set version of a romantic getaway. For the lace-curtain variety amour, book the Honeymoon Cottage, set not far from the cliff's near-vertical staircase leading to the sandy beach below. Under a cathedral ceiling, the living area—adjacent to a fully stocked kitchen—features a wood stove/fireplace and entertainment center, and is decorated with warm country antiques, a doll collection, and rare prints. Or check into the two-story double-decked Penthouse, the more sophisticated cousin of the cottage. Original oil paintings grace the 20-foot walls and airy loft of this luxuriously romantic getaway, where amenities include a hot tub, entertainment center, and various sundries that could be found in the dwellings of the rich and famous. ■ *Call ahead for directions; (360)221-8857; PO Box 758, Langley, WA 98260; $$$; AE, MC, V; checks OK.*

Galittoire ★★ Galittoire is a sleek, contemporary B&B that's almost sensual in its attention to detail. The decor is spare and deliberate: slanted ceilings, lots of windows, lovely oak trim throughout, and unexpected details, such as the variation on a four-poster bed in one of the suites—silky, snow-white fabric hanging from the ceiling to all corners of the bed. And if a deer wanders through the rolling yard past the gazebo, he may just seem like part of the perfect plan. Amenities abound—hot tub, spa, hors d'oeuvres in the evening—and owner Mahésh Massand is an accommodating host. Two-night minimum on weekends. Galittoire is also a catering company. ■ *Off Highway 525 on Coles Rd; (360)221-0548; 5444 S Coles Rd, Langley, WA 98260; $$$; AE, MC, V; local checks only.*

Log Castle ★★ This is the house that Jack built—literally. And whenever there's time, U.S. Congressman Jack Metcalf builds on it some more, to his wife Norma's newest designs. As a result, the beachside castle has a slightly unfinished air about it, which shouldn't in the slightest detract from what can be a distinctly unusual experience. Every log tells a story, and the place can feel quite cozy on a winter evening. The loft suite comes

▼

Whidbey Island: Langley

Lodgings

▲

with an antique ship's stove; two rooms on the other side of the house are built into an octagonal turret and feature remarkable views. The Metcalfs originally ran the facility as a Christian retreat center for many years; however, the religious ambience isn't fanatical. ■ *1 mile west of Langley on Saratoga; (360) 321-5483; 3273 E Saratoga Rd, Langley, WA 98260; $$; MC, V; checks OK.*

Villa Isola ★★ Tucked into a pine-studded pastoral landscape, Gwen and Gary Galeotti's version of an Italian country villa goes a long way in re-creating the slow, sweet life of the Old Country. Guests have this inspired space defined by walls stenciled with grape vines, floor-to-ceiling windows, and modern European furnishings all to themselves. Three large, sumptuous rooms named after legendary Italian towns continue the Mediterranean motif; each has an oversized bath (one has a Jacuzzi), queen-size bed, and down comforter. Espresso and delicacies are served cafe-style in the sunny dining room or on the adjacent deck. Borrow the inn's mountain bikes or engage in a game of bocce (Italian lawn bowling) on the regulation-size court beyond the fruit trees in the big backyard, where local senior citizens compete on Wednesday nights. Gwen keeps the living room flush with CDs and board games and the kitchen stocked with Italian desserts. ■ *2 miles southeast of Langley on S Coles Rd; (360)221-5052; 5489 S Coles Rd, Langley, WA 98260; $$$; MC, V; checks OK.*

Garden Path Inn ★ For an island getaway that feels more like an uptown city condo, book a weekend at one of the two upstairs suites above proprietress Linda Lundgren's interior design shop. A brick and trellis walkway leads to the tucked-away retreat off First Street. The exquisite back suite is equipped with a full gourmet kitchen, a long dining room table, bay window, four-poster bed, and Jacuzzi tub. Both suites show off Lundgren's decorative flair, an eclectic and intelligent blending of art and crafts, sophistication and comfort, and antique and contemporary pieces—most of which are for sale. ■ *Downtown Langley; (360)221-5121; 111 1st St, Langley; PO Box 575, Langley, WA 98260; $$-$$$; MC, V; checks OK.*

Harrison House Inn ★ It's a two-minute walk from downtown to the Harrison House with architectural touches reminiscent of New England. But the inn, opened recently by longtime hoteliers (and Brits) John and Kathleen Harrison, sets the Anglophile's standard of comfort plus privacy. Indeed, the trappings of respect and graciousness extend to the 15 distinctive view rooms, each festooned in warm plaids and prints and furnished with gas fireplaces, armoires, and entertainment centers. Have the first meal of the day delivered to your chambers. Serious solitude seekers can opt for the separate Carriage

▼
Whidbey Island: Langley

Lodgings
▲

House ($225), with a full kitchen, stone fireplace, and king-size sleigh bed. Conferences sometimes monopolize the richly appointed Library Boardroom. But everyone's welcome in the tea room, where you can socialize over civilized beverages. ■ *Take 1st St to Cascade Ave; (360)221-5801; 201 Cascade Ave, Langley; PO Box 428, Langley, WA 98260; $$$; MC, V; checks OK.* &

Lone Lake Cottage and Breakfast ★ Dolores Meeks's place is still one of the most interesting B&Bs around. The estimable resort may have outlasted its interior design motifs, but not its eccentric charm. One of the four lodgings is aboard the *Whidbey Queen*, a beamed-ceiling stern-wheeler, permanently moored on the lake. Guests staying on the *Queen* enjoy the same extras found in the two lakeside cottages: fireplace, soaking tub for two, VCR, and CD player. Pore over the boat's years-long stack of guest books filled with poetry and endearments. The one-bedroom Terrace Cottage is the nicest of the landlubber's accommodations; it looks into the domed top of a stunning aviary housing some 300 rare birds from around the world. A honeymoon suite near the lake in front of the main house is cool and comfortable and sports a grand lake view, fireplace, kitchen, and double Jacuzzi. Exotic ducks, pheasant, quail, peacocks, and swans mingle in an outdoor pen. Each room has a full kitchen stocked with breakfast makings, plus seasonings for the barbecue should you get lucky and land a trout or two. Guests are welcome to use the private beach, canoes, rowboat, and bikes. ■ *5½ miles from the Clinton ferry, off Hwy 525 on S Bayview; (360)321-5325; 5260 S Bayview Rd, Langley, WA 98260; $$$; no credit cards; checks OK.*

Eagle's Nest Inn Bed and Breakfast In 1994, innkeepers Jerry and Joanne Lechner took over this four-story octagonal getaway tucked into the forest on a knoll overlooking scenic Saratoga Passage, Camano Island, and Mount Baker. And while a handful of complaints concerning a lack of honest hospitality on the part of the new innkeepers were borne out on our visit, its physical charms are still undeniable. Guests may enjoy the view from the four spotless, floral-motifed upstairs rooms. The best is the Eagle's Nest, an eight-sided penthouse suite rimmed with windows (and a balcony) offering a 360-degree view. The library-lounge is stocked with local art, books, videotapes, and CDs. On the main floor, the high-ceilinged living room is dominated by a white wood stove and flanked by a baby grand piano and stained-glass windows. Breakfast is at 9am, the hot tub and the cookie jar are open all day. ■ *Call ahead for directions; (360)221-5331; 3236 E Saratoga Rd, Langley, WA 98260; $$$; MC, V; checks OK*

WHIDBEY ISLAND: FREELAND

The unincorporated town of Freeland, population 1,544, is home to Nichols Brothers Boat Builders, manufacturers of cruise boats and stern-wheelers—and the town's largest employer. **Island Bakery** (Main Street, (360)321-6282) is a good spot for picnic supplies, or try the salubrious soups. **Freeland Park** on Holmes Harbor has picnic tables, a play area, and sandy beach.

LODGINGS

Cliff House ★★ Seattle architect Arne Bystrom designed this dramatic house, which makes an extraordinary getaway. The striking home on a cliff above Admiralty Inlet is full of light from lofty windows, centering on a 30-foot-high atrium filled with native plants (open to the weather), and a sunken fireplace. For $365 a night, you have use of the entire house and its 14 acres of woods. There are hammocks, bench chairs, and a platform deck with a hot tub built high on the cliff. The elfish Sea Cliff Cottage includes a queen-size feather bed, kitchenette, and a deck overlooking the water. Peggy Moore sets the country kitchen table (in both houses) with a continental breakfast. ■ *Bush Point Rd to Windmill Rd; (360)331-1566; 5440 Windmill Rd, Freeland, WA 98249; $$$; no credit cards; checks OK.*

WHIDBEY ISLAND: GREENBANK

Here on the narrowest part of the island, stop by **Whidbey's Greenbank Berry Farm**, at one time the largest loganberry farm in the country. After a short self-guided tour, sample their Loganberry Liqueur or Whidbey Port. Lots of pretty picnicking spots. And don't miss the two-day **Loganberry Festival** in July, featuring food and crafts booths and entertainment (and a pie-eating contest, of course); (360)678-7700.

LODGINGS

Guest House Bed & Breakfast Cottages ★★★ We love this place, partly because "playing house" here fulfills long-lost storybook dreams. Seven varied dwellings are set on a pastoral clearing fringed with woodland. The Farmhouse (closest to the swimming pool and hot tub) is perfect for two couples. The studio Carriage House offers a queen-size featherbed and a whirlpool bath. King-size featherbeds and river-rock fireplaces grace the pine-log Emma Jane Tennessee Cottage and the Kentucky Pine Cottage. Comparatively modest, less expensive, but just as cozy are the Farm Guest Cottage and the funky Hansel and Gretel Log Cabin with kitchen, whirlpool tub, and VCR. (The video library includes 400 flicks.) But everybody's favorite is the Lodge, a $285-a-night custom-built log home for two perched at the edge of a spring-fed wildlife pond with a broad deck and views of the Cascades and the Sound from the loft bedroom. A 24-foot-tall rugged stone fireplace plays center stage in a space that combines the old (a wood stove next to the greenhouse breakfast nook) with the new (two whirlpool tubs, a dishwasher). Breakfast makings are left in the fully equipped kitchens. ■ *1 mile south of Greenbank off Hwy 525; (360)678-3115; 3366 S Hwy 525, Greenbank, WA 98253; $$$; AE, MC, V; checks OK.*

WHIDBEY ISLAND: COUPEVILLE

The second-oldest incorporated town in the state dates back to 1852; no wonder the town has a strict agenda of historical preservation. Coupeville's downtown consists of a half-dozen gift and antique shops and several restaurants. A must-see gallery is the **Jan McGregor Studio**, (360)678-5015, open on weekends throughout the year and every day in the summer. McGregor has studied pottery around the world and specializes in rare porcelain techniques. **Toby's 1890 Tavern**, (360) 678-4222, is a good spot for burgers, beer, and a game of pool. Homemade breads, pies, soups, and salads make a memorable meal at **Knead & Feed**, (360)678-5431, and real coffee has come to Coupeville at **Great Times Espresso**, (360)678-5358. **Island County Historical Museum**, (360)678-3310, tells the story of Whidbey Island's early history. Annual community events include the **Coupeville Arts & Crafts Festival**, the second weekend in August, and the **Penn Cove Water Festival** in May; for information (360)678-5434. **All Island Bicycles**, 302 N Main, (360)678-3351, sells, rents, and repairs bikes and equipment. An extra bike lane follows Engle Road 3 miles south of Coupeville to **Fort Casey**, a decommissioned fort with splendid gun mounts, beaches, and commanding bluffs. Explore the magnificent bluff and beach at the 17,000-acre **Ebey's Landing** and **Fort Ebey State Park**. The **Keystone ferry**, (360)678-6030, connecting Whidbey to Port Townsend, leaves from Admiralty Head, just south.

LODGINGS

Captain Whidbey Inn ★ Innkeeper John Colby Stone has gone to every effort to make sure that nothing much changes about this old Penn Cove inn, built in 1907 of sturdy and shiny-with-use madrona logs. In such a beloved place, history sometimes outranks comfort and quiet. The walls are so thin they seem to talk, and sniffle, and sneeze. Upstairs, the 12 smallish, almost shiplike original hotel rooms (two suites) have marble sinks but share two separate bathrooms. Stay clear of those above the bar. Wooden pews, ancient travel chests, and old-style ceramic washbasins connect the common areas. Four sparsely furnished cottages include fireplaces and baths. The best bets are the 13 lagoon rooms, with private baths and verandahs overlooking two calm inlets of water. The public rooms—a lantern-lit dining room with creaky wooden floors that seem to slope toward the sea, the deck (when the weather's warm), a cozy bar festooned with nautical maps, wine bottles, and business cards, a well-stocked library, and a folksy fireplace room—are quite attractive. The restaurant continues to feature, naturally, Penn Cove mussels—you're looking at the mussel beds as you indulge—fresh seafood preparations, and greens from the inn's elaborate gardens. ■ *Off Madrona Way on W Captain Whidbey Inn Rd; (360)678-4097; 2072 W Captain Whidbey Inn Rd, Coupeville, WA 98239; $$; full bar; AE, MC, V; checks OK; breakfast, lunch, dinner every day (lunch Sat–Sun only in winter).*

Fort Casey Inn ★ Built in 1909 as officers' quarters for nearby Fort Casey, this neat row of nine houses now offers tidy, no-frills accommodations with a historical bent. Houses are divided into two-bedroom duplexes, each kitchen stocked with breakfast makings. Decor consists mostly of tied-rag rugs, old military photographs, and renditions of early U.S. presidents. Garrison Hall, with a small reception area and its own private bedroom and bath, can be rented for weddings or private parties. Unlike most B&Bs on Whidbey, Fort Casey welcomes kids—and is truly a fun place to explore. Ask the manager anything you need to know about Fort Casey State Park, the bird sanctuary at Crockett Lake, or nearby Ebey's Landing National Historic Reserve. ■ *2 miles west of Coupeville; (360)678-8792; 1124 S Engle Rd, Coupeville, WA 98239; $$; AE, MC, V; checks OK.*

Inn at Penn Cove ★ This gracious inn consists of two historic pink homes, the Kineth House (built in 1887, and completely restored to its former grandeur) and the Coupe-Gillespie House (circa 1891, a decidedly more casual affair). The Kineth guest rooms are prettily furnished, if slightly overdecorated. The three rooms in the second house seem best for guests with children (there's a game room with puzzles). Breakfasts are a great send-off, with blueberry and lemon poppyseed muffins, seasonal fruits, cereal, Scandinavian-style breakfast cakes, waffles, or pancakes. ■ *Take Hwy 20 from Deception Pass or Hwy 525 from the ferry; (360)678-8000 or (800)688-COVE; 702 N Main St, Coupeville, WA 98239; $$; AE, DC, MC, V; checks OK.*

The Old Morris Farm ★ This is no old farmhouse by any means. Owners Mario Chodorowski and Marilyn Randock have successfully transformed their 1909 farmhouse into an elegant countryside B&B. The guest rooms are individual in style and decor that reflect the colonial feeling of the house. The Rose Room is done up in paisley, and has a private bath and a deck that leads out to the secluded spa. Enjoy a grand breakfast in the red, red dining room, and evening hors d'oeuvres in

▼

▲

the sunwashed living room. Stroll the grounds and enjoy the flower, vegetable, and herb gardens. A small gift shop includes locally made walking sticks. ▪ *Take Hwy 20, 3 miles from Coupeville overpass; (360)678-6586; 105 W Morris Rd, Coupeville, WA 98239; $$; MC, V; checks OK.* &

WHIDBEY ISLAND: OAK HARBOR

Named for the thriving Garry oak trees, Oak Harbor is Whidbey's largest city and home to **Whidbey Island Naval Air Station**, a large air base for tactical electronic warfare squadrons. For the most part, Oak Harbor is engulfed in new military and retired military folk.

An interesting stop is **Lavender Heart**, which manufactures floral gifts on a 12-acre former holly farm. From the Hendersons' gift store, you can peek at the impressive 1,000-square-foot production facility; 3 miles south of Deception Pass at 4233 N DeGraff Road, (360)675-3987. For the kids at heart, visit **Blue Fox Dri-Vin Theatre and Brattland Go-Karts**; 1403 Monroe Landing Road, Oak Harbor, (360)675-5667.

Deception Pass. The beautiful, treacherous gorge has a lovely, if crowded, state park with 2,300 acres of prime camping land, forests, and beach. **Strom's Shrimp/Fountain and Grill**, just north of the pass, sells fresh seafood for your cookout. They also grill up a mean oysterburger; (360)293-2531.

RESTAURANTS

Kasteel Franssen (Auld Holland Inn) ★ Half a mile north of Oak Harbor, this motel with the trademark windmill is just fine, if a shade close to the highway; however, the restaurant is quite delightful. Kasteel Franssen, owned and operated by Joe and Elisa Franssen, has quite a regal, European feel about it and a solid reputation among locals. There's a big gas fireplace and a lively piano bar. Chef Scott Fraser of Vancouver, BC, has taken over the toque and the results are pleasing. Dinner offerings include seafood, chicken, and beef, but Fraser is also preparing game—including caribou and pheasant. Particularly good is the beef tenderloin sautéed and served with a brandy Dijonnaise cream sauce. As for the inn, some upper-story rooms have antiques, and six impressive-looking rooms include hot tubs. There's a tennis court, hot tub, outdoor pool, and children's play area. Rates include a continental breakfast. ▪ *8 miles south of Deception Pass on State Rd 20; (360)675-2288; 5681 SR 20, Oak Harbor; $$; full bar; AE, DC, MC, V; local checks only; dinner every day (Mon–Sat in winter).* &

Lucy's Mi Casita It doesn't look like much, lined up along a strip of fast-food joints and automotive stores and decorated with old calendars, beer bottle-cap curtains, and cutouts of flamenco dancers, but Al and Lucy Enriquez keep locals coming back with their homemade Mexican food and lively atmosphere. Upstairs is a lounge with a balcony (watch out for the 27-ounce Turbo Godzilla margarita). The large menu includes shredded beef tacos, seafood burritos, chile poblano imported from Mexico, Lucy's authentic refried beans, tortillas shipped from California, and homemade hot sauce. Don't miss the entomatadas—a tortilla topped with tomato sauce, cheese, and onion—from Lucy's hometown of Chihuahua. ■ *On main drag of Oak Harbor; (360)675-4800; 1380 W Pioneer Way, Oak Harbor; $; full bar; AE, MC, V; local checks only; lunch, dinner every day.*

VASHON ISLAND

Faintly countercultural, this bucolic isle is a short ferry ride away from downtown Seattle (foot passengers only), West Seattle (take the Fauntleroy ferry), or Tacoma (from the Point Defiance ferry). It's a wonderful place to explore by bicycle, although the first long hill up from the north-end ferry dock is a killer. Few beaches are open to the public, although there are some public spots where you can take a stroll and enjoy the view.

Vashon Island has many of its own island-based companies that market their goods both locally and nationally; many of these offer tours (it's a good idea to call ahead): **K2 Skis, Inc**, (206)463-3631; **SBC** (popularly known as Seattle's Best Coffee), Island Highway, (206)463-3932; **Maury Island Farms**, with berries and preserves, at 99th and 204th on Island Highway, (206)463-9659. **Wax Orchards**, on 131st SW north of 232nd, is no longer open for tours, but you can stop by and pick up some fresh preserves, fruit syrups, and apple cider; (206)463-9735. Island arts are on display at the **Blue Heron Art Center**, (206)463-5131. **The Country Store and Farm** is an old-fashioned general store stocking most of the island-made products, along with natural-fiber apparel, housewares, sundries, dried herbs, and gardening supplies; (206)463-3655.

Lodgings. There are a myriad of small (one and two bedroom) bed and breakfasts on the island; call the Vashon Island Lodging Association for information (206)463-6737.

Vashon Island

Restaurants

RESTAURANTS

Back Bay Inn ★★ The restaurant at the Back Bay Inn, a treat for islanders, is beginning to make Vashon a destination for dinner (luckily there are four antique-filled rooms upstairs if you want to avoid the ferry ride home—ask for one of the bigger end rooms). While the dining room is prettied with white linens, candles, and flowers, and the service is knowledgeable, it is the food that stands out: start with a plate of unbelievably light gnocchi in a Gorgonzola sauce with toasted walnuts or meaty crab cakes loaded with the real thing. For dinner, satisfy yourself with the stuffed pork chops, roasted lamb shank, or grilled mahi mahi in a Thai curry broth, aromatic with coconut milk, lime, and hot peppers. Sunday breakfast is a new addition, with omelets (smoked salmon or shiitake mushroom, for example) and other great waker-uppers. Overnight guests play checkers in the downstairs fireplace library. ■ *In the community of Burton; (206)463-5355; 24007 Vashon Hwy SW, Vashon Island, WA 98070; $$$; full bar; AE, MC, V; checks OK; dinner Tues–Sun (Fri–Sun in winter). & (restaurant only).*

Dog Day Cafe and Juice Bar ★ Inside this stylish street-side cafe dolled up in gothic 1990s, there are tête-à-tête tables, great espresso (made with SBC, of course), and interesting lunch fixings (roasted eggplant sandwich with tapanade; chicken sandwich with chutney and apples; a chapati roll with black beans, brown rice, and sprouts). Some just saunter by in the afternoon for a tall glass of squeezed-to-order juice, and perhaps a dessert of vanilla bread pudding. At press time, new owners were settling in, but little is expected to change from the customer's vantage. ■ *Corner of Vashon Hwy and Bank Rd; (206)463-6404; 17530 Vashon Hwy SW, Vashon Island; $; beer and wine; no credit cards; local checks only; late breakfast, lunch daily. &*

Turtle Island Cafe ★ Just off the main drag through downtown Vashon is Turtle Island Cafe, a small, friendly restaurant—a favorite of many islanders. It's no wonder…the food here is wonderful. Chef Rick Tada puts together a menu with treats such as angel hair pasta tossed with sun-dried tomatoes and roasted garlic, oyster stew with polenta, or a hoisin-roasted chicken. The wine list offers a good selection of reasonably priced domestic and imported wines, by the bottle or by the glass. Little things—like a perfect, zesty vinaigrette dressing—contribute to good meals at Turtle Island Cafe. ■ *Near intersection of Vashon Hwy and SW Bank Rd; (206)463-2125; 9924 SW Bank Rd, Vashon; $$; beer and wine; MC, V; checks OK; lunch Mon–Fri, dinner every day. &*

PUYALLUP

At the head of the fertile Puyallup Valley, this frontier farm town serves as a major gateway to Mount Rainier. While much of the bulb, rhubarb, and berry farmland continues to be cultivated, a great part of it has been strip-malled and auto-row ravaged around the edges. Avoid the fast-food strip to the south and head east up the valley to Sumner, White River, Orting, Wilkeson, and Carbonado.

The **Ezra Meeker Mansion** is the finest original pioneer mansion left in Washington. Its builder and first occupant, Ezra Meeker, introduced hops to the Puyallup Valley. The lavish

17-room Italianate house (built 1890) now stands beautifully restored in the rear parking lot of a Main Street furniture store;
312 Spring Street, (206)848-1770, open Wednesday through
Sunday, 1pm to 4pm, March through mid-December.

Puyallup is big on old-time seasonal celebrations, and
it's home to two of the biggest in the Northwest: the **Daffodil Festival and Parade** in early April and the **Western
Washington Fair**, better known as the Puyallup Fair, in
September. It's one of the nation's biggest fairs; call (206)845-
1771 for dates and information. **Puyallup Downtown Farmers Market** is held every Saturday, starting at 9am, at Pioneer
Park. It runs throughout the growing season, usually late May
through September.

RESTAURANTS

Balsano's Tom Pantley has filled the menu at this congenial
restaurant with unusual regional dishes (preciously priced)
from his Sicilian roots. Photos of his mother's family line the
wall (many of the staff *are* family). Homemade sausage of
coarsely chopped pork and the subtle anise flavor of fennel is
served, traditionally, with golden-fried cauliflower. Thin slices
of tender veal are topped with mushrooms, onions, and dry,
sweet Marsala wine from the western region of Sicily; spinach
lightly braised with balsamic vinegar and hazelnuts is another
treat. ■ *Between Pioneer and E Main; (206)845-4222; 127
15th St SE, Puyallup; $$; beer and wine; DC, MC, V; checks
OK; lunch Mon–Fri, dinner every day.* ⚒

TACOMA

Sided by Commencement Bay and the Tacoma Narrows and
backed by Mount Rainier, Tacoma is no longer just a blue-
collar mill town, but a growing urban center with a thriving
cultural core.

Tacoma has fervently embraced the idea of preservation.
The historic buildings in the downtown warehouse district are
being converted from industrial use to residential and com-
mercial functions, and some of the old warehouses are slated
for a University of Washington branch campus. The stately
homes and cobblestone streets in the north end are often used
as sets for Hollywood's moviemakers, and students still fill the
turreted chateau of Stadium High School. Old City Hall, with
its newly coppered roof, Renaissance clock, and bell tower; the
Romanesque First Presbyterian Church; the rococo Pythian
Lodge; and the one-of-a-kind coppered Union Station—now the
much praised Federal Courthouse—delight history and archi-
tecture buffs. The old Union Station rotunda is now graced by
some spectacular work by glass artist and Tacoma native Dale
Chihuly. This common area exhibit is also an annex of the

Tacoma Art Museum, open to the public at no charge during business hours, so do drop in for a peak. The **Ruston Way Waterfront**, a 6-mile mix of parks and restaurants, is thronged with people in any weather.

Pantages Center, 901 Broadway Plaza; (206)591-5894. The restored 1,100-seat Pantages Theater, originally designed in 1918 by nationally known movie theater architect B. Marcus Priteca, is the focal point of the reviving downtown cultural life—dance, music, and stage presentations. And the nearby **Rialto Theatre** has been restored for smaller performance groups. **Tacoma Actors Guild**, Tacoma's popular professional theater—at the Commerce Street level atop the park-covered transit center, (206)272-2145—offers an ambitious and successful blend of American classics and Northwest premieres that draw an audience from throughout the Puget Sound region.

Tacoma

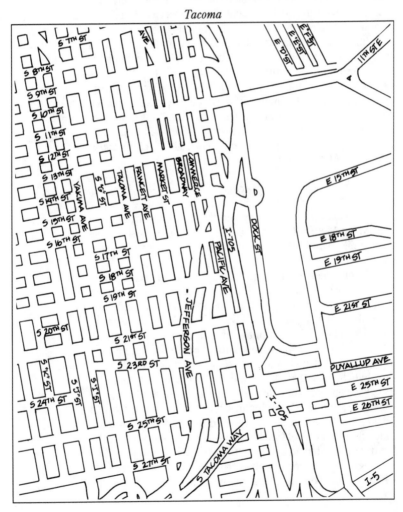

The **Tacoma Art Museum**, 12th and Pacific, (206)272-4258, is housed in a former downtown bank. The small museum has paintings by Renoir, Degas, and Pissarro, as well as a collection of contemporary American prints. The **Washington State Historical Museum**, (206)593-2830, has left its previous home near Stadium High School and will be opening just south of Union Station at 1911 Pacific Avenue in the summer of 1996. This new facility not only has many times the previous exhibit space, it will offer a state-of-the-art museum experience, providing history and innovation under the same roof. From the outside, however, the museum has been carefully designed to blend into its surroundings and complement the Union Station built in 1911.

OTHER THINGS TO DO

Point Defiance Park is situated at the west side of Tacoma, with 500 acres of untouched forest jutting out into Puget Sound. Aside from its many other attractions, this park is one of the most dramatically sited and creatively planned city parks in the country. The wooded 5-mile drive and hiking trails open up now and then for sweeping views of the water, Vashon Island, Gig Harbor, and the Olympic Mountains beyond. There are rose, rhododendron, Japanese, and Northwest native gardens, a railroad village with a working steam engine, a reconstruction of Fort Nisqually (originally built in 1833), a museum, a swimming beach, and the much acclaimed zoo/aquarium. Watching the almost continuous play of seals, sea lions, and the white beluga whale from an underwater vantage point is a rare treat; (206)591-5335. **Wright Park** at Division and I streets is a serene in-city park with many trees, a duck-filled pond, and a beautifully maintained, fragrant conservatory, built of glass and steel in 1890. One of the area's largest estates, and the former home of the late Corydon and Eulalie Wagner, is now **Lakewold Gardens** (12221 Gravelly Lake Drive SW, (206)584-3360), located on a beautiful 10-acre site overlooking Gravelly Lake in Lakewood, just 10 minutes south of Tacoma. Recognized nationally as one of the outstanding gardens in America, Lakewold Gardens is open Thursday through Monday for guided and nonguided tours (call for details). Take exit #124 off I-5 to Gravelly Lake Drive.

The **Tacoma Dome**, the world's largest wooden dome, is the site of many entertainment and trade shows as well as a sports center. The dazzling neon sculpture by Stephen Antonakos provides a dramatic background for events such as the **Tacoma Rockets** hockey games, championship ice-skating competitions, and many other regional activities. Call (206) 272-6817 for ticket information.

Fans who like their baseball played outdoors in a first-class ballpark arrive in enthusiastic droves at **Cheney Stadium** to watch the **Tacoma Rainiers**, the Triple-A affiliate of the Seattle Mariners; (206)752-7707.

Fishing/boating. With the waters of Puget Sound lapping at virtually half of Tacoma's city limits, it is to be expected that many Tacomans and visitors choose to spend their leisure time afloat or on the pier. There are two fishing piers along Ruston Way and public launches and boat rentals at Point Defiance.

RESTAURANTS

The Cliff House ★★ Over the years, this restaurant survived on its commanding view of Commencement Bay and Tacoma's north end, and its formal, pretentious airs. The food, though, was forgettable until chef Jon Brzycki came on board. Now there is homemade venison sausage with a wild rice pancake and dried fruit chutney for starters. Or the delicious smoked duck salad with a sesame dressing. For a main course, tough choices include pan-roasted pheasant with a light touch of port wine sauce accented with pears and cranberries, the braised rabbit with papayas and sun-dried tomatoes, or shrimp sautéed with pineapple and Chinese black beans. Desserts, less noteworthy, are a trip down memory lane with cherries jubilee and crêpes Suzettes flambéed tableside. Maybe just have a brandy and enjoy the view. ■ *Follow East Side Dr to the top of the hill; (206) 927-0400; 6300 Marine View Dr, Tacoma; $$$; full bar; AE, DC, MC, V; no checks; lunch Mon–Fri, dinner every day.* &

Tacoma

▲

Fujiya ★★ Absolute consistency continues to attract a loyal clientele from near and far to Masahiro Endo's stylish downtown Japanese restaurant. For years this has been a favorite spot for the best sushi and sashimi around, and the return of ace sushi chef Yutaka Saito, after an extended jaunt to Tokyo, means these offerings are better than ever. Begin your meal with a steamed gyoza (savory pork-stuffed dumplings). The real test of a Japanese restaurant is the tempura, and Endo makes certain that his is feathery crisp. And for those who prefer their seafood cooked, the yosenabe (seafood stew) is full of delicious things served in a small cast-iron pot. He's a generous and friendly man, Mr. Endo; seldom an evening goes by that he doesn't offer a complimentary tidbit of one kind or another. ■ *Between Broadway and Market on Court C; (206) 627-5319; 1125 Court C, Tacoma; $$; beer and wine; AE, MC, V; checks OK; lunch Mon–Fri, dinner Mon–Sat.*

Stanley and Seaforts Steak, Chop, and Fish House ★★ Every seat in this restaurant is provided with a panoramic view of Tacoma, its busy harbor, and, on a clear day, the Olympic Mountains. Here is a view restaurant that doesn't just rest on it's sunsetting laurels. The emphasis is on quality meats and seafood simply grilled over apple wood with flavorings of herbs and fruits. It's the combination of interesting menu

selections and dependability that has made Stanley and Seaforts a favorite for over 14 years. The spacious bar features distinctive Scotch whiskeys—and, well, a great sunset to boot.
■ *City Center exit off I-5, follow Hwy 7, take 38th west, right on Pacific Ave, right on 34th; (206)473-7300; 115 E 34th St, Tacoma; $$; full bar; AE, DC, MC, V; local checks only; lunch Mon–Fri, dinner every day.*

Bimbo's ★ A seedy name, a seedy location, but here's a family Italian restaurant that's been attracting regulars for almost 75 years. Members of the original owner's family are still cooking their native recipes with little regard for today's trends. Rabbit—once the most common source of meat in their region of Tuscany—is served year-round in a hearty, full-bodied tomato sauce. The pork ribs are meaty and luscious, and aficionados of that Italian favorite, tripe, will find it judiciously treated here. Their hallmark tomato sauce must cook for hours to reach that thick, rich flavor and deep color; it's a perfect partner for the hearty pasta dishes. ■ *15th and Pacific; (206)383-5800; 1516 Pacific Ave, Tacoma; $; full bar; AE, MC, V; local checks only; lunch Mon–Sat, dinner every day.* ₺

Cedars III ★ Tacoma is awash with restaurants of various ethnic bents, but Mediterranean cuisine is a rarity. For those baba ganouj and garlic-bathed chicken cravings, be thankful for Nadim Alawar and his Cedars III restaurant (his first two are in Seattle), not far from the Narrows Bridge. If you have trouble deciding between the baba ganouj (great smoky flavor) and the hummus, the chicken or the lamb (garlic galore!), try the "Cedars Delight"—a big platter of samplings from the menu, served family-style for two or more. Unfortunately, the pita is the same dry stuff you might find at the grocery store. The wine list consists of only four table reds from Lebanon, Spain, Morocco, and France. ■ *Take 6th Ave exit from Hwy 16, head west; (206)564-0255; 7104 6th Ave, Tacoma; $$; beer and wine; AE, MC, V; checks OK; dinner Tues–Sun.* ₺

Tacoma

Restaurants

East & West Cafe ★ What this restaurant lacks in location, it makes up for 10-fold in great food and charm. East & West Cafe is a haven of Asian delights on the busy thoroughfare south of the Tacoma Mall. Owner Vien Floyd—a Saigon native—has gained a very loyal following among locals. Her incomparable personality helps make meals here a treat. The emphasis is on Vietnamese and Thai cuisine, a mix that invites you to experiment: the Saigon Crêpe is a large curried crêpe filled with bean sprouts, strips of pork, shrimp, and vegetables, with dipping sauce alongside. The vegetables are always crisp and bright and full of fresh flavor, the sauces have character, meats are tender—you really can't go wrong. For the price, it's hard to have a better meal in Tacoma. ■ *Just west of I-5, take 56th St exit; (206)475-7755; 5319 Tacoma Mall Blvd,*

Tacoma; $; beer and wine; MC, V; local checks only; lunch, dinner, Mon–Sat. ♿

Engine House #9 ★ Things are changing at the old E-9; they're tapping their own kegs (reported six beers at a time), and serving their customers tableside (no more counter service). Don't let all this talk of change make you think the E-9 is any different. It really is still the friendly, neighborhood beer-lover's dream of a tavern (minus the smoke). Regulars can still pick from the famed worldwide selection of draft and bottle beers and they can still sink their incisors into Cheeseburger Chili. A sister brew-pub called the Powerhouse opened the summer of 1995. ■ *6th and Pine; (206) 272-3435; 611 N Pine St, Tacoma; $; beer and wine; MC, V; checks OK; lunch, dinner every day.* ♿

Harbor Lights ★ Decor is circa 1950, with glass floats, stuffed prize fish, and a giant lobster, but Tacoma's pioneer Ruston Way waterfront restaurant still packs them in (reserve early). Up-to-the-minute it may not be, but that doesn't seem to bother the seafood fans who regularly crowd into the noisy dining room to consume buckets of steamed clams and mounds of perfectly cooked pan-fried oysters. Grilled fillet of sole is done to perfection; halibut and chips are the best around, as are the crisp hashbrowns. The portions are so gargantuan that only an ace trencherman can dig his way to the bottom of the plate. ■ *City Center exit and follow Schuster Pkwy to Ruston Way; (206) 752-8600; 2761 Ruston Way, Tacoma; $$; full bar; AE, DC, MC, V; checks OK; lunch Mon–Sat, dinner every day.* ♿

Katie Downs ★ Katie Downs's Philadelphia-style deep-dish pizza is a winner. You place your own order at the counter for one of their classic combinations. Especially good is the "Fearless," which recklessly matches smoked bacon and provolone cheese with white onions, spicy peperoncini—and lots and lots of fresh garlic. Since the pizzas can take close to 30 minutes to make and bake, order some steamer clams to tide you over while you wait and watch the tugs, barges, freighters, and sailboats move across Commencement Bay. This place is noisy, boisterous, and fun, but remember it is a tavern (no minors). ■ *City Center exit off I-5, follow Schuster Pkwy onto Ruston Way; (206) 756-0771; 3211 Ruston Way, Tacoma; $; beer and wine; MC, V; local checks only; lunch, dinner every day.* ♿

Lessie's Southern Kitchen ★ Calorie counters might pass up this little cafe (and you might pass by anyway—it's located on a difficult and busy five-way corner). However, if you have a hankering for the authentic fare of the South, do stop. Abandon all restraint and order up some pork chops smothered with gravy or liver with lots of lovely onions, all sided by long-cooked collard greens served up in their own "pot likker,"

▼

Tacoma

Restaurants

▲

black-eyed peas, or sweet nuggets of yams. Alabama-born Lessie also dishes up some mighty fine fried chicken and barbecued ribs. Thin, light corn-batter cakes are served in lieu of rolls and most folks finish up their meal with a slice of homemade sweet potato pie. Breakfasts are great, too: pan-fried butterfish with eggs, buttery grits, home-fries, and genuine Southern biscuits. ■ *6th and Division; (206) 627-4282; 1716 6th Ave, Tacoma; $; no alcohol; AE, MC, V; checks OK; breakfast, lunch, early dinner Mon–Sat.* &

The Lobster Shop ■ The Lobster Shop South ★ The Dash Point Lobster Shop could just as well be set next to the moorings of Maine lobster trawlers as it is to the docks of the small public beach on Puget Sound. This sea-weathered restaurant is a welcome change from the increasing number of pricey, slick eateries blossoming along the waterfront. As could be expected, rich, oven-baked lobster (Australian rock lobster) is the house specialty. Large juicy crab cakes, often paired with panfried oysters, are another favorite. They have a full liquor license, at last.

The larger, swankier Lobster Shop South on the Ruston Way waterfront has a distinctly different atmosphere and menu. It provides good seafood dishes, a full bar, and elegant surroundings, but not quite the same charm of the original. There is a small smoking area in the dining room. ■ *Off Dash Point Rd; (206) 927-1513; 6912 Soundview Dr NE, Tacoma; $$; full bar; AE, MC, V; checks OK; dinner every day.* & ■ *Take Schuster Pkwy to Ruston; (206) 759-2165; 4015 Ruston Way, Tacoma; $$; full bar; AE, MC, V; checks OK; dinner every day, brunch on Sunday.* &

Antique Sandwich Company A visit here is a little like returning to a storybook grandma's house. Plastic bears filled with honey adorn the shared tables; a roomy couch usually has several students curled up on it studying and eating. On the way to Point Defiance Park, it's also a favorite luncheon gathering place for the diaper set and their parents. Toys abound on a carpet-covered platform, which doubles as a stage on open-mike Tuesdays. Peanut-butter-and-jelly sandwiches with bananas and fresh-fruit milk shakes share the menu with big-people food such as hearty homemade soups, quiches, and a variety of other tasty sandwiches. ■ *2 blocks south of Point Defiance Park main entrance; (206) 752-4069; 5102 N Pearl, Tacoma; $; no alcohol; AE, MC, V; checks OK; breakfast, lunch, dinner every day.* &

LODGINGS

Sheraton Tacoma Hotel ★★ This elegant hotel has filled a real need in Tacoma. Adjacent to the Tacoma Convention Center, it's quite suitable for conventions. Most rooms look out over Commencement Bay or have a view of Mount Rainier. The more expensive concierge rooms on the 24th and 25th floors include a continental breakfast and early-evening hors d'oeuvres. The mezzanine cafe, Wintergarden, is pleasant for casual meals, but for some of the excellent Italian food in the area, head up to **Altezzo** ("lofty" in Italian) on the top floor. Their treatment of veal is particularly good. The tiramisu is the real McCoy. Service remains the biggest stumbling block at Altezzo (although they are well-intentioned), but if you are patient with the servers, you'll be rewarded with great things from chef Charlie McManus in the kitchen. ■ *Downtown between 13th and 15th on Broadway; (206)572-3200; 1320 Broadway Plaza, Tacoma, WA 98402; $$$; AE, DC, MC, V; checks OK; breakfast, lunch, dinner every day (Altezzo: dinner, Mon–Sat). &*

The Villa Bed & Breakfast ★★ In the heart of Tacoma's historic residential North End is a home that stands out from the crowd. Built for a local businessman in 1925, it was designed with the Mediterranean in mind: open and airy, with high arched windows, tiled roof, and a palm tree out front. This spacious home has been transformed into a gracious bed and breakfast by Becky and Greg Anglemyer. Our favorite room is actually the relatively small Maid's Quarters on the top floor—utterly private with a grand view of Commencement Bay and the Olympics. Guests have more space in the Bay View Suite, with a fireplace, sitting area, and a bay-view verandah. A CD player in every room (and a good CD collection downstairs) is music to our ears. ■ *City Center exit from I-5, follow Schuster Pkwy exit to Stadium Way, follow Stadium to Tacoma St, right on Tacoma to N 5th, go left; (206)572-1157; 705 N 5th St, Tacoma, WA 98403; $$; MC, V; checks OK.*

Commencement Bay Bed & Breakfast ★ It's hard to find bigger fans of the South Sound than hosts Sharon and Bill Kaufmann. For business clients, they offer fax, modem, and other amenities. For diversion, they have a rec room with puzzles and games, a fireplace sitting room, and a hot tub on the back deck. Two of the three rooms—Myrtle's Room and Jessie's Room—offer Commencement Bay views (and TVs when the weather has shrouded the view). Breakfast is copious. An ideal spot for University of Puget Sound visitors. ■ *From Hwy 16, take Union exit north, west on N 26th, north on Proctor, east on N 34th, south on Union; (206)752-8175; 3312 N Union Ave, Tacoma, WA 98407; $$; AE, MC, V; checks OK.*

▼ **Tacoma**

Lodgings

▲

PARKLAND

RESTAURANTS

Marzano's ★ The reputation of Lisa Marzano's voluptuous cooking still has people arriving from miles away. When the weather turns fair, outside seating on two deck areas is an added plus to her relatively new larger space. The food hasn't changed—including the crusty bread at the beginning of each meal, ready to be topped with shredded Parmesan and herbed olive oil. The stubby rigatoni are perfect for capturing the extraordinary boscaiola sauce made with mushrooms and ham; the lasagne is sumptuous, as is the elegant chicken piccata pungent with capers and lemons. When all's said and done, we'd go back even if it were just for the many-layered chocolate poppyseed cake floating in whipped cream. Reservations are needed. ■ *Adjacent to PLU; (206)537-4191; 516 Garfield S, Parkland; $$; beer and wine; MC, V; checks OK; lunch Tues–Fri, dinner Tues–Sat.* &

GIG HARBOR

Gig Harbor, once an almost undisturbed fishing village (and still homeport for an active commercial fleet), is now part suburbia, part weekend destination. Boating is still important here, with good anchorage and various moorage docks attracting gunwale-to-gunwale pleasure craft. When the clouds break, Mount Rainier holds court for all.

A variety of interesting shops and galleries line Harborview Drive, the single street that almost encircles the harbor. It's a most picturesque spot for browsing and window-shopping.

Gig Harbor was planned for boat traffic, not automobiles (with resulting traffic congestion and limited parking), yet it is still a good place for celebrations. An arts festival in mid-July and a jazz festival in mid-August are two main events. May through October (on Saturdays) the **Gig Harbor Farmers Market** features locally grown produce, plants, and Northwest gifts; Pierce Transit Park and Ride, off Highway 16, (206)884-2665.

Nearby **Kopachuck State Park** is a popular destination, as are **Penrose Point** and **RFK state parks** on the Key Peninsula, all with numerous beaches for clam digging. (Purdy Spit and Maple Hollow Park are the most accessible spots.) At **Minter Creek State Hatchery** the public can watch the different developmental stages of millions of salmon of various species. About 15 minutes from downtown Gig Harbor, the facilities are open to the public every day, or for group visits by special arrangement. Call (206)857-5077 for directions or more information.

Performance Circle, 6615 38th Avenue NW, (206)851-7529, Gig Harbor's resident theater group, mounts eight enjoyable productions year-round, with summer shows staged outside in the meadow at 9916 Peacock Hill Avenue NW. Theatergoers bring picnics and blankets, and watch the shows beneath the stars. It's turning into a wonderful small-town custom.

Marco's Ristorante Italiano ★ Everyone in this area loves what Marco (Mark Wambold) and his wife, Mimi, have done for dining in Gig Harbor. It shows in the busy, crowded bustle of the place (so reserve early). Mimi's the star behind the stoves, her menu ranging from the traditional (spaghetti and meatballs, handmade tortellini in fresh pesto) to the more original specials (a dense, tender piece of tuna sautéed in red wine). Deep-fried olives are an unusual starter. Adjacent to the restaurant they have opened a retail shop featuring Italian specialty goods. At press time, the Wambolds opened a new restaurant a couple of blocks away on the harbor (see The Green Turtle review). ■ *2 blocks up Pioneer Way from the harbor; (206)858-2899; 7707 Pioneer Way, Gig Harbor; $$; beer and wine; AE, MC, V; checks OK; lunch and dinner Tues–Sat.* &

North by Northwest ★ This home on the top of Peacock Hill was once the Peacock family estate, where they used to raise chickens. Today it is a favorite among the growing collection of quality restaurants in the South Sound. Seasonal cuisine is the guide word here, with offerings such as an endive, walnut, and pear salad or a grilled portobello mushroom salad. Entrees include everything from ribs to Southwestern-inspired black bean ravioli. The mixed grill is quite good, a combination that might include halibut or salmon paired with lamb, chicken, or sausages. The burnt cream and fruit crisps are among the standout desserts. Friday nights you'll be treated to music in the bar. ■ *Left on Peacock Hill Ave NW to top of hill; (206)851-3134; 9916 Peacock Hill Rd NW, Gig Harbor; $$; full bar; AE, MC, V; checks OK; dinner Tues–Sun, brunch Sun (seasonal lunch).* &

Tides Tavern "Meet you at the Tides" has become such a universal invitation that this tavern perched over the harbor often has standing room only, especially on sunny days when the deck is open. And people do come, by boat, seaplane, and car. Originally a general store next to the ferry landing, the Tides doesn't pretend to be anything other than what it is—a self-service tavern (no minors) with pool table, Gig Harbor memorabilia, and live music on weekend nights. Indulge in man-sized sandwiches, huge char-broiled burgers, a gargantuan shrimp salad, and highly touted fish and chips (pizzas are only passable). ■ *Harborview and Soundview; (206)858-3982; 2925 Harborview Dr, Gig Harbor; $; beer and wine; AE, MC, V; checks OK; lunch, dinner every day.*

The Green Turtle [*unrated*] Just weeks before press time, this new restaurant overlooking the harbor opened. Mark Wambold of Marco's might be worried if he didn't own this place as

▼

Gig Harbor

Restaurants

▲

well. Here chef Mimi gets to stretch her wings a bit. After a few years of cooking Italian, she's off to the Pacific Rim. And early reports of her pan-fried wontons with a vibrant dipping sauce are creating tidal waves in the little harbor community. The spicy seafood sauté is a dressed up phad Thai with mussels, shrimp, scallops, clams. Although you can get Marco's famed cheesecake here, dessert dances to a different tune than usual, with mango ice cream or a poached pear bathed in chocolate sauce. It won't take much of a limb to stand on, to say this restaurant shows great promise. ■ *Just past the Tides on Harborview; (206) 851-3167; 2905 Harborview Dr, Gig Harbor; $$; beer and wine; AE, MC, V; checks OK; dinner Tues–Sat.* ⅃

LODGINGS

The Pillars ★★ From the windows of this landmark house, you can see Colvos Passage, Vashon Island, and Mount Rainier. And from the front door, you're just uphill from the harbor. All three guest rooms are beautifully decorated, with large private baths and separate reading areas furnished with writing desks and telephones. An added bonus is the covered, heated swimming pool and Jacuzzi. The master of the house is also a master baker, so you'll find breakfasts feature particularly tasty home-baked breads and muffins. ■ *Take the first Gig Harbor exit off Hwy 16; (206) 851-6644; 6606 Soundview Dr, Gig Harbor, WA 98335; $$$; MC, V; checks OK.*

▼
Steilacoom
▲

No Cabbages B&B ★ If you are looking for a relaxed environment in an old, well-loved beach house (filled with knotty pine and Northwest arts and crafts) with a friendly hostess who happens to be an accomplished cook, No Cabbages may be just right. After reluctantly getting out of your bed—which has an intimate view of the harbor—you might start the day with a large glass of freshly squeezed orange juice, a Brie and green apple omelet, and all the freshly ground coffee you can handle. There's boating, and it's a superb place for bird-watching—great blue herons nest nearby, and a clutter of gulls, terns, grebes, ducks, and cormorants are always around. ■ *Follow the bay, on the east side of the harbor; (206) 858-7797; 7712 Goodman Dr NW, Gig Harbor, WA 98332; $; no credit cards; checks OK.*

STEILACOOM

Once an Indian village and later Washington Territory's second incorporated town (1854), Steilacoom today is a quiet village of old trees and houses, with no vestige of its heyday, when a trolley line ran from Bair's drugstore to Tacoma. October's **Apple Squeeze Festival** and midsummer's **Salmon Bake**, with canoe and kayak races, are popular drawing cards.

The **Steilacoom Tribal Museum** is located in a turn-of-the-century church overlooking the South Sound islands and the entire Olympic mountain range.

Ferries run to rural **Anderson Island** with restricted runs to McNeil Island (a state penitentiary); call the Pierce County Ferry Information Number: (206)596-2766.

RESTAURANTS

ER Rogers ★ View restaurants on Puget Sound are not novelties, but views like this one are still exceptional, particularly when seen from a restored 100-year-old Queen Anne–style home. Much is noteworthy here, but the Steilacoom special prime rib, first roasted, then sliced and quickly seared, is still tops. You can't beat the huge Sunday buffet brunch, with its large selection of seafood: oysters on the half shell, cold poached salmon, flavorful smoked salmon, cracked crab, pickled herring, steamed clams, and fettuccine with shrimp. There is a beautiful upstairs bar with a widow's walk just wide enough for one row of tables. ▪ *Corner of Commercial and Wilkes, off Steilacoom Blvd; (206)582-0280; 1702 Commercial St, Steilacoom; $$; full bar; MC, V; checks OK; dinner every day, brunch Sun. &*

Bair Drug and Hardware Store Side orders of nostalgia are presented gratis when you step into Bair Drug. Except for the customers, little has changed since it was built—in 1895. Products your grandparents might have used—cigars, washtubs, perfume, and apple peelers—are still on display. Old post office boxes mask the bakery, which turns out pies and pastries such as flaky apple dumplings; the potbelly stove warms customers in the winter. Best of all, there is a 1906 soda fountain, where you can still get a sarsaparilla, a Green River, or a genuine ice cream soda. On weekday afternoons, by reservation only, you can enjoy a traditional high tea, complete with tiny tea sandwiches and tartlets. Friday nights, come to the Bair for a steak or crabcake dinner. ▪ *Lafayette and Wilkes; (206)588-9668; 1617 Lafayette St, Steilacoom; $; beer and wine; MC, V; local checks only; breakfast, lunch every day, dinner Fri. &*

ANDERSON ISLAND

LODGINGS

Anderson House on Oro Bay ★★ Anderson Island is a well-kept secret. A short ferry ride from Steilacoom and a few miles from the dock is a large house surrounded by 200 acres of woods. Randy and B. Anderson stay next door at grandfather's home, so guests have exclusive use of the whole house, with its four large bedrooms and antique furnishings. Full farm breakfasts feature breads hot from the oven, fruit pizzas, and other treats. Since this is isolated country with no restaurants, lunch and dinner are also served with advance notice. In addition, the Andersons rent a three-bedroom cedar fishing cabin (wood-stove heated but updated with full kitchen amenities, right down to a microwave) hidden away on outer Amsterdam Bay with a sweeping view of the Olympics from the deck. A short bike ride from the Anderson House brings you to a mile-long secluded beach. Arrangements can be made to pick up guests at the ferry dock. Boaters and those with seaplanes have their own dock, but check the tides. ▪ *Head south from ferry for 3½ miles to head of Oro Bay; (206)884-4088; 12024 Eck-enstam-Johnson Rd, Anderson Island, WA 98303; $$; no credit cards; checks OK.*

OLYMPIA

The capitol's centerpiece is the classic dome of the Washington State Legislative Building. Lavishly fitted out with bronze and marble, this striking Romanesque structure houses the offices of the Governor and other state executives. The State Senate and House of Representatives meet here in annual sessions that can be viewed by visitors.

Just opposite the Legislative Building rises the pillared **Temple of Justice**, seat of the State Supreme Court. To the west is the red brick Governor's Mansion, open to visitors on Wednesday afternoons from 1pm to 2:45pm. Reservations must be made in advance, (360)586-TOUR.

Handsomest of the newer state buildings is Paul Thiry's squarish **State Library**, directly behind the Legislative Building. Open to the public during business hours, it boasts artifacts from the state's early history. At 211 W 21st Avenue, the **State Capitol Museum**, (360)753-2580, houses a permanent exhibit that includes an outstanding collection of Western Washington native American baskets.

Downtown, on Seventh Avenue between Washington and Franklin streets, is the restored **Old Capitol**, whose pointed towers and high-arched windows suggest a late medieval chateau. In another part of the downtown, just off the Plum Street exit from I-5, and adjacent to City Hall, is the newly installed **Yashiro Japanese Garden**, which honors one of Olympia's sister cities.

There is also a triad of colleges here: **The Evergreen State College (TESC)**, west of Olympia, on Cooper Point; **St. Martin's**, a Benedictine monastery and college in adjacent Lacey; and **South Puget Sound Community College**, just across Highway 101. TESC offers a regular schedule of plays, films, and experimental theater, as well as special events such as its annual February Tribute to Asia. Its library and pool are public; (360)866-6000, ext. 6128.

In Olympia proper, the **Washington Center for the**

Performing Arts (on Washington Street between Fifth Avenue and Legion Way) has brought new life to the downtown. In the same block is the **Marianne Partlow Gallery**, a leading outlet for contemporary painting and sculpture. Across Fifth Avenue, the **Capitol Theatre** provides a showcase for the offerings of the active Olympia Film Society as well as for locally produced plays and musicals. Toward the harbor, at the corner of N Capitol Way and W Thurston Street, is the lively **Olympia Farmers Market**, which displays produce, flowers, and crafts from all over the South Sound; open Thursday through Sunday during the growing season.

Wholly different in character is **W Fourth Avenue** between Columbia and Water streets, a hangout for students and ex-students, artists and would-be artists, and counterculture members. Increasingly, Percival Landing (a new waterfront park) is becoming a community focal point, the site of harbor festivals of all kinds. The historic heart of the whole area (Olympia, Lacey, and Tumwater) is **Tumwater Falls**, where the Deschutes River flows into Capitol Lake. Established here today is the chief local industry, the Tumwater Division of the **Pabst Brewing Company**, with free daily tours.

The area's finest nature preserve lies well outside the city limits. This is the relatively unspoiled **Nisqually Delta**—outlet of a river that rises on a Mount Rainier glacier and enters the Sound just north of Olympia. Take exit 115 off I-5 and follow the signs to the **Nisqually National Wildlife Refuge**. From here, a 5-mile hiking trail follows an old dike around the delta, a wetland alive with bird life. Just south, a rookery of great blue herons occupies the treetops.

▼

Olympia

▲

RESTAURANTS

Bristol House ★★ Adolf Schmidt (of the Olympia Brewery founding family) is owner and chef at this cheerful place, located south of the Thurston County courthouse. There have been some new additions to the menu, such as the prawns in a light white wine sauce with lemon, sun-dried tomatoes, and spinach; and the blackened steak salad, served over greens with a caesar-style dressing. Regulars know the popular Bacardi beef is still the best in town. Go for dinner if you want to take full advantage of the chef's ingenuity; lunches are relatively uninspired. Service is fast and professional. ■ *Off Evergreen Park Dr; (360)352-9494; 2401 Bristol Ct SW, Olympia; $$; full bar; MC, V; checks OK; breakfast, lunch, dinner Tues–Fri, dinner only Sat, breakfast only Sun.* &

Gardner's Seafood and Pasta ★★ To loyal fans, Gardner's is the hands-down favorite in Olympia, with very good reason. This homey place—with its wood floors and profusion of fresh flowers on all the tables—makes you feel like you're in the home of a good friend who cooks like a dream. Owners Leon and Jane Longan offer good, simple food that always hits the spot. During the right season, you might find the true Puget Sound delicacy of a dozen Calm Cove Olympia oysters, each the size of a quarter, served on the half shell. Pastas can be bland, but the appetizers, such as the roasted rock shrimp with garlic, never is. Connoisseurs of ice cream won't want to pass up Gardner's homemade product. Reservations important. ■ *North on Capitol Way to Thurston; (360) 786 8466; 111 W Thurston St, Olympia; $$; beer and wine; AE, MC, V; checks OK; dinner Tues–Sat.*

La Petite Maison ★★ This tiny, converted 1890s farmhouse—now overshadowed by a beetling new office building—is a quiet, elegant refuge for Olympians seeking imaginative, skillfully prepared Northwest cuisine (the menu changes daily). Among its appetizers are steamed Kamiche clams and mussels, and delicate and flavorful Dungeness crab cakes served with a dill sauce. Entrees include perfectly sautéed medallions of pork with tangy Dijon mustard sauce and fresh poached petrale sole stuffed with salmon mousse. In spring or summer, it's pleasant to sit on the restaurant's glassedin porch—though the view of over-trafficked Division Street outside may make you long for the days when this place was truly a farm. ■ *1 block south of Division and Harrison; (360) 943-8812; 2005 Ascension Ave NW, Olympia; $$; beer and wine; DC, MC, V; checks OK; lunch Tues–Fri, dinner Mon–Sat.* ⅌

Seven Gables ★★ Visually, this dinner house is the most striking restaurant in Olympia, occupying as it does the fine old Carpenter gothic residence built by the city's turn-of-the-century mayor, George B. Lane. The site takes full advantage of a splendid Mount Rainier view. Steven and Glenda Taylor are the new owners of the delightful spot. Their elegant menu includes such items as a homemade seafood sausage with lobster sauce, red snapper in walnut crust with basil cherry sauce, and beef tenderloin with white mushroom essence. Daily specials include a vegetarian feature. ■ *¾ mile north of the 4th Ave bridge; (360) 352-2349; 1205 W Bay Dr NW, Olympia; $$; full bar; AE, MC, V; checks OK; dinner Tues–Sun.* ⅌

Ben Moore's ★ Ben Moore's plain exterior looks as though it hasn't changed much since the time of the New Deal, and inside there is good food to be had at very reasonable prices. If you order any of the prawn, oyster, or steak dinners, you'll get a lot to eat, and none of it is likely to disappoint. Prices are out of a bygone era; the costliest complete dinner is a New York steak with prawns at $13.95. ■ *On 4th Ave, east of Columbia; (360) 357-7527; 112 4th Ave, Olympia; $; full bar; AE, MC, V; checks OK; breakfast, lunch, dinner Mon–Sat.* ⅌

Budd Bay Cafe ★ There's no doubt about it: the Budd Bay Cafe, with its long row of tables looking out across Budd Inlet, is still a preferred after-hours haunt of many of today's legislators, lobbyists, and state government movers and shakers. Restaurateur John Senner is on hand most of the time, seeing that everyone is satisfied. Don't look for elaborate dishes here; the menu (steaks, sandwiches, pasta, salads, seafood) is designed for boaters and people to whom good talk matters more than haute cuisine. The bar is pleasant and lively with a long list of specialty beers. ■ *Between A and B on Columbia; (360) 357-6963; 525 N Columbia St, Olympia; $$; full bar; AE, DC, MC, V; checks OK; lunch Mon–Sat, dinner every day, brunch Sun.* &

Capitale ★ In downtown Olympia, across Sylvester Square from the old courthouse, is a tiny, casual place serving up interesting food in a pleasant atmosphere. The walls are lined with the work of local artists and jazz music often complements the meals; in good weather, a few tables are added outside, giving this place a nice neighborhood feel. The menu is Italian-esque, with interesting variations. Consider the tortellini with Brie and avocado, or the appetizer of a sweet potato gratin—tender little pieces of sweetness with a sprinkle of Parmesan cheese melted on top. The rectangular pizzas are excellent. Or try the goat cheese and sun-dried tomato tamales. ■ *Capitol Way and Legion St; (360) 352-8007; 609 Capitol Way S, Olympia; $$; beer and wine; no credit cards; checks OK; breakfast, lunch, dinner Mon–Fri lunch, dinner Sat.* &

Chattery Down ★ This small dining room, which began as an annex to Ann Buck's gift shop next door, has proven so successful that it has almost taken over the whole place. Many patrons prefer Fridays, when an oyster dish is always on the menu—perhaps in a stew or chowder, or raw on the half-shell. Others come in for high tea on Wednesdays and Saturday afternoons. Dinners offer Northwest products in traditional French preparations, such as paupiettes of sole stuffed with spinach and salmon mousse, or steak and prawns Monique, served in a dill cream sauce. Service needs a spanking. ■ *Across from the Capitol Theatre; (360) 352-8483; 209 5th Ave E, Olympia; $$; beer and wine; AE, MC, V; checks OK; lunch Mon–Sat, dinner Thurs–Sat, breakfast Sat.* &

Falls Terrace ★ It would be hard to find an Olympian who hasn't had at least one meal at this longtime Tumwater institution; anyone wanting to eat during regular hours should get reservations. Part of the reason for its popularity is its splendid setting overlooking the Tumwater Falls of the Deschutes River. There's a wide variety of steak, lamb, and chicken dishes, along with a fried version of the delectable Olympia oysters. Ice cream desserts are featured. The wine list is not for connoisseurs, even though the adjacent bar is one of the most agreeable drinking spots in town. ■ *Across the Deschutes River from the Olympia Brewery; (360) 943-7830; 106 Deschutes Way, Tumwater; $$; full bar; AE, DC, MC, V; checks OK; lunch Mon–Sat, dinner every day.* &

Sweet Oasis ★ This spot on Capitol Way is particularly informal, but offers some delicious foods of the Mediterranean. Among the daily specials are spanakopita and Lebanese baked vegetables. Friday and Saturday you can get kibby sineeyah, a deliciously offbeat dish combining ground lamb with bulgur, pine nuts, and spices baked in squares. Falafel, meat pies, and other traditional Mediterranean fare is available as well. The dessert pastries are house-made and very good. Saturday nights you get a bonus belly-dancing show—a very artful performance—winding casually among the tables. ■ *Capitol Way and 5th Ave; (360) 956-0470; 507 Capitol Way, Olympia; $; beer and wine; MC, V; local checks only; lunch and dinner every day.* &

Urban Onion ★ The site of many a power lunch for Olympia's rising breed of feminist politicians, the Urban Onion (originally called the "Herb and Onion") retains a faint flavor of the counterculture of the '60s. A signature dish is an especially satisfying lentil soup. The Mexican chicken grilled with mushrooms is also outstanding. Breakfasts include a hefty huevos rancheros. The Urban Onion has expanded into the lobby of the former Olympian Hotel, and meeting space is available. ■ *Legion and Washington; (360) 943-9242; 116 Legion Way, Olympia; $$; full bar; AE, MC, V; checks OK; breakfast, lunch, dinner every day.*

Wagner's European Bakery and Cafe ★ Almost as *echt deutsch* as an opera by that other well-known Wagner is the formidable collection of pastries regularly produced by Rudy Wagner's bakery, which effortlessly fabricates beautifully decorated cakes, apricot squares, raspberry mousse tortes, cream horns, several species of doughnuts, and all kinds of fresh-baked breads. Toothsome Black Forest tortes whirl temptingly in a display case. An attached cafe, featuring continental breakfast and lunch, has expanded to serve more customers. German-born Wagner, chief baker as well as owner, gets new ideas on trips back to Europe. ■ *Capitol Way and Union; (360) 357-7268; 1013 S Capitol Way, Olympia; $$; no alcohol; DC, MC, V; checks OK; continental breakfast, lunch Mon–Sat.* &

The Fish Bowl Aptly named the Fish Bowl, the Fish Tale Ales brew pub is full to the gills with fish paraphernalia, from real specimens swimming around in the large tank, to metal salmon sculptures and ceramic fish on the walls. The beers are the draw—all Fish Tale productions are made in the adjoining facilities. The beer's available to go as well. For nibbles (called "Fish Food") consider smoked oysters, cheeses, shrimp cocktail, antipasto, or oyster shooters. The whole-wheat–crust pizzas come from the wood-fired ovens of Levity Cafe next door. ■ *Downtown Olympia, corner of Jefferson and Legion; (360) 943-3650; 515 Jefferson, Olympia; $; beer and wine; no credit cards; checks OK; lunch, dinner Mon–Sat.* &

The Spar Above the restaurant's old-fashioned booths are blown-up Darius Kinsey photos of teams of old-time loggers beaming over unbelievably mammoth trees they've just brought to earth. Indeed, some 60-odd years ago, the Spar used to be known as a workingman's hangout. Today it's classless, with a volatile mixture of students, attorneys, businesspeople, artists, politicians, fishermen, tourists, and leisured retirees. The Spar's robust milk shakes and homemade bread pudding are locally acclaimed, although much of the menu is purely average. Willapa Bay oysters or fresh salmon from the Farmers Market are sometimes available; the prime rib dinner is popular on weekends. ■ *1 block east of Capitol Way; (360) 357-6444; 114 E 4th Ave, Olympia; $; full bar; AE, DC, MC, V; checks OK; breakfast, lunch, dinner every day.* &

LODGINGS

Harbinger Inn ★ Occupying a restored 1910 mansion, this B&B offers Edwardian furnishings, a fine outlook over Budd Inlet and the distant Olympic mountains, and four choice guest rooms (two with views, two without). Nicest is the two-room suite on the view side; but rooms on the back side are farther from the street, with only the sound of a small artesian-fed waterfall to disturb the tranquility. The inn is situated near excellent routes for bicycle riding; complimentary bicycles are available. A light breakfast is served. ■ *1 mile north of State St; (360) 754-0389; 1136 E Bay Dr, Olympia, WA 98506; $$; AE, MC, V; checks OK.*

Westwater Inn ★ Few urban hotels around Puget Sound take such striking advantage of the Northwest's natural beauty as this one, dramatically perched on a high bluff above Capitol Lake, with much greenery in view, and the Capitol dome—illuminated by night—rising to the north. There are fairly large rooms, a heated outdoor pool (seasonal), a year-round Jacuzzi, and occasionally music in the lounge. Some rooms can be noisy, so it's advisable to request one on the water side. Meals are served in the coffee shop and at Thurstons, a restaurant where a Sunday brunch concentrates on, well, dessert. ■ *Exit 104 from I-5; (360) 943-4000 or (800) 551-8500; 2300 Evergreen Park Dr, Olympia, WA 98802; $$; full bar; AE, DC, MC, V; no checks; lunch and dinner every day, brunch Sun.* &

Wolf Haven, 3111 Offut Lake Road, (360)264-4695, is an educational research facility that teaches wolf appreciation and studies the question of whether to reintroduce them into the wild. The public is invited to see the wolves or join them in a "howl-in."

RESTAURANTS

Alice's Restaurant ★ Located in a fine turn-of-the-century farmhouse on a lively little creek, Alice's serves hearty dinners, all including cream of peanut soup, a Waldorf salad, trout, an entree (baked ham with pineapple glaze, fresh oysters, a selection of game dishes, perhaps quail, and even catfish), and choice of dessert. In conjunction with the restaurant, Vincent de Bellis operates the Johnson Creek Winery, which is the exclusive wine list offering. (Ask about wine tastings when you call for reservations.) Advance reservations are required. ■ *Call for directions; (360)264-2887; 19248 Johnson Creek Rd SE, Tenino; $$; beer and wine; AE, DC, MC, V; checks OK; dinner Wed–Sun.* &

YELM

RESTAURANTS

Arnold's Country Inn ★ Long known as one of Olympia's most accomplished chefs, Arnold Ball has established his latest restaurant just outside Yelm on the road to Mount Rainier. Steaks and meat dishes dominate here. But besides steak Diane, there are familiar Arnold's specialties such as chicken sautéed with raspberry brandy, roast duckling à l'orange, and traditional escargots. Arnold is careful with small details: his rolls baked on the premises are warm and delicious, as are his fine pies. His wine list is adequate, but many patrons are happy to drive all the way from Olympia just for the food. ■ *Across from the Thriftway Shopping Center; (360)458-3977; 717 Yelm Ave E, Yelm; $$; full bar; AE, MC, V; local checks only; breakfast, lunch, dinner Tues–Sun.* &

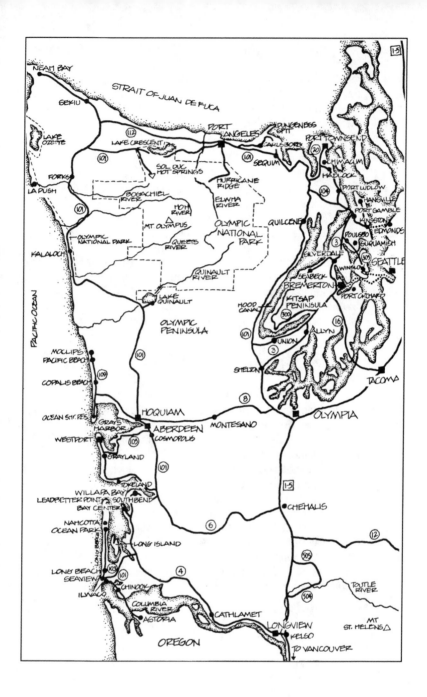

Olympic Peninsula

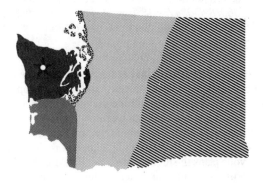

The Kitsap Peninsula north to Hansville and Foulweather Bluff, angling west across Hood Canal to Port Townsend, continuing westward along the Juan de Fuca shore to Cape Flattery, then southward along the Pacific coast to Ocean Shores. The southern boundary angles eastward to Shelton and northeast to Kitsap County.

PORT ORCHARD

The center of this small town hugs the southern shoreline of one of Puget Sound's many fingers of water—Sinclair Inlet. There are numerous antique shops, and **Sidney Galleries** displays Northwest art on the first floor of the Masonic Lodge Building. On Saturdays, from the end of April through October, the **Port Orchard Farmers Market** (Marina Park, one block from Bay Street) offers a tantalizing selection of cut flowers, fresh vegetables, baked goods, and crafts. Take home some Hood Canal oysters or ask the oyster lady to cook a few on her grill. With its boardwalk and beach access, the waterfront area is a true gathering place.

    Horluck Transportation, a privately owned foot ferry that runs every half hour, seven days a week, provides an economical means of travel between the main ferry terminal at Bremerton and downtown Port Orchard; (360) 876-2300.

RESTAURANTS

Hadi's Restaurant ★ Good Lebanese food—a marvelous mixture of Mediterranean influences—would be a welcome treat anywhere, and it's especially so in the west Sound area. Assad Nakkour and his wife, Samiha, serve tempting classic appetizers: hummus, baba ghanouj, tabouli, stuffed grape leaves, and cabbage rolls. Fresh, delicious ingredients go into these dishes. Beef, lamb, and chicken shish kabobs, cooked to order, make up the bulk of the entrees. Portions are plentiful, and Nakkour is happy to expound on Lebanese cuisine or Middle Eastern politics. ■ *On the main drag, next to the movie theater; (360)895-0347; 818 Bay St, Port Orchard; $$; beer and wine; no credit cards; checks OK; lunch Mon–Sat, dinner every day.* &

LODGINGS

Reflections Bed and Breakfast Inn ★★ Every cliché used to describe an excellent Northwest bed and breakfast applies to this sprawling B&B set on a hillside overlooking Sinclair Inlet, with the Olympic Mountains as backdrop. Former New Englanders Jim and Cathy Hall extend warm hospitality to their guests—complete with a hearty breakfast of regional dishes that everyone plans the night before. The Halls furnish the four guest rooms with family antiques, including heirloom quilts. The largest room, often used for honeymooners, has a private porch and Jacuzzi tub. The well-tended grounds include a hot tub, a gazebo, and always a multitude of birds eating and preening at various feeders. ■ *East of Port Orchard off Beach Dr; (360)871-5582; 3878 Reflections Lane E, Port Orchard, WA 98366; $$; MC, V; checks OK.*

BREMERTON

Bremerton and its naval station have been entwined since the early 1890s when a young German, one William Bremer, sold close to 200 acres of bay front to the U.S. Navy for $9,587. Today, the Navy shipyards are still right downtown and rows of moth gray ghost ships—all silent reminders of past naval battles—loom offshore, soon to include the 45,000-ton battleship *Missouri*. Only the destroyer USS *Turner Joy*, which saw action off Vietnam, is open for self-guided tours, Thursday through Monday. Adjacent to both the ferry terminal and the *Turner Joy*, the **Bremerton Naval Museum** depicts the region's shipbuilding history back to bowsprit-and-sail days; (360)479-7447; closed on Monday, Labor Day to Memorial Day; open daily in summer.

Farther north on Kitsap Peninsula is the **Trident Nuclear Submarine Base** at Bangor. Occasionally a pod of orcas can be glimpsed escorting one of the mammoth submarines through the local waters to deep-sea duty. Since 1915, Keyport has been the major U.S. site for undersea torpedo testing. Now it also is home to an extraordinary **Naval Underseas Museum**, housing the first Revolutionary War submarine. Open daily (closed Tuesday, November through April); (360)396-4148.

Washington State Ferries provide transportation to the Kitsap Peninsula and highway access to the Olympic Peninsula.

They run regularly between downtown Seattle and Bremerton, and Fauntleroy in West Seattle and Southworth near Port Orchard; (206)464-6400 or (800)84-FERRY.

RESTAURANTS

Boat Shed ★ This casual seafood restaurant overhanging the Port Washington Narrows is aptly named. Rough wood panels the walls inside and out and a solitary fish tank serves as decor. Scaups and scoters run and patter along the water while boats of every size pass by. Whenever possible, hit the deck and enjoy a pint of ale, a gigantic serving of tangled Cajun onion strings, and a cup of rich clam chowder, or the knockwurst piled with red onions and cheese on sourdough. A sesame seed–coated piece of tuna is topped with a pat of wasabe butter; lime enlivens the Dungeness crab cakes. Even most of the pasta dishes showcase the bounty of the local waters. ■ *East side of Manette Bridge, on the water; (360)377-2600; 101 Shore Dr, Bremerton; $; full bar; MC, V; local checks only; lunch, dinner every day, brunch Sat–Sun.* &

LODGINGS

Willcox House ★★★ Colonel Julian Willcox and his wife, Constance, once played host to such famous guests as Clark Gable at this copper-roofed, art deco, 10,000-square-foot manse on Hood Canal. Oak parquet floors, walnut-paneled walls, and a copper-framed marble fireplace—one of five throughout the house—grace the front rooms. Downstairs is a bar, a game room, and a clubby library, where you can look out over the canal, the impressive gardens, and a saltwater lap pool. Comb the beach for oysters, fish from the dock, or hike the hillside trails. A hearty breakfast is served, and lunch is offered to multinight guests, as is a prix-fixe dinner (open to nonguests on weekends by reservation). On Friday nights in summer there's a salmon barbecue served on the dusky terrace. It's about a half-hour drive from the Bremerton ferry, though some guests opt to arrive by boat or floatplane. ■ *9 miles south of Seabeck, call or write for directions; (360)830-4492 or (800)725-2600; 2390 Tekiu Rd, Bremerton, WA 98312; $$$; MC, V; checks OK.* &

SILVERDALE

RESTAURANTS

Bahn Thai ★★ Equally as good as (and arguably even better than) the highly esteemed Seattle Bahn Thai (which his wife and brother still run) is Benchai (Benny) Sunti's new version — which has the same name, same personal service, and similar menu, but a much different look. This is a place to come with a group of hungry eaters to share a wide variety of the brightly flavored dishes of Thailand. Tod Mun, spicy, crispy patties of minced fish, green beans, and lime leaves is served with a contrasting fresh cucumber relish, making an excellent starter before Tom Yum Goong, a favorite Thai soup of prawns and lemon grass. Try one of six different exotic curries, including Masuman—beef and potatoes sauced with a mildly hot curry infused with coconut milk and cloves, nutmeg, and cinnamon: not your everyday plate of meat and potatoes. ■ *½ block north of Bucklin Hill Rd; (360) 698-3663; 98811 Mickelberry Rd, Silverdale; $; full bar; AE, MC, V; local checks only; lunch, dinner every day.* ♿

Hakata ★ For those searching for sushi with a difference, chef Yoshiyuki Sugimoto, formerly at Bush Gardens in Seattle, offers some intriguing selections in his own immaculate restaurant in an out-of-the-way shopping plaza. Tobiko (flying fish roe) and wasabe (pungent Japanese horseradish) explode with flavor when you bite through a handroll. A tangy leaf of shiso adds a subtle surprise to a delicate nigiri sushi of flounder, and the spider roll—made with crunchy soft-shell crab—is a house favorite. In a class by itself is the fat, fancy futomaki roll with its pinwheel of contrasting ingredients. For lunch, try one of the popular meal-in-one dishes like donburi (big bowls of rice heaped with such delights as shrimp and vegetable tempura). ■ *Take the Kitsap Mall exit off Hwy 3, behind the post office in Pacific Linen Plaza; (360) 698-0929; 10876 Myhre Pl #108, Silverdale; $; beer and wine; MC, V; local checks only; lunch Tues–Sat, dinner Tues–Sun.* ♿

Yacht Club Broiler ★ A simple restaurant with some elegant touches and a water view: copper-covered tables, walls lined with delicate rice-paper fish prints, and bare wood floors softened by Oriental-style rugs. As might be expected by its name and location (on Dyes Inlet), seafood is a major menu item here. What is *unexpected* is the excellent quality of that seafood (as the commercial fishermen who eat here will attest), be it the sweet, moist Dungeness crab cakes, or a bucket of plump steamed clams. The prime rib special on Sunday and Monday nights makes scrumptious eating, too. ■ *From 305 take Silverdale exit, first right into town, then left on Bayshore; (360) 698-1601; 9226 Bayshore Dr, Silverdale; $$; full bar; AE, DC, MC, V; checks OK; lunch, dinner every day, brunch Sun.* ♿

LODGINGS

Silverdale on the Bay ★ This tastefully designed resort hotel serves equally well as a conference site or a getaway destination, although the encroaching shopping malls are a distraction. Many rooms have balconies with views over Dyes Inlet; mini-suites are the best. Extras establish it as the resort it aspires to be, with an indoor lap pool, large brick sun deck, sauna, weight room, video game room, and dock. The Mariner Restaurant offers white-linened tables, professional service, and nicely prepared meals that aren't too pricey. Enjoy breakfast par excellence, with boardinghouse-style biscuits and gravy or Belgian waffles piled with strawberries and cream. ■ *Turn east at the intersection of Silverdale Way and Bucklin Hill Rd; (360)698-1000 or (800)544-9799; 3073 Bucklin Hill Rd, Silverdale, WA 98383; $$; full bar; AE, DC, MC, V; checks OK; breakfast, lunch, dinner every day.*

POULSBO

Poulsbo was once a community of fishermen and loggers, primarily Scandinavian. Today its snug harbor is full of yachts, and the trees have given way to town buildings. The Scandinavian heritage, however, is still going strong—Front Street sports its "Velkommen til Poulsbo" signs and the architecture is a dolled-up version of the fjord villages of Norway.

The folks at the **Poulsbo Smokehouse** (18881C Front Street, (360)779-1099) are serious about the quality of their product, using king salmon from Alaska that they smoke with bleached alder. They skip the nitrates and keep their brine low in salt. The **Poulsbo Country Deli**, across from the Anderson Park gazebo, (360)779-2763, makes marvelous sandwiches, soups, quiche, and desserts (the park along the waterfront is a perfect spot for a picnic). Or go back to Front Street and try to select something from the overwhelming choices at **Sluy's Bakery** (18924 Front Street NE, (360)779-2798); take home a loaf of Poulsbo Bread, the local specialty. Finally, **Boehm's Chocolates** has an outpost here (18864 Front Street, (360)697-3318); it's worth walking into its quiet, dark interior just for the wonderful smell.

There's a growing population of antique dealers in Poulsbo as well as numerous gift shops. Farther afield, the **Kemper Brewing Company**, 2 miles north of town at 22381 Foss Road NE, (360)697-1446, follows the classic German brewing style and makes excellent lagers, on tap at the brewery's grill where a simple menu is served from 11am until early evening. Call ahead for tour time.

RESTAURANTS

Molly Ward's Gardens ★★ Sam and Lynn Ward's homespun establishment (which doubles as a dried-flower shop, with the latest pickings hanging above you) shines best when the sun does—when the open French doors welcome the garden scents, when the chefs can forage in the organic garden, and when you and your friends have time to savor the entire experience, maybe even wander through the garden between courses. Breakfast begins at a leisurely time and might be anything from fresh brioche and berries to pan-fried oysters. Lunch (a favorite of a local bridge club) might take up the rest of the afternoon. Whatever it is (decided at the whim of Sam Ward), it will be accompanied by delicate garden soup and fresh-picked salad. On Saturday eves, Sam designs a five-course feast. Don't expect much verbal elaboration when being served—efforts are put into the meal. Bring your own beer or wine: no corkage fee. ■ *Just past Manor Farm Inn on Big Valley Rd; (360) 779-4471; 27462 Big Valley Rd, Poulsbo; $$; no alcohol; MC, V; checks OK; breakfast starting at 10:15 Tues–Sun, lunch every day, dinner Fri–Sat.*

Judith's Tearooms and Rose Cafe ★ The small storefront of this charming spot disguises a large interior space that runs back through several rooms. The farther back you go, the more claustrophobic you feel, but decorations with a mix of antique furniture and false windows help. The food more than makes up for a bad seat. Judith's team of efficient waitresses serve homemade food along with tea brewed in tea pots. Sandwiches come on thick slices of delicious bread; soups, desserts, tea sandwiches, meat loaf, and quiche are prepared fresh every day. A special menu section offers Scandinavian delicacies and between 2pm and 4pm Judith's serves afternoon tea. ■ *At the east end of Front St; (360) 697-3449; 18820 Front St NE, Poulsbo; $; wine and champagne; MC, V; checks OK; lunch, tea every day.*

LODGINGS

Manor Farm Inn ★★★ A lavish retreat in the middle of nowhere, Manor Farm is a working farm with horses, pigs, sheep, cows, chickens, and a trout pond—a beguiling mix of the raw and the cultivated that succeeds in spoiling even the city-bred. Jill Hughes, a Los Angeles native, is the proprietor who runs a superlative accommodation. There are seven bright guest rooms (two have fireplaces) and a hot tub bubbles in a too central location. Best are the cottages. The farm cottage is across the road, with French country-pine antiques, down comforters, and a hot tub. Or there's the beach house a few miles away on Hood Canal with two bedrooms, decks, and hot tub. Adjacent to the farmhouse is a small conference center.

Breakfast happens twice at Manor Farm: first a tray of hot scones and orange juice is left at your door; then (for nonguests as well) at 9am, there are fresh fruit, oatmeal folded with whipped cream, eggs from the farm chickens, and rashers of bacon. The once legendary four-course dinners are now only special occasion affairs. Call ahead. ■ *½ hour from Winslow ferry dock off Hwy 3 on Big Valley Rd; (360) 779-4628; 26069 Big Valley Rd NE, Poulsbo, WA 98370; $$$; beer and wine; V; local checks only; breakfast every day (dinner, December and Valentine's Day only).*

SUQUAMISH

In Suquamish on the Port Madison Indian Reservation (follow he signs past Agate Pass), the **Suquamish Museum** in the Tribal Center is devoted to studying and displaying Puget Sound Salish Indian culture; (360)598-3311. **Chief Sealth's grave** can be found nearby, on the grounds of St. Peter's Catholic Mission Church. Twin dugout canoes rest on a log frame over the stone, which reads, "The firm friend of the whites, and for him the city of Seattle was named."

KINGSTON

RESTAURANTS

Kingston Hotel Cafe ★★ If every town had a spot like this, the world would be a better place. Judith Weinstock (formerly of Bainbridge Island's famed Streamliner Diner) adopted this two-story, Western-front building overlooking the Sound and turned it into one of the most inviting eateries (with some of the most enticing food) on the peninsula: a delightful sorrel and potato soup comes dressed with a confetti of rose petals; salmon and halibut—beautifully braided—might be enhanced with a light lemon and caper sauce. When the mood's right, Judith's husband (and custom jeweler), David Weinstock, plays music—occasionally joined by others. It's so much more than a cafe—it's a meeting place. Bring the kids and let them play in the sandbox while you sit on the deck and enjoy another latte with your breakfast. ■ *A block north of the ferry terminal at Washington Blvd and 1st Ave; (360)297-8100; 25931 Washington Blvd, Kingston; $; beer and wine; V; checks OK; breakfast, lunch, and dinner Tues–Sun.*

Port Gamble

PORT GAMBLE

Built in the mid-19th century by the Pope & Talbot timber people, who traveled here by clipper ship from Maine, this is the essence of the company town. Everything is company-owned and -maintained, and the dozen or so Victorian houses are beauties and in splendid repair. The town, which was modeled on a New England village, also boasts a lovely church, a vital and well-stocked company store, and a historical museum that is a gem; (360)297-3341. An ideal presentation of a community's society and industrial heritage, it was designed by Alec James, who designed the displays for the Royal Provincial Museum in Victoria. The lumber mill, incidentally, is still in operation.

HANSVILLE

Just beyond the unassuming fishing town of Hansville are a couple of the prettiest, most accessible, and least explored beaches on the peninsula. To the east is **Point No Point**, marked by a lighthouse and great for families with kids. Follow the road from Hansville to the west and you'll come across **Cape Foulweather**. The short trail through the woods is tough to find, so look for the Nature Conservancy sign on the south side of the road.

SHELTON AND HOOD CANAL

The logging community of Shelton sells thousands upon thousands of Christmas trees nationwide each year. In the nearby bays and inlets, the oyster and clam populations are making a comeback, and vacation homes line the miles of scenic shoreline. Traveling on 101, which hugs the west side of the Hood Canal through tiny towns with names like Duckabush, Liliwaup, Dosewallips, or Hamma Hamma, you should stop at a roadside stand or store for fresh crab and oysters. Sample Hoodsport Winery's selection at their cottage tasting room (N 23501 Hwy 101, (360)877-9894).

This stretch of highway serves as the jumping-off spot for many recreational areas in the **Olympic National Forest and Park**, including Lake Cushman with its state park. Numerous hiking trails lead to remote cloud-draped alpine lakes and meadows. Every summer weekend, concerts are given by the internationally acclaimed, Seattle-based Philadelphia String Quartet and world-class guest artists at the **Olympic Music Festival**, where music lovers sit on hay bales in an 80-year-old Dutch colonial barn or stretch out on the gentle hillside while listening to chamber music. (Directions: 11 miles west of the Hood Canal Bridge on Highway 104, then a quarter mile south from the Quilcene exit; (360)728-6411.)

RESTAURANTS

Cafe Luna ★★ There is nothing about Shelton to prepare you for Cafe Luna—Alice must have felt the same sense of unreality when she fell into Wonderland. Cafe Luna is an intimate, muted, art deco room with moons of magic. The real magic, though, is in the simple Italian dishes that emerge from the kitchen. Pasta dishes could serve as object lessons in balancing the heady flavors of sauces with just the right pasta. There are only a very few meat or fish dishes from which to choose, but you can seldom go wrong; bear in mind there are still the desserts to enjoy—perhaps a chocolate-rich rum fig cake. The high quality of the cuisine and the service may have something to do with the fact that Cafe Luna is open only three nights a week—so the cook's creativity never dulls. ■ *In the Mercantile Mall at 3rd and Railroad; (360)427-8709; 221 W Railroad St, Shelton; $$; beer and wine; no credit cards; checks OK; dinner Thurs–Sat.* ♿

UNION

RESTAURANTS

Victoria's ★★ There is a stone-and- log structure on the east bank of Hood Canal that has been a stopover spot since the early 1930s. Locals remember it as a lively dance hall and tavern, but in the last decade it has evolved into one of the better eateries on the Canal. High-beamed ceilings, a fireplace, and large windows that look upon a nearby brook and sheltering trees set the scene for equally appealing food. The seafood can be exceptional and the ample portions of prime rib make for good eating. Desserts are imaginative—and rich. ■ *1 mile west of Alderbrook Inn on Hwy 106; (360)898-4400; E 6791 Hwy 106, Union; $$; full bar; MC, V; checks OK; breakfast Sun, lunch, dinner every day.* ♿

BRINNON

RESTAURANTS

Half-Way House Restaurant ★ Brinnon is a town you can miss if you blink, but keep your eyes open for the Half-Way House, especially on Tuesday around dinnertime. That's the night that chef Joseph Day puts on a gourmet five-course champagne dinner. The tiny cinder-block cafe is packed with loggers and others in the know who come for his escargots in mushroom caps and lobster with wild rice (lobster is served every third Tuesday). The meal ends, properly, with a cheese plate and sinfully rich desserts. If you can't get a table on Tuesday, the food is still good the rest of the time, especially the homemade soups and pies. Reservations required on Tuesday nights only. ■ *On the west side of Hwy 101 in Brinnon next to post office; (360)796-4715; Hwy 101 and Brinnon Lane, Brinnon; $ ($$ on Tues); full bar; AE, MC, V; local checks only; breakfast, lunch, dinner every day.* ♿

QUILCENE

RESTAURANTS

Timber House Surrounded by cedar and hemlock, the Timber House resembles nothing so much as a hunting lodge gussied up to make it comfortable for the womenfolk. Descriptive

logging scenes are painted on the hand-carved tables and coun-
terledges: a nice touch. The local seafood is the main reason
to eat here. Quilcene oysters come from right down the road,
and there's much more from the waters around the Sound.
Dungeness crab is a winner: sautéed, as a sandwich filling, in
an omelet or a salad. Locals swear by the roast beef dinners. ■
*About ½ mile south of Quilcene on Hwy 101; (360) 765-3339;
Highway 101 S, Quilcene; $$; full bar; MC, V; checks OK;
lunch, dinner, Wed–Mon.* &

PORT LUDLOW

LODGINGS

Inn at Port Ludlow ★★ The new Inn at Port Ludlow (a sister
establishment to Pam and Paul Schell's Inn at Langley and Fri-
day Harbor House) guards the head of Hood Canal on a sandy
bar across from the Resort at Port Ludlow. It exudes the at-
mosphere of a New England estate—a place to go and be
peaceful. The rooms are retreats in themselves, or you can play
chess in the living room, or hold your own private wine-tasting
in the wine nook. Unfortunately, erratic reports about service
(exemplary one night, aloof another) leave us slightly tentative
about Schell's place number three; we know they're capable of
more careful consistency. The inn's restaurant is quietly be-
coming one of the better places to dine on the peninsula. Chef
Colleen Herrick has been receiving accolades for her careful
executions of roasted duck and simple renditions of crab
cakes. ■ *6 miles north of Hood Canal Bridge on west side;
(360) 437-0411; 1 Heron Rd, Port Ludlow; PO Box 65460,
Port Ludlow, WA 98365; $$$; AE, MC, V; checks OK.* &

Port Ludlow Golf & Meeting Retreat ★★ Pope and
Talbot's legendary 1880s sawmill manager's "biggest
damn cabin on the Sound" (actually a splendid Victorian
home) once shared this site overlooking the teardrop bay with
the busy Port Ludlow mill. Still owned by Pope and Talbot, it
is now a popular resort facility, catering especially to groups,
with a marina, tennis courts, 27-hole championship golf course,
hiking and cycling trails, and year-round swimming pool on
1,500 developed acres. The individually decorated suites—all
privately owned as second homes by out-of-town families—are
very livable, with fireplaces, kitchens, and private decks, many
with views of the harbor. But stay away from the standard
rooms, which resemble a budget motel, complete with paper-
thin walls and noisy heaters. The Harbormaster Restaurant has
a pleasant bar and a delightful deck. ■ *6 miles north of Hood
Canal Bridge on west side; (360) 437-2222; 9483 Oak Bay Rd,
Port Ludlow, WA 98365; $$$; AE, MC, V; checks OK.*

PORT HADLOCK

RESTAURANTS

Ajax Cafe ★ The old-timers living in Port Townsend, Port Ludlow, and points in between are glad to see this longtime eating establishment flourishing again. This waterside cafe is funky in the truest sense—complete with live, bluesy music, shiny black table coverings, and unmatched chairs painted in bright primary colors. Owner/chef Rudy Valiani has given Ajax a style all its own. Most everyone agrees that Tennesseans are right at the top when it comes to barbecuing pork, and the tender barbecue pork ribs, here blessed with a thick barbecue sauce containing a goodly splash of Jack Daniel's Tennessee whiskey, reflect this tradition. From time to time, the vegetables show signs of old age—but what the heck, everyone is having fun and nobody seems to mind. ▪ *In Lower Hadlock on the waterfront, off Oak Bay Rd; (360) 385-3450; 271 Water St, Port Hadlock; $$; beer and wine; AE, MC, V; local checks only; dinner every day.*

MARROWSTONE ISLAND

Marrowstone Island is just off the northeast corner of the Olympic Peninsula. To get there, drive across the southern end of Indian Island. **Fort Flagler State Park**, an old coastal fortification, is a beautiful spot for walks and picnics. A large group of seals hangs out at the very end of the sand spit and often surround kayakers paddling by. Several local establishments farm oysters and harvest clams.

LODGINGS

The Ecologic Place A great spot for families who'd rather spend more time out than in, this is your basic gathering of rustic cabins in a natural setting. And what a setting. The Ecologic Place borders on a tidal estuary that flows into Oak Bay and then Puget Sound, and offers a view of the Olympics and Mount Rainier, conditions permitting. The cabins, each with its own character, have never been acquainted with an interior decorator, but have everything you need to enjoy the simple beauty of the place—wood stoves, equipped kitchens, comfortable mattresses on the queen-size beds, and fine-for-the-children bunks and twins. Bring bikes, boats, books, bathing suits, binoculars, children, and groceries too. ▪ *Turn right at Welcome to Marrowstone sign; (360) 385-3077; 10 Beach Dr, Nordland, WA 98358; $$; MC, V; checks OK.*

During the early days of the clipper ships, Port Townsend was the official point of entry to Puget Sound. Vessels from around the globe landed, and the foreign consuls added a cosmopolitan flavor to the social life of the wealthy folk who settled here. This early prosperity gave rise to the construction of more than 200 Victorian homes, reflecting the reign of Queen you-know-who. When the mineral deposits petered out, the rail never came, and the elite investors left, Port Townsend became a land of vanished dreams and vacant mansions. The restored buildings, now forming a National Historical Landmark District, and the wraparound views lie at the heart of the town's charm.

Chetzemoka Park, a memorial to the Indian chief who became a friend of the first white settlers, in the northeast corner of town, has a charming gazebo, picnic tables, tall Douglas firs, and a grassy slope down to the beach. **Fort Worden**, along with sister forts on Marrowstone and Whidbey islands, was part of the defense system established to protect Puget Sound. The 433-acre complex overlooking Admiralty Inlet now incorporates turn-of-the-century military structures, campgrounds, gardens, a theater, and a concert hall (see review). A huge central field is perfect for games or kite flying. This setting may look familiar to those who saw the movie *An Officer and a Gentleman*, which was filmed here. At the water's edge, an enormous pier juts into the bay—it's the summer home to the **Marine Science Center**, with touch tanks and displays of sea creatures. There's a safe, protected swimming beach on one side of the pier, and access to miles of beaches. Above on the hillside you can spend hours exploring the deserted cement bunkers.

Fort Worden is also home to **Centrum**, a sponsor of concerts, workshops, and festivals throughout the year. Many of these take place in the old balloon hangar, reborn as McCurdy Pavilion. The **Centrum Summer Arts Festival**, one of the most successful cultural programs in the state—with dance, fiddle tunes, chamber music, a writers conference, jazz, blues, and theater performances—runs from June to September; (360)385-3102.

A historic homes tour happens the first weekend in May and again the third weekend in September. The **Rhododendron Festival** in May, with a parade and crowning of the queen, is the oldest festival in town. The **Wooden Boat Festival** at Point Hudson Marina, (360)385-3628, the weekend after Labor Day, is a celebration of traditional crafts and a showcase for everything from prams to kayaks to yachts to tugboats.

The Jefferson County Historical Society has a fascinating museum at 210 Madison Street, (360)385-1003, with old jail cells; the Society's collection of Northwest Indian artifacts is extensive. Colorful shops line Water Street: **North by Northwest**

▼
Port
Townsend
▲

(918 Water Street, (360)385-0955) has a wide selection of historic and contemporary Indian baskets; wood, ivory, and soapstone carvings; jewelry; and related books. Next door is **Melville and Co.** (914 Water Street, (360)385-7127), offering an extensive selection of English mysteries, old comics, and rare books. **William James Bookseller** (829 Water Street, (360)835-7313) has a vast and well-organized inventory of used books. **Earthen Works** (702 Water Street, (360)385-0328) specializes in high-quality Washington craft items. The best ice cream cones can be had at **Elevated Ice Cream** (627 Water Street, (360)385-1156); the best antique selection at **Port Townsend Antique Mall** (802 Washington Street, (360)385-2590), where about 40 antique merchants have convened under one roof. The best pastry is to be had at **Bread and Roses Bakery** (230 Quincey Street, (360)385-1044). At **Riley's General Store** (1020 Water Street) you can buy incredible chocolates. For wines, try **The Wine Cellar** (940 Water Street, (360)385-7673), a place to pick up food for a gourmet picnic. For live music and local color, check out the historic **Town Tavern** (Water and Quincey streets), where the enormous historical back bar, pool tables, and the owner's great taste in music draw an interesting assortment of people. **Sirens** (823 Water Street, (360)379-0779), hidden way up three flights of stairs in the historic Bartlett Building, is a delightful place to enjoy a glass of wine, have a snack, and listen to music from the Bay View deck. Don't overlook the revitalization of uptown, especially **Aldrich's** (Lawrence and Tyler streets, (360)395-0500), an authentic 1890s general store come to life with an upscale twist; the **1004 Gallery** (1004 Lawrence Street, (360)385-7302), for excellent contemporary art; **Jack and Jill** (1044 Lawrence Street, (360)385-3166), for tasteful children's clothing displayed in a historical setting.

Washington State Ferries make daily trips to Whidbey Island; (206)464-6400 or (800)84-FERRY. The Puget Sound Express (431 Water Street, (360)385-5288) runs a daily ferry to Friday Harbor on San Juan Island.

RESTAURANTS

Belmont ★★ In a town where good seafood is almost "hohum," the Belmont is a special treasure. And in a town where sweeping water views are as common as seagulls, the Belmont stands out. The ideal place to be seated in this three-level restaurant is up the stairs to the back or out on the deck overlooking the bay. And the ideal dish to order is an exquisite fillet of Northwest salmon, broiled exactly. Taking further advantage of the availability of impeccably fresh seafood, chef Bill Severin now offers up an appetizer of sushi. Excellent lunch salads include a very large and distinctively Asian-influenced chicken salad. Ask about staying in one of the renovated

Victorian-era hotel rooms (two overlook the water). ▪ *Center of town, waterside; (360)385-3007; 925 Water St, Port Townsend; $$; full bar; AE, DC, MC, V; local checks only; lunch, dinner every day.*

Lanza's ★★ Lanza's offers no view, no fancy decor, and little out of the ordinary, menu-wise. But this long, narrow pizzeria is so popular because the food is top-notch. Wise customers scan the menu for the velvety polenta drizzled with a companionable sauce, or the sumptuous vegetarian lasagne. Whenever possible, organically grown scallops and vegetables are used. Try anything made with house-smoked salmon (say, the Northwest pizza—a traditional roasted garlic-heavy Neapolitan-style pie topped with not-so-traditional smoked salmon and fat prawns). Live music on Friday. ▪ *Uptown on the bluff; (360)385-6221; 1020 Lawrence, Port Townsend; $$; beer and wine; MC, V; checks OK; dinner Mon–Sat.*

Blackberries ★ A delightful little restaurant attached to the conference center dining hall in Fort Worden State Park, Blackberries features ingredients utilized by the Makah, S'Kallam, and other native Northwest tribes. Among the unusual offerings: a braid of salmon and halibut with a tangy salal berry sauce and a tasty ragout made from hormone-free, lower-fat beefalo (a cross between beef and buffalo). You'll find a definite emphasis on healthy food served in portions that won't leave you hungry. ▪ *Fort Worden State Park Conference Center, 1 mile north of downtown; (360)385-9950; 200 Battery Way, Building 210, Port Townsend; $$; no alcohol; MC, V; checks OK; dinner every day, May–September (Thurs–Sat only in winter), brunch Sun.*

Cafe Piccolo ★ Owner/chef Farnham Hogue, with the help of his wife, Nancy, presents consistently good, high-quality Italian food whose inspiration comes from all over Italy's boot. Expect dishes tweaked with a personal (and sometimes improbable) touch, evident in such fare as polenta with a spicy black bean salsa. There's always a selection of special individual-size pizzas in original combinations. Pastas are nicely prepared, with a judicious choice of ingredients. ▪ *On Hwy 20, about a mile outside of town; (360)385-1403; 9793 Hwy 20, Port Townsend; $$; beer and wine; MC, V; checks OK; dinner every day May–Sept (Wed–Sun Oct–Apr).* &

Fountain Cafe ★ Locals like to bring their out-of-town guests here, especially for lunch. And they'll line up several deep in the tiny storefront dining room to inspect the art on the walls while waiting for a table. This really is good cafe food—an Asian-style ginger chicken is pleasantly piquant, while a vegetarian pasta with artichokes, olives, and feta is a longtime favorite with the regulars. The wine list is short, but includes some good selections, and you should save room for the loganberry fool, a wondrous blend of custard, fruit, and whipped cream. Service is courteous, even with patrons queued up in front. ■ *At the Port Townsend fountain steps; (360) 385-1364; 920 Washington St, Port Townsend; $$; beer and wine; AE, MC, V; checks OK; lunch, dinner every day.*

Kho Laub Thai ★ This gracious restaurant with its muted cool greens is a welcomed balance to the tingling heat and vibrant flavors that unmistakably identify the food as Thai. One of the best of the aromatic curries is a gently steamed salmon fillet with cabbage and a slightly sweet but still spicy sauce. Delicious chicken wings stuffed with ground pork and shrimp look like fat crispy lollipops. The helpful, attentive staff carefully explains how to order a balanced selection of dishes. ■ *Off Water Street on Adams; (360) 385-5023; 225 Adams St, Port Townsend; $$; beer and wine; MC, V; local checks only; lunch, dinner every day from May–Oct (closed on Wed Oct–May).* ♿

The Public House ★ The Public House is a large space with soaring ceilings, brought into human scale by clever interior design. It's both comfortable (with antique light fixtures, wood floors, and dark green wainscoting, and a nonsmoking bar that's a marvel of the cabinetmaker's art) and casual (a great place for ribs or a burger with a side of sweet, crispy onion rings). Whenever possible, try the house favorite, cioppino, a wine-based fish stew made with fresh local seafood. Select a beer from the impressive list of drafts and watch the world go by through the big front windows. Live music at night. ■ *On the north side of Water Street; (360) 385-9708; 1038 Water St, Port Townsend; $; full bar; MC, V; local checks; lunch, dinner every day.* ♿

Salal Cafe ★ Breakfasts are justly famous here, with a couple of morning newspapers circulating and locals trading stories back in the solarium. The omelets are legendary—both in quality and variety (we like the Greek, with basil, spinach, and feta). Other morning starters, such as cheese blintzes, honey crêpes, or an occasional smoked salmon frittata, are equally satisfying. The light, cheerful cafe serves lunch with a smattering of basic Mexican plates, but breakfast is where the Salal Cafe really shines. ■ *Quincy and Water sts; (360) 385-6532; 634 Water St, Port Townsend; $; beer and wine; no credit cards; checks OK; breakfast, lunch Wed–Mon.* ♿

Silverwater Cafe ★ If you consider seafood one of life's great pleasures, the Silverwater Cafe shares your passion, providing simple preparations of whatever is in season—and if it is fresh frozen, the waitstaff will point that out. For those who love oysters, the Canterbury oysters harvested from nearby beds are remarkably sweet and briny. At lunch, the shrimp burger is tasty and the salmon salad quite refreshing. And on the meat side, the pepper steak comes highly recommended by the locals. The Silverwater is slated to move a couple of blocks to a new location on Taylor Street, next to the Rose Theater and beneath the historic Elks Club. ■ *On Quincy St, near the old ferry dock; (360) 385-6448; 237 Taylor St, Port Townsend; $$; beer and wine; MC, V; local checks only; lunch Mon–Sat, dinner every day.*

LODGINGS

The James House ★★★ The first bed and breakfast in the Northwest (1889) is still in great shape, though when a gale blows off the strait and hits the high bluff, you are glad to be in one of the three rooms with a fireplace or wood-burning stove. This fine B&B rests in the competent hands of Carol McGough, who is still improving it, continually freshening the 12 rooms and the delightful garden. Rooms in the front of the house have the best views across the water. Not all rooms have private baths, but the shared facilities are spacious and well equipped. The main floor offers two comfortable parlors, each with a fireplace and plenty of reading material. Breakfast is served either at the big dining room table or in the kitchen with its antique cookstove. ■ *Corner of Washington and Harrison; (360) 385-1238; 1238 Washington St, Port Townsend, WA 98368; $$; AE, MC, V; checks OK.*

Ann Starrett Mansion ★★ The most opulent Victorian in Port Townsend, this multi-gabled Queen Anne hybrid was built in 1885 by a local building contractor who just had to build himself a home with more of everything than his neighbors. He succeeded. The spiral stairway, octagonal tower, and "scandalous" ceiling fresco are visually stunning. All rooms are antique-furnished and have lovely decorative touches, though some may find the florid color scheme, appropriate to the rococo decor, a bit unsettling. The Drawing Room (with a tin claw-footed bathtub) opens to views of the Sound and Mount Baker, while the newer, romantic Gable Suite, which occupies the whole third floor, has a skylight (also with a knockout view) and spacious seating area. Ample breakfasts. The house is open for public tours from 1pm until 3pm, when unoccupied bedrooms are tied off for viewing (this creates somewhat of a "living museum" atmosphere). ■ *Corner of Clay and Adams; (360) 385-3205; 744 Clay St, Port Townsend, WA 98368; $$; AE, MC, V; checks OK.*

Hastings House/Old Consulate Inn ★★ This ornately turreted red Victorian on the hill is one of the most frequently photographed of Port Townsend's "Painted Ladies." It is also one of its most comfortable. A large collection of antique dolls is displayed in the entryway and new arrivals are often greeted by the aroma of freshly baked cookies to be nibbled later at afternoon tea. All of the immaculate rooms have closet-size private baths, but guests in the enormous Master Suite can soak in a claw-footed bathtub, later warming themselves in front of their own antique fireplace. The third-floor Tower Suite, with a sweeping bay view and swathed in lace, is the essence of a Victorian-style romantic valentine. There's a new hot tub for guest use. Owners Rob and Joanna Jackson serve a mammoth seven-course breakfast—over which Joanna will be more than delighted to wittily recount the inn's history. ■ *On the bluff, at Washington and Walker; (360)385-6753 or (800)300-6753; 313 Walker St, Port Townsend, WA 98368; $$$; AE, MC, V; checks OK.*

Quimper Inn ★★ The light from all the windows plays across richly hued walls, suffusing every corner of the house with a mellow glow. A first-floor bedroom resembles a library with a comfortable bed and a bath (with tub), and upstairs there is a lovely suite with period decor and a private bath. The room with bay windows and a brass bed has its own commodious bath with a 6-foot-long tub, a pedestal sink, and wicker furniture. Sue and Ron Ramage treat their inn and their guests with thoughtful care. Breakfasts are well executed. ■ *Corner of Franklin and Harrison; (360)385-1060 or (800)557-1060; 1306 Franklin St, Port Townsend, WA 98368; $$; MC, V; checks OK.*

Ravenscroft Inn ★★ A nonconformist among the surrounding Victorians, Ravenscroft Inn was built in 1987, with a design borrowed from historic South Carolina. The structure is large and impressive with a long front porch, redwood-stained clapboards, and graceful end chimney. A suite on the third floor sports dormer windows that overlook the town and harbor. Thick, warm carpeting throughout the house deadens sound and creates immediate coziness. The color scheme in every room is unique; each has wicker or antique reproduction furniture and custom upholstery (and one romantic room on the second floor has its own fireplace). Breakfast is the high point of a stay here, when guests enjoy a gourmet meal from the immense open-style kitchen, often with a piano accompaniment. ■ *On the bluff at Quincy and Clay; (360)385-2784; 533 Quincy St, Port Townsend, WA 98368; $$; AE, DC, MC, V; checks OK.*

 Fort Worden ★ Fort Worden was one of three artillery posts built at the turn of the century to guard the entrances of Puget Sound. The troops are long gone, and the massive gun mounts on the bluff have been stripped of their iron, but the beautifully situated fort now is a state park, a conference center, a youth hostel (especially for teenagers biking the Peninsula), the site of the splendid Centrum Arts Festival, and an unusual place to stay. Twenty-four former officers' quarters—nobly proportioned structures dating back to 1904—front the old parade ground. These houses have been made into spacious lodgings, each with a complete kitchen, at bargain rates. The most coveted of the one-bedroom lodgings is Bliss Vista, perched on the bluff, with a fireplace and plenty of romantic appeal. The three-story brick turret called Alexander's Castle, built in the 1890s, is lots of fun. Reservations should be made at least a year in advance. ■ *1 mile north of downtown; (360) 385-4730; Fort Worden State Park Conference Center, 200 Battery Way, Port Townsend, WA 98368; $$; no credit cards; checks OK.*

Lizzie's ★ Lizzie, the wife of a tugboat captain, put the deed of this model of Victorian excess in her own name; her name now also graces a line of bath lotions created by owners Patti and Bill Wickline. Breakfast, served around an old oak table in the cheerful kitchen, can turn into a friendly kaffeeklatsch; a soak in the tub in the black-and-white corner bathroom—especially if the sun is slanting in—is a Victorian treat. There are views from half of the eight bedrooms, and flowered decor. Lizzie's room comes with its own fireplace. Two parlors seem to have been plucked from the past; in one you'll even find a vintage stereoscope. ■ *Near the corner of Lincoln and Pierce in the Historic District; (360) 385-4168 or (800) 700-4168; 731 Pierce St, Port Townsend, WA 98368; $$; DC, MC, V; checks OK.*

Palace Hotel ★ The 1889 Romanesque Palace places visitors in the midst of Port Townsend's shopping and gawking district. The 15 rooms retain the building's ex-bordello atmosphere; Marie's (the venerable madame of the house until the mid-1930s) Room is decorated in original shades of burgundy and forest green. Warning: Long flights of stairs, though handsome reminders of another era, can be a challenge, and nightlife noises from a nearby tavern can make for a restless sleep. Still, it's worth the challenge. There's complimentary breakfast and off-street parking available. Cafe Ptarmigan is located off the front lobby. ■ *On the corner of Water and Tyler; (360) 385-0773 or (800) 962-0741; 1004 Water St, Port Townsend, WA 98368; $$; AE, MC, V; checks OK.*

Heritage House [*unrated*] Visitors to this hillcrest Victorian bed and breakfast will find a sprightly variety of refinished antiques matching guest rooms with names like Lilac and Morning Glory. Five of the seven rooms have private baths; the Peach Blossom has an oak-and-tin claw-footed bathtub that folds away when not in use. Relax in the evenings on the porch swing, in the mornings perhaps over a breakfast of decadent French toast. The views over the north Sound and the business district come close to rivaling those of Heritage's venerable neighbor, the James House. Children over eight years are permitted, but pets are not. At press time, new owners were making some cosmetic changes, as yet unfinished. ■ *Corner of Washington and Pierce; (360)385-6800 or (800)385-6867; 305 Pierce St, Port Townsend, WA 98368; $$; AE, MC, V; checks OK.* &

SEQUIM AND DUNGENESS VALLEY

Sequim (pronounced *skwim*) was once a carefully kept secret. The town sits smack in the middle of the "rain shadow" cast by the Olympic Mountains: the sun shines 306 days a year with only 16 inches of rainfall. Now Sequim's been discovered, especially by the retiree population, and is growing fast. Farms have become subdivisions and golf courses sprout in what used to be pastures. There is still lots to do and see nearby.

On Sequim Bay, near Blyn, the S'Kallam Indians operate the unique **Native Art Gallery** (E Sequim Bay Road). Across the highway, they have recently opened **Seven Cedars**, a truly mammoth gambling casino with valet parking and good food (270756 Hwy 101, 1-800-4LUCKY7). **Cedarbrook Herb Farm**, (open March through December 23, daily), Washington's oldest herb farm, has a vast range of plants, scented geraniums, fresh-cut herbs, and a pleasant gift shop; 1 mile toward the mountains off Highway 101 (1345 Sequim Avenue S, (360)683-7733). **Olympic Game Farm** breeds endangered species and raises a few animals for Hollywood roles. An hour-long guided walking tour is available mid-May to Labor Day, with a driving tour available year-round; 5 miles north of Sequim (1423 Ward Road, (360)683-4295).

Dungeness Spit, 6 miles northwest of Sequim, is a national wildlife refuge for birds (more than 275 species have been sighted) and one of the longest natural sand spits in the world; (360)457-8451. The driftwood displays are extraordinary, the winds are often good for kite flying, and a long walk down the 5½-mile narrow beach takes you to a remote lighthouse (check a tide table before planning your walk). Two small but notable wineries are in the vicinity: **Lost Mountain Winery** (3174 Lost Mountain Road, (360)683-5229) offers tastings mainly by arrangement or chance; **Neuharth Winery** (885 S Still Road, (360)683-9652) is open daily for tastings in summer (winter, Wednesday to Sunday).

Sequim and
Dungeness
Valley

Restaurants

RESTAURANTS

Anything Goes ★ "Anything goes," indeed. Word of the casual Italian, off-beat Thai, and soon-to-be French food—all at reasonable prices—is slowly spreading, with regulars finding the relaxed atmosphere and friendly service a particular treat. You might start with a soothing cup of chunky chicken soup soothed with coconut milk, followed by a contrasting curry of prawns, asparagus, and mushrooms. Or consider a calzone, those puffy, folded-over pizzas, stuffed with unusual ingredients like sea scallops or tender strips of steak. A delicate Key lime pie makes a cooling finish to a spicy curry. ■ *In Creamery Square, east of the center of town on Hwy 101; (360) 683-1061; 235 E Washington, Sequim; $; beer and wine; MC, V; checks OK; lunch, dinner, Mon–Sat.*

Eclipse ★ Eclipse is now in its second incarnation at a new location. Tom Wells, a former physicist and now co-owner, host, and sole waiter, and his wife, Cambodian-born Lay Yin, start cooking and serving at 8am and close by 3pm—and many or all of the dishes may disappear even before noon. (In-the-know locals phone ahead and have Yin set aside their order.) Diners enter through the back door of this tract home, sit at a minuscule counter or at one of the two tables, and consider themselves blessed to eat whatever is available from the predominantly Southeast Asian menu: chicken congee, a thick and savory rice soup (and breakfast favorite), and that universal snack, the spring roll—here delicate and delicious. Good-value group dinners, with 20 or more dishes, can be arranged. ■ *3 blocks north of Washington (Hwy 101), corner of 3rd and W Alder; (360) 683-2760; 139 W Alder, Sequim; $; no bar; no credit cards; checks OK; breakfast and lunch Sat–Tues.* ఈ

Oak Table Cafe ★ Good, old-fashioned meals of Nebraska-raised beef and mashed potatoes or a serving of fresh-caught fish are the Friday and Saturday night dinner specialties of this cafe owned by one of the Nagler family (who also own the Chestnut Cottage and First Street Haven in Port Angeles). Breakfast is a feast of huge omelets, fruit crêpes, or the legendary puffy apple pancakes. Service is friendly and efficient—the coffee keeps coming—and the cream is the real thing. It's noisy and boisterous and chatty. ■ *1 block south of Hwy 101 at 3rd and Bell; (360) 683-2179; 292 W Bell St, Sequim; $$; no alcohol; no credit cards; checks OK; breakfast every day, lunch Mon–Sat, early dinner Fri–Sat.*

The Buckhorn Grill It may be a motel restaurant, but the Buckhorn Grill—which shares 17 wooded acres with the Best Western Sequim Bay Lodge—brings in hungry eaters from nearby Sequim and Port Angeles. The reason is simple: enjoyable food, well-presented, served quickly and politely. The menu may not run to fancy food, but you can count on such dishes as braised lamb shank. Vegetables and salads are handled with finesse; the wine list is comprehensive. The adjacent **Sequim Bay Lodge** is an attractive 54-unit resort with a putting course and outdoor heated pool, hot tub, and fireplace suites;

(800)622-0691, (360)683-0691. ▪ *Hwy 101 east of Sequim;*
(360)683-9010; 268522 Hwy 101, Sequim; $$; full bar; MC,
V; checks OK; breakfast, lunch, dinner Thurs–Tues. ⚹

Hiway 101 Diner Welcome to the Hiway 101 Diner, a neon-lit nostalgic kind of place where the back end of a '56 T-bird serves as a jukebox playing old "Hit Parade" songs. You can sit in a booth with sweet June Allyson smiling down on you, listen to "Two to Tango," and wrap your fist around a juicy "Awful Awful Burger." Expect the usual diner food at breakfast, but it's the burger-and-pizza offerings that have the edge here. ▪ *On Hwy 101; (360)683-3388; 392 W Washington, Sequim; $; no alcohol; MC, V; checks OK; breakfast, lunch, dinner every day.*

Jean's Mini Mart and Deli An old corner minimart is what you see from the road, but what you can't see is the cozy little cafe tucked in the back where Jean started baking a little here and making soup there for the odd customer. The word got around, and now her cooking is in demand full-time during the weekdays. A piece of carrot cake or something called "lemon lush" is the best choice for dessert. Good muffins, cinnamon rolls, and honey buns are offered as early as 5am. ▪ *At Hwy 101 and Carlsborg Rd; (360)683-6727; 20 Carlsborg Rd, Sequim; $; beer and wine; no credit cards; checks OK; breakfast, lunch Mon–Fri.*

▼

LODGINGS

Greywolf Inn ★ In a peaceful gray frame home on the east side of Sequim, transplanted Southerners Bill and Peggy Melang built this B&B offering six tasteful guest rooms. Their hospitality is always evident (especially at the hearty breakfast often featuring North Carolina country ham). The wooded hillside has a trail for walkers and bird-watchers, and a small herd of elk, wandering through, has been known to startle breakfasting guests. A small courtyard with an enclosed hot tub is right next door, along with various exercise machines for the more ambitious. ▪ *One mile east of Sequim, on Keeler Rd; (360)683-5889; 395 Keeler Rd, Sequim, WA 98382; $$; AE, MC, V; checks OK.*

▲

Groveland Cottage ★ At the turn of the century this was a family home in Dungeness, a wide spot in the road, just a half mile away from the beach. Now, the place has the comfortable salty-air feel of an old beach house where you might have spent a summer holiday with a favorite aunt, with four cheerful rooms over a country-style store that sells a bit of everything. A one-room cottage out back may not be as special, but many like having their own cooking space. The place fills up in the summer with guests addicted to owner Simone Nichols's little luxuries—such as receiving the newspaper and coffee in your room before sitting down to her four-course breakfast. ▪ *Follow* *signs from Sequim toward Three Crabs; (360) 683-3565; 4861 Sequim Dungeness Way, Dungeness, WA 98382; $$; AE, MC, V; checks OK.*

Juan de Fuca Cottages ★ Any of these five comfortable cabins—either overlooking Dungeness Spit or with a view of the Olympics—is a special hideout, whether for a winter weekend or a longer summertime sojourn. (A two-bedroom suite has both views and a welcoming fireplace.) All are equipped with a Jacuzzi, kitchen utensils, games, and reading material, as well as cable TV, VCR, and a 250-film library from which to choose. Outside is the spit, begging for beach walks and clam digging. Two-night minimum stay July and August (and weekends year-round). ■ *7 miles north of Sequim; (360) 683-4433; 182 Marine Dr, Sequim, WA 98382; $$; MC, V; checks OK.*

PORT ANGELES

The north shore of the Olympic Peninsula was home to several thriving native American tribes long before outside explorers laid claim to the area. Today this blue-collar mill town is known as Port Angeles, "where the Olympics greet the sea." **Port Angeles Harbor**, protected against wind and waves by Ediz Hook sand spit, is the largest natural deepwater harbor north of San Francisco. It is also a jumping-off point to **Victoria**, 17 miles across the straits on Canada's Vancouver Island via the ferry *Coho*, operated by Black Ball Transportation, (360) 457-4491; or the much quicker *Victoria Express*, a foot-passenger ferry that runs two or three times daily during summer and early fall; (800) 633-1589, (360) 452-8088.

Port Angeles is also the north (and most popular) end of the **Olympic National Forest**. The park, as big as Rhode Island with a buffer zone of national forest surrounding it, contains the largest remaining herd of the huge Roosevelt elk, which occasionally create "elk jams" along Highway 101. Follow the signs to the visitors center; (360) 452-0330. Then drive 17 miles along winding precipices to mile-high **Hurricane Ridge** and breathtaking views that mountains with twice the altitude seldom offer. Restrooms and snack facilities are available. There are many hiking trails; (360) 452-0330. In winter there is good cross-country skiing, a Poma-lift downhill skiing and tubing area (weekends only), and snowshoe rental and guided snowshoe nature walks through March. Check current road conditions by calling a 24-hour recorded message, (360) 452-9235, before you set out. For a different way to travel, Al and Sara Courtney lead guided llama tours into the park; (360) 452-4475. Olympic Raft and Guide Service offers easy Class I and Class II floats on the Elwha, Hoh, and Queets rivers; (360) 452-1442.

Downtown, at the **Arthur D. Feiro Marine Laboratory** on the city pier, 80 species from nearby waters—including octopi, wolf eels, sculpins, and sea slugs—have been collected, and a touch tank keeps children occupied. An expanded **Port Book and News** at a new location (104 E First, (360)452-6367) sells a wide selection of magazines and the daily *New York Times* and *Wall Street Journal*. **Mombasa Coffee Company** (113 W First, (360)452-3238) serves excellent fresh-roasted coffee. **Bonny's Bakery** (502 E First, (360)457-3585), housed in a lovely old church, is a good place to stock up for picnic and ferry-ride food, especially cinnamon rolls and freshly made sandwiches. Browse **Swain's General Store** (602 E First, (360)452-2357), which sells virtually everything.

RESTAURANTS

C'est Si Bon ★★ Yes, it *is* good—especially if you're yearning for classic pre-nouvelle French cooking with its splendid sauces. Dine leisurely in an attractive setting (the best tables, in window bays, overlook the rose garden). If the food is slow in coming, host Juhasz Norbert will regale waiting guests with tales of his musical experiences in France and Hollywood. A big bowl of onion soup, bubbling under a brown crust of cheese, can serve as a meal in itself for those easily sated, particularly when followed by a refreshing salad. The classic steak au poivre is fabulous, as are the fresh halibut and salmon served in season. The chocolate mousse is wickedly rich, and the wine list has good choices for those who aren't. Plans are on the drawing board for an adjacent 60-room chateau-type hotel. ■ *4 miles east of Port Angeles on Hwy 101 E; (360)452-8888; 2300 Hwy 101 E, Port Angeles; $$$; full bar; AE, MC, V; local checks only; dinner Tues–Sun.*

Chestnut Cottage ★ Owners Diane Nagler and Ken Nemirow (who also run First Street Haven) are very particular when it comes to quality food and service. It definitely shows. Their Chestnut Cottage is *the* place to go for an exceptional breakfast in delightful country Victorian–style surroundings. A custardy apple and walnut French toast is only one of several morning treats; others include: Belgian waffles, pancakes, quiches, frittatas, or lemon blintzes drizzled with raspberry purée. On the simpler side, a bowl of porridge and berries will surely satisfy. Or go exotic with a breakfast pizza (ham and eggs on pita). ■ *On Hwy 101, east of the center of town; (360)452-8344; 929 E Front St, Port Angeles; $$; beer and wine; MC, V; checks OK.; breakfast and lunch every day.* ﺏ

Chihuahua ★ Typical of small towns across the country, Port Angeles has its share of Mexican restaurants. A notch or two above most is the Chihuahua—a small, busy spot that specializes in the foods of northern Mexico. Although most of the dishes cater to Tex-Mex tastes, owners Raphael and Juan Hernandez offer other more regional dishes such as chili Colorado—a comforting pork stew, thick with chiles, herbs, and spices; or machaca con huevos—shredded beef scrambled with eggs, onions, and tomatoes. Occasionally, wonderful soups are bubbling away in the kitchen. On Sunday, ask for the menudo, a hearty soup of tender tripe in a well-flavored broth (especially recommended for hangovers). ■ *1 block south of the old Clallam County Courthouse, between 4th and 5th; (360)452-8174; 408 South Lincoln, Port Angeles; $; beer and wine; MC, V; checks OK; lunch, dinner every day.*

First Street Haven ★ It's just a skinny slot of a restaurant, easily missed among the storefronts if you're not paying attention. The cinnamon rolls are what draw the locals—in addition to the socializing on Saturday or Sunday morning. Fresh and unusual salads with homemade dressings, hearty sandwiches, pastas, and quiche dominate the menu, and the chili is great on a cold winter day. Expertly made espresso and their own coffee blend are fine jump-starters, especially with a fresh blueberry muffin or sour cream coffee cake. Prices are reasonable, and service is friendly and attentive. ■ *1st and Laurel, next to the Toggery; (360)457-0352; 107 E 1st St, Port Angeles; $; no alcohol; no credit cards; checks OK; breakfast, lunch Mon–Sat, brunch Sunday.*

Swan ★ Pasta and oysters. Oysters and pasta. There are other things on the menu, but these, in one combination or another, are the way to go. Oyster Dorado combines a medley of sautéed oysters, mushrooms, and eggplant on a bed of pepper linguine. There are lots of oyster appetizers, too; in one of the best, the oysters are gently steamed on the half shell, infused with ginger and garlic. There is sometimes a tendency to combine too many conflicting ingredients: an excellent clam chowder overpowered by a heavy-handed shot of sherry or the walnut and Gorgonzola ravioli with two taste-confusing sauces. Seasonal dessert specialties end the meal. In the spring the rhubarb or raspberry fools are standouts. Efficient service goes with the simple atmosphere. ■ *Half block from the ferry dock in Harbor Town Mall; (360)452-2965; 222 N Lincoln St, Port Angeles; $$; beer and wine; AE, MC, V; local checks only; lunch, dinner every day.*

LODGINGS

Domaine Madeleine ★★★ Set on a bluff overlooking the Strait of Juan de Fuca among tall firs, lawns, and gardens, this modern home is an ideal spot to get away and let someone pamper you. Of the four sleeping areas, the spacious upstairs Ming Suite with its own large balcony and antique Oriental furnishings is our favorite. There is a nicely appointed cottage for those desiring even more privacy. Steer clear of the smallest room. The living quarters are dominated by a mighty basalt fireplace and views of distant Victoria, the Canadian coastal range, and Mount Baker. Soft sofas, antique and Oriental furnishings, and a harpsichord fill the room. Breakfast is a thorough indulgence, always starting with baskets of John's freshly baked tiny French rolls, and Washington cheeses and fresh fruit served with coffee, tea, or hot chocolate. The main course, served on porcelain, may be a rich dish of poached egg and salmon on a bed of spinach, cloaked with a cheese sauce, and garnished with mushrooms and artichoke hearts. ■ *North of Hwy 101 between Sequim and Port Angeles (call for directions); (360)457-4174; 146 Wildflower Lane, Port Angeles, WA 98362; $$$; AE, MC, V; checks OK.*

Tudor Inn ★★ One of the best-looking buildings in town, a completely restored Tudor-style bed and breakfast, is located 12 blocks from the ferry terminal in a quiet residential neighborhood. Owners Jane Glass and her daughter, Katy, are friendly hosts, well-versed in Port Angeles political and cultural life. Their house boasts a library, fireplace, crisp linens, and antique touches here and there. The five rooms have been spruced up, and the best one has a balcony with wonderful views, a fireplace, and a claw-footed bathtub, as well as a shower. Jane serves a traditional full breakfast with none of the forced conviviality around the dining table that sometimes afflicts other B&Bs. Your hosts will gladly provide transportation to and from the ferry dock, and arrange for fishing charters, horseback rides, or winter ski packages. ■ *11th and Oak; (360)452-3138; 1108 S Oak St, Port Angeles, WA 98362; $$; AE, MC, V; checks OK.*

Olympic Lodge ★ This Best Western hotel just seems to offer the right combination of comfort and rustic atmosphere that fits in Port Angeles—and if you don't have the time to hike the backcountry, just walk the halls to see what you are missing. Sequim photographer Ross Hamilton has a large collection of work on permanent display. The 106 rooms are spacious and well-appointed with cherry furniture; many have views of the mountains. There is a large heated swimming pool as well as a Jacuzzi spa. ■ *On Hwy 101, east side of Port Angeles; (360)452-2993 or (800)600-2993; 140 Del Guzzi Dr, Port Angeles, WA 98362; $$–$$$; AE, DC, MC, V; no checks.* &

Pond Motel Six spare but exceptionally clean rooms overlook an acre-big pond where bufflehead ducks and mallards float by and two pet rainbow trout occasionally stir the serene water. There are also two bigger cabins equipped with vintage '40s kitchenettes and two single rooms (dark, but sort of cozy) next to the office. Highway 101 runs right by, but Young Chung, the friendly owner of this unassuming arrangement, has maintained quiet little meadows and peaceful gardens here and there so it hardly seems to matter. ■ *Half-mile west of city limits; (360)452-8422; 1425 Hwy 101 W, Port Angeles, WA 98362; $; MC, V; checks OK.*

LAKE CRESCENT

The south shore of 600-foot-deep Lake Crescent skirts Highway 101, with numerous scenic pullouts. The Fairholm store and boat launch are on the far west end of the lake with East Beach 10 miles away on the other. Crescent Lake is home to rainbow trout and steelhead, to Beardslee and the famous Crescenti trout, which lurk in its depths. Rental boats are available. In summer, take an interpretive boat tour of Lake Crescent aboard the paddle wheeler MV *Storm King,* named after the original 1916 ferry. Tickets and reservations are available from Shadow Mountain General Store, one mile east of the park on Highway 101; (360)452-4520. An easy one-mile hike takes you to the 90-foot Marymere Falls.

LODGINGS

Lake Crescent Lodge ★ Built 80 years ago, the well-maintained Lake Crescent Lodge has also been well-worn since the days when it was known as Singer's Tavern. The historic main building has a grand verandah overlooking the deep, crystal blue waters of Lake Crescent, a so-so restaurant, and a very comfortable bar. The upstairs rooms are noisy and rustic—a euphemism that means, among other things, that the bathroom is down the hall. The motel rooms are the best for the money, but the cabins, with their porches and fireplaces, can be fun (if you bear in mind that they were built in 1937, back when President Franklin Roosevelt came to visit Olympic Park). The service is just fine—mainly enthusiastic college kids having a nice summer. ■ *20 miles west of Port Angeles on Hwy 101; (360)928-3211; 416 Lake Crescent Rd, Port Angeles, WA 98362; $$; AE, DC, MC, V; checks OK; (closed mid-Nov–Apr).*

Log Cabin Resort Located on the "sunny side" of Lake Crescent, this venerable resort has served visitors for over a century, although none of the present buildings are over 70 years old, and some a great deal younger. Whatever the age, the secluded grounds are well-maintained, as are the wide variety of shoreside accommodations. No frills, but very livable. The lakeside chalets sleep six when using the upstairs loft, and although there is a refrigerator, cooking must be done outside on a barbecue. Some cabins have full kitchenettes. It's pleasant to sit out on the porch in your rocker and watch the fish jump and the sun drop behind the mountain peaks. For campers, the one-room log cabins with electricity but no indoor plumbing work fine. ■ *3 miles north of Hwy 101 on East Beach Rd; (360) 928-3325; 3183 East Beach Rd, Port Angeles, WA 98363; $$; DC, MC, V; checks OK; closed Oct–May.*

SOL DUC HOT SPRINGS

Whether you arrive by car after an impressive 12-mile drive through old-growth forests, or on foot after days of hiking mountain ridges, these hot springs are the ideal trail's end. The Quileute Indians called the area "Sol Duc"—a land of "sparkling water." In the early 1900s, Sol Duc became a mecca for travelers seeking relief from their aches and pains. For about $6, you can have a hot soak, followed by a swim in a cold pool. You can also opt for a lengthy massage. Open daily mid-May to end of September; weekends only, October to April; (360) 327-3583. The hike to nearby Sol Duc Falls passes through one of the loveliest stands of old-growth forest anywhere.

LODGINGS

Sol Duc Hot Springs Resort Surrounded by forest, 32 small cedar-roofed sleeping cabins are clustered in the grassy meadow. The favorites are those with their porches facing the river. Up to four adults and two kids can share a cabin (it'll be a pretty cozy fit). The duplex units have kitchens, and in keeping with the natural serenity, there are no TVs anywhere (and there's a no smoking policy everywhere). Camping and RV sites available. The Springs Restaurant is open for breakfast and dinner—a snack deli is open midday. Hot springs and pool use is included in the cabin rental fee. ■ *12 miles south off Hwy 101, west of Lake Crescent; (360) 327-3583; PO Box 2169, Port Angeles, WA 98362; $$; AE, MC, V; checks OK.*

Sekiu

Lodgings

SEKIU

Twenty-one miles south on Hoko-Ozette Road from Sekiu is **Lake Ozette**, the largest natural body of fresh water in the state. At the north end of the lake there are campgrounds and trails leading to several beaches where you can see the eerie eroded coastal cliffs looming out of the water. It was near here that tidal erosion exposed a 500-year-old village, with homes perfectly preserved. The archaeological dig was closed in 1981 after 11 years of excavation; artifacts are on display at the Makah Museum in Neah Bay.

LODGINGS

Van Riper's Resort The only waterfront hotel in Sekiu, or anywhere in the area, Van Riper's is a comfortable family-operated place. The smaller, street-side rooms are nothing special, but those facing Clallam Bay can look out at fishing boats moored at the docks or to the strait and the rugged coastline of

Vancouver Island beyond. Two of these units are large apartments with complete kitchens—suitable for a family or group of friends. A small house up the hill is also available. Owners Chris and Val Mohr also operate the small store on the premises with bait and tackle, charter service, and launch ramp.
- *Corner of Front and Rice on the main street; (360) 963-2334; PO Box 246, Sekiu, WA 98381; $; MC, V; checks OK.*

NEAH BAY

This is literally the end of the road: Highway 112 ends at this small waterside town on the northern edge of the **Makah Indian Reservation**. Ten miles of unimproved road, known as the End of the World Loop, continues to Cape Flattery. The Makah allow public access across their ancestral lands—a half-mile walk on what is usually a muddy trail—to Land's End, the far northwestern corner of Washington's seacoast. From these high-cliffed headlands, cow-calf pairs of gray whales can often be seen migrating north in April and May. Salmon-fishing charters are available at Big Salmon Resort, (360) 645-2374; Farwest Resort, (360) 645-2270 or 2240; and Raven Charters, (360) 645-2121. Sandy **Hobuck Beach**, near **Cape Flattery Resort**, is open for picnics (no fires), surfing, and horseback riding, and farther on, the Tsoo-Yas (Sooes) Beach is accessible (if you pay the landowners a parking fee). Call the parks department for coastal access information; (360) 452-4501.

The Makah Nation has opened **Cape Flattery Resort** in the former air base barracks. It's nothing fancy, but rooms are clean and reasonably priced (in winter, a family pays a flat fee of $35). A great base for bird-watchers and sea kayakers; (360) 645-2251.

FORKS

From this little town on the west end of the Olympic Peninsula, you can explore the wild coastal beaches, hook a steelhead, or go mountain biking, camping, or hiking. Ask at **Olympic Sporting Goods**, next to the liquor store, for information on fishing guides, licenses, or where best to land the Big One; (360) 374-6330.

The **Hoh Rain Forest**, 30 miles south of Forks, is the wettest location in the contiguous United States, with an average yearly rainfall of 133.58 inches. This steady moisture nurtures the dense vegetation—more than 3,000 species of plant life—including the **Rain Forest Monarch**, a giant Sitka spruce over 500 years old towering close to 300 feet over the moss- and fern-carpeted forest floor. Take the spur road off Highway 101, 13.2 miles south of Forks to the Visitors

Center; (360)374-6925. For those with more time, one- to three-day round-trip hikes up Mount Olympus provide some of the best hiking experiences in the world. The longer trip to Glacier Meadows is best mid-July through October.

RESTAURANTS

Smoke House Restaurant Stop at this big blue building north of Forks for a sampling of what the food in this part of the state is all about. Owner Steve Torgesen alder-smokes all his salmon here, and this moist, lightly smoked fish is the star ingredient on the restaurant's menu. Try it as an entree, in sandwiches or salads, or tossed with pasta. Liver, with plenty of onions, is another staple. The waitresses know almost everyone, go out of their way to make strangers welcome, and dispense lots of travel advice. ▪ *North of town at the junction of Hwy 101 and La Push–Quillayute Rd; (360)374-6258; 193161 Hwy 101, Forks; $; full bar; MC, V; checks OK; lunch, dinner every day.*

LODGINGS

Eagle Point Inn ★★ Cradled on 5 acres in a bend of the Sol Duc River, this spacious lodge built of logs was especially designed by Chris and Dan Christensen to provide a perfect combination of comfort and style. The two downstairs bedrooms, each with queen-size beds covered with thick down comforters, have commodious bathrooms. The open two-story common living quarters house Chris's collection of kerosene lamps and other interesting antiques, leaving enough room to spread out, perhaps to relax in front of the fireplace made of rocks from the Sol Duc River. Even if you need to get up before dawn to fish, a hearty breakfast will be ready when you are (and ever-attentive Chris also fixes picnic lunches on request). A covered outdoor kitchen down near the river is ideal for barbecuing your own meal at night. ▪ *Between Forks and Sappho on Hwy 101; go east on Stormin' Norman Rd at milepost 202; (360)327-3236; 384 Stormin' Norman Rd, Beaver; PO Box 546, Beaver, WA 98305; $$; no credit cards; checks OK.*

Miller Tree Inn ★ Though set back from the road in a cluster of large trees encircled by pastures and wooded hills, Miller Tree Inn is just a few blocks east of Highway 101. One of the original homesteads in Forks is run by Ted and Prue Miller, a retired logger and his wife from Yorkshire, England. The atmosphere is relaxed; fresh lemonade is served on the lawn in summer, and the kitchen is not off-limits if you just ask. Though very comfortably furnished, some of the bedrooms may prove a bit small. Fisherfolk will appreciate the pre-dawn breakfasts, the Millers' knowledge of local river conditions, the room set aside to clean and freeze your catch, and the hot tub to relax in after a day on the river. Kids and well-mannered pets are welcome. ■ *6th St and E Division, next to City Hall; (360)374-6806; 654 E Division St, Forks; PO Box 953, Forks, WA 98331; $; MC, V; checks OK.*

River Inn A secluded private chalet right on the banks of the Bogachiel River—one of the finest steelhead-fishing rivers on the peninsula—now serves as a guest house. Playful otters can often be seen in the river, and browsing deer are a common sight on land. The bedroom on the upper-floor loft has its own entrance, large deck, and private bath. Owner Joanne Klontz, who lives next door with her husband, Les, fixes country-style breakfasts. There is a spacious outdoor hot tub. Best deal is to rent the whole house and come with friends or family. ■ *2½ miles west of downtown Forks; (360)374-6526; 2596 Bogachiel Way, Forks, WA 98331; $; no credit cards; checks OK.*

LA PUSH AND OCEAN BEACHES

The Dickey, Quillayute, Calawah, and Sol Duc rivers all merge and enter the ocean near La Push. To the north and south extend miles of wilderness coastline—the last such stretch remaining in the United States outside of Alaska. It is home to the Quileutes. Today, the small community still revolves around its fishing heritage, although plans are afoot to bring in a gambling casino. The lure of wild ocean beaches, with their jagged offshore rocks and teeming tide pools, bring those seeking adventurous solitude. The only nearby lodging is the **Ocean Park Resort** in La Push, (360)374-5267, which is getting a bit too worn to recommend.

Several miles to the north, Mora Road leads to Rialto Beach and a three-day wilderness beach hike to **Cape Alava** off Ozette Lake. A shorter but more strenuous hike leads from Third Beach, south of La Push, 16 miles to the Hoh River (an extraordinarily dramatic stretch). Warning: All ocean beaches can be extremely dangerous due to fluctuating tides and unfordable creeks during periods of heavy rain. Be sure to stop in at the ranger station in nearby Mora to get a use permit and tide tables; (360)374-5460.

Along Highway 101, just south, is the wide stretch named **Ruby Beach** for the tiny garnet crystals that compose much of the sand, ideal for walking. A mile farther is the viewpoint for **Destruction Island**, a wildlife sanctuary topped by a lighthouse. Nearby, a trail leads to the world's largest Western red cedar. There are several more beaches to explore as you continue south—particularly at **Kalaloch**, which has a campground and fine clamming beach.

KALALOCH

LODGINGS

Kalaloch Lodge Ask any of the longtime regulars why they keep returning year after year and they'll tell you it's because Kalaloch offers comfort and camaraderie in one of the most isolated beachside resorts in Washington. A wide range of accommodations includes rooms in the lodge that are surprisingly quiet (four have ocean views). Seacrest, a modern two-story lodging set amid wind-shaped trees, has some rooms with ocean-view decks and four two-bedroom suites with wood-burning fireplaces (these are in great demand, especially during the holidays). Equally sought after are the newer log cabins with their small kitchen area (no utensils) and Franklin stove complete with a stack of wood by the door. Couples favor the duplex cabins on the edge of the bluff. The older cabins should be a last choice. No phones or TVs except in the bar or stuck away in the upstairs library (where guests prefer the piano or quiet reading in front of the large fireplace). The restaurant staff is friendly and competent, but don't expect anything more than standard fare. Pets allowed in cabins only.
■ *Hwy 101, 34 miles south of Forks; (360) 962-2271; 157151 Hwy 101, Forks, WA 98331; $$; AE, MC, V; checks OK.*

LAKE QUINAULT

Lake Quinault, at the inland apex of the Quinault Indian Reservation, is usually the first or the last stop on Highway 101's scenic loop around the Olympic Peninsula's National Park and Forests. The glacier-carved lake is surrounded by cathedral-like fir forests, the fishing is memorable, and there are several easy trails, including one to **Campbell Grove** with its enormous old-growth trees. The ranger station will provide information on other more strenuous hikes up the North Fork of the Quinault River or to **Enchanted Valley**, a glorious several-day round-trip journey. A large 1930s log chalet at the end of the trail can accommodate 50 to 60 hikers overnight.

LODGINGS

Lake Quinault Lodge ★ A massive cedar-shingled structure, this grand old lodge was built in 1926 in a gentle arc around the sweeping lawns that descend to the lake. The rustic public rooms are done up like Grandma's sun porch in wicker and antiques with a massive stone fireplace in the heart of the lobby; the dining room overlooks the lawns, and the bar is lively at night. Rooms in the main building are small but perfectly nice; half have lake views. Though the adjoining wing has balconies and plasticky fireplaces in each unit, the decor leaves quite a bit to be desired. The choice lodgings are the 36 newer lakeside rooms a short walk from the lodge. Amenities consist of a sauna, an indoor heated pool, a Jacuzzi, a game room, canoes and rowboats, and well-maintained trails for hiking or running. Summer reservations take about two months' advance notice. The dining room puts up a classy front, but the food is uninspired. On occasion there are conventioneers around, drawn by the spalike features of the resort, but somehow the old place still exudes the quiet elegance of its past. ■ *South Shore Rd; (360) 288-2571 or (800) 562-6672 (from Wash. only); PO Box 7, Quinault, WA 98575; $$–$$$; AE, MC, V; checks OK.*

MOCLIPS

LODGINGS

Ocean Crest Resort ★ Nestled in a magnificent stand of spruce on a bluff high above one of the nicest stretches of beach on the Olympic Peninsula, the Ocean Crest has always offered rooms with memorable views. Now there's a wing featuring even more spectacular views and modern units done up in cedar paneling with fireplaces and European-style showers. A recreation center is just across the road, with a swimming pool, sauna, Jacuzzi, and weight room, and there's access to the beach along a winding walkway through a lovely wooded ravine. An annex a quarter mile down the road offers two apartments, each with complete kitchen, porch, and two bedrooms. Unfortunately, maids are hard-pressed to trek the extra distance and may need to be requested. In fact, attention to detail and housekeeping at the resort have slipped all around since our last visit.

There are few views on the Northwest coast that can rival the panorama from the dining room at the Ocean Crest, but the furnishings are old and the food (with the exception of the excellent breakfasts) has suffered from inconsistency of late. Upstairs is a cozy bar, furnished with Northwest Coast Indian artifacts. ■ *18 miles north of Ocean Shores; (360) 276-4465; Hwy 109, Moclips; PO Box 7, Moclips, WA 98562; $$$; AE, MC, V; checks OK.*

PACIFIC BEACH

LODGINGS

Sandpiper ★★ Here's the place to vacation with four other couples, or to bring the kids, the grandparents, and the family dog: miles of beach, a fleet of kites, and volleyball players. The spotless resort consists of two four-story complexes containing large, fully equipped suites—usually a sitting room with a dining area and a fireplace, a compact kitchen, a small porch, and a bedroom and bath. There are splendid views of the beach (and a childrens' play area) from every deck. Penthouse units have an extra bedroom and cathedral ceilings. The rooms in the older complex are a tad larger than the others. There are also cottages and one-room studios. This resort knows enough not to try to compete with the draws of the Pacific: there's no pool, no TV, no restaurant, no in-room telephones, no video machines—but the large gift shop does sell board games, kites, and sand buckets, plus condiments and sportsware. Prices are reasonable and the staff is very hospitable. Minimum stays are imposed on weekends and summers, and reservations are best made months in advance. Housekeeping drops by every day to see if you need anything (but you'll need to pay extra for logs for the fireplace); otherwise you're on your own...just like home. ■ *Hwy 109, 1½ miles south of Pacific Beach; (360)276-4580; 4159 Hwy 109, Pacific Beach; PO Box A, Pacific Beach, WA 98571; $$; MC, V; checks OK.*

OCEAN SHORES

Ocean Shores is finally outgrowing its schlocky past. The push for big-time gambling has waned and the convention center is busy year-round with trade shows, collectors fairs, and art exhibits. There's an annual jazz festival, a photography show with a statewide following, and sand castle and kite-flying competitions. McDonald's put up its golden arches in 1994 and building is booming.

To get away from it all, and avoid downtown altogether, reserve one of the private beach houses that owners occasionally rent. Reservations need to be made weeks in advance; (360)289-2430 or (800)562-8612 in Washington only. The same numbers can also take motel reservations.

RESTAURANTS

Alec's by the Sea ★ Ocean Shores has never been a restaurant town, but two new arrivals merit mentions. Alec's by the Sea does a lot of things well, including grilled razor clams, chicken fettuccine, and steaks. The delicious Philadelphia Prime Sandwich features sliced prime rib, grilled with onions and juicy bell peppers, topped with Swiss cheese, and served on a toasted French roll. A large menu, generous portions, efficient waitstaff, and crayons for the kids add up to a high-quality, friendly family restaurant. ■ *Point Brown Rd, left onto Chance a la Mer Blvd; (360)289-4026; 131 E Chance a la Mer Blvd NE, Ocean Shores; $$; full bar; DC, MC, V; local checks only; lunch, dinner every day.*

Galway Bay Restaurant & Pub Guinness on tap (which everyone knows is good for you) and authentic Irish stew, with lamb, potatoes, carrots, and succulent sautéed onions, plus soda bread and real butter. Need we say more? This is surely

the best way to warm up after a day of beachcombing. ■ *In
town on Ocean Shores Blvd, ½ block from Shilo; (360)289-
2300; 676 Ocean Shores Blvd NW, Ocean Shores; $$; full bar;
AE, DC, MC, V; checks OK; lunch, dinner every day.* &

LODGINGS

The Best Western Lighthouse Suites Inn ★★ This handsome,
hospitable new hotel is the best on the beach—at least until the
reviews are in on the big, new Shilo. Each tastefully decorated,
spacious room features a fireplace, wet bar, microwave,
refrigerator, and coffeepot, plus cable TV and VCR. Sixty of
the 76 rooms have a full ocean view. There's an indoor pool
and spa and a cozy library. No restaurant, but a continental
breakfast is free. ■ *At the north city limits; (360)289-2311
or (800)757-SURF; 491 Damon Rd NW, Ocean Shores;
PO Box 879, Ocean Shores, WA 98569; $$$; AE, DC, MC,
V; checks OK.* &

The Grey Gull ★ This condominium-resort looks like a ski
lodge (a rather odd style here on the beach), with jagged angles, handsome cladding, and a front door to strain the might-
iest triceps. There are 36 condominium units, facing the ocean
at a broad stretch of the beach (although not all have views;
prices are calibrated accordingly), each outfitted with a balcony, fireplace, kitchen, TV, VCR, and attractive furnishings.
The resort has a pool, a sauna, and a spa. You are right on the
beach, the main plus, and the lodge has been built with an eye
for good Northwest architecture. Prices for the suites get fairly
steep, but there are smaller rooms and you can save money by
doing your own cooking in the full kitchen. ■ *In town on
Ocean Shores Blvd; (360)289-3381; 651 Ocean Shores Blvd
SW, Ocean Shores; PO Box 1417, Ocean Shores, WA 98569;
$$$; AE, DC, MC, V; checks OK.*

Shilo Inn *[unrated]* Our jury's still out on Shilo Inns' $10 mil-
lion, 113-suite "convention resort"—opened just before press
time on the site of the landmark Ocean Shores Inn. Destined
to be the mother of all Ocean Shores overnight accommoda-
tions (if we're to believe the PR hoo-ha), each of its suites fea-
tures a beachfront balcony, fireplace, microwave, refrigerator,
and wet bar. Facilities include an indoor pool, sauna, steam
room, and fitness center. ■ *In town on Ocean Shores Blvd;
(360)289-4600 or (800)222-2244; 707 Ocean Shores Blvd
NW, Ocean Shores, WA 98569; $$$; AE, DC, MC, V; checks
OK.* &

Southwest Washington

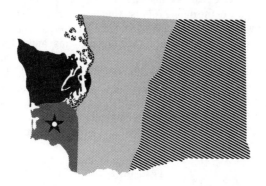

A clockwise route: southward on the southern half of I-5, west along the Columbia River, north along the Long Beach Peninsula and the south coast, and eastward at Grays Harbor.

CENTRALIA

The Chehalis-Centralia Railroad offers round-trip steam-train rides between these twin cities weekends from Memorial Day through September. Shoppers will find a bargain mine of factory outlet stores along I-5 outside Centralia, and the 80 antique dealers who work the downtown area offer good finds too. The Kulien Shoe Factory (611 N Tower (360) 736-6943) is a tiny company that crafts handmade shoes. Train buffs will love the Lewis County Historical Museum, open Tuesday through Sunday (599 NW Front Street, Chehalis, (360)748-0831).

RESTAURANTS

Winter Kitchen ★ Julie Norman owns this little green house decorated year-round in tasteful Christmas attire. The lunch menu is short and sweet—cheap too, with sandwiches, salads, and an oyster stew, all (except a seafood salad) less than $5. Red floats, green floats, apple cider, and hot chocolate make this a fun spot to stop on a wearying highway drive. Friday-night candlelight dinners (until 8pm) come complete with a candle on your plate. ■ *2 blocks east of exit 81 off I-5;*

(360) 736-2916; 827 Marsh St, Centralia; $; no alcohol; no credit cards; checks OK; lunch Mon–Sat, dinner Fri.

CHEHALIS

RESTAURANTS

Mary McCrank's Good, homemade value. The 1935 dinner house occupies a large home, with fireplaces in some of the dining rooms; windows overlooking the garden, lawns, and stream; and armchairs scattered around the comfy rooms. Dinner starts with breads, jams, and a tray of homemade relishes (soups and salads, however, are perfunctory). Offerings include chicken with dumplings, pork chops, and other country fixings. A glorious pie comes for dessert: we never turn down the sour-cream raisin. ■ *4 miles east of I-5 on the Jackson Hwy, 4 miles south of Chehalis; (360) 748-3662; 2923 Jackson Hwy, Chehalis; $; beer and wine; MC, V; checks OK; lunch and dinner Tues–Sun.*

LONGVIEW

RESTAURANTS

Henri's The Longview big shots all come here for lunch, when the large place can be fun and reliable; at dinner, when the pretension level rises and the number of customers dips, things can be rather lonely. Still, the steaks are perfectly good, you can have some nice seafood bisques, and the rack of lamb with béarnaise is quite tasty. There is a fancy wine room, into which guests are escorted by owner Henry Paul, who learned how to do this kind of thing years ago at Seattle's Golden Lion. ■ *45th and Ocean Beach; (360) 425-7970; 4545 Ocean Beach Hwy, Longview; $$; full bar; AE, MC, V; local checks only; lunch Mon–Fri, dinner Mon–Sat.* &

LODGINGS

Monticello Hotel It fronts on Civic Center Park with an impressive facade of brick and terra-cotta. But the 1923 edifice has suffered a loss of confidence over the years; now the hotel rooms are rented out as senior housing and offices. However, four executive suites have opened in the hotel, or you can stay in a motel-like wing to one side, where the low-priced rooms are perfectly standard. ■ *Larch and 17th; (360) 425-9900; 1405 17th Ave, Longview, WA 98632; $$; AE, MC, V; no checks.*

VANCOUVER

Vancouver, long known as a bedroom community of Portland, is coming into its own with the advent of new industry, including a number of up-and-coming restaurants. Among the

modest tourist attractions is the Northwest's oldest apple tree
(in Old Apple Tree Park, east of I-5 on Columbia Way).

Fort Vancouver was the major settlement of the Hudson's Bay Company until the 1860s, when it passed to the
Americans. The stockade wall and some of the buildings have
been reconstructed, and the visitors center has a decent museum; 1501 E Evergreen Boulevard, (360)696-7655. On your
way to Officers Row, you'll pass the active military post, **Vancouver Barracks**. The Heritage Trust of Clark County gives
tours of the restored officers' quarters nearby; (360)737-6066.
The Grant House on Officers Row now houses the **Folk Art
Center**, a tribute to regional art. It's open Tuesday through
Sunday; (360)694-5252. **Clark County Historical Museum**
reconstructs pioneer stores and businesses; 1511 Main Street
at 16th, (360)695-4681. **Covington House** is the oldest log
house (1846) in the state; 4201 Main Street, (360)695-4106.
Ridgefield National Wildlife Refuge, 3 miles west of I-5 exit
14, has nature trails leading to the bird refuge on the lowlands
of the Columbia River; (360)887-3883.

RESTAURANTS

Grant House Cafe ★★ The 1849 Grant House, named for
Ulysses Grant, doubles as a folk art museum and cafe. Its

Vancouver

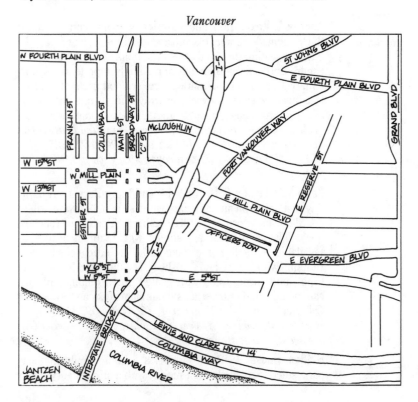

location, with verandah and herb garden, is quite charming, and the food is rapidly catching up. For lunch, soups, salads, quiches, seafood, and sandwiches are the bill of fare; for dinner, a Northwest bistro menu tempts—pasta, salmon, Willapa Bay oysters, and grilled duck breast, with apple crisp or praline gingerbread for dessert. We'd come back any time for the sesame potato soup and the free regional folk art exhibit. ■ *Midtown Vancouver on Officers Row off Evergreen Blvd; (360)699-1213; 1101 Officers Row, Vancouver; $$; beer and wine; AE, MC, V; checks OK; lunch Tues–Sat, dinner Thurs–Sat.*

Pinot Ganache ★★ Downtown Vancouver, forever struggling to buff up its image, shows off a glimmer of panache at the Pinot Ganache. The interior is slick with well-spaced tables and live jazz on Tuesday nights. Multiethnic meals such as Asian-style game hen, Arabic falafel pita, and enchiladas con pollo are as much of a draw as the juicy sirloin burger with sautéed onions and mushrooms. Desserts are equally impressive: caramel custard pear tart, chocolate cappuccino coffee cake, and tiramisu. The place brightens in summer, when pink geraniums bloom in the sidewalk cafe. ■ *Corner of Washington and Evergreen; (360)695-7786; 1004 Washington St, Vancouver; $$; beer and wine; AE, MC, V; checks OK; lunch, dinner Tues–Sat.*

Andrew's Restaurant and Catering ★ Some come here for the homemade almond biscotti and good coffee, others like the outdoor seating that lends this little Italian cafe in Vancouver a more European air. Lunch is refreshingly unpretentious—polenta with pesto or marinara sauce; seafood pasta or spinach lasagne; a focaccia sandwich; an array of fresh, imaginative salads (from roasted eggplant to an Asian noodle variation). Best of all, nothing exceeds $7. ■ *Between Grant and Franklin sts across from the courthouse in Vancouver; (360)693-3252; 611 W 11th St, Vancouver; $; no alcohol; MC, V; checks OK; breakfast, lunch Mon–Fri.*

Bernabe's Family Cafe ★ Pedro and Mary Bernabe run this tiny restaurant on an undistinguished strip of highway, where the Mexican flavors would fill a sombrero. Traditional rellenos, quesadillas, and fajitas are served with homemade tortillas (available by the dozen for take-out). Let Pedro's posole stew (hominy with lettuce and radishes), Menudo (made with beef tripe), and carne asada with grilled green onions and guacamole take you into perhaps unfamiliar Mexican territory. ■ *Off Hwy 99 north of Vancouver; (360)574-5993; 9803 NE Hwy 99, Vancouver; $; beer and wine; MC, V; checks OK; breakfast, lunch, dinner every day.*

Hidden House ★ The Hiddens, a leading family in these parts since 1870, made their money with a brick factory. Their handsome brick home was opened by Susan Courtney as a restaurant in 1976, and she has succeeded in turning it into a reliable, if old-fashioned, place for an intimate dinner. You are offered a combination of slightly dated small-city standards (pasta primavera, scampi, tenderloin, pork loin medallions with plum sauce). A "beggar's banquet" of soup, salad, and homemade poppyseed or pumpkin bread is a midday favorite. There's a fairly inclusive Northwest wine list. A satellite cafe, the Paradise Cafe, is open for breakfast and lunch next door; 304 Main Street, (360)696-1612. ■ *Corner of 13th and Main in downtown Vancouver; (360)696-2847; 100 W 13th St, Vancouver; $$–$$$; beer and wine; AE, MC, V; checks OK; lunch Mon–Fri, dinner Tues–Sun.*

Thai Little Home ★ It's not as fancy as similar joints across the river in Portland, but Serm Pong and his family prepare fresh, home-cooked Thai food that locals think is just fine. Yum Nuer (sliced beef salad with cucumber, seasoned with chile and lime juice) rivals the popular Pra Koong (shrimp with chile paste, lemon grass, and lime juice); we've enjoyed both mee krob (Thai crispy noodles) and chicken satay at the beginning of meals. Service is friendly, informed, and fast. ■ *Just north of downtown Vancouver and Clark College; (360)693-4061; 3214 E 4th Plain Blvd, Vancouver; $; beer and wine; AE, MC, V; local checks only; lunch, dinner Mon–Sat.*

▼

Cathlamet

▲

Who-Song and Larry's Cantina If you wondered, wandering around downtown Vancouver, where all the *people* were: they're here. The entire basketball team is packing in enchiladas by your side, families are rounding the large buffet with dedicated zeal, there's lots of chat to make you feel part of a large, homey party. The menu patter is a bit of a delusion: this place is yet another link in the vast El Torito chain. Mexican buffet is no great shakes, but there are great margaritas and swift service. A jolly cantina away from the hubbub lets you nibble nachos with your Corona and watch the grain ships force the Vancouver-Portland bridge to open. ■ *Take the Camas (Hwy 14) exit off I-5, go east 1 mile, turn right at light; (360)695-1198; 111 E Columbia Way, Vancouver; $; full bar; AE, DC, MC, V; local checks only; lunch, dinner every day, brunch Sun.*

CATHLAMET

Cathlamet, seat of Wahkiakum County, is an old-style river town, tied almost as closely to the Columbia as Mark Twain's Hannibal was to the Mississippi. Fishing is everyone's recreation—in season, for trout, salmon, and steelhead; all year round for the Columbia's mammoth, caviar-bearing sturgeon. Nearby **Puget Island**, reachable by bridge, is flat dairyland, ideal for cycling; a tiny ferry can take you from there directly across to Oregon. Wahkiakum County is the sort of place where nostalgia buffs discover round barns and covered bridges. You can camp right on the river beach at **Skamokawa Vista Park** (say Ska-MOCK-away).

LODGINGS

The Bradley House Country Keeper ★ It's not exactly in the country (Main Street, Cathlamet, is more exact), but it's certainly a keeper. This former town library is an immaculate 1907 mansion—original decorative hardwood floors, Oriental rugs, light fixtures, and all. It's handsomely furnished with period pieces. As a tribute to the mansion's former incarnation, the comfortable bedrooms are filled with books. A porch with a distant view of the Columbia invites long afternoon visits in summer. ▪ *Just off SR 4, on Main St, north end of town; (360) 795-3030; 61 Main St, Cathlamet, WA 98612; $$; MC, V; checks OK.*

CHINOOK

Nestled on the shores of Baker Bay, part of the broad Columbia River estuary, Chinook was formerly a profitable salmon fish-trapping center. The too-efficient fish traps were outlawed earlier this century; today, most of the thousands of wooden pilings visible in the bay at low tide are all that remains of these harvesting contraptions.

Nearby, on Scarborough Hill, **Fort Columbia State Park** is a collection of restored turn-of-the-century wooden buildings that once housed soldiers guarding the mouth of the Columbia River from the threat of foreign invasion. The former commander's house is now a military museum (nearby is the youth hostel); foreboding concrete bunkers once held huge cannons. The park also claims some of the area's largest rhododendron bushes. Open daily, mid-May to September, but hours vary; (360)777-8221.

RESTAURANTS

The Sanctuary ★ You dine in a deified setting, an old Methodist church complete with pump organ, stained-glass windows, statues of angelic cherubs—even pews to sit in, for God's sake. Amid the finery, owner/chef Joanne Leech serves an eclectic array of food, from steak and seafood to *svenska kottbullar* (Swedish meatballs) and *fiskekaker* (Scandinavian fish cakes)—both of which can be sampled as appetizers. She also purveys the area's best fresh-baked bread. Innovative preparations include fresh snapper fillet coated with a crunchy, potato-pancake crust; or a filet mignon served with a zingy Jack Daniel's mustard sauce. For dessert, homemade sherbet—blackberry one time, lemon another—is, er, heavenly. Ditto for the "sinful sundae." Light lunches, and some weekend pizzas, are served in the herb house. ▪ *Hwy 101 and Hazel; (360) 777-8380; Hwy 101 and Hazel St, Chinook; $$; full bar; AE, MC, V; checks OK; dinner Wed–Sun, brunch Sun (winter hours vary).* &

LONG BEACH PENINSULA

The slender finger of land dividing Willapa Bay from the Pacific is famous for its 37-mile-long flat stretch of public beach (reputedly the longest such stretch worldwide); its gentle marine climate; its exhibition kite flying; its cranberry bogs, clamming, and rhododendrons; and for its food, which is unequaled by any like-size area on the Northwest Coast.

Willapa Bay's **Long Island**, reachable only by boat, harbors a 274-acre old-growth cedar grove. Some trees are over 200 feet tall, with trunks 11 feet in diameter. Campsites are available. The island is part of the **Willapa National Wildlife Refuge**, with headquarters on Highway 101, back on the mainland and 10 miles north of Seaview; (360) 484-3482.

LONG BEACH PENINSULA: ILWACO

Named after a Chinook Indian chief, Ilwaco is best known as the sport-fishing hub of the lower Columbia River. Two popular sport-fishing operators, both located at the port docks, are **Sea Breeze Charters**, (360) 642-2300, and **Coho Charters**, (360) 642-3333. Because of intermittent ocean closures for sport fishing, many charter operators are now offering "eco" tours. Phone ahead for information.

The **Ilwaco Heritage Museum** is a fine example of a small-town museum. It offers not only a look at Southwest Washington history (including native American artifacts and a scale-model glimpse of the peninsula in the 1920s) but also contains an excellent research library, art gallery, and a whole separate building of train memorabilia; 115 SE Lake Street, in the Convention Center, (360) 642-3446.

Fort Canby State Park covers 2,000 acres stretching from North Head south to Cape Disappointment at the Columbia's mouth. Good surf fishing and wave watching can be had from the North Jetty, 2 miles of massive boulders separating the ocean and river, with an observation platform for good views. The park also includes hiking and biking trails and 250 campsites; open all year, (360) 642-3078.

Also in the park is the **Lewis and Clark Interpretive Center**, which depicts the explorers' journey from St. Louis to the Pacific, explains the history of Cape Disappointment and North Head lighthouses, and enjoys the best view of the

Columbia River bar—a great storm-watching spot. The light-houses are not open to the public, but may be approached on foot; (360)642-3029.

RESTAURANTS

Bubba's Pizza It's not much to look at, inside or out, but the aroma of fresh-baked pizza dough, garlic, provolone, and pepperoni will entice you through the door. Once inside, chef Bubba Kuhn's artistry, wit, and showmanship (every pie is hand-tossed, and Kuhn keeps a running commentary throughout) will keep you entertained. And as soon as you taste one of Bubba's creations, well, you'll be hooked. All the usuals are here, plus the Man Overboard (10 toppings); the Farm (olive oil instead of sauce with garlic, herbs, and a ton of vegies); and the Lower East Side (cream-cheese-and-pastrami–covered crust sprinkled with onions, tomatoes, and olives). ▪ *On Ilwaco waterfront at SE Howerton; (360)642-8750; 177 SE Howerton Way, Ilwaco; $; beer and wine; AE, MC, V; checks OK; dinner every day.*

LODGINGS

Chick-a-dee Inn at Ilwaco ★ Located on a quiet dead-end street overlooking the town, this bed and breakfast is housed in the old Ilwaco Presbyterian Church. The sanctuary has been transformed into a performing arts center that hosts a myriad of community theater productions (and is still a good place for a wedding), while the former Sunday school has been converted into nine guest rooms (seven with private bath) with plush bedding, lacy curtains, and original wood floors. Privacy seekers will find the walls unfortunately thin. A couple of rooms can accommodate two twin beds, a good choice for families. In the spacious public room, guests take their ample breakfast and read the morning papers. New innkeepers Chick and Delaine Hinkle plan renovations and perhaps the addition of a couple of guest rooms. ▪ *Off 4th at Williams; (360)642-8686; 120 Williams St NE, Ilwaco; PO Box 922, Ilwaco, WA 98624; $$; MC, V; checks OK.*

LONG BEACH PENINSULA: SEAVIEW

Some of the peninsula's prettiest stretches (and a couple of its finest restaurants and lodgings) are tucked into this small, beachfront, bedroom community. Almost every westward road leads to the beach, where you can park your car to stroll the quaint neighborhoods and traverse the rolling dunes. The Charles Mulvey Gallery displays quintessential peninsula watercolors of ocean, beach, and bay; 46th Place & L Street, (360) 642-2189. Campiche Studios, 3100 S Pacific Way, (360)642-2264, features watercolors, sculptures, and photography.

The Shoalwater (The Shelburne Inn) ★★★★ The Shoal-

water is the finest eating establishment on the Northwest coast. Under the direction of owners Ann and Tony Kischner and head chef Francis Schafer (who also oversees the Lightship's kitchen, see review) this exquisite eatery has helped to establish Northwest cuisine as a nationally recognized method of choosing and preparing food. Inside, the atmosphere is understated but elegant. The main dining area, with tongue-in-groove walls and ceiling, brass light fixtures, finely brushed watercolors, and a grandfather's clock, resembles a first-class captain's cabin. Service is purposeful without being pretentious, attentive but never pushy, and courses are generally well-paced. The seasonal menu is a treat to peruse, and the wine list is superlative. Schafer continually produces imaginative, artful offerings, always using the Northwest's finest ingredients. Northwest salmon, in one of its finer incarnations, comes bathed in a sublime spiced pear sauce. Dungeness crab is fashioned into mouth-watering cakes and served with garlic-pepper cheese, an understated red bell pepper mayonnaise, and mai-fun noodles. Rabbit sausage is flavored with garlic and herbs, grilled, and presented on a bed of tomato-onion-cumin fettuccine while halibut is graced by a swath of cran-blueberry mustard sauce. Even a simple salad, accented with chopped hazelnuts and dressed with a salal berry vinaigrette, is superb. Anything composed with local Willapa Bay oysters is worth a taste. As for dessert, lemon cheesecake is heavenly, bread pudding is perfection, and anything with cranberries (say, white-chocolate cheesecake in a cranberry purée) is out of this world.
■ *Pacific Hwy 103 and N 45th; (360) 642-4142; 4415 Pacific Hwy, Seaview; $$$; full bar; AE, DC, MC, V; checks OK; lunch, dinner every day, brunch Sun.* ⅃

▼

**Long Beach
Peninsula:
Seaview**

Restaurants

42nd Street Cafe ★★ Cheri and Blaine Walker, late of Shoal-

water restaurant fame (she ran the kitchen; he was the manager), have taken over this popular dinner house just down the highway from the Shelburne Inn. Cheri is transforming the kitchen, slowly but surely. Expect more imaginative offerings than the Americana fare formerly served; a recent menu's appetizers like garlic shrimp and sherry-cooked mushrooms and an Italian fish stew entree offered more than a fleeting glance toward the Mediterranean. But never fear: the comfy-cozy decor, the cheerful waitresses, and the hearty portions of home cooking (berry conserves and corn relish, iron-skillet–fried chicken) are still here. Only the freshest fish is used (and it won't be breaded). Local oysters will no doubt be featured in a number of creations, and desserts (sour cream raisin pie, bread pudding) are terrific. The Walkers have found their niche: comfort food with lots of flair. ■ *42nd St and Pacific*

Hwy; (360) 642-2323; 42nd Pl, Pacific Highway 103, Seaview; $$; beer and wine; MC, V; checks OK; dinner every day (winter hours vary). &

The Heron and Beaver Pub ★ There's a feeling of serendipity here. You might slip in for a beer as you wait for your table at the Shoalwater, across the foyer, then discover that most of the pub's patrons aren't going anyplace else. They're here because the handsome, pint-size Heron and Beaver is a destination in its own right. If only it weren't so small. Just think of it as cozy, as you sip something with a head on it, select from the excellent wine list, or savor a single-malt Scotch. Light meals are available—pasta, sandwiches, soup, a delectable cheese fondue, or a stout chicken cordon bleu burger—all prepared with the same meticulousness as the food next door. ■ *In the Shelburne Inn, Pacific Hwy 103 and N 45th; (360) 642-4142; 4415 Pacific Hwy, Seaview; $$; full bar; AE, DC, MC, V; checks OK; dinner every day, lunch Mon–Sat, brunch Sun.* &

LODGINGS

The Shelburne Inn ★★ You can't see the ocean from here, but you most definitely can feel its allure throughout the historic Shelburne, a creaky but dignified century-old structure. Trouble is, there's a busy highway out front, with a well-lit supermarket across the way. Consequently, request a west-facing room to assure peace and quiet. They're bright and cheerful, with antiqued interiors, private baths, and cozy homespun quilts covering queen-size beds. Don't expect the modern amenities (sauna, Jacuzzis) that have become de rigueur at so many chic hideaways. The third floor offers the best buys, lots of tongue-and-groove woodwork, and gently slanted floors (the entire building was pulled across the street by a team of horses in 1911). Breakfasts are superb: innkeepers David Campiche and Laurie Anderson whip up satisfying eye-openers of razor-clam cakes or scrambled eggs with smoked salmon, chives (from the herb garden out front), and Gruyère cheese—not to mention the pastries. The separately owned Shoalwater (see review) is the dinner restaurant. ■ *Pacific Hwy 103 and N 45th; (360) 642-2442; PO Box 250, Seaview, WA 98644; $$$; AE, MC, V; checks OK.* &

Sou'wester Lodge ★ This place is definitely not for everyone, but those who appreciate good conversation, a sense of humor, and rambling lodgings on the beach will find Leonard and Miriam Atkins's humble, old-fashioned resort just what the doctor ordered. The main structure was built in 1892 as a summer home for U.S. Senator Henry Winslow Corbett; you can also stay in fully equipped cabins or a collection of classic trailers. The hosts are as much a draw as the lodgings. Originally from South Africa, they came to Long Beach by way of Israel

Long Beach Peninsula: Seaview

Restaurants

▲

and Chicago. The view from the lodge's balcony—across wind-swept, grassy dunes to the sea—is enough to keep them here permanently. Interesting books and periodicals clutter the living room, which also occasionally hosts lectures, chamber music concerts, and informal (but stimulating) conversations. Leonard has deemed this joint the official outpost of the "B & (MYOD)B club"—Bed and (Make Your Own Damn) Breakfast. ■ *1½ blocks southwest of Seaview's traffic light on Beach Access Rd (38th Pl); (360)642-2542; PO Box 102, Seaview, WA 98644; $; MC, V; checks OK.*

LONG BEACH PENINSULA: LONG BEACH

After many years of dormancy, Long Beach is bustling. New buildings are going up at warp speed and new businesses abound. Increased tourism is inevitable, so if you visit during the summer, prepare for the onslaught. A popular hang-out is the half-mile-long elevated boardwalk (with night lighting) stretching between S 10th and Bolstad streets, accessible by wheelchairs, baby strollers, and, of course, by foot.

Kite lovers can visit the **Long Beach World Kite Museum and Hall of Fame**, Third and N Pacific Highway, (360)642-4020, or buy their own at Long Beach Kites, at the stoplight, (360)642-2202; or Stormin' Norman's, one block south, (800)4-STORMIN. August's **International Kite Festival** brings thousands of soaring creations to the skies. The entire peninsula swells with visitors for this event, so plan ahead; (360)642-2400. Milton York Candy Company, on the main drag, purveys chocolates and ice cream, (360)642-2352, while nearby Plain Jane's offers tasty chocolate chip cookies and other sweets, (360)642-4933. For some Tex-Mex fast food, also on the main drag, head for Dos Amigas Cafe (Second and Pacific Highway, (360)642-8365). Farther out, Clark's Nursery grows fields of rhododendrons, (360)642-2241.

RESTAURANTS

The Lightship Restaurant and Columbia Bar ★★ The Lightship is a rare find: a view restaurant with good food. It's housed on the top floor of a boxy Nendel's Inn, and looks like just another poor-quality, high-priced, ocean-front eatery, the type of establishment that seems to proliferate wherever land and sea meet. Disregard all that, because the ocean view, fair prices, and, especially, the food make it all worthwhile. Begin with something as unusual as grilled scallops wrapped in bacon with citrus-jalapeño sauce. Pan-fried Willapa Bay oysters are served either lightly floured or heavily dusted with herbed cornmeal. Linguine is fresh, the sauces herby and flavorful. There's breakfast (try the hangtown fry), and lunch selections are extensive; everything done here must pass muster with owners

Ann and Tony Kischner (who also own the acclaimed Shoal-water Restaurant). ■ *Between 10th St and the beach; (360) 642-3252; at Nendel's Inn on S 10th, Long Beach; $$; full bar; AE, DC, MC, V; checks OK; lunch, dinner every day, breakfast Sat, brunch Sun.* ⅃

My Mom's Pie Kitchen The name says it all. This is a small establishment that serves a host of homemade pies. Banana cream, pecan, sour cream, chocolate-almond, raisin, rhubarb, raspberry, and myriad other concoctions are offered, depending on the time of year and, in some cases, the time of day. Arrive too late (especially in summer), and this sweetnick's haven might be sold out of your favorite (but it's easy enough to find a satisfying replacement). Before savoring a slice, satisfy yourself with a steamy bowl of chowder or a silky Dungeness crab quiche. ■ *Pacific Hwy and 12th St; (360) 642-2342; Pacific Hwy and 12th St, Long Beach; $; no alcohol; MC, V; checks OK; lunch Tues–Sun.*

Pastimes What began as a hip espresso house with lots of books and board games is now a restaurant, too. Actually, this place with the glassed-in eating (and sipping) area and the gift shop up front is a pocket of serenity in bustling downtown Long Beach. The ambience is laid-back, the soups and salads (try the wild rice with hazelnuts in an orange-fennel vinaigrette) are super, and the coffee-drink selection is the best around. Luscious scones and gooey thick cinnamon rolls are baked daily, and there's even a quote du jour to keep you thinking. Imaginative dinner entrees (chicken with a hazelnut crust, for example) are offered during the summer months. ■ *5th and Pacific Hwy; (360) 642-8303; 504 Pacific Hwy S, Long Beach; $; wine available with dinner; MC, V; checks OK; breakfast, lunch every day (dinner Fri–Sun in summer).*

LODGINGS

Boreas Bed & Breakfast ★ Boreas is a picturesque lodging in a postcard-perfect setting. A remodeled 1920s beach house, it's tastefully decorated with art and antiques and appointed with handsome furnishings. Four rooms are available, three upstairs and one down. Two enjoy private baths and ocean views. There's a hot tub inside a glassed-in sun deck for year-round soaking and a cozy backyard deck that's private and out of the wind. The beach is a short walk through the dunes. ■ *On N Boulevard, 1 block west of the main drag; (360) 642-8069; 607 N Boulevard, Long Beach; PO Box 1344, Long Beach, WA 98631; $$; MC, V; checks OK.*

LONG BEACH PENINSULA: OCEAN PARK

Ocean Park, founded as a religious settlement, is now a tranquil retirement community with a quiet beach—except in June, when the **Garlic Festival** takes over the town. Needless to say, there's lots of stinkin' good food at this event, (800)451-2542. The **Wiegardt Watercolors Gallery**, 2607 Bay Avenue, (360) 665-5976, displays Eric Wiegardt seascapes in a restored Victorian house. Nearby (at 25712 Sand Ridge Rd, (360)665-4382) the Shoalwater Cove Gallery, exhibits nature scenes in soft pastels.

RESTAURANTS

La Petite Maison ★ Be prepared for some unusual creations from this diminutive, rustic restaurant tucked into a grove of trees. For instance, you'll be served tasty, fresh-baked bread shaped like a hedgehog (or a turtle, or a sand dollar). There are also imaginative, made-from-scratch meals, such as shrimp Creole, rabbit and veal in various preparations, and some excellent pan-fried oysters. Soups—hearty corn chowder, savory sweet pea—and some humongous hamburgers (sandwiched between two slices of sand dollar bread) are always a good bet. ■ *Off Bay Ave, across from Sentry Market; (360)665-6525; 26108 R Pl, Ocean Park; $$; wine; no credit cards; checks OK; dinner Thurs–Mon.* &

Back Porch Garden Cafe Not quite a full-fledged restaurant, but a lot more substantial than roadside fast food, this place is as delightful as the fresh sea breeze that blows daily in these parts. It's a homey, mellow, one-woman kitchen connected to a seven-table deck area out back (and mostly out of the wind). The limited menu is well-suited to a summer's day at the beach, and includes scratch-made soups such as curried sweet corn or chicken tortilla, pasta and chicken salads, and a variety of small (8-inch), custom-made pizzas. Great baked goods for dessert. ■ *On Bay Ave, across from Jack's Country Store; (360)665-5732; 1517 Bay Ave, Ocean Park; $; no alcohol; no credit cards; checks OK; lunch Thurs–Mon; (closed Nov–Mar).*

Long Beach
Peninsula:
Nahcotta

LODGINGS

Klipsan Beach Cottages ★ This cozy operation, a row of nine small, separate, well-maintained older cottages, stands facing the ocean in a parklike setting of pine trees and clipped lawns. Since these are individually owned condominiums, interior decoration schemes can vary widely, but all of the units feature fireplaces (or wood stoves), full kitchens, and ocean-facing decks just a couple of hundred feet from the beach. Children are fine, but no pets. ■ *Hwy 103, 2 miles south of Ocean Park; (360)665-4888; 22617 Pacific Hwy, Ocean Park, WA 98640; $$-$$$; MC, V; checks OK.* &

LONG BEACH PENINSULA: NAHCOTTA

Nahcotta has become almost synonymous with oysters. At the **Nahcotta Oyster Farm**, 270th and Sandridge Road, on the old rail line, you can pick up some pesticide-free 'sters (or gather your own for half-price); **Jolly Roger Seafoods**, across from The Ark, (360)665-4111, is also a good bet. The **Nahcotta Natural Store**, at 270th and Sandridge Road, (360)665-4449, is a pleasant stop for beverages and grub. Two places help explain the oyster story: The Willapa Field Station (267 Sand Ridge Road, (360)665-4166) has outdoor interpretive signs, maps, and info; Willapa Bay Interpretive Center (on the Nahcotta pier, open in summer only) features a viewing deck and indoor exhibits.

RESTAURANTS

The Ark ★★ Accolades from up and down the West Coast have built The Ark up to legendary status; unfortunately, such renown is hard to uphold, and in the process, the restaurant has gained some snob appeal but lost some epicurean excitement. To wit: the clam chowder barely rises above ho-hum, and an otherwise delicate sauté of Dungeness crab meat—deglazed with sherry and cream and paired with mushrooms and artichoke hearts—can come overwhelmed by the needless addition of a béarnaise sauce. But most of the time the restaurant with the picture-perfect setting is still quite good. Calamari Dijonnaise and traditional French onion soup are heavenly starters; salmon (try it pan-sautéed with chanterelles, lime, cilantro, and sherry, or sauced with a reduction of Scotch and orange juice and finished with a hit of Drambuie) is a solid entree, as are the ouzo-enhanced prawns. The legendary Ark oyster feed, an unlimited amount (the record is 100) of Willapa Bay bivalves lightly breaded and pan-fried, continues to be the best in, at least, our universe. ■ *On the old Nahcotta dock, next to the oyster fleet; (360)665-4133; 273rd and Sandridge Rd, Nahcotta; $$$; full bar; AE, MC, V; checks OK; dinner Wed–Sun, brunch Sun.*

LODGINGS

Moby Dick Hotel Although it looks fairly institutional at first glance, this friendly place is one of those that grows on you. Fritzie and Edward Cohen of the Tabard Inn in Washington, DC, first spied the Moby Dick from a window table at the Ark and knew it just needed the care of good innkeepers. So today the hotel, originally built in 1929 by a railroad conductor with his gold-prospecting money, is under their careful ownership. It's quite beachy (without really having a beach), with a couple of spacious public rooms, 10 small and modest bedrooms (most with shared bath), and a rambling bay front (loaded with oysters). In the afternoon, join the innkeepers for a few Pacific oysters on the halfshell. Full breakfasts (included) make use of the hotel's own garden produce. Like virtually every other place in Nahcotta, you can buy oysters here too. Pets welcome. Dinners are offered (for guests and others) off and on depending on whether the chef is in residence. Call ahead to find out. ▪ *South of Bay Ave on Sandridge Rd; (360) 665-4543; PO Box 82, Nahcotta, WA 98637; $$; MC, V; checks OK.*

LONG BEACH PENINSULA: OYSTERVILLE

Oysterville dates to 1854 and was the county seat until (legend has it) a group from South Bend stole the county records in 1893. South Bend remains the county seat to this day, but Oysterville has its own charm. It's listed on the National Register of Historic Places and features a distinctive row of shoreside homes, surrounded by stately cedars and spruce trees. (Follow Sandridge Road north to the Oysterville sign.)

Oysterville is, of course, known for its bivalves, and **Oysterville Sea Farms**, at the old cannery in Oysterville, sells 'em by the dozen (open weekends, year-round).

Leadbetter Point State Park, on the northern tip of the peninsula, is a stopover site for over 100 species of birds, and a nature-lover's paradise with miles of sandy trails as well as un-trampled ocean beaches. Hiking trails abound (3 miles north of Oysterville on Stackpole Road).

SOUTH BEND

This picturesque burg is perched on the evergreen bluffs along Willapa Bay, one of America's most pristine estuaries. Ruling over the town is the historic **County Courthouse** with its splendid stained-glass dome. (It was denounced by some fiscal sourpusses as a "gilded palace of extravagance" when it opened in 1910.) On Highway 101 just north of town, the **H & H Cafe**, (360) 875-5442, is still the place to stop for pie.

RESTAURANTS

Gardner's ★★ South Bend, the sleepy county seat of Pacific County, bills itself as "The Oyster Capital of the World." That's a classic bit of boosterism, but the Willapa Bay oysters *are* world-class. After the courthouse, the next best roadside attraction is Gardner's, where succulent pan-fried oysters, and almost everything else, from cheeseburgers to cannelloni, are prepared with wonderful attention to detail. Gene and Libet Gardner, who operated the much admired Gardner's Seafood & Pasta in Olympia for 10 years, bought this former hamburger stand and transformed it into a friendly knotty pine cafe that seats 35. Gene is in a perpetual swoon over the raw materials at his doorstep: seafood fresh from the ocean and Willapa Bay, mushrooms often served the day they're plucked from the forests nearby; cranberries fresh from the bogs. ▪ *On Hwy 101; (360) 875-5154; 702 Robert Bush Dr, South Bend; $$; beer and wine; AE, DC, MC, V; checks OK; dinner Wed–Sun.*

TOKELAND

Set on the long peninsula reaching into northern Willapa Bay, this crabbing community, named after 19th-century Chief Toke, is the loneliest part of the southwest coast, where the omnipresent tackiness of contemporary resort life is least apparent. The tiny Shoalwater Bay Indian Tribe hopes to open a casino, so don't bet on the status quo. In the meantime, pick up a container of crabmeat and some cocktail sauce from **Nelson Crab** (open daily 9am–5pm) to enjoy while sitting on a driftwood log at the beach across the street.

LODGINGS

Tokeland Hotel ★ This chaste, century-old structure teetered for several years on the edge of genteel collapse until a series of rescues. A Seattle couple bought "the oldest resort hotel in Washington" and made major improvements in both the food and plumbing. The remodeling's probably never complete, but all 18 rooms are open. Some offer views of pristine Willapa Bay. Mind you, they're somewhat spartan, and bathrooms are shared, but the rooms have an old-fashioned charm that doesn't include a lumpy mattress. The creaky-floored restaurant is often filled with folks from the surrounding community who take advantage of large helpings of good food at reasonable prices. Breakfast is included in the price of a room (kids will love the pigs in a blanket). ▪ *Kindred Ave and Hotel Rd; (360)267-7006; 100 Hotel Rd, Tokeland, WA 98590; $$; beer and wine; MC, V; local checks only; breakfast and dinner every day, lunch Mon–Sat.*

GRAYLAND

RESTAURANTS

The Dunes ★ Turn off Highway 105 at the sign of the giant razor clam and follow the bumpy gravel road a quarter of a mile down to the dunes. You will discover a funky kind of place that's as comfortable as an old windbreaker: a beachcomber's hideaway, decorated with shells, ship models, and stained glass. With a fireplace in the middle and linen-draped oak tables, the main dining room is warm and enticing after a walk on the beach. The aptly named restaurant offers a front-row seat on the ocean just beyond the dunes. Quality control isn't what it was when the moderately eccentric owners were in their prime, but most of the time you won't find fresher seafood. ▪ *Off Hwy 105; (360)267-1441; 783 Dunes Rd, Grayland; $$; beer and wine; AE, DC, MC, V; checks OK; breakfast, lunch, dinner every day (winter hours vary).*

GRAYS HARBOR

The debate over the spotted owl and widespread negative publicity in the wake of native son Kurt Cobain's suicide ("Aberdeen is not Nirvana!" was the refrain) left the locals in a temporary funk. But this county, with natural resources to match its natural beauty and real estate bargains galore, is on the rebound after a rough decade. The wild beauty of the expansive bay and the obvious attractions of the coastal beaches draw retirees, tourists, surfers, and migrating shorebirds.

A half million Arctic-bound shorebirds migrate from as far south as Argentina and congregate on the tidal mudflats at the wildlife refuge of **Bowerman Basin** each spring from about mid-April through the first week of May. At high tide, the birds rise in unison in thick flocks that shimmer through the air, twisting and turning, before settling back onto their feeding grounds. There are trails through the marsh (located just beyond the Hoquiam airport). Be sure to wear boots. For more information and peak migratory days, call the Grays Harbor National Wildlife Refuge, (360)753-9467.

WESTPORT

For a small coastal town that regularly endures flood tides of tourists, Westport remains surprisingly friendly, scenic, and uncondominiumed. Most "fishers" rise early and join the almost comically hasty 6am exodus from the breakwater to cross the bumpy bar and head for the open sea. The unpredictable **salmon fishing** seasons of recent years have changed charterboat marketing. Bottomfishing trips for halibut, lingcod, and rockfish are increasingly popular, and many charter operators now feature whale-watching cruises as well. **Gray whales** migrate off the coast March through May on their way toward Arctic feeding waters, where they fatten up for the trip back down to their breeding lagoons in Baja, come fall. Breakfast cafes are open by 5am, some much earlier (especially those down by the docks).

You can drop by and pick up a bushel of **Brady's Oysters** (a shack at water's edge) or take home some great chorizo, kielbasa, or beef jerky, all made on the premises of **Bay City Sausage Company**.

Charter rates vary little from company to company. Some of the **best charters** include Cachalot, (360)268-0323; Deep Sea, (800)562-0151 or (360)268-9300; Westport, (800)562-0157 or (360)268-9120; Islander, (800)322-1740 or (360)268-9166; Washington Charters, (800)562-0173 or (360)268-0900; Salmon Charters, (800)562-0157; Travis, (360)268-9140. (Toll-free numbers are often in operation only during the season.)

Things quiet down until the 3:30pm return of the fleets. You can explore the town during this lull, or head for the expansive beaches—open for driving, jogging, clamming, or picnicking—along the coast from Grayland to Westport. Wetsuited **surfers** can be found year-round hoping to catch their own Big One along the jetty at Westhaven State Park, where there's a new concrete walkway cresting the dunes all the way to the historic Westport Lighthouse.

RESTAURANTS

Constantin's ★★ Constantin "Dino" Kontogonis, who came to Westport in 1987 to get away from Seattle, is a gregarious Greek with a gift for cooking. Dino's place is only a stone's throw from the Westport docks, so there's fresh seafood galore, including salmon, oysters, crab, and squid. Just park alongside the charter boats and follow your nose to a tiny cafe with a big heart. Olive oil, garlic, shallots, onions, and fresh herbs mingle in the saucepan with tomatoes, mushrooms, and wine; linguine comes laced with mizithra cheese, ensuring that the aromas wafting past the plastic grapes are heavenly. A new menu is twice as long and a lot more adventurous than its predecessor and the wine list is one of the most ambitious on the Olympic Peninsula. Locals might complain of high prices, but by city standards they're really quite reasonable. And no one ever leaves hungry. ■ *½ block from the dock; (360) 268-0550; 320 E Dock St, Westport; $$; beer and wine; AE, MC, V; local checks only; lunch, dinner every day (call for winter hours).* &

LODGINGS

The Chateau Westport ★ This is considered the fanciest motel lodging in Westport—though it bears no resemblance to any chateau we know. Prices for the 108 units are moderate, especially in the off season when the beachcombing is the best; indoor pool and hot tub are available. Studio units have fireplaces and can be rented alone (with a queen-size hideabed) or in conjunction with adjoining bedrooms to form a suite. It's not the quietest place, and the continental breakfast is nothing to get excited about, but the ocean views are magnificent; those from the third and fourth floors are best. ■ *W Hancock and S Forest sts; (360)268-9101; 710 Hancock, Westport; PO Box 349, Westport, WA 98595; $$; AE, DC, MC, V; no checks.* &

Glenacres Inn Turn-of-the-century entrepreneuse Minnie Armstrong ran a horse 'n' buggy service from the docks of Westport to her bed and breakfast long before B&Bs became the latest thing in overnight accommodations. The trees are taller now (so you don't have a sense of the ocean) and you probably won't be arriving by carriage, but the place is a gabled gem with lots of lodging alternatives and a hot tub, no less. In addition to the five plush bedrooms there are three simpler "deck" rooms and two cottages with fully stocked kitchens. ■ *1 block north of the stoplight on N Montesano; (360) 268-9391; 222 N Montesano, Westport; PO Box 1246, Westport, WA 98595; $$; MC, V; checks OK.*

COSMOPOLIS

LODGINGS

Cooney Mansion ★★ For many years this 1908 manse housed timber tycoon Neil Cooney, his servants, and his out-of-town guests. There's a very masculine feel to the place (Cooney was a bachelor and a J. Edgar Hoover–style taskmaster who had 1,200 workers under his thumb): spruce wainscoting in the living room, large windows with dark wooden frames, heavy Craftsman furniture throughout. A clubby feel prevails: from the deck on the second floor you can sit and watch golfers on the newly expanded public course next door. Tennis courts are visible as you head up the driveway (they are part of Mill Creek Park, but are available for guests' use). Jim and Judi Lohr are fastidious hosts, offering eight guest rooms and a bounteous "Lumber Baron's Breakfast." ■ *Follow C St to 5th; (360) 533-0602; 1705 5th St, Cosmopolis, WA 98537; $$; AE, DC, MC, V; no checks.*

ABERDEEN/HOQUIAM

With the timber industry in slow decline, these old Siamese-twin lumber towns are in transition, as they have been since the sawmilling and shipping glory days of the early 1900s. The **Grays Harbor Historical Seaport**, east side of Aberdeen, (360) 532-8611, provides tours of a splendid replica of Captain Gray's *Lady Washington*, a 105-foot floating museum. The ship is often on tour to other ports of call, so be sure to call ahead.

Tour **Hoquiam's Castle**, a 20-room mansion built for a prominent lumberman in 1897; 515 Chenault Avenue, Hoquiam, (360) 533-2005. Right next door is the equally splended house his brother built—now the **Lytle House Bed and Breakfast** (see Lodgings).

Polson Park is a fine house by Arthur Loveless, with a rose garden; 1611 Riverside Avenue, Hoquiam, (360) 533-5862.

RESTAURANTS

Parma ★★★ Mario Andretti once said, "The closest thing to heaven is eating my mother's gnocchi." In Aberdeen, the closest thing to heaven is when Pierre Gabelli's mother brings you a plate of his gnocchi. The dimpled potato dumplings melt in your mouth, and the French-Italian chef is always experimenting. One night it's a spicy arrabbiata, the next it's spinach gnocchi expertly sauced with Gorgonzola. The nightly specials are often adventurous and never disappointing: wild boar with polenta; mussels, clams, and saffron with spinach fettuccine. The pasta is housemade and a charcoal grill produces succulent steaks, chops, and sausages. In between courses, Gabelli's pop, a retired electronics engineer, will bring you up to date on Ferrari's wind tunnel tests. Mama, meanwhile, keeps busy baking bread so rich it could be dessert and desserts so rich you'll wish you hadn't eaten all that rigatoni. ■ *On Heron, 1 block west of Broadway; (360)532-3166; 116 W Heron St, Aberdeen; $$; beer and wine; AE, MC, V; checks OK; dinner Tues–Sat.* ᕯ

Billy's Bar and Grill ★ The best little whorehouse in town used to be right across the street from this historic pub, and the walls at Billy's sport some original artwork that recalls Aberdeen's bawdy past. The place is named after the infamous Billy Gohl, who terrorized the Aberdeen waterfront in 1907. Billy shanghaied sailors and robbed loggers, consigning their bodies to the murky Wishkah River through a trapdoor in a saloon only a block away from the present-day Billy's—where you get a square-deal meal (thick burgers and ranch fries) and an honest drink, without much damage to your pocketbook. ■ *Corner of Heron and G; (360)533-7144; 322 E Heron St, Aberdeen; $; full bar; AE, DC, MC, V; local checks only; lunch, dinner every day.* ᕯ

Bridges ★ Sonny Bridges started out with a corner cafe 30 years ago and kept expanding his horizons—both in space and in taste. A recent remodel produced an airy, pastel-hued setting with casual class. The diverse menu contains few surprises, but Sonny owns a piece of the best seafood market in town, and the clams and salmon can't be beat. There's also prime rib that's really prime and pasta that hasn't been overcooked. The busy bar is first-class, with espresso drinks, and Northwest wines and beers. The staff, as always, is extraordinarily professional. ■ *1st and G; (360)532-6563; 112 N G St, Aberdeen; $$; full bar; AE, DC, MC, V; local checks only; lunch, dinner Mon–Sat, dinner Sun.* ᕯ

The Levee Street ★ Though Roy Ann Taylor spent 12 years as a cook at a logging camp, her restaurant has nothing in common with a cookhouse save generous portions of good, real food. We're talking ambience here: plum-colored carpets, soft music, and a great view of tugboats and seabirds. And this is one of the few nonsmoking restaurants in timber country. The extensive and eclectic menu offers everything from the "Raging Bull"—a logger's portion of medium-rare prime rib coated with a port and peppercorn sauce—to fresh salmon, veal Marsala, and bouillabaisse. Great, chewy bread sticks. ■ *7th*

LODGINGS

Lytle House Bed & Breakfast ★ In 1897, when timber baron Robert Lytle built what was to become Hoquiam's architectural landmark, Hoquiam's Castle, his brother Joseph erected a smaller version next door. This has become Lytle House, decorated throughout with the almost requisite Victorian embellishments. (The latest acquisition is a magnificent square grand piano.) The front parlor feels too formal for anyone to hunker down in a big chair for reading, but there are more than enough parlors for all and the eight guest rooms are quite spacious. On the second floor the Windsor Room has a small library, an antique wood stove, and a balcony overlooking the town. Guests share the bathrooms, with huge claw-footed tubs. Breakfasts are excellent, with granola, yogurt, fresh fruit, and omelets. Owners Robert and Dayna Bencala—two young refugees from California—are B&B hosts of the best kind: genuinely hospitable yet unobtrusive. ■ *West on Emerson, right on Garfield, up hill to Chenault; (360)533-2320 or (800)677-2320; 509 Chenault, Hoquiam, WA 98550; $$; MC, V; checks OK.*

MONTESANO

RESTAURANTS

Savory Faire ★★ Savory Faire grew out of Candi Bachtell's popular cooking classes at Montesano's award-winning Community School. Today, marvelous aromas come wafting out of Candi and Randy Bactell's charming place just a block away from the handsome and historic Grays Harbor County Courthouse. Breakfasts feature flawlessly cooked omelets, country-fried potatoes, fresh-baked breads, and wonderful cinnamon rolls. The coffee is as good as you'll find anywhere in Seattle. At lunchtime, try the turkey pesto sandwich or an exceptional French dip. There is now a wine boutique on the premises, as well as specialty coffees, cookbooks, condiments, and kitchenware. ■ *Take Montesano exit off Hwy 12; (360)249-3701; 135 S Main St, Montesano; $; beer and wine; AE, MC, V; checks OK; breakfast, lunch Mon–Sat.*

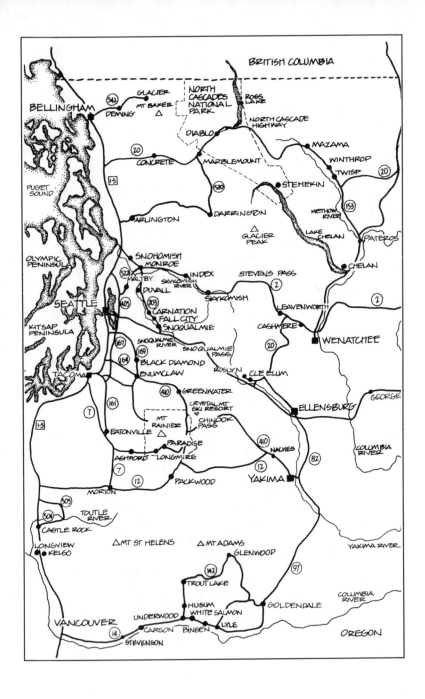

Washington Cascades

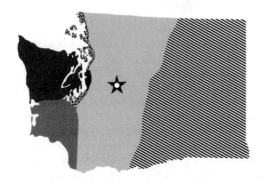

Easterly crossings, starting in the north from Deming to Mount Baker, then to the Methow Valley along the North Cascades Highway. Farther south in the Cascade Loop: eastward along Highway 2 to Cashmere on Route 2, south to Cle Elum, westward again on I-90, then north through dairy country to Duvall. The two Mount Rainier approaches— Maple Valley to Chinook Pass; Eatonville to Ashford —followed by a southward route through the heart of the Cascades, past Mount St. Helens, and a short easterly jog along the Columbia River (including Mount Adams).

DEMING

RESTAURANTS

Deming Restaurant and Lounge ★ In operation since 1922, this is one of the few real steak houses left hereabouts. It's not a fancy place, but everyone (a mix of loggers, suburbanites, and Bellingham city slickers) comes for the steak. You can get a tender, well-aged 6-ounce tenderloin for $9.25, a 16-ouncer for $15.95. The ultimate challenge here: you can have a 72-ounce steak, with a baked potato and spaghetti, for *free*—provided you can eat the whole thing in half an hour. If you can't, it's $44.95. So far, everyone has paid up. ■ *Off Mount Baker Hwy at Deming Rd and 1st St; (360) 592-5282; 5016 Deming Rd, Deming; $$; full bar; MC, V; checks OK; lunch, dinner every day.*

Carol's Coffee Cup Carol's is a local institution: a pleasant little hamburger joint/bakery/cafe, long a favorite with loggers, skiers, and hikers. The hamburgers are fine, but the big cinnamon rolls and homemade pies are best. Be prepared for a long wait on summer weekends and during the peak of the Koma Kulshan (Mount Baker) ski season. ▪ *1½ miles east of Deming at Mt Baker Hwy; (360)592-5641; 5415 Mt Baker Hwy, Deming; $; no alcohol; MC, V; checks OK; breakfast, lunch, dinner every day.* ௹

LODGINGS

The Logs ★ Five log cabins nestled among dense stands of alder and fir at the confluence of the Nooksack River and Canyon Creek comprise this rustic retreat. Cabins are comfortable, not luxurious: they sleep up to 10 people in bunk-bedded rooms and on pull-out couches. The centerpoint of each cabin is the large fireplace (built from river cobbles and slabs of Nooksack stone), stocked with firewood. Each cabin has a fully equipped kitchen and a charcoal grill. There's a pool and a volleyball court for summer. A great place to bring the kids and the family dog. ▪ *30 miles east of Bellingham on Mt Baker Hwy; (360)599-2711; 9002 Mount Baker Hwy, Deming, WA 98244; $$; no credit cards; checks OK.*

▼

▲

GLACIER

RESTAURANTS

Innisfree ★★ Discriminating folks are lured from Seattle and Vancouver to Fred and Lynn Berman's Innisfree. The Bermans are organic farmers, and they opened the restaurant as a reliable outlet for their produce (you'll find fresh berries and lightly steamed vegetables tossed in creative combinations). Over the years they've honed their cooking skills to the point of excellence at this cabin-in-the-woods experience. The menu is simple but intriguing, ever-changing Northwest eclectic: Ellensburg lamb, Alaskan scallops, or halibut. The finishers, poached pears with mascarpone cream or chocolate hazelnut torte, are exceptionally flavorful. You can sit up front, but it's better to wait for a seat in the light and airy dining room. ▪ *31 miles east of Bellingham on Mt Baker Hwy; (360)599-2373; 9393 Mt Baker Hwy, Glacier; $$; beer and wine; AE, MC, V; checks OK; dinner Thurs–Tues (summer) Thurs–Sun (winter).*

Milano's Market and Deli ★ Popular with locals and carbo-loading hikers and skiers alike, this tiny, clean restaurant is really three: a deli (with meats and sandwiches), a casual Italian restaurant (with hearty pastas and a well-priced wine selection), and a nice place for dessert and coffee. The pasta is made fresh daily and stars in two different lasagnes, a filling chicken Gorgonzola, or a slew of wonderful raviolis. ▪ *Mt Baker Hwy*

in Glacier; (360)599-2863; 9990 Mt Baker Hwy, Glacier; $$;
beer and wine; MC, V; checks OK; lunch, dinner every day,
breakfast Sat and Sun.

MOUNT BAKER

Mount Baker Ski Area, 56 miles east of Bellingham, has
gained quite a reputation with snowboarders. It's open mid-
November through April (the longest season in the state).
The mountain never lacks for snow, and runs are predomi-
nantly intermediate, with bowls, meadows, and trails. Call
(360)734-6771.

Hiking in the area is extensive and beautiful, especially in
the late summer when the foliage is turning, the wild blueber-
ries are ripe, and the days are hot and dry. The end of the road
(which, in winter, doubles as the Mount Baker Ski Resort) is
a jump-off point for some easy day hikes and spectacular views
of both Mount Baker and the most photographed mountain in
the world, the geographically eccentric **Mount Shuksan.**
For trail and weather conditions call the Glacier Public Service
Center, (360)599-2714.

MARBLEMOUNT

Hundreds of bald eagles perch along the Skagit River from De-
cember through March. The best area to view these scav-
engers is along Route 20 between Rockport and Marblemount
(bring your binoculars). You'll be able to spy a number from
the road; however, the best way to view them is from the river;
call **Downstream River Runners,** (206)483-0335; **Northern
Wilderness River Riders,** (206)448-RAFT; or **Orion Expe-
ditions,** (206)547-6715. The adventuresome may want to canoe
downriver from Marblemount to Rockport (an easy 8 miles);
the river appears tame, but can be deceptively swift.

RESTAURANTS

Buffalo Run This serve-yourself restaurant makes for a nour-
ishing stop along the North Cascades Highway. Homemade
breads and organically grown vegetables become big sand-
wiches; soups, salads, and quiches round out the menu (but
never anything deep-fried). For dessert, try a slice of fresh
berry pie. Northwest microbreweries and vintners are well rep-
resented. The feeling is rustic and faintly countercultural
(with a sometimes crabby waitstaff). A pleasant, tree-ringed
garden outside. ▪ *In middle of town on Hwy 20; (360)873-
2461; 5860 Hwy 20, Marblemount; $; beer and wine; AE,
DC, MC, V; local checks only; breakfast, lunch, dinner every
day May to Sept; (closed Nov to Mar; open part-time Apr
and Oct).*

DIABLO

Since the only road access to Ross Lake is south from Hope, BC, the best way to get to the southern end of the lake—save by a 3½-mile hike—is on the Seattle City Light tugboat from Diablo. Here Seattle City Light built an outpost for crews constructing and servicing the dams on the river. The tugboat leaves twice daily (8:30am and 3pm), runs from mid-June through the end of October, and the ride costs $2.50; (360)386-4393.

Worth visiting are the dams themselves, built by a visionary engineer named James Delmage Ross. **Skagit Tours** offers 4-hour journeys through the Skagit Project, including an informative slide presentation, a ride up an antique incline railway to Diablo Dam, then a boat ride along the gorge of the Skagit to Ross Dam, a construction of daring engineering in its day. Afterward there is a lavish chicken dinner back in Diablo. There are also 90-minute mini-tours available. Six miles down the road in Newhalem are inspirational walks to the grave of Ross and to Ladder Creek Falls, with plantings gathered from around the world. Tours are arranged through Seattle City Light, 1015 Third Avenue, Seattle, WA 98104, (360)684-3030; summer only; reserve well in advance.

MAZAMA

With a sociable espresso counter, products from Tim's chips to Orvis fishing rods, a clever goat logo on everything from water bottles to T-shirts, and a picnic area (complete with grillmeister in the summer), **Mazama Country Store**, the only store in town, has become a favorite hangout for valley locals and travelers alike; (509)996-2855.

LODGINGS

Mazama Country Inn ★★ With a view of the North Cascades from nearly every window, this spacious 6,000-square-foot lodge makes a splendid year-round destination (especially for horseback riders and cross-country skiers), with 14 good-size rooms of wooden construction with cedar beams. Some of the guest rooms (all fairly standard) have air conditioning, nice on hot summer Eastern Washington nights. Each room has a private bath, thick comforters on the beds, and futonlike pads that can be rolled out for extra guests. The four rooms behind the sauna have individual decks, two with views of Goat Peak and two looking out into the woods. Winter packages include three family-style meals, but summers are à la carte (salmon to prime rib to spaghetti). Make a reservation for meals. Four cabins with kitchen and bath are available for families or groups of up to 14. ■ *14 miles west of Winthrop just off Hwy 20 in Mazama; (509)996-2681 or (800)843-7951; HRC 74*

Box 89, Mazama, WA 98833; $$; beer and wine; MC, V; checks OK; breakfast, lunch, dinner every day.

Early Winters Cabins [*unrated*] What were once six dark, rustic cabins on Early Winters Creek are now six classy country cabins with handsome river-rock fireplaces, all oriented toward the river and touched with originality such as locally crafted wrought-iron fixtures and artwork. It's all just the beginning of something more grand (a lodge is scheduled to open in early 1996 a little farther south on the property). ■ *15 miles west of Winthrop just off Hwy 20 in Mazama; (509) 996-2355; PO Box 505, Winthrop, WA 98862; $$; MC, V; checks OK.*

WINTHROP

Stroll through this Western-motif town and stop in at the **Shafer Museum**, housed in pioneer Guy Waring's 1897 log cabin on the hill behind the main street. Exhibits tell of the area's early history and include old cars, a stagecoach, and horse-drawn vehicles. It is said that Waring's Harvard classmate Owen Wister came to visit in the 1880s and found some of the material for *The Virginian* here.

The valley offers fine whitewater rafting, spectacular hiking in the North Cascades, horseback riding, fishing, and cross-country or helicopter skiing (call Methow Valley Central Reservations for more information; see below). An excellent blues festival in the summer brings in such talents as John Mayall and the Bluesbreakers and Mick Taylor (see Calendar). And after you've had a big day outside, quaff a beer at the Winthrop Brew Pub, (509) 996-3174, in an old schoolhouse in downtown Westernville, a favorite local hangout.

Methow Valley Central Reservations is a booking service for the whole valley—Mazama to Pateros—as well as a good source of information on things to see and do and on current ski conditions. Write PO Box 505, Winthrop, WA 98862, or call (800) 422-3048 or (509) 996-2148.

The Methow Valley Touring Association keeps the valley's excellent cross-country ski trails groomed and available to visitors. Write to the association at PO Box 327, Winthrop, WA, 98862, or phone Central Reservations for conditions.

Hut-to-Hut Skiing offers miles of cross-country ski trails connecting with three spartan huts in the Rendezvous Hills. Each hut bunks up to eight people and comes equipped with a wood stove and a propane cookstove. Open for day skiers—a warm, dry lunch stop. For Rendezvous Huts information, call the Central Reservations office listed above.

RESTAURANTS

Duck Brand Cantina, Bakery, and Hotel Built to replicate a frontier-style hotel, Duck Brand is a Winthrop standby for good, filling meals at decent prices: bulging burritos to fettuccine to sprout-laden sandwiches on whole-grain breads. The American-style breakfasts feature wonderful cheesy Spanish potatoes and billowing omelets. The in-house bakery produces delicious baked goods from biscotti to giant cinnamon rolls to 3-inch-thick berry pie. When you're not in the mood for painfully slow service, just take the sweets to go. Upstairs, the Duck Brand Hotel has six sparsely furnished rooms, priced right. ■ *On the main street; (509) 996-2192; 248 Riverside Ave, Winthrop; $; beer and wine; AE, MC, V; local checks only; breakfast, lunch, dinner every day.*

LODGINGS

Sun Mountain Lodge ★★★ The location has always been dramatic, set on a hill high above the pristine Methow Valley and backed by the North Cascades. Now the massive timber-and-stone resort is equally impressive (thanks to the $20 million remodel). Ask for one of the rooms in the 28 Gardner unit. They are dressed in natural colors, from the hand-painted bedspreads to the bent-willow headboards. Each new room has a gas fireplace (only those in the suites burn wood) and a view of the spectacular Methow Valley. Rooms in the main lodge are more standard. In addition, there are 13 spankingly new cabins available just down the hill at Patterson Lake. In winter, over 50 miles of well-groomed cross-country trails make this a haven for Nordic skiers (with 150 miles available throughout the valley). Expert instructors are available for skiers of any level. Close by are a heated pool (closed in the winter), two hot tubs, and tennis courts. In summer there are also guided nature hikes through the wilderness, brisk breakfast trail rides, and outfitter pack trips as well. The restaurant now offers a great table to every guest, whether it's a warm spot by the massive stone fireplace or a window table with a sweeping view of the valley. The best choices are those that don't challenge the kitchen. The wine list is well-chosen. ■ *9 miles southwest of Winthrop on Patterson Lake Rd; (509) 996-2211; PO Box 1000, Winthrop, WA 98862; $$$; full bar; AE, MC, V; checks OK; breakfast, lunch, dinner every day.*

WolfRidge Resort ★ The resort (12 condo-style units in three log buildings) sits both literally and metaphorically somewhere between the home-style Mazama Country Inn and the more showy Sun Mountain Lodge. The lodgings are tastefully, if simply, furnished and provide families and small groups with a full kitchen in each unit. The design allows the flexibility of being able to rent an entire unit (complete with kitchen) or a suite or just a single room. Whatever suits your needs. There's one separate cabin for groups up to six. The 50-acre setting includes a pool, hot tub, playground, and barbecue area (and in the winter a warming hut for skiers). Horseback riders are referred to the local outfitters. ■ *5 miles northwest of Winthrop on Wolf Creek Rd; (509) 996-2828; Wolf Creek Rd, Rt 2, Box 655, Winthrop, WA 98862; $$; MC, V; checks OK.* ⅋

TWISP

RESTAURANTS

The Queen of Tarts and Confluence Gallery ★ This cafe with adjoining gallery makes for a new twist in Twisp, a town dominated by hardware and feed stores. The breakfast-and-lunch cafe features delicious homemade soups such as curried lentil served with a crusty chunk of bread, and fresh salads and sandwiches, as well as the specialty, quiche tarts (try tomato, mushroom, and artichoke heart or crab and shrimp). The gallery showcases works of local and regional artists. ■ *On the main street; (509) 997-1335; 104 Glover St, Twisp; $; no alcohol; no credit cards; checks OK; breakfast, lunch Mon–Fri, Sat from May to Oct.*

METHOW

RESTAURANTS

Cafe Bienville ★ Jim and Louise Swickard might be newcomers to the area, but they're not newcomers to the restaurant scene. You might recognize some of the dishes (blackened catfish, gumbo, or bouillabaisse) from their New Orleans Kitchens in Wenatchee or South Lake Tahoe. You can find select Creole, Cajun, or classic French eats on the menu, which has more entrees than the restaurant has tables. There's lots of flavor here, and it's not all in the food. Jim Swickard loves to pour you a glass of one of his great wines. ■ *Can't miss it; (509) 923-2228; Hwy 20, Methow; $; beer and wine; no credit cards; checks OK; dinner Wed–Sat.*

PATEROS

LODGINGS

Amy's Manor ★★ Built in 1928, the enchanting manor is dramatically situated at the foot of the Cascades overlooking the Methow River, and the rooms are country-quaint, with patchwork quilts tossed over rocking chairs and comfortable beds. The 170-acre estate includes a small farm with chickens and rabbits. When you combine a harvest from their organic garden with a former Seattle chef, the table's bounty, be it breakfast or dinner, never disappoints. Your best bet for miles. ■ *5 miles north of Pateros on Hwy 153; (509) 923-2334; PO Box 411, Pateros, WA 98846; $$; MC, V; checks OK.*

PLAIN

LODGINGS

Natapoc Lodging ★★ For any city dweller who has ever dreamed of a weekend home on the Wenatchee River, Natapoc is the next best thing. Each log cabin claims one to five piney acres and at least 200 feet of riverfront. All are stocked with everything from a VCR to a microwave oven. And they come in all sizes from an utterly romantic twosome to a rambling twentysomething. Lots of outdoorsy things to do, from fly-fishing to cross-country skiing, but frankly, all we really want to do is soak in the cabin's hot tub and make angels in the snow. ■ *4 miles from Lake Wenatchee on Hwy 209; (509) 763-3313 or (800) 775-3313; 12338 Bretz Rd, Leavenworth, WA 98826; $$$; AE, MC, V; checks OK.*

LEAVENWORTH

A railroad-yard-and-sawmill town that lost its industry, Leavenworth, with its stunning alpine setting in the Cascade Range, decided years ago to recast itself as a Bavarian-style town with tourism as its primary industry. The architecture in the city center features some excellent craftsmanship in the Bavarian mode. Popular festivals are the Autumn Leaf Festival the last weekend in September and the first weekend in October, the Christmas Lighting Festival the first two Saturdays in December, and Maifest the second weekend in May.

Shopping. We recommend browsers head to the Gingerbread Factory (828 Commercial Street) for authentic decorated gingerbread cookies and a delightful village of gingerbread houses; Images and Sounds (Ninth and Commercial) for distinctly non-Bavarian posters, prints, and notecards; the Black Swan and Ugly Duckling (827 Front Street) for boutique fashions and children's wear; Village Books (215 Ninth Street) for an excellent collection of books about the Northwest, books by Northwest authors, and cookbooks; the Wood Shop (719 Front Street) for colorful wooden children's puzzles and Christmas tree ornaments; Die Musik Box (837 Front Street) for a dazzling (and sometimes rather noisy) array of music boxes; the Alpen Haus's (downstairs at 807 Front Street) for a fascinating collection of dollhouse furniture and miniatures; and Country Things (221 Eighth Street) for folk art, antiques, furniture, tinware, and linens.

Oberland Bakery and Cafe relies largely on whole-grain breads, but also does a great raspberry Danish. The restaurant is spare, but they also serve hearty soups and sandwiches on their substantial breads (703 Front Street, (509) 548-7216). Other attractions include **Homefires Bakery**, where visitors can see the German-style wood-fired oven (the nine-grain

▼

Plain

▲

bread is the thing to get, but don't pass up the dark German rye bread) and during fair weather can sit at the picnic table on the lawn and have cinnamon rolls and coffee (outside of town, 13013 Bayne Road, off Icicle Road). There's also the new **Leavenworth Brewery** (636 Front Street, (509) 548-4545), which has six or seven beers made on the premises on tap (the types of beers rotate with the season), and offers daily tours of the small brewery itself.

Outdoor activities include river rafting on the Wenatchee; fishing and hiking at Icicle Creek; touring the fish hatchery on Icicle Creek (12790 Fish Hatchery Road, off Icicle Road, (509) 548-7641) to watch the chinook salmon run (June and July) and spawn (August and September); golfing at the scenic 18-hole Leavenworth Golf Club, (509) 548-7267; downhill skiing at Stevens Pass, (360) 973-2441, or Mission Ridge, (509) 663-6543; fabulous cross-country skiing around the area, at the golf course, on Icicle Road just past the fish hatchery, or at the Leavenworth Nordic Center, (509) 548-7864; horseback riding at Eagle Creek Ranch, (509) 548-7798; sleigh rides behind Belgian draft horses at Red-Tail Canyon Farm, (509) 548-4512; walking along the river on a new city center trail system which leads via wheelchair-accessible ramps to Blackbird Island; mountain biking with rentals available at Icicle Bicycle at the Leavenworth Nordic Center, (509) 548-7864; and rock climbing in **Peshastin Pinnacles State Park**, just 10 miles east of Leavenworth (no camping, just climbing).

Now run by Don and Chris Hanson and Mark and Linda Wells, **Scottish Lakes Back Country Cabins**, 8 miles into the backcountry west of Leavenworth, is a cluster of primitive plywood cabins at the edge of one of the nation's finest wilderness areas. You can ski the 8 miles or be carted up in a heated 12-seat snow-cat and ski the 3,800-foot descent home; High Country Adventures, PO Box 2023, Snohomish, WA 98291-2023, (800) 909-9916, by reservation only.

RESTAURANTS

Edel Haus Inn ★ Edel Haus got its start as a bed and breakfast; however, today it's a quiet, pleasant restaurant with an international menu. The caesar salad remains true to the original recipe. The menu changes about once a month, and its biggest fault is that it tries to do too much. The Cajun sampler of blackened steaks, shrimp, and yellowfin tuna is savory and delicious; the chicken piccata, though tasty, could benefit from a lighter sauce. Upstairs, there are several pretty guest rooms, and next door there's a cottage suite with a Jacuzzi and gas fireplace. The Edel Haus Inn doesn't serve breakfast to its overnight guests, but does offer them a 50 percent discount on the other meals. ■ *On 9th between Commercial and the river; (509) 548-4412; 320 9th St, Leavenworth, WA 98826; $$;*

beer and wine; MC, V; local checks only; dinner every day (Wed–Sun from Jan–Apr), lunch Sat and Sun only (brunch Sat and Sun in winter).

Reiner's Gasthaus For the quintessential Bavarian culinary experience in Leavenworth, Reiner's is the place. The smoked Bavarian-style farmer's sausage with sauerkraut and German rye bread is a safe selection for the uninitiated. More adventuresome eaters can try the homemade dumplings (boiled liver, egg, and bread) served with melted cheese for lunch; or the schnitzel topped with paprika sauce or the Hungarian goulash for dinner. Seating is European-style (which means tables are sometimes shared); service is prompt and knowledgeable. There's a wide selection of imported wines and beers. Have dessert somewhere else. ■ *Across from the gazebo; (509)548-5111; 829 Front St, Leavenworth; $; beer and wine; MC, V; local checks only; lunch, dinner every day; (winter hours vary).*

LODGINGS

All Seasons River Inn ★★ Each of the six guest rooms in this outstanding inn takes advantage of the Wenatchee River view with a private deck or patio and an indoor seating area in front of sliding glass doors. Rooms are furnished with unusual antiques and have spacious, gleaming private baths and Jacuzzis. A hearty, filling breakfast is served family-style at 8:30am. Mountain bikes are available, and the owners have a wealth of knowledge about the area. ■ *1 mile off Hwy 2 on Icicle Rd; (509)548-1425 or (800)254-0555; 8751 Icicle Rd, Leavenworth; PO Box 788, Leavenworth, WA 98826; $$$; MC, V; checks OK.*

Run of the River ★★ Built on the bank of the Icicle River, this log-construction bed and breakfast boasts such solitude and comfort that you may want to spend the entire day on the deck, reading or watching the wildlife in the refuge across the river with the provided binoculars. Hosts Monty and Karen Turner run Leavenworth's finest B&B. There are six rooms, each with hand-hewn log bed, private bath, TV (cable), deck, and complimentary robes. Best rooms face the river. The Aspens Room, warmed by a wood stove, has perhaps the best river view, but the Jacuzzi in the Pinnacles Suite is a nice attribute. Hearty breakfasts emphasize the seasonal discoveries from a local organic farmer and the Turners' own herb garden. There's a Jacuzzi on the deck near the river, and mountain bikes are available for off-road explorations (ask the Turners for where-to-go tips). The in-room massage gives a new meaning to R & R at the R of the R. ■ *1 mile east of Hwy 2; (509)548-7171 or (800)288-6491; 9308 E Leavenworth Rd, Leavenworth; PO Box 285, Leavenworth, WA 98826; $$; AE, MC, V; checks OK.*

Haus Lorelei Inn ★ Here's a rarity: a bed and breakfast that not only welcomes kids but is run by several (and their mom). The 2-acre site, surrounded by towering pines and flanking the Wenatchee River, is only two blocks from Leavenworth's main street. Elisabeth Saunders and her children offer eight bedrooms furnished in comfortable European tradition. Each of the rooms affords gorgeous views of the Cascades; at night you can hear the river rushing over the boulders. Guests may use the private tennis court. There's a hot tub overlooking the river, and a sandy swimming beach isn't far. ■ *2 blocks off Commercial on Division; (509) 548-5726; 347 Division St, Leavenworth, WA 98826; $$; no credit cards; checks OK.*

Haus Rohrbach Pension ★ It's a true European-style pension, with alpine architecture, gracious hosts, and breakfast included. The lodge is tucked into the base of Tumwater Mountain, so it has a nearly Bavarian view over the valley farmland back toward town and the snow-clad mountains. Most rooms open onto a flower-decked balcony facing the majestic vista. The rooms on the uppermost floor facing the valley have the most light and appeal, unless you want to spring for one of the very appealing suites, which offer king-size beds, whirlpool tubs, gas fireplaces, and private decks. Bring the kids—there's a swimming pool, and a sled hill (the suites, however, are reserved for adults and children over 12). ■ *About ½ mile off Ski Hill Dr; (509) 548-7024; 12882 Ranger Rd, Leavenworth, WA 98826; $$; AE, MC, V; checks OK.*

Mountain Home Lodge ★ Although you can drive to this lodge in the summer (over 3 miles of rough dirt road), in the winter a heated snow-cat picks you up from the parking lot at the bottom of Mountain Home Road. Miles of tracked cross-country ski trails leave from the back door; you can snowshoe and sled, and there's a 1,700-foot toboggan run. Complimentary cross-country ski equipment loaners are available at the lodge. There's a Jacuzzi on the deck looking out to a broad meadow and the mountains across the valley. Summer activities include hiking, horseshoe pitching, badminton, swimming, and tennis. And that's a good thing, because there aren't many places to gather when the weather's not cooperating. The nine rooms themselves are very plain (almost motelish), and noise travels from bedroom to bedroom. No kids. Simple meals are included in the price during the winter. ■ *Mountain Home Rd off E Leavenworth Rd and Hwy 2; (509) 548-7077 or (800) 414-2378; 8201-9 Mountain Home Rd, Leavenworth; PO Box 687, Leavenworth, WA 98826; $$$; MC, V; checks OK.*

Mrs. Anderson's Lodging House ★ Although it originally opened in 1903 as a boardinghouse for sawmill workers, this nine-room inn right in the center of Leavenworth has charm to spare and very friendly operators. Rooms are minimally, crisply

▼

▲

furnished, boardinghouse-style—but sparkling clean. It's a bargain. (All prices include breakfast of muffins, cereal, juice, tea, and coffee.) We fancy the room upstairs with the deck facing town, or the room with the splendid view of the North Cascades. ■ *Just off the center of town at Commercial St; (509)548-6173 or (800)253-8990; 917 Commercial St, Leavenworth, WA 98826; $$; AE, MC, V; checks OK.*

River Chalet ★ An ideal vacation spot for groups of couples, this contemporary guest house on the east side of Leavenworth gives the visitor a real feel for the Northwest. It's right on the Wenatchee River, and large windows look out toward the mountains. Four bedrooms sleep 10 comfortably (but slumber parties of 22 sleeping-baggers have occurred); wood stoves keep you warm. Outside there's a hot tub. A large kitchen makes gourmet collaborations a pleasure. Cost is $200 for four, $20 for each additional person. Catering can be arranged on request. ■ *4 miles west of Leavenworth off Hwy 2; (509)663-7676; 1131 Monroe St, Wenatchee, WA 98801; $$$; no credit cards; checks OK.*

Enzian Motor Inn This is the best hotel/motel place in town (and the price includes your breakfast). Built by former contractor Bob Johnson and his son, Rob, it is now owned and operated by Rob and his wife, Nancy. The Johnsons were meticulous about detail throughout. Stair rails and ceiling beams are hand-carved by a true Bavarian woodworker. The suites offer in-room spas and fireplaces; even the standard rooms are tasteful and a cut above most "motor inns." During the summer Rob plays the alpenhorn on the balcony outside the dining room. ■ *On the north side of Hwy 2 in the center of town; (509)548-5269 or (800)223-8511; 590 Hwy 2, Leavenworth, WA 98826; $$; AE, DC, MC, V; checks OK.* &

Sleeping Lady [*unrated*] At press time, this former CCC camp from the 1930s will have been transformed into what could be the Northwest's foremost conference facility. Designed to be extremely efficient, Harriet Bullitt's retreat is built with an acute awareness of nature, using nontoxic materials and wood from the original cabins for many of the board-and-batten clusters. The original fieldstone chapel is now a 200-seat performing arts theater; those looking for more solitude will gravitate toward the library building. Although conferences will have first dibs on the place, there will be some flexibility for other guests on a space-available basis, especially during concerts performed by the Kairos Quartet. ■ *2½ miles south of Leavenworth on Icicle Creek Rd; (509)548-6344; Icicle Creek Rd, Leavenworth; PO Box 1060, Leavenworth, WA 98826; $$; MC, V; checks OK.* &

If you're not in a Bavarian mood, this little orchard town gives cross-mountain travelers an alternative to stopping in Leavenworth. The main street has put up Western storefronts; the town's bordered by river and railroad.

Chelan County Historical Society and Pioneer Village (600 Cottage Avenue, (509)782-3230) has an extensive collection of Indian artifacts and archaeological material; the adjoining pioneer village puts 19 old buildings, carefully restored and equipped, into a nostalgic grouping.

Aplets and cotlets, confections made with local fruit and walnuts from an old Armenian recipe, have been produced in Cashmere for decades. You can tour the plant at Liberty Orchards and (of course) consume a few samples (117 Mission Street, (509)782-2191).

RESTAURANTS

The Pewter Pot Here you can get Early American food such as apple country chicken topped with owner Kristi Biornstad's own apple cider sauce, Plymouth turkey dinner, and New England boiled dinner. Desserts are tasty. The restaurant, short on atmosphere, has been prettied with lace curtain dividers which help soften the lone room. Biornstad works hard to serve dishes that reflect the area, using local ingredients. Try one of the daily specials. But if you want dinner, arrive early; the place closes promptly at 8pm even on Saturdays. ▪ *Downtown Cashmere in the business district; (509)782-2036; 124 Cottage Ave, Cashmere; $$; beer and wine; MC, V; checks OK; lunch, dinner Tues–Sat.* &

▼

Cashmere

Lodgings

▲

LODGINGS

Cashmere Country Inn ★★ In the middle of Aplet-and-Cotlet country, consummate innkeepers Patti and Dale Swanson have created a first-class inn. The Swansons are energetic but never intrusive, full of enthusiasm about the area, and genuinely concerned for the well-being of their guests; the farmhouse and its gardens are fitted out with a keen eye for aesthetics. The five guest rooms are a bit smaller than what you might expect for a place of such ambitions, but we'll trade in extra dimension for such attention to details any day (a lit fire in the fireplace, complimentary Saturday night dessert). A fifth room, with French doors opening to the swimming pool and hot tub area, is also available. Breakfasts are an accomplished cook's delight: pineapple with fresh mint sauce or eggs Florentine with country inn potatoes and fresh raspberry muffins. Patti will also do a lovely candlelit five-course dinner with advance notice (by the pool if you'd like). Take advantage of this place any time of the year: in summer for poolside lounging, in fall for apple picking (and fresh cider). ▪ *Off Hwy 2, follow Division to Pioneer;*

(509)782-4212 or (800)291-9144; 5801 Pioneer Dr, Cashmere, WA 98815; $$; AE, MC, V; checks OK.

THORP

LODGINGS

Circle H Holiday Ranch ★★ Sweeping views of the Kittitas Valley and the Cascade foothills and a small herd of horses are the big draws to the Circle H, located an easy hour and a half from Seattle. The sprawling, modern ranch house was bought out of bankruptcy from an agriculture baron who hit hard times; Betsy Ogden converted the bunkhouses into two-room suites, decorated with the overflow from her collection of Westernalia. Each sleeps four and contains a kitchenette and bath; books, puzzles, and playing cards fill the shelves, but no phones or TVs (there's a big-screen TV in the day room). Meals, included in the price of your stay, are served family-style (breakfast only in winter).

The corral supports a small menagerie, from rabbits to burros. Oliver, the ranch collie, playfully herds guests around the landscaped grounds. The Ogdens welcome young hands to help with ranch chores, while others opt for a trail ride on one of the horses. The 100,000-acre L.T. Murray Wildlife Area backs up to the ranch and is prime for hiking, biking, and riding (bring your own horse, if you like). The nearby Yakima River provides quality fly-fishing and lazy-day river rafting. ■ *Exit 101 off I-90; (509)964-2000; 810 Watt Canyon Rd, Thorp, WA 98946; $$$; MC, V; checks OK.*

CLE ELUM

Easy access brings travelers from the freeway to Cle Elum, a former coal-mining town now undergoing a modest rediscovery.

Cle Elum Bakery is a longtime local institution, doing as much business these days with travelers as with locals. From one of the last brick-hearth ovens in the Northwest come delicious torchetti, cinnamon rolls, and great old-fashioned cake doughnuts. Closed Sundays. First and Peoh, (509)674-2233.

Cle Elum Historical Telephone Museum. Open Memorial Day to Labor Day only, this museum incorporates the area's original phone system, which was operating well into the 1960s; First and Wright, (509)674-5702.

RESTAURANTS

Mama Vallone's Steak House & Inn ★ Talk to the regulars and they'll tell you about the warm welcomes, great steaks, and good homemade pasta at Mama Vallone's. One of the biggest deals is bagna cauda, a "hot bath" of garlic, anchovy, olive oil, and butter into which you dip strips of steak, chicken breast, vegetables, or your favorite seafood. Another favorite is the Sicilian-spiced steak slices tossed with homemade fettuccine. Wines are okay; service is exceptional. Upstairs, two bedrooms with private baths and antique reproductions. ▪ *On the main drag at the west end of town; (509)674-5174; 302 W 1st St, Cle Elum, WA 98922; $$; full bar; AE, DC, MC, V; checks OK; dinner Weds–Sun.*

LODGINGS

Hidden Valley Guest Ranch ★ A short hour from Seattle is the state's oldest dude ranch. Bruce and Kim Coe have brought a little pride of ownership back to this pastoral 700 acres. The 13 cabins are still quite rustic and thin of wall (the ones with the fireplaces are the best in the winter), but miles of wildflower-lined trails, horseback riding, nearby trout fishing, a pool, a hot tub, and splendid cross-country skiing terrain make up for the basic accommodations. All meals are taken in the cookhouse, a dining room serving country-style buffets (open to the public by reservation). Here you'll also find treats such as cookies and lemonade. On Wednesday and Sunday mornings they load up the chuck wagon with blueberry pancakes, muffins, and wrangler-style coffee for a hearty breakfast out in the fields (don't forget the bug repellent). ▪ *Off SR 970 at milepost 8, Hidden Valley Rd; (509)857-2322; 3942 Hidden Valley Rd, Cle Elum, WA 98922; $$; MC, V; checks OK.*

The Moore House ★ This bed and breakfast was originally built in 1913 to house employees of the Chicago, Milwaukee, St. Paul & Pacific Railroad. Now on the National Register of Historic Places, the bunkhouse with 10 guest rooms and a honeymoon suite is light, airy, and pleasantly furnished with reproduction antiques. Railroad memorabilia—vintage photographs, model trains, schedules, and other artifacts—are displayed in the hallways and the public rooms. Two cabooses in the side yard are fully equipped with baths, fridges, queen-size beds, and private sun decks. Unfortunately, the current owners aren't the railroad buffs the former owners aimed to be. There's an outdoor hot tub that the proprietors will rev up for your use. ▪ *Adjacent to Iron Horse State Park Trail at 526 Marie St; (509)674-5939 or (800)22-TWAIN; 526 Marie St, South Cle Elum; PO Box 629, South Cle Elum, WA 98943; $$; AE, MC, V; checks OK.*

ROSLYN

Until the TV series "Northern Exposure" introduced Roslyn to the nation (and called it Cicely), it was just a sleepy reminder of its rough-and-tough days as a thriving coal-mining town. Today, people come from all over the world in search of the fictitious Cicely, Alaska. Modest turn-of-the-century homes have become weekend places for city folk, and the former mortuary is now a video store and movie theater, but the main intersection still offers a cross-section of the town's character: the historic Northwestern Improvement Company building (which once housed the company store) occupies one corner, while the old brick bank across the way still operates behind the original brass bars and oak counters. It will be interesting to watch what happens to this town now that the series is over.

"Northern Exposure" fans will recognize the old stone tavern, inexplicably called **The Brick**, which has a water-fed brass spittoon running the length of the bar; (509)649-2643. Down the road, behind the town's junkyard, you'll find **Carek's Market**, one of the state's better purveyors of fine meats and sausages. Notable are the Polish sausage, the pepperoni, and the jerky; 4 South A Street, (509) 649-2930.

RESTAURANTS

Roslyn Cafe ★ The Roslyn Cafe remains the kind of funky eatery that every picturesque, slightly chic town like Roslyn should have. It's an old building with high ceilings, a short bar that is now a counter, neon in the window, hard chairs, a jukebox with original 78s—full of a sense of different types belonging. Dinners try to be a bit fancier—grilled halibut with dill sauce, Chinese pepper steak. But it's best at lunch, when you can get really good burgers, a fine corn chowder, or a super Philadelphia steak sandwich. Breakfast is also worth the side trip. ■ *2nd and Pennsylvania; (509)649-2763; 28 Pennsylvania Ave, Roslyn; $; beer and wine; MC, V; local checks only; breakfast and lunch every day, dinner Wed–Sun (winter hours vary).*

Roslyn

Village Pizza ★ You've found the local hangout, run by a couple of real characters, Nan and Darrel Harris, a mother/daughter team from San Francisco. Their urban literary passions (they'll have copies of the *New York Review of Books* and *Architectural Digest* arrayed on the tables) are well in evidence. This is good pizza too, some (like the pungent fresh garlic pizza) are *molto delizioso*. Everyone is here—gangs of wild children with their bicycles piled outside, longhairs, local ranchers, yuppies—peacefully coexisting. ■ *1st and Pennsylvania; (509)649-2992; 105 Pennsylvania Ave, Roslyn; $; beer and wine; no credit cards; checks OK; dinner every day.*

SNOQUALMIE

This lovely country, where the dairyland folds into the mountains, was once best known for its falls. Today it's familiar to most as the setting for "Twin Peaks." The series is long since over, but the town's diner still serves Twin Peaks pie, and Peakers can still purchase a T-shirt almost anywhere (even at the bank). The 268-foot **Snoqualmie Falls** just up the road is, as it has always been, a thundering spectacle. There is an observation deck; better is to take a picnic down the 1-mile trail to the base of the falls.

Puget Sound Railway runs a scenic tour up to Snoqualmie Falls gorge most Saturdays and Sundays from April through October. There's also a good railroad museum. Call Snoqualmie Depot for schedule; (206)746-4025.

The **Snoqualmie Winery**, under the ownership of Stimson Lane, is a splendid stop on the way through the Cascades, with tours, tastings, and a marvelous view; 1000 Winery Road, (206)888-4000.

Snoqualmie Pass. The four ski areas—Alpental, Snoqualmie, Ski Acres, and Hyak, (206)434-6161—are all under the same ownership, and offer the closest downhill and cross-country skiing for Seattle buffs (with a free shuttle that runs between the areas on weekends). Alpental is the most challenging; Snoqualmie (with one of the largest ski schools in the country) has excellent instruction for beginners through racers; Ski Acres has some challenging bump runs; and the smallest of the four, Hyak, is a favored spot for downhill telemark skiers, with lighted, groomed cross-country tracks and many miles of trails. In summer, the relatively low-lying transmountain route is a good starting point for many hikes.

LODGINGS

The Salish Lodge ★★★ The falls may be the initial draw. But since you really can't see much of them from many of the rooms, it's a good thing the owners have rebuilt the lodge with rooms that are as much a selling point as the falls themselves. Each room is designed in a tempered country motif: light, clean-lined wooden furnishings, pillowed window seats (or balconies in some), flagstone fireplaces (and a woodbox full of split wood and kindling), and a cedar armoire. The details are covered here: TV cleverly concealed, bathrobes and even a telephone in the bathroom. Jacuzzis are separated from the bedrooms with a swinging window. The rooftop open-ceiling hot tub is another nice feature. There are five banquet rooms downstairs and every detail is well attended to.

The excessive multicourse brunch lives on—though we can live without it, opting instead for dinner and praying for a table with a view of the falls. A significant change was under way in the kitchen at press time, with the arrival of chef Dean Ecker. Ecker hopes to lend a lighter touch to the Northwest-inspired menu, which had earlier produced such gems as a sweet potato bisque floating a tender mouthful of lobster, and a mix of fresh salad greens tossed with a shallot vinaigrette and topped with a "sheep cheesecake." The wine list is almost legendary; good thing a helpful sommelier is at hand. ■ *Exit 27* *off I-90, follow signs to Snoqualmie Falls; (206)888-2556; 37807 SE Fall City–Snoqualmie Rd, Snoqualmie, WA 98065; $$$; full bar; AE, DC, MC, V; checks OK; lunch Mon–Fri, breakfast and dinner every day.*

FALL CITY

RESTAURANTS

The Herbfarm ★★★★ What began as a front-yard wheelbarrow filled with a few extra chives for sale has become a trustworthy haven of *gourmandaise* in the Cascade foothills. (The legendary difficulty in securing reservations has been slightly alleviated since the proprietors began leaving a quarter of their 32-seat dining room unreserved until 1pm Friday of the week before the weekend in question.) What the Herbfarm presents is not simply a meal, but an opportunity for tasting, learning, and talking about what you have eaten. Meals generally begin with a short tour of the herbal gardens, and the education continues throughout, as owner Ron Zimmerman and chef Jerry Traunfeld narrate from the open kitchen. Unfortunately, co-owner Carrie Van Dyck brings a stuffed bear named Herb into the act, providing the only oversweetened moments of the whole feast. And a feast it is. A dinner might begin with sparkling wine perfumed with a sweet herbal extract and move to a sorbet made from champagne and Douglas fir needles, a soufflé of Oregon white truffles served in a fresh brown egg–cup, and a risotto rich with wild boletus mushrooms and shavings of Sally Jackson's handcrafted sheep cheese. The entree—an herb-crusted Ellensburg lamb—keeps company with wild hedgehog and black trumpet mushrooms. Each course comes with a matched wine, including a rare dessert wine such as 1915 Cossart-Gordon Madeira. Plan on three hours for luncheon, four to five for dinner, and plan on paying dearly (though you'll never regret it) for this extraordinary celebration of Northwest bounty. ■ *3½ miles off I-90 from exit 22; (206)784-2222; 32804 Issaquah–Fall City Rd, Fall City; $$$; wine only; AE, MC, V; checks OK; lunch and dinner Fri–Sun; (closed in March).*

CARNATION

Carnation is a lovely stretch of cow country nestled in the Snoqualmie Valley, where a stop for a giant cinnamon roll at **The River Run Cafe** is practically mandatory; 4366 Tolt Avenue, (360)333-6100.

At **MacDonald Memorial Park**, meandering trails and an old-fashioned suspension bridge across the Tolt River provide a great family picnic setting; Fall City Road and NE 40th Street.

Biking. The Cascade Bicycle Club sponsors rides all over the region. The Carnation–North Bend ride leaves from Mac-Donald–Tolt River Park and winds its way up to Snoqualmie Falls, the Herbfarm in Fall City, and George's Bakery in North Bend. Free to anyone who wants to ride; call (206)522-BIKE.

Remlinger Farms. The sky's the limit for your favorite fruits and vegetables at this U-pick farm. The Strawberry Festival in mid-June starts off the season. Throughout the summer you can choose from the best in raspberries, apples, corn, and grapes. The kids, young and old alike, love tromping through the fields in search of the perfect jack-o'-lantern-to-be in October; (206)333-4135 or (206)451-8740.

BLACK DIAMOND

Black Diamond Bakery, now much more than just a bakery, boasts the last wood-fired brick oven in the area. The bread that comes out of it is excellent: 26 different kinds, including raisin, cinnamon, sour rye, potato, seven-grain, honey-wheat, and garlic French. To get there, take the Maple Valley exit from I-405; at Black Diamond, turn right at the big, white Old Town sign; at the next stop sign, veer left; the bakery is on the right; 32805 Railroad Avenue, (360)886-2741, closed Monday.

ENUMCLAW

Stop in at the Lindon Bookstore, 1522 Cole Street, Enumclaw, (360)825-1388, for an espresso and a browse through the large, well-considered selection of books.

RESTAURANTS

Amanda's ★ Stop here to collect picnic supplies for a trip to Mount Rainier, or sit at a pink-draped table in the atrium for an early supper after a day at the mountain. It's a full delicatessen, formerly called Baumgartner's, with a range of European sausages and cheeses, coffee beans, teas, spices, and Boehm's chocolates. The friendly staff make up delectable sandwich combinations on fresh bread and croissants (huge). Try a poor boy with ham, pastrami, salami, Swiss, provolone, and the works. The freshly baked desserts have made a name for themselves. ■ *On Hwy 410, ½ block west of the Pickle Factory; (360)825-1067; 1008 Roosevelt E, Enumclaw; $; beer and wine; MC, V; checks OK; breakfast and lunch every day.* &

GREENWATER

RESTAURANTS

Naches Tavern Now *this* is the way to do a country tavern. The fireplace is as long as a wall and roars all winter long to warm the Crystal Mountain aprés-ski crowd. The group assembled is a peaceable mix of skiers, hunters, loggers, and locals. The food is homemade and modestly priced—deep-fried mushrooms, chili, burgers, pizza, four-scoop milk shakes. There's a countrified jukebox, pool tables, a lending library (take a book, leave a book) of yellowing paperbacks, and furniture so comfortable that the stuffing is coming out. Play a little cribbage, stroke the roving house pets, nod off in front of the hearth. ■ *North side of Hwy 410; (360) 663-2267; 58411 SR 410E, Greenwater; $; beer and wine; no credit cards; no checks; lunch, dinner every day.*

CRYSTAL MOUNTAIN

The ski resort is the best in the state, with runs for beginners and experts, plus fine cross-country touring. Less well known and less used are the summer facilities. You can ride the chair lift and catch a grand view of Mount Rainier and other peaks; rent condominiums with full kitchens, balconies, or other facilities from Crystal Mountain Reservations, (360) 663-2558, and play tennis. Other than that, there's just a grocery store, a sports shop, and Rafters, the bar-and-buffet restaurant atop Crystal's lodge. In summer, the Summit House offers weekend dinners. Off Highway 410 just west of Chinook Pass.

ELBE

The advent of the Morton Dinner Train (and an enterprising restaurateur) has turned this onetime sawmill town into more of a museum (some say graveyard) for antique cabooses. The **Morton Dinner Train**—$55 per person, (360) 569-2588—is a 4-hour, 40-mile round-trip train ride from Elbe to Morton. The dinner (shrimp cocktail, prime rib, and the works) is surprisingly good, and the conductor is well versed in the area's lore. You don't get dinner on the hour-long **Mount Rainier Scenic Rail-road**—summers only, (360) 569-2588—but the scenery (to Mineral and back) is equally attractive. A new convention resort is in the works on 300 acres just outside of Elbe. More next edition.

EATONVILLE

Northwest Trek is a "zoo" where animals roam free while people tour the 600-acre grounds in small open-air trams. The buffalo herd steals the show. You can also combine your visit with breakfast at the in-park food service concession, the Fir Bough. Open daily February through October, weekends only the rest of the year. Group rates available. Seventeen miles south of Puyallup on Route 161, (360) 832-6116.

ASHFORD

LODGINGS

Alexander's Country Inn ★★ This quaint country inn (circa 1912) has gained such a following that it now rivals the mountain itself as the best reason to visit Ashford. Best is the Tower Room: a lofted suite in the turret of the manor. A large wheelchair-accessible suite has been added on the second floor—very private, with its own deck. Indeed, this blending of old and new is the real genius here; it feels turn-of-the-century, but the comforts are pure 1990s. Complimentary wine is served in the parlor in the evening, and there's an outdoor Jacuzzi. The dining room is your best bet in these parts for a fine meal that includes a perfectly pan-fried trout—caught out back in the holding pond. During the summer, get a table on the brick patio. ▪ *4 miles east of Ashford on Hwy 706; (360)569-2300 or (800)654-7615; 37515 Rt 706 E, Ashford, WA 98304; $$; beer and wine; MC, V; checks OK; breakfast (summer only), lunch, dinner every day (weekends only in winter).*

Mountain Meadows Inn and B&B ★ Logger-turned-innkeeper Chad Darrah saved this 1910 mill superintendent's home from fading away in the ghost town of National, Washington. It is now situated near a trout pond on 14 acres of landscaped grounds in Ashford. Five large guest rooms are filled with antiques, books, and extensive train memorabilia. Nothing kitschy here; trains are conductor Darrah's passion. There's a VCR with rare train footage in the living room, if you're so inclined, and a player piano if you're not. If you need more space, ask about the guest house with two studio apartments. Full breakfasts of homemade sausage and muffins baked in a wood stove are fuel enough for a locomotive. ▪ *¼ mile west of Ashford; (360)569-2788; 28912 SR 706 E, Ashford; PO Box 291, Ashford, WA 98304; $$; MC, V; checks OK.*

Ashford

Lodgings

Nisqually Lodge ★ Reasonably priced and clean, this lodge just a few miles before the west entrance to Mount Rainier offers welcome respite from the train-memorabilia theme that's pervading the area. This 24-room, two-story lodge (owned by the same folks who run the Cowlitz River Lodge in Packwood and the Seasons Motel in nearby Morton) is well visited—returnees like the stone fireplace in the lobby, the air conditioning in the summer, and the hot tub outside (though we hear reports about the thin walls). Coffee and pastries are served for breakfast. ▪ *Hwy 7 to Rt 706, 5 miles from park entrance; (360)569-8804; 31609 Rt 706, Ashford, WA 98304; $$; AE, DC, MC, V; no checks.*

Wellspring [*unrated*] For more than a decade, Wellspring has quietly greeted outdoor enthusiasts with two spas nestled in a sylvan glade surrounded by evergreens. A soothing hour or two at Wellspring has become almost de rigueur for folks coming off Mount Rainier. Trouble is, no one wanted to leave. So recently, owner Sunny Thompson built three log cabins (no kitchens but woodstoves, featherbeds, baths, and small refrigerators) on her wooded south slope. Now you don't need to drive home in the cold and you can wake up to a basketful of breakfast. ■ *On Kernahan Rd 2¼ miles east of Ashford; (360)569-2514; Kernahan Rd, Ashford, WA 98304; $$; MC, V; checks OK.*

MOUNT RAINIER

The majestic mountain is the abiding symbol of natural grandeur in the Northwest and one of the most awesome mountains in the world. Its cone rises 14,410 feet above sea level, thousands of feet higher than the other peaks in the Cascade Range. The best way to appreciate the mountain is to explore its flanks: 300 miles of backcountry and self-guiding nature trails lead to ancient forests, dozens of massive glaciers, waterfalls, and alpine meadows, lush with wildflowers during its short summer. Chinook and Cayuse passes are closed in winter; you can take the loop trip or the road to Sunrise only between late May and October. The road from Longmire to Paradise remains open during daylight hours in winter. It is advisable to carry tire chains and a shovel during winter, and it is always wise to check current road and weather conditions by calling a 24-hour information service: (360)569-2211. Obligatory backcountry-use permits for overnight stays can be obtained from any of the ranger stations.

Longmire. A few miles inside the southwestern border of the park, the little village of Longmire has the simple **National Park Inn**, (360)569-2275, a small wildlife museum with plant and animal displays, a hiking information center, and a crosscountry skiing rental outlet. It also has the only place that sells gas in the park.

Paradise. At 5,400 feet, Paradise is the most popular destination point on the mountain. On the way to this paved parking lot and visitors center, you'll catch wonderful views of Narada Falls and Nisqually Glacier. The visitors center, housed in a flying saucer–like building, has a standard cafeteria and gift shop, extensive nature exhibits and films, and a superb view of the mountain from its observation deck. Depending on the season, you could picnic (our advice is to bring your own) among the wildflowers, explore some of the trails (the rangers offer guided walks), let the kids slide on inner tubes in the snow-play area, try a little cross-country skiing, or even take a guided snowshoe tromp. The ice caves, 3 miles northeast of Paradise, still exist, but entering the deteriorating caves has become extremely dangerous.

Sunrise. Open only during the summer months, the visitors center at Sunrise (6,400 feet) is the closest you can drive to the peak. The old lodge here has no overnight accommodations, but it does offer a snack bar and exhibits about the mountain. Dozens of trails lead from here, such as the short one leading to a magnificent viewpoint of Emmons Glacier Canyon.

Climbing the Mountain. There are two ways to do it: with Rainier Mountaineering, the concessionaire guide service, or in your own party. Unless you are qualified to do it on your own—and this is a big, difficult, and dangerous mountain on which many people have been killed—you must climb with the guide service. Call Paradise (360)569-2227 in the summer, Tacoma (206)627-6242 in the winter. If you plan to climb with your own party, you must register at one of the ranger stations in Mount Rainier National Park, (360)569-2211. Generally, the best time to climb the mountain is from late June through early September.

LODGINGS

Paradise Inn ★ The hotel at Paradise, just above the visitors center, is a massive, old-fashioned 1917 lodge, full of exposed beams, log furniture, and American Indian rugs. Unlike the modest inn at Longmire, the Paradise Inn has 125 rooms, a comfortable full-service dining room, a small, smoky bar, and a lobby with two big stone fireplaces. The greatest advantage to staying here, however, is the proximity to the summit; the rooms are nothing grand, the bathrooms can be antiquated, and the expensive meals in the restaurant tend toward routine beef and frozen seafood dishes. ■ *Hwy 706 to Paradise in Mt Rainier National Park; (360)569-2275; PO Box 108, Ashford, WA 98304; $$; full bar; AE, DC, MC, V; checks OK; breakfast, lunch, dinner every day, brunch Sun; (open late May to October only).*

PACKWOOD

LODGINGS

Packwood Hotel Just 10 miles west of White Pass Ski Area, Packwood makes a good base camp for wintertime skiers and summer hikers into the Goat Rocks Wilderness. A couple of motels in town may have more modern appliances, but this spartan lodge (open since 1912) remains a favorite. The woody aroma from the wood stove in the lobby permeates the place just enough to make you feel like you're really in the middle of the mountains (as opposed to downtown Packwood). A small narrow staircase climbs up to the simple shared-bath rooms.

■ *Main St; (360)494-5431; 104 Main St, Packwood, WA 98361; PO Box 130, Packwood, WA 98361; $; no credit cards; checks OK.*

MOUNT ST. HELENS

The temperamental **Mount St. Helens** simmers about 2 hours south of Seattle off I-5. On a clear day it is well worth the trip to see the 8,365-foot remains as well as the mountain's regrowth since the incredible eruption of May 18, 1980 (it's 1,300 feet shorter than before the blast). A visitors center (cafe, gift shop, bookstore) now sits on top of Coldwater Ridge; (360)274-2131. It's a multimillion-dollar facility with a million-dollar view—of the black dome that rests in the 2-mile-wide steaming crater like a phoenix egg, of the debris-filled North Fork of the Toutle River valley, and of new lakes formed by massive mudslides. The speed and heat of the blast, estimated at 600 miles an hour and up to 500 degrees in temperature, scalped at least 150,000 acres surrounding the mountain. The Coldwater Ridge center's focus is on the astounding biological recovery of the landscape. From the visitors center, you can hike the short distance to Coldwater Lake—where there is a picnic area and a boat launch—or take a guided interpretive walk. Two new visitors centers—the **Hoffstadt Bluff Rest Area and Viewpoint** (milepost 27 on the Spirit Lake Memorial Highway), which explores the lives and deaths of those most directly affected by the blast, and **North Fork Ridge** (at milepost 33.5), which focuses on the land's recovery in the wake of the eruption—opened in 1995. Closer to the mountain is the **Johnston Ridge Observatory**, due to open in 1996, with an even better view directly into the crater.

▼

Packwood

Lodgings

▲

To get there, take the Castle Rock exit from I-5 and travel 43 miles east on the recently completed Spirit Lake Memorial Highway (Highway 504). Oldest of the visitors centers in the Mount St. Helens area is the U.S. Forest Service's wood-and-glass center, 5 miles east of I-5 along Highway 504, (360)274-2100. Built shortly after the eruption, it commemorates the blast with excellent exhibits, a walk-through volcano, hundreds of historical and modern photos, geological and anthropological surveys, and a film documenting the destruction and rebirth.

Close to the freeway, before you begin the ascent to the ridge, you can stop in to see the Academy Award–nominated film *The Eruption of Mount St Helens* projected onto the Cinedome's three-story-high, 55-foot-wide screen. The rumble alone, which rattles your theater seat, is worth the price of admission. It's just off I-5 at the Castle Rock exit; (360)274-8000.

For climbing information (permits required, and no cheating; fines are doled out—at the top), call (360)750-3691.

MOUNT ADAMS

Mount Adams and its surrounding area are a natural splendor largely overlooked by visitors from Portland and Seattle, who seldom venture in from the Columbia Gorge. Besides climbing to the summit of the 12,276-foot mountain—greater in mass than any of the five major volcanic peaks in the Northwest—hikers and skiers can explore miles of wilderness trails in the Mount Adams Wilderness Area and the Gifford Pinchot National Forest.

Volcanic activity long ago left the area honeycombed with caves and lava tubes, including the **Ice Caves** near Trout Lake with stalactites and stalagmites formed by dripping ice. To the southwest of Trout Lake is **Big Lava Bed**, a 12,500-acre lava field filled with cracks, crevasses, rock piles, and unusual lava formations. Contact the Mount Adams Ranger Station in Trout Lake, (509) 395-2501, to register for ascents and for information on area activities.

In the warm months, Klickitat County is a land of abundance: morel mushrooms in the Simcoe Mountains (April through June), wildflowers in the Bird Creek Meadows (part of the only area of the Yakima Indian Reservation open to the public) in late July, and wild huckleberries—reputedly the best in the state—in and around the Indian Heaven Wilderness (mid-August to mid-September).

Trout Lake

Lodgings

TROUT LAKE

LODGINGS

Mio Amore Pensione Tom and Jill Westbrook's restored 1904 farmhouse sits alongside Trout Lake Creek, with a view of Mount Adams from the Jacuzzi. The inside is decorated with memorabilia collected from around the world. Our only quibble is that everything here is a little *too* precious (even more so with the on-premises gift shop of local crafts). Bedrooms are small, but the Venus Room is the most spacious, with a private bath and a two-seat sitting room with a view of Adams. The converted stone icehouse in the corner of the yard is quiet and rustic, and it sleeps four—but you have to go into the main house for a bathroom. Breakfast includes a bountiful array of Jill's award-winning baked goods. Tom, a trained chef, prepares a four-course dinner for $25 extra. You don't need to be a pensione guest to sample these savories, but reservations are required. ■ *Just off Hwy 141, take a sharp right onto Little Mountain Rd; (509) 395-2264; 53 Little Mountain Rd, Trout Lake, WA 98650; PO Box 208, Trout Lake; $$; wine ; MC, V; checks OK; dinner every day.* &

GLENWOOD

LODGINGS

Flying L Ranch ★ We love the Flying L; this 160-acre ranch is like a big kids' camp in some of the most spectacular country around. Except that here, you're on your own. Bicycle the backroads, hike the trails, observe the birds in the Convoy Wildlife Refuge, or ski Mount Adams. The Lloyd family have lived here all their lives. Darvel and Darryl Lloyd can point you in the right direction for anything. Or just stick around. The pace here is relaxed. You'll feel quite comfortable putting on some classical music and curling up with an old issue of *National Geographic* by the fireplace in the main lodge's spacious living room or watching evening fall over Mount Adams from the hot tub in the gazebo. The bedrooms are nothing fancy—but we like 'em that way. The Charles Russell room, the George Fletcher room, and the Mt. Adams suite have fireplaces. Two cabins back in the woods offer the most privacy. You might have huckleberry pancakes for breakfast; lunch and dinner you'll have to do yourself in one of the two well-equipped community kitchens. Dinners for large groups can be prepared with advance notice. ■ *½ mile off Glenwood-Goldendale Hwy; (509)364-3488; 25 Flying L Lane, Glenwood, WA 98619; $$; AE, MC, V; checks OK.* ⅊

STEVENSON

Stop by the newly opened **Columbia Gorge Interpretive Center** for a history of the Gorge, including a nine-projector slide show that re-creates the Gorge's cataclysmic formation, native American fishing platforms, and a 37-foot-high replica of a 19-century fish wheel. Just west of Stevenson off Hwy 14, (509)427-8211.

LODGINGS

Skamania Lodge ★★ The Gorge's grand lodge was constructed by a $5 million grant to spur on the economic development of Washington's side of the gorge—the side forgotten by windsurfers and left behind by timber companies. The lodge was not meant to be a luxury resort: you won't encounter nightly turndown service or private decks. It's best to think of it as a park resort or a conference center, and go and enjoy without expectations of grandeur. Its massive stone-and-wood lobby absorbs the warm glows of morning and evening, and a little library nook on the second floor offers guests more quiet respite with the same view. Still, with 195 rooms, this place is meant for people—lots of people. Even on days absent of conventions there are many echoes in the restaurant and many voices through the walls (some of the most expensive view suites are located directly above the bar with live music on weekends). Guests have use of an 18-hole golf course, tennis courts, a lap pool, saunas, and an appealing outdoor hot tub. The U.S. Forest Service's information center in the lobby provides maps and information on Gorge activities. New executive chef Emmanuel Afentoulis gets high praise for dishes like Skamania Lodge hash (poached eggs on smoked salmon hash), spicy chicken quesadilla, and roasted sturgeon. The Friday night Gorge Harvest Buffet serves a variety of Northwest favorites. ■ *Just west of Stevenson; (509) 427-7700 or (800) 221-7117; 1131 Skamania Lodge Way, Stevenson; PO Box 189, Stevenson, WA 98648; $$$; AE, DC, MC, V; checks OK; breakfast, dinner every day, lunch Mon–Sat, Sunday brunch.* &

HOME VALLEY

RESTAURANTS

Sojourner Inn ★★ At the Sojourner, breakfast and bed is just the beginning. Co-owner Bob Davis, a Cordon Bleu chef, cooks what might be some of the best dinners on the Washington side of the Gorge. At first you won't believe it, driving up to this modest-looking home on the hill. And at 7:30pm sharp, it could be an awkward moment of just the two of you or a festive group of 20 others. Either way, the evening continues smoothly with, perhaps, a salad tossed with Oregon blue cheese, perfectly ripened pears, and a light minty dressing; roasted chicken roulade with oyster pecan stuffing served with fresh, buttered green beans; and a sweet finish of apple pie loaded with thinly sliced apples and baked with a cheddar cheese crust. At $25 (including two glasses of wine), you'll never care that everyone else in the room is getting the same thing. Call before noon for same-day dinner reservations. A new wing has been added to the house, so all five guest rooms now have nice views—of the Gorge (the best view), a small garden, or the ridge behind the house. ■ *Follow signs from Hwy 14 in Home Valley; (509) 427-7070; 142 Lyons Rd, Home Valley; $$; MC, V; checks OK; dinner by reservation only.* &

Carson

CARSON

The eccentric 1897 **Carson Hot Springs**—PO Box 370, Carson, WA 98610; (509) 427-8292)—reminiscent of days when the sickly "took the waters" to improve their health, is today a bit worn; but we still recommend the hot mineral bath ($8), after which you're swathed in towels and blankets for a short rest. The women's side is much more crowded than the men's, so if you go in a mixed group, the men will finish sooner. To avoid this problem, you can reserve a massage in advance ($32 per hour) and a bath time will also be reserved for you. Don't expect as healthy a treatment from the restaurant.

HUSUM

LODGINGS

Orchard Hill Inn ★★ You're asked to leave your shoes by the doormat (and they might even get a shine) at this B&B on 13 acres overlooking pear and apple orchards and the National Wild and Scenic White Salmon River valley. The two bedrooms, decorated with family antiques, offer refreshing respite. Bathrooms—one with a whirlpool bath—are shared. The bunkhouse out back sleeps four. A sideboard breakfast includes homemade breads, huckleberry bran muffins, baked apples, eggs, local produce, and excellent coffee. Children are welcome at Orchard Hill and have a place of their own in a two-story tree house. There's a fabulous swing, a great porch for lounging, a sandbox, a volleyball court, and a Frisbee golf course. ■ *2 miles up Oak Ridge Rd out of Husum, milepost 2; (509)493-3024; 199 Oak Ridge Rd, White Salmon, WA 98672; $; MC, V; checks OK.*

BINGEN

RESTAURANTS

Fidel's ★ This Mexican restaurant seems transplanted straight from California; in fact, Fidel and Martha Montanez brought their family recipes from San Diego. Lively Mexican music sets the mood. Enormous margaritas go with the warm chips and salsa. The menu offers carne asada, a chili verde, a chili colorado, and machaca (a shredded beef, chicken, or pork omelet). Portions are generous (often big enough for two), and the chile relleno—encased in a thick layer of egg whites so that it resembles a big pillow—is *muy bueno.* ■ *1 mile east of the Hood River toll bridge on Hwy 14; (509)493-1017; 120 E Stuben St, Bingen; $; full bar; MC, V; local checks only; lunch, dinner every day; (call ahead in winter).* ঌ

LYLE

RESTAURANTS

Lyle Hotel ★★ The Lyle Hotel is a very modest place in a very humble town, but its most recent incarnation by owner Cal Wood has convinced people to give Lyle a second chance. Upstairs are nine clean and serviceable guest rooms, but the restaurant is the real reason for stopping here. Wood uses not only produce from the fertile Hood River Valley and a variety of Northwest seafood, but also locally grown pheasant from just up the Klickitat River. Much of his culinary inspiration comes from the Southwest—king salmon glazed with a chile-flavored sauce, Yucatan-style chicken skewers with papaya tomatillo salsa, grilled prawn black bean taco. Be sure to save room for a berry shortcake or the creamy smooth hazelnut cappuccino mousse with raspberry sauce. The wine list is more extensive than you would expect in such an out-of-the-way place; several local microbrews are on tap. Call ahead for reservations, especially if you're coming from a long way—weekends are crowded, and once in a while the restaurant closes unexpectedly. ■ *10 minutes east of the Hood River toll bridge, turn south on 7th St in Lyle; (509)365-5953; 7th and Lyle Ave, Lyle; $$; full bar; MC, V; checks OK; dinner Wed–Mon, Mar to Sept; Wed–Sun, Oct to Dec; closed Jan to Feb. &(restaurant only)*

GOLDENDALE

Maryhill Museum, a stately Palladian mansion, perches rather obtrusively upon the barren Columbia River benchlands. Constructed in 1917 by the eccentric Sam Hill, son-in-law of railroad tycoon James J. Hill, Maryhill began as the European-inspired dream home for Hill and his wife, Mary, but became instead what it is today: a fine art museum. With one of the largest collections of Rodin sculptures in the world, a whole floor of classic French and American paintings and glasswork, unique exhibitions such as chess sets and Romanian folk textiles, and splendid Northwest tribal art, the museum makes for quite an interesting visit. A cafe serves espresso, pastries, and sandwiches; peacocks roam the lovely landscaped grounds; Highway 14, 13 miles south of Goldendale, (509)773-3733. Up the road is another of Sam Hill's bizarre creations: a not-quite-life-size replica of **Stonehenge**, built to honor World War I veterans.

Goldendale Public Observatory, on a hill overlooking town (20 minutes north of Goldendale on US 97), was a popular spot when Halley's comet dropped in. High-powered telescopes give incredible celestial views through unpolluted skies. Open daily April through September, 2pm to 5pm and 8pm to midnight; in winter, open weekend afternoons and Saturday evenings, (509)773-3141.

LODGINGS

Highland Creeks Resort ★★ New owners have done wonders for this sheltered, backwoods resort (formerly call Three Creeks Lodge) nestled in the Simcoe Mountains. All rooms have been renovated with skylights, new carpeting, locally made Ponderosa pine furniture, new insulation for quiet, and private hot tubs—the most romantic are on private porches overlooking the river. Guests take advantage of the wilder-ness—hiking and fishing in summer, cross-country skiing and sleigh riding in winter. The dining room in the main lodge makes splendid use of its situation at the confluence of three creeks, with glass and cedar walls that seem to bring the trees inside. Salmon is cooked on a cedar plank; and soups are made from scratch every day. ■ *18 miles north of the Columbia River on Hwy 97; (509)773-4026 or (800)458-0174; 2120 Hwy 97, Goldendale, WA 98620; $$; full bar; AE, MC, V; checks OK; breakfast, lunch, and dinner every day.* &

Eastern Washington

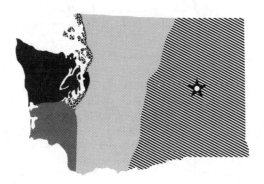

*An eastward route along I-90, Ellensburg to Spokane,
then a northwesterly arc through the northeast corner of the
state to the Okanogan and Colville national forests. The
Wenatchee loop begins in Okanogan and continues clockwise
through Grand Coulee, Soap Lake, and north again to
Wenatchee and Chelan (and Stehekin, accessible from
Chelan). Finally, an eastward drive along the
bottom of the state—Yakima to Pullman.*

ELLENSBURG

If you get away from the tourist ghetto by the freeway, as you
should, this college-and-cowboy town projects a pleasant ease.
Its famous Labor Day rodeo draws many for its slice-of-life view
of rural America.

Architecture. Ellensburg has more than its share of interesting buildings. The downtown area was rebuilt after a dev-
astating fire in 1889. Among the handsome structures still
standing are the Davidson Building, on the corner of Pearl and
Fourth, and the Masonic Temple, with its intriguing asym-
metrical facade. On the fringes of town, at Third and Wenas,
is a prime example of the Great American Train Station, built
late in the last century for the Northern Pacific. Art deco is represented by the Liberty Theater, at Fifth and Pine, and by the
Valley Cafe.

Central Washington University. To see modern

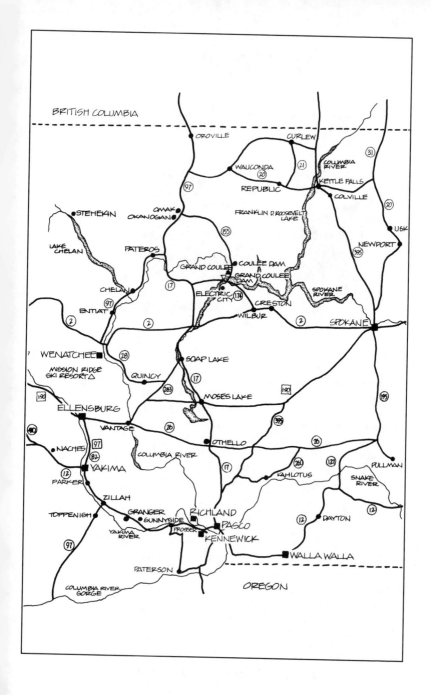

architecture, turn to the campus of Central Washington University, which displays Fred Bassetti's library and dormitory compound and Kirk/Wallace/McKinley's fine-arts complex. The campus makes for a wonderful stroll, especially through the serene Japanese Garden, designed by Masa Mizuno. The curious should call ahead and arrange a Saturday or Sunday workshop with the Chimpanzee and Human Communication Institute (at 14th and D at the north end of campus). Here you can observe a human and chimps communicating through American Sign Language. Call in advance for workshop times and prices; (800)752-4380.

Art. Sarah Spurgeon Gallery, on 14th Street in the fine-arts complex at Central, presents regional and national exhibits in all media, Monday through Friday (closed in September), (509)963-2665. The Clymer Museum and Gallery, at 416 N Pearl Street, honors Ellensburg's own chronicler of the Western frontier, John Clymer, whose work appeared several editions of *Saturday Evening Post*, (509)962-6416. Community Art Gallery, 408½ N Pearl, (509)925-2670, has nice quarters in an old building, displays good contemporary art, and sells local crafts; open 11am to 5pm Monday through Saturday.

Theater. Central Washington's only professional repertory theater presents over 35 performances by the energetic Laughing Horse Company during July and August (Wednesday through Saturday at 8pm); for reservations, call (509)963-3400. Plays are staged in the architecturally stunning Tower Theater on the Central campus.

Ellensburg Oddities. Close to the Central Washington campus along Ninth Street are tree-lined blocks of attractive turn-of-the-century homes. For something a bit out of the ordinary, check out the *Ellensberg Bull* statue by Richard Beyer, located in the historic downtown business district; the cowboy sculpture by Dan Klennard that guards the corner of Fifth and Pearl; or stop by 101 N Pearl for a gander at Dick & Jane's Spot, a blend of unusual yard art, including reflector gyros, statues, and other unique offerings. Treat the kids to an ice cream straight from the dairy at Winegar Family Dairy, 419 W 15th, (509)925-1821 (Monday to Saturday 11am to 6:30pm). Or down an espresso while sitting in the saddle at the Cowboy Espresso Bar in Jaguar's clothing store, 423 N Pearl, (509)962-6081.

The hills surrounding Ellensburg are speckled with blue agates found nowhere else in the world but in the Kittitas Valley. If you don't stumble upon any, you can purchase some at any of the local gem shops, particularly the Ellensburg Agate Shop, 201 S Main; (509)925-4998.

Olmstead Place, 4 miles east of town on Squaw Creek Trail Road (off I-90), is a cottonwood log cabin from an 1875 cattle ranch now coming back to life; tours Saturday and Sunday noon to 4pm, and by appointment; (509)925-1943. Not too far from Ellensburg is the Thorp Mill, an 1883 gristmill still in mint condition after 110 years. Open for tours by appointment; (509) 964-9500 or write PO Box 7, Thorp, WA 98946.

The big event in Ellensburg is the **Ellensburg Rodeo**, held Thursday through Monday of every Labor Day weekend at the fairgrounds (see calendar); (509) 962-7639.

Yakima River. There are fine canoe and raft trips to be made through the Yakima River's deep gorges. Fly fishermen know this to be one of the finest trout streams in the country. Highway 821, south of town, follows the gorge. Information about floats and river trips: (509) 925-3137.

RESTAURANTS

The Valley Cafe ★★ This 1930s-built bistro, with mahogany booths and back bar, would be an oasis anywhere—but is especially so in cow country. People traveling to Ellensburg arrange to arrive around lunchtime just to eat at this airy art deco spot. Salads are the choice at lunch, or one of the deli sandwiches. For breakfast you'll find French toast or a breakfast sauté of vegetables, chiles, eggs, and cheese. Eclectic concoctions, fresh seafood, and Ellensburg lamb compose most of the dinner menu. There's a well thought-out list of Washington wines, and some bracing espresso drinks. If you require faster service, a take-out branch is next door. ■ *Near the corner of 3rd and Main; (509) 925-3050; 105 W 3rd, Ellensburg; $$; beer and wine; AE, DC, MC, V; checks OK; breakfast Sat–Sun, lunch, dinner every day.*

Ellensburg

Giovanni's on Pearl ★ Welsh-born owner John Herbert started in the food and hotel business at age 12 in his parents' hotel on the Isle of Jersey. He landed here not too long ago and took over the fledgling Carriage House—and Ellensburg is all the better for it. The prime rib is gone (replaced by the oft-requested Ellensburg lamb), but there's a good sampling of fish and lotsa pasta. A chef's special might feature pan-fried oysters over fettuccine alfredo or smoked salmon in a blue cheese cream sauce with penne. Candlelight, flowers on the tables, and green chintz tablecloths add a slight English country air to a fresh and relaxing atmosphere. The college-bound servers are knowledgeable and prompt. Desserts (blackberry cobbler and an unmatched Dutch apple pie) are outstanding. ■ *1 block east of Main in the historic district; (509) 962-2260; 402 N Pearl, Ellensburg; $$; full bar; AE, MC, V; checks OK; lunch, dinner Tues–Sat.* &

VANTAGE

Situated on a splendid stretch of the Columbia, Vantage has nothing much in the way of food, but the view from the parking lot of the A&W surpasses that of all other known root-beer stands. Nearby **Ginkgo Petrified Forest State Park** has an interpretive center—open daily in summer, 10am to 6pm (by appointment only otherwise), (509)856-2700—that takes you back to the age of dinosaurs; then you can go prospecting for your own finds. It's a great spot for a picnic.

GEORGE

A naturally terraced amphitheater looking west over the Columbia Gorge offers a spectacular summer-evening setting for musical events, attracting thousands of people with big-name artists and performances from Lollapalooza to Boyz 2 Men, Def Leppard to Crosby, Stills, and Nash, Bonnie Raitt to George Thorogood. You can bring a picnic, but no booze (they'll search your packs and toss it, so don't bother). Arrive early; the one country road leading to George is not fit for crowds of this kind. For tickets, call Ticketmaster in Seattle, (206)628-0888. George is a 3-hour drive from Seattle; although you may find camping nearby (for a small fee, you may camp at a partitioned area just above the concert site), the closest lodgings are found in Ellensburg, Vantage, or Ephrata.

MOSES LAKE

It's the RV capital of the state, with many campers and boaters lured by the fishing and hunting around the lakes. The anglers come for trout and perch. You can rent a boat, then motor out to a sandy island in Potholes Reservoir for a picnic or camping.

SPOKANE

The friendly city by Spokane Falls is far more attractive to visit than is generally recognized. It is full of old buildings of note, marvelous parks, and splendid vistas, and the compact downtown is most pleasant for strolling. The Gold Rush of the 1880s brought it wealth and railroads brought it people.

Architecture. The three blocks on W Riverside Avenue between Jefferson and Lincoln contain a wealth of handsome structures in the city—doubtless the loveliest three blocks around. The Spokane Club on W Riverside is a fine example of the work done by Kirtland Cutter, who rebuilt most of the city after the fire of 1889; the Spokesman-Review Building, also on W Riverside, is everybody's idea of what a newspaper building should look like, especially one that is the seat of power for the dominant Cowles family. The Spokane County Courthouse, north of the Spokane River on W Broadway is a Loire Valley clone built in 1895 by Willis A. Ritchie. City Hall, on Spokane Falls Boulevard, occupies an old Montgomery Ward building, now elaborately restored in an award-winning blend of the

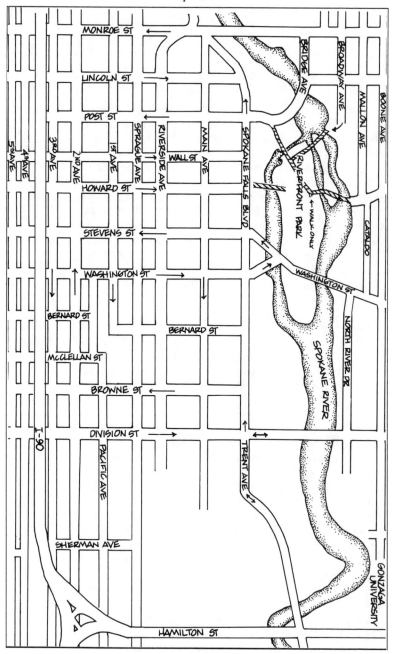

profoundly practical and the aesthetic to full art deco elegance.

Old Homes. Tour Overbluff Drive to see the small palaces of the upper crust, and Cliff Drive or Sumner Avenue on the South Hill to view some splendid older homes. Browne's Addition, west of downtown, is full of late-Victorian homes.

Parks. Riverfront Park is the pleasant green heart of the old city. Developed from old railroad yards by Expo '74, the park is now an airy place full of meandering paved paths, with entertainments ranging from ice-skating to an IMAX theater. The 1909 carousel is a local landmark, hand-carved by master builder Charles Looff. The music is too loud for children under about four (and most adults), but older kids love riding the menagerie. Manito Park, at Grand Boulevard and 18th, has a splendidly splashable duck pond and theme gardens. Finch Arboretum (west of downtown Spokane), a pleasant picnic site, hosts a modest but attractive collection of trees and shrubs among ravines and a stream. For a panoramic vista of Spokane, visit Cliff Park at 13th and Grove.

Nature. Two natural areas just a couple of miles outside Spokane's city limits offer excellent places to hike and see birds and wildlife: the Little Spokane Natural Area, (509)456-3964, and the Spokane Fish Hatchery, (509)625-5169. The fishery is at 2927 W Waikiki Road; for the Natural Area, look for the Indian Rock Paintings parking lot on Rutter Parkway. The Dishman Hills Natural Area, a 460-acre preserve in the Spokane Valley, has a network of trails with mixed wildlife habitats. Take I-90 east to Sprague Avenue exit, go east 1½ miles to Sargent Road; turn right ½ mile to parking area. Just 25 miles south of Spokane you'll find the 15,000-acre Turnbull National Wildlife Refuge, especially interesting during fall and spring migration. Take I-90 west, exit at Cheney, go through the town, and turn left on Smith Road.

Spokane

Culture. Brazilian-born conductor Fabio Machetti has been working with the Spokane Symphony since June 1993, and programs, including a pops series, are lively and innovative. An annual free Labor Day concert in Comstock Park draws thousands of picnicking spectators; (509)326-3136. The Spokane Civic Theatre, 1020 N Howard, (509)325-2507, offers a mixed bag of amateur performances each season; the Interplayers Ensemble Theatre, 174 S Howard, (509)4550-7529, is a professional company with a full season. Riverfront Park often hosts concerts of jazz, bluegrass, and popular music during the summer; call (509)456-4386 for information. The new 12,000-seat Spokane Veterans Arena, opened in mid-1995 is big enough to attract major entertainers and bands to the city; most of the tickets are sold through a local ticket agency, G&B Select-a-Seat, (509)325-7328 or (800) 325-7328. A Best of Broadway touring performance series is held at the Opera House at the south edge of Riverfront Park.

Museums. Cheney Cowles Museum displays pioneer and mining relics, and one of the fine old mansions from Spokane's mining era, Clark Mansion, is open for viewing; 2316 W First Avenue, (509)456-3931.

Sports. Golf is very good here. Indian Canyon, (509)747-5353, and Hangman Valley, (509)448-1212, two of the most beautiful public courses in the nation, have recently attracted a number of professional tournaments. The Creek at Qualchan, (509)448-9317, is the newest and most challenging of the city courses. There are no less than nine others. Spokane's parks and hilly roads and the Centennial Trail (flanking the river from Riverside State Park to Coeur d'Alene) offer great bicycle riding. Runners will find themselves in good company, especially during Spokane's annual Bloomsday Run (see Calendar). The Spokane Veterans Arena is the home of the Western Hockey League Spokane Chiefs. The good ski areas nearby are 49 Degrees North, 58 miles north of Spokane near Chewelah, (509)935-6649, a good place for beginners; Mount Spokane, 31 miles north on Highway 206, (509)238-6281, with fair facilities and some challenging runs; Schweitzer Mountain Resort in Sandpoint, Idaho, (208) 263-9555, with excellent facilities for family skiing; and the region's newest destination ski resort, Silver Mountain at Kellogg, Idaho, (208) 783-1111. Mount Spokane also has 17 kilometers of groomed cross-country ski trails along with two warming huts; a SnoPark pass is required. Summers, Mount Spokane State Park, (509)456-4169, is prime huckleberry terrain.

Brewery tour. Hale's Ales, which now has breweries in Spokane and Kirkland, is a microbrewery that welcomes visitors—when the day's brewing work is done. Call ahead for a reservation for a tour and a taste of their pale ale, bitter, porter, Moss Bay ale, and seasonal specialties: E 5634 Commerce Street, Spokane, (509)534-7553.

RESTAURANTS

Luna ★★ It didn't take long for local diners to embrace this new restaurant. The eclectic menu crosses the boundaries of ethnic cuisine with the emphasis on fresh herbs and seasonal fruits and vegetables. The restaurant is in a renovated one-story former produce market that features an open kitchen and booths with marbletop tables. The food is innovative and delicious. One of our favorites is the grilled prawns with Parmesan-flavored polenta, surrounded by a showy ring of red pepper sauce. A fair-weather patio awaits summer. Reservations recommended. ■ *South on High Dr to 56th, right 1 block to Perry; (509)448-2383; 5620 S Perry, Spokane; $$; AE, DC, MC, V; beer and wine; checks OK; breakfast, lunch, dinner Tues–Sun.*

Milford's Fish House and Oyster Bar ★★ Spokane's oldest fish house is simply decorated—exposed brick, red-and-white checkered tablecloths, a few green plants—and offers good food at reasonable prices. Check the fresh list and don't hesitate to ask the waiter for recommendations. Fresh salmon, baked or poached, is available in season, and the halibut is always a winner. On the weekend, service can be slow, especially in the trendy Oyster Bar. Reservations are highly recommended. ■ *Corner of Broadway and Monroe; (509)326-7251; 719 N Monroe St, Spokane; $$; full bar; MC, V; checks OK; dinner every day.* &

Clinkerdagger's ★ Clinkerdagger's has broadened its menu from the basic chicken and steak selections to include more Northwest-oriented dishes, but in the end, it's the basic but well-handled (and attractively presented) food that wins us over—especially when fresh seafood is available. Reservations recommended; request the coveted window seats (but there are no guarantees) in the spring, when the Spokane River is rushing. ■ *East of Monroe in Flour Mill; (509)328-5965; 621 W Mallon Ave, Spokane; $$; full bar; AE, DC, MC, V; local checks only; lunch Mon–Sat, dinner every day.*

The Downtown Onion ★ The magnificent old bar is a relic of the days when the building that houses this eatery was a fine hotel, the St. Regis. Some of the furnishings—the pressed-tin ceiling, the wooden dividers—are from the original hotel. The Onion set the standard in Spokane for gourmet hamburgers, and they're still local classics. The beer selection would be outstanding anywhere; fruit daiquiris (especially the huckleberry) are a specialty. A young, informal crowd dominates on most nights, especially on Monday nights during NFL season. Being part of the chaos is part of the fun of this place, so don't take a booth in the sun room. The same menu is served at the North Onion at 7522 N Division, (509)428-6100. ■ *On Riverside at Bernard; (509)747-3852; 302 W Riverside Ave, Spokane; $; full bar; AE, MC, V; checks OK; lunch, dinner every day.* &

Knight's Diner ★ Eggs the way you want them and crispy hashbrowns have been served up in this renovated circa-1900 railroad car for four decades, with only a brief interruption when the diner was moved to its new site at the south end of Hillyard. Those seeking an old-fashioned breakfast flock to this former Pullman passenger car where they sit on stools and eat at a mahogany counter that runs the length of the car. Those on grill-front stools get to watch the cook keep the dozens of orders all cooking at once. Hungry diners can order the 24 dollar-size pancakes. Few bother with the lunch menu. ■ *At the intersection of N Market and Green St; (509)484-0015; 2909 N Market, Spokane; $; no alcohol; no credit cards; checks OK; breakfast, lunch Tues–Sun.*

▼

Spokane

Restaurants

▲

Marrakesh ★ This Moroccan restaurant (in a former used appliance store), which expanded here from Seattle and Portland, does much to broaden Spokane's ethnic offerings. Diners sit on benches along the walls or on tippy hammocks. The meal begins with a traditional finger-washing routine and ends with the sprinkling of fragrant rose water over your hands, practical since your fingers are your utensils. A set price of $14.50 buys a five-course meal in which you choose only the entree. The execution of the food is never quite as good as the dining ceremony itself. Plan to go with at least a group of four; if it's crowded and there are only two, you may be seated with another couple or a larger group. ■ *West of Monroe on Northwest Blvd; (509)328-9733; 2208 Northwest Blvd, Spokane; $$; beer and wine; MC, V; checks OK; dinner Tues–Sun.*

McGowen's ★ This cafe's an adjunct to Auntie's Bookstore and Uncle's Games in the historic Liberty Building. On the second floor there's a spacious area for readings, and an art gallery specializing in the work of local artists. The brightly lighted cafe makes a great place to settle with a latte and a book. The fare includes soups, salads, and desserts; there's also a modest menu of daily hot entrees that might include lasagne and spanakopita. Breakfast is perfunctory. ■ *On the corner of Washington and Main; (509)624-1870; 404 W Main Ave, Spokane; $; no alcohol; MC, V; local checks only; breakfast, dinner Mon–Sat, lunch every day.*

Niko's Greek & Middle Eastern Restaurant ★ Niko's is deservedly popular locally for traditional Greek food, much of which is homemade in this modest taverna-style restaurant. Lamb is well-treated here, and the garlicky, smooth hummus can be ordered as an entree at lunch with a plate of vegetables or pita. Niko's Favorite, with chicken, tomatoes, and vegetables over rice with tahini sauce, is ours, too. The Greek salads have plenty of salty, strong feta and Greek olives; the baklava is loaded. Thursday is belly-dancing night. Niko II, downtown at W 725 Riverside Avenue, (509)624-7444, is a popular lunch spot. ■ *2 blocks off Sprague; (509)928-9590; 321 S Dishman-Mica Rd, Spokane; $; beer and wine; AE, MC, V; local checks only; lunch Mon–Fri, dinner Mon–Sat.*

Patsy Clark's ★ Patrick F. Clark, "Patsy" to his friends, arrived in America in 1870 at the age of 20, and by the time he was 40 he was a millionaire many times over, thanks to the success of Montana's Anaconda Mine. Naturally anxious to display his success, he instructed architect Kirtland Cutter to build him the finest mansion he could conceive—never mind the cost. Marble was shipped in from Italy, wood carvings and clocks from England, a mural from France, and a spectacular stained-glass window (with more than 4,000 pieces) from Tiffany's of New York. Locals like to show off Patsy's, but not so much for its dinners. An elegant spot it is, and you should find some excuse to stop by, even if it's only for a drink (the wine list is one of the best in the area). Sunday brunch—a memorable experience based on sheer quantity—requires reservations. ■ *15 blocks west of downtown at 2nd and Hemlock; (509) 838-8300; 2208 W 2nd Ave, Spokane; $$$; full bar; AE, DC, MC, V; local checks only; lunch Mon–Fri, dinner every day, brunch Sun.* &

Thai Cafe ★ You won't just stumble into this off-the-beaten-track ethnic oasis in the Eastern Washington desert. A waft of curry greets patrons at the door; and you'll find such seasonings, along with coconut milk and peanuts, in most of the entrees. We've yet to be disappointed with any of the chicken selections. Try the pra ram long song—chicken with peanut sauce, served on a bed of fresh spinach—or the squid. And don't miss the desserts—black rice pudding over ice cream or warm bananas in coconut milk. ■ *Sprague at Washington; (509) 838-4783; 410 W Sprague Ave, Spokane; $; Thai beer only; no credit cards; local checks only; lunch Mon–Fri, dinner Mon–Sat.* &

Coyote Cafe The walls of this recently remodeled Mexican place are covered with offbeat art, and the service is prompt and relentlessly cheerful. If you want to be in and out in 20 minutes, that's no problem. Food includes reasonably priced, standard south-of-the-border fare—tacos and burritos, refried beans and fajitas—all of which is enhanced by the large, icy margaritas. Try the fish tacos. ■ *Corner of 3rd and Wall; (509) 747-8800; 702 W 3rd Ave, Spokane; $; beer and wine; MC, V; checks OK; lunch, dinner every day.* &

Spokane

Lodgings

Europa Pizzeria Restaurant Exposed brick walls and bare wood give this place a certain Old World charm, and the relaxed atmosphere attracts good-tempered students from downtown college branch campuses. With the addition into the adjacent former antique shop, the bar area is now one of the best in town. Couches and wingbacked chairs divide the space into conversation areas, and generous portions of baked pasta entrees and calzone are served by a cheerful staff. Bar-side advice is reliable and the pace relaxed (sometimes too much so for those on a lunch hour). ■ *North side of the railroad trestle downtown, next to the Magic Lantern Theater; (509) 455-4051; 125 S Wall St, Spokane; $; beer and wine; MC, V; checks OK; lunch, dinner Mon–Sat.*

LODGINGS

Fotheringham House ★★ Owners Graham and Jackie Johnson restored this quintessential Victorian house to the grandeur intended by its builder, David B. Fotheringham, the first mayor of Spokane. The details inside and out—pressed tin ceilings, brass feet on the big claw-footed tub, Americana quilts, hundreds of daffodils in the lawn, Victorian-style perennial gardens—make all the difference in this 1891 Browne's Addition house. Location next to Patsy Clark's mansion doesn't hurt either. The former mayor's bedroom has views of Coeur d'Alene Park. The Museum and Mansion rooms are smaller and share a bath. Summers, guests can relax in the wicker swing on the wraparound porch, stroll the cobblestone paths through the butterfly and bird gardens, or play tennis on the courts in the park. ■ *Maple St exit from I-90, north to 2nd, turn west, stay in right lane; (509) 838-1891; 2128 W 2nd Ave, Spokane, WA 99204; $$; MC, V; checks OK; (closed Christmas).*

Waverly Place ★★ Across the street from what was a racetrack, Waverly Place retains the elegance of the Victorian era, inside and out. The track is now Corbin Park, a lovely oval with a couple of tennis courts, a shady tree canopy, and walking trails. Add Waverly Place's own pool and a tall glass of lemonade and call it vacation. There are four guest rooms. The Skinner Suite is decorated with oak furnishings—including a sleigh bed—and is the only room with a private bath. Anna's Room has a window seat that overlooks the park; the small Garden Room has a full view of the pool and backyard. Fresh fruit, Swedish pancakes with huckleberry sauce, sausages, and coffee are breakfast samplings. ■ *Exit I-90 at Division St, north on Division and Ruby to North Foothills Dr, west to Washington, north to Waverly; (509) 328-1856; 709 W Waverly Pl, Spokane, WA 99205; $$; AE, D, MC, V; checks OK.*

Cavanaugh's Inn at the Park ★ This hotel on the bank of the river across from Riverfront Park has 402 rooms, many with southern views of downtown Spokane (and a few, of the hydropower weir). All seven stories of rooms open out to the spacious lobby; it can be noisy, so specify a quiet corner room or perhaps one in the wing at the east end of the hotel, away from the lobby and busy Washington Street, or in the tower at the west end of the complex. The attractive Windows on the Seasons restaurant overlooks the river. ■ *Division St exit from I-90, north to North River Dr; (509) 326-8000 or (800) 843-4667; 303 W North River Dr, Spokane, WA 99201; $$; AE, DC, MC, V; checks OK.* &

West Coast Ridpath Hotel ★ The 340 rooms are pleasant and spacious, and those in the tower overlook the city. The downtown location is convenient. This place is popular with conventioneers and tourists, and some of the public areas can be crowded, but the mood here is always convivial. The rooftop restaurant, a predictable Ankeny's, boasts a grand view of Spokane. At night, the town glitters in the smoked glass and mirrors of the interior decor. ■ *In the heart of downtown; (509) 838-2711 or (800) 426-0670; 515 W Sprague Ave, Spokane, WA 99204; $$; AE, DC, MC, V; checks OK.*

COLVILLE

The Colville River valley has tiny farming communities, but outdoor recreation—fishing and cross-country skiing, primarily—
is beginning to draw many to the pristine area. Highway 20 from
Colville to Tonasket is a National Scenic Byway. It climbs over
Sherman Pass, amazingly the highest pass in Washington.

KETTLE FALLS

LODGINGS

My Parent's Estate ★ This 120-year-old house has also been
a mission school, an abbess's home for a Dominican convent,
a home for troubled boys, and a private residence; it's now a
quiet haven in the woods. The 49-acre estate on the Colville
River boasts a gym, a barn, a caretaker's house, and a ceme-
tery; more modern additions include a Jacuzzi and private
baths. Hosts Al and Bev Parent are proud of their home; Bev's
arts and crafts collection is displayed around the house. The
three guest rooms encourage quiet country relaxation, with
comforters on the queen-size beds, refinished vanities, and antique washbasins. The lofty living room is dominated by a floor-
to-ceiling stone fireplace. What to do? Cross-country ski in the
winter; float the Colville River in summer, hike, or play in the
water at nearby Franklin D. Roosevelt Lake. ■ *7 miles past
downtown Colville on Hwy 395; (509) 738-6220; PO Box 724,
Kettle Falls, WA 99141; $$; no credit cards; checks OK.*

▼

Wauconda

Restaurants

▲

CURLEW

RESTAURANTS

The Riverside Restaurant and Lounge ★ An oasis in Wash-
ington's northeastern corner. The setting is pleasant: wooden
tables and chairs and a wooden bar. The dining room has a
large wood stove. There's a view of the river, and the produce
is fresh, and the food is fairly simple but always good. You can
get the all-American thick sirloins, but there's a better bent to-
ward Mexican, and where else in this territory can you get
shredded beef enchilada sided by gently steamed asparagus?
■ *On the main drag; (509) 779-4813; 813 River St, Curlew;
$$; full bar; MC, V; checks OK; dinner Wed–Sun.*

WAUCONDA

RESTAURANTS

The Wauconda Cafe, General Store, and Post Office If you
want atmosphere, here it is in this small general store cum gas
station cum post office cum restaurant. A lunch counter with a

few booths is squeezed between the general store and the dining room. It's a popular hangout for the local folk, both rancher types and counterculturalists. The view is out across the rolling meadows so typical of the Okanogan Highlands, with a few weatherbeaten barns enhancing the horizon, and wildflowers in the spring. The food is fresh and simple: tasty burgers, milk shakes, sandwiches, and homemade soups for lunch; sautéed prawns, prime rib, and big salads for dinner. Owners Dennis and Lucy Smith have added Chinese food to the menu on weekend nights. Breads and desserts are homemade. ▪ *The only place in town; (509)486-4010; 2432 Hwy 20, Wauconda; $; beer and wine; MC, V; local checks only; breakfast, lunch, dinner every day.*

OMAK

The famous—and controversial—Suicide Race is the climax of the Omak Stampede the second weekend each August. At the end of each of the four rodeos that take place over the three-day weekend, a torrent of horses and riders pours down a steep embankment, across the Okanogan River, and into the arena. No one's ever been killed during the races since the event started in 1933, but plenty of horses have broken their legs.

▼

Wauconda

Restaurants

▲

RESTAURANTS

Breadline Cafe ★ Here in the heart of steak and Stampede country, the Breadline offers a choice of fare. In the front of an old bottling-works building, owner Paula Chambers has expanded her eatery to include a low-tech bistro/nightclub offering full dinners and live music—from small folk bands to big-name blues artists like Charlie Musselwhite. The country-style menu includes steak and scampi, Cajun chicken, and pasta. We like the big, informal market in the back, with fresh baked breads, pastries, and deli items. Watch the whole-grain bread come out of the oven as your hearty sandwich or salad is prepared. Hot apple fritters with cream maple sauce finish you off. ▪ *Ash and 1st; (509)826-5836; 102 S Ash St, Omak; $; full bar; AE, MC, V; checks OK; lunch Mon–Sat, dinner Tues–Sat.*

OKANOGAN

LODGINGS

U and I Motel The name suits this family-run place's folksiness. It's not much to look at from its front on the old backroad between Okanogan and Omak, but a closer look uncovers a pleasant little nook for hiding away from it all. The two-room cabinettes are less than spacious, but they're clean and cozily done up in rustic paneling. They are a deal, starting at $32, as are one-roomers with a double bed for $25. Best of all, the whole backyard of the motel is a grassy lawn and flower garden fronting the tranquil Okanogan. Grab a deck chair, cast a fishing line, and watch the river flow. Pets okay. ■ *Off Hwy 97 on old 97 at 838 2nd Ave N; (509) 422-2920; 838 2nd Ave N, Okanogan, WA 98840; $; MC, V; local checks only.*

COULEE DAM

LODGINGS

Coulee House Motel Dam good view and decent amenities—a pool, and refrigerators in some of the large, clean rooms, to name a few—earn our favor. At night you can sit on the tiny lanai outside your room (smoking or non) and watch the animated laser light show (summers only) over one of the largest dams on earth as the water cascades past. ■ *Birch and Roosevelt; (509) 633-1101; 110 Roosevelt Way, Coulee Dam, WA 99116; $$; AE, DC, MC, V; no checks.*

Four Winds Once a dormitory for dam engineers, the Four Winds is now Coulee Dam's most personable inn *and* within walking distance of the dam itself. There are 11 spotlessly clean rooms with many combinations of baths (shared with one other, down the hall, etc.). At one end of the building is a foyer for reading, conversation, or board games. Nothing fancy here, but all competently overseen by Richard and Fe Taylor, who at 8:30am serve a virtual smorgasbord. ■ *Lincoln St is across from Coulee Dam City Hall; (509) 633-3146 or (800) 786-3146; 301 Lincoln St, Coulee Dam, WA 99116; $$; MC, V; checks OK.*

GRAND COULEE

Grand, yes—this is a wonderful area from which to appreciate the outsize dimensions of the landscape and the geological forces that made it. The Columbia, as it slices through central Washington, has an eerie power: the water rushes by in silky strength through enormous chasms. The river, the second largest in the nation, traverses a valley of staggering scale; in prehistoric times glacier-fed water created a river with the largest flow of water ever known.

Grand Coulee Dam is one of the largest structures on the earth—tall as a 46-story building, with a spillway twice the height of Niagara and a length as great as a dozen city blocks. The dam, completed in 1941, was originally intended more to irrigate the desert than to produce electricity; so much power was generated, however, that the dam became a magnet for the nation's aluminum industry. The north-face extension (completed in 1975) was designed by Marcel Breuer, a great practitioner of the International Style, and the heroic scale of the concrete is quite magnificent, especially when illuminated by the inspirational laser light show. There are daily self-guided tours of the dam; hours vary according to season: (509) 633-9265.

Eccentric inventor Emil Gehrke amassed an oddly compelling **windmill collection** at North Dam Park on Highway 155 between Electric City and Grand Coulee. Four hard hats tilted sideways catch the wind, cups and saucers twirl around a central teapot—it's whimsical and fascinating.

Houseboating. Until two years ago, Lake Roosevelt was untapped by the RV-on-pontoons fleet. Now there are 40 houseboats available to explore the 150-mile-long lake, and most book up early for the summer. The sun's almost guaranteed, and all you need to bring is food, bed linens, towels, and your bathing suit; boats are moored at Kelly Ferry Marina, 14 miles north of Wilbur, 1-800-648-LAKE.

CRESTON

RESTAURANTS

Deb's Cafe The glory days of Deb Cobenhaver, a world-champion rodeo rider back in the mid-1950s, are kept in a kind of time capsule here. Outside there is a wooden porch, like a stage-set saloon; inside, the place is strewn with trophies, photos, and saddles. Cowboy-hatted men and women shoot pool in the bar or line up at the lunch counter. The main cafe opens at 6am for hearty breakfasts with homemade cinnamon rolls; at lunch there are a few decent sandwiches, served with home-cut fries. Dinner? Steaks, natch. ■ *Hwy 2; (509) 636-3345; 600 Watson, Creston; $; full bar; MC, V; local checks only; breakfast, lunch, dinner every day.* ♿

SOAP LAKE

Early settlers named the lake for its unusually high alkali content, which gives the water a soapy feel.

Dry Falls, off Route 17 north of town, is the place where the prehistoric torrential Columbia once crashed over falls 3 miles wide and 400 feet high; an interpretive center (Wednesday through Sunday, 10am to 6pm, summer) explains the local geology, which has been compared to surface features of Mars. From this lookout, you can also see **Sun Lakes**, puddles left behind by the ancient Columbia. It's RV territory, but the waters are prime spots for swimming and fishing; (509) 632-5583.

LODGINGS

Notaras Lodge On the shores of Soap Lake, you can stay in the Norma Zimmer Room (the bubble lady on the "Lawrence Welk

Show") or the Bonnie Guitar Honeymoon Suite (named for a local country-western celeb whose own guitar is memorialized in an epoxied table along with other souvenirs of the singer's career). Such memorabilia are owner Marina Romary's passion; the Western Nostalgia Room boasts a pool table as well as a whirlpool. The healing waters of Soap Lake are available to guests on tap in the bathrooms (eight of which have Jacuzzis). Romary also owns nearby Don's Restaurant, 14 Canna Street, (509)246-1217, a popular steak-and-seafood-and-Greek eatery, where macho meals are served in a dark, slightly seamy interior. ■ *4 miles after Ephrata on Hwy 28, 1 block west on Main St; (509)246-0462; 236 E Main St, Soap Lake, WA 98851; PO Box 987, Soap Lake, WA 98851; $$; MC, V; checks OK.* &

WENATCHEE

You're in the heart of apple country, with an Apple Blossom Festival the first part of May. **Ohme Gardens**, 3 miles north on Route 97A, is a 600-foot-high promontory transformed into an Edenic retreat, with a fastidiously created natural alpine ecosystem patterned after high mountain country. Splendid views of the valley and the Columbia River; (509)662-5785.

Mission Ridge, 13 miles southwest on Squilchuck Road, offers some of the best powder snow in the region, served by four chair lifts (cross-country skiing, too); (509)663-7631. On the third Sunday in April, the Ridge-to-River Pentathlon is an impressive sporting event.

Rocky Reach Dam, 6 miles north on Route 97, offers a beautiful picnic and playground area (locals marry on the well-kept grounds), plus a fish-viewing room. Inside the dam are two large galleries devoted to the history of the region.

RESTAURANTS

John Horan's Steak & Seafood House ★★ Many of the orchards that once surrounded this turn-of-the-century home, built by Wenatchee pioneer Mike Horan, are gone. Yet the roundabout drive to the house near the confluence of the Wenatchee and Columbia rivers sets the tone for an evening that harkens back to more gracious times. The feel of the early 1900s remains in the dark floral wallpaper, the lace-draped windows, and the original Horan family furnishings and photographs. Proprietors Inga and John Peters offer country hospitality while their chef makes his mark with fresh fish and meat dishes, including a marvelous Columbia River sturgeon in season. We were even impressed with the rather plebian-sounding (and less expensive) beef tips—a flavorful combination of sautéed beef, mushrooms, and bell pepper with hints of garlic and red wine. The lemon swirl cheesecake proved refreshing and light. The Peters's newest addition is the Carriage House Pub next door to the main restaurant, where lighter fare is the mainstay. This is a friendly stop for those seeking a glass of wine, a Northwest microbrew, or a game of cribbage. ■ *Just south of the K-Mart plaza along the Wenatchee River; (509)663-0018; 2 Horan Rd, Wenatchee; $$$; full bar; AE, MC, V; checks OK; dinner every day (restaurant); lunch and dinner Tues–Fri (pub), dinner only Sat (pub).* &

Steven's at Mission Square ★★ Steven's is a handsome place where Wenatchee's premier chef Steve Gordon serves Northwest cuisine with a few international excursions. The split-level dining room with potted plants is elegant in a trendy sort of way; full-length mirrors reflect the well-dressed clientele. Pasta and seafood dishes are served here with pride and a flourish, from fettuccine with asparagus and prosciutto to apricot-honey-mustard chicken with sweet basil on a bed of spinach, pecans, and Bermuda onions. The lunch menu is highlighted by a grilled prawn sandwich and a red Thai curry. Bread is freshly baked and warm, and desserts are first-rate. ■ *1 block off Wenatchee at 2nd and Mission; (509)663-6573; 218 N Mission St, Wenatchee; $$; full bar; AE, MC, V; checks OK; lunch Mon–Fri, dinner every day.* &

The Windmill ★★ A constantly changing number on a blackboard keeps track of the steaks sold at this celebrated steak house. On our last visit it was 316,700. That's not the number of steaks sold since the Windmill opened 72 years ago—that's since January 1982, when Pat and Linda Jackson took over as owners, and we haven't heard of even one that wasn't terrific. Waitresses here don't come and go—they stay and stay, sporting pins that proudly declare the number of years they've served. The meals, too, are time-tested and classic. There are seafood and pork chops, but don't be a fool. Ritual dictates that you finish with a piece of one of the magnificent pies. ■ *1½ blocks west of Miller, on the main thoroughfare; (509)663-3478; 1501 N Wenatchee Ave, Wenatchee; $$; beer and wine; AE, MC, V; checks OK; dinner Mon–Sat.*

Garlini's Ristorante Italiano ★ There's nothing fancy about the outside of this niche restaurant tucked away on one of the main streets in East Wenatchee. But inside, the dark, heavy wood, dim lighting, and festive music bring Italy to the senses. The Garlini family cooks up all the old Italian favorites: seafood fettuccine, chicken and veal parmigiana, and lasagne just like Mamma's. Large, round tables and ample space accommodate families and large parties. Expect to wait a little longer for your meals on busy weekends. Busy or not, the servers keep a ready smile. ■ *1 block north of the Wenatchee Valley Mall; (509)884-1707; 810 Valley Mall*

Parkway, East Wenatchee; $; beer and wine; AE, MC, V; checks OK; dinner Tues–Sat.

Mickey O'Reilly's Sports Bar & Grill ★ Modeled after Seattle's Jake O'Shaughnessey's, this sports bar doubles as a family restaurant and gathering place. It's a take-me-out-to-the-ball game kind of place. The bar is separate from the main dining area, but TV screens with the hottest sporting events are visible from any perch. The courteous young waitstaff trot around in shorts and T-shirts while the menu runs from a multitude of burgers to a mixed grill. Don't blow your chance to try an Ice Cream Potato, spud-shaped vanilla ice cream rolled in powdered chocolate "peel." ■ *Across from the Wenatchee Valley Mall in East Wenatchee; (509) 884-6299; 560 Valley Mall Parkway, East Wenatchee; $; full bar; AE, MC, V; checks OK; breakfast buffet Sat and Sun, lunch and dinner every day.*

Visconti's Italian Restaurant ★ All the standards are on the menu, from spaghetti to caesars to thick slabs of lasagne. Fresh garlic and herbs permeate each generously sized dish. Try the mostaccioli (a tube-shaped noodle) with Italian sausage and mushroom sauce. Reports on dessert are good, especially the white chocolate raspberry truffle cheesecake. ■ *At the west end of town on Wenatchee; (509) 662-5013; 1737 N Wenatchee, Wenatchee; $; beer and wine; AE, DC, MC, V; checks OK; lunch Mon–Fri, dinner every day.*

The Wenatchee Roaster and Ale House ★ High atop the West Coast Wenatchee Center Hotel, the Roaster serves up a variety of home-away-from-home-cooked meals in a venue that shouts "corporate chain." The spit roaster and fruit-wood smoker display fragrant whole chickens and turkeys rotating slowly over aromatic apple wood. Crowd-pleasers like prime rib (guaranteed to be the best in Wenatchee or your money back) and "all-clam clam chowder" are keeping the customers satisfied. Even the weight-conscious get the nod here; low-cal chicken and veggie entrees give you an excuse to make up the calories with one of 24 beers on tap. Watch out for slower-than-usual service on busy weekend nights. ■ *1 block north of the Wenatchee Convention Center; (509) 662-1234; 201 N Wenatchee Ave, Wenatchee; $; full bar; AE, DC, MC, V; checks OK; breakfast and dinner every day, lunch Mon–Sat, brunch Sun.* ♿

Golden East A remodeled bank is now a vault of red vinyl booths, paper lanterns, and Chinese food. George Chang and his wife, Marisa, prepare both Cantonese and more potent Sichuan favorites (even so, you might need to tell them you like it hot). Chang trained and worked in Seattle before going east to seek his fortune. He has a light hand with oil and favors cook-to-order preparation. The combination plates are fine, but you'll do better to order mu-shu pork with tender rice pancakes or chicken with cashews, soul-warming with hot peppers. Ask for a window table with a view of the Wenatchee River and Mission Ridge beyond. ■ *Across the Columbia River and up Grant Rd; (509)884-1510; 230 Grant Rd, East Wenatchee; $; beer and wine; MC, V; local checks only; lunch, dinner Tues–Sun.* &

Greathouse Springs Cafe The noontime hot spot for local 9-to-5'ers. Belly up to the sandwich bar and place your order, or have a seat at one of the cedar picnic benches where the owner himself will be glad to do the honors. Panini—grilled focaccia combined with cheeses, meats, and seasonings alla Italia—ubiquitous in the big city—are the *new* rage here in farm country. ■ *Follow Wenatchee Ave till it branches at N Miller; (509)664-5162; 1505 N Miller St, Suite 130; $; no alcohol; checks OK; no credit cards; continental breakfast Mon–Fri; lunch Mon–Sat.* &

LODGINGS

The Warm Springs Inn ★ The Wenatchee River is a perfect backdrop, and the pillared entrance and dark green and rustic brick exterior lend a certain majesty to Janice and Dennis Whiting's B&B. Four guest rooms with private bath are dressed in floral accents. A path behind the two-story inn (which served as a hospital in the 1920s) leads through a wooded area to the river's edge. Guests can relax in the naturally lit sitting room or enjoy the company of others on the verandah. Janice keeps coffee brewed at all times. ■ *Head toward Cashmere and turn left off Hwy 2 onto Lower Sunnyslope Rd; (509)662-8365 or (800)543-3645; 1611 Love Lane, Wenatchee, WA 98801; $$; MC, V; local checks only.*

West Coast Wenatchee Center Hotel ★ This is the nicest hotel on the strip, with its view of the city and the Columbia River. It's Eastern Washington–elegant, but not overdone. The nine-story hotel has three nonsmoking levels. Rates may rise if most rooms are already booked the day you call, so do make advance reservations and be sure to ask about package rates. The Wenatchee Roaster and Ale House is on the top floor (see review) and the city's convention center is next door, connected by a sky bridge. The outdoor pool is great under the hot Wenatchee sun (the indoor pool's for the other season). ■ *Center of town on Wenatchee Ave; (509)662-1234; 201 N Wenatchee Ave, Wenatchee, WA 98801; $$; AE, DC, MC, V; checks OK; breakfast, lunch, dinner every day.* &

The Chieftain The motels all line up along Wenatchee Avenue, but this one stands out for its dependable quality year after year (since 1928). It may need a new paint job, but it's popular with the locals who come for the famous prime rib evenings. The rooms themselves are larger than those of the Chieftain's cousins down the pike. Ask for a room in the newer wing, the "executive rooms," surprisingly spacious quarters for about $55. There's a swimming pool, a hot tub, and a helicopter pad (that is used more often as a basketball court). You can bring your pet with advance notice. Ugly views. ▪ *On Wenatchee off 9th; (509) 663-8141 or (800) 572-4456; 1005 N Wenatchee Ave, Wenatchee, WA 98801; $$; full bar; AE, DC, MC, V; checks OK; breakfast, lunch, dinner every day.* &

CHELAN

This resort area is blessed with the springtime perfume of apple blossoms, a 55-mile lake thrusting like a fjord into tall mountains, 300 days of sunshine a year, and good skiing, hunting, fishing, hiking, and sailing. It's been trying to live up to its touristic potential since C. C. Campbell built his hotel here in 1901, but with mixed success so far. Now that time-share condos are springing up near the golf course and B&Bs are blooming near the cross-country trails, the amenities are improving. No one need improve the scenery.

The top attraction is the cruise up the lake on an old-fashioned tour boat, *The Lady of the Lake*, or the newer *Lady Express*. The lake is never more than 2 miles wide (it's also one of the deepest in the world), so you have a sense of slicing right into the Cascades. At **Stehekin**, the head of the lake, you can visit craft shops, take a bus tour, eat a barbecue lunch, and get back on board for the return voyage. The tour boat departs Chelan at 8:30am daily in summer, three or four days a week off-season, and returns in the late afternoon; rates are $21 per person round-trip; kids 6 to 11 years old travel half price. No reservations needed. The faster *Lady Express* shortens the daily trip to just over 2 hours, with a 1-hour stop in Stehekin before heading back; round-trip tickets are $38, and reservations are suggested. More info: The Lake Chelan Boat Company, (509) 682-2224. Or fly up to Stehekin, tour the valley, and be back the same day via Chelan Airways, (509) 682-5555.

Chelan Butte Lookout, 9 miles west of Chelan, provides a view of the lake, the Columbia River, and the orchard-blanketed countryside.

Sports. Echo Valley, northeast of Chelan, offers rope tows and a poma lift on gentle slopes; Lake Chelan Golf Course, call (509) 682-5421 for tee times, is an attractive, sporting course near town; fishing for steelhead, rainbow, cutthroats, and chinooks is very good in Lake Chelan, with remote, smaller lakes particularly desirable.

Nostalgia. St. Andrew's Church, downtown Chelan, is a log edifice, reputedly designed by Stanford White in 1898 and still in service; from the Chelan Museum (Woodin Avenue,

▼

Chelan

1pm to 4pm in summer) you can learn about other restored houses nearby, such as the old Lucas Homestead.

RESTAURANTS

Goochi's Restaurant ★ After years of abuse as a tavern in the historic Lakeview Hotel building, this pretty space with its huge antique cherrywood back bar is now a smart dinner stop. Classic rock 'n' roll plays on CDs, and neon sculpture decorates the cedar-planked walls. Burgers and pasta selections are popular with children; for the adults, however, the restaurant strives for a slight twist on the usual, offering black-eyed peas in lieu of potatoes or rice pilaf. A moist chicken breast may come with a tart lemon-thyme cream sauce. Soups (such as Southwestern beef) are often spicy and flavorful. Chelan's Riverfront Park, just around the corner, is good for a postprandial stroll. ▪ *Across Woodin from Campbell's Lodge; (509) 682-2436; 104 E Woodin, Chelan; $; full bar; AE, MC, V; local checks only; lunch, dinner every day, brunch Sat and Sun.* ᇈ

LODGINGS

Campbell's Lodge ★★ Chelan's venerable resort (whose history goes back to 1901 and includes the absorption of its once-rival to the north, Cannon's) continues to be the most popular place for visitors, with prime lakeside properties and 148 rooms, many with kitchenettes. Among the facilities, you'll find three heated pools and an indoor Jacuzzi, a sandy beach, and moorage should you arrive by boat. The convention center services up to 250 people. Campbell House, the most dependable restaurant at the lake, is here. Off a crowd-pleasing dinner menu one can order grilled chicken, beef stroganoff, breaded trout, a selection of seafoody pastas with sometimes unbalanced sauces. Soft sourdough rolls, desserts, and informed service are all first-rate. Reservations here, as at the lodge, can be scarce in high season. ▪ *On the lake at the end of the main street through Chelan; (509) 682-2561; 104 W Woodin, Chelan; PO Box 278, Chelan, WA 98816; $$$; full bar; AE, MC, V; checks OK; breakfast, lunch, dinner every day.* ᇈ

Darnell's Resort Motel ★ Situated right on the shore of the lake, this is a resort especially suited to families. Suites are large and attractive and all have views ($75 to $145 for a suite for four). Lots of amenities are included with the price of the room: putting green, heated swimming pool, sauna, hot tub, exercise room, shuffleboard, volleyball, badminton, tennis, barbecues, bicycles, rowboats, and canoes. Down the road from Campbell's and the center of town, Darnell's is removed from the seasonal hurly-burly. ▪ *Off Manson Hwy at 901 Spader Bay Rd; (509) 682-2015; 901 Spader Bay Rd, Chelan,; PO Box 506, Chelan, WA 98816; $$$; AE, MC, V; checks OK.*

▼

Chelan

▲

Kelly's Resort ★ Kelly-owned for about 45 years, this resort is a favorite among families who prefer the location on the shore and away from town. The original 10 fully equipped cabins are set back in the woods; they're dark and rustic, but they're great for those on a budget ($90 for four) and families seeking a playground. We prefer one of the four condo units on the lake (from the lower units you can walk right off the deck into the water). There's a nice deck near the grocery store (a good spot to have a beer) and a knotty-pine common area with table tennis and a fireplace. ■ *14 miles uplake on the south shore; (509)687-3220; Rt 1, Box 119, Chelan, WA 98816; $$–$$$; MC, V; checks OK.*

STEHEKIN

A passage to Stehekin, a little community at the head of Lake Chelan, is like traveling back in time. This jumping-off point for exploring the rugged and remote North Cascades National Park can be reached only by a 4-hour *Lady of the Lake* boat trip or the faster *Lady Express* (daily from mid-April to mid-October, less frequently in winter), (509)682-2224; by Chelan Airways floatplane, (509)682-5555; by hiking (write Chelan Ranger District, PO Box 189, Chelan, WA 98816); or by private boat. The boat and the plane will take you to Stehekin from Chelan. For a shorter boat ride, catch the *Lady Express* uplake at Field's Point.

Exploration is the prime reason for coming here. There are several day hikes, including a lovely one along the lakeshore and another along a stream through the Buckner Orchard, and many more splendid backcountry trails for the serious backpacker. In winter there are some fine touring opportunities for cross-country skiers or snowshoe enthusiasts, although the town pretty much shuts down then. The ranger station at Chelan (open year-round), (509)682-2576, is an excellent source of information for these activities. A National Park Service shuttle bus provides transportation from Stehekin to trailheads, campgrounds, fishing holes, and scenic areas mid-May to mid-October; for information, call either (206)856-5700 or (509)682-2549. Rent bikes or boats at the North Cascades Lodge.

Stehekin Valley Ranch. The Courtney family pick you up at Stehekin in an old bus and take you to the farthest end of the valley for seclusion and hearty family-style meals at their ranch. Open in the summer months, their rustic tent-cabins offer a place to bunk and just the basics (a kerosene lamp, showers in the main building), plus hearty, simple food at a decent price ($49 per night per person). **Cascade Corrals**, also run by the family, arranges horseback rides and mountain pack trips; (509)682-4677, or write Stehekin Valley Ranch, Box 36, Stehekin, WA 98852.

The **Stehekin Pastry Company** fills the void the Honey Bear Bakery left when it migrated to Seattle; this spot is a local favorite for sweet desserts and rich conversation.

LODGINGS

Silver Bay Inn ★★ The Silver Bay Inn, located where the Stehekin River flows into Lake Chelan, is a wonderful retreat for those who want to explore the Stehekin Valley. Friendly Kathy and Randall Dinwiddie welcome their guests to this passive solar home with hikes and stories only the locals know. Guests get a continental breakfast, and for an afternoon snack, the Stehekin Pastry Company is just a short stroll down the road. The setting is spectacular: 700 feet of waterfront with a broad green lawn rolling down to the lake. The main house has a master suite (with a two-night minimum to ensure you'll take time to enjoy yourself) decorated in antiques, with a separate sitting room, two view decks, a soaking tub, and a faraway view. Two separate lakeside cabins are remarkably convenient (dishwasher, microwave, all linens) and sleep four and six. Bicycles, canoes, croquet, and (for the less active) hammocks are available. A hot tub has a 360-degree view of the lake and surrounding mountains. Silver Bay is a perfect place for families with kids over 12. ■ *Take the* Lady of the Lake *to Stehekin; (509)682-2212; PO Box 43, Stehekin, WA 98852; $$; no credit cards; checks OK.*

▼
Stehekin
▲

NACHES

LODGINGS

Whistlin' Jack Lodge ★★ There are a number of fishing lodges nestled in the pines on the Naches River, but this one, just on the east side of Mount Rainier's Chinook Pass, is our favorite. Ideal for all manner of outdoor activity, from hiking and fishing to alpine and cross-country skiing, this mountain hideaway (originally built in 1957) has all the comforts of home and then some. There are six cabins, two bungalows, and eight motel units here, but best are the cabins—specifically, the Naches (with a riverfront lawn and hot tub on the deck) or the Grandview (so close to the rushing river you could almost fish from your deck). If you book a bungalow or room without a kitchenette, try the pan-fried trout in the restaurant. Access via Chinook Pass near Mount Rainier is restricted almost seven months a year, but lodge patrons (many families) are used to driving the winding road from Yakima instead. ■ *40 miles west of Yakima on SR 410; (509)658-2433 or (800)827-2299; 20800 SR 410, Naches, WA 98937; $$; MC, V; checks OK.*

If your last visit to the Napa Valley recalled rush-hour traffic on the freeway to Disneyland, you may be ready for the less traveled, more organic pleasures of the Yakima wine country. Get off the freeway at virtually any point between Union and the Tri-Cities and you'll find a scene of unspoiled pastoral splendor. (See also Tri-Cities Wine Country.) Vineyards and orchards follow the meandering Yakima River. Cattle graze the pastures. And the small towns scattered here and there provide constant surprises and unexpected small pleasures. The burgeoning wine industry (there are close to two dozen wineries in the valley, and more on the way) has encouraged small businesses to go after the tourist trade. Warm welcomes in the shops and tasting rooms are genuine; they really are glad to see you.

Since vineyards were first planted about two decades ago, the valley's unique weather patterns—warm days, cool nights, with seemingly more daylight than down in Napa—have encouraged winemakers to develop new approaches to winemaking. A Northwest style has emerged: bright fruit flavors underscored by crisp acids. The white wines are mostly dry (even the rieslings tend that way) and firmer than their counterparts in California, while the reds are rich and textured, with the structure of fine Bordeaux. Prices are low, and wineries often sell special bottlings unavailable elsewhere.

The Yakima Valley Wine Growers Association (PO Box 39, Grandview, WA 98930) publishes a useful brochure that lists member wineries along with tasting-room hours, easy-to-follow maps, and a bit of history. Big or small, all offer a taste of what's new and a chance to chat about the vintage in the most relaxed circumstances. Here's a quick rundown, as you head east from Yakima. **Thurston Wolfe**, 27 N Front, Yakima, (509)452-0335, dessert wine specialists, including a Sauternestyle "Sweet Rebecca" and a landmark zinfandel port. **Staton Hills**, 71 Gangl Road, Wapato, (509)877-2112, in an attractive building, with a view of Union Gap, picnic grounds. **Bonair Winery**, 500 S Bonair Road, Zillah, (509)829-6027, a small, friendly, family-run winery, with a flair for chardonnay. **Hyatt Vineyards Winery**, 2020 Gilbert Road, Zillah, (509)829-6333, fine dry white wines and a lovely view. **Zillah Oakes Winery**, Zillah, (509)829-6990, off-dry white wines, gift shop, and a tasting room with a Victorian motif, faces Highway 82. **Covey Run**, 1500 Vintage Road, Zillah, (509)829-6235, one of the larger wineries, expansive tasting room, picnic grounds, view, and a full line of well-made wines. Check out new line of Reserve and Vineyard Designated wines. **Portteus Vineyards**, 5201 Highland Drive, Zillah, (509)829-6970, new, family-owned, with estate-bottled reds—cabernet, merlot, and lemberger. **Horizon's Edge Winery**, 4530 E Zillah Drive, Zillah, (509)829-6401, another spectacular view and good lineup of wines. **Washington Hills Cellars**, 111 E Lincoln Avenue, Sunnyside, (509)839-9463, large selection of pleasant wines in a no-frills facility. **Eaton Hill Winery**, 530 Gurley Road, Granger, (509)854-2508, new winery and B&B in a restored homestead and cannery, all white wines so far. **Stewart Vineyards**, 1711 Cherry Hill Road, Granger, (509)854-1882, one of the oldest vineyards in the state; rieslings and cabernets are worth noting. **Tefft Cellars**, Outlook, (509)837-7651, produces a small number of hand-crafted wines. **Tucker Cellars**, Sunnyside, (509)837-8701, a family enterprise offering an extensive selection of Yakima valley fruit and produce as well as wines. Excellent tours at **Chateau Ste Michelle**, W Fifth and Avenue B, Grandview, (509)882-3928; where the state's biggest winery set up shop in the late '60s, and the highly regarded reds are still made in a facility dating back to the repeal of Prohibition. **Yakima River Winery**, Prosser, (509)786-2805, riverside location, full-blown reds and superb dessert wines. **Pontin del Roza**, Prosser, (509)786-4449, family-owned and operated. **Hinzerling Winery**, 1520 Sheridan, Prosser, (509)786-2163, one of the state's pioneering wineries; look for tannic reds and fine late-harvest "Die Sonne" gewürztraminer. **Chinook Wines**, Prosser, (509)786-2725, a charming, intimate setting in which small quantities of some of Washington's best wines are produced. Don't miss the merlot. The **Hogue Cellars**, Wine Country Road, Prosser, (509)786-4557, spectacularly successful family enterprise making superb whites and cellar-worthy reds; look for "Reserve" wines. **Oakwood Cellars**, Benton City, (509)588-5332, one of the newer additions to the growing number of wineries in the vicinity of Red Mountain. **Kiona Vineyards Winery**, Benton City, (509)588-6716, a small estate winery, the first to plant on Red Mountain, making remarkable cabernet, lemberger, and dry and sweet rieslings. **Seth Ryan Winery**, Benton City, (509)588-6780, a winery whose first bottlings of riesling and chardonnay gained recognition. **Blackwood Canyon**, Benton City, (509)588-6249, just up the road from Kiona, a no-frills facility making controversial but distinctive wines; the late-harvest wines are excellent. **Columbia Crest Winery**, Paterson, (509)875-2061; off the beaten track a half hour south of Prosser, this impressive facility showcases sophisticated winemaking on a grand scale.

YAKIMA

Irrigation (first tried by the Indians and missionaries here in the 1850s) has made this desert bloom with grapes, apples, mint, asparagus, and hops. The town also blooms with small conventions.

Front Street Historical District includes a 22-car

train that houses shops and restaurants, and the renovated Pacific Fruit Exchange Building, which holds a local farmers market.

The Greenway Bike Path winds along the Yakima River for 7 miles. Start out in Sherman Park on Nob Hill and go to the Selah Gap. Along the way, look for bald eagles and blue herons, or pick out a fishing hole; (509)453-8280.

The Wine Cellar is a fine place to sample local vintages and orient yourself for a more extended foray into the wine country. You'll find beer-making supplies, specialty food products, and gift baskets, too. 5 N Front Street, (509)248-3590.

Interurban Trolley. A restored 1906 trolley provides summer-evening and weekend rides around Yakima. Call (509)575-1700 for schedules.

Yakima

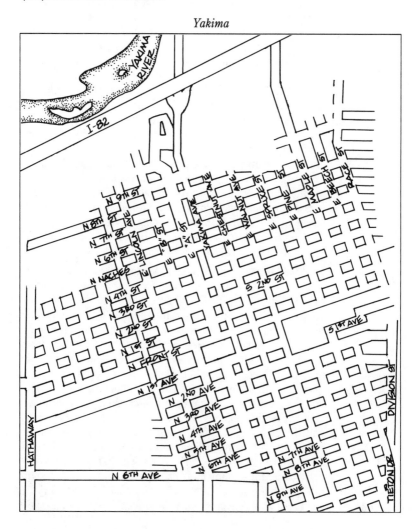

Horse racing. Yakima Meadows has live races November through March. It's a dandy place to see small-town, Old West racing; 1301 S 10th, (509)248-3920.

Yakima Valley Museum has handsome pioneer pieces, plus a collection from Yakima's most famous native son, Justice William O. Douglas. Open every day; 2105 Tieton Drive, (509)248-0747.

RESTAURANTS

20 YEARS **Gasperetti's Restaurant** ★★★ John Gasperetti's Northern Italian restaurant continues to be one of the most innovative in the region, despite the departure of long-time chef Brad Patterson. You feel well cared for the moment you step into the foyer of this intimate, casually elegant establishment. A somewhat formal dining room is set with elegant banquettes, linen-covered tables, and low lights. In the new Bar Giovanni, palms nestled in Italian terra-cotta create privacy between tables covered with wine-bottle motif brocade and glass tops. Small table lamps create a romantic glow, enhanced by large soft-toned murals. Appetizers of note include roasted garlic and Rollingstone chèvre and calamari with spicy oil. Among a listing of pastas and meats, tender fresh Dungeness crab comes wrapped in canelloni and sauced with a flag of mornay and marinara, or generously tossed with penne and garlic tomato cream sauce: impressive in either guise. Desserts are expertly prepared, and the expansive new wine list offers excellent bottlings of Washington wines, including many hard-to-find reds, in addition to a solid selection of Italian labels. Service is informed, unobtrusive, and a world away from the busy street outside. ■ *6 blocks south of the N Front St exit off I-82; (509)248-0628; 1013 N 1st St, Yakima; $$; full bar; AE, MC, V; checks OK; lunch Tues–Fri, dinner Tues–Sat.* ♿

Birchfield Manor ★★ Birchfield Manor offers elegant French country dining. When you arrive for your appointed seating, owners Wil and Sandy Masset greet you at the door and show you to your table in the large living room of their antique-filled historic home. Meals here are preceded by their reputation, which is taken *very* seriously. Trained in Europe, Wil produces an ambitious, imaginative meal, letting the food set the mood for a formal evening, and offering a one-of-a-kind experience here in Central Washington. You may choose from one of six entrees, perhaps a double breast of chicken Florentine or a very authentic bouillabaisse. Washington wines are featured, and the courses—dutifully explained by a friendly waitperson—are both individualistic and complementary. There are five B&B rooms upstairs ($75 to $100 with baths) and two fireplace suites for a chunk more change. An outdoor pool and hot tub are for guests only. ■ *Take exit 34 off I-82 onto Hwy 24, head east 2 miles, then south on Birchfield; (509)452-1960;*

2018 Birchfield Rd, Yakima; $$$; beer and wine; AE, DC, MC, V; checks OK; dinner Thurs–Sat. ⑀

Cafe European and Coffee Company ★★

What started out as Jerry Pardo's Viennese and French pastry shop has grown into one of Yakima's favorite eateries. Breakfast comes in the form of fluffy omelettes, quiche, homemade scones, or waffles. Lunch includes a number of sandwiches, but you'll do best to choose from the list of other selections—such as a cold curry chicken and pasta salad or a true-to-the-anchovies caesar salad. Of course, you can't leave without sampling a homemade truffle. Chef Frank Comito has charged up the dinner menu, and a series of spring and summer winemaker dinners offer ambitious prix-fixe fare hosted by Yakima Valley vintners. ■ *Between 31st and 32nd on Summitview; (509)248-5844; 3105 Summitview Ave, Yakima; $$; full bar; AE, MC, V; checks OK; breakfast, lunch Mon–Sat, dinner Wed–Sat, brunch Sun.* ⑀

Vannini's Italian Restaurant ★★

Fourth-generation restaurateur Matthew Vannini and partner Aaron Burks opened this Italian cafe in 1994. Together with spouses Lesley Burks Vannini and Devin Burks, they have created a culinary jewel in a most unlikely setting. Soft jazz and deep green faux marble tabletops and walls create an atmosphere that belies the dusty farm town and railroad tracks outside. A meal begins with warm herb-and-garlic breadsticks served with a spicy red sauce. Perfectly cooked angel hair pasta arrives gently tossed with tomatoes, crumbled feta, and a hit of garlic and crushed red pepper. Local and Italian wines are available and kids get a discount on real Italian sodas. ■ *Sunnyside/Outlook exit from I-82, follow the signs to Sunnyside; turn right on N 6th; (509)837-2225; 111 N 6th St, Sunnyside; $$; beer and wine; AE, MC, V; local checks only; lunch and dinner Mon–Sat.* ⑀

The Brewery Pub ★

Bert Grant, one of the creators of the Northwest's boom in microbreweries, has brought back full-flavored, fresh, locally made ales and stouts. The pub is in the old train station where small experimental batches are brewed; the bulk of the beer is made two miles south (tours by reservation only). It's a popular place that serves up a British pub menu to accompany Grant's brews. Homemade soups and Mexican food occasionally appear at lunch. A good place to meet friendly residents. ■ *Head west on Yakima, turn right on Front; (509)575-2922; 32 N Front St, Yakima; $; beer and wine; MC, V; checks OK; lunch, dinner every day.*

Deli de Pasta ★

The North Front Street area is a comfortable blend of the old, the funky, and the hip. A half block south of the Brewery Pub, this intimate Italian cafe is quite popular with the locals. Owners Bob and Diane Traner have a flair for decor, making simple touches (red wooden chairs, red tablecloths, white linen napkins) seem somehow extraordinary. Fresh pastas and sauces, made on the premises, can be mixed and matched to suit your mood. The service is friendly, the coffee's fine, and the congenial atmosphere encourages many happy returnees. ▪ *½ block off Yakima on N Front St; (509) 453-0571; 7 N Front St, Yakima; $; beer and wine; AE, MC, V; checks OK; lunch, dinner Mon–Sat.*

Santiago's ★ The high ceiling, dramatic brick walls, huge mural in the bar, and Southwestern art are festive; the enormous skylight creates the exotic atmosphere of a Mexican courtyard (albeit in downtown Yakima). The chalupas and the tacos Santiago (with beef, guacamole, and two kinds of cheese) are especially popular. Steak picado (their version of fajitas) was on the menu long before the sizzling sirloin strips became chic at every other Mexican restaurant. ▪ *Close to the intersection of 1st and Yakima; (509) 453-1644; 111 E Yakima Ave, Yakima; $; full bar; MC, V; checks OK; lunch, dinner Mon–Sat.*

LODGINGS

37 House ★★ Washington's first woman architect, Elizabeth Ayer, designed this elegant mansion for the Plath family, prominent Yakima orchardists. It remained their family home for 50 years and is now a bed and breakfast fantasy for lovers of unique and historic architecture—complete with the Plaths' original wallpaper and gracious furnishings. A sweeping hardwood staircase leads the way to five unique guest rooms. All share the charm of the '30s, with window seats and full mosaic-tile baths. In the morning, you're treated to a full country breakfast. ▪ *Take the 40th Ave exit off Hwy 12, turn right on Englewood Ave; (509) 965-5537; 4002 Englewood Ave, Yakima, WA 98908; $$$; AE, MC, V; checks OK.*

Rio Mirada Motor Inn ★ This Best Western motel, just off the I-82 freeway and right next to the shimmering Yakima River, doesn't look like much from the road. Once inside, you'll find 96 attractive, moderately priced rooms, each with a small balcony and a view of the river (second-story rooms are the best). Most rooms have tiny refigerators and a few have kitchenettes. For exercise there's an indoor heated pool and a pleasant 7-mile path that runs along the riverbank. ▪ *Exit 33 off I-82; (509) 457-4444; 1603 Terrace Heights Dr, Yakima, WA 98901; $$; AE, DC, MC, V; Wash State checks only.* &

TOPPENISH

Western artist Fred Oldfield was raised here and returns occasionally at the request of the Toppenish Mural Society, (509) 865-6516, to lead a mural-painting posse. As a result, the whole town is an art gallery, with 10 large walls covered in murals and more planned. Clusters of Western shops, antique

stores, and galleries make strolling and shopping pleasant, and
there are rodeos scheduled throughout the summer months.

Yakima Nation Cultural Center, located on ancestral
grounds, houses an Indian museum and reference library, plus
a gift shop, a native American restaurant, a commercial
movie/performing arts theater, and the 76-foot-tall Winter
Lodge, for conventions and banquets. Open every day (closed
January and February). On Fort Road off Highway 97, Toppenish, (509)865-2800. **Fort Simcoe** was built in 1856, and its
gothic revival officers' quarters still stand in desolate grandeur;
28 miles west of Toppenish on Route 220.

ZILLAH

RESTAURANTS

El Ranchito ★★ Here in hops- and fruit-growing country, home to many Mexican-Americans, is a jolly tortilla
factory-cum-cafeteria that makes a perfect midday stop.
You eat in the large dining area or in the cool, flower-shaded
patio during the summer. After lunch you can browse in the gift
shop, a minimercado with Mexican pottery, rugs, and hard-to-
find Mexican peppers, spices, canned goods, fresh tortilla
chips, and even south-of-the-border medicines. The authentic
food is ordered à la carte. The smooth burritos, tasty nachos,
and especially the barbacoa, a mild, slow-barbecued mound of
beef served in a tortilla shell or a burrito, are generous and recommended. There is a Mexican bakery on the premises, but
no cerveza. ■ *Exit 54 off I-82, follow the signs; (509)829-
5880; 1319 E 1st Ave, Zillah; $; no alcohol; no credit cards;
checks OK; breakfast, lunch, dinner every day.*

▼
Sunnyside
Lodgings
▲

SUNNYSIDE

RESTAURANTS

Taqueria La Fogata A small, simple roadside Mexican taqueria doing a lot of things right. The clientele is clearly local, the
help clearly Mexican, and the menu expansive enough to include specialties such as pozole (Michoacán stew of pork back
and feet and hominy) and menudo (Michoacán tripe and cow's-
feet stew in a spicy sauce) along with all the usual tacos
and burritos. The service is friendly and prices prehistoric. ■
*In Sunnyside; (509)839-9019; 1204 Yakima Valley Hwy,
Sunnyside; $; no alcohol; MC, V; checks OK; breakfast, lunch,
dinner every day.*

LODGINGS

Sunnyside Inn Bed and Breakfast ★ The eight bedrooms in
this 1919 home are huge (so big they sometimes feel empty),
four have outside entrances, and all come with phones, cable

TV, air conditioning, and enormous private baths with Jacuzzi tubs. On the main floor, ask for the Jean room (king-size bed, outside entrance) or the Karen room (gas fireplace). Upstairs, the cheerful Viola room is decorated in peach, and the Lola room features a pleasant sun porch. For those who like the friendliness of B&Bs but need their fair share of privacy, this place is a godsend. Breakfast is a bountiful affair of blueberry pancakes, warmed syrups, fruit, and classical music.

On weekend evenings, the Sunnyside Inn offers a prix-fixe gourmet dinner prepared by former Waldorf-Astoria chef James Graves. Call for reservations. ■ *Exit 63 or 69 off I-82; (509)839-5557; 800 E Edison Ave, Sunnyside, WA 98944; $; no alcohol; AE, MC, V; checks OK; dinner Fri–Sat (reservations required).* ♿

GRANDVIEW

RESTAURANTS

Dykstra House Restaurant Who can resist a restaurant that features bread made from hand-ground whole wheat grown in the Horse Heaven Hills? Rich desserts and a few choice Washington State wines complement this mansion's simple menu, which changes daily. If you go with an open mind, you won't be disappointed. Proprietor Linda Hartshorn takes the time to make visitors feel at home in the gray stone 1914 home of Grandview's former mayor and in the town at large. Local groups often reserve the upstairs for meetings or parties. Reservations are required for Saturday dinner. ■ *Exit 73 off I-82, 1½ miles on Wine Country Rd; (509)882-2082; 114 Birch Ave, Grandview; $$; beer and wine; AE, DC, MC, V; checks OK; lunch Tues–Sat, dinner Fri–Sat.*

▼ Sunnyside *Lodgings* ▲

PROSSER

Cherries have always grown well in the Yakima Valley, except when the weather doesn't cooperate. Too much rain cracks cherries, too little leaves them small. **Chukar Cherries** turns imperfect cherries into a year-round delicacy—dried cherries. In the showroom of their production center you'll also see chocolate-covered cherries, cherry poultry sauce, and even cherry waffle mix; 306 Wine Country Road, Prosser, (509)786-2055.

LODGINGS

Wine Country Inn Bed & Breakfast A welcome addition to the limited overnight options in Prosser, this riverside home has three rooms upstairs and one down. The river winds lazily by the front door and the adjoining restaurant, from which owners/innkeepers Chris Flodin and Audrey Zuniga turn out terrific country breakfasts, lunches, and ample, hearty dinners. The thin-walled rooms are clean and comfortable. A deck and gazebo open onto the river, with outside restaurant seating on warm summer nights. ■ *Exit 80 off I-82, near bridge in Prosser; (509) 786-2855; 1106 Wine Country Rd, Prosser, WA 99350; $; beer and wine; AE, MC, V; checks OK; lunch, dinner Wed–Sun.* ♿

TRI-CITIES WINE COUNTRY

The Tri-Cities wine country is the hub of the huge Columbia Valley viticultural appellation, which includes both the Yakima Valley and Walla Walla Valley appellations within its borders. Here its three principal rivers (Columbia, Snake, and Yakima) converge. A few miles to the west, at Red Mountain, the Yakima Valley wineries begin; and a few miles to the east is the small cluster of Walla Walla Valley wineries. The Tri-Cities Visitor and Convention Bureau, (509) 735-8486, can provide up-to-date wine-touring maps and tasting-room schedules, and visitors will find some of the state's oldest wineries and vineyards located nearby (90 percent of the state's vineyards are reportedly located within a 50-mile radius of Red Mountain). In the immediate area are **Bookwalter Winery**, 2708 Commercial Avenue, Pasco, (509) 627-5000, a small facility located just off the cloverleaf joining Highway 395 and I-82; **Gordon Brothers Cellars**, 531 Levey Road, Pasco, (509) 547-6224, one of the state's best vineyards, with a special flair for merlot and a nice view of the Snake River; **Preston Wine Cellars**, 502 E Vineyard Drive, Pasco, (509) 545-1990, a large, family-owned enterprise with an expansive tasting room and park; and **Quarry Lake Vintners**, 2520 Commercial Avenue, Pasco, (509) 547-7307, another big operation, whose success is built on the excellent Balcom & Moe Farms vineyard. Southwest of Tri-Cities is Stimson Lane's $25 million showcase **Columbia Crest Winery**, Highway 221, Paterson, (509) 875-2061.

TRI-CITIES: RICHLAND

Richland was once a secret city, hidden away while the atomic bomb workers did their thing in the 1940s; now "the Atomic City" is the second largest of the Tri-Cities. Interestingly, Hanford now employs more people to dismantle the site than it ever did in its heyday. However, as nuclear reactors close and the controversy over hazardous waste continues, civic leaders are working hard on industrial diversification. **Hanford Science Center** in downtown Richland tells a bit of the saga of atomic energy; the energy displays are quite instructive; 825 Jadwin Avenue, (509) 376-6374.

Howard Amon Park, along the bank of the Columbia, is

a great spot for picnics, tennis, golf, jogging, or just ambling. **Allied Arts**, 89 Lee Boulevard, (509)943-9815, located at the edge of the park, displays the work of mostly local artists in the oldest building in Richland.

RESTAURANTS

The Emerald of Siam ★★ One of the most authentic Thai restaurants in Eastern Washington is improbably located in a converted drugstore in a Richland shopping center. Thai-born Ravadi Quinn and her family run a cultural center for visiting school groups, a display of Thai handicrafts for sale, and an Oriental grocery. In the small restaurant, delicious native recipes include curries, satays, and noodles. All get high marks. Quinn's many projects include occasional cooking classes and her own cookbook, *The Joy of Thai Cooking.* ▪ *William and Jadwin; (509)946-9328; 1314 Jadwin Ave, Richland; $; beer and wine; MC, V; local checks only; lunch Mon–Fri, dinner Mon–Sat.*

Giacci's ★ In Richland's oldest building (1906), wonderful aromas waft from the busy kitchen and Puccini arias float through the air. Good salads and Italian sandwiches comprise the lunch menu at this attractive deli/restaurant. A similar menu makes for a rather ordinary dinner. Still, you'll finish on a fine note if you add a glass of Chianti and one of their excellent desserts. Outdoor tables in summer. ▪ *Corner of George Washington and Lee; (509)946-4855; 94 Lee Blvd, Richland; $; beer and wine; MC, V; local checks only; lunch, dinner Mon–Sat.* ♿

LODGINGS

Red Lion Hanford House ★ Location, location, location. For conventions you might do better at the Best Western Tower Inn down the street, but the Hanford House has secured Richland's finest piece of real estate right on the Columbia (aka Lake Wallula) stretched with more miles of park than most guests can manage in an afternoon jog. Due to the unusual shape of the hotel there aren't many riverfront rooms (best bets are 175 to 187 and 275 to 287). Or ask for one of the large rooms facing the attractive grassy courtyard and the dandy pool area (a must on the broiling Tri-Cities summer days). This is *the* place to stay in the Tri-Cities. ▪ *Take Richland exit off I-82 to George Washington Way; (509)946-7611; 802 George Washington Way, Richland, WA 99352; $$; AE, DC, MC, V; checks OK.*

TRI-CITIES: PASCO

This was the first of the Tri-Cities, a railroad town started in 1884. **Columbia Basin Community College**, near the airport, puts on shows and lectures; the Performing Arts

Building is a splendid, virtually windowless building in the brutalist mode.

LODGINGS

Red Lion Inn ★ The large, sprawling motel (279 rooms) in half-timbered style has several notable attractions. There are two outdoor pools, an exercise facility, and an 18-hole municipal golf course that runs right alongside the motel, making it appear to be set in a park—even though it's right on the freeway. The Red Lion is exceptionally convenient to the Tri-Cities airport and Columbia Basin Community College. Local residents like the dining room for "dressy" occasions where the blue flaming desserts and coffees can be seen clear across the dining room. This is one of the few restaurants in Eastern Washington that really knows how to cook seafood *and* beef. The service is unpolished but eager to please. ■ *Take 20th St exit off Hwy 395; (509)547-0701; 2525 N 20th St, Pasco, WA 99301; $$; full bar; AE, DC, MC, V; checks OK; breakfast, lunch, dinner every day.*

TRI-CITIES: KENNEWICK

RESTAURANTS

Chez Chaz ★ A fun collection of salt shakers sits on the counter and every table has its own sodium centerpiece, but that's as whimsical as this restaurant in an office building on Clearwater Avenue gets. The dinner menu is quite limited, probably because most people choose to do Chez Chaz for a well-executed lunch. There is a long list of sandwiches, like a great hot version of the Smoky Tom (turkey, cream cheese, provolone, and barbecue sauce on sourdough). But chef Chaz can do so much more—as evidenced by the specials: a spicy, peanuty Thai beef sauté on gently cooked vegetables, linguine with a light tomato and basil cream sauce, and Moroccan vinaigrette with couscous. Few diners leave without taking a sweet treat with them. ■ *Between Edison and Union on Clearwater; (509)735-2138; 5001 Clearwater Ave, Kennewick; $$; beer and wine; no credit cards; checks OK; lunch, dinner Mon–Sat.*

The Blue Moon Owners Linda, Dale, and Dean Shepard opened this restaurant with first-class food as an adjunct to their catering business. Unfortunately, it's tough to pay such prices for such good food and receive nothing in the sense of surroundings in return. But if you don't need atmo to enjoy your dinner, you'll appreciate this seven-course prix-fixe meal (one seating at 7:30pm Friday, 7:00pm Saturday; private parties of 15 or more can book Tuesday through Thursday). The lobster bisque is full-flavored, rich, and spicy. After a good caesar salad, a tasty cabernet sorbet cleanses the palate. Entree

Tri-Cities: Kennewick

Restaurants

selections might include a rack of lamb Provençal, tournedos Blue Moon, and sautéed pork Dijon. Reservations essential.
■ *A block from Washington; (509)582-6598; 21 W Canal Dr, Kennewick; $$$; wine only; MC, V; checks OK; dinner Fri–Sat.* ♿

Casa Chapala Tri-Cities' most endeared Mexican eatery is run by a couple so young that when they opened, they couldn't legally get a liquor license. They're old enough now and have maintained this very festive place where the help speak little English. Come Wednesday through Saturday between 5pm and 8:30pm and request a seat near the tortilla factory. Tortillas are that fresh, and you can be sure anything inside of them is too. ■ *Columbia and Washington; (509)586-4224; 107 E Columbia Dr, Kennewick; $; full bar; AE, MC, V; checks OK; lunch, dinner every day.*

LODGINGS

Quality Inn on Clover Island It's truly on an island, and thus offers wonderful river views from many of its 150 rooms. The Quality Inn gains our favor for its comparitively inexpensive rates. Otherwise, there's not much to distinguish this well-situated link in the chain (lodgings) from its Red Lion and Holiday Inn cousins. Avoid dining here. ■ *Columbia Dr and Washington; (509)586-0541; 435 Clover Island, Kennewick, WA 99336; $; AE, DC, MC, V; checks OK.* ♿

WALLA WALLA

The Walla Walla valley is an important historical area: the Lewis and Clark Expedition passed through in 1805, fur trappers began traveling up the Columbia River from Fort Astoria in 1811 and set up a fort in 1818, and in 1836 missionary Marcus Whitman built a medical mission west of the present town (Whitman and his wife, Narcissa, and a dozen fellow settlers were slain by a band of Cayuse Indians in the famous massacre of 1847). The town was founded in 1856 by Colonel Edward Steptoe and later named Walla Walla, an Indian phrase for "small, rapid streams." Main Street was built on the Nez Percé Indian Trail. Walla Walla has grown into a pleasant vale of 26,000 with fecund wheatlands all around and Whitman College, a pretty private college anchoring the city (the campus is a nice place to stroll, (509)527-5176). The community boasts the oldest continuous symphony west of the Mississippi River, which performs a season of winter concerts.

Whitman Mission, 7 miles west of town, off Highway 12, sketches out the story of the mission and the massacre; there aren't any historic buildings, but the simple outline of the mission in the ground is strangely affecting. A hike up an adjacent hill to an overlook offers the best impression of what the area looked like to the Whitmans and fellow settlers. The mission became an important station on the Oregon Trail and Narcissa Whitman's arrival was notable in that she and Eliza Spalding, also with the Whitman party, were the first white women to cross the continent overland. Call (509)529-2761.

Fort Walla Walla Museum in Fort Walla Walla Park on the west edge of town has a collection of 14 historic buildings and pioneer artifacts. Call (509)525-7703 for hours; camping and picknicking available at the park adjacent to the museum. Summers only.

Old Houses. Kirkman House Museum, listed on the National Register of Historic Places, is a fine period-home museum; 214 N Colville Street, (509)529-4373. Mature trees and Colonial architecture lend a New England feeling to Catherine Street, S Palouse Street, and W Birch Street. Pioneer Park on E Alder Street is a good example of the urban-park style of 80 years ago and was designed by the Olmsted brothers, the landscape architects whose father created New York City's Central Park and Seattle's Lake Washington Boulevard. The park has an excellent open-air aviary with a fine collection of pheasants, pigeons, and native waterfowl.

Onions. Walla Walla Sweets are spendid, truly sweet onions, great for sandwiches; here you can get the "number ones," with thin skins.

Wines. Walla Walla is home to some of the state's most brilliant wineries. Most notable is Woodward Canyon, Lowden, (509)525-4129, which produced a cabernet in 1987 that was judged one of the top 10 in the world by *Wine Spectator*. Others are L'Ecole No. 41, Lowden, (509)525-0940; Leonetti Cellars, Walla Walla, (509)525-0940; Waterbrook Winery, Lowden, (509)522-1918; and Seven Hills Winery, (509)529-3331, with production facilities over the state line in Milton-Freewater, Oregon, (509)938-7710 (open by appointment only).

Juniper Dunes Wilderness. This 7,140-acre wilderness, protected under the 1984 Washington Wilderness Act, includes some of the biggest sand dunes—up to 130 feet high and a quarter-mile wide—and the largest natural groves of western juniper, some 150 years old, in the state. This pocket of wilderness is all that remains of an ecosystem that once stretched over nearly 400 square miles south to the Snake and Columbia rivers. The area is managed by the Bureau of Land Management. No camping or fires are allowed in the wilderness and there is no drinking water available. Hikers must park at the boundary of the area. The most scenic portion of the wilderness is 2-mile hike northeast from the parking area toward the junipers and largest dunes. Getting to the parking area, which is 15 miles northeast of nearby Pasco, involves driving some unmarked back-roads through farmland; for directions to the parking area, contact the BLM, (509)353-2570.

RESTAURANTS

Merchants Ltd. ★★ It's a cluttered New York–style deli, with culinary merchandise piled ceiling-high on broad shelves, a deli counter loaded with breads, cheeses, sausages, salads, and caviars, and a glass-fronted bakery. The homemade soups are deservedly popular, but you won't be disappointed in the chicken salad or tabouli. There are tables inside, or sit out front under the awning at a sidewalk table and watch Walla Walla waltz by. Upstairs is a more sedate dining room where the food is quite good. Lunch is served buffet-style Tuesday through Friday (as is a Wednesday spaghetti dinner). Excellent wine list. ■ *Take 2nd St exit off Hwy 12, turn left on Main; (509)525-0900; 21 E Main St, Walla Walla; $$; beer and wine; MC, V; checks OK; breakfast, lunch Mon–Sat, dinner Wed until 8pm.*

Jacobi's For dining with a historic ambience, head for the former Northern Pacific Railroad Depot, home to Jacobi's, a cafe partially located in a former railroad dining car. The college crowd hangs out here, where they talk over espresso and beer from regional microbreweries. The cafe boasts "specialties from the Walla Walla Valley and beyond," and lives up to the promise. For more elegant ambience, ask for a table in the railroad dining car. The 20-page menu includes local offerings such as Washington apples with Jacobi's caramelized dip (an appetizer), stuffed potatoes, an eggplant sandwich, steak, seafood—the works. The eatery offers an impressive array of Northwest wines and beers. ■ *Take 2nd St exit off Hwy 12 to the old Northern Pacific Depot; (509)525-2677; 416 N 2nd St, Walla Walla; $; beer and wine; MC, V; checks OK; lunch, dinner every day.*

▼

Walla Walla

▲

LODGINGS

Green Gables Inn ★★ Margaret Buchan and husband Jim, the sports editor at the local newspaper, converted this arts and crafts–style mansion to a bed and breakfast and reception facility close to Whitman College. True to the architectural style, a broad covered porch sweeps across the front of the mansion and around one side, an ideal setting for relaxing on a warm afternoon, lemonade and book in hand. Inside, the large foyer is flanked by two sitting areas, both with fireplaces and one with a TV where guests can watch ball games with Jim. Names for the five guest rooms are from the L. M. Montgomery book *Anne of Green Gables*. A favorite is Idlewild, the only one with a fireplace, private deck, and Jacuzzi. Another is Dryad's Bubble, a spacious room with a comfortable reading area and French doors that open to a small balcony. A remodeled garage is a good (though somewhat sterile) family option complete with a kitchen. ■ *Take the Clinton exit off Hwy 12 to Bonsella; (509)525-5501; 922 Bonsella, Walla Walla, WA 99362; $$; AE, DC, MC, V; checks OK.*

Stone Creek Inn ★ When built in 1883, the Moore mansion was a home in the country. Now the mansion is a 4-acre oasis surrounded by a modest residential neighborhood on a busy arterial. The mansion built by Miles Moore is notable as the home of the last governor of the Washington Territory. At the moment, the mansion only has two guest rooms: a bright first-floor room (with an opulent bath) and a second-floor room with a fireplace and screened porch. Those interested in insects and butterflies will be interested in owner Greg Petersen's extensive collection in the parlor and library. Another passion? Classic cars, which Petersen restores. Ask him to take you for a spin or borrow one of their bicycles to tour on your own. ■ *Call ahead for directions; (509)529-8120; 720 Bryant, Walla Walla, WA 99362; $$; no credit cards; checks OK.*

DAYTON

An impressive 88 Victorian buildings on the National Register of Historic Places makes Dayton worthy of a stop, although don't expect to find all of the buildings restored. The town profited from a gold rush in 1861 in Idaho, as Dayton was on the main stage route between Walla Walla and Lewiston. Merchants and farmers built lavish houses during the boom years. Dayton boasts the oldest family-run hardware store in the state, Dingle's; the state's oldest volunteer fire department and oldest rodeo; and the state's first high school graduating class.

Skiing. In season, skiers can head for the Blue Mountains and Ski Bluewood, (509)382-4725, 21 miles southeast of Dayton (52 miles from Walla Walla) for cross-country and downhill skiing. The area, with the highest base elevation in the state, gets more than 300 inches of snow a year on its 26 runs.

RESTAURANTS

Patit Creek Restaurant ★★★ Bruce and Heather Hiebert have achieved the seemingly impossible: they've turned a small rural cafe into an excellent regional restaurant. Serving good food to the locals (both conservative farmers and more liberal college types) has been an experience—at times frustrating and educational—but the effort has paid off. There is now a steady and very appreciative clientele who don't mind driving long distances to eat superbly roasted meat at Patit Creek, located in what was a service station in the 1920s and later a soda fountain. Appetizers are notable, particularly the smoked salmon cheesecake (nonsweet) and the chèvre-stuffed dates wrapped in bacon and broiled. Bruce uses only the freshest vegetables and herbs. In the spring, fresh morel mushrooms are offered in a different entree each night. A little later in the season, he'll wander into the hills in search of extraordinarily sweet wild onions to use in some of his sauces. The wine list is short, but includes the finest Walla Walla area vintages. Heather's homemade pies and desserts provide a proper conclusion to such delightful fare. Reservations are crucial on weekends. Urbanites may sneer at fine food being served in a room with such folksy decor, a small gripe that easily disappears shortly after the first bite. Call for reservations. ▪ *On Hwy 12 at north end of town; (509) 382-2625; 725 E Dayton Ave, Dayton, WA; $$; beer and wine; MC, V; local checks only; dinner Tues–Sat.* ⅊

LODGINGS

The Purple House B&B A native of Southern Germany, owner Christine Williscroft brought her passion for Chinese antiques and Oriental rugs to her bed and breakfast. Breakfasts reflect Williscroft's heritage: streudel or huckleberry crêpes. She can pack a picnic lunch for explorers and on request will cook a European dinner, served family style. A typical dinner (guests only) would be Hungarian goulash, or trout in season when Williscroft goes fishing in the Touchet River. French doors in the first-floor guest room (decidedly feminine) open to a patio and swimming pool. The two upstairs rooms get quite hot in summer (at least the south-facing room has a ceiling fan). Small pets allowed with advance warning. A studio bedroom above the garage is cozy but dark; however, it has a freestanding fireplace and a kitchenette. ▪ *1 block off Hwy 12 in downtown Dayton; (509) 382-3159; 415 E Clay, Dayton, WA 99328; $$$; MC, V; checks OK; (closed October).*

PULLMAN

Pullman's population swells in the fall with Washington State University students, while the permanent residents are a mix of wheat farmers and university faculty. The largest of the Palouse towns, Pullman retains some of its cowpoke image, but covets an international reputation as a university town. The central business district consists mostly of one main street crowded with shops and some restaurants. There is abundant free parking just off the main street. Browsers might visit the **Nica Gallery** for an excellent representation of Eastern Washington artists, 246 E Main Street, (509) 334-1213; **Bruised Books** for used books that sometimes include hard-to-find first editions, 105 N Grand, (509) 334-7898; and **The Combine** for deli sandwiches, salads, desserts, espresso, and teas and herbs, 215 E Main, (509) 332-1774.

Washington State University. The campus is expanding constantly. The Fine Arts Center is a showcase with a spacious gallery that attracts exhibits of notable artists. Martin Stadium, home of the WSU Cougar football team, holds Pac 10 Conference–size crowds; the baseball team plays on Bailey Field near the 12,000-seat Beasley Performing Arts Coliseum, which houses both the basketball team and frequent rock concerts; (800)325-SEAT for tickets and an events calendar. Visitors might want to drop by Ferdinand's, located in the Agricultural Science Building and open weekdays only, which offers ice cream, milk shakes, and Cougar Gold cheese, made from milk and cream from WSU's own dairy herd, (509)335-4014. Tours of the university, (509)335-4527, can keep visitors busy for a couple of days. For an impressive insect collection, visit the **Museum of Anthropology** and Maurice T. James Entomological Collection in Johnson Hall. Other campus destinations include the Marion Ownbey Herbarium in Herald Hall for a quick-course on herbs; the Beef, Dairy, and Swine centers; and the Jewett Astronomical Observatory; call (509)335-6868 for tours. Pick up a campus map and a visitor's parking pass from the visitors center adjacent to the fire station (follow the signs on Stadium Way).

Kamiak Butte, 13 miles north on Route 24, offers a good place for a picnic and nice overlooks of the rolling wheat country. About 30 miles north of Pullman on Highway 195, **Steptoe Butte** towers above the Palouse and affords an impressive panoramic view as well as unobstructed stargazing. There's a picnic area at the top but plan for wind, which is constant. History buffs will find **Steptoe Battlefield** near Rosalia interesting; as at the Little Bighorn, the U.S. Cavalry lost this one, too.

Palouse Falls. Just north of the confluence with the Snake River, the Palouse River gushes over a basalt cliff higher than Niagara Falls and drops 198 feet into a steep-walled basin. Hiking trails lead to an overlook above the falls and to streamside below the falls. The falls are best during spring runoff starting in late March. Camping allowed. Just downstream from the falls is the Marmes Rock Shelter, where remains of the earliest known inhabitants of North America, dating back 10,000 years, were discovered by archaeologists. At the confluence of the Snake and Palouse rivers, there is a public boat launch at Lyons Ferry State Park. The Marmes site is accessible via a 2½-mile unmaintained trail from Lyons Ferry State Park and by canoe. Much of the actual shelter area is flooded by the backwaters of Lower Monumental Dam, but the area is still popular with canoeists.

RESTAURANTS

 The Seasons ★★ No doubt Pullman's finest dining experience. This elegant eatery occupies a renovated old house atop a flower-covered cliff. Dinner is presented in a proper and elegant fashion; chicken and seafood are good choices. Salad dressings are made on the premises and salads are served with scrumptious homemade breads such as whole-wheat with cornmeal, poppy seeds, and sesame seeds.

■ *On the hill about ½ block off Grand; (509)334-1410; 215 SE Paradise St, Pullman; $$; beer and wine; AE, DC, MC, V; checks OK; dinner Tues–Sun.*

Swilly's ★★ Located in what was a 1920s photography studio, Swilly's flanks the Palouse River and sports a small outdoor cafe. Across the street is one of the 20 artesian wells, drilled between 1890 and 1909, that were the deciding factor in locating a state college in Pullman. Inside, the warmth of the hardwood floors, the exposed brick walls, and the rich smell of espresso invite lingering. Works by area artists decorate the walls. The eatery boasts fresh local ingredients, right down to cream from a nearby dairy and bread from a local bakery. A separate calzone menu is billed as "the freshest and finest in the Palouse." The regular seasonal menu offers pastas with tempting ingredients such as marinated artichoke hearts, a lemon-caper combination, or an Oriental fish sauce. Swilly's has a modest selection of imported beers and a wine list with a good representation of Washington wines. ■ *1 block east of Grand; (509)334-3395; 200 NE Kamiaken St, Pullman; $$; beer and wine; AE, MC, V; checks OK; lunch, dinner Mon–Sat.*

Hilltop Steakhouse This motel and restaurant has probably the best steaks in Pullman, family-style chicken dinners Sunday afternoons, Sunday brunch, and a wonderful view of the university and surrounding hills. The food is consistently good, albeit predictable, fare. ■ *At city limits off Hwy 195 between Olsen and Davis Way; (509)334-2555; 928 Olsen, Pullman; $$; full bar; AE, DC, MC, V; checks OK; lunch Mon–Fri, dinner every day, brunch Sun.*

LODGINGS

Paradise Creek Quality Inn Just far enough off Route 270 to afford guests quiet nights away from traffic noise, this motel is also within easy walking distance of the WSU campus. It's situated over the meandering creek for which it's named. ■ *¼ mile east of the WSU campus near the junction of Hwy 270 and Bishop; (509)332-0500 or (800)669-3212; SE 1050 Bishop Blvd, Pullman, WA 99163; $$; AE, DC, MC, V; checks OK.*

BRITISH COLUMBIA

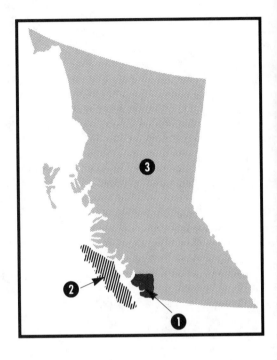

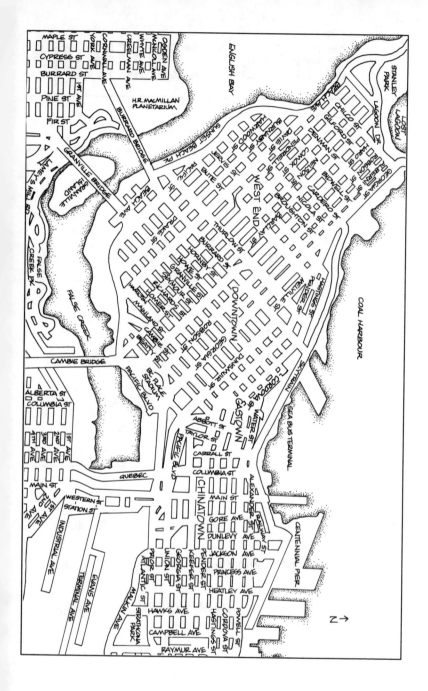

Vancouver and Environs

Vancouver restaurants and lodgings, including Greater Vancouver (Richmond, West Vancouver, and North Vancouver).

VANCOUVER

Vancouver has long touted itself as Canada's gateway to the Pacific Rim. But only when Hong Kong billionaire Li Ka-shing scooped up the old EXPO site, two hundred acres of prime development land, did the realization sink in that the city was also becoming the Pacific Rim's gateway to Canada. The new arrivals, especially those from Hong Kong, have taken advantage of immigration regulations designed to lure investors and have bought up billions of dollars worth of real estate since 1985.

Yet Vancouver has always accepted the waves of immigrants that have broken on its shore. Indeed, the city seems living proof that a benign environment will produce an easygoing disposition. Despite a stiffening of the work ethic of late, this is still a place of leisure and relaxed enjoyment.

Glance away from the opulence of the shops as you saunter along Robson and you will see why; at the end of a side street lap the peaceful waters of Burrard Inlet. Beyond, the mountains on the north shore glitter with snow for half the year. Vancouver, residents are fond of saying, is one of the few cities in the world where you can go skiing and sailing on the same day. How remarkable, then, that it should also be one of the few where, sitting ouside a Neapolitan cafe, you can eavesdrop on an impassioned argument in Hungarian and see graffiti in Khmer.

Vancouver's chameleon identity is that of home to the children of the dispossessed, whether they be Scottish Highlanders or Hmong tribespeople. For the sculptors and the screenwriters, the dancers, jugglers, retired war correspondents and exiled aristocrats, and the drifters and dreamers who have settled here in such disproportionate numbers, this is as close to the Promised Land as it's possible to get.

THE ARTS

Visual Arts. Francis Rattenbury's elegant old courthouse is now the Vancouver Art Gallery, which holds more than 20 major exhibitions a year and whose permanent collection includes works by Goya, Carr, Gainsborough, and Picasso (750 Hornby, (604)682-4668). Many of the city's commercial galleries are located on the dozen blocks just south of the Granville Bridge, and Granville Island, site of the Emily Carr Institute of Art and Design, has a number of potteries and craft studios. The avant-garde is most often found on the east side of the city, at spaces such as the Pitt International Gallery (317 W Hastings, (604)681-6740). The Museum of Anthropology at the University of British Columbia (UBC, 6393 NW Marine Drive, (604)228-5087) has an extensive collection of native American cultures of coastal British Columbia (including an impressive display of totem poles), as well as artifacts from Africa to the Orient.

▼

Vancouver

▲

Music. Thanks to vigorous fund raising by the musicians and their supporters, and injections of government cash, the Vancouver Symphony Orchestra is still on its feet. The main season starts in October at the Orpheum, an old vaudeville theater (884 Granville). The Vancouver Opera puts on five productions a year at the Queen Elizabeth Theatre (Hamilton at Georgia); the program is a balance of popular and traditional. For information about any musical event, call Ticketmaster, (604)280-4444.

Theater. The Vancouver Playhouse Theatre Company explores contemporary and classical theater, offering six plays each season, October to May, in the Vancouver Playhouse (Hamilton and Dunsmuir, (604)873-3311). The Arts Club is a commercial theater with two locations and, usually, less production panache than the Playhouse; Granville Island, (604)687-1644. Contemporary theater in Vancouver is largely centered in the VECC—Vancouver East Cultural Center, 1895 Venables Street, (604)254-9578.

OTHER THINGS TO DO

Parks and Gardens. The city is blessed with a climate—very similar to Britain's—well-suited for flowers and greenery. Take a walk through the quiet forest in the heart of Stanley

Park. The western edge is rimmed by three swimming beaches; you'll find tennis courts, a rose garden, an aquarium, and kiddie attractions on the southern fringes. Also great for kids is Science World British Columbia, across town at the old EXPO site. Here, hands-on exhibits, films, and working models will keep families busy for hours; 1455 Quebec Street, (604)687-7832. At Queen Elizabeth Park, dramatic winding paths, sunken gardens, and waterfalls skirt the Bloedel Conservatory, (604)872-5513 (stop in for lunch at Seasons in the Park). The University of British Columbia campus boasts three superb gardens — the Botanical Garden, Nitobe Memorial Gardens, and Totem Park—along with a top-drawer Sunday-tea setting at Cecil Green Park House, 6251 Cecil Green Park Road, (604)228-6289. The Chinese Classical Garden within Dr. Sun Yat-Sen Park (E Pender and Carrall streets) is a spectacular reconstruction of a Chinese scholar's garden, complete with pavilions and water-walkways. Near Queen Elizabeth Park, the VanDusen Botanical Garden stretches over 55 acres. Each part of the garden offers flora from a different region of the world, as well as those native to the Pacific coast. Open every day, year-round; 5251 Oak Street, (604)266-7194.

Shopping. Vancouver has always been bursting with storefronts. Robson Street has a pleasant, European feel, with colorful awnings, few high rises, and a proliferation of delicatessens, boutiques, and restaurants. Downtown is full of outstanding shops. In poor weather, head underground for the Pacific Centre and Vancouver Centre malls, with shops like Holt Renfrew, Eatons, and The Bay. At Granville Island Public Market on the south shore of False Creek, you can get everything from just-caught salmon to packages of fresh herbs to a wonderful array of fresh produce. Or visit the lesser-known public market at Lonsdale Quay in North Vancouver with two levels of shops and produce right at the North Shore SeaBus terminal. It's a 15-minute SeaBus ride from the terminal near Canada Place across Burrard Inlet. Gastown is a restored 1890s precinct, once touristy, now anchored by some really good shops of more use to locals. Book Alley, the 300 and 400 blocks of West Pender, has bookstores specializing in everything from cookbooks to radical politics to science fiction.

Nightlife. On a warm summer night, the music spilling out from Vancouver's clubs and bars will range from down-and-dirty R&B at the suitably raunchy Yale Hotel (1300 Granville, (604)681-9253) and the sprung-floored Commodore Ballroom (870 Granville, (604)681-7838), through local alternative bands at the Town Pump (66 Water, (604)683-6695) and disco thump at Richard's on Richards, the yuppie meat market (1036 Richards, (604)687-6794). The Railway Club (579 Dunsmuir, (604)681-1625) has a remarkably varied membership and presents consistently good music, whether pop or rock. Top names perform at BC Place Stadium (777 Pacific Boulevard S, (604)669-2300). To find out who's playing where, pick up a copy of the *Georgia Straight* or Thursday's *Vancouver Sun*. Jazz fiends can call the Jazz Hotline, (604)682-0706.

Sports. The Vancouver Canucks, who made the playoffs in 1993, are the obvious draw when they play (Pacific Coliseum, (604)280-4400). The Vancouver 86ers, the local soccer team, has a devoted following (1126 Douglas, in Burnaby; (604)299-0086). The BC Lions football team can boast a modest success of late, kindling hopes for greater glory in seasons to come (BC Place, (604)669-2709). Visiting baseball enthusiasts should try to catch a Vancouver Canadians game at the Nat Bailey Stadium, a venue of which many locals have fond memories (Queen Elizabeth Park, (604)872-5232). But most Vancouverites would rather play than watch. Golf, sailing, hefting weights, exploring the local creeks and inlets by any kind of boat you can name—the city has first-rate facilities for these activities and many more. For information, contact Sport, BC (1367 W Broadway, (604)737-3000).

Ethnic Vancouver. The oldest and biggest of Vancouver's ethnic communities is Chinatown. The 200 block of E Pender is the main market area; to get started, try Yuen Fong for teas or the Dollar Market for barbecued pork or duck. A growing number of Asians are moving into Richmond, as evidenced by the increasing number of outstanding Chinese restaurants and the New Aberdeen Centre, where you can get ginseng in bulk or durian from Thailand, and eat home-style Chinese food while you bowl. Italian commercial and cultural life thrives in the distinctive neighborhood around Commercial Drive, east of downtown. A second, less discovered Italian district is on Little Italy's northern border—the 2300 to 2500 blocks of E Hastings. Vancouver's 60,000 East Indian immigrants have established their own shopping area called the Punjabi Market in south Vancouver at 49th and Main streets, where you can bargain for spices, chutney, and sweets. One of Vancouver's longest-established groups of ethnic inhabitants, the Greeks, live and shop west of the intersection of MacDonald and W Broadway; and a large Iranian population has settled in North Vancouver, as the many Iranian markets and saffron-scented restaurants will attest.

RESTAURANTS

The Alabaster Restaurant ★★★★ With three former Four Seasons Hotel cooks in the kitchen, those in the know and with the dough refer to this Yaletown restaurant as a mini Chartwell. Central to the decor in this surpassingly elegant yet informal spot is a thoughtful alabaster statue of Venus. It's as sensuous and cerebral as the food that Markus Wieland serves here. A young chef, Wieland has experience—stints in some of the city's best restaurants, a grand tour of Europe—that many chefs twice his age might envy. His European approach is implicit in everything from the *amuse-gueule* (a "tastebud tickler") that prefaces dinner to a starter of fried polenta layered with bocconcini, Roma tomatoes, roasted peppers, and pesto. Whether you choose the salmon with pink grapefruit and Cinzano yogurt sauce or the ambrosial tomato risotto with mushrooms or the flawless saltimbocca, you can't go wrong here. Top things off with the buttery soft panna cotta with caramel—it's an Italian heart-stopper. Soothing service. Brava, Chef Wieland. ■ *Davie and Hamilton; (604)687-1758; 1168 Hamilton St, Vancouver; $$$; full bar; AE, DC, MC, V; no checks; lunch Mon–Fri, dinner Mon–Sat.* &

Bishop's ★★★★ Year in, year out, near flawless, with superlative standards of service and cuisine, closely watched by master host John Bishop. When the 1993 Summit came to Vancouver, the White House summoned Bishop to create his wonderful grilled Pacific salmon fillet for Presidents Clinton and Yeltsin (he now has a standing invitation to the White House). Hollywood knows about Bishop's as well—Glenn Close, Robin Williams, Joan Rivers, and others have been spotted here. Bishop warmly greets his guests (celebrity and otherwise) and, assisted by the most professionally polished young staff in the city, proceeds to demonstrate that he understands the true art of hospitality. Attention to detail is important in this minimalist Kitsilano restaurant. Entrees are uncomplicated. Lamb is always tender and excellent, as is daily fish (recently, ginger steamed salmon). We favor pan-seared scallops scented with lemon grass and topped with a crisp potato pancake. Everything bears the Bishop trademark of light, subtly complex flavors and bright, graphic color. His desserts, especially the Death by Chocolate, are legendary. ■ *Corner of Yew and 4th; (604)738-2025; 2183 W 4th Ave, Vancouver; $$$; full bar; AE, DC, MC, V; no checks; lunch Mon–Fri, dinner every day (closed for 2 weeks in Jan).*

Chartwell (The Four Seasons) ★★★★ Chartwell evokes an upper-class English men's club atmosphere. The new hand at the helm is Marc Miron, former executive chef of the award-winning Four Seasons resort in Nevis. Miron's food is generous in proportion and inspiration. Begin with his house-smoked candied salmon loin with horseradish crème fraîche and onion-dill bannock and move on to Miron's vanilla and mango dressing drizzled on mesclin greens and pink grapefruit. The rosy calf's liver with double-smoked bacon and garlic-roasted onion confit with buttermilk herb mashed potatoes is world-class. Master host Angelo Cecconi and his talented staff give Chartwell its distinctive stamp of personal service—warm, discreet, and attentive. A pre-theater dinner

Vancouver and Environs

▼

Vancouver

Restaurants

▲

menu with valet parking is an outstanding value. An award-winning wine list. ■ *W Georgia between Howe and Granville; (604)689-9333; 791 W Georgia St, Vancouver; $$$; full bar; AE, DC, MC, V; no checks; breakfast every day, lunch Sun–Fri, dinner every day.* ⅃

Le Crocodile ★★★★ France without a passport—that's Le Crocodile. Chef and owner Michel Jacob named his bistro after his favorite restaurant in his hometown of Strasbourg, and his Franco-German culinary heritage is obvious. He accompanies a wonderfully savory onion tart with chilled Alsatian wine in green-stemmed glasses. Salmon tartare and sautéed scallops in an herb sauce are both showstoppers. Luscious Dover sole, duck (crisp outside, moist inside) accompanied by a light orange sauce, calves' livers with spinach butter—it's a trauma to choose. The best desserts are the traditional ones. The well thought-out wine list and European atmosphere make a dinner at Le Crocodile an affair to remember. ■ *Burrard St (enter off Smithe St); 669-4298; 100-909 Burrard St, Vancouver; $$$; full bar; AE, DC, MC, V; no checks; lunch Mon–Fri, dinner Mon–Sat.* ⅃

Tojo's ★★★★ Tojo Hidekazu *is* Tojo's. This beaming Japanese chef has a loyal clientele that regularly fills his spacious upstairs restaurant, though most people want to sit at the 10-seat sushi bar—not big enough for all his devoted patrons. He's endlessly innovative, surgically precise, and committed to fresh ingredients. Show an interest in the food, and he might offer you a bit of this and that from the kitchen: Tojo tuna or perhaps special beef (very thin beef wrapped around asparagus and shrimp). Getting to be a regular is not difficult, and it's highly recommended. The dining room has a view of the stunning North Shore mountains and plenty of table seating; Japanese menu standards like tempura and teriyaki are always reliable, and daily specials are usually superb: pine mushroom soup in the fall, shrimp dumplings with hot mustard sauce from October to May, cherry blossoms with scallops and deep-fried sole with tiger prawns in the spring. Plum wine and fresh orange pieces complete the meal. ■ *Broadway and Willow; (604)872-8050; 202-777 W Broadway, Vancouver; $$$; full bar; AE, DC, MC, V; no checks; dinner Mon–Sat.* ⅃

Bacchus Ristorante (The Wedgewood Hotel) ★★★ A glaring game of musical chefs went on for a few years until dedicated hotelier Eleni Skalbania discovered Alan Groom. The emergence of executive chef Groom as a first-rate talent put Bacchus on the culinary map. Geographically speaking, the chef is decidedly British, but the climate is distinctly Northern Italian. Bacchus is an extraordinarily pretty place, with a striking open kitchen. You're relaxed, and you feel everyone in the kitchen is too: timing is superb. Raw Tofino oysters escorted by a papaya-lime salsa are outstanding, as are the grilled salmon with citrus dill and cracked-pepper butter sauce and the tiger prawns with asparagus lemon risotto. A crisp, roasted free-range chicken with lime butter served with a mountain of garlic mashed potatoes and fresh greens competes with an exemplary osso buco. Surrender to a homey summer pudding. ■ *Between Robson and Smithe; (604)689-7777; 845 Hornby St, Vancouver; $$; full bar; AE, DC, MC, V; no checks; breakfast, lunch, dinner every day, brunch Sat and Sun.*

Beach Side Cafe ★★★ With their creative and varied approach to regional cuisine, owner Janet McGuire and chef Carol Chow have turned this little Ambleside haunt into one of the area's more serious kitchens. The summertime deck rates among the city's best, with views of Stanley Park and Kitsilano across the water. Choices are plentiful, with emphasis on daily specials as well as a cutting-edge list of better West Coast wines. In season, look for grilled squid with purée of fava beans, or seared scallops and prawns in a zesty garlic, sundried tomato, and wine sauce. Definitely order the goat cheese salad, with crispy pancetta, frisée, and pine nut vinaigrette. Dessert lovers swear by the lemon meringue pie. ■ *Between 13th and 14th, West Vancouver; (604)925-1945; 1362 Marine Dr, West Vancouver; $$; full bar; AE, MC, V; no checks; lunch Mon–Fri, dinner Mon–Sun, brunch Sat and Sun.*

Caffe de Medici ★★★ As you enter Caffe de Medici, you are immediately made to feel like a favored guest. The high molded ceilings, serene portraits of members of the 15th-century Medici family, chairs and drapery in Renaissance green against crisp white table linen, and walls the color of zabaglione create a slightly palatial feeling that is businesslike by day, romantic by night. Skip the soups and order the beautiful antipasto: a bright collage of marinated eggplant, artichoke hearts, peppers, olives, squid, and Italian meats. Pasta dishes are flat-out *magnifico*—a slightly chewy plateful of tortellini alla panna comes so rich with cheese you'll never order any others. Although it's mostly a Florentine restaurant (with a knockout version of beefsteak marinated in red wine and olive oil), we've also sampled a fine Roman-style rack of lamb. ■ *Between Burrard and Thurlow on Robson; (604)669-9322; 1025 Robson St, Vancouver; $$$; full bar; AE, DC, MC, V; no checks; lunch Mon–Fri, dinner every day.*

CinCin ★★★ *Cin-Cin* is a hearty Italian toast, a wish of health and good cheer, all of which is implied in this sunny Mediterranean space. The scent from wood-burning ovens, the warm surroundings—what more could one need? Best seats are in the northeast corner by the window. CinCin's breadsticks and flatbreads (rosemary and garlic oatmeal) are irresistible. Launch your meal with a saffron-scented cioppino, or carpaccio.

Noodles are made fresh daily. Rigatoni is tossed with house-made sausage, artichokes, and sweet onions; linguine rib-bons are laced with a mingling of sea creatures; and rotini is dotted with juicy morsels of roast chicken and porcini mushrooms. The well-crafted wine list is uncompromising in quality. Desserts are all homemade in the best sense of the word. A great place to sip wine with the gang in the lounge (food's served until midnight). ■ *Between Bute and Thurlow; (604)688-7338; 1154 Robson St, Vancouver; $$$; full bar; AE, DC, MC, V; no checks; lunch Mon–Fri, dinner every day.*

The Fish House at Stanley Park ★★★ Located in the old Beach House Restaurant close by the tennis courts is high-profile restaurateur Bud Kanke's best restaurant. The all-new Fish House reopened after a face lift that has added continuity and expanded the country-cottage theme. Unlike most sequels, Fish House II is much better than the original, mainly because of the deal that saw Karen Barnaby, current Queen of West Coast Cuisine, enthroned in the kitchen. Here, seafood rules (salmon, sea bass, shellfish of all kinds)—everything you'd expect and some that you wouldn't. It's the whole plate that impresses. Barnaby's vegetables aren't an afterthought; each is a discovery in itself: red cabbage with fennel, spaghetti squash with poppy seeds, and buttermilk mashed potatoes. Ahi tuna comes as fist-sized loins (a pair), barely grilled through, and fork-tender in a green pepper sauce. Yucatán peppered oysters have an incendiary blast that doesn't disguise the flavor. Desserts are equally memorable, especially the oven-baked apple galette with lemon curd and cinnamon crème fraîche. The service is friendly, but could use some polish. ■ *At the entrance to Stanley Park; (604)681-7275; 2099 Beach Ave, Vancouver; $$; full bar; AE, DC, MC, V; no checks; lunch Mon–Fri, dinner every day, brunch Sat and Sun.* &

Five Sails (Pan Pacific Hotel) ★★★ From this restaurant's perch the view of the city is magic, gentled in the daylight, jeweled by nighttime. Facing the harbor from your table, you could be aboard a luxury liner sailing to Alaska. This taut ship runs with a balance of warmth and snap and the hearty, flavorful cooking of chef Robert Sulatycky. Begin with smoky BC salmon and warm potato pancake, or share a goat cheese flan, then choose among the grilled tuna fillet with a winning wasabe potato Napoleon, or peppered sirloin with addictive thick potato fries, or crispy chicken roasted with garlic. Set sail on an individual baked Alaska. Free parking. ■ *On the waterfront at the north end of both Burrard and Howe; (604)662-8111; 999 Canada Pl, Vancouver; $$$; full bar; AE, DC, MC, V; no checks; dinner every day.* &

Grand King Seafood Restaurant (Holiday Inn) ★★★ Chef Lam Kam Shing's celebrated stint at the Dynasty Restaurant in the Vancouver Renaissance Hotel earned him a reputation as one of the best chefs in Vancouver. Now, once again, an appreciative crowd is frequenting his restaurant, located in the Holiday Inn on W Broadway. The decor here is no match for the elegant Dynasty, but the service—led by the ever-courteous Simon Lee and affable Peter Ling—is correspondingly less formal, equally helpful, and somehow more comfortable. The menu is trademark Lam—a creative assimilation of Chinese cuisines with innovative touches gleaned from Japanese and other Asian cooking styles. Local ingredients become new classics in dishes such as shrimp, ham, and duck in cabbage. Above all, ideas both simple and complex are backed by thoughtful and impeccable execution in the kitchen. Examples are the steamed rock cod, barely off the bone and doused with Lam's secret blend of soya, and crispy roasted suckling pig trimmed to present just the right balance of skin, fat, and lean meat. The chef's special menu changes monthly, ensuring that the kitchen's creative juices continue to flow—and that you'll be coming back for more. ■ *Between Heather and Willow on W Broadway; (604)876-7855; 705 W Broadway, Vancouver; $$$; full bar; MC, V; no checks; lunch, dinner every day.* &

Il Giardino di Umberto ★★★ Stars, stargazers, and the movers and shakers come to Umberto Menghi's Il Giardino to mingle amid the Tuscan villa decor: high ceilings, tiled floors, winking candlelight, and a vine-draped terrace for dining alfresco (no better place in summer). The emphasis is on pasta and game, with an Italian nuova elegance: farm-raised pheasant with roasted-pepper stuffing and port wine sauce, tender veal with a mélange of lightly grilled wild mushrooms. Be warned: The prices on the specials are in their own category. For dessert, go for the tiramisu—the best version of this pick-me-up in town. ■ *Pacific and Hornby; (604)669-2422; 1382 Hornby St, Vancouver; $$$; full bar; AE, DC, MC, V; no checks; lunch Mon–Fri, dinner Mon–Sat.*

Imperial Chinese Seafood Restaurant ★★★ The Imperial may lay claim to being the most opulent Chinese dining room around: a central staircase leads to the balustrade-lined mezzanine, diplomatic dignitaries and rock stars dine in luxurious private rooms, and large windows command expansive views of Burrard Inlet and the North Shore mountains. The food can be equally polished, as in the superb pan-fried prawns in soy, beef sautéed in chile with honey walnuts, and crunchy-sweet gai lan with garlic and bonito. Dim sum is consistently good. If it weren't for a bit of unevenness in the service, this could be a perfect restaurant. Reservations recommended on weekdays. ■ *Burrard and W Hastings; 688-8191; 355 Burrard St, Vancouver; $$; full bar; AE, MC, V; no checks; lunch, dinner every day.* &

Kirin Mandarin Restaurant ▪ Kirin Seafood Restaurant
★★★ Kirin's postmodern decor—high ceilings, slate green walls, black lacquer trim—is oriented around the two-story-high mystical dragonlike creature that is the restaurant's namesake. The menu reads like a trilingual (Chinese, English, and Japanese) opus spanning the culinary capitals of China: Canton, Sichuan, Shanghai, and Beijing (live lobsters and crabs can be ordered in 11 different preparations). The northern Chinese specialties are the best. Peking duck is as good as it gets this side of China, and braised dishes such as sea cucumber with prawn roe sauce are "royal" treats. Atypical of Chinese restaurants, desserts can be excellent—try the sweet fried red-bean pie. The Western-style service is attentive though sometimes a tad aggressive. The Cognac cart is for splurgers only.

The second, equally fine outpost is in City Square with a passable view of the city. It focuses more on seafood and has great dim sum. ▪ *Alberni St at Bute; (604)682-8833; 1166 Alberni St, Vancouver.* ▪ *12th Ave at Cambie; (604)879-8038; 201-555 W 12th Ave, Vancouver; $$$; full bar; AE, DC, V; checks OK; lunch, dinner every day (breakfast in summer at Alberni St location).* &

Landmark Hot Pot House ★★★ Hotpotting—traditionally for the warming of body and soul on long wintry nights—seems to have transcended its seasonal limits to emerge as a Chinese culinary trend. In the Landmark, the center of each table is cut out for the built-in natural-gas stove and its settings, which include a personal strainer and chopsticks. The menus are simply lists of available ingredients and prices; the rest is up to you. This is heartwarming, healthy food at its simplest, embellished only by the chef's exquisite knife work and perfect presentation. ▪ *Cambie St near Queen Elizabeth Park; (604)872-2868; 4023 Cambie St, Vancouver; $$; full bar; MC, V; no checks; dinner every day.* &

Le Club (Sutton Place Hotel) ★★★ Hidden just a few steps behind the bustling Gerard Lounge in Vancouver's venerable Sutton Place Hotel is this wonderfully romantic setting with salmon-colored fabric walls, original artwork, and European furnishings. Although it's rather old-fashioned looking, a hip, casually dressed crowd brings its appetite here. Stick to the $36 table d'hôte menu and you'll get a brilliant dinner at a reasonable price, orchestrated by talented chef Kai Lermen. Anything from the dessert trolley is worth hailing. ▪ *On Burrard between Robson and Smithe; (604)682-5511; 845 Burrard St, Vancouver; $$$; full bar; AE, DC, MC, V; no checks; dinner Mon–Sat.* &

Le Gavroche ★★★ Arguably the most romantic restaurant in the city, Le Gavroche has re-emerged as one of the city's leading French kitchens, enhanced by a discreet upstairs room, complete with blazing fire and glimpses of the harbor and mountains. Chef Scott Kidd's cooking comfortably melds traditional favorites with Northwest Coast influences. For starters, try the endive, pear, and Stilton salad with port orange vinaigrette. Kidd's approach to seafood is simple and beguiling: sea bass comes with leek confit. Service is formal, but friendly and subtly attentive. Le Gavroche has one of the city's better wine cellars with a range of Bordeaux and Burgundies. ▪ *Alberni at Cardero; (604)685-3924; 1616 Alberni St, Vancouver; $$$; full bar; AE, DC, MC, V; no checks; lunch Mon–Fri, dinner every day.*

Phnom Penh Restaurant ★★★ Once Vancouver's best-kept secret, these restaurants (there are now two) are winning a steady stream of accolades from sources as diverse as local magazine polls and Julia Child. The decor is still basic, but the menu has expanded from its original rice and noodle dishes to include the cuisines of China, Vietnam, and Cambodia. Hot and sour soup with sablefish is richly flavored, redolent of lime and purple basil. An excellent appetizer of marinated beef sliced carpaccio-thin is seared rare and dressed with nuoc mam (a spicy, fishy sauce—the Vietnamese staple). Sautéed baby shrimp in prawn roe and tender slivers of salted pork cover hot, velvety steamed rice paste—a real masterpiece. The oyster omelet is a dream. Service is knowledgeable and friendly. ▪ *Near Chinatown at Main and Georgia; (604)682-5777; 244 E Georgia St, Vancouver. ▪ Near Oak on W Broadway; (604)734-8898; 955 W Broadway, Vancouver; $; full bar; AE, MC; no checks; lunch, dinner Wed–Mon.*

Quattro on Fourth ★★★ Antonio Corsi took over the westside space that had been home to Montri's Thai Restaurant and turned it into one of the most comfortable Italian restaurants in the city. There's a high sense of *abbondanza* here. An impressive selection of antipasti includes no less than eight different carpaccio offerings; razor-thin sliced raw swordfish is superb, so too the grilled radicchio bocconcini and portobello mushrooms. Spaghetti Piga ("for Italians only") rewards with a well-spiced sauce of chicken, chiles, black beans, and plenty of garlic. Food prepared with lots of TLC from son Patrick and staff. At press time, Quattro added a heated patio to serve 35. ▪ *4th and Trafalgar; (604)734-4444; 2611 W 4th Ave, Vancouver; $$; full bar; AE, DC, MC, V; no checks; dinner every day.*

Raintree ★★★ Even though executive chef Karen Barnaby has defected to the Fish House in Stanley Park, chef Andrew Skorzewski has been running the show successfully. The concrete-walled space is prettied with huge flower arrangements, decorated with a simple sophistication, and offers a spectacular view of the North Shore skyline. "BC first and fresh" is still the

▼

hallmark of this pioneer of regional cooking. Fennel and cucumber salad with cilantro mint dressing and a venison carpaccio are light starters. There's a bounty of salmon: kippered, smoked wild sockeye, and spring salmon, Indian candy, or the seafood bowl. For dessert, order the sampler and taste everything or have Raintree's signature apple pie, which contains 3 kilograms (7 pounds) of Okanagan fruit. The wine list echoes the Northwest Coast theme and is augmented to match a busy schedule of winemaker dinners. ■ *On Alberni between Bidwell and Cardero; (604)688-5570; 1630 Alberni St, Vancouver; $$$; full bar; AE, DC, MC, V; no checks; dinner every day.* ⅋

Seasons in the Park ★★★ Considerable attention in the kitchen has contributed to Seasons in the Park's rapidly rising reputation. Although the park setting and the stunning view of downtown and the North Shore mountains still guarantee a line of tour buses outside, today's visitors to Seasons come as much for the food as the view. Diners are treated to chef Pierre Delacorte's menu of just-picked produce, succulent seafood, and local wines. ■ *Inside Queen Elizabeth Park; (604)874-8008; W 33rd Ave at Cambie, Vancouver; $$; full bar; AE, MC, V; no checks; lunch Mon–Fri, dinner every day, brunch Sat and Sun.* ⅋

Star Anise ★★★ Here in the heart of the trendy South Granville quarter, Sam Lalji and Adam Busby's chic Star Anise has nothing to do with Chinese seasoning and everything to do with exemplary service and endlessly inventive cooking. Elegant surroundings attract anyone who is passionate about food. Dictated by the season and chef Busby's whim, the menu is honest and unpretentious, leaning to lightness or deep, earthy comfort, with a constant theme of fresh ingredients. Lunchtime is a steal with grilled Merguez sausage and steamed coastal mussels atop angel hair pasta, tandoori lamb brochette with couscous and minted yogurt or an omelet of Gruyère and pancetta. Dinner starters can range from a purple plum relish to an inspired trio of ocean tartare (made with fresh seafoods). The pan-roasted chicken and the quince marinated medallions of deer have their own devout following. ■ *12th Ave east of Granville; (604)737-1485; 1485 W 12th Ave, Vancouver; $$$; full bar; AE, DC, MC, V; no checks; lunch Mon–Fri, dinner every day, brunch Sat and Sun.* ⅋

Sun Sui Wah Seafood Restaurant ★★★ These sister restaurants are actually an extension of a Hong Kong chain. Consequently, preparations are tried and true: crisp, tender roasted squab; deftly steamed scallops on silky bean curd topped with creamy-crunchy tobikko (flying-fish roe) sauce; and kirin fish—steamed rock cod slices interwoven with paper-thin slices of ham and fleshy mushrooms on a fresh lotus leaf. The Richmond location has dim sum at lunch and is renowned for its platter of deep-fried "milk"—fragrant, sweet coconut in a fluffy crust. With only a few minor lapses in service, Sun Sui Wah's success is richly deserved. ■ *Alderbridge Plaza, Richmond; (604) 273-8208; 4940 No. 3 Rd, Richmond.* ■ *Main near 32nd; (604) 872-8822; 4818 Main St, Vancouver; $$; full bar; AE, MC, V; no checks; lunch, dinner every day.* &

Villa del Lupo ★★★ Owners Julio Gonzalez Perini and Vince Piccolo boast culinary pedigrees, and it shows. The "House of the Wolf" is a simple, elegant space warmed with a sunny Tuscan palette that balances heritage with contemporary. Prices tend to be high, but portions are generous. Almost everything is wonderful: a simply broiled lamb chop with a carrot and basil reduction is accompanied by herb mashed potatoes to soak up the juices; fresh salmon and shrimp cakes are served with a piquant saffron and lime mayonnaise. The osso buco is a constant and for serious appetites only. Italy isn't the only region on the wine list and grappa and eaux-de-vie are available as well. Service is always correct. ■ *Hamilton and Smithe; (604) 688-7436; 869 Hamilton St, Vancouver; $$$; full bar; AE, DC, MC, V; no checks; dinner every day.*

The William Tell (The Georgian Court Hotel) ★★★ The elegance and charm of this Old World restaurant are a reflection of Erwin Doebeli, its dedicated owner. Doebeli, a consummate restaurateur, seems to be here, there, and everywhere, enthusiastically greeting arrivals at the door or flamboyantly whipping up a cafe diablo. Outstanding appetizers include Swiss-style air-dried beef and BC salmon tartare enhanced with fennel; if you crave soup, order the shellfish bisque. We recommend the Fraser Valley duck flavored with apples and cucumbers in a wine sauce or the chateaubriand. The desserts just get better: an unequaled meringue glacé au chocolat, perfect hot fruit soufflés, and opulently rich crêpes Suzette prepared at your table. Sunday night is family dining with a Swiss farmer's buffet. One of the best wine cellars in the city (aficionados should ask to see the "reserved wine menu"). ■ *Corner of Beatty and Robson, across from BC Place Stadium; (604) 688-3504; 765 Beatty St, Vancouver; $$$; full bar; AE, DC, MC, V; no checks; breakfast every day, lunch Mon–Fri, dinner Mon–Sun.* &

Bandi's ★★ You'll exit in a fog of garlic. At Bandi's, chef/owner Bandi Rinkhy produces the robust country food of Hungary, with maître d' and co-owner Kader Karaa's sense of humor providing the dash of paprika. Start with an excellent sour-cherry soup and the dangerously addictive langos, a deep-fried peasant bread served with raw garlic (order one for your friends, one for yourself, and one to take home). Duck aficionados who haven't experienced Bandi's signature dish—crisp duck served with red cabbage braised in Tokay wine—should by all means do so. Goulash is presented in a little kettle set over a portable flame. Hungary's best whites are on the wine list. ■ *Howe between Beach and Pacific; (604)685-3391; 1427 Howe St, Vancouver; $$; full bar; AE, MC, V; no checks; lunch Mon–Fri, dinner every day.*

Bianco Nero ★★ Bianco Nero's bold black-and-white decor and its proximity to the Queen Elizabeth Theatre never fail to impress. Though the service doesn't always live up to the surroundings, the well-prepared food remains consistent. The kitchen has a healthy regard for garlic, onions, and olive oil (and a macho disregard for presentation). Every Italian dish imaginable makes an appearance here. The place is for lovers of Italian wine, with one of the most comprehensive selections in Canada, including a full range of vintage Barolo. ■ *Corner of W Georgia and Richards; (604)682-6376; 475 W Georgia St, Vancouver; $$$; full bar; AE, MC, V; no checks; lunch Mon–Fri, dinner Mon–Sat.*

Bridges ★★ One of the city's most popular hangouts has a superb setting on Granville Island. Seats on the deck, with sweeping views of downtown and the mountains, are at a premium on warm days. Bridges is actually three separate entities: a casual bistro, a pub, and a more formal upstairs dining room. The bistro's casual offerings are the best bet; upstairs, the kitchen takes its seafood seriously, but expect to pay for more than what you get. ■ *Near Cartwright St on Granville Island; (604)687-4400; 1696 Duranleau St, Vancouver; $$; full bar; AE, MC, V; no checks; lunch, dinner every day, brunch Sun.* ♿

Cafe Fleuri (Sutton Place Hotel) ★★ In the afternoon, blissfully tranquil surroundings and a very civilized tea await those who venture through Sutton Place Hotel's chandeliered lobby. Hotel guests—corporate types and movie stars (celeb-spotting is a popular sport)—converse over a classic English tea or a traditional Japanese tea ceremony with hand-whisked macha tea and bean jelly. For $15, you can nibble on finger sandwiches, pastries, and scones and cream. Buffets are a specialty—Friday and Saturday, tables are laden with seafood for the "Taste of Atlantis." On Thursday, Friday, and Saturday, the Chocoholic Bar has become a legend. ■ *On Burrard between Robson and Smythe; (604)682-5511; 845 Burrard St, Vancouver; $$; full bar; AE, DC, MC, V; no checks; breakfast, lunch, dinner.* ♿

Cafe Norte ★★ Tucked away in Edgemont Village, this friendly spot is just minutes away from the north end of the Lions Gate Bridge. Peruse the menu while sampling the house salsa and tortilla chips. There's a full range of serious nachos: warm black bean guacamole, chile con queso topped with chorizo, sweet pineapple with jalapeño, and more. Smooth, rich cream of crab soup comes with a garnish of finely chopped red peppers and parsley. Fajitas arrive with tender pieces of still-sizzling chicken nudged up against onions and green peppers. For diehard traditionalists, the refried beans are great and the margaritas perfectly slushy. Of the too few Mexican restaurants in Vancouver, Cafe Norte reigns supreme. ■ *Corner of Edgemont and Highland, North Vancouver; (604)255-1188; 3108 Edgemont Blvd, North Vancouver; $$; full bar; AE, MC, V; no checks; lunch Mon–Sat, dinner every day.* &

The Cannery ★★ A Vancouver original, serving "salmon by the sea" for more than 20 years. Salmon selections run the gamut, from house-smoked items to the restaurant's hallmark, salmon Wellington. The seared salmon fillet, infused with flavors imparted from a cedar plank, has a subtle quality; by contrast, a mesquite-grilled smoked fillet has a lovely, truly strong barbecued flavor. Service can be rushed and inconsistent. ■ *Victoria Dr and Commissioner St, East Vancouver; (604)254-9606; 2205 Commissioner St, Vancouver; $$$; full bar; AE, DC, MC, V; no checks; lunch Mon–Fri, dinner every day.*

Capers ★★ Healthy, holistic, fresh, inventive—pick practically any current buzzword and Capers fits the bill. Two locations serve up West Coast cuisine, pure and simple, but what sets them apart is that you can shop in a country store setting for glorious produce, unusual condiments, and a broad assortment of take-out dishes. Less than a half hour from downtown, the Dundarave location wows with water and city views from the outdoor terrace. Generous helpings and low prices draw local residents, who come for the apple and pear chutney, organic beef burgers, or pita pockets stuffed with organic turkey. At the Kitsilano location, expect to find local fresh seafood and chicken and pastas, which include corn- and rice-based noodles and soba. Vegetarian emphasis translates into big-flavored dishes. ■ *25th and Marine Dr, West Vancouver; (604)925-3374; 2496 Marine Dr, West Vancouver; $; beer and wine; AE, MC, V; no checks; lunch, dinner every day, brunch Sat and Sun.* ■ *Corner of 4th and Vine (upstairs); (604)739-6685; 2285 W 4th Ave, Vancouver; $; beer and wine; AE, MC, V; no checks; breakfast, lunch, dinner Mon–Sat, breakfast, lunch Sun.* &

Chez Thierry ★★ Restaurateur Thierry Damilano shops at the market in the morning, goes off windsurfing, and returns later in the day to roll out the red carpet for regulars. He presides over his cozy restaurant with sunny good nature and flirtatious French charm. Chef François Launay leaves experimentation to the nouveaux chefs and instead prepares simple, traditional meals without a lot of ornamentation. The house pâté is good but not outstanding; try a watercress and smoked salmon salad instead. A find: fresh prawn tails in a mild curry cream sauce served with artichoke bottoms. This is one of the few places in town that has a decent cheese plate. The tarte Tatin is superb, served upside down and flamed with Calvados. For an unusual show, order a bottle of champagne and ask Damilano to open it for you—his favorite party trick is slashing off corks with a military saber, decked out in his flashing Napoleonic uniform. ■ *Robson between Bidwell and Cardero; (604) 688-0919; 1674 Robson St, Vancouver; $$; full bar; AE, DC, MC, V; no checks; dinner every day.*

Chili Club ★★ Despite the name, Chili Club's fare is not particularly hot; however, if you want it hot the informed staff members will gladly oblige. We've enjoyed pork satay and tom yum kung soup (prawns and mushrooms married in a good broth with hot spices and deep-scented lemon grass). Order the giant smoked New Zealand mussels stuffed with a mild, thick curry paste or the solidly spiced chicken curry, made with coconut milk and bite-size Thai eggplant. For the best view of False Creek, try the bar upstairs with ceiling-to-floor windows on all sides. Even when the food *is* fiery, the decor is rather cold. ■ *Under the Burrard St Bridge (near the water); (604) 681-6000; 1000 Beach Ave, Vancouver; $$; full bar; AE, MC, V; no checks; lunch, dinner every day.* ዿ

Chiyoda ★★ In a town full of sushi restaurants with robata grills on the side, Chiyoda is a robata restaurant with a sushi bar. Built on a generous scale, the robata bar was designed in Japan. Robata selections are arranged in wicker baskets on a layer of ice that separates the customer's side of the bar from the cook's side. Order from the simple menu (snapper, squid, oysters, scallops, eggplant, and shiitake). The cook prepares your choices and hands you the finished dishes across the bar on the end of a long wooden paddle. Seafood is excellent, but don't miss a foray into the cross-cultural world of robata-cooked garlic, potatoes, and corn. A popular spot for downtown businesspeople, the Chiyoda also attracts Japanese visitors exhausted from shopping in the huge gift shop downstairs. ■ *Alberni and Thurlow; (604) 688-5050; 1050 Alberni St, Vancouver; $$; full bar; AE, MC, V; no checks; lunch Mon–Fri, dinner Mon–Sat.* ዿ

Cipriano's Ristorante & Pizzeria ★★ This compact pasta-pizza house is approaching institution status for its basic and most plentiful portions. Strains of Tony Bennett and Frank Sinatra fill the air as straightforward Italian home cooking arrives at your table, preceded by fabulous garlic bread, dripping with butter and deluged with Parmesan. The giant caesar salad (made to share), an exercise in excess, is garlic-laden and crammed with croutons. Deep-dish pizza, pasta puttanesca, and chicken cacciatore are all worth your attention, though some sauces can be remarkably similar. Short routines from owner and onetime standup comedian Frank Cipriano punctuate the meal. For atmosphere and value, few places compare—reservations are a must. ■ *24th and Main; (604)879-0020; 3995 Main St, Vancouver; $$; full bar; V; no checks; dinner Tues–Sat.*

Corsi Trattoria ★★ This little family-run trattoria makes a great excuse for a mini-cruise via the SeaBus. The Corsi family was here on the North Shore before the SeaBus terminal and Lonsdale Quay Public Market existed. The family ran a trattoria in Italy, and the old-country touches still show. Twenty-odd homemade pastas include the house specialty, rotolo—pasta tubes stuffed with veal, spinach, and ricotta and topped with cream and tomato sauces. Or try trenette al salmone affumicata—pasta with smoked salmon, cream, olives, and tomatoes. Adventurous eaters might try the Roman food orgy (for a minimum of two big appetites): four pastas, mixed salad, a platter of lamb, veal, and prawns, followed by coffee and dessert. ■ *Across from the Lonsdale Market, North Vancouver; (604)987-9910; 1 Lonsdale Ave, North Vancouver; $$; full bar; AE, DC, MC, V; no checks; lunch Mon–Fri, dinner Mon–Sat.* &

Delilah's ★★ The three-martini lunch may be gone (unlamented), but let's hear it for the one-martini cocktail hour with hors d'oeuvres at Delilah's. At the original location (at press time Delilah's was planning a move to Coast Plaza), you started with valet parking (the quickest in town) and, if early enough, grabbed a red plush banquette. People lined up to get in (or arrived early enough—shortly after 6pm). At Delilah's it really doesn't matter what you eat—the place is a giggle. Your menu is your bill; simply check off your selections and hand it to your waiter. The house specialties are the 30-plus varieties of martinis, which you shake (or stir) yourself. At the original location, every possible set used to gather at the bar under frescoed ceilings—will they still do so at the new location? ■ *Haro and Gilford; (604)687-3424; 906 Haro St, Vancouver; $$; full bar; MC, V; no checks; dinner every day.* &

Griffins (Hotel Vancouver) ★★ The eminently respectable Hotel Vancouver (one of the historic Canadian Pacific chateaus that dot Canada) houses a bright and lively bistro. With taxi cab yellow walls, griffin-motif carpet, and a feeling of urban action, the place has energy to burn. Three meals a day (plus high tea) are served à la carte, but the buffet meals are the way to go. The breakfast buffet lets you veer toward the healthy—muesli, fresh fruit compote, and such—or the hedonistic: carved Pepsi Cola–glazed ham or smoked chorizo. An Asian corner supplies early birds with a fix of grilled salmon and

toasted nori. Make a dinner of smoked salmon or roasted peppers with basil at the appetizer bar, or work your way through entrees of silver-dollar scallops in garlic sauce, an exemplary steak, or a pasta dish, then take a run or three at the pastry bar.
■ *Burrard and W Georgia; (604) 662-1900; 900 W Georgia St, Vancouver; $$; full bar; AE, DC, MC, V; no checks; breakfast, lunch, dinner every day.* &

Kamei Sushi ★★ With five locations, Kamei may no longer be the best Japanese restaurant in town, but its simple, Westernized dishes certainly make it one of the most popular. The luxury-class Kamei Royale on W Georgia Street seats over 300, with open and private tatami rooms. Combination platters contain all the standards, or try the red snapper usuzukui, thinly sliced and fanned on the plate, accompanied by a citrus sauce. Robata dishes are the special focus at the Broadway Plaza location (601 W Broadway, (604) 876-3388) and can be very good.
■ *Burrard and W Georgia; (604) 687-8588; 1030 W Georgia (and branches), Vancouver; $$; full bar; AE, DC, MC, V; no checks; lunch Mon–Sat, dinner every day.* &

Koji Japanese Restaurant ★★ In our opinion, Koji has the most beautiful garden in a downtown Vancouver restaurant— an island of pine trees and river rocks on a patio above Hornby Street. The best seats are either the nonsmoking ones by the windows looking out onto the garden or at the sushi and robata bars. The rest of the restaurant is a crowded, smoky room often full of Japanese tourists. The sushi is not the best in town, but selections from the robata grill are dependable; grilled shiitake, topped with bonito flakes and tiny filaments of dry seaweed, are sublime. Finish with green-tea ice cream. ■ *Hornby and Georgia; (604) 685-7355; 630 Hornby St, Vancouver; $$; full bar; AE, DC, MC, V; no checks; breakfast, dinner every day, lunch Mon–Fri.* &

La Cucina Italiana ★★ Stuck rather incongruously in the middle of North Vancouver's strip of car dealerships and video shops, La Cucina overcomes its surroundings with its rustic character. The attractive dining room has Italian opera playing at just the right volume. When it's available, try bresaola—air-dried beef imported from Switzerland—as an appetizer, or the cold antipasto. Pastas range from traditional spaghetti with tomato and meat sauce to fettuccine with squid and sweet red peppers. Fish specials are usually good. Don't leave without sampling the homemade ice cream. ■ *Corner of Marine Dr and McGowan, North Vancouver; (604) 986-1334; 1509 Marine Dr, North Vancouver; $$; full bar; AE, MC, V; no checks; dinner Mon–Sat.* &

La Toque Blanche ★★ This cozy, '70s-retro woodsy retreat tucked away behind the Cypress Park Mohawk gas station is still a well-kept culinary secret. Owner John-Carlo Felicella has a passion for detail, manifest in appetizers such as tiger prawns in a chile spinach pesto, and wickedly rich lobster bisque. His entrees are equally impressive, as proved by breast of duckling glazed with Calvados, and morsels of lamb, cooked perfectly pink in a mustard sauce. A moderately priced winelist complements the menu. Prices are almost a bargain by today's standards—especially considering the quality, detail and presentation. ■ *Next to the Cypress Park Market, West Vancouver; (604) 926-1006; 4368 Marine Dr, West Vancouver; $$; full bar; AE, MC, V; checks OK; dinner Tues–Sun.* &

Mescalero ★★ The very good Mescalero has become a most popular hangout (especially on Thursday nights) for Southwestern food and atmosphere. For best value, order from the tapas list; you can piece together a meal from garlic prawns, alder-baked stuffed sweet pepper; roasted mussels in sun-dried tomato chipotle cream; and grilled eggplant salad with fresh spinach leaves and tangy blue cheese dressing, generously garnished with pine nuts—among others. Roll out after a dark chocolate pizza with pistachios and walnuts in ginger and nutmeg chocolate sauce. Lots of Chilean wines by the glass. ■ *Bidwell between Davie and Denman; (604) 669-2399; 1215 Bidwell St, Vancouver; $$$; full bar; AE, E, MC, V; no checks; lunch, dinner every day, brunch Sat and Sun.* &

Monterey Lounge & Grill (Pacific Palisades Hotel) ★★ The bounty of the BC harvest and a well thought-out award-winning wine list star in this newly renovated room on Robson, where jazz pianists tickle the ivories six nights a week. Chef Rod Butters, a devotee of regional farming and organic foodstuffs, layers flavors and textures with sophistication. For starters, order the meaty crab cakes with red pepper lime mayonnaise or the wild mushroom and turnip chip torte. For entrees select the luscious lasagne—layers of sweet potato, onion, and scallions—or Butters' oat-crusted Arctic char with maple butter. Don't skip dessert—especially if the divine double-chocolate mashed brioche is featured. ■ *Robson and Jervis; (604) 684-1277; 1277 Robson St, Vancouver; $$; full bar; AE, DC, MC, V; no checks; breakfast, lunch, dinner every day.* &

Ouzeri ★★ Traditionally, the Greek Ouzeri is a place to go to drink and eat appetizers before going to dinner. In Vancouver, the Ouzeri is where you can go any time of day and compose a meal of appetizers. Chicken livers are wonderful—crisp on the outside and tender on the inside. Prawns dressed with ouzo and mushrooms are simply amazing. Friendly, casual, happy, Ouzeri proves that being Greek doesn't mean you can't be trendy. Nibble until midnight, 2am on weekends. ■ *Corner of Trucht and W Broadway; (604) 739-9378; 3189 W Broadway,*

Vancouver; $$; full bar; AE, DC, MC, V; no checks; lunch, dinner every day. ₠

The Pink Pearl ★★ Tanks of fresh fish are your first clue that the Cantonese menu is especially strong on seafood. The crab sautéed with five spices—sometimes translated as crab with peppery salt—is a spectacular dish, crisp, chile-hot, and salty on the outside, moist on the inside. A good dim sum is served every day (be sure to arrive early on weekends to avoid the lineups). Table clearing is an event in itself: the tablecloth is actually a stack of thick white plastic sheets; when you finish eating, a waiter will grab the corners of the top sheet and with a quick flip scoop everything up, dishes and all. A great place for kids. ■ *1 block west of Clark; (604)253-4316; 1132 E Hastings St; Vancouver; $$; full bar; AE, MC, V; no checks; lunch, dinner every day.* ₠

Raincity Grill ★★ English Bay from Raincity's patio is stunning; inside, a clean, contemporary look with natural wood and lots of greenery is most inviting. Owner Harry Kambolis and chef Gregory Walsh have created an imaginative menu based on Granville Island produce. Salmon chowder (with plenty of fish and flavor) is worth a taste, as are the littleneck clams. For entrees, try a healthy, al dente portion of black Thai rice rissoto with toasted cumin yogurt and vegetables; juicy halibut swims in a warm lavender vinaigrette. Desserts are paired with wines (optional), such as a blockbuster frozen bitter chocolate and lemon soufflé served with a glass of Quady Essencia. ■ *Corner of Mortan and Denman; (604)685-7337; 1193 Denman St, Vancouver; $$; full bar; AE, DC, MC, V; no checks; lunch, dinner every day, brunch Sat and Sun.* ₠

Raku Kushiyaki ★★ This almost-too-stark restaurant sports an innovative fusion menu. It offers skewered tidbits and tiny preparations from the Far East, the Middle East, India, Thailand, France, and the Caribbean. There are some delicious surprises here, and some pitfalls as well. Those looking for the unusual will find perfectly prepared asparagus spears with mustard butter, an excellent spicy grilled calamari with lime, barbecued squid yaki, and grilled tofu packages with teriyaki sauce. Raku stocks four brands of sake. You can nibble, nosh, and share at Raku, but watch out—it adds up. ■ *10th and Trimble; (604)222-8188; 4422 W 10th Ave, Vancouver; $$; full bar; DC, MC, V; checks OK; dinner every day.*

The Red Onion ★★ Forget drive-ins and head to Kerrisdale for the best double dogs, cheeseburgers, and fries (with a sour cream and dill dip) in town. The menu is designed to please everyone (we like the hot chicken salad; others pick the veggie soup). The wieners are the Onion's own, and so are the buns. At breakfast, the muffins (blueberry, chocolate chip, or banana) and aromatic cinnamon buns are baked on the premises. The best of its kind in the city. Take-out, too. ▪ *W 41st Ave between E Blvd and Maple; (604) 263-0833; 2028 W 41st Ave, Vancouver; $; beer and wine; MC, V; no checks; breakfast, lunch, dinner every day.* &

Romano's Macaroni Grill ★★

Meals are served with aplomb by singing waiters in this heritage West End mansion that's great theater. Pizzas, toothsome pasta dishes (ask for extra sauce), and a hearty breaded veal with tomato sauce, asiago cream, and pasta are good bets. Wine is measured by the inch and just about everything is worth the fair price. A great family place. Don't miss the frozen bellinis. On Sundays, there's a midday All You Can Eat Pasta Bar for under $9. ▪ *Corner of Davie and Nicola; (604) 689-4334; 1523 Davie St, Vancouver; $$; full bar; AE, DC, MC, V; no checks; lunch, dinner every day.* &

The Salmon House on the Hill ★★

West Coast native arti-facts reflect the origins of the Salmon House menu. The hallmark dish at Salmon House is BC salmon cooked over green alder-wood, which delivers the distinctive, delicate, and smoky flavor—certainly worth the drive halfway to Horseshoe Bay. There's a fresh sheet every day—try the mussels, they're perfectly prepared. Although recent renovations have added a striking entrance area, the lounge is smoky and somewhat uninviting despite the incredible view. Service is friendly and correct. ▪ *Corner of Folkestone Way and Ski Lift Rd, West Vancouver; (604) 926-3212; 2229 Folkestone Way, West Vancouver; $$$; full bar; AE, DC, MC, V; no checks; lunch, dinner every day, brunch Sun.*

Salute ★★

This relaxed spot joins the growing number of excellent eateries sprouting alongside West Vancouver's Marine Drive. Owner/chef Gamal Hanna spent several years at one of Vancouver's respected trattorias honing his skills, as reflected in his version of carpaccio: lean and moist, attractively arranged, drizzled with piquant, grainy mustard, and garnished with capers and fresh parsley. Salads can sometimes be too oily, though the carciofi—a colorful mix of greens with shrimp, chopped marinated artichoke hearts, and sun-dried tomatoes—is commendable. A good list of pastas is punctuated by some more rustic dishes, such as ciocicara—a gutsy, earthy combination of fusilli pasta with potatoes and spicy sausage. A predominantly Italian wine list leans toward the high end. ▪ *17th and Marine, West Vancouver; (604) 922-6282; 1747 Marine Dr, West Vancouver; $$; full bar; AE, MC, V; no checks; lunch Mon–Fri, dinner every day.*

Shijo Japanese Restaurant ★★

Shijo is a pleasant, uncluttered sushi bar serving excellent sushi, sashimi, and robata.

Oysters, grilled on the half shell and painted with a light miso sauce, are a good bet, as are butterflied tiger prawns or shiitake foilyaki—mushrooms sprinkled with lemony ponzu sauce and cooked in foil. Meals end in a refreshing manner, with orange sherbet served in a hollowed-out orange. ■ *Between Cypress and Maple (on 2nd floor); (604) 732-4676; 1926 W 4th Ave, Vancouver; $$$; full bar; AE, DC, MC, V; no checks; lunch Mon–Fri, dinner every day.* &

Sophie's Cosmic Cafe ★★ Where "Leave It to Beaver" meets Pee Wee Herman—this funky diner-cum–garage sale is a fun place to be. Don't worry about the wait—there's plenty to look at, including Sophie's collection of colorful lunch boxes and hats that were once stashed in her attic. People rave about the huge spicy burgers and chocolate shakes, but the best thing here is the stick-to-the-ribs-style breakfast: Mexican eggs (with sausage, peppers, and onions and spiced with hot pepper sauce poured from a wine bottle). ■ *W 4th between Arbutus and Maple; (604) 732-6810; 2095 W 4th Ave, Vancouver; $; beer and wine; MC, V; no checks; breakfast, lunch, dinner every day, brunch Sat and Sun.* &

The Teahouse at Ferguson Point ★★ This stunning location is a magnet for tourists, with its park setting and spectacular view of English Bay, but a faithful following of locals attests to the consistency of fare. Appetizers run the gamut from mussels in a white wine cream sauce to Pernod-spiked fresh seafood soup. Salmon is always a good bet, sometimes served with a rich topping of crab and shrimp in a dill hollandaise. Rack of lamb in fresh herb crust is also a perennial favorite—even without the view attached. Recent interior changes include a sunset patio overlooking English Bay. ■ *In Stanley Park; enter Stanley Park from Georgia St, follow road to Ferguson Pt; (604) 669-3281; 7501 Stanley Park Dr, Vancouver; $$; full bar; AE, MC, V; no checks; lunch Mon–Fri, dinner every day, brunch Sat and Sun.* &

Top Gun Chinese Seafood Restaurant (Aberdeen Centre) ★★ Located in an area known as "Little Asia," Top Gun has as its neighbors a Japanese mall, education center, and Buddhist temple. The menu is generic Cantonese with steamed sea scallops in black bean sauce or chicken, curried or lemon sauced. Specials, though, are really special, such as sautéed spiced frogs' legs with fagara. For dessert, amble across the mall to the Rhino Cafe (next to the bowling alley) and try some of the unusual Eurasian cakes and pastries that are featured there. ■ *Aberdeen Centre, between No. 3 Rd and Cambie St; (604) 273-2883; 2110-4151 Hazelbridge Way, Richmond; $$; full bar; V; no checks; lunch, dinner every day.* &

Vassilis Taverna ★★ You'll feel transported to the Mediterranean: the paper place mats are even adorned with maps of the Greek islands. Vassilis, one of Vancouver's original Greek restaurants, is located in what is loosely referred to as "Little Greece." The menu is quite traditional, but the quality is consistent. Worthy starters include lightly battered calamari and rich, salty, scalding-hot saganaki (Greek kefalotiri cheese fried in oil and sprinkled with lemon juice). The house specialty is a perfectly juicy kotopoulo—chicken pounded flat, simply seasoned with lemon juice, garlic, and oregano, and then barbecued. The Greek salad makes a meal in itself, especially with a succulent pile of quick-fried baby smelts on the side. In summer, the restaurant opens onto the sidewalk. ■ *Between McDonald and McKenzie; (604) 733-3231; 2884 W Broadway, Vancouver; $$; full bar; AE, MC, V; no checks; lunch Tues–Fri, dinner Tues–Sun.* ⅀

Vij's ★★ A civilized change from ersatz curry houses. Vikram Vij dishes up home-cooked Indian fare that evolves at whim. His menu changes every 10 days or so, but almost always includes a mean curry or a killer saag. Courtesy and simplicity rule as Vik waits carefully on all who arrive early enough to get in—first greeting them with a glass of chai before discussing the menu. At about $10 a head, the prices are civilized too. ■ *W Broadway between Granville and Hemlock; (604) 736-6664; 1453 W Broadway, Vancouver; $; no alcohol; no credit cards; no checks; lunch Mon–Fri, dinner Mon–Sat.* ⅀

Vong's Kitchen ★★ With new upscale Chinese restaurants cropping up all over the city, one could get positively nostalgic about Vong's. It seems to have been around forever and has just moved down the street (and doubled its size). If you are serious about food and don't care that much about atmosphere, then Vong's family place will fill the bill. Order the jade chicken with deep-fried spinach, orange beef, or spicy garlic prawns. Although the execution of some dishes can be inconsistent, you are getting as close to a home-cooked Chinese meal as you can without heading west. Those without reservations should plan to arrive before 6pm on weekends. ■ *Fraser and 27th; (604) 879-4298; 4298 Fraser St, Vancouver; $; no alcohol; no credit cards; no checks; dinner Tues–Sun.*

Bo-Jik Vegetarian Restaurant ★ As part of a well-established Buddhist vegetarian tradition—there are hundreds of these restaurants in Hong Kong—Bo-Jik brings all the force of Chinese culinary tradition to bear on the problem of eating well without eating meat. Generally, you want to avoid the gluten dishes, which substitute textured soy protein for meat, and steer toward the vegetable dishes—the Bo-Jik veggie pancake, for example. It's a tangle of stir-fried vegetables, a generous stack of paper-thin Mandarin pancakes, and a Hoisin sauce—mu-shu pork without the pork. Pair it with big fresh shiitake mushrooms on a bed of brilliant green sautéed gai lan, and you have, with a few bowls of rice and some tea, a splendid dinner for under $25. Service is friendly, if somewhat disorganized. Unfortunately, the restaurant has all the atmo of a mall record store. ▪ *W Broadway at Willow; (604) 872-5556; 820 W Broadway, Vancouver; $; no alcohol; MC, V; no checks; lunch, dinner every day.*

The Bread Garden ★

The Bread Garden is Vancouver's original bakery-cafe; it opened in 1981 as a croissant bakery and quickly turned into an all-night coffee bar. Now there are nine Bread Gardens, and many are open 24 hours a day. As the Bread Gardens proliferate, the deli cases grow bigger and bigger. The First Avenue Bread Garden is still the scene for early weekday coffee and (much later) weekend brunch, but now you can also eat a quick and entirely satisfying dinner of wholesome foods such as shepherd's pie, lasagne, or black bean and corn salad. Rice Krispies treats and a croissant-bread pudding send you home. ▪ *W 1st between Burrard and Cypress; (604) 738-6684; 1880 W 1st Ave (and branches), Vancouver; $; beer and wine (1st Ave location only); MC, V; no checks; breakfast, lunch, dinner every day.* ♿

Cafe Roma ★

Mario Corsi (also of the Park Royal Hotel and Corsi Trattoria) operates this friendly, casual room. The food is good—and very Italian. Excellent focaccia appears first. Some of the pasta dishes, like the ultra-spicy spaghetti trasteverini sauced with minced chicken, black beans, garlic, and pepperoncini, are rarely seen outside the old country. There are several choices of pizza, as well as many nicely prepared fish and meat dishes. The deck is superb in summer, with an impressive view of downtown. ▪ *On Semisch St and Esplanade St in North Vancouver; (604) 984-0274; 60 Semisch St, North Vancouver; $$; full bar; AE, DC, MC, V; no checks; lunch Mon–Fri, dinner every day.* ♿

English Bay Boathouse ★

The Boathouse presides over the sands of English Bay and, at day's end, some of the best sunsets in the world. The decor is ship-shape and lean. Downstairs, a casual bistro with a summertime deck is a favorite spot. Upstairs the serious eating takes place (but forget the wine list). A house specialty, mesquite-grilled and rosemary-brushed salmon comes crispy outside, moist within. A sight to behold is a foot-and-a-half–long, piping-hot, cast-iron platter of well-sauced, barbecued back ribs with a mountain of curly fries and a generous portion of vegetables. A good spot for family dining, beachside. ▪ *Beach between Denman and Burnaby; (604) 669-2225; 1795 Beach Ave, Vancouver; $$; full bar; AE, DC, MC, V; no checks; lunch Mon–Sat, dinner every day, brunch Sun.* ♿

Flying Wedge ★ Pizza is all they sell, but it's arguably the best in town in all four locations. Join the lunchtime business crowd on Robson Street or the Kitsilano beach bunch on Cornwall Avenue, just south of the Burrard Street bridge. You'll find funky, Crayola-colored surroundings in all venues, as well as generous wedges of thin-crusted pizza, served cafeteria-style, for $3 a pop. Old faves: Deep Purple, heady with marinated eggplant, and a good spicy Sichuan chicken. New tastes: peaches and Black Forest ham. There is a wide choice of nonalcoholic drinks. Open till 1am weekends. Sundays, all you can eat for $5.95. ■ *Robson between Bute and Thurlow; (604) 681-1233; 1175 Robson St, Vancouver (and branches); $; no alcohol; no credit cards; no checks; lunch, dinner every day.* &

Isadora's ★ Isadora's children's menu (clown-faced pizzas and grilled cheese with potato chips), in-house play area, and tables next to the outdoor water park in summer make this a family favorite. The wholesome menu also features more grown-up items, such as smoked wild salmon sandwiches, organic salads, great nut burgers, and plenty of choices for vegans. Isadora's is busiest at Sunday brunch. Service is generally slow. ■ *Granville Island; (604) 681-8816; 1540 Old Bridge St, Vancouver; $; full bar; MC, V; no checks; breakfast, lunch, dinner every day, brunch Sat and Sun.* &

Moutai Mandarin Restaurant ★ The menu at this tiny restaurant was modeled after the one at the well-patronized Szechuan Chongqing (see review); now West Enders don't have to leave their territory to get good versions of Szechuan Chongqing favorites such as green beans with pork and plenty of chile pepper. We particularly like the specials: spicy clams in black bean sauce and the blistering stir-fry with tiger prawns. Moutai's acid green tabletops and arborite trim in a pebble-pattern gray are miles removed from red-dragon tacky or Hong Kong slick, which seem to be the city's dominant Chinese restaurant styles. ■ *Davie and Denman; (604) 681-2288; 1710 Davie St, Vancouver; $; full bar; AE, MC, V; no checks; dinner every day.* &

Nazarre BBQ Chicken ★ There are rubber chickens on the turntables decorating the new storefront location, but only tender barbecued chicken finds its way onto your plate. French-born and Mexican-raised owner Gerry Moutal bastes the birds in a mixture of rum and spices in the rotisserie—the chickens drip their juices onto potatoes roasting and crackling below and are delivered with mild, hot, extra-hot, or hot garlic sauce. There are a few other goodies, but it's the chicken you really should not miss. Four tables—or take it to go. ■ *Commercial between 2nd and 3rd; (604) 251-1844; 1859 Commercial Dr, Vancouver; $; no alcohol; no credit cards; no checks; lunch, dinner every day.*

▼

Olympia Fish Market and Oyster Co. ★ The Olympia is first and foremost a fish shop, but it purveys some of the best fish 'n' chips in the Lower Mainland. Eight years ago, Robson Street fish merchant Carlo Sorace decided that what the street really needed was a good place to get fish 'n' chips. Whatever is on special in the store, which might be halibut cheeks, scallops, catfish, or calamari, is the day's special at the 12-seat counter (or take out). Soft drinks include chinotto (an Italian herbal and fruit-flavored sparkling water). ■ *Corner of Thurlow and Robson; (604) 685-0716; 1094 Robson St, Vancouver; $; no alcohol; DC, MC, V; no checks; lunch, dinner every day.*

Pho Hoang ★ As common in Vietnam as the hamburger is here, pho is a quick meal or snack, and a great bargain besides. A large bowl of broth with rice noodles and your choice of flank, rump, brisket, tripe, or a dozen other beef cuts and combinations will cost you less than $5. You're served a side dish of bean sprouts, fresh basil, sliced green chiles, and lime to garnish as you see fit. A cup of strong Vietnamese coffee, filter-brewed at the table, is the only other thing you need. A second location is at 238 Georgia Street in Chinatown. ■ *Corner of 20th and Main; (604) 874-0810; 3610 Main St, Vancouver; $; no alcohol; no credit cards; no checks; lunch, dinner every day.*

Shinla Korean Restaurant ★ Shinla is a Korean restaurant for Koreans. The second-story location on E Broadway has minimal signage, giving it the feeling of a private club. Private rooms surround a center area with booth seating—all functionally decorated—with bulgogi grills on every table. The special combination for two (a hearty undertaking) is a bargain: rib-eye steak slices, short ribs, chicken, prawns, and pork come neatly arranged on a large platter ready to be seared to taste, complemented by interesting side dishes of kimchi, pickled garlic, grilled dry minnows, sesame spinach, and other vegetables. The execution of sushi and tempura is sometimes inconsistent. ■ *At Kingsway and E Broadway; (604) 875-6649; 208-333 E Broadway, Vancouver; $$; full bar; MC, V; no checks; lunch, dinner every day.*

Szechuan Chongqing ★ For a long time, Chongqing was the only Chinese restaurant offering authentic Sichuan specialties. The robust flavors, the piquant sauces, and the searing heat of fresh and dry chiles quickly became familiar signposts of Chinese food in Vancouver. Live seafood tanks filled with lobster and crab line one wall, and a couple of VIP salons are available in the back. The fried prawns with chile sauce are quite simply magnificent: sweet and masterfully seasoned. The rich, smooth-crunchy tan tan noodles, the lingering orange-peel beef, and, of course, those worth-their-weight-in-gold beans—are all there to attest that the Chongqing dynasty is going to be long-lived. ▪ *12th and Commercial; (604) 254-7434; 2808 Commercial Dr, Vancouver; $$; full bar; AE, MC, V; no checks; lunch, dinner every day.*

Tio Pepe ★ Tio Pepe—a shoebox of a restaurant, one long, narrow room crammed full of tables, with the kitchen at the back—has reasonable prices and food unlike any other Mexican food in town. Start with margaritas and a double order of chicken flautas. Charbroiled lamb is marinated in wine and spices with a haunting, bittersweet taste of Seville oranges. Pascaya con huevo—date-palm shoots fried in an egg batter and served with tomato sauce—is an unusual appetizer, with a pleasantly astringent taste. The food has a flavorful mildness typical of Yucatán cooking. If fire is your style, however, shake on some habañero hot sauce, distilled from the hottest peppers known to anyone. ▪ *Between the pier and Williams; (604) 254-8999; 1134 Commercial Dr, Vancouver; $; full bar; MC, V; no checks; dinner Mon–Sat.* &

The Tomahawk ★ The Tomahawk must be the original inspiration for all those hokey, totem-pole theme restaurants on highways across North America. In Vancouver, it's a 74-year institution, famous for its hungry man–size meals. Everybody comes here for the eye-opening Yukon breakfast—five rashers of bacon, two eggs, hashbrowns, and toast—served all day. For lunch, there are several hamburger platters (named after native chiefs), sandwiches, fried chicken, and fish 'n' chips. Pies (lemon meringue, Dutch apple, banana cream) are baked on the premises, and the staff will gladly wrap one to go. ▪ *Marine and Philip, North Vancouver; (604) 988-2612; 1550 Philip Ave, North Vancouver; $; no alcohol; AE, DC, MC, V; no checks; breakfast, lunch, dinner every day.* &

Tomato Fresh Food Cafe ★ Tomato is two experiences, both noisy. One is a row of tables and chairs down the center of the restaurant, placed so close that your elbows touch your neighbor's. The other (our choice) is a set of roomy booths around the edge, with plenty of space to lounge. For years this was an undistinguished diner; now it has an overlay of young, retro energy, most lucidly expressed in the big, chunky, wildly colored bowls used for serving specialties such as "teapuccino"— cappuccino made with tea. Young waitstaff serve a variation of mom food: vegetarian chili with really good corn bread, a whacking slab of turkey in the turkey sandwich, and real milk shakes. There's also great take-out from Tomato To Go (open Monday through Saturday, just around the corner). ▪ *17th and Cambie; (604) 874-6020; 3305 Cambie St, Vancouver; $; beer and wine; MC, V; no checks; breakfast, lunch, dinner Tues–Sat, brunch Sat and Sun.*

Ezogiku Noodle Cafe If it weren't for the word *noodle* in its name, one would expect to find a trendy espresso bar here; instead, ramen dishes are the order of the day at this 14-seater. Ramen comes in regular (pork), miso, or soy broth, a fried rice dish, a fried noodle dish, a curried dish, and gyozas—and that's it. Ezogiku's size and focus are the secret to the large bowls of perfectly cooked chewy noodles in rich, steaming broth. Do what the old master in the movie *Tampopo* instructed: study, sniff, and savor. A larger location at 1329 Robson Street (685-8606) now accommodates 70 noodle fanatics with equally focused food. Other branches are in Honolulu and Tokyo. ■ *Robson at Bidwell; (604)687-7565; 1684 Robson St, Vancouver; $; no alcohol; no credit cards; no checks; lunch, dinner every day.*

The Only Seafood Cafe Vancouver's oldest restaurant, the Only opened for business in 1912 when out-of-town loggers came to E Hastings Street to spend their wages on liquor and flesh. Today, amid a neon sea of pawnshops and peep shows, a diverse sampling of humanity convenes for fresh no-frills fish. A periodic scrub and a coat of paint have brightened this greasy spoon over the years, but the time-worn design remains. There are two booths and a counter with stools, and you've got to be quick to nab one. Halibut, sole, and lingcod are snatched from the deep fryer at the instant of just-cooked perfection and served with a side of fries. One bite tells you why this diner has become a Vancouver legend. ■ *E Hastings between Columbia and Carrall; (604)681-6546; 20 E Hastings St, Vancouver; $; no alcohol; no credit cards; no checks; lunch, dinner every day.*

LODGINGS

The Four Seasons ★★★★ The upscale chain of Four Seasons hotels is well known for pampering guests, and the Vancouver hotel only enhances that reputation. Arrival is awkward, however, since guests must enter from a small driveway wedged between concrete pillars and then ride an elevator to the lobby, which is also connected to the Pacific Centre shopping mall. Once the hurdle of checkin has been overcome, guests wallow in luxury. Although the hotel is located smack-dab in the center of high-rise downtown, many of the guest rooms offer surprising views of the city. Amenities include bathrobes, hair dryers, VCRs, a complimentary shoeshine, 24-hour valet service, a year-round indoor-outdoor pool, and a rooftop garden. Kids are welcomed with complimentary milk and cookie on arrival. Chartwell is one of the best dining rooms in the city. The Garden Lounge, just off the lobby, is a place to see and be seen. ■ *Howe and W Georgia; (604)689-9333; 791 W Georgia St, Vancouver, BC V6E 2T4; $$$; AE, DC, MC, V; no checks.* &

The Sutton Place Hotel (formerly Le Meridien) ★★★★ Le Meridien may have changed its name to something more British- than French-sounding than, but little else has changed at Vancouver's most elegant hotel. All 397 soundproofed rooms in this sumptuous residential-style hotel in the heart of the city are designed and decorated to look and feel like a beautiful home, and they do. The king-size beds are extra large: the furnishings are reproductions of European antiques. Maids faithfully appear twice a day; expect all the amenities one could wish for—including fresh flowers, umbrella, and complimentary shoeshine. The lobby recalls a European manor and posts a 24-hour concierge service, and the bellhops snap to attention whether you arrive in a beat-up truck wearing blue jeans or in a limo dressed for a black-tie event. The restaurants and lounges have been popular with locals since the day they opened, with the richly paneled Gerard Lounge ranking as one of the best watering holes in the Northwest. Le Spa offers a swimming pool, fitness room, and a world of beauty-care treatments. Room rates in season range from $180 for a standard double to $1,250 for the Presidential Suite; however, special getaway weekend packages are available.

The best rental condominiums in the city are located in a separate building connected to the Sutton Place Hotel. La Grande Residence provides all the amenities of a luxury hotel in 162 spiffy one- and two-bedroom suites with kitchens and balconies. Valet parking, concierge, and secretarial, maid, laundry, and room services are all available. Telephone calls and visiting guests are received by the hotel's front desk. The minimum stay is a month (starting at $3,500 for 30 days). ■ *Corner of Smithe and Burrard; (604) 682-5511 or (800) 543-4300; 845 Burrard St, Vancouver, BC V6Z 2K6; $$$; AE, DC, MC, V; no checks.*

Delta Place ★★★ Mandarin International built this richly appointed, 197-room hotel in time for Vancouver's world exposition in 1986, but sold it shortly thereafter to Delta Hotels. Nonetheless, the hotel remains worthy of the Mandarin name. From the Italian marble in the bathrooms to the silk draperies and the exquisite art throughout, the Delta Place is a jewel in every respect—some consider it one of Vancouver's best-kept secrets. Located in the heart of the downtown business and financial districts, it offers oversize, soundproofed deluxe rooms with balconies and peekaboo views of the city. There are 18 palatial suites, outstanding concierge service, nightly turndown service on request, 24-hour room service, a full-scale business center, and one of the finest hotel health clubs. (There are even television sets in the saunas.) Delta Place also offers a club floor and several programs for families with children (kids six years and under eat free). Le Café serves breakfast, lunch, and dinner. The Clipper Lounge's weekday Asian luncheon buffet is a holdover from the Mandarin days that has proved too popular to change. Rates start at $220, but special weekend rates plunge to $99. ■ *Dunsmuir and Howe; (604) 687-1122 or (800) 877-1133; 645 Howe St, Vancouver, BC V6C 2Y9; $$$; AE, DC, MC, V; no checks.* 초

English Bay Inn ★★★ Owner Bob Chapin devotes meticulous attention to his romantic five-room English Bay Inn. Down comforters rest atop Louis Phillipe sleigh beds beneath alabaster lighting fixtures. The pièce de résistance is a two-level suite on the top floor with a fireplace in the bedroom. Extras include terrycloth robes, evening sherry, and phones in each guest room. All rooms have a private bath, and two back rooms open onto a small garden. A fabulous breakfast is served in a formal dining room with gothic dining suite in front of a crackling (albeit gas) fire. Stanley Park and English Bay are just minutes away by foot. ■ *1 block from English Bay on Comox at Chilco; (604) 683-8002; 1968 Comox St, Vancouver, BC V6G 1R4; $$$; AE, MC, V; checks OK.*

Georgian Court Hotel ★★★ Compared with the other pricey hotels in the city, this intimate and luxurious 180-room European-style hotel situated across from BC Place Stadium and the Queen Elizabeth Theatre offers much in the way of value. All rooms feature desks, minibars, three telephones, nightly turndown service, and (at last) good reading lamps. The health club offers a whirlpool, sauna, and fully equipped fitness area. Among Vancouverites, the Georgian Court Hotel is best known as the home of the William Tell Restaurant (see review), where for years flamboyant owner Erwin Doebeli has set the standard for fine dining in Vancouver. ■ *Cambie and Beatty; (604) 682-5555 or (800) 663-1155; 773 Beatty St, Vancouver, BC V6B 2M4; $$$; AE, DC, MC, V; checks OK.* 초

Hotel Vancouver ★★★ This is one of the grand French château–style hotels built in 1939 by the Canadian Pacific Railway barons to entice visitors to ride the train across Canada. The green, steeply pitched copper roof that dominated the city's skyline for decades remains a less obvious landmark today. The 508-room hotel is popular with conventions; nonetheless, service remains quite good and includes complimentary coffee and newspapers in the morning. Dinner dances take place in the Roof Restaurant and Lounge—it's that kind of hotel. An executive floor called Entrée Gold includes premium rooms with a dedicated reception desk and concierge, secretarial services, and continental breakfast and canapés. The hotel has a health club with a sky-lit lap pool. Try for a room high above the street noise. ■ *Georgia and Burrard; (604) 684-3131 or (800) 441-1414; 900 W Georgia St, Vancouver, BC V6C 2W6; $$$; AE, DC, MC, V; checks OK.* 초

Pacific Palisades ★★★ The internationally celebrated Shangri-La chain purchased the Pacific Palisades in 1991 and promptly began a complete renovation of what was already a good hotel. The 233 rooms, most of which are one-bedroom suites, have long been popular with the many movie production crews that visit Vancouver. Part of the appeal comes from the hotel's personal attention to guests' needs, but the major draw is spacious rooms, all with a mini-kitchen that includes a fridge, microwave, and coffee-maker. There's a health club and a swimming pool. The location on Robson Street is tough to beat if you want to be where the action is. ■ *Between Bute and Jervis on Robson; (604) 688-0461 or (800) 663-1815; 1277 Robson St, Vancouver, BC V6E 1C4; $$$; AE, DC, MC, V; no checks.*

Pan Pacific Hotel ★★★ No hotel in Vancouver has a more stunning location, a better health club, or a more remarkable architectural presence. As part of Canada Place, the Pan Pacific juts out into Vancouver's inner harbor with its five giant white signature sails. The building is also the embarkation point for the thriving summertime Alaska cruise ship market. The first four floors comprise the World Trade Centre Vancouver, but up on the eighth, where the guest rooms begin, things become more diminutive. Standard guest rooms (high-season rates start at $315) are among the smallest of Vancouver's luxury hotels, and the decor is all a bit disappointing after such a grand facade. But the spectacular views make up for any shortcomings. The best views face west, but you can't beat a corner room (with views from your tub). A complete range of guest services is offered. The fine dining restaurant, the Five Sails, has achieved a fair bit of attention for its exquisite Pacific Rim cuisine. The Cascades Lounge, just off the lobby, is a must-stop if you want to watch ships sail into the sunset and sea-planes land—all against the backdrop of the North Shore mountains. ■ *At the north foot of Burrard St, across from Stanley Park; (604) 662-8111 or (800) 937-1515; 300-999 Canada Pl, Vancouver, BC V6C 3B5; $$$; AE, DC, MC, V; no checks.* ᓚ

Vancouver

Lodgings

Vancouver Renaissance Hotel ★★★ Hong Kong–based New World Development brought this former Holiday Inn up to the level of the better hotels in the city. A wavelike design (the hotel is just above Coal Harbour) is carried throughout—from the confetti-patterned rug in the lobby to the contoured hall-ways (leading to the meeting rooms) to the rotating dining room on the top floor. The rooms are standard hotel-size with extra features such as hair dryers and heated bathroom floors, even in the most inexpensive. Ask for a room with a view of the North Shore, and if you want extra-special treatment, request a room on the exclusive 18th floor. The ballroom is one of the few in the city, with a spectacular entryway and view of the harbor. A pool, sauna, workout room, and sun deck are on the fourth floor. Vistas, the revolving rooftop restaurant, serves West Coast continental cuisine. ▪ *Above Burrard Inlet between Bute and Thurlow; (604) 689-9211 or (800) 468-3571; 1133 W Hastings St, Vancouver, BC V6E 3T3; $$$; full bar; AE, DC, MC, V; no checks; breakfast, lunch, and dinner every day.* &

Waterfront Centre Hotel ★★★ The tasteful rooms in the newish 23-story Waterfront Centre are among the best in the city. Their size and rich appointments clearly outclass the Pan Pacific Hotel, just across the street on Vancouver's inner harbor. Underground passageways connect the Waterfront Centre to Canada Place and the convention and trade center. Expect wonderful surprises, such as third-floor guest rooms with private terraces and gardens concealed from the street level. A club floor called Entrée Gold caters to every whim, offering a private concierge, continental breakfast, nightly hors d'oeuvres, and private conference room. Of the 489 guest rooms, there are 29 suites, including one fit for royalty. Operated by Canadian Pacific, it ranks among the top hotels in Vancouver, and as new as it is, it has the most Canadian feel. There is an excellent health club, complete with outdoor pool (a view-and-a-half), nightly turn-down service, nonsmoking floors, and rooms designed for people with disabilities. The works of Canadian artists are prominently displayed throughout the hotel's public spaces and guest rooms. Don't miss the upbeat gospel music at Sunday brunch. ▪ *Across the street from Canada Place; (604) 691-1991 or (800) 441-1414; 900 Canada Pl Way, Vancouver, BC V6C 3L5; $$$; AE, DC, MC, V; no checks.* &

The Wedgewood Hotel ★★★ Owner and manager Eleni Skalbania takes great pride in the Wedgewood. And Skalbania has much to be proud of. Ideally located in the heart of Vancouver's finest shopping district, and across the street from the Vancouver Art Gallery, the gardens of Robson Square, and the courthouse built of glass, the Wedgewood offers Old World charm and scrupulous attention to every detail of hospitality. From the complimentary Belgian chocolates (fruit baskets during the summer months) on arrival to the potted flowers flourishing on the balcony of every room to the renowned Bacchus Ristorante, this 93-room hotel is all that a small urban luxury hotel should be. This is the only luxury hotel in the city where you won't find tour buses unloading swarms of visitors. The finely appointed rooms, which are surprisingly large and decorated with vibrant colors and genuine English antiques, feel like a grand home. There is nightly turn-down service, a bare-essentials fitness room, and 24-hour room service. This is the place to spend your honeymoon (and many do), but any week-end at the Wedgewood is a weekend to savor. ■ *On Hornby between Smithe and Robson; (604)689-7777 or (800)663-0666; 845 Hornby St, Vancouver, BC V6Z 1V1; $$$; AE, DC, MC, V; no checks.*

Coast Plaza Inn ★★ Situated just off the main artery through the vibrant West End, this former apartment tower offers 267 large rooms, including a dozen two-bedroom suites. All have balconies, and more than two-thirds of the rooms have complete kitchens, making this a great place for vacationing families and Hollywood film crews working in Vancouver (the stars stay elsewhere). Amenities include 24-hour room service, a minibar, and a small fridge. But the hotel's strongest point is its proximity to Stanley Park. Request a room with a park view. Guests are welcome at the adjoining health club. ■ *At Stanley Park; (604)688-7711 or (800)663-1144; 1733 Comox St, Vancouver, BC V6G 1P6; $$$; AE, DC, MC, V; checks OK.*

Delta Vancouver Airport Hotel ★★ The closest hotel to Vancouver International Airport (formerly called the Delta River Inn) spreads along the banks of the Fraser River. All in all, not a bad place to lay over if you are passing through Vancouver. East-facing rooms front the river and marina. Downtown is 15 minutes away. The 400-plus guest rooms and over a dozen meeting rooms are popular for conventions and corporate travelers. Recreational facilities include an outdoor pool, bar, and barbecue, as well as bicycle and running trails. Kids under six eat free in the hotel's dining facilities. There are other hotels in the vicinity of the airport, but the Delta Vancouver Airport Hotel is the best of the lot. ■ *On Cessna Dr before airport; (604)278-1241; 3500 Cessna Dr, Richmond, BC V7B 1C7; $$$; AE, DC, MC, V; no checks.*

Granville Island Hotel and Marina ★★ The Granville Island Hotel is a bold combination of an old stucco building (now pink) and a dramatic new complex of glass and corrugated iron, the latter reminiscent of Granville Island's industrial past. A glass atrium, extending toward the water like the bow of a ship, splits the building down the middle and lets in a stream of natural light. The small 54-room hotel has a lot to recommend it: the custom-furnished rooms are decorated in muted tones with light wood accents; some have shutters that open onto small balconies. Avoid rooms that face the atrium: the nightclub can make for a sleepless night. Prices range from $150 for a double to $250 for a one-bedroom suite. Boats can moor at the dock and hook up to the hotel's television and telephone system, power and water lines, and order from room service. There are two restaurants here: the casual Pelican Pub and Grill and the more formal Pelican Bay. ■ *Far eastern* *corner of Granville Island; (604)683-7373; 1253 Johnston St, Vancouver, BC V6H 3R9; $$$; AE, MC, V; no checks.* &

Hyatt Regency ★★ No surprises here. This is a good Hyatt Regency, like all the others around the world. It's popular with conventions and tour groups, yet continues to offer personalized service. Good views of the harbor and mountains are available from north-facing upper floors. Try for a corner room with a balcony. The Regency Club floor, with special keyed access, has its own concierge, complimentary breakfast, late afternoon hors d'oeuvres, and evening pastries. Standard rooms (among the largest standards in the city) start at $175. A health club and pool are available to all guests. ▪ *Burrard and Georgia; (604)687-6543 or (800)233-1234; 655 Burrard St, Vancouver, BC V6C 2R7; $$$; AE, DC, MC, V; checks OK.*

Laburnam Cottage Bed and Breakfast ★★ This elegant country home is set off by an award-winning English garden, tended with care over the past four decades by innkeeper Delphine Masterton, who raised five children here before opening the home to lodgers. The main house, furnished with antiques and collectibles, features four guest rooms, each light and airy with private bath and garden view. The Summerhouse Cottage—situated in the midst of the garden and accessed by a footbridge that traverses a small creek—is perfect for honeymooning couples. Another, larger cottage, with private entrance, kitchen, fireplace, and children's loft, sleeps six. Masterton's warm gift for welcome and ability to weave strangers into friends over the cheerful breakfast table make a stay here all it should be. ▪ *6 km from downtown, 1 block East of Capilano, North Vancouver; (604)988-4877; 1388 Terrace Ave, North Vancouver, BC V7R 1B4; $$$; MC, V; checks OK.*

Park Hill Hotel ★★ This urban hotel, owned by Mainami Canada, is lovely and coolly sophisticated. Rooms are large and nicely furnished; each has a balcony, and from the 18th floor, there is an incomparable view of English Bay and the islands beyond. Extras include sauna, outdoor swimming pool, and exercise room. Prices are competitive. You're a 15-minute walk from the hub of the city, but the lively street life right outside your door in Vancouver's West End is a show in itself. ▪ *Davie and Thurlow; (604)685-1311 or (800)663-1525; 1160 Davie St, Vancouver, BC V6E 1N1; $$$; AE, DC, MC, V; no checks.*

Park Royal Hotel ★★ A perfect setting for an ivy-covered 30-room Tudor-style hotel. Too bad the rooms aren't a little nicer, or the staff a little friendlier. Located just off the north end of Lions Gate Bridge along the quiet backwaters of Capilano River, the Park Royal Hotel offers a bit of old

England just minutes from downtown and with quick access to the road to Whistler. During summer reservations can be hard to get, especially for a riverfront room. The dining room is extremely pleasant, opening onto a lovely garden fronting the river. ■ *6th and Clyde, West Vancouver; (604) 926-5511; 540 Clyde Ave, West Vancouver, BC V7T 2J7; $$; AE, DC, MC, V; checks OK.*

Penny Farthing Inn ★★ This 1912 Edwardian home is a historic treasure in Vancouver's trendy westside Kitsilano district. Request the attic room, which overlooks the overgrown English garden backdropped by the North Shore mountains. Owner Lyn Hainstock is a professional innkeeper with a wealth of information about Vancouver. Breakfast is a gourmet's feast. ■ *On 6th Ave near McDonald; (604) 739-9002; 2855 W 6th Ave, Vancouver, BC V6K 1X2; $$; no credit cards; checks OK.*

River Run Floating Cottage ★★ River Run Floating Cottage is a jewel on the Fraser River. Located in historic Ladner, 30 minutes south of downtown Vancouver and close to the ferries to Victoria, this floating cottage docked among a community of houseboats offers a closeness to nature—ducks, swans, leaping salmon, and bald eagles all put on a show. Views from the rear deck include the North Shore mountains and Vancouver Island. Open all year round, the cottage is nicely appointed with a claw-footed tub, wood-burning potbelly stove, and cooking facilities. A hot breakfast is delivered on board. Two one bedroom cottages on shore have wood-burning stoves; one has a Jacuzzi tub, the other has a soaker tub out on the deck. ■ *5 km west of Hwy 17, through town to River Rd; (604) 946-7778; 4551 River Rd W, Ladner, BC V4K 1R9; $$; MC, V; checks OK.*

(20 YEARS) **Sylvia Hotel** ★★ A favorite for price and location. This ivy-covered eight-story historic brick hotel is a landmark adjacent to English Bay, Vancouver's most popular beach and strutting grounds. Try for a south-facing room. A low-rise addition was built to compensate for the busy summer season when you might just need to settle for *any* room. Doubles begin at $55, and reservations are required well in advance. All 116 rooms (quite standard) have baths. Families or small groups should request the large two-bedroom suites with kitchens ($85 to $120). The hotel also offers a restaurant and a lounge—reportedly the first cocktail bar in Vancouver (opened in 1954)—and on some winter afternoons it looks like the original clientele is still there. Pets permitted. ■ *Beach and Gilford; (604) 681-9321; 1154 Gilford St, Vancouver, BC V6G 2PG; $; AE, DC, MC, V; checks OK.*

Wall Center Garden Hotel ★★ This stunning 35-story glass tower houses a wonderful addition to Vancouver's already rich

luxury lodging scene. What distinguishes this hotel from the competition is the very stylish decor. The lobby area features furnishings in playful primary colors set amid dramatic marble. Standard double rooms are small, although expansive views from the higher floors help them feel larger. Check into a one-bedroom corner suite with a two-vista view (05 series); floor-to-ceiling windows face north up Burrard Street with Grouse Mountain in the distance, and west to English Bay and the Coast Mountains beyond. Even the lighting adds visual interest: torchères, wall sconces, and distressed-metal table lamps in interesting geometric shapes. The suites feature deep soaking tubs in the marble bathrooms, even a wet bar and microwave. There's a full health club, with swimming pool, in the complex. Certain luxuries that we've come to take for granted at other hotels are absent here, however, such as turn-down service or morning newspapers. The two restaurants—Azure, featuring Mediterranean cuisine, and Indigo, a more informal bistro—are gorgeous. All in all, this is a wonderful place to stay.
■ *At Burrard and Nelson; (604) 331-1000 or (800) 223-5652; 1088 Burrard St, Vancouver, BC V6Z 2R9; $$$; AE, DC, MC, V; no checks; breakfast, lunch, dinner every day.* &

West End Guest House ★★ Don't be put off by the blazing pink exterior of this early-1900s Victorian home, located on a residential street close to Stanley Park and just a block off Robson. Owner Evan Penner runs a fine nine-room inn, and during summer a vacancy is rare. Rooms are generally small but nicely furnished, with antiques throughout the house. The staff have all worked in major hotels and know what hospitality is. Sherry is served in the afternoon. Nightly turn-down service, feather and lambskin mattress covers, terrycloth robes, TV, and telephones are provided in every room. Breakfast is a bountiful cooked meal served family style or delivered to your room. There is guest parking (a rarity in the West End). Families with well-behaved children are welcome. ■ *1 block south of Robson, between Jervis and Broughton; (604) 681-2889; 1362 Haro St, Vancouver, BC V6E 1G2; $$; AE, MC, V; checks OK.*

Westin Bayshore Hotel ★★ The Bayshore sits on the southern shore of Coal Harbour next to the main entrance to Stanley Park. Set back from busy Georgia Street, this is the only downtown hotel that resembles a resort (children love it here). Rooms look out over a large outdoor pool, with Coal Harbour's colorful marina as a backdrop and the North Shore mountains beyond. The Hertz counter in the hotel rents bicycles, and if you're up for a one-hour ride, you can't beat the scenery along the connecting Stanley Park seawall. Amenities include all that you'd expect from a Westin. Tower rooms all have balconies. There's also a health club with

20 YEARS

both indoor and outdoor pools. The major business and shopping areas of downtown are a pleasant 15-minute walk away. The staff could use a week or two at the Wedgewood or the Sutton Place for some advanced training. ■ *Georgia and Cardero, just south of Stanley Park; (604)682-3377 or (800)228-3000; 1601 W Georgia St, Vancouver, BC V6G 2V4; $$$; AE, DC, MC, V; checks OK.*

 Hotel Georgia ★ This attractive stone 12-story hotel, built in 1927, offers old-fashioned charm, with its small oak-paneled lobby, elaborate brass elevators, and comfortable rooms furnished with contemporary oak furniture, but it has the feel of a hotel for traveling salespeople and bus tours. The rooms with the best views face south to the Vancouver Art Gallery, but they are on a busy, noisy street. Executive rooms have a seating area that is useful for conducting business. The hotel's location couldn't be more central. The Georgia has two bars that are popular with locals (especially for their pub-style lunches). ■ *Howe and Georgia; (604)682-5566 or (800)663-1111; 801 W Georgia St, Vancouver, BC V6C 1P7; $$$; AE, DC, MC, V; no checks.*

Lonsdale Quay Hotel ★ Few visitors take the time to explore the North Shore, which has the best wilderness parks of perhaps any major North American city. The pleasant Lonsdale Quay Hotel, located inside the enjoyable Lonsdale Quay market across the harbor from downtown Vancouver (only 15 minutes away via the SeaBus), offers a comfortable place to stay (as long as you don't need to be pampered). French doors on south-facing rooms open up to the Vancouver skyline, a dazzling sight at night. ■ *Bottom of Lonsdale Ave in North Vancouver; (604)986-6111 or (800)836-6111; 123 Carrie Cates Ct, North Vancouver, BC V7M 3K7; $$$; AE, DC, MC, V; no checks.*

▼

Vancouver

Lodgings

▲

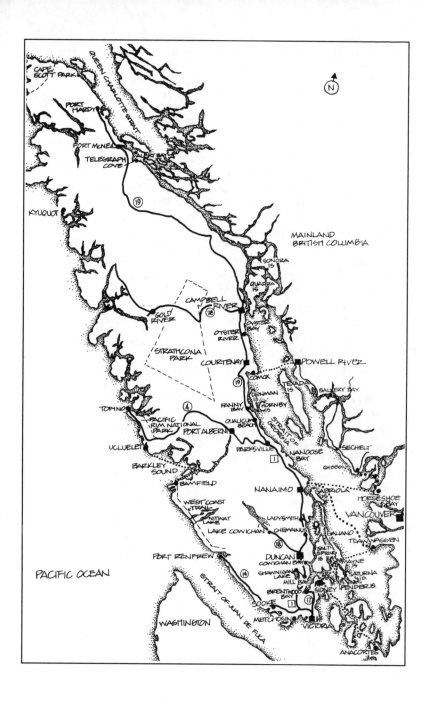

Victoria and Vancouver Island

*From Victoria and environs—westward to Sooke,
northward to Sidney—up-island along the east coast to
Parksville. From there a short jog inland to Port Alberni
(and access to west coast towns); then back to Qualicum
Beach and north along the coast to Port Hardy.
Finally, the Gulf Islands, north to south.*

VICTORIA

Romantic as Victoria may be, with its delightful natural harbor
and the Olympic Mountains of Washington State on the horizon, the provincial capital of British Columbia is less a museum
piece nowadays than it is a tourist mecca. Visitors pour in to
gawk at vast sculptured gardens and London-style double-deck
buses, to shop for Irish linens and Harris tweeds, sip afternoon
tea, and soak up what they believe is the last light of British im-
perialism to set on the Western hemisphere. Raves in the travel
press have brought a new crop of younger residents to upset
Victoria's reputation as a peaceful but dull sanctuary for retir-
ing civil servants from eastern Canada. The quality and variety
of restaurants is improving as a result, and no longer are Victoria's streets silent after 10pm.

   Ferries. From Seattle, the passenger-only **Victoria Clipper,** a jet-propelled catamaran, makes its 2½-hour voyages up
and back four times daily in summer (one of which goes via
the San Juan Islands) and once or twice daily off-season ($89

round-trip). The good seats on the upper deck by windows are quickly taken, so board early; from Vancouver, call (604)382-8100; from Seattle, (206)448-5000; or (800)888-2535 (outside Seattle or outside BC). Other ferry services **from Washington** to the Victoria area: Washington State ferries run year-round, departing Anacortes, north of Seattle, to Sidney, BC, 27 kilometers north of Victoria), one of the most scenic water routes in the Pacific Northwest; (206)464-6400 or (604)381-1551, $36 round-trip in summer or $30 in winter. Ferries to Victoria also leave Port Angeles on the Olympic Peninsula (via the privately run Black Ball ferry), a 1½-hour voyage (year-round) on which cars are allowed, but for which no reservations are taken (call a day in advance to find out how long the wait will be); (206)457-4491 or (604)386-2202; $26 one-way car and driver, $6.50 for foot passengers. Ferries **from British Columbia** mainland depart from Tsawwassen to Swartz Bay, 32 kilometers north of Victoria, every hour from 7am to 10pm in summer, following a scenic route through the Gulf Islands; $54 round-trip car and driver; call BC Ferries at (604)386-3431.

Air Transportation. The fastest link from Seattle (Lake Union) to Victoria (Inner Harbour) is provided by seaplane several times daily for about $142 round-trip on scenic Kenmore Air, (800)826-1890. You also can fly from Vancouver via Air BC, (604)688-5515, or Helijet Airway, (604)273-1414.

▼

Victoria

▲

Attractions. First stop should be Tourism Victoria, a well-staffed office dispensing useful information on the sights; 812 Wharf Street, (604)953-2033. The **Royal British Columbia Museum** is one of the finest of its kind in the country, offering dramatic dioramas of natural landscapes and full-scale reconstructions of Victorian storefronts. Of particular interest is the Northwest Coast Indian exhibit, rich with spiritual and cultural artifacts. Watch for special seasonal and touring exhibitions and an intriguing "undersea" show. Open every day, Belleville and Government, (604)387-3701. The **Art Gallery of Greater Victoria** houses one of the world's finest collections of Oriental art (including the only Shinto shrine in North America), with special historical and contemporary exhibits on display throughout the year. Open every day, 1040 Moss Street, (604)384-4101. **McPherson Playhouse**, a former Pantages vaudeville house done up with baroque trappings, offers evening entertainment throughout the summer. The box office, (604)386-6121, also has information about plays and concerts at the Royal Theatre and other sites. The free *Monday Magazine* offers the city's best weekly calendar of events. Spreading out over 184 acres, **Beacon Hill Park** provides splendid views of the water, but the real interest here is in the landscaping (much of it left wild) and the hand-holding couples who stroll the walkways and give retirement a good name. A lovely spot to get away from the shopping mania downtown.

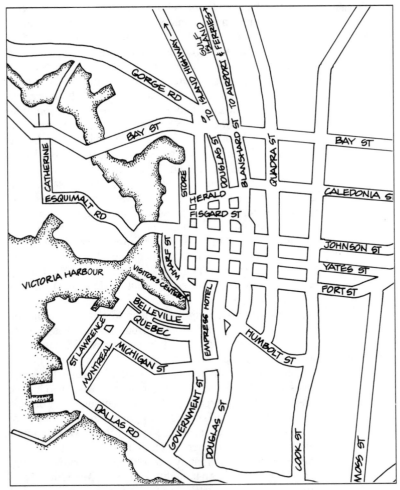

Victoria

Crystal Garden is a turn-of-the-century swimming-pool building converted into a glass conservatory with a tropical theme (lush greenery, live flamingos and macaws). It's a fine place to spend a rainy day; admission is $5. Open every day, 713 Douglas Street, (604)381-1213. Just across the street is the **Victoria Conference Centre**, linked to the Empress Hotel by a beautifully restored conservatory and accommodating 1,500 delegates. **Butchart Gardens**, 21 kilometers north of town, shows what can be done with dug-out limestone quarries (with help from a small army of Chinese workers). The 50 acres of gardens are beautifully manicured, lovely displays in many international styles; they're lighted after dark. Take the time to look beyond the profusion of blooms to the landscape structure and its relationship to the setting of rocky bays and tree-covered mountains. In the summer it's best to go late in the afternoon, after the busloads of tourists have left. Concerts, fireworks on summer evenings, a surprisingly good afternoon tea, and light meals provide diversions. Open every day, (604)652-5256. **Craigdarroch Castle** puts you back into an era of unfettered wealth and ostentation. Vancouver Island coal tycoon Robert Dunsmuir built this 19th-century mansion to induce a Scottish wife to live in faraway Victoria. Open every day, 1050 Joan Crescent, (604)592-5323. You can visit five of the better restored **Victoria heritage homes**, (604)387-4697: Helmcken House, behind Thunderbird Park, east of BC Royal Museum; Point Ellice House, at Bay Street and Pleasant Street; Craigflower Manor, 110 Island Highway; Craigflower Schoolhouse at Admirals and Gorge Road W; and Carr House, at Government and Simcoe. Admission to all five is $3.25. The **Esquimalt and Nanaimo (E&N) Railway** leaves early in the morning from a mock-Victorian station near the Johnson Street bridge and heads up-island to towns with fine resorts. The trip is slow but scenic; no food service. Call Via Rail, (604)383-4324 or (800)561-8630.

Specialty Shopping. For British woolens, suits, and toiletries, the downtown area north from the Empress on Government Street is the place to shop. **George Straith Ltd.** is the best of the clothing stores, and you can be measured for a suit here that will be tailored in England; **Piccadilly Shopper British Woolens** specializes in good-quality women's clothes; **W & J Wilson Clothiers** sells English wool suits and women's clothes; **Sasquatch Trading Company Ltd.** offers some of the best of the Cowichan sweaters; **EA Morris Tobacconist, Ltd.** carries a very proper, Victorian mix of fine pipes and tobaccos; **Munro's**, a monumental 19th-century bank-building-turned-bookstore, has a thoughtful selection; **Murchie's Teas and Coffee** offers the city's finest selection of specially blended teas and coffees; and don't forget **Roger's Chocolates** and the **English Sweet Shop** for chocolates, almond brittle, black currant pastilles, marzipan bars, Pontefract cakes, and more; and **Bernard Callebaut Chocolaterie** for picture-perfect chocolates in the Belgian style. Market Square is a restored 19th-century courtyard surrounded by a jumble of shops, restaurants, and offices on three floors. A few blocks farther at Fisgard Street, the entrance to Victoria's small and seemingly shrinking **Chinatown** is marked by the splendid, lion-bedecked Gate of Harmonious Interest. Visit the tiny shops and studios on Fan Tan Alley and check out Morley Co. Ltd., a Chinese grocery. **Antique hunters** should head east of downtown, up Fort Street to Antique Row—block after block of shops, the best of which are the Connoisseurs Shop and David Robinson, Ltd., with excellent 18th-century English pieces. Visit **Bastion**

▼ **Victoria** ▲

Square for sidewalk restaurants, galleries, the Maritime Museum, the alleged location of Victoria's old gallows, and a great gardener's shop called Dig This; Trounce Alley for upscale clothing; and Windsor Court for boutiques and gifts.

RESTAURANTS

Camille's ★★★ Chef and wine columnist David Mincey, together with partner Paige Robinson, has carefully created Victoria's most romantic basement, with soft lights, music, and wine from a selection of over 200 stored in a huge, walk-in vault. Dishes are based on fresh local produce, seafood, rabbit, and lamb. The Old South–style jambalaya is deliciously rich and smoky, and loaded with chicken, prawns, sausage, and vegetables in a spicy tomato sauce. For those not chained to a low-fat diet, the three-cheese soup is a creamy delight. Wine-tasting dinners (monthly, Sundays) are highly popular—reserve early. Camille's has a faithful local following. ▪ *Fort and Langley in Bastion Square; (604)381-3433; 45 Bastion Square, Victoria; $$; full bar; MC, V; no checks; dinner Tues–Sun.* ₺

Chez Daniel ★★★ Chez Daniel is one of Victoria's finest French restaurants, tucked in Oak Bay a long way off the tourist track. Chef/owner Daniel Rigollet has garnered a fine reputation, and has been pleasing people here for years. The decor in the two small dining rooms is pleasant, and the award-winning wine list shows great care in selection, with bottles running from $20 dollars to several hundred. The expensive menu, though traditionally French in approach, is rich and wide-ranging in flavor, from salmon in vermouth and cream sauce to duck in a fine chestnut sauce. The bisque is excellent. Daniel works alone in the kitchen and the waitstaff takes time to deliver their polite, knowledgeable service. Plan to make an evening of it. ▪ *Estevan and Beach, 10 minutes from downtown; (604)592-7424; 2524 Estevan Ave, Victoria; $$$; full bar; AE, MC, V; checks OK; dinner Tues–Sat.* ₺

Da Tandoor Restaurant ★★★ Authentic cuisine from Northern India doesn't come any better around Victoria. Da Tandoor (no connection with Vancouver's similiarly named establishment) is everything most of us expect from an Indian restaurant—glitzy decor and an atmosphere so rich with spice and aroma you could slice it with a knife. Service is polite, prompt, and especially helpful when it comes to advice for the spice neophyte. All the classics are here and well presented: pappadums and chutney, chicken tandoori, lamb curry, curried lentils, basmati rice. Try a glass of sweet lassi, flavored with rose water, or Kingfisher, the "authentic" Indian beer that's actually brewed under license in England. ▪ *Fort and Vancouver; (604)384-6333; 1010 Fort St, Victoria; $$; full bar; MC, V; no checks; dinner every day.*

Cecconi's Pizzeria and Trattoria ★★ Cecconi's is one of several restaurants owned by Mike Murphy (others include Pescatore's and Il Terrazo, both downtown), a man who knows how to create atmosphere. Suppertime's a noisy affair, with occasional live jazz and lots of families and shoppers seeking refuge from the nearby mall. The wood-fired oven turns out some of the best pizza and focaccia around. A simple pizza pomodoro is a fine example of how rich and satisfying a meal at Cecconi's can be. Enjoy one of Victoria's better pastas like Rotini alla Barese (with spicy Italian sausage) topped off with a hard-working chunk of Reggiano Parmesan, which staff will grate over almost everything except drinks and dessert. ■ *Shelbourne and N Dairy Rd, across from Hillside Mall; (604)592-0454; 3201 Shelbourne, Victoria; $$; full bar; MC, V; no checks; lunch, dinner every day.* &

The Met Bistro ★★ The Met is a long, narrow restaurant that's broad on service—a place where martini fans can indulge in over a dozen original variations on their favorite theme. Need we say it's a trendy, post-theater kind of spot? We've liked roasted tomato and gin soup, as well as a generous dish of steamed clams and mussels in white wine with garlic, tomato, shallots, and fresh herbs. The biggest change between lunch and dinner is the cosmopolitan atmosphere that arrives around sunset. ■ *Herald and Government; (604)381-1512; 1715 Government St, Victoria; $$; full bar; AE, MC, V; no checks; lunch Mon–Fri, dinner every day.* &

▼

Victoria

Restaurants

▲

Pagliacci's ★★ Hip Victorians of all ages come to see and be seen here. The famous clown about town, Howie Siegel, is a movie buff whose menu reads a bit like a Cannes festival guide; Al Capone Prawns sit next to Damon Runyon New York Steak. Hollywood mug shots and Manhattan murals on deep pink walls, live music, and Amateur Night, where anything goes, add to an always boisterous atmosphere. Service can take a while, but portions are generous. Modest food comes reasonably priced. Factory-made croutons are a small flaw in otherwise great salads. One of few places in town where folks seem to enjoy waiting to be let in. Pag's weekend brunches are legendary. ■ *Between Fort and Broughton on Broad near Eaton Centre; (604)386-1662; 1011 Broad St, Victoria; $$; full bar; MC, V; checks OK; lunch Mon–Sat, dinner every day, brunch Sun.* &

San Remo Restaurant ★★ Hungry customers are still lining up to eat at San Remo. The Mediterranean, Greco-Italian theme is wearing well, and the Greek influence on the menu here is what gives San Remo the edge. A filling introduction to this cuisine is the $37.50 combination platter for two (moussaka, lamb chops, chicken souvlaki, calamari, spinach pie, tzatziki, Greek salad, rice, and fresh veggies). The pita is superb and perfect for dipping tzatziki or hummus. Saganaki—pan-fried goat cheese flamed at your table with brandy and lemon—will excite the youngsters in your party. Conservative diners can depend on charbroiled chicken salad. Ask for a table in the many-windowed glassy back room on a sunny day. ■ *Quadra and Hillside; (604)384-5255; 2709 Quadra St, Victoria; $$; full bar; AE, MC, V; no checks; lunch Mon–Sat, dinner every day.*

Siam ★★ Moving to this location from Government Street has only improved Victoria's best Thai restaurant, giving it an airier atmosphere. The food is star rated, from one-star mild to four-star painful—Thai food has a temper. The Yum Talay salad of mixed seafood cooked with onions, cilantro, and mint leaves in lime juice is excellent. Also recommended are Siam Curry (red curry with coconut milk, bamboo shoots, sweet basil, and your choice of meats) and, as an appetizer or small lunch, the Satay (grilled chicken marinated with curry powder and coconut milk served with peanut sauce). Big-screen karaoke on occasional weekend evenings. ■ *Near the foot of Fort St; (604)383-9911; 512 Fort St, Victoria; $$; full bar; AE, MC, V; no checks; lunch Mon–Sat, dinner every day.* &

Spinnakers Brew Pub ★★ Spinnakers has become a local institution, setting the standard for pubs and brew pubs across Vancouver Island. The selection of natural beers, most of which are made in the pub's own brewery (inspect it as you enter from the parking lot) gets bigger and more adventurous every year. Regulars and visitors mingle here to enjoy a great view in a cheerful, noisy atmosphere with discreet live music and traditional pubs games. Minors are welcome downstairs in the restaurant, where they (and their majors) will enjoy the same good view and a touch more dining sophistication than is offered with the pub fare upstairs. A few low-fat dishes have been added, but there's still plenty of the good old fish 'n' chips, burgers, potpies, and the odd Mexican-style treats. ■ *Travel west over the Johnson St Bridge to Catherine, or water taxi from the Inner Harbour; (604)386-2739; 308 Catherine St, Victoria; $; full bar; AE, MC, V; no checks; breakfast, lunch, dinner every day.* &

Szechuan ★★ There's nothing pretentious about this basic little restaurant right across the street from Memorial Arena and Victoria's spanking new police station. Szechuan offers good spicy food with lightning-quick service. Try the Pon Pon Chicken appetizer—a tender breast with thick sesame sauce; crispy, whole rock cod with a choice of hot bean, sweet-and-sour, or fermented rice sauce, or the tongue-tantalizing ginger beef. ■ *Across from the Memorial Arena parking lot; (604)384-5651; 853 Caledonia Ave, Victoria; $$; full bar; AE, MC, V; no checks; lunch, dinner Tues–Sun.*

Barb's Place ★ If the weather behaves and you don't mind lineups, eating at Barb's is an alfresco treat: fresh fish caught by the local fleet that bobs nearby. The fish 'n' chips are first-rate—tender halibut (ask for cod during midsummer) encased in crisp batter accompanied by home-fried chips with skins left on. Sit at one of two dockside picnic tables or tour the docks as you nibble. Grassy park nearby for sun worshippers and boisterous kids. ■ *At Fisherman's Wharf; (604) 384-6515; 310 St. Lawrence St, Victoria; $; no alcohol; no credit cards; no checks; breakfast, lunch, dinner every day.* &

Blethering Place ★ "Blethering" is Scottish for voluble, senseless talking, so settle down for just that amid the civilized clatter of authentic British crockery, where one of Victoria's best teas comes at a reasonable price. (Here behind the "tweed curtain" in fussy Oak Bay, things can be more British than the real thing.) The roomy tea shop is quaint without being gimmicky, and popular with locals shopping the high street and tourists who've ridden the double-decker Oak Bay Explorer from downtown. Enjoy a decent pot of tea with a choice of pastries. ■ *Oak Bay and Monterey; (604) 598-1413; 2250 Oak Bay, Victoria; $; beer and wine; AE, DC, MC, V; local checks only; breakfast, lunch, dinner, tea every day.* &

Demitasse ★ Despite the price of beans and number of tearooms, coffee is still a big deal in Victoria and Demitasse has helped set the standard. The hipper-than-thou set mingles with businessfolk and tourists. Fans arrive early for long breakfasts (and delicious croissants), but staff are kept busy all day plying snacks and lunches—homemade soups, doorstep-sized sandwiches, and excellent desserts. There's a bar for people-watching or magazine reading. If you want to sit outside and absorb the atmosphere of this busy street corner, move quickly—there's only one small table. ■ *Corner of Blanshard and Johnson; (604) 386-4442; 1320 Blanshard St, Victoria; $; beer and wine; no credit cards; checks OK; breakfast, lunch, dinner every day.* &

Futaba ★ Locals will tell you Futaba is more than a Japanese restaurant. It's a promoter (but not a preacher) of healthy eating, a favorite place for some discriminating vegetarians and macrobiotic eaters, and a good spot to try some Japanese dishes that you won't find anywhere else in Victoria. Appetizers are interesting, but sushi here is fundamental (brown rice is the norm, though white is offered). The Westernized atmosphere might disappoint camera-toting tourists seeking kimono-clad waitresses, but eating here is a casual, not ceremonial, pleasure. ■ *Quadra and Pandora; (604) 381-6141; 1420 Quadra St, Victoria; $$; full bar; MC, V; no checks; lunch Mon–Sat, dinner every day.* &

Grace Bistro ★ Tucked into a narrow corner of Chinatown, the Grace offers healthy fare with a touch of class in a nonsmoking environment appointed with funky couches and overstuffed armchairs. Walls hung with large canvases and guitars set the scene for what is a popular lunch and coffee spot during the day and a hip bustling bistro at night, with live music every weekend—including a jazz jam Sunday evening. There's always a vegetarian soup (the black bean scented with lime and cilantro and served with a generous salad and slab of multi-grain bread is a deal) and handmade vegetarian samosas are a hit. Rich desserts come piled high and the coffee's first rate. ■ *Toward the lower end of Chinatown; (604)385-5677; 533 Fisgard St, Victoria; $; no alcohol; V; local checks only; lunch every day, dinner Fri–Sun.* &

Re-bar ★ People come here for the healthy food and drink and the smoke-free environment, not for the lime green walls, purple bar, and garish vinyl tablecloths. The house salad, one of many offered, sports an especially good basil vinaigrette. Health-conscious patrons sip a variety of vegetable juices and cocktails, some of them fortified with wheat grass (growing in a rack of trays), bee pollen, amino acids, electrolytes, protein powder, or other dietary shots-in-the-arm. The on-site bakery uses organic grains to produce all baked goods, and take-out business is brisk. ■ *Langley and Bastion Square; (604)361-9223; 50 Bastion Square, Victoria; $; beer and wine; AE, V, MC; local checks only; breakfast, lunch, dinner Mon–Sat, brunch Sun.* &

Sweet Pea Cafe ★ The Sweet Pea, just a few minutes away from Butchart Gardens, is run by a women's cooperative that cares about low-fat, tasty snacks and meals. Inside, you'll find a delightful country cafe serving wholesome food that's locally grown and just about 100 percent organic. The decor leans toward diner-style, with white vinyl stools and low red counter—just an arm's reach from the open kitchen. Outside, relax at a picnic bench in a pretty yard where blackberries overrun a glassless old greenhouse. The roasted potato wedges are a hit with kids. Sumptuous desserts and take-out service provide great picnic fare. ■ *Durrance and W Saanich Rd; (604)652-3132; 6002 W Saanich Rd, Saanich; $; no alcohol; MC; checks OK; lunch Wed–Sun, call for dinner hours.*

Yoshi Sushi ★ Originating in Southeast Asia as a means of preserving fish in salted rice, sushi has become *the* "healthy heart" food of the '90s. Yoshi's expertise and years of experience show in the way he treats delicate flavors with care and sensitivity. At the sushi bar, the robata bar, or in one of the 12 tatami rooms, you'll get prompt, courteous service and great Japanese food. If sushi's not your thing, try one of the many vegetarian, chicken, or beef dishes, or concoct your own meal around udon or soba noodles. All of the entrees are preceded by miso soup, sunomono, and an appetizer of yakitori or sushi. ■ *In Gateway Village Mall just outside of town on Hwy 17; (604) 474-3900; 602-771 Vernon Ave, Victoria; $$; full bar; AE, MC, V; no checks; lunch Mon–Sat, dinner every day.*

Four Mile Roadhouse The Four Mile has been catering to travelers since it opened as a roadhouse in 1858. The restaurant and tearoom occupy the quaint original section of the building where leaded windows and brick fireplaces add Old World charm. The neighborhood pub takes up the rear half of the premises, opening to a small deck and flower-filled garden. The restaurant menu is versatile, offering Mediterranean angliotti and Caribbean trout in addition to the requisite steak, chicken, and ribs. Pub food includes hearty burgers and Tex-Mex-Cajun cuisine. Live music in the pub Wednesday evenings. ■ *Old Island Hwy past Craigflower; (604) 479-2514; 199 Old Island Hwy, Victoria; $; full bar; AE, MC, V; no checks; lunch, dinner every day.* ♿

Herald Street Caffe It's not quite the restaurant it used to be, but the busy Caffe at the edge of Chinatown still enjoys a loyal following. Happy regulars settle beneath pink stucco walls and huge flower arrangements to enjoy noisy conversation. Food is adventurous, though it occasionally misses the mark (an improperly cooked seafood risotto). The stuffed roast pork tenderloin with a sweet apple-based sauce comes with an interesting combination of vegetables. Shaker lemon pie wins raves. Herald Street Caffe uses a professional wine consultant, and it shows—the wine list has won prestigious awards and offers several good wines by the glass. Make reservations or be prepared to wait. Late hours (until midnight) are handy for patrons of nearby Kaleidoscope and McPherson theaters. ■ *Government and Herald, 1 block past Chinatown; (604) 381-1441; 546 Herald St, Victoria; $$; full bar; AE, MC, V; no checks; lunch Wed–Sun, dinner every day, brunch Sun.* ♿

John's Place John's Place is usually bustling with a youngish crowd who come for the price and the portions—the bottomless bowl of soup is legend. Don't expect fast service, especially during brunch. Eggs are a big deal here, as are John's famous Belgian waffles. This is also a heritage building, so enjoy the Victoriana floors and walls, accented, not affronted, by decor of the '90s. ■ *Douglas and Pandora; (604) 389-0711; 723 Pandora Ave, Victoria; $; full bar; MC, V; no checks; breakfast Mon–Sat, lunch, dinner every day, brunch Sun.* ♿

Pounder's It's a bit gimmicky, but it's fun. You arm yourself with a stainless steel bowl, select meats and vegetables from a long table, have them weighed (and charged to your bill), then stir-fried Mongolian-style and served to you with rice and salad. Talk about international menu: mako shark, Australian bluenose, kangaroo, smoked eel, wild boar, ostrich, musk ox, and even some tough and bony rattlesnake; however, most folks settle for the prawns, sea bass, or chicken. Best to make several trips with your bowl and work through the light, then dark fish, and then tackle the meats. Desserts are far less exotic. ■ *Near the bottom of Yates St at Wharf; (604)360-1875; 535 Yates St, Victoria; $$; full bar; AE, MC, V; no checks; lunch and dinner every day.* &

Soho Village Bistro Now under the careful guidance of original owner Clarke Fowler, Soho's menu has simplified and come down a bit in price and variety. It's still a sophisticated little black-and-white bistro adorned with lots of colorful artwork, a cafe by day (with its own doughnut maker), and a jumping, sometimes smoky bistro by night (especially when the Belfry Theatre has a performance across the street). Organic greens come tastily dressed, and there are individual pizzas, appetizers such as filo-baked Brie with a sharp raspberry coulis, and a range of good burgers and sandwiches. ■ *Gladstone and Fernwood, across from the Belfry Theatre; (604)384-3344; 1311 Gladstone, Victoria; $; full bar; MC, V; no checks; lunch, dinner every day, brunch Sun.* &

LODGINGS

Abigail's ★★★ The feminine counterpart of the Edwardian Beaconsfield, just two blocks away, the Tudor Abigail's is all gables and gardens and crystal chandeliers, with three floors of odd-shaped rooms: third-floor guest rooms are grandest. Not a lavish detail is missed: crystal goblets sit in each room; the halls smell faintly of good coffee and beautiful women. Practicalities, too, are all well in place—a light shines in the shower, the walls are well soundproofed (light sleepers, however, may want to request a room as far from noisy Quadra Street as possible). In short, Abigail's combines the beauty of the Old World with the comforts of the New. The guest library is inviting, especially with a glass of sherry after a day about Victoria. ■ *Vancouver and McClure; (604)388-5363; 906 McClure St, Victoria, BC V8V 3E7; $$$; MC, V; checks OK.*

The Beaconsfield ★★★ Of all the imitation England spots, this is the best. Tree-lined Humboldt Street is closer to the hub of downtown than its quiet demeanor would suggest, so the Beaconsfield's location just two blocks from Beacon Hill Park is prime. It's meant to convey a sense of romance and hideaway and does, with nine antique-filled bedrooms, all with private baths and down comforters. The Attic Room, Jacuzzi and all, is exceedingly private. The Duchess Room has a half-canopied queen-size bed, with inlaid mahogany pieces and an unusual wood-enclosed period bathtub. The antiques are offset by rediscovered "modernities" such as steam-heated towel racks. There is so much dark, gleaming mahogany in this Edwardian home that one can feel a bit cloistered on a sunny day, but this is easily remedied in the conservatory (where breakfast is often served). ■ *Vancouver and Humboldt; (604) 384-4044; 998 Humboldt St, Victoria, BC V8V 2Z8; $$$; MC, V; checks OK.* &

Holland House Inn ★★★ The house is a modern beauty (just the antidote to the endless Olde England theme so prevalent in Victoria), decked with rose trellises and a picket fence outside, skylights and stark white walls inside. Fine art and sculpture, many of the pieces by owner Lance Olsen, fill the 10 sparkling guest rooms. The result is as startlingly chic as you're likely to find in Quaintville. Rooms 20 and 30 have fireplaces and all but one have their own balcony or patio. The service is never fawning. ■ *2 blocks behind the Parliament buildings, at Government and Michigan; (604) 384-6644; 595 Michigan St, Victoria, BC V8V 1S7; $$$; AE, DC, MC, V; checks OK.* &

Laurel Point Inn ★★★ Laurel Point's angular construction means that all of the 200 rooms and suites offer views of the harbor or the ship channel. Be sure to ask for a room in the massive brick-and-glass ziggurat addition; all are beautifully appointed with graceful Japanese accents and private deck. Spacious marble bathrooms are fitted with deep-soak tubs and sexy, peek-a-boo stall showers. The channel-side rooms offer the best view of the comings and goings of boats and seaplanes and the gracious Japanese garden at channel's edge. The dining room, Cafe Laurel, is a wicker-and-fern affair with better-than-adequate food. Sunday brunch is the best in town. ■ *On the west side of Inner Harbour; (604) 386-8721; 680 Montreal St, Victoria, BC V8V 1Z8; $$$; AE, DC, MC, V; no checks.* &

The Bedford Regency Hotel ★★ The liveried doorman is gone, but the carefully maintained flower boxes, thick and pillowy bed quilts, private Jacuzzis, and a dozen rooms with fireplaces are still here. In a renovation that proved frogs can still become princes, Victoria's reigning dukes of hospitality transformed what used to be downtown's shoddiest hotel, the Alhambra, into a small showcase of European-style elegance. Most of the 40 rooms are pricey and without a view, but the hotel's central downtown location is hard to beat for shoppers. Afternoon tea is an extra $11.95, but breakfast is complimentary.

1½ blocks north of Fort St; (604)384-6835 or (800)665-6500; 1140 Government St, Victoria, BC V8W 1Y2; $$$; AE, MC, V; no checks. &

The Coast Victoria Harbourside Hotel ★★ The Coast Victoria features Victoria's only indoor/outdoor pool and a view of the Olympic Mountains, the Strait of Juan de Fuca, or the Inner Harbour. The penthouse suites offer much in the way of comfort (sleeping quarters flank cushy sitting rooms, though the decor—bold, dark colors, expensive, high-gloss furnishings, and gigantic wide-screen TVs—may strike some as seriously overblown. Standard guest rooms have small bathrooms and silly little Mr. Coffee machines. Other features are underground parking, whirlpool, sauna, and exercise rooms, and a 42-slip marina. ■ *Between Laurel Point and Fisherman's Wharf; (604)360-1211; 146 Kingston St, Victoria, BC V8V 1V4; $$$; AE, DC, MC, V; no checks.* &

The Haterleigh ★★ The Haterleigh House was built in 1901 by Thomas Hooper, an architect who designed many of Victoria's Victorian homes. The house has been well preserved and finely restored. Fine curved, stained-glass windows grace the parlor. Breakfasts include eggs goldenrod (a variation of eggs Benedict), a fruit plate, homemade baked goods, juice, and coffee. Guests enjoy a glass of sherry and samples of rich Rogers chocolates, made in Victoria, upon arrival. ■ *Take Belleville west to Pendray until it dead-ends; (604)384-9995; 243 Kingston St, Victoria, BC V8V 1V5; $$$; MC, V; no checks.*

▼

Victoria

Lodgings

▲

Joan Brown's B&B ★★ Joan Brown may monopolize the conversation at the breakfast table, but most visitors enjoy listening to her tales. This lovely house draped with wisteria is in the renowned Rockland neighborhood, but the spacious rooms (a few are ballroom-size) and Joan's quirky ways of running an inn make this stately bed and breakfast a very comfortable stay. Our pick for rooms is the one with a Second Empire flavor furnished with a king-size bed, fireplace, bath, and bay window. Nothing could be better for a rainy afternoon than the well-stocked library. ■ *Pemberton and Fort; (604)592-5929; 729 Pemberton Rd, Victoria, BC V8S 3R3; $$; no credit cards; checks OK.*

 Oak Bay Beach Hotel ★★ Presiding over the Haro Strait, this Tudor-style hotel is the loveliest part of Anglophile Victoria, a nice place to stay if you want to be removed from downtown. Even so, it's a very busy spot—especially its bars. Still it evokes another world: handsome antiques dot the comfortable rooms full of nooks and gables. The best rooms are those with private balconies and a view of the sea. The garden-side dining room, Bentley's on the Bay, is prettily done, but isn't up to the rest of the place. Opt for the inviting Snug where you can sit before the fire. Across the street is the private Victoria Golf Club dramatically bordered by the sea. And do enjoy the hotel's afternoon tea—a proper affair that deserves proper attire. ■ *Near the corner of Oak Bay Ave and Beach Dr; (604)598-4556; 1175 Beach Dr, Victoria, BC V8S 2N2; $$$; AE, DC, MC, V; checks OK.*

The Prior House ★★ No imitation here: this grand B&B occupies an English mansion built during the Edwardian period for the king's representative in British Columbia. It is in a quiet neighborhood about 1½ miles from downtown. Five of the six rooms have fireplaces and views of water; the Lieutenant Governor's suite has a luxurious Jacuzzi bath, gold fixtures, and crystal chandeliers. Innkeeper Candis Cooperrider fixes simple breakfasts and serves tea at 4pm. Well-behaved children okay in selected suites. ■ *St. Charles and Rockland; (604)592-8847; 620 St. Charles, Victoria, BC V8S 3N7; $$$; MC, V; checks OK.*

Victoria Regent Hotel ★★ For those with a taste for very luxurious condo living, the modern Victoria Regent is a posh apartment hotel with grandstand views of the harbor from the north. Don't let the unadorned exterior put you off. Inside, you'll find huge, nicely decorated one- and two-bedroom suites. Each apartment has a living room, dining room, deck, and kitchen, and most have two bedrooms and two bathrooms. Most have views of city and harbor. Full room service from the Water's Edge Cafe and Lounge is available. ■ *Corner of Yates and Wharf; (604)386-2211; 1234 Wharf St, Victoria, BC V8W 3H9; $$$; AE, DC, MC, V; checks OK.*

The Captain's Palace ★ What was once a charming one-guest-room B&B with a mediocre restaurant is now a charming 20-guest-room B&B (in three Victorian houses) with a mediocre restaurant. The B&B outgrew the original handsome 1897 mansion near the harbor and spread into the adjacent property, where the quarters are newer and decorated in florals and muted pastels. Some have balconies; all have private baths—some with cute claw-footed tubs. The orange-blossom-special breakfast is served in the dining room of the main house. ■ *2 blocks west of the Empress; (604)388-9191; 309 Belleville St, Victoria, BC V8V 1X2; $$$; AE, DC, MC, V; no checks.*

Craigmyle Guest House ★ Built as a guest house early in the century, the Craigmyle stands next to Craigdarroch Castle (a grand, well-preserved mansion). Best rooms are those with views of the neighborhood castle. A large breakfast with homemade preserves and good coffee is served, and the main lounge features traditional wainscoting, lofty ceilings, an enormous fireplace, and annoying easy-listening music. Rooms are quite reasonable, but you're 1½ kilometers from city center. One of the few guest houses in Victoria that allows children. ■ *1½ kilometers up Fort St from city center, look for the castle; (604)595-5411; 1037 Craigdarroch Rd, Victoria, BC V8S 2A5; $$; MC, V; no checks.*

The Empress ★ The hotel that once stood as the quiet, ivy-clad dowager of the Inner Harbour had a $45 million facelift in 1989. In the years since then, that lovely facade has proven to be a facelift that only the Queen Mother could love. First the good news: a separate guest entrance pavilion was added, the Palm Court and the Crystal Ballroom were polished up, and 50 new rooms brought the total to 482. The grounds were landscaped, and a restored conservatory at the rear of the hotel now connects it to the Victoria Conference Centre. And now for the bad: many of the rooms received little or no attention, the hall carpets are already terribly stained, and you pay a lot for the view. A harbor-view suite might offer up a tiny bedroom, and even the "new" rooms sport furnishings in need of serious updating. Nevertheless, the Empress is the most notable landmark in town and is worth a stroll (take the excellent historic tour). High tea is served daily by reservation, and while it may be overpriced, it's still the best value at the Empress. ■ *Between Humboldt and Belleville; (604)384-8111 or (800)441-1414; 721 Government St, Victoria, BC V8W 1W5; $$$; AE, DC, MC, V; checks OK.* ⅏

▼

Victoria

Lodgings

▲

Heritage House ★ This 1910 beauty is 5 kilometers from the center of town. The four rooms (which share three baths) have been redecorated to the original Craftsman style of the house, and are enchanting, as is the Garden Room, a reading room with three walls of windows. Downstairs the fireplace parlor is a cozy place; a wraparound porch provides ample seating for garden appreciators (the garden is splendid). Gourmet breakfasts consist of several courses and—if you're lucky—Sandra's much-praised salmon quiche. Two-day minimum stay. ■ *Hwy 1 north, right on McKenzie, left to Heritage Lane; (604)479-0892; 3808 Heritage Lane, Victoria, BC V8Z 7A7; $$; MC, V; no checks.*

Huntingdon Manor Inn ★ A comfortable antique-furnished parlor with a blazing log fireplace and an indoor whirlpool and sauna make for a pleasant stay at the Huntingdon. Unfortunately, it's behind the very touristy stuff near the harbor and views can be rather odd. Rooms are nicely furnished, some with four-poster beds, and the spacious two-story gallery suites have bedroom lofts. This is a full-service hotel, but some rooms have kitchen facilities. Kids under 12 stay free in their parents' suite. ■ *Downtown across from the harbor; (604)381-3456;*

*330 Quebec St, Victoria, BC V8V 1W3; $$$; AE, DC, MC, V;
no checks.* ♿

SOOKE

This relatively undiscovered area, half an hour west of Victoria, offers spectacular beach scenery and seclusion. The road at Port Renfrew peters out into the famous **West Coast Trail**, one of the greatest (and most demanding) hikes in the Northwest (see Pacific Rim National Park in Ucluelet).

Botanical Beach, just west of Port Renfrew, has exceptionally low tides in the early summer that expose miles of sea life and sculpted sandstone. The entire coast has excellent parks, with trails to the beach or into the forest and good waves for surfers.

Royal Roads Military College, on the road to Sooke, is a Dunsmuir family castle turned military college; the beautiful grounds are open to the public each day 10am to 4pm; call (604)363-4660.

East Sooke Park, a wilderness park, offers hiking trails in the forest, spectacular views, and good swimming beaches.

Sooke Region Museum mounts some interesting displays of logging and pioneer equipment, Indian artifacts, and a fully restored historic cottage showing turn-of-the-century lifestyles. The museum also sponsors BC's largest juried fine arts show, held every August in the Sooke Arena. Museum open daily; call (604)642-6351 for more information.

Between Sooke and Port Renfrew are dozens of trails leading down to ocean beaches (Mirror Creek is a favorite), all of which offer fine beachcombing possibilities. Ask at the Sooke Region Museum for details.

Lester B. Pearson College of the Pacific, on Pedder Bay, has a two-year program to foster international understanding; the setting and the architecture are both worth seeing. Call (604)478-5591.

RESTAURANTS

Sooke Harbour House ★★★ This white clapboard farmhouse, perched waterside at the end of the road in a modest Sooke neighborhood, is home to one of British Columbia's finest inns. The country-cozy dining room with a central stone hearth and candle-lit tables offers a stunning view of the Strait of Juan de Fuca. For more than a dozen years, owners Sinclair and Frederica Philip, along with their team of chefs, have gained international attention for their rare dedication to the freshest local ingredients blended with a good deal of energy and flashes of searing innovation. While the focus is the freshest of seafood, the menu extends to locally farmed meats and some 200 varieties of herbs, grown in decorative profusion around the grounds. These herbs, along with a tangle of wild greens and a sprinkling of edible flower petals, comprise the famous Sooke house salad, kissed with a refreshingly tart dressing. The desserts here will please even the most discriminating palate. Still, we're sorry to report that in recent visits, style seems to have overtaken substance, causing us to hold back that fourth star. For example, an otherwise delightful smoked black sablefish poached in a vibrant carrot juice is marred by the presence of fine bones and a garnish of barely edible onion and Parmesan–flavored polenta. The wine list is in need of a significant update: too many were simply unavailable. Here's hoping that these problems will be remedied, and soon.

The accommodations, however, still merit four stars. The original 1931 inn features three spectacularly angular upstairs suites (the Blue Heron Room has the best view, a Jacuzzi, and a fireplace) and sits adjacent to a sparkling new house with 10 rooms. Each room is lovingly, singularly decorated: the Victor Newman Longhouse Room creates a theme rich in the spirit of the Northwest with a vaulted ceiling, native American accoutrements, and an enormous bathtub positioned before a breathtaking view; the Herb Garden Room, in shades of mint and parsley, opens out through French doors onto a private patio with a broad vista over the green lawn and the pewter harbor toward the Olympic Mountains. Views, decks (or patios), and artful extras such as bouquets of fresh flowers in every room, a decanter of fine port, and terrycloth bathrobes are a given. A platter of lavish breakfast (delivered to your room) and a light lunch are included in the cost of a night's stay. ■ *At the very end of Whiffen Spit Rd; (604) 642-3421; 1528 RR4 Whiffen Spit Rd, Sooke; $$$; full bar; AE, MC, V; checks OK; dinner every day.* &

Good Life Bookstore and Cafe ★ The good life is, indeed, good food served among books. This is a funky establishment with a mishmash of furnishings in an old house where the former living room is now the dining room and a couple of the bedrooms a bookstore. Locals will tell you the food is not anything fancy but it's quite good and well priced. Breakfast is just coffee and muffins (and occasionally eggs). Lunches usually entail two soups served with homemade soda bread and a number of vegetarian entrees (lots of seafood too). Seafood and chicken star at dinner. ■ *In downtown Sooke; (604) 642-6821; 2113 Otter Point Rd, Sooke; $$; beer and wine; MC, V; checks OK; lunch Tues–Sun, dinner Tues–Sat.* &

Margison House ★ An elegant cottage just off the highway in downtown Sooke serves up the best afternoon tea in these parts, along with light lunches of seafood chowder, raisin scones, sausage rolls, and the like. The view is fine, the grounds are pretty, and amiable owner Sylvia Hallgren has a charming B&B cottage next door. Hallgren stocks the cottage's fridge with freshly laid eggs and breakfast goodies from her garden. ■ *In the center of Sooke Village, look for signs; (604)642-3620; 6605 Sooke Rd, Sooke; $; beer and wine; V; local checks only; lunch, tea Thurs–Sun (cottage available May–Sept only).* &

LODGINGS

Malahat Farm ★★ Diana Clare's 45-acre "gentleman's farm" is a perfect escape for any city slicker longing for a little taste of the country. From the charming upstairs rooms, you can keep an eye on the well-grazed fields of Herefords, sheep, chickens, and a couple of peacocks. The two downstairs rooms have fireplaces but lack the pastoral view of the upstairs ones. Clare lives in the cottage next door, but in the morning comes over to prepare an abundant farmhand's spread of which virtually everything from the blackberry jam to the eggs and potatoes comes from the farm. The tranquil setting provides sweet rejuvenation (especially with the addition of a hot tub in the gazebo), but if you're inclined to explore, Clare is a wealth of local knowledge and will point out the best walks, loan you a good mountain bike, and maybe even pack you treats to go. ■ *15 minutes west of Sooke off W Coast Rd at Anderson Rd; (604)642-6868; RR2, Sooke, BC V0S 1N0; $$; no credit cards; checks OK.*

Richview House ★★ Francois and Joan Gething's farmhouse is a three-minute walk from its famous neighbor, the Sooke Harbour House—and a pleasant, low-key alternative to the often-booked inn. Two matching guest rooms, complete with private entrance, sitting area, fireplace, and a deck—with a Jacuzzi tub and a view of the strait—are nestled upstairs in the farmhouse's new B&B addition, with its handsome fir floors, hardwood furnishings, and tasteful, simple appointments. Joan's three-course breakfast can be delivered to your room. ■ *Take Whiffen Spit Rd to Richview Rd, turn right; (604)642-5520; 7031 Richview Dr, RR4, Sooke, BC V0S 1N0; $$$; MC, V; local checks only.*

Ocean Wilderness ★ This log cabin (with a nine-room wing for guests) is a good choice if you want to leave pretensions behind. The rooms are big and filled with an odd assortment of furnishings. Best rooms for the view are those on the top floor. The place swarms with honeymooners who come primarily for the location, set back in a cove with a nice trail to the beach. There's a separate Jacuzzi in its own Japanese-style gazebo (reserved soakings), and three rooms have private soaking tubs. Aside from breakfast, guests may choose to enjoy a beachside seafood fest of steamed shellfish and grilled salmon, and a bonfire, held twice weekly. ■ *10 minutes west of Sooke; (604)646-2116; 109 W Coast Rd, Sooke, BC V0S 1N0; $$$; MC, V; checks OK.* ⅁

Point No Point Resort ★ The Soderberg family owns a mile of beach and 40 acres of wild, undeveloped, quintessentially Northwest coastline facing the Strait of Juan de Fuca and the Pacific. They rent 20 reasonably priced rustic cabins among the trees on or near the cliffside, catering to those who eschew TV and telephones and seek remote beauty and tranquillity (Cabins 3 and 4 allow pets). Four of the pricier cabins have hot tubs; four hang right over the water. The only distractions here are the crashing of the rolling swells and the crackle of the fireplace. Firewood is supplied, but stop on the way to Point No Point and buy your own food. Meals and afternoon tea (with mediocre pastries) are served in a convivial but tired dining room. ■ *Hwy 14, 24 km west of Sooke; (604)646-2020; 1505 W Coast Rd, RR2, Sooke, BC V0S 1N0; $$$; V; checks OK; dinner Thurs–Sun.* ⅁

BRENTWOOD BAY

LODGINGS

Brentwood Bay Bed & Breakfast ★ Inside this restored Victorian you'll find four guest rooms with antique furniture, glossy wood floors, lace curtains, colorful braided rugs, and handcrafted coverlets. There's also a cottage (summers only), a suite designed especially for the handicapped with a kitchenette and a full bath. Most rooms have bathrooms. Ask for a room away from the fairly busy highway. Owner Evelyn Hardy serves spicy sausage and pear cobbler for breakfast in a glassed-in sun porch. ■ *Corner of Stelly and W Saanich; (604)652-2012; 7247 W Saanich Rd, Brentwood Bay, BC V0S 1A0; $$; no credit cards; checks OK.*

SIDNEY

RESTAURANTS

[20 YEARS] Deep Cove Chalet ★★★ Scrupulously manicured lawn rolls down to the cove. Even in winter the fragrance of an extravagant English flower arrangement greets you at the door. The service is professional without being stuffy. Pierre Koffel is one of the most gifted chefs on Vancouver Island—and one of the most entertaining. He's not above taking on whatever task needs attention in the Chalet: on any given night he might be spied clearing a table, ceremoniously decanting a bottle of wine, or greeting a guest with the warmest of welcomes. As eccentric as he is, regulars know he's a stickler for freshness and quality. The wine list touts lots of high-priced California bottlings. Finish with classic crêpes Suzette, prepared tableside. ■ *40 km north of Victoria on the Trans-Canada Hwy; (604)656-3541; 11190 Chalet Rd, Sidney; $$$; full bar; AE, MC, V; checks OK; lunch, dinner Tues–Sun.*

Cafe Mozart ★★ James and Marietta Hamilton have a fascination with Mozart; they even married on the anniversary of his death. So it's not surprising that the couple, with their Austrian ties and Swiss training, named their small European cafe after the maestro. It's stark with lots of shiny black furniture, the walls covered with musical instruments and framed prints to match, and guess who's playing on the stereo? The food remains quite good with such outstanding items as smoked goose breast and kiwi salad or prawns and scallops Amoureuse —a brochette marinated with fresh herbs and served with a Cognac- and lobster-flavored butter sauce. Reservations are essential. ■ *Downtown Sidney, between 2nd and 3rd; (604)655-1554; 2470 Beacon Ave, Sidney; $$; beer and wine; MC, V; local checks only; lunch Fri–Sat, dinner every day.*

Blue Peter Pub and Restaurant Blue peter is the international flag yachtsmen use to signal their ship is about to sail. There are plenty of boats here, but the sailors are often found moored to the deck of this pub. Pub dining is fun with fare that's a cut above average, including the requisite burgers, club sandwiches, and fish 'n' chips. The more formal dining room doesn't always meet expectations; however, the promise of sunsets in summer fill the restaurant to capacity inside and out. ■ *3 km north of Sidney on Harbour Rd; (604)656-4551; 2270 Harbour Rd, Sidney; $; full bar; MC, V; no checks; lunch, dinner Tues–Sun (Mon in summer only).*

MALAHAT

LODGINGS

The Aerie ★★ Maria and Leo Schuster's "Castle in the Mountains" roosts on a hill some 400 feet above the Malahat summit looking out over Saanich Inlet's Finlayson Arm. On a clear day Mount Baker looms in the east and the Olympics are spread out across the south. The building is impressive, with nooks and crannies, odd angles, and arched doorways. Some rooms have private decks and built-in Jacuzzis or fireplaces (rooms with all three weigh in at $320). Prepare yourself for a pampering with attentive service and such amenities as sauna, hot tubs, multilevel lounging decks, and a helipad for those arriving in style. There's an indoor pool and an outdoor tennis court. Recently added accommodations and small massage spa attest to the Aerie's popularity as a near-to-Victoria getaway destination. An excellent complimentary breakfast is especially bountiful on Sunday.

Cooked by Leo (originally of Innsbruck, Austria), meals are many-coursed and beautifully sauced with excellent starters such as shrimp bisque, asparagus vichyssoise, and seasonal greens. The poached salmon is capably cooked; black tiger prawns—accompanied by angel hair pasta and basil—come firm and tender. Desserts are not to be missed. Presentation is unfailingly pleasing; the piano player is a nice thought. Ask for a window table in advance. ■ *Trans-Canada Hwy, at Spectacle Lake turnoff; (604) 743-4055 or (604) 743-7115; PO Box 108, Malahat, BC V0R 2L0; $$$; full bar; AE, MC, V; no checks; breakfast, dinner every day.*

SHAWNIGAN LAKE

RESTAURANTS

Jaeger House Inn An informal pub-style eatery in a massive building with a big stone fireplace and a charming outdoor garden. The 65-item menu is just as substantial, offering German standbys such as a mushroom-laden veal cutlet with brown gravy side by side with teriyaki chicken and seafood casserole. It's still good, though, and situated near popular Shawnigan Lake. ■ *Follow Shawnigan/Mill Bay Rd off Trans-Canada Hwy to Renfrew; (604) 743-3515; 2460 Renfrew Rd, Shawnigan Lake; $$; full bar; MC, V; no checks; breakfast Sun, lunch, dinner every day.*

DUNCAN

The **Native Heritage Centre** is a must-see for admirers of native arts and crafts. In summer you can watch the famous Cowichan sweaters as they are hand-knit in one piece, their unique patterns reflecting the knitter's family designs (some even spin their own wool). The Centre also features an open-air carving shed, where a native carver with handmade tools crafts a traditional 12- to 20-foot totem pole; each pole represents a tribal design in the carver's own artistic interpretation. There are, at present, 66 such totem poles in Duncan, both downtown and along a half-kilometer section of the Trans-Canada Highway. On the way to Duncan, stop at one of the pullouts along the way for stunning views of the Saanich Peninsula and Salt Spring Island. The Native Heritage Centre is at 200 Cowichan Way, (604) 746-8119; call for schedule.

RESTAURANTS

The Quamichan Inn ★★ Set amid several acres of lawn and garden, this comfortable turn-of-the-century home has been nicely transformed into a bed-and-breakfast-cum-dinner-house for boaters moored at the nearby marinas. Dinner might include escargot Bourguignon, Indian curry, or roast prime rib with Yorkshire pudding. There are Fanny Bay oysters, locally produced clams, and imported wines (from a list far less sophisticated than the menu). Take your after-dinner coffee in the garden among fragrant wisteria, blooming fuchsias, and colorful dahlias. You may stay in one of three guest rooms and start your morning with an English hunt breakfast. If you're staying on your boat, the proprietors will pick you up at Maple Bay or Genoa Bay and drop you off again when dinner's over. ■ *Just east of Duncan; (604) 746-7028; 1478 Maple Bay Rd, Duncan; $$$; full bar; AE, MC, V; checks OK; dinner every day.*

LODGINGS

Fairburn Farm Inn ★★ Originally an Irish millionaire's country estate; it's now a 130-acre organic sheep farm and country inn overlooking a vista reminiscent of southern England. The working-farm orientation is the charm of the place, especially for families. Six large guest rooms feature Jacuzzi tubs in the baths and comfortable furniture. There's also a six-person cottage available in summer. Guests are welcome to use two downstairs parlors (family reunions often book Fairburn) and to roam the grounds, where a sheepdog minds the lambs and a creek flows idly by. The hearty breakfast always begins with porridge. Arrange ahead for other meals. In this modern-day Eden you can witness a stunning example of how it is still possible to live off the land: almost everything you eat is organically homegrown. ■ *11 km south of Duncan at 3310 Jackson Rd; (604) 746-4637; 3310 Jackson Rd, Duncan; RR 7, Duncan, BC V9L 4W4; $$$; MC; checks OK; (closed Nov to Mar).*

Grove Hall Estate ★★ Tough for the curious to find, but an undisturbed retreat for guests. Seventeen wooded acres surround this 1912 Tudor manse near Lake Quamichan. From the outside it looks as if there would be far more than three rooms—until you see the size of the rooms. Each room has an Oriental theme (Indonesian, Singapore, Siamese) and magnificent rugs (you're provided with Chinese slippers), but no private baths. The master bedroom, decorated with pieces from Djakarta and Bali, expands into a sitting area and then onto a balcony. Play tennis on the private court or games in the billiards room, or stroll along the quiet lakefront. ■ *Call for directions; (604) 746-6152; 6159 Lakes Rd, Duncan, BC V9L 4J6; $$$; no credit cards; checks OK.*

Duncan

Restaurants

CHEMAINUS

Faced with the shutdown of its mill in 1981, this logging town bucked up and hired artists to come paint murals telling the story of the town—all over everything. Chemainus is now a tourist attraction, and with each passing year it takes on more class and less tackiness, managing to project an air of old-fashioned small-town charm.

RESTAURANTS

The Waterford Inn & Restaurant Ltd. ★★ You might take it for a tearoom in this town of tearooms and funky cafes, but the Waterford offers the finest dining for the thinnest dollar in this neck of the woods. Service is personal and prompt, while the food more than lives up to its billing. Linda (who runs the front of house) and Dwayne Maslen (he's the chef) have accomplished much in the two years since they opened. You can expect to pay as much here for a lunch of delicate sole amandine, New York steak, or seafood crêpes as you'd pay elsewhere for a burger and fries. Dinner, a tad more formal, includes such specialties as bouillabaisse, duck with fresh blackberries, or rack of lamb. Ask if they have frog legs (they do), then ask "How do you walk?" ▪ *5 minutes north of downtown Chemainus on Maple St; (604)246-1046; 9875 Maple St, Chemainus; $$; AE, MC, V; local checks only; lunch, dinner Tues–Sun; (closed Mon–Tues in winter).* &

LODGINGS

The Little Inn on Willow ★★ If you have an ounce of romance in your soul, find somebody and come here. For a bit more than a song you can book this fairy-tale cottage all to yourselves, where comfort and romance are at a premium with a private yard and deck, Jacuzzi, fireplace, and refrigerator stocked with champagne and orange juice. A little storybook place you wish you never had to leave, but if you do, it's all just a pebble toss from the heart of pretty downtown Chemainus. Bookings in advance are a must. Next door is the more family-oriented Pacific Shores Inn (same owners) with three rooms with kitchens. ▪ *2 blocks from the water in downtown Chemainus; (604)246-4987; 9849 Willow St, Chemainus; PO Box 985, Chemainus, BC V0R 1K0; $$; MC; checks OK.* &

LADYSMITH

RESTAURANTS

Crow and Gate Neighbourhood Pub ★ This magnificent English country pub makes a nice destination for a lazy summer afternoon or a rainy winter one. It is set back from the road, with a rose-arbor entrance, a backyard patio, and a duck pond replete with exotic waterfowl. The homesick fellow who built the pub remembered the English original well. A blazing hearth, dart board, and a wonderful store of English magazines complete the scene. The pub food is top-notch, especially the flaky Cornish pasties, the steak-and-kidney pie, and the buttery

Yorkshire pudding. The draughts are foamy and at night everyone's having a ruddy good time. ■ *About 13 km south of Nanaimo; (604)722-3731; 2313 Yellow Point Rd, Ladysmith; $; full bar; MC, V; checks OK; lunch, dinner every day.*

LODGINGS

Yellow Point Lodge ★★★ On a rocky, gently forested promontory is Yellow Point Lodge, perhaps the most serendipitous of all the classic British Columbia resorts. It's creaky and delightful, not exclusive in any sense of the word. The hours pass with six wholesome meals a day—as if you were on a cruise ship—and one could easily describe the place as summer camp for grown-ups (though it's popular year-round): you eat family-style at shared tables in the lodge, with no kids under 16 to detract from the mood. Many of the comfort-sized rooms have private baths; two have balconies. You'll want a cabin, however; the best are the small White Beach cabins with wood stoves and beds with tree-trunk bases. There are two kinds of cabins: those on the beach (the Cliff Cabin is most remote, and the nicest) and the field cabins (Eve's is the most private). And there are the very popular beach barracks, ramshackle quarters with thin walls, built right on the shoreline rocks, with a "tree shower."

Best of all is the site: two good tennis courts, a huge seawater pool, 130 acres of meadow and forest for strolling, a hot tub, a sauna, a classic 32-foot boat for picnic cruising, and big slabs of rock jutting into the sea for sunbathing. ■ *Yellow Point Rd, 14½ km east of Ladysmith; (604)245-7422; RR3, Ladysmith, BC V0R 2E0; $$$; MC, V; checks OK.*

Inn of the Sea Inn of the Sea's nicest feature is the scenery, especially the long stretch of beach along Stewart Channel. Deluxe suites have fireplaces, kitchens, and balconies; large parties can request rooms that connect vertically via a spiral staircase. Many of the rooms are smaller than standard. There is a pleasant dining room with a touch of formality. The owners offer a range of beach and boating activities, and you might play tennis, or swim in the large heated pool at the water's edge. A pier out front allows for boat moorage, with water and power hookup. ■ *Yellow Point Rd, 14½ km east of Ladysmith; (604)245-2211; 3600 Yellow Point Rd, Ladysmith; RR3, Ladysmith, BC V0R 2E0; $$; full bar; AE, MC, V; no checks; dinner every day.* ⅖

NANAIMO

This former coal-mining town is evolving into something very different. It now has a clean, accessible waterfront, cultural festivals in the summer, a university campus with a marvelous view, and vastly improved dining. Of the new attractions,

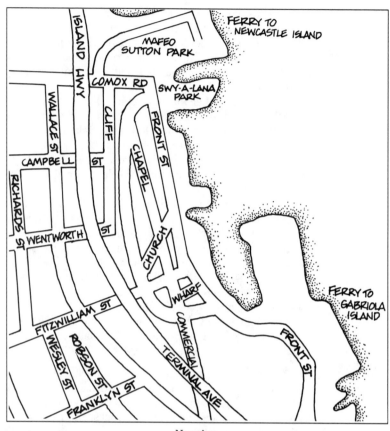

Nanaimo

Nanaimo claims itself as the home of North America's first (and only) bridge built specifically for **bungee jumpers**. You can watch or jump ($95) from this 140-foot bridge above the Nanaimo River; contact Bungy Zone, (604)753-5867. Or for $3, ferry over to the **Dinghy Dock Pub**, a very nautical floating bar off Protection Island. Other attractions are: **The Bastion**, one of the few Hudson's Bay Company forts still standing, built in 1853. There's a cannon-firing every day at noon in the summer. **The Nanaimo District Museum**, 100 Cameron Road, (604)753-1821, has a to-scale replica of a coal mine entrance, among other displays.

    Wandering. The waterfront promenade extends from the downtown harbor, past the modern seaplane terminal, through Swy-a-lana Lagoon Park (Canada's only man-made tidal lagoon), over the new pedestrian bridge, by the Nanaimo Yacht Club, and as far as the BC Ferry Terminal. The **Bastion Street Bookstore**, 76 Bastion Street, (604)753-3011, houses an impressive collection of children's books, natural history texts, guidebooks, and Canadian authors. On nearby Commercial Street, the Scotch Bakery concocts the namesake **Nanaimo bar**. Several companies offer wildlife and harbor tours; **Bastion City Wildlife Cruises**, (604)754-8474, provides informative commentary, and fresh fruit and baked goodies too.

Parks. Pipers Lagoon, northeast of downtown, includes a spit that extends into the Strait of Georgia backed by sheer bluffs great for bird-watching. **Newcastle Island**, (604)753-5811, is an autoless wilderness island reached by ferries that leave hourly from behind the civic arena; it has a long shoreline trail, a trail that accommodates wheelchairs, and some fine old-growth timber.

Golf. Nanaimo and the area to the north have seen the proliferation of golf courses with a view. Most noteworthy is the **Nanaimo Golf Club**, 5 kilometers north of the city, a demanding 18-hole course with beautiful views of the water; (604)758-6332. Others include Pryde Vista Golf Club in Nanaimo, (604)753-6188; FairWinds at Nanoose, (604)468-7766; and Morning Star, (604)248-2244, and EagleCrest, (604)752-9744, near Parksville/Qualicum.

Gabriola Island. A 20-minute ferry ride from Nanaimo will take you to this rural spot (see Gulf Islands).

RESTAURANTS

Nanaimo

Old Mahle House ★★ It's off the beaten track, but once discovered, it impresses guests who come back again and again. Three elegant, airy rooms are done in a country motif. The affable owners, Delbert and Ginny Horrocks, and Del's sister, Maureen Loucks, emphasize fresh, locally produced ingredients. A dozen daily specials fill a whiteboard: thick, savory carrot-and-ginger soup; homemade pasta tossed with salmon and cream, capers, and scallions providing a tart counterpoint; or grilled beef tenderloin with prawns in a black bean sauce. The regular menu competes with fresh Australian rack of lamb with black currant cassis. End the meal with one of a battery of homemade desserts—the silken chocolate banana cheesecake alone was worth the drive. Delbert is a wine connoisseur who is delighted to discuss the more than 200 varieties in his cellar. ■ *Corner of Cedar at Hemer Rd; (604)722-3621; Site 01-C6, RR 4, Nanaimo; $$; full bar; MC, V; local checks OK; dinner Wed–Sun.*

Gina's Cafe ★ Gina's is a colorful place with all the downhome ambience of a Tex-Mex roadside cafe. A healthy, imaginative menu reflects the owners' vegetarian leanings. Chimichangas are served spicy hot, a young crowd comes for the friendly, informal atmosphere, and aficionados of south-of-the-border fare show up for authentic-tasting eats.

■ *1 block from the waterfront; (604) 753-5411; 47 Skinner St, Nanaimo; $; full bar; MC, V; no checks; lunch Mon–Sat, dinner every day.*

Maffeo's ★ Well-known to Nanaimo residents, this was once the home of former mayor Pete Maffeo and now houses Nanaimo's most *real* Italian restaurant. A deli—where you may buy housemade pastas and Italian cheeses and meats— occupies the main floor. Dine upstairs in one of the two rooms furnished with antiques. Great pastas. The cioppino with a dash of saffron is a local favorite. ■ *Prideau and Wentworth; (604) 753-0377; 538 Wentworth, Nanaimo; $$; full bar; AE, MC, V; no checks; lunch Mon–Fri, dinner Mon–Sat.*

The Grotto The Grotto, a Nanaimo perennial for over 30 years, has outgrown its wharfish name. Its ample menu has many proven favorites—fresh barbecued salmon, Tofino shrimp curry and Zum Zum (a seafood platter)—and cafe entrees such as gourmet burgers, ribs, and exotically sauced chicken. ■ *On the waterfront near the BC ferries; (604) 753-3303; 1511 Stewart Ave, Nanaimo; $; full bar; AE, MC, V; no checks; dinner every day.*

LODGINGS

Coast Bastion Inn ★★ All 179 rooms of this popular hotel have views of the restored Hudson's Bay fort; all are tastefully styled in postmodern hues. There's a formal meeting room, and a trio of formula eateries—the family-style Cutters Cafe, the Offshore Lounge, and Sgt. O'Flaherty, a New York–style deli. A sauna, a hot tub, and a cool tub make the Bastion a self-sustaining entity. It's right in the middle of things downtown. ■ *Bastion St and Island Hwy; (604) 753-6601 or (800) 663-1144; 11 Bastion St, Nanaimo, BC V9R 2Z9; $$$; AE, DC, MC, V; no checks.*

The Dorchester Hotel ★★ Though it was built in the late 1880s on the site of an opera house and the residence of a coal baron, there's little hint of the past at this refurbished Nanaimo landmark. That's partly because the original third floor, with its archways and detailing, was removed after a fire in the '50s and replaced with utilitarian block architecture. The rooms are tastefully decorated; many have lovely views of the harbor and the Bastion. The lobby is light and airy, with a warming fireplace; the restaurant, Café Casablanca, offers good food at surprisingly reasonable rates (and a view too). It is popular with locals, who venture in for the smoked-on-the-premises scallops with saffron and lime or the rack of lamb. Service is prompt and attentive; the wine list is touted even in Vancouver. ■ *Church and Front sts; (604) 754-6835; 70 Church St, Nanaimo, BC V9R 5H4; $$; full bar; AE, DC, MC, V; no checks; breakfast, lunch, dinner every day.*

PARKSVILLE

Parksville offers good sandy beaches; the annual Brant Festival (early April) and the annual Sandcastle Competition (in July); lovely picnic sites on Cameron Lake, Englishman River Falls, and Little Qualicum Falls; and fine fresh- and saltwater fishing. **MacMillan Nature Park**, 32 kilometers west of Parksville on Route 4 heading for Port Alberni, has preserved Cathedral Grove, a haunting old-growth forest of Douglas firs and cedars that range up to 200 feet high and to 1,000 years old.

LODGINGS

Tigh-Na-Mara Hotel Owners Jackie and Joe Hirsch's complex of log cottages can no longer claim the term "rustic" since they've acquired more acreage and added beachfront condominiums, all with views of the Strait of Georgia, some with Jacuzzis. The 40-or-so log cabins are spread among the 22 acres of natural arbutus and fir. Some people feel the addition of the condominiums has taken away some of the atmosphere, but that said, the 12 viewless suites in the lodge are surprisingly cozy with a fireplace, fridge, and full bath; a few have their own kitchenettes. With the indoor pool and Jacuzzi, outdoor tennis courts, volleyball, and 700 feet of beachfront, you'll have no problem working up an appetite. ■ *2 km south of Parksville on Island Hwy; (604) 248-2072; 1095 E Island Hwy, Parksville, BC V9P 2E5; $$; AE, DC, MC, V; local checks only.*

▼
Parksville
▲

PORT ALBERNI

The **Lady Rose** departs from the Harbour Quay at the end of Argyle Street in Port Alberni and voyages to Bamfield on Tuesdays, Thursdays, and Saturdays, with special Sunday trips during July and August. Round-trip fare is $36. Early June to late September, she sails for Ucluelet on Mondays, Wednesdays, and Fridays. Round-trip fare is $40. Besides being a better way to reach these remote towns than over rough roads, the 5-hour cruise down Alberni Inlet and through the Broken Islands Group is breathtaking. Breakfast and lunch are served. Or take along a loaf of cheese bread from the Flour Shop, (604) 723-1105. Other half-day wildlife-viewing cruises will appeal to a younger crowd who enjoy powerboat speed; (604) 723-8313 or (800) 663-7192.

BAMFIELD

Bamfield is a tiny fishing village heavily populated by marine biologists. The *Lady Rose* from Port Alberni comes on Tuesdays, Thursdays, and Saturdays (and Sundays in summer); see above. You are advised to take the boat rather than the bumpy dirt road, which has some frightening logging traffic. For hikers, it's the end (or the start) of a five- to six-day beach trek along the **West Coast Trail** from Port Renfrew (see Pacific Rim National Park under Ucluelet). It is one of the premier places for finding a wilderness beach all to yourself, all week long. Photographers, bring your cameras. In Bamfield you can rent boats for fishing or exploring the islands.

Whale watching. During March and April, pods of migrating gray whales can be seen off the coast: book whale-watching trips through Ocean Pacific Whale Charters Ltd., Box 590, Tofino, BC V0R 2Z0, (604)725-3919; or SeaSmoke Sailing Charter & Tours, Box 483, Alert Bay, BC V0N 1A0, (604)974-5225.

LODGINGS

Aguilar House ★★ Far and away the most spectacular setting and guest ambience in Bamfield is this hidden-away resort run by Andreas Artz and Andrea Ernst. While the village focuses on the harbor, Aquilar House faces almost due west out into Barkley Sound. Sunsets here are mind-benders, especially when viewed from the modest guest rooms and cabins. The cuisine joins in the enthusiasm. The chefs prepare a properly paced feast that may begin with two huge platters of shrimp, smoked salmon, fresh oysters, and baked clams in the living room. Move to the dining room where you'll be presented with a mini-smorgasbord. An Ohiaht guide gives historical tours of the area by boat. ■ *Guests are met at the ferry from Port Alberni; (604)728-3000; Bamfield West, Bamfield, BC V0R 1B0; $$; MC, V; checks OK.*

UCLUELET

Pacific Rim National Park, the first National Marine Park in Canada, comprises three separate areas—Long Beach, the Broken Islands Group, and the West Coast Trail—each conceived as a platform from which visitors can experience the power of the Pacific Ocean. Long Beach, an 11-kilometer expanse of deep sandy beaches and rocky outcrops, backed by forest and mountains, can be reached by car from Port Alberni over a winding (take care if you're driving) mountain highway. The Broken Islands Group—more than 100 in all, at the entrance to Barkley Sound—is accessible only by boat. This area is famous for sea lions, seals, and whales, and is very popular with fishermen, scuba divers, and kayakers. The West Coast Trail is a rugged 72-kilometer stretch that was once a lifesaving trail for shipwrecked sailors. It can be traveled only on foot, and it's a strenuous but spectacular five- to six-day hike for hardy and experienced backpackers. It's quite regulated now: you have to write Parks Canada to reserve your hiking time. The number of hikers is now limited in order to preserve the fragile ecology of the area. For more information on the park, go to the information center at the park entrance on Highway 4 or call (604)726-4212. Pacific Rim National Park, Box 280, Ucluelet, BC V0R 3A0.

The Wickaninnish Interpretive Center has interesting oceanic exhibits and an expansive view; (604)726-7333, 10 kilometers north of Ucluelet off Highway 4. The same building houses the Wickaninnish Inn (see review).

RESTAURANTS

Wickaninnish Inn ★ In a dramatic setting on an otherwise untouched 3-kilometer-long beach, it's a striking building with glass on three sides, a beam-and-stone interior, and a rock fireplace serving as excellent backdrop for white linen tablecloths and pastel-cushioned chairs. Unfortunately, by the time you're seated you've seen the best of the Wick. In the height of summer, service can be slow and forgettable, but once your food arrives, most is forgiven. It will be well prepared, from the Wickaninnish salad with a raspberry vinaigrette to a saffron-laced bouillabaisse, fresh halibut with pesto, or tender veal draped in a savory black currant and mushroom sauce. ■ *10 km north of Ucluelet in Pacific Rim National Park; (604)726-7706; $$; full bar; AE, MC, V; no checks; lunch, dinner every day (closed mid-Oct to mid-Mar).* ♿

(20 YEARS badge shown beside listing)

LODGINGS

Canadian Princess Fishing Resort ★ A retired 235-foot survey ship in the Ucluelet Boat Basin has been converted to 30 cabins for lodging and a below-decks dining room for meals. The accommodations are comfortable but not at all luxurious: the small cabins have from one to six berths and share washrooms. The captain's cabin, with adjoining bathroom, is a little more spacious. Nautical gear has been left in place—the ship's mast goes right through the dining room—but the conversion is rather spiffy. The 46 newer shoreside units, a little roomier and more modern, are for dry-land sailors. The galley serves reasonable food and opens at 4:30am for breakfast during the fishing season. The *Canadian Princess*, with 10 charter boats, serves as a base for fishermen. ■ *In the boat basin; (604)726-7771; Peninsula Rd, Ucluelet; PO Box 939, Ucluelet, BC V0R 3A0; $; full bar; AE, MC, V; no checks; breakfast, lunch, dinner every day (closed Oct–Feb).*

TOFINO

Literally at the end of the road on the west coast of Vancouver Island, Tofino, once a timber and fishing town, is quietly becoming a favored destination for Northwest and European travelers alike. Local environmentalists and artists have banded together to suspend destruction of one of the last virgin timberlands on the west coast of Vancouver Island and halt the rapid development for which the area is prime. It boasts miles of sandy beaches, islands of old-growth cedar, migrating gray whales (March through April, September through October), natural hot springs, colonies of sea lions, and a temperate climate.

Tofino Sea-Kayaking Company offers guided day trips with an experienced boater and naturalist; or explore the wilds of the west coast with one of the eight charter **water taxi companies** (which are as available as their four-wheeled counterparts in New York City); or contact the seaplane company, **Tofino Air Lines**, to venture out to the sea lion caves or other remote places on the west coast of Vancouver Island. The new **Nuu-chah-nulth Booking & Info Centre** in the Himwitsa Building is operated by knowledgeable First Nations members and offers water taxi service, Meares Island interpretive tours, Pacific Rim National Park Eco Tours, and wilderness adventures; call (604)725-2888 or (800)665-WHALE.

Galleries. There are two excellent native-run galleries in town: Roy Henry Vickers's hand-hewn longhouse called **Eagle Aerie Gallery** and the newer **House of Himwitsa** (which includes a gallery, restaurant, and lodging facilities).

RESTAURANTS

Himwitsa Lodge and the Sea Shanty Restaurant ★★ What began as the House of Himwitsa is now the native-run enterprise of Lewis and Cathy George. They've got one of the best locations in town, a new log building on the waterfront right near the government dock. Great place to watch seaplanes take off and land (or maybe spot an occasional whale), whether you're devouring Tofino's most outstanding steamed crab on the patio of the Sea Shanty or soaking in the sunset from your private deck above. The menu is Northwest Coast with a French twist, and the crab is so good and so fresh, if this is your first time here, just order it. Upstairs there are five rooms, three with kitchens. We recommend you reserve one of the three with a harbor view; but of those, the one with a hot tub on the deck is hands-down the best (especially after a rain-soaked day on the beach). ■ *Across from the main dock; (604)725-2902 (restaurant) or (604)725-2888 (lodge) or (800)665-WHALE; 300 Main St, Tofino; PO Box 453, Tofino,*

BC V0R 2Z0; $$; MC, V; no checks; breakfast, lunch, dinner every day. ⅃ (restaurant only)

Alley Way Cafe ★ Christina Delano-Stephens thinks the way of life in Tofino is the closest thing to her Latin American roots she'll ever see in Canada. She's livened up a little sun-filled house with some pink and turquoise paint, put two picnic tables outside, and opened one of the most heart-filled spots north of Victoria. Vancouver Island's only organic restaurant outside Victoria is thriving with a menu that just won't stop growing: vegetarian burritos; clam burgers; organic rice salad; excellent enchiladas; and, if you're lucky, pickled geoduck. ■ *Behind the bank; (604) 725-3105; 305 Campbell St, Tofino; $; no alcohol; no credit cards; no checks; breakfast, lunch, dinner every day; (call for seasonal closing in winter).* ⅃

Common Loaf Bake Shop ★ A perennial town-meeting place, to which visitors are referred long before they set foot in Tofino, where there are save-the-whale buttons at the cash register and save-the-trees pleas on the bulletin board. Wonderful cinnamon buns and healthful peasant bread tempt year-round; come summer, pizza's the thing and the Common Loaf is the busiest nook in town. A fabulous seafood combo pizza is topped with smoked sockeye salmon, shrimp, and mushrooms; a European version has beer sausage and cheese. Waitstaff is young and may be easily distracted. ■ *Just behind the bank; (604) 725-3915; 180 1st St, Tofino; $; beer and wine; no credit cards; no checks; breakfast and lunch every day (dinner summer months only).* ⅃

Orca Lodge Restaurant ★ There's no view, the dining room is only moderately attractive, and service is rather slow and confused, but the *food* is wonderful and prices reasonable. Grilled slices of focaccia are served with a plate of olive oil. Try one of the delicious pasta dishes such as linguine pescatore, served with lots of fresh seafood. Perhaps they'll offer grilled halibut and salmon, served with a basil purée and crisp shoestring potatoes: simple and exquisite. The adjoining pub offers a fireplace and an English-style pool table (smaller balls and even smaller pockets) and draws a mellow local crowd. ■ *Just south of Tofino on Rte 4; (604) 725-2323; 1258 Pacific Rim Hwy, Tofino; $$; full bar; AE, DC, MC, V; no checks; dinner every day (closed Jan to Feb).*

LODGINGS

Middle Beach Lodge ★★ This 26-room lodge, with its forest-green and natural-wood color scheme, blends nicely into its wooded setting on rocks above a private beach. The common room has floor-to-ceiling windows, beautiful wood floors, and a huge stone fireplace. There are multilevel decks from which to enjoy the ocean views. Rooms are small, but nicely appointed with crisp cotton sheets, fluffy duvets, and colorful throws on the beds (the best are the west-facing balcony rooms). Friends traveling together will probably be more comfortable taking two adjoining rooms than sharing one small one. A bunk room with four twin beds is available for guests looking to save a few bucks. No children under 12. ■ *South of Tofino off Rt 4, look for signs; (604) 725-2900; 400 MacKenzie Beach Rd, Tofino; PO Box 413, Tofino, BC V0R 2Z0; $$; MC, V; no checks (closed Jan).*

Wilp Gybuu (Wolf House) Bed & Breakfast ★★
A spotlessly clean and shining west coast contemporary home with comfortable beds and absolutely all the amenities (slippers, candies, magazines, and thoughtful toiletries in the en suite bathroom). And all rooms have their own private entrance. Hosts Wendy and Ralph Burgess have much more to offer than delicious breakfasts—sparkling conversation, for one. An early morning tray of coffee is left outside your door. Wendy makes every guest feel as though they are the first and only guest she's ever had. Thanks. ■ *Hwy turns into Campbell, turn left onto 1st, right on Arnet Rd, left onto Leighton Way; (604) 725-2330; 311 Leighton Way, Tofino; PO Box 396, Tofino, BC V0R 2Z0; $$; no credit cards; no checks.*

Chesterman's Beach Bed and Breakfast ★
With its location on Chesterman's Beach, you can't go wrong: kilometers of beach stretch out at low tide to nearby islands, with ever-changing tidepools. Joan Dublanko designed her home around driftwood and travelers. Each space is different and very much your own: a romantic nook for two, a separate one-bedroom cabin (no view, sleeps up to four), or the main floor of the house with its own entrance (two bedrooms, kitchen, and sauna). Showers should be quick: the hot water sometimes runs low. In the evening, you can have beach bonfires long into the night. ■ *First left after Pacific Sands Resort on Chesterman's Beach Rd; (604) 725-3726; 1345 Chesterman's Beach Rd, Tofino; PO Box 72, Tofino, BC V0R 2Z0; $$$; MC, V; checks OK.*

Paddler's Inn Bed and Breakfast ★
Bliss after a few days exploring Clayoquot Sound. White cotton sheets, down comforters, clean-lined Scandinavian-style furnishings. The five rooms in Tofino's original hotel are as basic and lovely as Tofino itself: no phones, no TVs, no distractions (and no common areas). Owner Dorothy Baert (whom you'll often find in her Tofino Sea-Kayaking Company downstairs) comes in to cook you a fitting breakfast in the kitchen. (If you think you'll want to cook, request the suite with its own kitchenette.) Check in at the kayak shop. ■ *Just above the 1st St dock; (604) 725-4222; 320 Main St, Tofino; PO Box 620, Tofino, BC V0R 2Z0; $; MC, V; no checks.*

Ocean Village Beach Resort It's too bad this motel—like the other large motels on the Esowista peninsula—doesn't live up to its setting (could any motel?): a kilometer and a half of marvelous beach with a tiny island reached by sandbar at low tide, secluded rocky coves a short walk away where you can gather mussels. Just north of Pacific Rim National Park, Ocean Village is the best of the on-the-beach motels. It has three rows of odd-shaped cedar-shake housekeeping units for families of four; all units face the beach. The heated indoor pool and hot tub are very welcome should you be enjoying a winter getaway vacation. In summer, minimum stay is two days and the indoor pool and hot tub are often full of children. ■ *4 km south of Tofino, look for signs; (604) 725-3755; 555 Hellesen Dr, Tofino; PO Box 490, Tofino, BC V0R 2Z0; $$; MC, V; no checks.*

Vargas Island Inn Where else can you find an inn on an island all to itself? You're a couple of hours by kayak or a half hour by skiff from Tofino, so you should expect a few sacrifices: there aren't any refrigerators or chefs (though owner Marilyn Buckle is an expert on cookies and crab). But that's a small price to pay to be so far from civilization and so close to the warmth of a living-room fireplace, sipping tea in the wood stove–heated kitchen or sleeping in absolute silence. Upstairs there are five modest rooms. What more? There's a wood-burning sauna, a hobbitlike A-frame nearby (great—and cheap—for groups of six or so), not to mention all the crab or cod you (and the Buckles) happen to catch. ■ *Accessible only by water taxi from Tofino; (604) 725-3309 or call the Village Gallery, (604) 725-4229; PO Box 267, Tofino, BC V0R 2Z0; $; MC, V; checks OK.*

QUALICUM

RESTAURANTS

Old Dutch Inn It's a funny place—a motel and dining room done in a Dutch motif with a spectacular view of the expansive Qualicum Bay. The 34 rooms that make up the hotel portion of the inn are comfortable enough; some feature views, but be aware that there's a major highway between the motel and the beach. The real draw is the Dutch cuisine. The chef is something of a celebrity, having cooked for Her Majesty Queen Elizabeth on two occasions when she stayed in private homes nearby. We liked the uitsmyter—an open-faced sandwich topped with Dutch smoked ham and Gouda cheese—and the lekkervekje—Dutch-style fresh fish 'n' chips. Be sure to save room for dessert: the traditional Dutch apple cake with fresh whipped cream is delicious. ■ *On Island Hwy; (604) 752-6914; 2690 Island Hwy W, Qualicum Beach; $$; full bar; MC, V; no checks; breakfast, lunch, dinner every day.*

FANNY BAY

RESTAURANTS

The Fanny Bay Inn Ever wonder what a real roadhouse looks like? Come to the "FBI," an unassuming haunt with local clientele, a fine fireplace, the obligatory collection of tankards, a dart board, and hearty pub fare (great hamburgers). A low-key, convenient stop on the trek north from Parksville. Stop in for a pint and a game of darts at this classic slice of Canadiana whose blue roof is a local landmark. ▪ *Center of town; (604)335-2323; 7480 Island Hwy, Fanny Bay; $; full bar; MC, V; no checks; lunch, dinner every day.* ♿

COURTENAY/COMOX

The Comox Valley has skiing in winter, water sports in summer, some of the best restaurants around, and scenic access to Powell River on the Sunshine Coast via the *Queen of Sidney*, which leaves four times daily from Comox, (604)339-3310. Cross-country and downhill skiers flock to a pair of surprisingly decent hills: **Mount Washington**, where four chair lifts operate over 140 days of the year and there are 29 kilometers of cross-country tracks, (604)338-1386; and **Forbidden Plateau**—named for an Indian tale—a half hour from downtown Courtenay, (604)334-4744.

RESTAURANTS

La Crémaillère ★★ Courtenay is fortunate to have this restaurant capable of answering the challenge of the Old House. La Crémaillère, a two-story Tudor with a Puntledge River view, relies on the culinary skills of Michel Hubert, a menu that transforms the region's delicacies into fine French cuisine, and an ambience that offers more intimacy than the bigger restaurant down the road. Start your meal with huîtres Rockefeller (using local oysters) or an extraordinarily delicate pheasant pâté. Opt for the plush private dining room for two if you like. The emphasis on regional products stops at the wine cellar—La Crémaillère features an excellent selection of French wines. ▪ *Take 17th St Bridge Rd off Island Hwy; (604)338-8131; 975 Comox Rd, Courtenay; $$$; full bar; AE, DC, MC, V; no checks; lunch Wed–Fri, dinner Wed–Sun.*

The Old House Restaurant ★★ This carefully restored pioneer-style home is set amid lovely trees and colorful flower gardens. Cedar shakes cover the outside; inside, the exposed heavy ceiling beams, large stone fireplace, copperware, and old porcelain combine to create an air of simple, rough-hewn charm. The Old House is actually two restaurants in one: a formal upstairs dining room with linen, fresh flowers, and a pricier, more innovative menu; and the more casual downstairs restaurant with latticed deck and simpler fare. Upstairs or down, it's a popular dining spot, though lunch can be disastrously slow. The upstairs menu reflects the freshest of local seafood, fruit, vegetables, meat, and herbs. Dinner's invention may yield veal timbales stuffed with sweetbreads or roasted pecan chicken with peaches and apricot tarragon sauce. You'll also do well with the time-tested French classics. ■ *Turn right on 17th from Island Hwy north, take the first right before the bridge; (604)338-5406; 1760 Riverside Lane, Courtenay; $$; full bar; AE, DC, MC, V; checks OK; lunch, dinner every day, brunch Sun.* ᕕ

LODGINGS

Greystone Manor ★ Conveniently close to the booming ski scene at Mount Washington and Forbidden Plateau, midway between boaters' havens of Nanaimo and Campbell River, this elegant four-room B&B is a welcome alternative to a night in a featureless Island Highway hotel. Authentic Victoriana and other splendid period furnishings and an English flower garden that's the envy of the island. ■ *5 km south of Courtenay on Island Hwy, watch for signs; (604)338-1422; 4014 Haas Rd, Courtenay; 4014 Haas Rd, Site 684/C2, Courtenay, BC V9N 8H9; $$; MC, V; no checks.*

Kingfisher Beach Resort Set off the highway among a grove of trees, 5 minutes south of Courtenay, this motel with its clean lines, cedar-shake roof, and white stucco walls is pleasing to the eye after the dozens of run-of-the-mill places that line the route. The lobby invites with a large fireplace, skylight, and hanging plants; and the rooms are spacious with striking, simple furnishings, refrigerators, and decks overlooking the pool and the Strait of Georgia. Diversions include a tennis court and whirlpool. ■ *On S Island Hwy, 8 km south of Courtenay; (604)338-1323; 4330 S Island Hwy, Courtenay; mail: RR6, Site 672, C-1, Courtenay, BC V9N 8H9; $$; AE, DC, MC, V; no checks.* ᕕ

OYSTER BAY

RESTAURANTS

Gourmet-by-the-Sea ★ Chef Michel Rabu has made a name for himself with townspeople and travelers alike, who return for the fresh leeks wrapped in prosciutto and cheese sauce, a simple watercress salad sprinkled with a lovely raspberry vinaigrette, and a mousseline of scallops in a sauce of puréed lobster reduced in whipping cream and accented with Cognac. His seafood specialties are utterly fresh—don't miss the bouillabaisse. All the tables look out to a magnificent view, and the bistro menu, served in a separate dining area, offers lighter fare. ▪ *14½ km south of Campbell River on Discovery Bay;* *(604)923-5234; 4378 S Island Hwy, Oyster Bay; $$; full bar; AE, MC, V; no checks; dinner Wed–Sun.*

CAMPBELL RIVER

A town of over 16,000 people, Campbell River is big as island cities go. It's completely ringed with shopping malls, yet the city center still looks and feels as it undoubtedly did in the '50s. Here you'll find some of the best fishing outfitters on the island; during the Salmon Festival in July, the town is abuzz with famous and ordinary sportsfisherfolk. An excellent new museum is worth a visit, and you can rent a rod and reel and try your luck on the town's 600-foot-long fishing pier. For information on the region's wealth of short trails and dive sites, call the Chamber of Commerce, (604)287-4636.

Strathcona Provincial Park, to the west, is a park of superlatives. It has Canada's highest waterfall, Vancouver Island's highest mountain, and offers a wide variety of landscapes to explore, including a glacier, alpine meadows and lakes, and large stands of virgin cedar and Douglas fir. Easily accessible by road (take Highway 28 from Campbell River), the park has campgrounds and boat-launching facilities at Buttle Lake, and a surprisingly deluxe lakeside accommodation, **Strathcona Park Lodge** (see review). The park also has fine trout lakes and an extensive trail system for backpacking.

Campbell River

Restaurants

RESTAURANTS

Koto ★★ It makes sense: a very fresh sushi bar smack in the middle of fishing country. Still, it's tough to find essential Japanese ingredients in a place where most people opt for loggers' cuisine. In his pleasant Campbell River restaurant, Takeo Maeda (Tony) is single-handedly turning that around. Locals are becoming familiar with (and fond of) his sushi specialties and other Japanese fare from teriyaki to sukiyaki. It's a nice meal, especially if you pull into town late. There's only one sushi chef—so when it's busy (especially in summer) the service can be slow. ▪ *Behind the Bank of BC building; (604)286-1422; 80 10th Ave, Campbell River; $$; full bar; AE, MC, V; no checks; lunch Tues–Fri, dinner Tues–Sat.*

Royal Coachman Inn ★★ We like everything about this place, from the hearth bearing soccer trophies to the savory aroma of the soup du jour (if it's French onion, order it) to the practiced pouring arm of the bartender. A steady stream of regulars crowds the Coachman from lunch into the wee hours, and the chef meets demands with a small, hard-working kitchen staff. A blackboard menu changes daily. Meals include surprisingly ambitious dishes that you don't expect to see in a pub: crêpes; schnitzel cordon bleu; sole topped with asparagus, shrimp, and hollandaise. Tuesday and Saturday nights are prime rib nights—come early. ■ *2nd and Dogwood; (604)286-0231; 84 Dogwood St, Campbell River; $; full bar; AE, MC, V; no checks; lunch, dinner every day.*

LODGINGS

Painter's Lodge ★ You'd never know this was a 60-year-old fishing lodge. Due to a fire in 1985, the place is brand-spanking-new. Old photos of big-name types and their award-winning fish line the plush lobby, lounge, and dark Tyee pub, where salty fishermen seem almost out of place—but aren't. Pandemonium breaks out at 4am as the seaplanes and 50 Boston whalers zoom in to pick up the anglers and shatter any non-fisherman's sleep. Packages run from $305 to $379 for two nights, which includes eight hours of fishing. Painter's is a growing resort with four buildings (in addition to the main lodge) totaling 80 rooms, and more in the works. Best are rooms in the main lodge (no longer for anglers only), with two steps down into the bedroom and a porch overlooking Discovery Passage and Quadra Island. In the evening, appetizers in the lounge are our choice. Dinners may be inconsistent and service less than competent. ■ *McDonald Rd and Island Hwy, 4 km north of Campbell River; (604)286-1102; 1625 McDonald Rd, Campbell River; Box 460, Campbell River, BC V9W 5C1; $$; full bar; AE, MC, V; no checks; open Apr–Oct.*

Strathcona Park Lodge A week-in-the-woods experience on lovely Upper Campbell Lake: canoeing, day hikes, lake play. Amenities are simple but certainly adequate. Stay in one of the camper-style cabins with kitchens or one of the modest motel units—a bit overpriced for what you get, but you couldn't ask for a better location. (On a recent visit, however, the roomy honeymoon suite proved in need of a good vacuuming.) There are lots of outdoor activities (including rock climbing and rope courses) perfect for families seeking fresh-air fun. Paddle your own canoe or rent theirs. Family-style buffet meals at strictly regulated hours feature healthful food. Don't be late for meals—other guests have extremely hearty appetitites. ■ *At the edge of Strathcona Park, 45 km west of Campbell River; (604)286-8206; PO Box 2160, Campbell River, BC V9W 5C9; $$; full bar; MC, V; checks OK; (limited facilities during winter months).*

GOLD RIVER

The **Uchuck III** will take you for a magnificent 10-hour chug from Gold River along Vancouver Island's broken western coastline to the remote settlement of Kyuquot. You spend the night at a bed and breakfast and return the next day ($260 couple, $154 single, all-inclusive); PO Box 57, Gold River, BC V0P

1G0; (604)283-2325. Book these tours well in advance. Gold
River also offers fine caving for spelunkers.

PORT MCNEILL

The major asset of this remote spot is proximity to all things
wild and wonderful—great boating, diving, whale watching,
salmon fishing, and tidepooling.

The U'mista Cultural Centre in Alert Bay, an inspiring
Kwagiulth museum, is a short ferry ride from Port McNeill.
This one examines cultural origins and potlatch traditions. Sea-
sonal hours: (604)974-5403.

Whale watching is superior (July through October only)
from Telegraph Cove, 16 kilometers south of Port McNeill.
Stubbs Island Charters, (604)928-3185, takes groups out for
morning and afternoon cruises to view the cetaceans on their
migration down Johnstone Strait, and can accommodate
groups of five or more in a cluster of modest harborfront cabins. Old homes at Telegraph Cove have been refurbished and
gaily painted and are also available for overnight stays.

LODGINGS

Hidden Cove Lodge ★★ A spacious log retreat just north of
Telegraph Cove in its very own secluded cove on 9½ acres. No
TVs, no phones, no fancy amenities—just acres of woodsy, waterfront property, with nature trails for walking. Hosts Dan and
Sandra Kirby will key you in to the best of what's to do in the
area, or ask them to plan something for you and they might
sign you up for a whale-watching trip, saltwater fishing, or a no-
holds-barred heli-venture (like flying out to a salmon stream
where they have exclusive fishing rights). The six rooms (with
private baths) are simply furnished in pine, and accommodations can include continental breakfast or three meals, all prepared by Sandy. A wrap-around, window-lined lounge invites
convivial gatherings, quiet reading, and frequent sightings of
herons, eagles, whales, and even bears. ▪ *From Hwy 19, take
Beaver Cove/Telegraph Cove cutoff and watch for sign;
(604)956-3916; PO Box 258, Port McNeill, BC V0N 2R0;
$$$; beer and wine; V; checks OK (closed Oct to Apr).*

PORT HARDY

You'll feel as though you're on the edge of the world in Port
Hardy—to venture any farther north, you'll need a boat or
plane. It's a town of loggers, fishermen, and miners—as well
as travelers stopping long enough to catch the 15-hour ferry
to Prince Rupert. The boat leaves every other day in summer
and once a week in winter; for information, call BC Ferries,
(604)949-6722.

The famous Edward S. Curtis film *In the Land of the War Canoes* was filmed in nearby **Fort Rupert**, still one of the best places to purchase authentic native American art.

Cape Scott Park. A drive of 1½ hours on a gravel road west of Port Hardy and then a 20-minute hike on a boardwalk through old-growth forest bring you to spectacular San Josef Bay. (Don't leave valuables in the car.) For exact directions or information on other hikes at the northernmost tip of the island, contact the Chamber of Commerce, (604)949-7622.

THE GULF ISLANDS

Stretching for 240 kilometers up the broad expanse of the Strait of Georgia are clusters of forested islands, Canada's more remote version of the U.S. San Juans. Development is sparse—a shop or two at the ferry terminal, some farms and pastureland, a smattering of lodgings. Well-stocked stores, bank machines, gas stations, and even restaurants are scarce to nonexistent (plan accordingly). But natural beauty and recreational opportunities abound—all in the rain shadow of Vancouver Island's mountains.

Often collectively referred to as the Gulf Islands, these gems fall into three groups. The best known and most populous are the southern Gulf Islands—Gabriola, Galiano, Mayne, Salt Spring, Saturna, and Pender—tucked along Vancouver Island's shore between Victoria and Nanaimo. Visited several times daily by ferries, the southern Gulfs offer the widest choices of inns, eateries, and enhancements. Farther north, Denman and Hornby are a short hop from the big island. East of Campbell River is the dense grouping of the Discovery Islands—Quadra, Cortes, and Sonora—fishing and boating meccas.

BC Ferries from Tsawwassen and numerous spots on Vancouver Island service most of the islands. If you're in a car, don't expect simply to arrive at the terminal and drive aboard. The perplexing web of schedules, routes, and fares makes advance planning (and often, reservations) a must. Or spare yourself the stress and expense by leaving your car at home; most inns and B&Bs will pick you up at the terminal (and the islands are great for cycling). Inter-island ferries ply the waters of the southern Gulfs, operating on a first-come, first-served basis. For more information, call BC Ferries, (604)669-1211.

Although there are numerous inns and lodges throughout the islands, the best lodgings are often the B&Bs—a room and delicious breakfast in a stunning home, a converted farmhouse, or a quaint cottage. Have **Canadian Gulf Islands B&B Reservation Service**, (604)539-5390, find one exactly suited to you.

THE GULF ISLANDS: SONORA

LODGINGS

Sonora Lodge ★★ Sonora is big and it's posh—a multimillion-dollar resort catering to those who want to fish from the lap of luxury. You'll pay more than $1,000 per night (two-night minimum), but *everything* (well, except the professional massage) is included: airfare from Vancouver, guided fishing (fly fishing has recently been added to the agenda), gourmet meals, drinks, fishing rods, rain gear, and more. Luxurious suites—some with their own Jacuzzis—are housed in five different lodges; each lodge has a common room with hot tub, steam bath, and complimentary bar. Other amenities include world-class billiards tables, a small convention center, a lap pool, and tennis courts. The kitchen is competent and serves a well-selected variety of fresh fish. Occasionally a special chef is brought in for a fête around the Teppan cooker. ■ *48 km north of Campbell River (accessible by boat or plane only); (604)287-2869; 625-B 11th Ave, Campbell River, BC V9W 4G5; $$$; full bar; DC, MC, V; checks OK.*

THE GULF ISLANDS: QUADRA

Quadra is a 10-minute ferry ride from the salmon-fishing mecca of Campbell River. Resident artists and craftspeople make the island a fine place to sleuth around for pottery and other wares. You can pick up a detailed map of the island at the **Kwakiutl Museum**, 3 kilometers south of the ferry dock on Green Road, (604)285-3733. Their outstanding collection of native American masks, blankets, and carvings rival displays in the finest international museums.

LODGINGS

April Point Lodge ★★★ Between April and October this famous resort draws serious fisherfolk and celebrities from all over the world for the extraordinary salmon fishing—bluebacks in April and May, tyee July through September, coho throughout the summer. The staff expertly pairs guides with guests. Fishing is the primary activity (although the cost of it is not included in the room rate), but recently April Point has become more family oriented, offering bicycle and kayak rentals and opportunities for horseback riding. Lovely beach walks are available about 8 kilometers in either direction: the lighthouse to the south, Rebecca Spit Provincial Park to the east. The resort's accommodations—spacious and beautifully appointed—range from large guest houses to lodge suites to comfortable cabins; most have fireplaces, hot tubs or Jacuzzis, sun decks, kitchens, separate sitting/living areas, and water views. Reserve at least three or four months in advance. The

main lodge is sunny and cheerful; the food is always very good.
■ *10 minutes north of the ferry dock on April Point Rd;*
(604)285-2222; PO Box 1, Campbell River, BC V9W 4Z9;
$$$; AE, DC, MC, V; checks OK (open Apr–Oct for full ser-
vice; cabins available in off season). &

Tsa-Kwa-Luten Lodge ★★ The Cape Mudge band of the
Kwakiutl built this contemporary lodge in the spirit of a long-
house. The 33 rooms (including three fully equipped beach
cabins) all overlook Discovery Passage; some have fireplaces.
Fishing is the primary attraction here, although nonfishers can
also explore the beach, with its ancient petroglyphs, as well as
the nearby Cape Mudge Lighthouse. Mountain bikes are avail-
able for rent, and the staff can arrange transportation for ex-
ploring other parts of the island. Local seafood is the catch in
the dining room. In summer, the lodge offers a weekly buffet
of regional foods, with a tribal dance following; breakfast in-
cluded in off season. ■ *About 10 minutes south of the ferry
dock off Lighthouse Rd (look for signs); (604)285-2042 or
(800)665-7745; PO Box 460, Quathiaski Cove, BC V0P 1N0;
$$$; AE, DC, MC, V; checks OK; breakfast, lunch, dinner ev-
ery day (open mid-Apr–Oct).*

THE GULF ISLANDS: DENMAN AND HORNBY

Tranquil and bucolic, the sister islands of Denman and Hornby
sit just off the coast of Vancouver Island. Denman, the larger
of the two (10 minutes by ferry from Buckley Bay, south of
Courtenay), is known for its pastoral farmlands and its population of talented artisans. The relatively flat landscape and un-
traveled roads make it a natural for cyclists. Hornby (10
minutes by ferry from Denman) boasts Helliwell Park, with
dramatic seaside cliffs and forest trails, as well as a lovely long
beach at Tribune Bay.

LODGINGS

Sea Breeze Lodge Catch the ferry from Denman before 6pm
(10pm Fridays) and stay in one of these 13 beachside cottages. Owned for more than 20 years by the Bishop family,
Sea Breeze has evolved into a comfortable family retreat.
There have been reports of less than satisfactory service and
maintenance, but the resort still boasts a loyal following.
From June to the end of September, cabin rates include three
home-cooked meals. The rest of the year, the rustic dining
room is open only on weekends, so reserve a cabin with a
kitchen. Soak in the hot tub (glass-enclosed in winter, open
in summer) and enjoy the view. ■ *Tralee Point; (604)335-
2321; Hornby Island, BC V0R 1Z0; $$; full bar; MC, V;
checks OK.*

THE GULF ISLANDS: GABRIOLA

Although this most accessible island has become a bedroom community for nearby Nanaimo (20 minutes by ferry), it manages to remain fairly rustic and beachy. Highlight of the fine beach walks along the west shore is the **Malaspina Gallery**, weird rock formations and caves carved by the sea. You'll have to look elsewhere for recommended accommodations.

THE GULF ISLANDS: GALIANO

Despite being the first stop off the Tsawwassen ferry, Galiano retains an undeveloped, secluded character. Dedicated residents have worked hard to protect the natural features that extend along the island's narrow, 30-kilometer length: densely forested hillsides, towering bluffs, wildflower meadows, and sheltered harbors. On **Bodega Ridge,** trails wind through old-growth forests and skirt fields of often rare wildflowers; views extend as far as the Olympic Mountains in Washington. From **Bluffs Park** and **Mount Galiano**, you can watch eagles, ferries, and sweeping tides on Active Pass, and walk or cycle forested roads and trails. Most Galiano roads (and in particular the partially paved eastern route) allow you to pedal untroubled by traffic. Or explore the islands by water; contact Gulf Islands Kayaking, (604)539-2442, or Canadian Gulf Islands Kayak and Catamaran, (604)539-5390. **Montague Harbour** is a lovely, sheltered bay with beaches, picnic and camping areas, boat launch, and stunning sunset views. At the northern tip of Galiano is ruggedly beautiful **Dionysio Point Provincial Park**, which offers more primitive camping.

With barely 1,200 permanent residents, Galiano has one gas station, no bank, and only a few stores, all clustered at the southern end. Eateries are scarce, although you'll find hearty pub food and local color at the popular Hummingbird Inn (junction of Sturdies Bay and Georgeson Bay roads, (604)539-5472).

RESTAURANTS

La Berengerie ★ Popular with locals and visitors alike, this quaint, 40-seat restaurant occupies the main floor of a two-story, wood-sided house, set back from the road amid huge cedars. Owner/chef/hotelier Huguette Benger, who learned the trade running a small hotel in Paris, offers a four-course menu that might include gingered beef with saffron rice, and crisp vegetables harvested from the restaurant's own garden. The service and atmosphere are casual (Benger is often your server as well as chef). Reservations are a must. When the weather's nice, enjoy a simple lunch in the atrium out back. Upstairs are five modest guest rooms, two with private bath, and all with paper-thin walls. The hot tub on the deck up at Benger's house and the good breakfast make up for any flaws. ■ *On the corner of Clanton and Montague Harbour rds; (604)539-5392; Montague Harbour Rd, Galiano Island; $$; full bar; V; checks OK; lunch, dinner every day in summer, Thurs–Sun off season (closed Nov to Mar).*

LODGINGS

Galiano Lodge ★★ After much anticipation (and several false starts), the remodeled Galiano Lodge seems to have hit its stride. This and Woodstone Country Inn figure as the upscale lodgings on Galiano; Woodstone is the more formal, Galiano the more plush. The new, two-story building may not look impressive from the outside, but the 10 deluxe rooms within have it all: wood-burning fireplaces, down comforters, private balconies, soaker tubs or Jacuzzis in elegant bathrooms, and pretty French country accoutrements. Seven modest rooms with sitting areas and private baths are in the original beachside building. The property is right on Sturdies Bay, with views of Active Pass and Mount Baker (although the ferry terminal occupies the immediate foreground). Rates include a full breakfast. In the evening, guests and islanders alike partake of the Northwest cuisine served in the dining room. The reasonably priced menu might include an appetizer of West Coast cod cakes and a main course of rainbow trout stuffed with Brie and apples. Brunch on weekends. ■ *On the water, first left from ferry terminal; (604)539-3388; 134 Madrona Dr, Galiano Island; PO Box 247, Galiano Island, BC V0N 1P0; $$$; MC, V; checks OK.* ᕕ

The Laidlaws ★★ You'll have a hard time deciding which accommodations to choose at Sally and Joe Laidlaw's B&B. Will it be the spacious room in their home, or one of the two charming stone cottages on their woodsy 10 acres? Regardless, you're guaranteed a perfect island getaway, with delightful hosts and spectacular views over Trincomali Channel. The graciously appointed room in the Laidlaws' home has floor-to-ceiling windows, stone fireplace, and a bath with a 5x7-foot tiled shower (*not* your typical B&B bath). The larger of the two cottages perches on a high rock ledge, its deck suspended over the water. It has a full kitchen, woodstove, sleeping alcove, and loft with a king-size foam mattress. Farther up the hill is the smaller cottage—a former greenhouse, now an intimate hideaway for two. The Laidlaws serve a full breakfast to room guests, and deliver a continental breakfast to the cottages. Their quintessential island home is so private the windows need no curtains. ■ *Take Porlier Pass Rd 4½ km from the ferry to Ganner Dr; (604)539-5341; RR #2, Ganner Dr, Galiano Island, BC V0N 1P0; $$$; MC, V; checks OK.*

Mount Galiano Eagle's Nest ★★ Just about the time you think you must have turned onto a logging road by mistake, you finally come upon Francine Renaud and Bernard Mignault's unusual home, nestled in its roost at the foot of Mount Galiano with an eagle's-eye view of Trincomali Channel. Built from a combination of slash wood and salvaged architectural elements, the house sits on 75 acres of land and a whole kilometer of waterfront—all abutting the Galiano Mountain Wilderness Park. Renaud and Mignault's garden is a work of art (and a prolific producer). And the breakfasts: melon and grapefruit served with nasturtium blossoms, followed by waffles accompanied by all manner of toppings. Our favorite of the three rooms is the romantic, peach-colored upstairs chamber that looks out over the water. An absolute treat unless you have something against shared bathrooms or friendly cats. ▪ *Call for directions; (604)539-2567; 2-720 Active Pass Dr, Galiano Island, BC V0N 1P0; $$; V; checks OK.*

Woodstone Country Inn ★★ On rustic Galiano, Woodstone Country Inn offers a more elegant and formal alternative. Business retreats are encouraged (a small conference room was recently added); children are not. The service can be stiff, even cool. But the pastoral setting, straddling woods and fields, is lovely, and the 12 rooms are spacious and bright. All have tall windows, sitting areas, private baths (some with Jacuzzis or soaker tubs), and such touches as hand-stenciled wallpaper or original artwork. Most have fireplaces. The best possess a dreamy view of green pastures. In the comfortable common room are a piano and well-stocked bookshelves. For breakfast (included in the rate), expect something rich and delicious; in the afternoon, guests regroup for tea.

The dining room here gave Galiano its first taste of elegant cuisine: a deliciously hot spinach salad with curry vinaigrette, freshly baked soda bread laced with thyme, pasta in a red pepper sauce, and an exquisite, lightly braised salmon in béarnaise sauce. ▪ *Bear left off Sturdies Bay Rd to Georgeson Bay Rd, follow signs to turnoff; (604)539-2022; RR 1, Georgeson Bay Rd, Galiano Island, BC V0N 1P0; $$$; full bar; AE, MC, V; no checks; dinner every day (except January).* &

Bodega Resort ★ On a high, westward-facing bluff in the center of Galiano is a Western-style resort, ideal for families or large, casual groups. There are seven two-story log chalets, with fir and cedar paneling and touches such as lace country curtains, custom cherry-wood cabinets, and cast-iron wood stoves. Each has three bedrooms, two baths, a fully equipped kitchen, and two view decks; the ranch-style unit has one bath and a large sun deck surrounded by a rose garden. The lodge has a conference room and a few additional rooms. For fun there's horseback riding, a trout pond, hiking trails, and Bodega Ridge and Dionysio Point nearby. Turn your back to the recently logged hillside and soak up the unobstructed views to the west. ■ *Follow Porlier Pass Rd 22½ km north of Sturdies Bay to Cook Rd; (604)539-2677; 120 Monasty Rd, Galiano Island, BC V0N 1P0; $$; MC, V; checks OK.*

THE GULF ISLANDS: SALT SPRING

Named for the unusually cold and briny springs on the north end of the island, Salt Spring is the largest, most populated, and most visited of the Gulf chain. It's serviced by three ferry routes: Tsawwassen–Long Harbour, Crofton–Vesuvius, and Swartz Bay–Fulford. The island is known for its sheep-raising; be sure to tour the rolling pastures on the north end (visit in the spring, and you'll never order rack of lamb again). Salt Spring is also known as a center for arts and crafts; pick up a map of the studios from the tourist bureau, (604)537-5252.

All roads lead to **Ganges**, the biggest and most bustling town in the Gulfs. There are more stores, services, restaurants, and galleries (not to mention tourists and cars) crammed into Ganges than exist on most islands. Even non-shoppers, however, will enjoy historic **Mouat's Mall**, a rickety, white-and-green building where you can browse a fine art collection at **Pegasus Gallery**, (604)537-2421, or enjoy the soup du jour at **Stella's Boardwalk Cafe**, (604)537-1436). On Saturday mornings in the summer, wander the farmers market in the park. For local ambience, harbor views, and great pub food, visit **Moby's Marine Pub** (at the head of the harbor, (604)537-5559).

In contrast to Ganges, **Fulford**, at the southern end, consists mostly of a few crafts shops, a Mexican cafe, the ferry terminal, and a decidedly laid-back atmosphere. Next to the ferry dock at the island's northern end is **Vesuvius Inn**, (604)537-2312. The food ranges from good to so-so, but the view from the verandah fully compensates.

Good camping facilities are available at St. Mary Lake, the waterfront Ruckle Provincial Park, and Mouat Provincial Park on the southeastern tip of the island, where you'll find a spectacular mixture of virgin forest, rock-and-clamshell beach, and rugged headlands. Or drive Cranberry Road up to the top of **Mount Maxwell** for a panorama of the archipelago from Salt Spring to the U.S. mainland.

RESTAURANTS

House Piccolo ★★ Some of the best food in Ganges can be had at this cozy house restaurant right in the middle of things. The menu is European with a decidedly Scandinavian slant, with herring in many guises, fresh seafood, local venison, and other enticing entrees. The seafood on the fried combo platter is lightly breaded and greaseless and served with a spicy aioli, the shrimp pasta is delicate and topped with fontina cheese, the stuffed trout is light and subtly flavored. Do not miss dessert, which is Piccolo's coup de grace: particularly the homemade cheesecake, flavored with cloudberries. Friendly service. ■ *At 2nd main intersection in town, near Thrifty; (604)537-1844; Hereford Rd, Ganges; $$; full bar; AE, D, MC, V; local checks; dinner every day.*

LODGINGS

Hastings House ★★★★ Standing in all its gentrified splendor and imbued with an almost formidable air of genteel hospitality, Hastings House aspires to being the ultimate country retreat. It very nearly achieves that goal. The setting is postcard-perfect, the accommodations both luxurious and distinctive, and under the watchful eyes of managers Patricia Gibson and Ian Cowley, the service is impeccable. Four restored farm buildings, surrounded by meadows, gardens, gnarled fruit trees, and rolling lawns, overlook a peaceful cove. The suites are all beautifully furnished, each with fireplace or wood-burning stove, wet bar, sitting area, and touches such as down comforters and artwork. We like the Post—a charming garden cottage with antique wicker furniture. In the reconstructed barn, we prefer the Hayloft, with its bay window seat, Franklin stove, and quaint folk art. Perfect for two couples is the two-story, two-suite, stucco and half-timbered Farmhouse. In the Tudor-style Manor House, the two upstairs rooms have prime water views through leaded casement windows; the only drawback is that the kitchen and dining room are directly below. The suites in the Cliff House are the least inspired in decor, and suffer from traffic noise drifting across the cove. Included in the stiff tariffs are wake-up coffee and muffins delivered to your room, afternoon tea seated around the huge stone hearth in the Manor House, and a delectable breakfast.

Whether you stay at Hastings House or not, you should reserve a place at chef Ian Cowley's table d'hôte dinner, served in the handsome Tudor dining room. It begins with cocktails on the lawn or in the parlor, and progresses through five expertly prepared and beautifully presented courses, all served by a knowledgeable and gracious staff. An appetizer might be cured Gulf Island salmon served with nugget potatoes, fresh dill, and a touch of lime; the entree (you have five choices), slices of richly flavored Fraser Valley duck breast, with a counterpoint of spiced cranberries and apples, or a BC venison loin surrounded by chanterelles and shiitakes. The ingredients are local (Gulf Island salmon, Fraser Valley duck, Salt Spring lamb), and the fruit, vegetables, and herbs often from the inn's own gardens. ■ *Just north of Ganges on Upper Ganges Rd;*

(604)537-2362; 160 Upper Ganges Rd, Ganges; PO Box 1110, Ganges, Salt Spring Island, BC V0S 1E0; $$$; AE, MC, V; local checks only; dinner every day, brunch Sun. &

The Old Farmhouse ★★★ On this island boasting nearly 100 bed and breakfasts, the Old Farmhouse stands out. German-born hosts Gertie and Karl Fuss have turned their heritage farmhouse into an inn worthy of *House Beautiful*: four guest rooms, each with a private bath and a patio or balcony, are charmingly decorated. Brilliant whitewashed wainscoting, crisp floral wallpaper, stained-glass and leaded windows, French doors, polished pine floors, feather beds and starched duvets, a bouquet of fresh roses—it's all here, and scrupulously maintained by very professional hosts (who know everything about the island down to all the ferry times). A gazebo, a hammock, and a couple of porch swings abet the appearance and reality of near-perfect relaxation. There's a canoe to take across the street to St. Mary Lake.

Morning coffee is delivered to your room, followed by an elegant and copious breakfast at the country dining room table. There's not a detail these hosts miss: they even supply doggie bags (so you can take the inevitable extras on with you for an afternoon picnic), then suggest the best picnic spot. ■ *4 km north of Ganges; (604)537-4113; RR 4, 1077 North End Rd, Salt Spring Island, BC V0S 1E0; $$$; MC, V; checks OK.*

The Beach House on Sunset Drive ★★ This extraordinary property a few kilometers north of Vesuvius is in a league of its own. Jon De West, an affable, gregarious expatriate from the Vancouver rat race, and his wife, Maureen, a former instructor from the Cordon Bleu, were born to be B&B hosts. Coffee is delivered to each room in the morning. Maureen's four-course breakfasts, served around the big table in the view dining room, are legendary. The sprawling home lies right on the ocean, enjoying warm currents sweeping up from the south that heat the surf to bathtub temperature in spring and summer. Two large guest rooms are in a private wing of the main house, but best is the namesake Beach Cottage, a cozy refurbished boathouse with a wraparound deck, kitchenette, bedroom, and breathtaking sunset vista. This one has honeymoon written all over it. ■ *Up Sunset Dr from Vesuvius Bay; (604)537-2879; 930 Sunset Dr, Salt Spring Island, RR #1, Ganges, BC V0S 1E0; $$$; MC, V; checks OK.*

Green Rose Farm and Guest House ★★ Hosts Ron Aird and Tom Hoff have restored this 1916 farmhouse on 17 acres of orchard, meadow, and woods, and the result is classic and inviting. The decor serves as welcome antidote to the chintz-and–Laura Ashley style of so many other B&Bs. Here it's sort of farmhouse-nautical, surehandedly decorated with yachting accoutrements, painted pine floors, crisp white duvets on the beds, and handsome pinstriped wallpaper. All three guest rooms now have private baths. In the guests' living room are comfortable couches and a beautiful renovated fireplace. Hoff, who attended culinary school, makes a full breakfast each morning. ■ *Take Upper Ganges Rd, stay right until Robinson; (604)537-9927; 346 Robinson Rd, Salt Spring Island, BC V0S 1E0; $$$; MC, V; local checks only.*

Weston Lake Inn ★ The owners of this contemporary farmhouse just above Weston Lake—Susan Evans, Ted Harrison, and Wilson (their sheep dog)—have become experts at fading into the background and letting their guests enjoy the comfortable space. Their touches are everywhere: in Harrison's petit-point embroideries, framed and hanging in the three guest rooms; in Evans's excellent, hearty breakfasts (with vegetables from their organic garden); and in the blooming results of their gardening efforts. Evans knows and loves her island and is a fount of local knowledge. Guests have access to a comfortable lounge with fireplace, library, TV, VCR (including a decent collection of videos), and the Jacuzzi out on the deck. ■ *3½ km east of Fulford Harbour on Beaver Point Rd; (604)653-4311; 813 Beaver Point Rd, Fulford Harbour; mail: C34 Beaver Point Rd, Fulford Harbour, BC V0S 1C0; $$$; MC, V; checks OK.*

THE GULF ISLANDS: MAYNE

Rolling orchards and warm rock-strewn beaches abound on this rustic 13-square-kilometer island. It's small enough for a day trip, but pretty enough for a lifetime. Sink your teeth into a burger or savor a caesar salad at the comfortably dilapidated **Springwater Lodge** (400 Fernhill Drive, (604)539-5521), hike out to the grassy point of the Indian reservation, drop by the lighthouse, or stroll up to the top of Mayne's mountain for a view of the Strait of Georgia, and you'll begin to discover what Mayne's all about. By ferry the island's usually the second stop from Tsawwassen (1½ hours), and the fourth or second from Swartz Bay (1½ hours).

LODGINGS

Oceanwood Country Inn ★★★ Most of us thought Oceanwood was just fine the way it was; innkeepers Jonathan and Marilyn Chilvers were of a different mind. They've completely renovated the existing building of their beautiful inn and added a new wing. The dining room (made justifiably famous by chef Chris Johnson) has been moved to the front to take advantage of the water views. French doors open onto the terrace. The new wing—built at an angle to maximize the views down the channel—has seven suites: best is Wisteria, which is double the size of the others, with a soaking tub on its deck. Most of

Oceanwood's rooms now have fireplaces, a soaking tub or whirlpool, and private deck.

And what hasn't changed? The lovely setting with tree-webbed views of Navy Channel and distant islands. The innovative and hearty breakfasts. Teatime, with the buttery cookies, eagle watching, and convivial atmosphere. And best of all, the outstanding hospitality of the Chilvers—truly innkeepers' innkeepers. They seem as accustomed as ever to meeting the needs of their guests, thinking of everything, right down to a written list of nearby scenic walks. Also unchanged is the attention Chris Johnson lavishes on dinner. The new location of the restaurant only enhances this special meal in four courses. The wine list is carefully chosen, and the dining room suitably intimate. Coffee (or something off the admirable list of ports and single-malt Scotches) by the fire in the library is the perfect finale. ■ *Right on Dalton Dr, right on Mariners, then left onto Dinner Bay Rd; look for sign; (604) 539-5074; 630 Dinner Bay Rd, Mayne Island, BC V0N 2J0; $$$; full bar; MC, V; local checks only; dinner every day.*

Fernhill Lodge ★ The Crumblehulmes' eccentric taste permeates every corner of this unusual hilltop retreat, from Mary's vast collection of English pewter to the eclectic selection of books in the library to the eight guest rooms, each decorated in a period theme—Jacobean, 18th-century French, Victorian, Oriental, Canadiana, farmhouse. Most of the rooms are dark and a bit severe (steer clear of the garish Moroccan room), but guests are welcome to stroll through the herb garden, relax on the discreetly placed benches or gazebo along the hillside, or enjoy the wood-fired sauna under the trees. Brian Crumblehulme's passion is historical cookery. An unusual evening feast is prepared on prior notice (the first party to reserve gets to select one of five menus). Breakfasts are copious. The Crumblehulmes' hospitality is boundless—from loaning bikes to sharing a soothing cup of tea out on the patio. It's not on the water, but a good swimming beach is not too far. ■ *Left onto Village Bay Rd from the ferry terminal, go about 5½ km to Fernhill Rd; (604) 539-2544; C4 Fernhill Rd, Mayne Island, BC V0N 2J0; $$–$$$; MC, V; checks OK; dinner every day, brunch Sun.* &

THE GULF ISLANDS: NORTH AND SOUTH PENDER

Green, rural North and South Pender islands are separated by a canal and united by a bridge. The population is decidedly residential; don't expect many restaurants, lodgings, or shops. Beaches, however, abound, including **Mortimer Spit** and **Gowland Point Beach**, both on South Pender. Hike up **Mount Norman**, one of three provincial parks, for spectacular views. During the summer, you can oogle the hundreds of cruising boats that pass through **Bedwell Harbor**, location of Canadian customs. South Pender's gentle topography is especially inviting to bikers. Rent bikes at Otter Bay Marina, (604) 629-6659, on North Pender, or a kayak from Mouat Point Kayaks, (604) 629-6767, next door. The ferry lands at the dock at Otter Bay, where the **Stand**, (604) 629-3292—an unpresupposing trailer—grills the best burgers around.

LODGINGS

Cliffside Inn-on-the-Sea ★★ Rarely does a place invoke such disparity of opinion. Some cringe at the dolled-up house and the rules to ensure privacy, while others swoon; however, no one disputes the location. You're perched at the edge of a bluff beside a staircase leading down to a mile-long beach, with a sweeping view of the channel, the islands, and Mount Baker beyond. The emphasis here is on privacy: each of the four bedrooms has a private entrance, deck, and bath. Three face the ocean. The hot tub on the cliff-hanger deck with the 280-degree view can be reserved for private sessions well into the night. Hostess Penny Tomlin will prepare gourmet dinners for guests and arrange boat excursions and the occasional island cookout. Breakfast served promptly at 9am in the solarium dining room (warning: late sleepers receive a wake-up holler). A recent addition to the roster is the two-bedroom, cedar-sided Edgewater Cottage next door—ideal for a longer stay. ■ *Follow signs to Hope Bay, government dock, turn on Clam Bay Rd to Armadale; (604) 629-6691; Armadale Rd, North Pender Island, BC V0N 2M0; $$$; MC, V; no checks.*

Corbett House B&B ★ Owners John Eckfeldt and Linda Wolfe run a fine B&B in a beautiful pastoral setting. The Yellow, Red, and Blue rooms are all equally cozy. The Yellow Room is the only one with a full bath (though water pressure is minimal) and a private balcony. The parlor is open to guests, who often gather round the fireplace for evening coffee or quiet reading. The hosts provide an ample breakfast of fresh-baked goods, fruit, coffee, and varying entrees, all generally from local sources. Long country walks fit in well here. ■ *1½ km from the ferry on Corbett Rd, call ahead for directions; (604) 629-6305; Corbett Rd, RR1, Pender Island, BC V0N 2M0; $$; MC; checks OK.*

Bedwell Harbour Resort [*unrated*] Consider the ideal location of this South Pender Island resort—a perfectly sheltered cove and marina, backed by a gentle, wooded hillside, with stunning sunset views. It would seem to guarantee success. Yet this sprawling complex—which includes a marina, rooms, cabins, a pub, a restaurant, and villas in a new condo—has been in transition for years. The latest formula, with new owners,

▼

The Gulf Islands: North and South Pender

Lodgings

▲

manager, and chef, may be the winner. The rooms and cabins (long a part of the resort) have been upgraded and repainted. They have woodstoves, balconies or decks, kitchens or kitchenettes, and sweeping views. Newer, more luxurious accomodations are available in the condominium—two-bedroom villas done in broad pine, with fully equipped kitchens, fireplaces, and decks. A breakfast package (served in the dining room) is available with all of the lodgings. The restaurant (and the pub) has been redone, with the menu now stressing affordable, West Coast fare. ■ *On the main street above the harbor; (604)629-3212; 9801 Spaulding Rd, South Pender Island, BC V0N 2M0; $$; full bar; AE, MC, V; no checks; breakfast and dinner every day (lodgings closed Jan–Feb; restaurant closed Nov–Mar).*

THE GULF ISLANDS: SATURNA

Rural, sparsely populated, and difficult to reach, Saturna is easily the least spoiled of the Gulf Islands. **Winter Cove Marine Park** is a naturalist's paradise—an inviting place to beachcomb, meander deep into forests, or picnic above the Strait of Georgia (but no camping, here or anywhere else on Saturna). A hike up **Mount Warburton** will reward you with dazzling views. Or drive remote East Point Road out to the tidal pools and sculpted sandstone of **East Point**. Saturna's big social event is the annual lamb barbecue, held on Canada Day (July 1).

RESTAURANTS

Boot Cove Lodge and Restaurant ★★ With Claude Croteau as manager and chef at Boot Cove, you're guaranteed top-of-the-line dining and hospitality. The lovely frame lodge sits high on a hill overlooking an inlet and oyster farm. Windows wrap the simple, comfortable dining room; a crackling fire makes it even more inviting on a cool evening. Croteau insists on the freshest local ingredients, so his menu—always reasonably priced—changes according to what's best at the time. His rack of lamb (from Salt Spring, of course) has quite a following, and his sure hand also wields magic in the form of pan-fried goat cheese salad with a scallion vinaigrette, or an extraordinary blackened snapper with a delectable, not-too-rich Cajun cream sauce. Don't miss the in-season strawberries in Devonshire cream. The service is islandy, the food worldly, and reservations a must.

The four bright and sunny B&B rooms upstairs are contemporary in feel, with pleasant sitting areas and serene views. Two have private baths; the honeymoon suite ($130) has a soaker tub and private balcony. Chef Croteau's breakfast will start your day in sumptuous style. ■ *Follow signs from the* *ferry; (604)539-2254; PO Box 54, Saturna Island, BC V0N 2Y0; $$; beer and wine; MC, V; checks OK; dinner every night (guests only).*

LODGINGS

Stone House Farm Resort ★★ Derrick and Pip Woodcock have brought a touch of olde England to Saturna. Their white-stone farmhouse still looks a bit stark on its perch above Narvaez Bay, but landscaping will eventually soften the effect. Inside, Tudor post-and-beam construction, low ceilings, warm wood paneling, plaster walls, and period furniture transport you to a 17th-century English inn. Every window opens onto peaceful views of the bay and distant Mount Baker; a comfortable sitting room with soapstone fireplace invites quiet contemplation. The three B&B rooms upstairs, with private baths and balconies, are pleasant and simply adorned. In the game room, you can curl up in front of the VCR or play billiards. Bring a big appetite to Pip's hearty English breakfast, then wander the Woodcocks' 25 acres in search of eagles and deer. ■ *From ferry take East Point Rd to Narvaez Bay R, follow nearly to end; (604)539-2683; Box 10, 207 Narvaez Bay Rd, Saturna Island, BC V0N 2Y0; $$–$$$; MC, V; checks OK.*

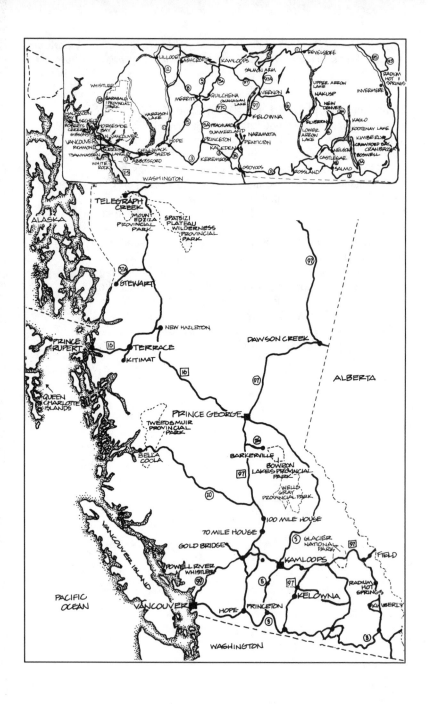

Mainland British Columbia

First, north from the U.S./Canada border (skipping Vancouver) along the Sunshine Coast to Powell River, then inland to Whistler, Lillooet, and Gold Bridge. North to Prince George, then west to Prince Rupert and the Queen Charlotte Islands. Then the eastward route out of Vancouver from Fort Langley, through Harrison Hot Springs and Hope, turning northward at Manning Provincial Park, through Kamloops and Ashcroft. The Okanagan Valley at Osoyoos, then north along Lake Okanagan, east to the Rocky Mountains, turning south, then westward again along the southern rim of the province.

WHITE ROCK

RESTAURANTS

Giraffe ★★ This delightful, elegant neighborhood restaurant with a view of Semiahmoo Bay strongly believes in the three G's of California-style cooking—garlic, goat cheese, and grilling. As you peruse the menu, a basket of crisp pappadums is delivered to the table. Nobody will rush you through luxurious appetizers of crispy wonton skins filled with fresh crab, or a layered torta basilica of cream cheese, pesto, pine nuts, and sun-dried tomatoes with garlic crostini. The lamb loin in mustard-herb sauce with caramelized onions is outstanding—ditto the boneless chicken breast with mixed berries. Be sure to graze the dessert menu. A heated patio opens in spring. ■ *Across from the pier; (604)538-6878; 15053 Marine Dr,*

White Rock; $$; full bar; AE, MC, V; local checks only; dinner every day, lunch Mon–Fri, brunch Sun. ⅃

THE SUNSHINE COAST

The southernmost end of the Sunshine Coast is only about 32 kilometers from downtown Vancouver, but the glittering waters of Howe Sound set the two places a world apart. Take the 45-minute ferry ride from Horseshoe Bay to Langdale, and it's easy to feel that you have entered a more benign region altogether.

Once a logging and fishing center, the Sunshine Coast has long been a magnet for artists and writers, as well as retired people. It's always been a place to relax, but relaxing, we suppose, is beginning to catch on. **Gibsons**, just west of Langdale, became widely known some years ago as the setting for "The Beachcombers," a popular TV series, and has not been slow to cash in on its fame. And 17 kilometers farther up Highway 101 is **Sechelt**, the third-fastest-growing town in Canada. As well as the Rockwood Centre, site of the renowned annual Festival of the Written Arts, Sechelt now has a mall, a McDonald's, and a rash of condominiums.

Turn off the main highway and you discover a scattering of small coastal communities where life still unfolds at a leisurely pace. Roberts Creek, between Gibsons and Sechelt, is a favorite haunt of painters and craftspeople. Pender Harbor, north of Sechelt, was once the winter headquarters of the Sechelt nation, and on nearby Mount Daniel you can see the remains of Moon Rings (stone circles built by Sechelt girls as they entered womanhood); Sechelt pictographs mark the cliffs above Sakinaw Lake.

If you want to get away from the highway and explore the attractions of the Sunshine Coast in more intimate detail, there are plenty of hiking trails from pleasant strolls to all-day tramps and longer. The really adventurous might launch an overnight expedition to climb the 6,200-foot Mount Drew, known locally as Red Top.

The 50-minute ferry ride north from Earl's Cove, at the top of the Sechelt Peninsula, will bring you to the final stretch of Highway 101, which continues from the ferry landing at Saltery Bay, through Powell River, to the village of Lund, where the highway ends. This is pretty rugged terrain, home of the martin and the bobcat and the black bear. As well as excellent hiking, this last stretch of the coast has some fine lakes for canoeing.

Getting there. For information about getting to the Sunshine Coast, call BC Ferries: (604)921-7414.

RESTAURANTS

Ernie and Gwen's Drive-In If your kids think that the only hamburgers are found under golden arches, this is a good place to introduce them to the real thing. No longer run by Ernie and Gwen, this old, established hamburger/fries/milk shake joint is still going strong with fast and filling food, made more to satisfy a voracious appetite than to flirt with the palate. ■ *On Hwy 101, in the middle of town; (604)886-7813; 812 Hwy 101, Gibsons; $; no alcohol; no credit cards; local checks only; lunch, dinner every day; (closed over Christmas).*

Howl at the Moon If you get on the ferry hungry enough to howl, forgo the notoriously bad ferry food, and hold your appetite to Gibsons. The newly opened Howl at the Moon frightens away those hunger pains with Tex-Mex staples augmented by steaks, burgers, and six imaginative chicken dishes. Stick with the Tex-Mex (load up your fajita with lots of the spicy marinated steak or try something different like the Fajita Caesar). Service is prompt and friendly, portions generous, and water view is almost as if you were back on that ferry (balcony tables, too). ■ *On the 1st block of Marine Dr going back from the harbor toward Langdale; (604)886-8881; 8-450 Marine Drive, Gibsons; $; full bar; MC, V; no checks; lunch, dinner every day (closed Mon in winter).* &

▼

Gibsons

Lodgings

▲

LODGINGS

Rosewood Bed and Breakfast ★★ Owner Frank Tonne felled and milled the timber growing on his steep slope overlooking Georgia Strait and combined it with classic doors and windows rescued from older Vancouver houses. The result harks back to the spacious elegance of earlier times: an Edwardian-style mansion, but filled with light. White walls and blond wood give the house a warm, honeyed glow, and provide a perfect setting for the Oriental rugs and period furniture. Of the three rooms, the room with the bay-window bath looking out to the sea is the best. Wake up to champagne and orange juice in the airy sun room. Breakfast can be pretty much whatever the guests would like, and, like dinner, is provided after prior discussion. ■ *Two hundred yards down Pine Rd, which starts at Lower Rd turnoff from Hwy 101, about 6½ km west of Gibsons; (604)886-4714; 575 Pine Rd, Gibsons; mail: S46C21, RR2, Gibsons, BC V0N 1V0; $$; no credit cards; checks OK; dinner available if booked in advance.* &

Bonniebrook Lodge This simple yellow clapboard house on the water has been a guest house since 1922. Its combination of inn with campground and RV sites is not for everyone, but the owners have made extensive renovations and redecorated it from top to bottom. Request either of the two rooms facing Georgia Strait. If you prefer, there are a few campsites behind the lodge and on the water. Breakfast is served in Chez Phillipe restaurant (for guests only). ■ *Outside Gibsons at Gower Point; (604)886-2887; 1532 Ocean Beach Esplanade, Gibsons; mail: RR4, S10 C34, Gibsons, BC V0N 1V0; $$; full bar; AE, MC, V; no checks; dinner every day (summers only); (closed Jan).*

Cattanach Bed and Breakfast To stay with the Cattenachs is to taste what life was like for the early settlers. The log house and its 5 acres are not theme-park reconstructions. They are the real thing, from the smell of saddle soap and the beehives on the roof to the rifle rack by the door and the unbroken colts in the paddock. Owner Ian Cattanach is a horsebreaker, a hunter, a logger, and a bewitching storyteller. Catch him at home and there's a good chance he'll give even the most dogmatic environmentalist/animal rights activist/vegetarian pause for thought. Children are welcome, and it's hard to imagine a better way to show a child a way of life that has now almost entirely vanished. ■ *Exit Lockyer Rd from Hwy 101 (just west of Roberts Creek Rd) to Hanbury Rd, 2½ km on left; (604)885-5444; 1756 Hanbury Rd, Gibsons; mail: S18C7, RR2, Gibsons, BC V0N 1V0; $; no credit cards; checks OK; (closed mid-Oct to mid-Mar).*

ROBERTS CREEK

RESTAURANTS

The Creek House ★★ Here's a restaurant with continental cooking—by which we mean the continent of today, not the one enshrined in mediocre hotel cooking. Situated in a house with a view of a tree-filled garden, Yvan Citerneschi's restaurant (former chef at Vancouver's Le Bistro) is decorated simply with white walls, light wood floors, flowers on the tables, and original contemporary art. On a given night, you may choose from 10 entrees that change seasonally, such as roasted duck, rack of lamb Provençal, sautéed prawns, or locally caught rabbit. Mango mousse lightens up the evening. ■ *Beach Ave and Roberts Creek Rd; (604)885-9321; 1041 Roberts Creek Rd, Roberts Creek; $$; full bar; MC, V; local checks only; dinner Wed–Sun.* &

Gumboot Garden Just around the corner from the Creek House is an old maroon house with a simple sign: Cafe. Inside, a terra-cotta sun on the yellow-painted wall radiates warmth and the menu shows a strong Mexican influence. Try the Huevos Gumboot, a hearty breakfast dish that's actually available all day: eggs and black beans on a tortilla with Monterey jack, green onions, and homemade salsa. Breads and

cheesecakes are baked daily and organic produce is used when possible. Locals come to hang out and listen to music as well as to eat—there are plans to add a small stage—and, in keeping with the community and the clientele, service is laid back.
▪ *At the junction of Lower Rd and Roberts Creek Rd; (604)885-4216; 1057 Roberts Creek Rd, Roberts Creek; no alcohol; $; no credit cards; checks OK; breakfast, lunch Tues–Sun.* &

LODGINGS

Country Cottage Bed and Breakfast ★ Philip and Loragene Gaulin's charming butterscotch farmhouse is surrounded by a cherry orchard and over 100 rosebushes, and a field of grazing sheep that Loragene raises for wool. There are three very different options here: you can stay in a pretty one-bedroom cottage, the sunny Rose Room, or best is the newest addition of a spectacular Adirondack-style cedar lodge (sleeps six), complete with river-rock fireplace. Your uncommonly genial hostess will prepare you a breakfast from what's in season, such as garden-fresh asparagus crêpes with cheese and fresh fruit. Later on, join them for afternoon tea. You're a pleasant five-minute stroll from a sandbar beach. There are bikes to borrow and a wood-fired sauna. ▪ *14½ km from the ferry off Hwy 101; (604)885-7448; 1183 Roberts Creek Rd, Roberts Creek; General Delivery, Roberts Creek, BC V0N 2W0; $$; no credit cards; checks OK.*

The Willows Inn ★ Just behind John and Donna Gibson's lovely log house on a wooded lot is this charming cedar cottage. Guests are invited onto the Gibsons' terrace for a late afternoon glass of wine or pot of tea. The cottage has cedar plank floors, skylights, a wood stove, and rustic furnishings. Donna provides a muffin-and-fruit breakfast. The beach (two blocks away) or the pretty country road make good places for a morning stroll. ▪ *Beach Ave and Marlene Rd; (604)885-2452; 3440 Beach Ave, Roberts Creek, BC V0N 2W0; $$; no credit cards; checks OK.*

HALFMOON BAY

LODGINGS

Jolly Roger Inn ★ This once-seasonal resort (now open all year) consists of a cluster of one- and two-bedroom dark brown townhouses with fireplaces, kitchens, and decks; most have sweeping bay views. Boaters and fishermen find this spot enchanting: good fishing, a first-rate marina, pleasing accommodations. ▪ *Hwy 101, 5 minutes from Halfmoon Bay at Secret Cove; (604)885-7778 or (800)663-8755; Box 7 RR1, Halfmoon Bay, BC V0N 1Y0; $$$; MC, V; checks OK.* &

POWELL RIVER

Powell River is another boat ride away from Earl's Cove at the north end of the Sunshine Coast, but you don't necessarily have to drive up from Langdale to get there: there's a ferry from Comox on Vancouver Island; call (604) 485-2943. Powell River is home to 18,000 people and traditionally dependent on the logging industry for its survival. Tourism is developing quickly, though—thanks in part to an abundance of sun and fewer trees. The clarity of the water makes this a diver's paradise, while the nearby mountains have plenty of uncrowded slopes and trails. For hikers, the Inland Lake Trail is fully accessible by wheelchair; (604) 485-4051.

RESTAURANTS

Blackberry Cafe ★ You don't expect to come across this kind of culinary innovation in Powell River, but locals are captivated enough to keep Massimo Pagani and Ross Robertson in business cooking up delights such as orange and red onion salad with cumin, kitchen middens clam chowder, spiedini (marinated Italian sausage and chicken grilled on a skewer), or a delightful focaccia with onion, mushroom, pepper, sun-dried tomato, artichoke, and cheese filling. Appetizers are equally adventurous—try the blue-corn and shrimp quesedilla. Takeout service is available. ■ *Turn right off Hwy 101 (Marine Ave) at Alberni St; (604) 485-0080; #4, 7030 Alberni St, Powell River; $; full bar; MC, V; no checks; lunch, dinner Mon–Sat (call for winter hours).* &

LODGINGS

Beach Gardens Resort Hotel ★ Sitting on a protected section of the Strait of Georgia, the Beach Gardens Resort is a mecca for scuba enthusiasts, who come for the near-tropical clarity of the water and the abundant marine life. Off-season, it's often booked with conventions or seminars. There are tennis courts and an indoor swimming pool in the fitness center. A marina accommodates boaters. The rooms are comfortable—nothing sensational, except the views of all that clear water. Divers prefer the less expensive cabins without views. A decent dining room offers reliable seafood entrees, and a popular neighborhood pub. ■ *½ hour north of Saltery Bay ferry on Hwy 101; (604) 485-6267; 7074 Westminster Ave, Powell River, BC V8A 1C5; $$; AE, DC, MC, V; no checks.* &

WHISTLER

Whistler, nestled at the base of two mountains in British Columbia's Coast Range, two hours from Vancouver and 20 miles from the Pacific, has been ranked the number one ski resort in North America for three years, the number one snowboarding mountain in the world, and Japanese skiers' favorite international destination for four years. Whistler is also turning into a great four-season getaway (although May and October still have a definite off-season feel).

The drive along Highway 99, running north from Vancouver to Whistler, is an adventure in itself. The aptly named **Sea-to-Sky Highway** hugs fir-covered mountains that tumble sharply into island-filled Howe Sound. The views are breathtaking (look for the spectacular **Tantalus Range** pull-off north of Squamish). But don't get carried away—the curves of the road are often demanding, with occasional delays caused by rock slides.

As alternatives to driving, there are trains, planes, and buses from Vancouver to Whistler: Maverick Coach Lines ($13 one way, $25 return), BC Rail from North Vancouver ($26 one way, $52 return), or Whistler Air (604)932-6615. You can charter a four-passenger sea or ski plane (depending on the season) starting at $432 one way from the Vancouver International Airport or $408 from the Vancouver Harbour downtown. Call (800)WHISTLER for details.

En route, worth checking out: Brittania Beach's Flea Market/Native Crafts, Mountain Woman Burgers, and the Ninety-Niner Restaurant (favorite cheap dinner spot for returning Vancouver skiers); the rock climbers on Smoke Bluffs outside Squamish (lobbying to be the first Canadian National Park designated for climbers); and at Brackendale, **Rivers & Oceans Unlimited Expeditions**, offering unique rafting trips, (604)898-2774.

But the main event is waiting as you enter spectacular Garibaldi Provincial Park, crowned by the toothed Black Tusk Peak. Surrounded by 10,000-foot peaks, Whistler offers some of the finest skiing in the world. Canada's first resort municipality is actually two cheek-by-jowl communities (and two mountains)—**Whistler Village**, (800)WHISTLER (with a new adjoining Upper Village), and **Blackcomb Resort**, (604)932-3141 (often called the Benchlands). Walking in the pedestrian-only villages used to have a faintly European feel, with sociable plazas, broad boulevards, and unexpected alleyways. With continuous expansion, the resort now buzzes with the sound of multimillion-dollar condo and retail construction, including fine art galleries and designer stores (Ralph Lauren is here; Armani is not—yet). For a quick area overview and a chance to chat up locals for tips, ride the free shuttle buses that link the three village areas, or the local bus (exact fare $1.25), which connects outlying residential areas to them.

Friendly rivalry between Whistler and Blackcomb mountains pays off for the skier, with high-speed lifts and gondolas added regularly to provide better access to North America's largest high alpine area and longest vertical drop. Whistler's

Mainland British Columbia

▼

Whistler

▲

new $6 million high-speed quad, Harmony Express, and Blackcomb's new Excalibur Gondola will mainline you out of the Village. Don't miss the view from **Seventh Heaven**, Whistler's peak chair lift to Horseman Glacier. Sign up for the many adult clinics for bumps or powder—popular even with expert local skiers—or free twice-daily introductions to the mountains offered by the resort's **Ski Esprit** ski school, (604)932-3400. Heli-skiing is available from several private outfits; 15 kilometers of cross-country ski trails begin just outside Whistler, winding through the adjacent countryside (stop off for an inexpensive, casual dinner and a beer at the Chateau Whistler Golf Course clubhouse just off the trail); 50 kilometers of groomed trails can be found 20 minutes to the south of Whistler, (604)932-2394. Adventure activities include snowboarding (rentals and lessons are available) and paragliding lessons (with or without skis), dogsledding, snowshoeing, snowmobiling, ice-skating, and sleigh rides. There's even a fine-dining restaurant atop mile-high Blackcomb Mountain (**Christine's** on Rendezvous Ridge); make reservations. Call Whistler Activity and Information Centre, (604)932-2394.

Advance reservations are recommended for all lodging and restaurants in Whistler Village or the Blackcomb Resort. Call Central Reservations, (604)932-4222; from Vancouver, (604)685-3650; from the U.S. and Canada (except BC), (800)944-7853. Many of the rooms in the area, as well as condos, are owned by different management companies. The most high-profile management company (offering some of the resort's glitzier accommodations) is Whiski Jack Resorts, 4227-#14 Village Stroll, (604)932-6500. Whistler Chalets, 45211 Sunshine Place, (604)932-6699 or (800)663-7711, can arrange for a group to stay in a deluxe log home. New this year, and the only hotel on Green Lake (ideal summer and winter setting, with a new golf course, cross-country and bike trails, skating and canoeing nearby), is **Edgewater**, Box 369, (604)932-0688. For a simpler, less expensive stay, ask about the hotels, pensions and "budget" (remember, it's all relative in Whistler) accommodations outside the Village. Many lodgings now require 30 days' cancellation notice in high season, with a three-day minimum stay. As usual, the best does not come cheap. But come summer, prices are drastically reduced and may be even lower in the "shoulder" seasons. Ask Central Reservations for cancellations and special deals; they change daily. If you're tempted to buy in, don't miss the luxe Intrawest Resort Club at Blackcomb; (604)938-3030.

New in the heart of the Village where Ralph Lauren and the Christmas at Whistler shop thrive: a condo-retail complex housing Hot Rock Cafe, Helly Hansen, Eddie Bauer, Starbucks' latest cappuccino bar, Bestsellers (top CDs, magazines and books), a nifty hat store, and an underground adventure center with 18 bowling lanes, a fitness center, a large sports bar with batting cage, and a one-on-one basketball court. Add five restaurants and, hey, you need never leave the Village. Some don't.

Come summer, do what the locals do. Turn your back on the Village square and head for the hills (diehards ski June to mid-August on Blackcomb Glacier from noon to 3pm), the lakes (this is where board-sailing started in Canada), or the rivers (by raft, canoe, or kayak). Whistler Outdoor Experience Co., (604)932-3389, is broker for guided hikes, mountain horseback riding, river rafting, and fly-in fishing. Favorite local excursions include: Rainbow Lake (with optional side trip to Gin and Tonic lakes); **Helm Creek Trail** across Cheakamus River in a self-propelled cable car to Garibaldi Lake's cinder cones and meadows; and the 1½- to 4-hour round-trip walk (depending on route)—or bike ride—into the 1,000-year-old cedar grove at Cougar Mountain.

Golfers can try scenic Arnold Palmer–designed **Whistler Golf Club**, recently rated one of the best new courses in the world by *Golf* magazine, or the **Robert Trent Jones** linkcourse at Chateau Whistler (open to the public). This year a new Jack Nicklaus–designed course opens in the Emerald Lake area. Beyond Whistler, there is wickedly tough **Furry Creek** (just north of West Vancouver) and Pemberton's **Big Sky** (north of Whistler; voted runner-up best new Canadian course in 1994 by *Golf Digest*).

Many consider Whistler-Pemberton area the best mountain-biking terrain in the world, offering logging road access into the mountains and trails like Cut Yer Bars, No Girlie Mans, and Black Tusk, the black diamond of mountain biking. The mostly paved, mostly flat Valley Trail, which links to Lost Lake's 24 kilometers of connecting trails, is easy for novice riders. Whistler allows bikes on their lifts for the ultimate mountain descent. For other cheap thrills on wheels, rent in-line skates from Whistler Blades in Delta Whistler Resort, (604)932-9669 (bargain instruction packages from as little as $6 each for a half-hour lesson for four people), or Blackcomb Ski & Sport, (604)938-7788.

Drive beyond Whistler to dreamy, mountain-ringed Pemberton for cheap golf, great horseback riding, and Mount Currie, home to the Lil'wat people and the annual May (and sometimes September) Lillooet Lake Rodeo, (604)894-6507. Don't miss the **Spirit Circle Art, Craft and Tea Company** (604)894-6336, a native arts-and-crafts coffeehouse and restaurant in Mount Currie. Check September spawning salmon runs on the Gates and Birkenhead rivers.

The good times roll year-round in Whistler, with concerts performed daily on the Village stage from June to September. Highlights: country and blues festival (mid-June), Canada's

Birthday (July 1), Bastille Day (July 14), complete with classic French dinner hosted by Chez Joel restaurant, and Octoberfest. Mid-August, the hills are alive with the sound of the **Vancouver Symphony Orchestra** atop Whistler Mountain; (604) 932-2394.

RESTAURANTS

Val d'Isere ★★★★ Val d'Isere is the savvy skiers' number one restaurant. If you want to impress or be impressed, you can't go wrong in this sophisticated dining room. Superchef Roland Pfaff presides over the kitchen, while maîtres d'hôtel Mark Taylor and Cori Ross reign in the restaurant. Reserve a window seat and start with a slice of Onion Pie, a dense, smoky specialty, or warm smoked salmon in a horseradish cream. For entrees it's difficult to decide between the artful concoction of baked sea bass (topped with layers of potato slices arranged like the scales of a fish) served with a pinot noir sauce and Pfaff's classic loin of venison with sautéed chanterelles. An extravagant chocolate gâteau with a peppermint sauce towers over the dessert plate. Pfaff is planning a wraparound patio for summer lunches. ▪ *Upstairs in St. Andrews House in Whistler Village; (604) 932-4666; 4433 Sundial Pl, Whistler; $$$; full bar; AE, DC, MC, V; no checks; dinner every day; (closed after Canadian Thanksgiving and open before American Thanksgiving).* &

La Rua (Le Chamois) ★★★ Mario Enero runs a stylish but comfortable restaurant in Le Chamois Hotel that prides itself on snap-of-the-finger service and a great wine list. The food, nuova Mediterranean with Asian tweaks, offers some of the best cooking in Whistler. No one makes better lamb, Washington State rack with mint pesto and or a shank set atop root vegetables and lentils. There's also an unforgettable vegetarian dish, inspired pastas, and butternut squash agnolotti with smoked duck in a curry cream sauce. Save room for homemade biscotti and chocolate truffles. When the weather warms up, cigar aficionados hit the deck for ice wine or port with their stogies. ▪ *Upper Village on Blackcomb; (604) 932-5011; 4557 Blackcomb Way, Whistler; $$$; full bar; AE, DC, MC, V; no checks; dinner every day, lunch in summer (closed Tues in spring); (closed Nov 15 to Dec 15).* &

Rim Rock Cafe and Oyster Bar ★★★ Filled to the '70s-style rafters with a hip local crowd, this cozy cafe (with stone fireplace) has been dishing out great food for years. Split into two levels (smokers in the downstairs bistro), the Rim Rock is housed in an unprepossessing hotel outside of the Village proper. Bob Dawson and Rolf Gunther's restaurant is remarkable proof that fresh seafood and wondrous cuisine are not anomalies in the mountains. The freshest seafood appears on the specials sheet in all sorts of lovely incarnations. Begin with opulent oysters, raw (of course) with vodka, crème fraîche, and caviar. And for the main event, choose between such delicacies as an herb-infused salmon or pan-fried mahi-mahi in an almond ginger crust. The Death by Chocolate can make grown men cry. Service is top-drawer—knowledgeable without the airs. Reservations are a must in high season. ■ *Whistler Creek in the Highland Lodge; (604)932-5565; 2101 Whistler Rd, Whistler; $$$; full bar; AE, MC, V; no checks; dinner every day.*

Ristorante Araxi ★★★ A cousin to Vancouver's top-rated CinCin, Araxi has become one of Whistler's culinary corner-stones. It also offers a good view of all the action in Whistler Village Square; few vantage points can compare with Araxi's summer patio. The Italian menu speaks with a decidedly West Coast accent: an outstanding black pepper linguine intertwined with black beans and slices of house-smoked chicken; penne puttanesca sports a spicy tomato sauce, but is not quite as wicked as its name promises. The wine list (awarded several Vancouver International Festival medals) is impressive but a bit pricey. The good service, consistent quality, and ever-entertaining scenery make Araxi a Whistler experience worth sliding into. ■ *Central Whistler Village; (604)932-4540; 4222 Village Square, Whistler; $$$; full bar; AE, DC, MC, V; no checks; lunch and dinner every day, May–Oct; brunch only Sat–Sun, Nov–Apr.* &

Wildflower Restaurant (Chateau Whistler Resort) ★★★ Splashy Chateau Whistler's restaurant melds a big, formal space with folk-arty touches, and likewise combines a seriousness about food with personable service. Chef Bernard Casavant, formerly of the Four Seasons in Vancouver, uses local Northwest products—free-range chicken and lamb, wild salmon, and organic beef and produce—to create inspired dishes such as warm smoked chicken and Brie turnovers with roasted corn ratatouille, or seared sockeye with sun-dried cranberry vinaigrette. Dip into the Bailey's chocolate fondue for dessert. Brunch on Sunday is popular. ■ *At the base of Blackcomb Mountain, in the Chateau Whistler; (604)938-8000; 4599 Chateau Blvd, Whistler; $$$; full bar; AE, DC, MC, V; no checks; breakfast, lunch, dinner every day, brunch Sun.* &

Il Caminetto di Umberto ★★ The ubiquitous Umberto Menghi is at Whistler, too. Not surprisingly, this is a great place to go in the Village; few things can top fresh pasta and a bottle of red wine after a day on the mountains. The tables at this perennial favorite are too tightly packed together, and noise from the bar and cabaret interferes with table talk. Aside from pasta, aim for the specials such as the roasted rack of lamb with rosemary and garlic crust. Leave room for the mascarpone cheesecake. The less expensive Trattoria di Umberto in the Mountainside Lodge, (604)932-5858, appeals to the more informal crowd for pasta and rotisserie items. ■ *Across from the Crystal Lodge; (604)932-4442; 4242 Village Stroll, Whistler; $$; full bar; AE, DC, MC, V; no checks; dinner every day, lunch Sat–Sun during busy season (Thurs–Mon off-season).* &

La Fiesta (Chateau Whistler Resort) ★★ Festooned with piñatas and sombreros, the colorful and friendly La Fiesta is home to hot and cold tapas and Whistler's finest roll-your-own fajitas, which are cooked and assembled by you on sizzling rocks brought to the table—certainly festive, especially in a group. There are also dishes that arrive already cooked, such as lamb chops with a Caribbean twist and paella. Chock-full of chorizo, prawns, chicken, mussels, and more, the paella easily serves two, particularly if those two have initiated their meal with some tapas. ■ *On the 1st floor of Chateau Whistler; (604)938-2040; 4599 Chateau Blvd, Whistler; $$; full bar; AE, DC, MC, V; no checks; dinner every day (Wed–Sun off-season (closed Oct 10–Nov 21).* &

Sushi Village ★★ Sushi Village is a welcome reprieve from the boundless activity that Whistler offers. A civilized hush hovers over this refreshingly modest Japanese eatery, where the staff is knowledgeable and gracious. Consistently delicious sushi and sashimi plates are prepared by animated experts at the counter. It's straightforward and dependable. Reservations accepted only for parties of four or more. Tatami rooms available. ■ *2nd floor of the Westbrook Hotel; (604)932-3330; 4272 Mountain Square, Whistler; $$; full bar; AE, DC, MC, V; no checks; lunch, dinner every day, lunch weekends only off- season.* &

Anasazi ★ If Anasazi were any more authentically New Mexican, you'd walk out with red clay dust all over your shoes. The large, beamed two-story room boasts a warm Southwestern decor, accented by suitable paraphernalia such as saddles, bull whips, spurs, and sombreros. Chef Eric Rogers (formerly of Vancouver's Mescalero) serves an enormous tapas assortment—the menu's mainstay. Accompanied by his wife Susan's recipes for excellent homemade breads, the generous servings quickly add up to a meal. You gotta try the fresh mussels steamed with a spicy chipotle cream sauce or the clams in a red chile broth. There's also an imaginative wine-and-drink list that features real fruit margaritas and vodka infusions made with raspberries packed in a giant jar. Occasional lapses in service are part of the local flavor. ■ *In Whistler Village; (604)932-3000; 2021 Karen Crescent, Whistler; $$; full bar; AE, DC, MC, V; no checks; dinner every day; (call for off-season closures).*

LODGINGS

Chateau Whistler Resort ★★★ This is the place to see and be seen on Whistler—where else will a valet park your ski gear?

This Paul Bunyan–sized country mansion has 343 rooms (would Canadian Pacific construct anything small?). The lobby, appropriately termed the Great Hall, sets you amid a floor of giant slate slabs covered with oversize hooked rugs, walls decorated with huge hand-painted stencils of maple leaves, two mammoth limestone fireplaces, and a 40-foot-high beamed ceiling. The funky collection of folk art birdhouses and weathered antique furnishings warm up the grandeur. The health spa is especially swank: a heated pool flowing both indoors and out, allowing swimmers to splash away under the chair lifts or soak in the Jacuzzi under the stars. Other services include a multilingual staff, baby-sitting, room service, and a dozen or so shops. The rooms themselves are a bit disappointing (if only because your expectations are set so high in the grand entrance); nonsuite rooms are surprisingly small and undistinguished. Do it right and ask for a "ski-view" room. (See reviews of their restaurants, La Fiesta and Wildflower.). ■ *At the base of Blackcomb Mountain; (604) 938-8000 or (800) 441-1414; 4599 Chateau Blvd, Whistler, BC V0N 1B4; $$$; AE, DC, MC, V; no checks; breakfast, lunch, dinner every day, brunch Sun.* &

Durlacher Hof ★★★ Erika and Peter Durlacher's reputation as Whistler's most welcoming and generous innkeepers is legendary. This Austrian pension complete with edelweiss is a short ride from the base of Whistler-Blackcomb. Erika's painstaking attention to detail is evident in the cozy après-ski area and the immaculate rooms (some suites) with hand-carved pine furniture and comfortable beds with goose-down duvets. Part Mother Theresa who just can't do enough for her guests and part sergeant-major with a relentless drive for perfection, Erika never stops. Her lavish breakfasts are a new reason to smile when the sun comes up—a groaning sideboard holds a feast. And then comes the dishes she prepares for each guest, perhaps Kaiserschmarren, pancakes with stewed plums, or apfelschmarren, fresh apple pancakes. From the moment the Durlachers get up before daybreak to bake the day's bread to making the last cup of Glühwein late at night, sharing the Hof with them is a joy. ■ *Call for directions; (604) 932-1924; 7055 Nesters Rd, Whistler; PO Box 1125, Whistler, BC V0N 1B0; $$$; MC, V; no checks.* &

Brew Creek Lodge ★★ A quiet, welcome retreat a few kilometers south of Whistler. The lodge and two guest houses are decorated in a rustic style with post-and-beam timber frames, a huge stone fireplace, and nostalgic touches of Westernalia here and there. The lodge rooms with sumptuous beds covered with folksy spreads are spacious (room 1 is best, room 6 is over the kitchen). Still, Brew Creek is best suited for groups—a wedding party, a family reunion, or a corporate retreat—who reserve the entire place or at least a portion of

▼

Whistler

Lodgings

▲

it. Our favorite is the guest house (sleeps 13) with a tiny tree-house for lovers. The Brew House reminds one of something from *The Hobbit*. A separate conference room is built right over trout-filled Brew Creek. Food is prepared with advance notice (and they're often catering dinner here); the breakfasts we've sampled have been satisfying, if a tad ordinary. Affable hosts Peter and Susan Vera are hard at work keeping the lodge a comfortable, attractive place to stay, and Cinders the cat is hard at work finding a warm lap in which to lie. ■ *Off Hwy 99 just before Brandywine Falls, south of Whistler Village; (604) 932-7210; 1 Brew Creek Rd, Whistler, BC V0N 1B1; $$$; MC, V; checks OK.*

Edelweiss ★★ Regardless of how brisk, friendly, and accommodating the hosts are, if you're in a room downstairs, you may be awakened by guests clomping around in their ski boots. Ursula and Jacques Morel's nonsmoking Bavarian-style guest house, run in a European fashion, is one of our favorites of its kind (there are many around Whistler). The eight rooms are simple and spotlessly clean, with down comforters and private baths. Extras include the shared sauna, Jacuzzi, and massage on request. Jacques (a former competitive skier) and Ursula cook a variety of ample breakfasts with an international flair in their sunny breakfast room. Twice a week, the Morels prepare a raclette (a fonduelike treat made by wrapping melted cheese over ham, baby potatoes, bread, or vegetables) and serve it with French or German wine and espresso drinks. If your legs are strong, Edelweiss is within walking distance of the Village; elsewhere hop the free bus (it's easier than parking in the Village). ■ *1½ km north of Whistler Village in White Gold Estates; (604) 932-3641; 7162 Nancy Greene Dr, Whistler; PO Box 850, Whistler, BC V0N 1B0; $$; AE, MC, V; checks OK.*

Le Chamois ★★ The inviting six-story condo/hotel, though somewhat dwarfed by its gargantuan neighbor, the Chateau Whistler, has a sleek, refined air. Rooms are large and aesthetically pleasing. Light, airy, and clean, they feature simple Euro-style furnishings and smart color schemes. Single bedrooms are built to accommodate four; each includes a living area with either a fold-out sofa bed or a Murphy bed (and every room has a view, though that of the mountain costs more). During high season the hotel requires a minimum stay of two nights. All rooms are privately owned—this is a condo, after all—and some have special touches (one three-bedroom corner suite is furnished with a piano). The compact kitchens stock all the things you need for preparing quick meals: microwave, refrigerator, and all utensils, and some larger suites offer full kitchens (with dishwasher and oven). Downstairs, the elegant La Rua (see review) specializes in Mediterranean cooking with a continental flair, while more casual dining can be found at the new Thai One On. There are also a small conference area, a very small fitness room with an outdoor pool, and a Jacuzzi. Children under 12 stay free. ■ *At the base of Blackcomb Mountain; (604)932-8700 or (800)777-0185; 4557 Blackcomb Way, Whistler; PO Box 1044, Whistler, BC V0N 1B0; $$$; AE, MC, V; no checks.* &

Delta Whistler Resort ★ It may not be as grand as Chateau Whistler nor as chic as Le Chamois, but the Delta Whistler Resort, one of the oldest and largest hotels in the resort area, offers nearly 300 rooms, restaurant and bar, exercise room, swimming pool, and dome-covered year-round tennis courts. It's a good spot for hosting business meetings, with a conference area that holds 400. The rooms are plain; the better ones offer kitchen, fireplace, balcony, Jacuzzi, mini-bar, and view of the mountains; a snazzy restaurant, Evergreens, has some innovative items on its menu. Delta sits just 50 yards from Whistler's base lift. Dogs allowed. ■ *Whistler Village; (604)932-1982 or (800)877-1133; 4050 Whistler Way, Whistler; PO Box 550, Whistler, BC V0N 1B0; $$$; AE, DC, MC, V; checks OK; breakfast, lunch, dinner every day, brunch Sun.* &

Timberline Lodge ★ The enormous moose head that greets you in the lobby tells you this place has more of a sense of humor than the other big-name hotels. It's the kind of spot where you feel at home clomping into the lobby to warm your toes by the enormous fireplace. Timberline's 42 rooms are simple and rustic, with four-poster beds of rough-hewn wood—some rooms have fireplaces, others have balconies, and a few have both. A heated pool and Jacuzzi are also available. Full breakfast included during ski season. ■ *Adjacent to Conference Center in Whistler Village; (604)932-5211 or (800)663-5474; 4122 Village Green, Whistler, BC V0N 1B4; $$$; AE, MC, V; no checks.* &

LILLOOET

Two hours north of Whistler on a gravel road, you'll happen upon Lillooet—mile 0 of the Cariboo Gold Rush Trail. The best thing about Lillooet is getting there. The **BC Rail** line between Lillooet and Vancouver is a vital link to the outside world for the loggers, miners, and farmers who live in remote areas of the Coastal Range. It's also one of the most scenic stretches in British Columbia, along pretty Howe Sound and into the jagged mountains. The route links Vancouver with Whistler, Lillooet, and Prince George; call BC Rail at (604)984-5246.

FRASER RIVER

The **Fraser River** and the **Thompson River** descend from Lillooet and Ashcroft, respectively, to converge in Lytton where they squeeze through the narrow walls of the **Fraser River Canyon**. British Columbia's mightiest river rushes through the canyon for 85 kilometers. You can get a good sense of the river's whirling rapids from the many roadside pullouts. It's far more fun to pick a hot summer day, call a raft company, and buy some wet thrills. The Thompson River (Spences Bridge to Lytton) throws the most whitewater rapids. The biggest fleet on the river is Kumsheen Raft Adventures Ltd. (Main Street, Lytton; (604)455-2296). Other companies include: Fraser River Raft Expeditions (PO Box 10, Yale, BC V0K 2S0; (604)863-2336) and the River Rogues in Spences Bridge; (604)452-2252.

Downriver the popular **Hell's Gate Airtram** (Boston Bar; (604)867-9277) takes you across the boiling waters of the Fraser at the narrowest part of the gorge (from May to mid-October) to a good restaurant with salmon chowder. The river turns sharply west and calms at **Hope**, 140 kilometers east of Vancouver.

GOLD BRIDGE

LODGINGS

Tyax Mountain Lake Resort ★ In the wilderness of the Chilcotin Range about a hundred miles north of Vancouver, floatplanes are seen dropping incoming guests off at Tyaughton Lake's dock and taking fishermen up to Trophy Lakes; a helicopter out back lifts thrill-seekers to enjoy heli-*anything* (heli-skiing, heli-hiking, and even heli–fossil hunting). But it's not all a high-tech adventure: you can be just as happy canoeing, gold panning, ice skating, horseback riding. There are 29 suites (with beamed ceilings, balconies, and down-filled quilts) in the freshly hewn spruce log lodge. We prefer one of the large chalets (each with kitchen, loft, and a balcony over-looking Tyaughton Lake and the mountains)—especially for longer stays. Unless you're in a chalet, you take all your meals in the dining room where the perfunctory food is overpriced. Other amenities include a sauna, an outdoor Jacuzzi, a game room, aerobics classes, and workout rooms. The only thing an active person might run out of in this paradise is energy (or money). ■ *If you're without a floatplane, take the train from Vancouver to Lillooet, the resort will pick you up; (604)238-2221; General Delivery, Gold Bridge, BC V0K 1P0; $$$; AE, MC, V; no checks.*

70 MILE HOUSE

LODGINGS

Flying U Guest Ranch ★ It's a working ranch, ideal for families who like to ride horses. There are 25,000 acres to explore, and cattle to round up if you wish. Back at the lodge, you can stay in log cabins, canoe on the nearby lake, and you'll dine at the over-140-years-old main building. Movies, bonfires, hayrides, or square dancing often follow the meal. A saloon features a full bar and snacks. Rates are $100 per day or $550 per week per adult, all-inclusive (three meals a day, all you can chow). ■ *20 km east of 70 Mile House on N Greenlake Rd; (604)456-7717; Box 69, 70 Mile House, BC V0K 2K0; $$; AE, MC, V; checks OK.*

100 MILE HOUSE

LODGINGS

Best Western 108 Resort ★ At what seems like the edge of civilization (8 miles north of 100 Mile House, hence its name), this full-scale Best Western–owned resort covers thousands of acres of rangeland. There is horseback riding, a large pool, tennis courts, mountain biking, canoeing, and a topflight 18-hole golf course. In winter, the cross-country skiing is some of the best in the Northwest, with over 200 kilometers of well-maintained trails. The restaurant has a fine view of the golf course and two lakes, but the menu is limited to the expected. ■ *Hwy 97, 13 km north of 100 Mile House; (604)791-5211; Box 2, 108 Mile Ranch, BC V0K 2Z0; $$; AE, DC, MC, V; no checks.*

BARKERVILLE

Billy Barker found lots of gold here in 1862, whereupon the town became the largest city north of San Francisco; then it became a ghost town, and now it's a place revived for the tourist trade. It's not bad, really: restored old buildings and a general store full of 5-cent jawbreakers and lots of retro '60s (that's 1860s) goods. The whole place shuts down after the summer season (May to September).

Canoe Trips. Six lakes form an amazingly regular rectangle in **Bowron Lake Park**, a scenic and challenging setting for a 120-kilometer canoe trip (with a number of portages in between). Plan on spending a week to 10 days. For outfitting, a couple of lodges offer canoe, paddle, and lifebelt rentals. Becker's Lodge also has campsites, cabins, and a dining room; contact the lodge at mobile phone N698 552, Wells YP, in winter (604)492-2390; PO Box 129, Wells, BC V0K 2R0.

RESTAURANTS

Wake Up Jake's There's nothing about this old-time saloon that isn't 1870s authentic: they don't serve french fries (which hadn't been invented yet); they don't use processed anything. Instead, it's all real: soups, caribou stew, sourdough-bread sandwiches, steaks, flaky fruit pies, and even the specials—

pheasant or perhaps cheese and potato pie—amid saloon decor. ▪ *In the center of town; (604) 994-3259; Box 29, Barkerville; $; beer and wine; MC, V; no checks; breakfast, lunch, dinner every day; (closed Oct–Apr).*

PRINCE GEORGE

Prince George is the hub of north and central British Columbia, and the jump-off point for brave souls heading up the Alaska Highway. The city sits between two mountain ranges on a dry plateau. Forestry is the main industry here, and loads of logging roads take hunters and fishermen back into remote and bountiful spots. The **Stellako River**, west of Prince George near Fraser Lake, is famous for its record trout. The **Cottonwood Island Nature Park**, along the Nechako River, has an extensive trail system suitable for hiking in the summer and cross-country skiing in the winter. Adjacent to the park is the **Prince George Railway Museum**. Two city galleries are of interest: **Prince George Art Gallery** features regional and national exhibits monthly; **Native Art Gallery** exhibits local native art and crafts.

Railroads. BC Rail will roll you through 462 miles of some of the most beautiful scenery in BC, from Vancouver to Prince George via Rail Canada in 13 hours; (604) 984-5246. Transfer to the passenger run to Prince Rupert, where ferries to the Queen Charlotte Islands, Vancouver Island, and Alaska depart regularly: (604) 669-1211 for ferries within BC; (800) 642-0066 for Alaska Marine Highway information.

RESTAURANTS

The Achillion Authentic Greek lunches and dinners can be found at Kostas Iliopulos's spot on Dominion Street. The combination plate is a good choice for two, with pan-fried shrimp, beef shish kabobs, roast leg of lamb, potatoes, rice, and Greek salad or soup, all for $35. ▪ *4th and Dominion; (604) 564-1166; 422 Dominion St, Prince George; $; full bar; AE, MC, V; no checks; lunch Mon–Sat, dinner every day.*

LODGINGS

Esther's Inn Bring your swimsuit to Prince George, even in the middle of winter, and pretend you're in the tropics. This Polynesian-style hotel brings the tropics to the North, with palm trees, swaying philodendrons, and waterfalls cascading around the warm indoor swimming pool. There are also three Jacuzzis, two indoor water slides that spiral into a separate pool, and a sauna. Rates are reasonable—so what if they lay it on a little thick. ▪ *Off Hwy 97 at 10th Ave; (604) 562-4131; 1151 Commercial Dr, Prince George, BC V2M 6W6; $$; AE, DC, MC, V; no checks.*

PRINCE RUPERT

Prince Rupert began as a dream. Founder Charles Melville Hays saw this island as the perfect terminus for rail as well as sea travel and trade. Unfortunately, on a trip back from Europe, where he was rustling up money to help finance his vision, he met with an untimely death aboard the *Titanic*. Seventy-five years later, a number of local folks rekindled Hays's dream. By the mid-1980s Prince Rupert had two major export terminals and a booming economy. With this newfound prosperity have come culture and tourism. The **Museum of Northern British Columbia** has one of the finest collections of Northwest Coast Indian art you're likely to find anywhere: First Avenue E and McBride, (604)624-3207.

Ferries. Prince Rupert is called the gateway to the north, but it's also a place where ferries can take you west (to the remote Queen Charlotte Islands — see listing) or south (through the Inside Passage to Vancouver Island—see Port Hardy). The Alaska ferry winds north through the panhandle to Skagway.

RESTAURANTS

Smile's Seafood Cafe ★ Since 1922, Smile's Cafe has been tucked unobtrusively among the fish-processing plants beside the railroad. Favorites still include the fresh Dungeness crab, halibut, and black cod; the french fries are a perfect nongreasy, brown-skinned complement to the fish. Service is small-town friendly. ■ *Follow 3rd Ave into George Hills Way; (604)624-3072; 131 Cow Bay Rd, Prince Rupert; $$; full bar; MC, V; no checks; breakfast, lunch, dinner every day.*

QUEEN CHARLOTTE ISLANDS

A microcosm of the British Columbia coast, the Galápagos of the Northwest, these sparsely populated, beautiful islands (150 in all) offer an escape to a rough-edged (and often rainy) paradise. There are countless beaches, streams, fishing holes, coves, and abandoned Indian villages to explore. Many unique subspecies of flora and fauna share these islands with the 6,000 residents.

The Haida Indians carve argillite—a rare black rock found only on the islands—into Northwest figurines.

Pacific Synergies offers sailing excursions in the area; (604)932-3107. Or explore the island via kayak with the help of **Ecosummer**; (604)669-7741.

Transportation. There are only 120 kilometers of paved roads in the Queen Charlotte Islands. Take the six-to-eight-hour ferry crossing from Prince Rupert, fly in to the small airstrip on Moresby Island, or take a seaplane. Food and lodging are available, mainly on Graham Island, but most people who come camp. For information, call the local Chamber of Commerce, (604)559-8188, or call Kallahin Expeditions (out of Queen Charlotte City) for island-related excursions—everything from a bus-tour package to a pick-up for you and your kayak; (604)559-8070.

QUEEN CHARLOTTE ISLANDS: MASSET

LODGINGS

Copper Beech House ★★★ The garden's a bit tangled, and so are all the memorabilia and rare collectibles inside this turn-of-the-century home. But come spring the garden smells wonderful and come morning so does breakfast. David Philips cans his summer fruits for year-round breakfasts and smokes his own seafood. Upstairs there are three guest rooms with mission-style oak furniture: one has its own living room. But most would prefer to spend time at Philips's table (dinner for guests upon request). On an island where fresh food is nearly impossible to obtain, Philips's bounty might include halibut from the local fishermen and tomatoes from the garden. An unusual soup (such as a buttery peach and tomato) proves Philips is not limited, but challenged, by local ingredients. His culinary improvisations and unparalleled hospitality would be appreciated anywhere. In the Queen Charlottes, they're a godsend. ■ *Right by the fishing boat docks at Delkatlah and Collison; (604)626-5441; 1590 Delkatlah, Masset, BC V0T 1M0; $; MC, V; checks OK.*

QUEEN CHARLOTTE ISLANDS: QUEEN CHARLOTTE CITY

LODGINGS

Spruce Point Lodge What started as just a lawn and a shower offered to the occasional kayaker who needed a place to stay is now a cedar-clad building wrapped with a balcony on Skidegate Inlet attracting families and couples alike—and still, most often, kayakers. There are seven clean rooms—each with a full bath, cable TV, and locally made pine furnishings. Reasonable rates include a continental breakfast and an occasional impromptu seafood barbecue. Mary Kellie and Nancy Hett's lawn is not available anymore, but adventurers on a budget will appreciate the hostel rooms (sheets and pillowcase provided). There's use of the kitchen and laundry. Kayaks for rent. Pets and kids welcome. ■ *5½ km west of ferry, left after Chevron station, then 2nd left; (604)559-8234; 609 6th Ave, Queen Charlotte City; PO Box 735, Queen Charlotte City, BC V0T 1S0; $; MC, V; checks OK.*

FORT LANGLEY

RESTAURANTS

Bedford House ★ A lovely place with a picturesque view of the Fraser River, this restored 1904 house is furnished with English antiques and has a pleasant, countrified elegance. The menu is rich with fancy continental cuisine: roast duckling with a fruit sauce, broiled fillet of salmon with hollandaise, or scallops and prawns served on puff pastry with a creamy champagne sauce. ■ *On the bank of the Fraser River in downtown Fort Langley; (604) 888-2333; 9272 Glover Rd, Fort Langley, BC V0X 1J0; $$; full bar; AE, MC, V; no checks; dinner every day, brunch Sun.*

CHILLIWACK

The name's not the only thing that's curious about this prosperous farming and dairy center: speakers set along the downtown portal blare easy-listening music, and antique cars seem plentiful. Local landmarks include an offbeat military museum at the **Canadian Forces Base**, open Sundays all year, midweek during the summer: (604) 858-1011; **Minter Gardens**, 10 large theme gardens, 14 kilometers east at the Highway 9 junction: (604) 794-7191; and **Bridal Falls Provincial Park**, 15 kilometers east on Highway 1.

RESTAURANTS

La Mansione Ristorante ★ There's a menu of mixed delights in this handsome mock-Tudor mansion with leaded-glass windows and a warm fireplace for winter evenings. (Beware the air conditioner in summer; sitting near it can easily ruin the meal.) Sample the delicious seafood chowder, brimming with shrimp, crab, and clams, or the veal, pan-fried in butter with lemon and capers. Specialties include chateaubriand, rack of lamb, and veal scalloppine Sergio (the legacy of the former owner). Owner Peter Graham carries an extensive selection of wines by the glass. ■ *Near Williams St at Yale; (604) 792-8910; 46290 Yale Rd E, Chilliwack; $$; full bar; AE, DC, MC, V; no checks; lunch Mon–Fri, dinner every day.*

The New Yorker Steak House ★ This popular steak house in the center of town serves up enormous portions and consistently good quality. Charcoal-broiled Alberta grain-fed beefsteaks come in four cuts and seven sizes, and the most expensive will only set you back $13. Chilliwack residents swear by the mushrooms Neptune (baked with cream cheese, shrimp, and crabmeat) and the hefty seafood platter. The decor is BC casual, with the usual fringed cloth lampshades. ■ *Near Ontario at Yale; (604) 795-7714; 45948 Yale Rd W, Chilliwack; $; full bar; AE, MC, V; no checks; lunch, dinner every day.*

Situated at the southern end of Harrison Lake, the town is a small, quiet row of low buildings facing the sandy beach and lagoon. The hot springs themselves are in a strangely enclosed temple with sulfur steam billowing out and an occasional Coke can strewn along the bottom of the pool. But don't be dismayed; the public soaking pool (which has cooled hot-spring water pumped into it) is large and wonderfully warm (100 degrees average). In addition, there are sailboards and bikes to rent, hiking trails nearby, helicopters to ride, and a pub or two. In winter, skiers use Harrison as their spa after a day on the slopes at Hemlock Valley (a 40-minute drive).

RESTAURANTS

Black Forest ★ Bavarian food seems a staple in BC, and here's an authentic restaurant serving more than just schnitzel. This is the place for goulash soup, schnitzel, and beef Rouladen—sirloin stuffed with onions, pickles, mustard, and bacon, braised in red wine, and served with red cabbage and spaetzle. Be sure to make a reservation. ■ *1 block west of Hwy 9 at Esplanade Ave; (604) 796-9343; 180 Esplanade Ave, Harrison Hot Springs; $$; full bar; AE, MC, V; checks OK; dinner every day.*

LODGINGS

The Harrison Hotel Located at the southern shore of long and beautiful Harrison Lake, this legendary hotel is really a better place to view than to visit. The first hotel was built here in 1885 to take advantage of the hot springs; it burned down, and the present "old" building dates back to 1926. Since then the additions have changed the hotel into a sprawling mishmash of unrelated architecture. Grounds are pretty and spacious, with tennis courts and exercise circuit, but the best part about the place is definitely the hot spring water: two indoor pools (103 and 90 degrees) and one outdoor (90 degrees)—open only to hotel guests. A scenic golf course is 3 kilometers away. Staying here is expensive (there are extra charges for almost everything). Most of the rooms in the old wing still have 1950s decor. And since the hotel won't guarantee lake views, a safer bet is to book a room in the newer tower (on the east side). Our advice would be to use the place for a short stay, arrive in time to enjoy the excellent pools and a poolside drink and then promenade down the street to eat. ■ *West end of Esplanade Ave; (604) 796-2244; 100 Esplanade Ave, Harrison Hot Springs, BC V0M 1K0; $$$; AE, MC, V; checks OK.* &

MANNING PARK

LODGINGS

Manning Park Motel Situated within the boundaries of this pretty provincial park, the simple lodge gives you easy access to both gentle and arduous hiking trails. With a short drive, you can be paddling a rented canoe on Lightning Lake or riding a horse through the surrounding country. Besides the 41 motel rooms, the low-key resort includes a restaurant, coffee shop, cabins, and triplexes—all in the same plain, functional style. If you have 49 friends, however, book the Last Resort a few yards down the highway, a real old-fashioned '40s charmer that sleeps 50. In winter (two-day minimum then) the park turns into cross-country and downhill ski heaven: Gibsons Ski Area is just out the back door. ■ *Just off Hwy 3 in Manning Provincial Park; (604)840-8822; Manning Park, BC V0X 1R0; $$; MC, V; no checks.*

PRINCETON

RESTAURANTS

The Apple Tree Restaurant ★★ The big crabapple tree across from the Esso station marks the site of Douglas and Mary Rebagliati's excellent restaurant in a small house filled with greenery and fussy wallpaper. Expect such appetizers as escargots cooked in mushroom caps (an Okanagan favorite) and good, hearty, homemade soups; hope for the deceptively simple oregano chicken, marinated in olive oil and herbs and broiled. Desserts receive just as much attention (the reputation of the Louisiana mud pie has spread to Vancouver). The primarily British Columbia wine list is award-winning. The patio in the back is pleasant come summer. Have an early supper here and make Osoyoos by nightfall. ■ *Vermilion Ave at Dixie Lee; (604)295-7745; 255 Vermilion Ave, Princeton; $; full bar; MC, V; no checks; lunch Tues–Fri, dinner Tues–Sat (Tues–Sun, July–Sept).* &

▼

Quilchena

Lodgings

▲

QUILCHENA

LODGINGS

Quilchena Hotel ★★ Remote Quilchena Hotel captures the ambience of southwestern BC's cattle country, and it attracts a motley assortment: moneyed urbanites who fly over (the Quilchena has its own landing strip) in search of relaxation; cattle barons who come to buy livestock; gentlemanly senior citizens in search of the perfect golf course; and cowboys, Canada–style. It's a delightful stew, and meant to be that way: there are no phones or TVs in the 16 rooms; guests share bathrooms and dine together in the parlor. It's not elegant, but guests happily gather around the piano for an impromptu recital. Daytime finds you riding horses, playing tennis, golfing on the adjacent course, or searching the nearby fossil beds. For extended stays there's a three-bedroom ranch house on the grounds. Expect lots of beef on the restaurant's menu. ■ *Take the 2nd Merritt exit off the Coquilhalla Hwy; (604)378-2611; Hwy 5A, Quilchena, BC V0E 2R0; $$; MC, V; no checks; (mid-Apr to mid-Oct only).*

MERRITT

LODGINGS

Corbett Lake Country Inn ★ French-trained owner and chef Peter McVey first came from England to British Columbia on a fishing trip. Today McVey's country inn caters to lovers of fly-fishing in the summer and cross-country skiers in the winter. There are three nondescript rooms in the lodge, but most guests choose to stay in one of the 10 simple cabins, each with its own kitchen. The two duplexes all have fireplaces and one has a separate bedroom/living room. Aside from the outdoor activities, the food's the thing here. Dinner (by reservation only) is something different every night. McVey creates wonderful four-course evenings starting with soup (perhaps fresh mushroom), a salad (caesar, hot German, or cucumber), and continuing to an entree which could be anything from loin of pork with Dijon mustard to beef Wellington with Yorkshire pudding. Corbett Lake holds plenty of fish, but an extra fee gains you the privilege of angling in two privately stocked lakes. ■ *16 km south of Merritt on Hwy 5A; (604)378-4334; Box 327, Merritt, BC V0K 2B0; $$; V; checks OK; breakfast, lunch, dinner every day; (closed Nov and Mar–May).*

KAMLOOPS

RESTAURANTS

Minos ★ Minos had a tradition of being a family-owned operation and new owner Gus Krokos hasn't changed a successful enterprise. Service is exceptionally friendly, prompt, and well-informed, helping to create a warm atmosphere. The menu still leans heavily toward Greek fare—souvlaki of lamb, chicken, and seafood. Try a piece of honey-sweet baklava with a strong cup of Greek coffee for dessert. ■ *1 km north of Overlander Bridge; (604)376-2010; 262 Tranquille Rd, Kamloops, BC V2B 3G3; $; beer and wine; MC, V; no checks; lunch Mon–Sat, dinner every day.*

Lac Le Jeune Resort ★ Well-equipped and pleasant, this lodge puts you right on the lake for fishing and at the edge of the wilderness for hiking. You can stay in the lodge, in a self-sufficient cabin (perfect for families), or in a chalet. The resort includes an indoor whirlpool and sauna and meeting rooms for up to 200. A breakfast and dinner buffet is served for guests only. Adjacent is a downhill ski area; more than 100 kilometers of cross-country skiing trails wind through the property. Boats and canoes are available for rent (the famous Kamloops trout are great to catch—and eat). Large tour groups tend to book the place en masse during the summer months, so reserve early or take a chance on a last-minute cancellation. ■ *Off Coquihalla Hwy, Lac Le Jeune exit, 29 km southwest of Kamloops; (604)372-2722; Lac Le Jeune Rd, Kamloops; 650 Victoria St, Kamloops, BC V2C 2B4; $$; full bar; AE, DC, MC, V; checks OK; breakfast, dinner every day; (open mid-Apr to late-Oct).*

ASHCROFT

LODGINGS

Sundance Ranch ★★ Here's a dude ranch set in high plateau country, with the Thompson River cutting a deep gorge just to the west. Low-lying buildings of dark-stained wood contain handsome pine-paneled rooms. Children can stay in their own wing or with their parents. The pool is quite grand, and there's now a new tennis court. But the real attraction is the corral, where 100 good horses await you for the two daily rides, morning and late afternoon (it can get very hot here during mid-day). More than a dozen buffalo live in the adjacent fields. During the evening, the excellent meals are often served on the barbecue patio; Saturday nights there's a dance. Rustic public rooms set the scene for drinks, parties, and games. You'll sleep well, breathing the cool, sage-scented air. ■ *8 km south of Ashcroft off Kirkland Ranch Rd; (604)453-2422; Kirkland Ranch Rd, Ashcroft; PO Box 489, Ashcroft, BC V0K 1A0; $$; MC, V; no checks; (open Mar–Oct).*

KEREMEOS

LODGINGS

Cathedral Lakes Resort ★★ To say this resort is remote is more than an understatement. First you have to get to base camp, which is a 21-kilometer gravel-road journey off Highway 3 along the Ashnola River. Once you're there, a four-wheel-drive vehicle from the resort picks you up and takes you on a one-hour, 14½-kilometer journey to the lodge. The resort is heavy on recreation (hiking, canoeing, fishing), light on modern conveniences (such as phones and TVs). All rooms have hot water and views of the lakes and peaks that surround the resort. Choose a cabin (which can accommodate up to eight) or a room in the chalet or the lodge. Showers and toilets are shared. Three big meals are served (box lunches available upon request). Make your reservations early, since the season is short and space is limited.

Located inside the Cathedral Lake Provincial Park, the entire area is a protected wildlife refuge and a unique geological region. At 6,000 to 8,000 feet, the air is cool and dry, the views of surrounding Cascade mountains spectacular. Mount Baker, Mount Rainier, the Coast Range, and the Kootenays are all visible from Lakeview Mountain, a day hike from the lodge. ■ *Call ahead for directions; (604)499-5848 (or cellular phone (604)492-1606 off-season); RR1, Cawston, BC V0X 1C0; $$; no credit cards; checks OK (open June–Oct).*

THE OKANAGAN VALLEY

The Canadian Okanagans, stretching from Osoyoos at the border to Vernon to the north, are a summer playground. The valley is laden with orchards, making it especially appealing in spring when the fruit trees are in full bloom. The best time to pick up some of the valley's bounty is mid-August through early September; however, beginning as early as late June the fruit starts ripening: cherries (late June to mid-July), peaches (mid-July through September), pears (August through September), apricots (mid-July through mid-August), plums (September), apples (August through October), and grapes (September through mid-October).

Wineries. Fruit aside, winemaking is the hot ticket in the Okanagan. British Columbians have long taken inordinate pride in their wines—even when those mostly came from a few largish factories like Kelowna's Calona, on Richter Street, (604)762-3332, and Penticton's Cartier, on Main Street, (604)492-0621. However, ever since British Columbia authorized estate and smaller farmgate wineries, many excellent small wineries have popped up. Some of the best estate offerings come out of Gray Monk, 8 kilometers west of Winfield off Highway 97, (604)766-3168; CedarCreek, 14 kilometers south of Kelowna in the Mission, (604)764-8866; Sumac Ridge, off Highway 97, just north of Summerland, (604)494-0451; and Hainle Vineyards in Peachland, (604)767-2525. A couple of farmgate vineyards to keep an eye on are Quail's Gate Vineyards in Kelowna, (604)769-4451, and Wild Goose Vineyards just south of Okanagan Falls, (604)497-8919. Other notable wineries to visit: Mission Hill, south of Kelowna in Westbank off Boucherie Road, (604)768-5125; Gehringer Brothers, 4 kilometers south of Oliver off Highway 97 on Road 8, (604) 498-3537; Brights Wines, between Oliver and Vaseaux Lake on Highway 97, (604) 498-4981; Summerhill, (604) 764-8000, south on Pandosy/Lakeshore Road in east Kelowna; Okanagan Vineyards, (604) 498-6663, 5 kilometers south of Oliver off Highway 97, and Lang Vineyards, (604) 496-5987, south of Naramata on Gammon Road. Most offer tastings and seasonal tours; call ahead for times and dates.

Skiing. The local climate is a powdery medium between the chill of the Rockies and the slush of the Coast Range, and the slopes are distributed along the valley. Silver Star east of Vernon, has full resort facilities; information: (604) 542-0224. Last Mountain is the nearest stop from Kelowna for day schussing, (604) 768-5189; but Big White, (604) 765-3101, to the east has many more runs (44, up to 1,850 vertical feet), full facilities, and even cross-country trails, and claims the greatest altitude of all the ski areas in the province. Apex Alpine, Penticton's full-facility resort known for its challenging terrain, has added a number of "family" runs to complement its harder stuff; (604) 292-8222. Southwest of Penticton on Highway 3A, the Twin Lakes Golf Club doubles as a cross-country course in winter; (604) 497-5359. There's more downhill at Mount Baldy west of Osoyoos, (604) 498-2262—one of the first mountains in the area to have snow.

OSOYOOS

Osoyoos bills itself as "the Spanish capital of Canada," but not because of any pioneer ethnic roots. It's purely a gimmicky town theme selected by city fathers. The climate is Canada's driest, with 10 inches of rain a year, and Osoyoos Lake is reportedly Canada's warmest freshwater lake. The **Cheshire Cat and Bakery** at the corner of 85th and 76th offers up fresh-baked croissants, cookies, brownies, and scones. A good short hike is up **Mount Kobau**, just west of Osoyoos off Kobau Road. Take the Kobau Lookout trail (2 kilometers) to the fire lookout or Testalinden Trail (5 kilometers) loop trail with views of the Similkameen Valley.

RESTAURANTS

Diamond Steak & Seafood House ★ Just about everyone in Osoyoos likes this casual steak, seafood, and pizza house on the main street of town. The decor carries off the town's ersatz Spanish theme better than most, and the pizzas are quite good, if you like crust that's crisp enough to snap. The Greek salad is the best in town—no wonder—the owner is Greek. The wine list shows a collection of labels (literally) from several valley wineries, and there are refreshing Okanagan apple and pear ciders, too. ■ *Main St near 89th; (604) 495-6223; Main St, Osoyoos; $$; full bar; MC, V; checks OK; dinner every day.* ㋐

LODGINGS

The Log House Bed & Breakfast ★ An apricot orchard separates this lodgelike building from the rumbling of traffic on Highway 97. Trophy heads—elk and deer—and black bear rugs give the authentic lodge ambience. A rough stone fireplace presides over the sizable family room. Ask for the room with deck access and that valley view. Time your visit right and you can indulge in picking ultra-fresh peaches, nectarines, and apricots. ■ *On Hwy 97 about 10 km north of Osoyoos and 10 km south of Oliver; (604)498-0414; 30864 Hwy 97, Oliver; RR 1, Site 36, Comp 24, Oliver, BC V0H 1T0; $$; no credit cards; local checks only.*

Reflections Guesthouse ★ Apple orchards crawl up the hill behind this new bed and breakfast, built by owner Gary Fox. Out front there's a small private lake (surrounded by homes). Four suites are complete with kitchens and balconies. The setting is quiet; the accommodations are contemporary. Guests can stroll through the orchard, sit in the garden, or soak in the hot tub. Breakfast is continental-style. ■ *From Osoyoos take Hwy 97 south to 74th Ave, turn west at 103rd St, follow the signs; (604)495-5229; RR 2, Site 82, Comp 7, Osoyoos, BC V0H 1V0; $; no credit cards; checks OK.*

Inkaneep Point Resort Down a steep, winding road to a little peninsula in Osoyoos Lake is this unassuming resort. The best thing about it is location: all 10 beach-level rooms face directly south (maximum sun) and open only feet away from the water's edge (the two dark cabins face north). Families (some in their third generation of vacationing here) don't mind the fact the accommodations are a bit campish, because they really come for the sun. Don and Esme Hellyer book rooms by the week in the summer (July and August get booked up early in the year), love kids, and eschew loud boats and pets. ■ *3 km north of Osoyoos off Hwy 97; (604)495-6353; RR 2, Osoyoos, BC V0H 1V0; $; no credit cards; checks OK; (open only mid-May through Canada's Thanksgiving in Oct).*

KALEDEN

LODGINGS

Ponderosa Point Resort ★★ Ponderosa Point's compound of 26 individually owned rental cabins on a peninsula extending out into Skaha Lake is an ideal spot to take a thick book for three days in the off-season or a week in the summer (minimum stays respectively). The most attractive units are the one- and two-bedroom Pan Abodes set on a ponderosa pine–covered bluff above the lake. There's a 600-foot sandy beach, boat rentals, tennis courts, a playground, and a big grassy central compound. The cabins, individually furnished

by the owners, are not plush or contemporary, but they're universally comfortable and clean. Greasewood cabin, for two, has furniture with a hand-hewn look—perfect for the setting.
■ *319 Ponderosa Ave; (604) 497-5354; 319 Ponderosa Ave, Kalenden; Box 106, Kalenden, BC V0H 1K0; $$$; no credit cards; checks OK.*

PENTICTON

Penticton takes full advantage of its dual lakefronts. The south end of town (with its go-cart tracks, amusement centers, miniature golf courses, water slides, and RV parks) touches the north shore of Skaha Lake. The north end of town sidles along the southern tip of the 70-mile-long Lake Okanagan.

RESTAURANTS

Granny Bogner's ★★ One of the province's best restaurants is also one of the most consistent, and it has just about everything—great food, great location, great building, and desserts that alone make the trip here worthwhile. The restaurant is located in a big Arts and Crafts–style house. Diners relax in wing chairs in front of the fireplace with a glass of wine or after-dinner coffee. The menu covers a broad spectrum from halibut to prime rib, but it's the presentation of the food that sets this place apart. Entrees arrive garnished with an eye for color and shape; vegetables are artfully arranged. The dessert specials, often using fresh local fruit, are the best choices. The bar with its comfy chintz chairs invites brandy and dessert. The wine list does a grand job of representing the best local estate wineries. ■ *2 blocks south of Main; (604) 493-2711; 302 Eckhardt Ave W, Penticton; $$$; full bar; AE, MC, V; no checks; dinner Tues–Sat.*

Theo's ★ The ever-popular Theo's sports a series of sun-dappled interior patios, roofed with heavy rough-sawn beams, floored with red tile, walled in white stucco. Patrons say Theo's cooks an excellent rabbit (from nearby Summerland) and swear by the octopus. We agree, but we wish the accompaniments (white rice, carrots, and overcooked potatoes) were a little more inspired. That said, by all means go in the late afternoon for an aperitif and a plate of excellent fried squid, or late at night to eat moussaka. ■ *Near the corner of Main and Eckhardt; (604) 492-4019; 687 Main St, Penticton; $$; full bar; AE, DC, MC, V; local checks only; lunch Mon–Sat, dinner every day.* &

LODGINGS

Coast Lakeside Resort The Coast Lakeside (formerly the Delta Lakeside), the flagship of the Lake Okanagan shore, is looking a little forgotten these days (it needs paint and some new landscaping), strange for the most expensive place in town. It's the only place with its own beachfront. There are 204 rooms with balconies; the north-facing rooms have lake views. There are outdoor tennis courts and an indoor pool and two restaurants (one with outdoor seating). ■ *Main and Lakeshore; (604)493-8221; 21 Lakeshore Dr W, Penticton, BC V2A 7M5; $$$; full bar; AE, DC, MC, V; checks OK; breakfast, lunch, dinner every day.*

Riordan House Built in 1920, this two-story bungalow/antique shop is only a six-block walk to the beach of Okanagan Lake and downtown Penticton. The Master Suite has a sitting area with a wood-burning fireplace and plenty of windows. Summers, however, windows are opened for ventilation and in comes the noise from the busy intersection. That's when we prefer the quieter, spacious Mountain View room with its sitting nook. A simple and fresh breakfast is served. ■ *From Main St, turn west on Eckhardt St, 2 blocks; (604)493-5997; 689 Winnipeg St, Penticton, BC V2A 5N1; $$; MC, V; checks OK.*

Castle Rock B&B [*unrated*] This is *the* place to stay in Penticton, so everyone tells us. It must be, since reservations proved quite hard to get, especially when arriving in the valley unannounced. So we thought it important to mention this massive hand-hewn log lodge located between Okanagan and Skaha lakes. Besides basking in the glories of Okanagan adventures, you could also borrow their mountain bikes for the morning and return for an afternoon of sunning beside the heated outdoor pool. More next edition. ■ *Just north of downtown Penticton off Naramata Rd on Sutherland Rd; (604)492-4429; 2050 Sutherland Rd, Penticton; mail: C22, S200, RR#1, Penticton, BC, V2A 6J6; $$; MC, V; checks OK.*

NARAMATA

RESTAURANTS

The Country Squire ★★★ Every meal becomes an event at this clubby old house. Dinner might take up to four hours; however long it is, the table's yours for the night—you can even take a walk in between courses if you'd like (a good idea if you want a view of the lake). Master of ceremonies is Ron Dyck, who owns and operates this shrine of Okanagan cookery with his wife, Patt. Some think the flourishes are simply too much; others like all of Ron's personal touches. The opening act takes place when you call for reservations, at which time you are asked to choose from among several seasonal entrees. Upon arrival you find a formal card detailing the courses to come: perhaps a coarse duck pâté surrounded with Cumberland sauce to begin; a soup; your entree; a platter of well-selected cheeses and fruit; and dessert, such as the chocolate ginger pear, poached in sauvignon blanc. The food is good, if rococo, with only the occasional inexplicable lapse. The price is a flat $39.50—and Ron is at your side throughout the meal, decanting one his 350 wines, flambéeing the steak Diane, or carving the beef Wellington. He's also a splendid resource on local wines, many of which reside in his own deep cellar. ■ *Take Naramata Rd, left on Robinson, right on 1st; (604) 496-5416; 3950 1st St, Naramata, BC V0H 1N0; $$; full bar; MC, V; local checks only; dinner Wed–Sun.* ⟨&⟩

LODGINGS

Sandy Beach Lodge ★★ Here is the archetypal summer-lodge-on-the-lake, where the same families have signed up for the same two weeks in the same cabin for as long as anyone can remember. The setting is just about perfect: a wide, green lawn, breezy with stately pines and shady maples, sloping down to a quiet cove with a sandy beach perfect for horseshoes, croquet, or shuffleboard. And the 13 newer log duplexes (tastefully decorated and furnished) are a vast improvement over the old brown bungalows that they replaced. Request one of the five closest to the lake (they all have decks and outdoor barbecues). There are also six small rooms in the newly remodeled pine-log lodge. Tennis courts, a small swimming pool, rental boats, and wooden lawn chairs provide ample diversions. During peak summer season, reservations may be necessary up to a year in advance (and priority is given to returning guests). ■ *Off Robson on Mill Rd; (604) 496-5765; 4275 Mill Rd, Naramata; PO Box 8, Naramata, BC V0H 1N0; $$; MC, V; checks OK.* ⟨&⟩

SUMMERLAND

A theme town done in the same spirit as Osoyoos, only this time they chose to do it Tudor-style. Old Summerland is down on the water, but most of the town's business now thrives up on the hill.

RESTAURANTS

Shaughnessy's Cove Shaughnessy's strong suits are its dramatic view of Lake Okanagan (it's built as close to the water as the law allows) and its airy atmosphere. The restaurant is tiered into four levels, with two outdoor decks, 20-foot ceilings, an old oak bar, skylights, three fireplaces, and pleasant decor. The menu ranges from fish 'n' chips to chimichangas to a filling stew served in a hollowed-out loaf of bread. The caesars are so powerful, you'll also get a stick of chewing gum for later. Owners go way out of their way to make it easy for you to dine here. They provide the Shaughnessy Shuttle, which picks customers up at their homes or inn and returns them at the end of the

evening, no charge. ■ *Lakeshore Dr N in Old Summerland;
(604)494-1212; 12817 Lakeshore Dr, Summerland; $; full
bar; AE, DC, MC, V; no checks; lunch, dinner every day.* &

KELOWNA

On the east side of Lake Okanagan, Kelowna is the largest and
liveliest of the Okanagan cities, with some noisy nightlife, some
culture (an art museum and summer theater), a growing range
of continental and ethnic restaurants, a big regatta in July, and
an interesting historical preserve at Father Pandosy's Mission,
(604)860-8369. Kelowna even has its own version of the Loch
Ness monster: Ogopogo. Keep a lookout for him (or her) while
supping on the gaily decked-out paddle wheeler *Fintry Queen*
or touring aboard the *Okanagan Princess*.

Houseboats. Floating on the 70-mile-long Lake Okanagan is a good three- to seven-day vacation alternative for the entire family—most houseboats sleep up to six ($2,100 per
week). No previous boating experience is necessary—you'll
get a "Captain's lesson" when you arrive; Bridge Bay Marina,
(604)769-4411.

RESTAURANTS

Vintage Room (Capri Hotel) ★★ Nobody really wants
to like this elegant, pricey restaurant on the ground floor
of the Capri Hotel. Maybe that's what makes the Vintage
Room try so hard—and most often succeed. The service is impeccable, and the restaurant bends over backward to accommodate your whims. It's some of the most sophisticated food
in the Okanagan with such vintage fare as escargots,
chateaubriand, and lobster tail. Avoid the mediocre desserts,
and watch out for the tour groups that can slow service. ■
*Gordon and Harvey; (604)860-6060, ext 229; 1171 Harvey
Ave, Kelowna, BC V1Y 6E8; $$; full bar; AE, DC, MC, V;
checks OK; lunch Mon–Fri, dinner every day, brunch Sun.*

Yamas Taverna ★ For authentic Greek fare, the locals rec-
ommend Yamas. The feeling is casual here, with cafe chairs for
seating, tables covered with blue-and-white checked table-
cloths, and Greek music in the background. It's easy to get in
a Greek mood with a plate of lamb moussaka or a heaping serv-
ing of garlicky chicken souvlaki. Most entrees are served with
delicious roasted potatoes and a Greek salad of cucumbers,
tomatoes, and feta. ■ *Lawrence and Leon; (604)763-5823;
1630 Ellis St, Kelowna; $$; full bar; AE, MC, V; no checks;
lunch Mon–Fri, dinner every day.*

LODGINGS

Hotel Eldorado ★★ Hands down, this is the best place to stay
on Lake Okanagan—that is, if a boardwalk along the shore will

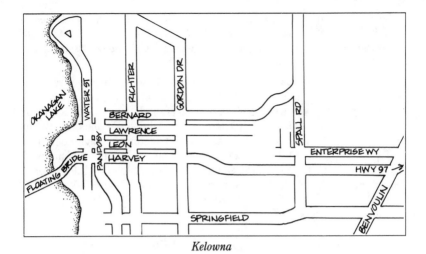

Kelowna

do instead of a sandy beach. (Rotary Beach is just a short walk away.) Eldorado Arms was originally built for a countess of Scottish descent; in 1989 it caught fire and burned almost to the ground. Consequently, the rebuilt manse feels very new, yet has the grandeur of a bygone era. Each of the 19 rooms has an antique armoire, most have balconies, and some have Jacuzzis. Best are the lakeside or corner rooms. The boardroom with a large patio is an excellent meeting place for 10 to 60 people. The round house nearby can hold up to 85 for banquets. There's not much of a lobby, as the restaurant and lounge take up most of the first floor. The restaurant, in the process of a menu change at our last visit, is consistently excellent. The wine selection is primarily British Columbian. Breakfast in the sun room is an extremely pleasant way to wake up. ■ *Follow Pandosy (which becomes Lakeshore) for 6½ km south of the Okanagan Floating Bridge; (604) 763-7500; 500 Cook Rd, Kelowna, BC V1W 3G9; $$$; full bar; AE,DC, MC, V; no checks; breakfast, lunch Mon–Sat, dinner every day, brunch Sun.*

Lake Okanagan Resort ★★ You reach the 300-acre resort via a beautiful, pine-clad winding road on the west side of Lake Okan-agan. The appointments are not first-class, but it's the best destination resort in the Okanagan. Now open year-round, it offers sailing, swimming, golf (nine holes), tennis (seven courts), and horseback riding to keep you busy. You can stay in a large condominium or a smaller chalet (both with wood-burning fireplaces), or any of four different inns. Since the resort is located on a very steep hillside, many of the rooms are a good climb from the activities, but a resort shuttle makes a quick job of it. The evening restaurant, Chateau, serves fancy continental-resort fare. A poolside lounge makes for an interesting social setting. ▪ *2751 Westside Rd, 17 km north of Kelowna; (604) 769-3511; 2751 Westside Rd, Kelowna, BC V1Y 8V2; $$$; full bar; AE, DC, MC, V; no checks; breakfast, lunch, dinner every day.* ᕁ

Capri Hotel All of the 185 rooms have seen a recent upgrade. The best still look out to the courtyard (with its outdoor hot tub and pool), but privacy is lacking on the ground floor. There are two dining options here, the informal Garden Cafe and the outstanding Vintage Room (see review). For relaxation there's an outdoor hot tub and pool, men's and ladies' saunas, and for a taste of nightlife, there's Angie's Pub. ▪ *Gordon and Harvey; (604) 860-6060; 1171 Harvey Ave, Kelowna, BC V1Y 6E8; $$$; AE, DC, MC, V; checks OK.*

VERNON

Vernon is the most commercialized tourist center in the valley, the main jumping-off point for skiers and the main landing pad for conventioneers. Nightlife is lively, but the dining scene is generally uninspired.

O'Keefe Historic Ranch, 11 kilometers north of Vernon, is one of the original cattle ranches from the late 1800s. Now a museum, the compound contains most of the original buildings and equipment from the era. Tours run April to October; (604) 542-7868.

RESTAURANTS

Intermezzo This musty green-colored restaurant looks as if it has been around for decades, and in fact, it has. Chef Jim Grady's been cooking here since its beginnings, so you can count on consistency and big servings. If you don't feel like eating in a windowless room, there are a few tables out on the patio or you can take your hefty order of cheesy lasagne, fettuccine pesto, or perhaps even some barbecued pork ribs to go. ▪ *On 34th Ave near 32nd St; (604) 542-3853; 3206 34th Ave, Vernon; $$; full bar; AE, MC, V; no checks; dinner every day.*

LODGINGS

Best Western Villager Motor Inn In terms of plush carpeting, contemporary accoutrements, and upkeep, this half-timbered-and-brick motel on the Highway 97 strip is the best in town. Of the 53 rooms, 24 open onto the atrium pool and hot tub, but the regular rooms are quieter. ▪ *At the north end of town, directly across from Village Green Mall; (604) 549-2224; 5121 26th St, Vernon, BC V1T 8G4; $$; AE, DC, MC, V; no checks.* ᕁ

SALMON ARM

RESTAURANTS

Orchard House ★ A retired British colonel built this lovely house in 1903, planting an orchard and tulips on its surrounding 20 acres. Now it's a restaurant, serving seafood almost any way—baked, fried, poached—but the rack of lamb shipped from Australia is the starring item. Four rooms have been converted into dining areas: try to get into the glassed-in verandah with a view of Shuswap Lake, or the living room with its glowing fire. ■ *22nd St NE; (604)832-3434; 720 22nd St NE, Salmon Arm; $$; full bar; DC, MC, V; checks OK; lunch, dinner every day.* ᕁ

SICAMOUS

Houseboating. You and your family can explore the 1,000 miles or so of the Shuswap Lake shoreline at the northern end of the Okanagan Valley on a houseboat—stocked with everything from microwave oven to a water slide. Seven-day trips run you between $2,000 and $4,000 depending on your boat choice, not including gas; Waterway Houseboats, (604)836-2505.

REVELSTOKE

Revelstoke's history is tied to the building of the Canadian Pacific Railway. Towering mountains rise all around Revelstoke and it's clear the town is trying to build a tourist industry that appeals to hikers and skiers. The four-block-long downtown on MacKenzie Avenue has been revitalized, with the restoration of historic brick buildings. Ambience Gallery & Frames carries the work of local artists; an espresso bar, Conversations, is filled with couches and easy chairs; Village Sports carries ski equipment winters, hiking gear summers.

Heli-skiing. For the serious skier, Revelstoke serves as a base camp to some amazing runs in and around the Albert Icefields. The catch: You need a helicopter to get there. Selkirk Tangiers Helicopter Skiing Ltd., (604)837-5378, boasts more than 200 runs. For a few grand, Canadian Mountain Holidays will take you out, for a week at a time, to one of their fully staffed lodges in remote hideaways for some great skiing and hiking; (403)762-4534.

RESTAURANTS

Black Forest Inn Inside this A-frame you'll find a bit of Bavaria, with cute cuckoo clocks and German souvenirs cluttering every spare inch of space. Fondue Provençal, British Columbia salmon fillets, and a variety of beef tenderloins round out a rather extensive menu; we recommend one of the Bavarian dishes such as sauerbraten or schnitzel. Swiss-born chef Kurt Amsler's specialty is rainbow trout from a local hatchery; the servings grow larger as summer and trout progress. ▪ *5 km west of Revelstoke on the Trans-Canada Hwy; (604)837-3495; Trans-Canada West #1, Revelstoke; $$; full bar; AE, MC, V; local checks only; dinner Wed–Mon; (closed Nov).*

The 112 Located in the Regent Inn downtown, the 112 is a unanimous favorite among locals. The masculine decor of dark cedar paneling, historical photographs of the Revelstoke region in the 19th century, and soft lighting blend well with the continental cuisine. Chef Peter Mueller specializes in veal dishes, but the cioppino and lamb Provençal also come with high recommendations. The wine list has been expanded to include some French and Australian labels, but still emphasizes British Columbia's own vintners. A variety of after-dinner flaming coffees are good for show but little else. ▪ *McKenzie and 1st; (604)837-2107; 112 E 1st St, Revelstoke; $$; full bar; AE, DC, MC, V; no checks; lunch, dinner Mon–Sat.* ♿

FIELD

LODGINGS

Emerald Lake Lodge ★★★★ In the heart of Yoho National Park, surrounded by the Rocky Mountains and stunning views, is the Emerald Lake Lodge. And a jewel it is, any time of year. You'll be well taken care of at this lodge on the lake. Now part of a trio of Rocky Mountain lodges, the complex includes 24 buildings as well as the main lodge. The lakeside buildings (12 to 15, 24 to 26, 32 and 33) have the best views; buildings 32 and 33 offer the most privacy. The big lodge, now remodeled, still retains the feel of an old parks lodge with wood beams and plenty of couches and chairs cozied up to big stone fireplaces. The bellmen won't let you lift a finger (except to light the match to the readied fire). Winter here is nearly as popular as summer; all rooms have a fireplace and twig chairs for curling up with a book on snowy days.

In the clubhouse building, there's a hot tub, sauna, and exercise facility; upstairs in the main lodge is a billiards room. The dining room menu boasts plenty of wild game—medallions of venison and buffalo, and barley soup for dinner; caribou or Alberta lake trout for breakfast. Hikers can order a sack lunch from the dining room. You're miles from anywhere, but no corners are cut.

Most people opt for horseback riding, fishing for trout, canoeing, hiking, or come winter, cross-country skiing (there's a nice trail around the alpine lake as well as more serious hikes to Takakkaw Falls, one of Canada's tallest waterfalls, with a free fall of more than 365 meters). The kids will never miss the TV.

- *In Yoho National Park, 8 km north of the Trans-Canada Hwy (no parking at the lodge, leave the car at parking lot and call the bellhop for transport); (604)343-6321; PO Box 10, Field, BC V0A 1G0; $$$; AE, DC, MC, V; checks OK.* &

RADIUM HOT SPRINGS

Radium Hot Springs makes an ideal soaking stop at the base of the Kootenay mountain range. The hot springs, open to the public year-round, are equipped with two pools: one heated, the other cooler for more athletic swimming. If you didn't pack your bathing suit, don't worry; they'll rent you one for a buck-and-a-half. On Highway 93, 3 kilometers from Radium Junction, (604)347-9485. Nearby you'll find golfing, camping, lodging, and tennis. Best motel in town is **Addison's Bungalows** (PO Box 56, Radium Hot Springs, BC V0A 1M0; (604)347-9545).

INVERMERE

RESTAURANTS

Strand's Old House ★★ Built in 1912 by pioneer Alexander Ritchie, this house has been converted to an idyllic setting for some of the finest dining in eastern British Columbia. Beyond the yard lined with beech trees are gardens with views to the mountains. Chef Tony Wood makes everything from scratch, right down to the mayonnaise served with the steamed artichokes. The elaborate leather-bound menu features page after page of outstanding appetizers and entrees. A cold, spicy avocado soup is a fresh starter; follow it with a well-prepared veal steak with a morel mushroom sauce or an exceptional creamy chicken Oscar, stuffed with crab. Regional wines and beers add gusto to occasional evenings of live music. Be sure to make reservations. ▪ *In the middle of town; (604)342-6344; 818 12th St, Invermere; $$; full bar; AE, DC, MC, V; no checks; dinner every day; (closed 2 days a week in Nov).*

LODGINGS

Panorama Resort ★ More than a resort, Panorama is its own village—a sprawling establishment in the Purcell Mountains that contains a seven-lift ski area, condos, and a hotel (even kennels for your dog), lots of restaurants and nightspots, and outdoor recreation aplenty. Eight well-maintained tennis courts, horses, hiking trails, and river rafting on Toby Creek relieve the resort from dependence on the winter ski trade. But ski season is still the time to go. The snow is deep, white powder (World Cup competitions have been held here), and if nature doesn't dispense the white stuff, machines will. We recommend the condos rather than the hotel units: they're more expensive, but they all have kitchens. Wherever you stay,

you're never more than a five-minute walk from the chair lifts.
- *18 km west of Invermere on Toby Creek Rd; (604)342-6941; Panorama Resort, Panorama; PO Box 7000, Invermere, BC V0A 1T0; $$; AE, DC, MC, V; checks OK.*

KIMBERLEY

Like many foundering mining towns in the early 1970s, Kimberley looked to tourism (and chose a Bavarian theme) to bolster a faltering economy. At 4,000 feet, Kimberley is the highest incorporated city in Canada. Views of the snowcapped Rocky Mountains are stunning, especially from the Kimberley Ski Resort, with more than 30 downhill runs. There are 26 kilometers of Nordic runs; 3 kilometers are lighted at night.

The town was named in 1896 after Kimberley, South Africa, because of a rich outcrop of minerals at the Sullivan Mine. Now owned by Cominco Ltd., Sullivan Mine is one of the largest lead, zinc, and silver mines in the world. It once employed 1,200; now half that many work there (the town's population is 6,700). The mountainside was initially mined as an open pit, and even though the pit has been filled in, it remains as an ugly scar. Ore is now mined 2 miles deep into the mountain and carried by railcar to the Cominco smelter in Trail, BC. **Gardeners** shouldn't miss the teahouse, greenhouse, and immaculately kept gardens, once maintained by Cominco and now under the care of the city, on the grounds of the Kimberly District Hospital.

The Heritage Museum, 105 Spokane Street, (604)427-7510, has an excellent display of the town's mining history and memorabilia, such as hockey equipment from the town team that won the World Senior Amateur Hockey Championships in 1937. For a good selection of regional books, try **Mountain High Book Store**, 232 Spokane Street, (604)427-7014. Skiers and mountain bike enthusiasts (roller bladers too) should check out **Rocky Mountain Sports**, 185 Deer Park Avenue, (604)427-2838. Accordion music is played on loudspeakers at the center of the Bavarian Platz (the town's three-block walking street). For a quarter, a yodelling puppet pops out of the upper window of Canada's largest cuckoo clock. The **Bauerhaus Restaurant** (280 Norton Avenue, Kimberley, (604)427-5133) has an outstanding view of the mountains; however, the well-reputed restaurant, dismantled in Austria and reconstructed here, is open only during ski season and for a few months in the summer; (604)427-5133.

RESTAURANTS

Chef Bernard's Kitchen ★ Originally a fresh pasta eatery, Chef Bernard's dishes up Lousiana specialties such as blackened catfish filet and Gulf shrimp étouffée. The steaks are named for celebrities: the Paul Newman steak is served with Atlantic scallops in cream and brandy; the Chi Chi Rodriguez steak is served with smoked salmon in cream and chablis. Nice tries; but the fresh pasta's the thing here. Try it with gingered chicken or the rainbow trout. An impressive German and Austrian wine list. ■ *On the Bavarian Platzl; (604)427-4820; 170 Spokane St, Kimberley; $$; full bar; AE, DC, MC, V; checks OK; dinner every day, breakfast after June 1 (dinner only in winter).*

The Snowdrift Cafe The local hangout for the young sporting crowd, this small eatery located in a 100-year-old converted house boasts plenty of healthful foods—homemade whole-wheat bread and muffins, vegetarian chili, spinach and caesar salads, a good carbo-loading lasagne for avid skiers and cyclers. The Hungarian mushroom soup, flavored with dill and filled with mushrooms, comes with thick slices of the whole-wheat bread. Locals claim this cafe has the best coffee and cheesecake in the Kootenays. ■ *On the Bavarian Platzl; (604)427-2001; 110 Spokane St, Kimberley; $; full bar; no credit cards; checks OK; lunch, dinner every day.*

LODGINGS

Kirkwood Inn/Inn West Five kilometers from Kimberley, adjacent to the ski and summer resort, is the Kirkwood Inn. There are hotel rooms, but we suggest opting for a condo instead. The condos have kitchens, fireplaces, access to laundry facilities and sauna, hot tub, and swimming pool (seasonal), and the balconies have views of the Rockies (through the trees in front of some). The trailhead of the Nordic ski-trail system is across the parking lot, and the ski lift at the downhill area is a block away. ■ *At the top of the hill at Kimberley Ski Resort; (604)427-7616; 880 North Star Dr, Kimberley; PO Box 247, Kimberley, BC V1A 2Y6; $$$; AE, MC, V; checks OK.*

BOSWELL

LODGINGS

Destiny Bay Resort ★★ German-born Rolf and Hanna Langerfeld brought a bit of Europe to the little town of Boswell on Kootenay Lake. You stay in one of the five sod-roofed cabins or in one of the suites in the lodge. Tall pines shadow the lake view from the decks and the road is a tad too close for such a remote place, but we don't mind the absence of TVs or phones. The reasonably priced restaurant offers some of the best food for miles. On sunny days the wraparound deck on the second floor is the spot—for seafood to schnitzels to herring salads, for the view. ■ *40 minutes from Creston on Hwy 3A; (604)223-8455; 11935 Hwy 3A, Boswell, BC V0B 1A0; $$; beer and wine; MC, V; no checks; breakfast, dinner every day; (open Apr–Oct only).*

CRAWFORD BAY

The tiny community of Crawford Bay, accessible via an hour's ferry ride from Balfour (32 kilometers east of Nelson), happens to be the home of one of BC's finest golf courses, **Kokanee Springs Golf Course**, (604)227-9226. Just up from the ferry dock is the Last Chance Restaurant, a local hangout with darn good sandwiches, (604)227-9477.

LODGINGS

Wedgwood Manor ★★ On 50 acres that tilt westward toward the Purcell Mountains, this lovely 1910 board-and-batten house is one of the finest lodgings in southeastern British Columbia. Downstairs there's a dining room and a parlor with a fireplace (where afternoon tea is served). There are six rooms (all with baths en suite). The four spacious upstairs rooms open onto a quiet, comfortable reading room; the Charles Darwin and Commander's rooms get most of the afternoon sun. The room off the parlor is too tiny, but has a big view of the garden from the double bed. In summer the large front porch is a very pleasant spot from which to gaze out over the big lawn and flower gardens to the Kokanee Glacier across the lake. The owners have taken over the former servants' quarters next door, so the house is entirely yours, so to speak. ■ *East of Nelson on Hwy 3A, take Balfour ferry to Kootenay Bay and head south; (604)227-9233; 16002 Crawford Creek Rd, Crawford Bay; PO Box 135, Crawford Bay, BC V0B 1E0; $$; MC, V; local checks only; (open Apr–Oct only).*

▼

Crawford Bay

▲

ROSEBERY

RESTAURANTS

Wild Rose Cafe It's no problem finding the restaurant, just tough to find the town of Rosebery (population: 50). A small side loop will get you to this tiny Mexican cafe. For the past 12 summers, people have been dropping in for some of Andrea Wright's great Mexican food. Everything's homemade, right down to the beans. Sit out on the porch and enjoy the evening. ■ *In Rosebery, 3 miles north of New Denver; (604)358-7744; Rosebery Loop Rd, New Denver; $; full bar; MC, V; local checks only; dinner Wed–Sun; (closed winters).*

SILVERTON

LODGINGS

Silverton Resort ★ You'll be pleased with this little resort in the heart of the Hidden Valley. Bill and Lorraine Landers's cabins on the shores of Slocan Lake are a great place if you like water play; bring your own or rent their canoes, windsurfer, or rowboat. There are a couple of mountain bikes available, too.

You stay in one of the five hemlock-log cabins—all spotlessly clean and simple and each named after a mythological hero. Some have sleeping lofts, all have kitchens and south-facing decks. They're all at the water's edge (though not far from the road), but Thor 4 is our favorite. A lakefront resort backed by a glacier in the Valhalla Provincial Park, ahhh. ■ *On the lakeshore in Silverton; (604)358-7157; Lake Ave, Silverton; Box 107, Lake Ave, Silverton, BC V0G 2B0; $$; MC, V; local checks only.*

NELSON

Nestled in a valley on the shore of Kootenay Lake, Nelson sprang up with the silver and gold mining back in the late 1890s and has retained its Victorian character. Its main street has changed little in a century, which has drawn more than one filmmaker to use the downtown as a set. More than 350 heritage sites are listed in this picturesque city of about 10,000. For the best overall view of Nelson, stroll to the vista point through **Gyro Park**, on the hillside just north of the town center. The park has picturesque gardens and a nice wading pool for children. An interesting pictorial exhibit of the region's history can be seen at the Nelson Museum, 402 Anderson St, (604)352-9813, which is open year-round. The mountains surrounding Nelson are a mecca for hikers, backcountry skiers, and sightseers; a popular destination is **Kokanee Glacier Provincial Park**, 29 kilometers northeast of Nelson (Ministry of Parks, RR 3, Nelson, BC V1L 5P6; (604)825-4421).

Shopping. Nelson has developed afternoon browsing to a fine art. In addition to the many galleries, there is a plethora of other interesting shops in the downtown area. Outdoor enthusiasts should stop in Snowpack, 333 Baker Street, (604)352-6411; for art and crafts by some of the many regionally based artists, visit the Craft Connection, 441 Baker Street, (604)352-3006. The Kootenay Baker, 295 Baker Street (604)352-2274, boasts one of the best selections of health foods in the region, including organic baked goods.

Art. The art shows and theater brought into Nelson by the town's arts council are well-selected. From theatrical productions to wildlife lectures to classical guitarists to nationally known folk-rock groups, there's almost always something going on at the Capitol Theatre, (604)352-6363. From June through August the entire town turns into an art gallery, with artists' work exhibited in almost 20 shops, restaurants, and galleries. Maps of Artwalk Gallery Tours can be picked up at the Tourist Information Bureau (225 Hall Street, (604)352-3433) or contact Artwalk (Box 422, Nelson, BC V1L 5R2; (604)352-2402). For a calendar of weekly events, pick up a free copy of the *Kootenay Weekly Express.*

Skiing. The small local ski area, Whitewater, provides some of the best (and most) powder in the lower Kootenays. There are only three chairs, with a high percentage of expert runs; call (604)354-4944 or (604)352-7669 (24-hour snow report). Good cross-country ski trails begin at the base of Mount Ymir, where the road to Whitewater leaves the highway.

A scenic day trip through sleepy villages follows Highways 31, 31A, and 6, then loops back into Nelson. On the way, take the 2-hour (round-trip) Balfour ferry across Kootenay Lake to Crawford Bay. It's a pretty trip and happens to be the **world's longest free ferry ride**. Don't miss **Ainsworth Hot Springs**, (604)229-4212, where for $5 you can explore caves of piping-hot (112 degrees), waist-deep water, or swim in the slightly cooler pool (open 365 days a year). The restaurant offers a stunning view of Kootenay Lake and, we've heard (but have yet to confirm), some good food as well. Tour the S.S. *Moyie*, (604)353-2525, a sternwheeler that plied the waters of Kootenay Lake from 1898 until 1957; open summers only, hours vary.

RESTAURANTS

Fiddler's Green ★★ Summer dining is best. But regardless of the season, this is Nelson's favorite spot for a special-occasion dinner. Locals quibble over whether the food is really the best in town, but they agree unanimously that this old estate house has the best atmosphere—and the only garden dining. There are three intimate dining rooms, one larger area (if the season calls for inside dining, ask to sit next to the fireplace). The focus is definitely not on the food—but sometimes, when you're seated next to the fireplace (or at Sunday brunch in the summer garden), the conversation flows, regardless of

▼

Nelson

▲

Nelson

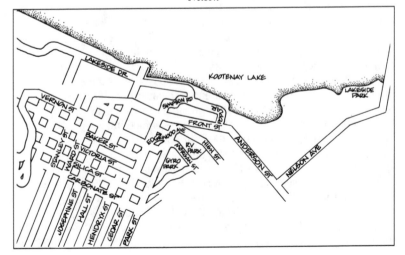

sometimes inconsistent food preparation. ■ *On the north lakeshore, 6 miles north of Nelson; (604)825-4466; Lower 6 Mile Rd, Nelson; $$; full bar; MC, V; local checks only; dinner every day, brunch Sun in summer (winter hours vary).*

Book Garden Cafe Cafe fare and books just seem to go together naturally and this bookstore-eatery combination is no exception. You can always get a fresh salad here; on hot summer days, we recommend the caesar, fresh lemonade, and dessert. The north-side parking lot has become an outdoor eating area and containers filled with blooms help soften the concrete look. Inside during winter, the cafe's a perfect place to while away the hours with a good book. The number of books available here about the Kootenays is impressive. ■ *1 block up the hill from Baker St on Josephine; (604)352-1812; 556 Josephine St, Nelson; $; no alcohol; MC, V; checks OK; breakfast, lunch every day, brunch Sun.*

Wild Onion Cafe Almost everyone in Nelson favors this comfortable downtown cafe for the bagel melts, garlicky caesars, and Heather's roast chicken sandwich served with homemade herb-wine jelly. And almost everyone orders the chocolate Frangelico cheesecake. Mealtimes are busy and service can be slow. ■ *Half block from Baker on Stanley; (604)352-6800; 536 Stanley St, Nelson; $; beer and wine; no checks; MC, V; breakfast, lunch Mon–Sat, dinner Thurs–Sat.*

LODGINGS

Willow Point Lodge ★★ You'll feel quite welcome in Sue and Alan Dodsworth's large, rambling 1922 Victorian perched on a hill amid 3½ spacious acres. The living room has a large stone fireplace. Of the six guest rooms, the spacious Green Room (our favorite) sports a large private, covered balcony looking out toward the Selkirk Mountains and Kootenay Lake. Breakfast is up whenever you are. ■ *4 km north of Nelson on Hwy 3A over Nelson Bridge to Taylor; (604)825-9411; Taylor Dr, Nelson; mail: RR1, S-21, C-31, Nelson, BC V1L 5P4; $$; MC, V; local checks only.*

Emory House ★ A quiet Arts and Crafts–style cottage at the north edge of downtown, the Emory House is perfectly situated for those who want to explore Nelson on foot. Vancouver, natives Michele Dupas and Colin Macrae moved to Nelson in 1993 looking for a house to convert to a bed and breakfast. They found the house's hardwood floors, woodwork, and built-in dining buffet beautifully preserved. Opt for the rooms overlooking the lake rather than the busy street—the home is adjacent to the Civic Centre. Breakfasts here are becoming an event. ■ *At the north end of Vernon St in downtown Nelson; (604)352-7007; 811 Vernon St, Nelson, BC V1L 4G3; $$; MC, V; checks OK.*

Mainland British Columbia

▼

Nelson

Lodgings

Inn the Garden ★ Toronto expatriates Lynda Stevens and Jerry Van Veen recently bought this Victorian (only a couple of blocks from downtown) and decorated it in a garden theme. In Toronto she was a genetics teacher, he was a graphic artist. Of the six guest rooms, three have views of the lake; the Tamarack Suite is a two-bedroom suite. The garden itself is the place for relaxing over afternoon tea, and perhaps for breakfast. ■ *One block south of Baker St between Stanley and Ward; (604) 352-3226; 408 Victoria St, Nelson, V1L 4K5; $$$; AE, MC, V; checks OK.*

KASLO

RESTAURANTS

The Rosewood Cafe The Rosewood adjoins Bayside Books, but it's hardly your typical bookstore cafe, which is why this new restaurant is drawing clientele from as far away as New Denver, a 40-minute drive. Decor is casual and prices reasonable, but the menu is ambitious, especially for the eastern reaches of British Columbia. Appetizers include calamari, Camembert fondue, and French onion soup with three cheeses; entrees range from blackened red fish to tortellini in curry sauce. Everything but the bread is homemade, and that comes from Kaslo's famed Rudolph's Bakery just down the street. ■ *At the end of Kaslo's main street; (604) 353-7673; 1435 Kaslo, Kaslo; $; full bar; MC, V; local checks only; breakfast, lunch, dinner every day.* ❧

NEW DENVER

This former mining town is now noted mainly for its spectacular location on Slocan Lake, with the peaks of the Valhalla Mountains rising more than 7,000 feet on the opposite shore. During World War II, New Denver was the site of an internment camp that housed some 2,000 Japanese-Canadians displaced from their West Coast homes. This shameful period of history has been commemorated with the **Nikkei Internment Memorial Centre**, on Josephine Street off of Third Avenue, (604) 358-2663; the center is open during the summer only, off-season by appointment. For such a small town, New Denver has a fine bookstore, The Motherlode, 317 Sixth Avenue, (604) 358-7274.

LODGINGS

Sweet Dreams Guesthouse The old Craftsman-style former municipal building across the street from Slocan Lake has been renovated and transformed into a delightful B&B comfortably decorated with pine wainscoting and wicker furniture. All five rooms share the bathrooms; room 4 upstairs has the best view of the lake and the breathtaking peaks of the Valhallas beyond. Breakfast is so big it's served in the former courtroom. ■ *One block off New Denver's main street across from the lake; (604)358-2415; 702 Eldorado Ave, New Denver; PO Box 177, New Denver, BC V0G 1S0; $–$$; MC, V; checks OK.*

ROSSLAND

This 1890s Gold Rush town has been experiencing a second boom recently. This time the gold is not in Red Mountain, but on it. **Red Mountain Ski Area**, 3½ miles southwest of town, is one of the more challenging ski areas in British Columbia, with runs steep enough to keep even the most adventurous skiers alert; (604)362-7700, (800)663-0105, or call (604)362-5500 for snow conditions. There are over 40 kilometers of cross-country ski trails (about half are groomed); for information, call **Black Jack Cross-Country Ski Club**, (604)362-5811.

In the summer, the colorful turn-of-the-century main street of tiny Rossland bustles with hikers bound for alpine lakes, mountain bikers en route to explore the numerous trails, or visitors seeking scenery. A good place to get a good look at the town (and its surrounding scenery) is from the rooftop cafe of **Rockingham's**, 2061 Columbia Street, (604)362-7373, with over 30 appetizers. **After the Gold Rush Espresso Bar and Book Store**, 2063 Washington Street, (604)362-5333, with live Celtic music most Sunday nights, is a good place to linger over a latte and a good book. For something a little stiffer, stop by the **Flying Steamshovel Inn and Onlywell Pub**, 2003 Second Avenue, (604)362-5323, a favorite local watering hole named after the unfortunate fellow who piloted—and then crashed—the first helicopter in North America.

Tour the fascinating **Le Roi Gold Mine**, Canada's only hard-rock gold mine open to the public. It's not just another roadside attraction (open May through September); (604)362-7722.

RESTAURANTS

Elmer's Corner The namesake of the elderly landlord, Elmer's Corner is run by two women from Quebec City, who missed the cafes there. Since opening in December 1994, Elmer's has won over locals with its funky atmosphere, homemade breads ,and mostly (but not all) vegetarian entrees. The thin-crust pizzas are excellent; the desserts are not. ■ *2 blocks up from Columbia on Washington; (604)362-5266; 1999 2nd Ave, Rossland; $; MC; local checks only; lunch and dinner Thurs–Sun, dinner only Mon–Wed.*

Sunshine Cafe Virtually anybody will feel comfortable in Rossland's favorite little cafe, which features a range of internationally inspired foods. Sit in the front of the restaurant or walk past the kitchen to the back room. The food doesn't try to be fancy—just good, and there's lots of it. You'll do well to start with the Malaysian egg rolls (ground beef, coconut, and spices) dipped in a plum sauce, and then go on to one of the Mexican dishes, the Budgie burger (boneless breast of chicken with ham and Swiss), or a simple entree such as the curried chicken. Huevos rancheros are a favorite of the breakfast crowd. Mealtimes are crowded, and during ski season, weekend reservations are recommended. No smoking. ▪ *In the middle of town on the main street; (604)362-7630; 2116 Columbia Ave, Rossland; $; beer and wine; MC, V; local checks only; breakfast, lunch, dinner every day.*

LODGINGS

Ram's Head Inn ★★ Dave and Doreen Butler's comfortable nonsmoking inn is the choice place to stay in this mountainous part of the province: it's just a few hundred yards' walk to the Red Mountain ski area. Of 12 rooms, the 3 new rooms in the recently built addition are the plushest, but as of press time the rest were scheduled for renovations. Still, it's the comfortable public room that's best, with a lofty ceiling, a stone fireplace, and big windows looking out to the wooded backyard. Package deals combine lift tickets with a bed and a full breakfast, not to mention the hot tub and sauna. Young children are quietly discouraged. ▪ *Red Mountain Rd, about 3 kilometers north of Rossland; (604)362-9577; Red Mountain Rd, Rossland; Box 636, Rossland, BC V0G 1Y0; $$–$$$; AE, MC, V; checks OK.*

Angela's Place British transplant Angela Wright "guarantees" her accommodations, casual and fun as they should be in this ski town. If you stay downstairs in the apartment with the fireplace, Wright will serve up a delicious skier's breakfast in her breakfast nook, meanwhile entertaining you with her brash brand of British humor; but if she likes you and isn't rushing out to the slopes herself, she might make you breakfast even if you stay in the upstairs suite, which has its own kitchen. The outdoor tub is for anyone. Prices are also flexible; she uses an honor-system sliding scale. This is a ski season–only place; Wright heads for the coast in the summers. ▪ *On Spokane, 4 blocks down the hill from the Uplander Hotel; (604)362-7790; 1520 Spokane St, Rossland; Box 944, Rossland, BC V0G 1Y0; $–$$; no credit cards; checks OK; (closed summers).*

Calendar of Events

Chinese New Year In January or February (depending on the lunar calendar) the International District greets the Chinese New Year with a fanfare of festivals and displays and a lively parade complete with lion dancers. ■ *International District, Seattle, WA; (206)623-5124.*

Great Northwest Chili Cook-off The chili cookoff benefits the Washington Park Zoo, raising funds for expansion and for the care of the animals. About 30 different chilis are sampled by no fewer than 2,500 visitors. ■ *Memorial Park Coliseum, Portland, OR; (503)226-1561.*

Women in View Festival This festival, whose mandate is to showcase work initiated by women, presents a variety of performances, workshops, and networking sessions highlighting the creative achievements of women in music, theater, dance, storytelling, and other art forms. ■ *Various venues around Vancouver, BC; (604)685-6684.*

Chilly Hilly Bike Ride Held the third Sunday in February, this 28-mile family ride sponsored by the Cascade Bicycle Club has come to be recognized as the opening day of bike season. Up to 4,000 cyclists fill the morning ferries to Winslow. Don't expect the weather to be warm or the road to be flat. ■ *Bainbridge Island, WA; (206)522-BIKE.*

Fat Tuesday Seattle's week-long Mardi Gras celebration brings a colorful parade and the beat of Cajun, jazz, and R&B to the streets and clubs of Pioneer Square. Nightclubs levy a joint cover charge, and proceeds from several events benefit Northwest Harvest, a local food bank. Held the week before Lent. ■ *Pioneer Square, Seattle, WA; (206)622-2563.*

Newport Seafood & Wine Festival Nearly 100 wineries from Oregon, Washington, California, and Idaho are the highlight of this seafood and wine festival on the central Oregon coast. ■ *Newport Marina, Newport, OR; (800)262-7844.*

Northwest Flower and Garden Show This enormous horticultural happening occupies almost 5 acres at the Convention Center for five days in mid-February. Landscapers, nurseries, florists, and noncommercial gardeners outdo themselves with over 300 demonstration gardens and booths. Shuttle bus service is available from Northgate and Longacres. General admission is $9, evenings $8. ■ *Washington State Convention and Trade Center, Seattle, WA; (206)789-5333.*

Oregon Shakespeare Festival An unassuming little college town, set in lovely ranch country, just happens to house one of the oldest and largest regional theater companies in the country. Almost 100,000 visitors a year (from February to October) attend the festival and crowd into the three theaters. Lectures, backstage tours, and Renaissance music and dance are other attractions. Last-minute tickets are rare but not nonexistent in the summer. ▪ *Citywide, Ashland, OR; (503)482-4331.*

Rain or Shine Dixieland Jazz Festival Every Presidents' Day weekend, rain or shine, Aberdeen hosts top Dixieland bands from up and down the West Coast. New bands take over every set. Multiple venues keep the town hoppin'. ▪ *Citywide, Aberdeen, WA; (360)533-2910.*

MARCH

Kandahar Ski Race Now in its 43rd year, this is possibly the last amateur-status, free-fall downhill race in existence. Anyone with the guts and a helmet can register. Generally held the first week in March. ▪ *Forbidden Plateau Resort, Courtenay, BC; (604)334-7944.*

Oregon State Special Olympics More than 400 developmentally disabled athletes compete in ice skating and downhill and cross-country skiing in preparation for the big international Special Olympics. ▪ *Mount Bachelor, Bend, OR; (503)382-2442.*

Pacific Rim Whale Festival Migrating gray whales can be observed during March and April just off the shores of the Long Beach section of Pacific Rim National Park. Numerous charter boats and a seaplane company offer close-up looks at the pods. The actual festival, including dances and education programs, begins the last week in March. ▪ *Tofino, BC; (604)725-3414.*

Vancouver Storytelling Festival Few events underline Vancouver's ethnic mix as well as the storytelling festival, held for three days at various West End locations. More than 20 participants, including First Nations and other storytellers spinning tales in five different languages (translators come too), hold audiences spellbound. ▪ *Vancouver, BC; (604)876-2272.*

Whale Migration From March to May, the gray whales return to Alaska from Baja California, where they winter and calve. Along the Washington and Oregon coasts are a number of excellent whale-watching spots; some towns, such as Westport, Washington, and Newport, Oregon, offer charters especially for whale-seekers. The return migration happens from October to December, a less favorable time for whale watching due to the weather. ▪ *For information, call the chamber of commerce, Westport, WA, (360)268-9422, or Newport, OR, (503)265-8801.*

APRIL

Brant Festival This festival celebrates the stopover of the brant (a species of geese) on their migration from Mexico to Canada. Staging areas provide fine opportunities to view the geese, once nearly extinct, as they feed. Wildlife art, photography exhibits, and carving competitions too. ▪ *Parksville, BC; (604)248-4117.*

Cherry Festival This week-long event has parades, cherry orchard tours, dances, a carnival, and golf and tennis tournaments. Held the second Sunday after Easter. ■ *The Dalles, OR; (503)296-2231.*

Daffodil Festival Grand Floral Parade The Daffodil Festival, a springtime tradition for over 60 years, celebrates the fields of gold in the Puyallup Valley. One of the largest floral parades in the nation visits downtown Tacoma, Puyallup, Sumner, and Orting—all in one day. ■ *Tacoma, WA; (206)627-6176.*

Hood River Blossom Festival The coordinators of this event assure us that any similarities between it and the one in The Dalles are purely coincidental. Altogether, there are 30 to 40 different things happening throughout the valley. Tours of the blossoming fruit orchards and wineries along a 40-mile loop are available. ■ *Hood River Valley, OR; (800)366-3530.*

International Wine Festival The largest and most prestigious wine event in Canada, the five-day festival attracted 7,000 visitors in 1995, when 12 countries were represented by 125 different wineries. Events include a Bacchanalia gala and complimentary palate cleansers. ■ *Vancouver Trade and Convention Center, Vancouver, BC; (604)873-3311.*

Seattle Mariners Baseball The crowd is predictably loyal—even to a team whose performance is not so predictable. Although the playing can be truly inspired (and Ken Griffey, Jr., is truly inspiring), the outlook for the next few seasons isn't particularly bright. The season lasts from early April through the first week of October. Bring your own peanuts (Kingdome food is too expensive and not too good) and prepare to get lively if you're sitting in the left-field stands. Tickets are cheap ($6 to $16). ■ *Kingdome, Seattle, WA; (206)628-3555.*

Skagit Valley Tulip Festival When the 1,500 acres of tulips burst into brilliant color in early April, Mount Vernon seizes the moment and entertains visitors with a street fair and the Taste of Skagit. Makes a nice—and flat—bicycle trip. ■ *60 miles north of Seattle via I-5, Mount Vernon, WA; (360)42-TULIP.*

TerrifVic Dixieland Jazz Festival Twenty Dixieland jazz bands from all over the world shake up the town for five days. Sixty dollars gets you an event badge good for every concert in every location. Shuttle service is available between participating hotels and the eight concert locations. ■ *Victoria, BC; (604)381-5277.*

Yakima Spring Barrel Tasting In late April, 20 wineries from Union Gap to Kiona hold special open houses to educate the public on the finer points of winemaking. Both owners and winemakers are on hand to explain the process, and wines from the barrel—some two or three years away from maturity—are available for tasting. Individual wineries add entertainment and food. ■ *Various wineries, Yakima, WA; call for map, (509)829-6027.*

MAY

Bloomsday Run Now the world's largest timed road race, Spokane's Bloomsday Run attracts thousands every year (over 50,000 runners) during the area's

Lilac Festival; (509)326-3339. Everyone who crosses the finish line gets an official Bloomsday T-shirt and his or her name in the city's major newspapers. Be sure to book hotel rooms well in advance (a year beforehand is advised). ■ *Spokane, WA; (509)838-1579.*

International Children's Festival This popular event brings in children's performers from all over the world. Crafts, storytelling, puppet shows, and musical and theater performances entertain kids and their parents for six days in early May. ■ *Seattle Center, Seattle, WA; (206)684-7346.*

National Western Art Show and Auction For nearly 20 years the three-day event has brought artists from all over the country to this college town off I-90. A hundred display rooms turned into mini-studios offer paintings and sculptures for sale. Three auctions are held as well, including one benefiting Elmview Industries for the community's developmentally disabled. ■ *Ellensburg, WA; (509)962-2934.*

Northwest Folklife Festival The largest folk fest in the nation runs throughout Memorial Day weekend and brings many ethnic groups and their folk-art traditions (dance, music, crafts, and food) to stages throughout the Seattle Center. A must. ■ *Seattle Center, Seattle, WA; (206)684-7300.*

Opening Day of Yachting Season Boat owners from all over the Northwest come to this festive ceremonial regatta, which officially kicks off the nautical summer. Arrive early to watch the world-class University of Washington rowing team race other nationally ranked teams through the Montlake Cut. Parade registration for watercraft is free. ■ *Lake Washington/Lake Union, Seattle, WA; Seattle Yacht Club, (206)325-1000.*

Poulsbo Viking Fest In mid-May, Puget Sound's "Little Norway" celebrates Scandinavian independence with a weekend of folk dancing and live music, a carnival and parade, and a lutefisk-eating contest (definitely an acquired taste). ■ *Poulsbo, WA; (360)779-4848.*

Rhododendron Festival This is the oldest festival in town, and it improves every year. Highlights of this two-week–long event include a Rover Run (dog and owner), beard contest (scruffiest, longest), adult tricycle race, carnival, senior citizen coronation and dance, and more. The "Grand Finale" is a classic parade; the "Anti-Climax Grand Finale" is the 12K Rhody Run. See all of the Rhododendron Queens' handprints in cement in downtown Port Townsend. ■ *Port Townsend, WA; (360)385-2722.*

Sand Castle Day Oregon's original and most prestigious sand castle contest began in 1964. Today, buckets, shovels, and squirt guns aid the 1,000-plus contestants in producing their transient creations. Upward of 15,000 spectators show up to view the masterpieces. ■ *Cannon Beach, OR; (503)436-2623.*

Seattle International Film Festival Founded in 1976 by Darryl Macdonald and Dan Ireland, the 3½-week Seattle International Film Festival brings films for every taste—high art to slapstick—to Seattle theaters every May and June. Fans of the obscure will appreciate SIFF's archival treasures and independent films. Series tickets (full and partial) go on sale in January

(Cinema Seattle, 801 E Pine Street, Seattle, WA 98122). ▪ *Citywide, Seattle, WA; (206)324-9996.*

Ski-to-Sea Festival A Bellingham civic festival over Memorial Day weekend that revolves around an 80-mile-plus, seven-event relay race that includes skiing, running, cycling, canoeing, and sailing. ▪ *From Mount Baker to Marine Park, Bellingham, WA; (360)734-1330.*

Slug Races In the Pacific Northwest, spring and slugs seem to go hand in hand. During Florence's Rhododendron Festival, the main attraction is the slug race. Watch the local gastropods slime their way toward victory. ▪ *Old Town, Florence, OR; (503)997-3128.*

Strawberry Festival The main attraction at this festive event is the world's largest strawberry shortcake (see the *Guinness Book of World Records*). Standing several feet tall and weighing a couple of tons, it's big enough for everyone to get a bite. Made with fresh strawberries, of course. ▪ *Lebanon, OR; (503)258-7164.*

Swiftsure Race Weekend Held every Memorial Day weekend, this event attracts boats from North America and foreign ports. Three races are held, the longest going west out the Strait of Juan de Fuca to the Pacific and back. Spectators can watch the vessels from Clover Point or Ogden Point. ▪ *Victoria, BC; (604)592-2441.*

U.S. Bank Pole, Pedal, Paddle Held mid-May, this grueling test of endurance is one of Central Oregon's most popular multisport events, complete with street fair and food. The six-leg relay begins with an alpine skiing run on Mount Bachelor; followed by 8 kilometers of cross-country skiing; a 22-mile, mostly downhill bike ride to Bend's Colorado Avenue; a 2-mile paddle on the Deschutes River; and, finally, a 400-meter footrace across the grass in Drake Park. Open to teams, pairs, and individuals. ▪ *Mount Bachelor, Bend, OR; (503)388-0002.*

Vancouver Children's Festival The first children's festival in North America is celebrating its 18th year in 1995, with kite-making, clay sculpture, papier-mâché, dance, music, and puppetry. Outdoors in Vancouver's Vanier Park. ▪ *Vanier Park, Vancouver, BC; (604)687-7697.*

Washington State Apple Blossom Festival When the apple trees burst into bloom in early May, Wenatchee hosts an 11-day festival (the oldest in the state) featuring arts, crafts, and plenty of food. ▪ *Citywide, Wenatchee, WA; (800)57-APPLE.*

JUNE

AquaSox Baseball The Seattle Mariners' farm team plays real baseball on real grass in real sunshine from mid-June through August. In 1990, the 1,800-seat Everett Memorial Stadium was enlarged to 3,000 seats to accommodate the ever-growing number of fans. Tickets are $7 for adults, $5 for kids 12 and under. Call for season schedule. ▪ *Everett Memorial Stadium, Everett, WA; (206)258-3673.*

BC Lions Football Some people feel that a wider field and one fewer down than in American ball make Canadian football more exciting. Action is the name of the game in this eight-team league. The season lasts from late June to late November and culminates in the Grey Cup Game, the Canadian version of the Super Bowl. ▪ *BC Place Stadium, Vancouver, BC; (604)280-4400.*

Britt Festival This musical extravaganza runs from mid-June through September in the hillside field where Peter Britt, a famous local photographer and horticulturist, used to have his home. A handsome shell has been constructed, and listeners sit on benches or loll on blankets under the stars. Programs run the gamut: classical, folk, country, jazz, musical theater, and dance. ▪ *Jacksonville, OR; (503)773-6077.*

Centrum Summer Arts Festival From June through September, one of the most successful cultural programs in Washington enlightens thousands with a multitude of workshops held by the nation's leading artists and musicians. For fiddlers, there's the Festival of American Fiddle Tunes. Jazz musicians can hone their skills at the Bud Shank Workshop or listen to the music at Jazz Port Townsend, one of the West Coast's foremost mainstream jazz festivals. Workshops are held at Fort Worden State Park; performances take place on the park grounds or at various locations around town. During the Marrowstone Music Festivals, young virtuoso musicians perform in two symphony orchestras. There are also a writers conference and theater performances. ▪ *Port Townsend, WA; (360)385-3102.*

Chamber Music Northwest One of the finest summer festivals in the country, distinguished by the caliber of its performances, takes place in Portland at Reed College and Catlin Gabel School from late June through late July. ▪ *Portland, OR; (503)223-3202.*

du Maurier Ltd. International Jazz Festival More than 500 musicians from Africa, Japan, Europe, and North and South America appear during the two-week festival, which presents the full spectrum of traditional and contemporary jazz. Happens at the end of June and beginning of July, including Canada Day weekend. ▪ *Vancouver, BC; (604)682-0706.*

Fremont Fair Fremont celebrates the beginning of summer with a solstice parade, music, craft booths, food, and dance. This event gets bigger, better, and crazier every year. Along the Fremont Ship Canal. ▪ *Seattle, WA; (206)548-8376.*

Northwest Garlic Festival This two-day affair attracts about 20,000 people each year. A street fair, live music, and a garlic-peeling contest are just a few of the events that will keep you busy all day. A garlic-eating contest may keep your enemies at bay. ▪ *Ocean Park, WA; (800)451-2542.*

Northwest Microbrewery Festival Thirty-six microbrews, live music, food, beer tasting, and forums are the highlights of this festival, held outdoors at the Herbfarm. ▪ *The Herbfarm, Fall City, WA; (206)784-2222.*

Olympic Music Festival The Philadelphia String Quartet opens its season with one of the Puget Sound area's premier music festivals, held in a turn-of-the-century barn nestled on 40 acres of pastoral farmland on the Olympic Peninsula. Sit in the barn on hay bales ($16) or spread a picnic on the lawn ($8). The festival spans 10 weekends. Bring a blanket. ▪ *Quilcene, WA; (206)527-8839.*

Rose Festival The Rose Festival is to auto racing what Seattle's Seafair is to boat racing. This 24-day celebration culminates in INDY CAR 200, a race featuring Indianapolis 500–style cars. Don't forget to catch the parade and stop in at the festival center. ▪ *Citywide, Portland, OR; (503)227-2681.*

Seattle. International Music Festival Previously known as the Santa Fe Chamber Music Festival, the SIMF (under new artistic director Dmitry Sitkovetsky) has plans to expand the format to include vocal and orchestral music as well as chamber music. ▪ *Various locations, Seattle and Bellevue, WA; (206)622-1392.*

Seattle-to-Portland Bicycle Ride (STP) There is a 10,000-rider limit for this 200-mile bike ride from Seattle to Portland sponsored by the Cascade Bicycle Club. Complete the course in one or two days (overnight facilities are provided at the halfway point). Registration is first come, first served. ▪ *Seattle, WA; (206)522-BIKE.*

Umpqua Valley Summer Arts Festival Over 100 booths, featuring every kind of art imaginable, sprout up in the park around the Art Center in Roseburg the last weekend in June. You'll find pottery, silk scarves, jewelry, teddy bears, quilts, folk art, porcelain, woven baskets, and stained-glass items (just to name a few). ▪ *Roseburg, OR; (503)672-2532.*

Washington State Special Olympics In 1968 an act of Congress created the organization known as the Special Olympics. It has since grown to be the world's largest sports-training and competition program for the developmentally disabled. The June event is the biggest competition in Washington. ▪ *Call for location; (206)362-4949.*

JULY

Bellevue Jazz Festival Top Northwest jazz artists entertain outdoors for two days, during the third weekend in July. Tickets are $10 (general admission), $8 (teens and seniors), and one concert is free. ▪ *Bellevue Downtown Park, Bellevue, WA; (206)451-6887.*

Bite of Seattle A chompfest that brings cheap nibbles from some 60 restaurants to Seattle Center on the third weekend in July. Admission is free. ▪ *Seattle Center, Seattle, WA; (206)232-2982.*

Camlann Medieval Faire Held on Saturdays and Sundays in July and August, this "faire" attracts thousands of people. Dancing, medieval food, performances, and a tournament of knights highlight the event. Admission $8. ▪ *Carnation, WA; (206)788-1353.*

Chinatown International District Summer Festival This mid-July extravaganza celebrates the richness and diversity of Asian culture with dancing, music, martial arts performances, food booths, and arts and crafts. A children's corner features puppetry, storytelling, and magic shows; various craft demonstrations (classical ikebana, a Japanese tea ceremony, basketry, calligraphy, and Hawaiian lei-making) take place in the cultural corner. ▪ *Hing Hay Park, Seattle, WA; (206) 728-0123.*

Coombs Country Bluegrass Festival A three-day weekend of gospel, country, and bluegrass. Performers such as Rural Delivery and the Rocky Mountain Boys have been major attractions in the past. Tickets are sold for each day. Rough camping is available on a first-come, first-served basis. ▪ *Coombs, BC; (604) 248-5142.*

Darrington Bluegrass Festival Every summer during the third weekend in July, bluegrass fans from all over the country turn their attention to the tiny town of Darrington, nestled in the Cascade foothills. Terrific foot-stomping, thigh-slapping bluegrass music is played outdoors by the country's best musicians. A convenient ticket package includes three nights of camping and three days of music: $60 for couples, $35 single. ▪ *Darrington, WA; (360) 436-1177.*

Folk Music Festival What better way to international peace and understanding than through the universal language of music? Last year over 200 performers from 12 countries came together for three days. There is a bewildering array of ticket options. The most economical is to form a group of 15 or more to qualify for a discount; a pass for the weekend is about $84 in advance, $90 at the gate. Buy early—admission is limited. ▪ *Jericho Park, Vancouver, BC; (604) 879-2931.*

Fort Vancouver Fourth of July Fireworks The best fireworks in Oregon are across the Columbia River in Washington. Portlanders flock to the National Historic Site of Fort Vancouver for a day of activities and stage entertainment, climaxing in the largest free aerial display west of the Mississippi. The bombardment lasts at least a full hour. ▪ *Vancouver, WA; (206) 694-2432.*

Harrison Festival of the Arts During this nine-day event, over 35,000 people visit Harrison Hot Springs to celebrate the musical, visual, and performing arts of a different set of countries each year. Activities include theater, lectures, workshops, and live entertainment. ▪ *Harrison Hot Springs, BC; (604) 796-3664.*

King County Fair The oldest county fair in the state is also its best, featuring five days of music by top country acts, a rodeo, 4-H and FFA exhibits, a loggers' show (remember ax-throwing contests?), crafts, and food. Begins the third Wednesday of July. ▪ *King County Fairgrounds, Enumclaw, WA; (360) 825-7777.*

McChord Air Show Come see pilots in action as the F-16s do their thing. Afterward watch military demonstrations—from an all-services attack demo to antique aircraft—and get your picture taken in the cockpit of a jet. In July or August; call for dates. ▪ *McChord Air Force Base, Tacoma, WA; (206) 984-5637.*

Pacific Northwest Scottish Highland Games Kilts are not the only thing you'll find here. Scottish piping, drumming, dancing, Parade of the Clans, and games are the major attractions, not to mention a chance to sample authentic Scottish food and drink. Seven dollars gets you in for the day. ▪ *King County Fairgrounds, Enumclaw, WA; (360) 522-2541.*

San Juan Island Dixieland Jazz Festival A three-day festival, $45 for all three days, sponsored by the San Juan Island Goodtime Classic Jazz Association, brings Dixieland fans out to enjoy the jazz of yesteryear, mid- to late July. ▪ *Friday Harbor, San Juan Island, WA; (360) 378-5509.*

Sand-Sations Sand Castle Contest Hundreds of children and children-at-heart flock to this annual event to build their sand castle masterpieces. With judging in all sorts of categories (teamwork, effort, intricacy, suitability to sand), there are prizes totaling $3,000. At least 10,000 people show up to watch the artists at work. ▪ *Long Beach, WA; (360) 642-2400.*

Seafair Seattle's frenzied summer fête has been around since 1950 and—to the chagrin of many locals—isn't likely to go away. The hoopla begins on the third weekend of July with the milk-carton boat races at Green Lake and ends the first Sunday in August, when the hydroplanes tear up the waters of Lake Washington. Bright spots include a couple of triathlons, some excellent ethnic festivals (International District Festival, mid-July; Bon Odori, late July; Hispanic Seafair Festival, late July), and the Torchlight Parade (the Friday before the hydroplane races), which is a full-scale march in the downtown area and a kids' delight. Almost all Seafair events are free. ▪ *Citywide, Seattle, WA; (206) 728-0123.*

Seattle Fourth of July Fireworks Dueling fireworks: the Lake Union version, sponsored by Cellular One, explodes to the sound of the Seattle Symphony at Gas Works Park, while Ivar's Elliott Bay show is best viewed from Myrtle Edwards Park. A lucky few who think to make reservations for a late dinner at the Space Needle can view them both. The pyrotechnics start just after dark. ▪ *Seattle, WA; Ivar's, (206) 587-6500; Cellular One, (206) 622-5123.*

Sweet Onion Festival Fort Walla Walla Park celebrates the sweetest onion around with the onion-slicing contest, the two-headed onion shot put, the onion hunt, the onion-dish recipe contest and cook-off, and the onion ringtoss. ▪ *Walla Walla, WA; (509) 525-0850.*

Vancouver International Comedy Festival Watch out, *Improv*, Vancouver has a 10-day shindig with international comedians that'll knock your socks off. You'll find roving street entertainers as well as scheduled shows. ▪ *Granville Island, Vancouver, BC; (604) 683-0883.*

Vancouver Sea Festival This festival has everything from puppet shows and sand castle contests to a whole slew of sports demonstrations and competitions. ▪ *English Bay, BC; (604) 684-3378.*

Victoria International Festival Artists from the Northwest gather at various Victoria venues to give classical music concerts, recitals, and ballet performances throughout the months of July and August. ▪ *Victoria, BC; (604) 736-2119.*

Waterfront Blues Festival National blues artists such as Charlie Musselwhite play at this four-day benefit for the Oregon Food Bank. The shows are free, although sponsors accept donations of food and money. A big event: in 1992, 60,000 fans turned out. ■ *McCall Waterfront Park, Portland, OR; (503)282-0555.*

Whistler Country & Blues Festival The third weekend in July, enjoy the sounds of country, blues, rockabilly, and zydeco onstage at Whistler. Don't miss the Whistler Chili Cook-off! ■ *Whistler, BC; (604)932-3928.*

Winthrop Rhythm and Blues Fest This late-July festival has attracted such national performers as Mick Taylor and John Mayall, as well as the best of the local bands. Now it has been expanded to three days, and events include a New Orleans–style street dance in the Old West streets of Winthrop and a full day of steamy blues under the blazing sun at Twin Lakes. A popular event with the Harley-Davidson crowd. ■ *Winthrop, WA; (509)996-2111.*

AUGUST

The Bite, A Taste of Portland Eat to your heart's content and help Special Olympics at the same time. Thirty restaurants and 20 wineries offer scores of delectables while performers at different venues entertain you. ■ *McCall Waterfront Park, Portland, OR; (503)248-0600.*

Evergreen State Fair For 11 days in late August through Labor Day, this fair features country music headliners, roping and riding, stock-car races, a lumberjack show, a carnival, and a chili cook-off. Great fun. ■ *Monroe, WA; (360)794-7832.*

Filburg Festival This sophisticated arts and crafts festival continues to grow in reputation as one of the region's finest juried shows. Woodwork, glass, pottery, and woven goods are just a few of the things on display. ■ *Comox, BC; (604)334-3234.*

Fine Arts Show Residents of southern Vancouver Island display their paintings and sculptures in the largest juried art show and sale in BC. A $10 admission is good for the entire 10-day event. ■ *Sooke Region Museum, Sooke, BC; (604)642-6351.*

Gig Harbor Jazz Festival The grassy natural amphitheater makes a great setting for a festival that draws national jazz artists. Boat owners can sail up to the site. ■ *Celebrations Meadow, Gig Harbor, WA; (206)627-1504.*

International Airshow Want to see a Russian MIG up close or watch wingwalkers defy gravity? How about the flying aerobatics of the U.S. Thunderbirds and the Canadian Snowbirds? Abbotsford International Airshow has it all and more. ■ *Abbotsford Airport, BC; (604)852-8511.*

Mount Hood Festival of Jazz Definitely one of the premier festivals around, this weekend affair has featured such greats as Diane Schuur, Lou Rawls, and the Count Basie Band. Tickets are around $27.50 a day. ■ *Gresham, OR; (503)666-3810.*

Omak Stampede and Suicide Run A hair-raising and controversial horse race: horses plunge down a 255-foot hill with a 120-foot vertical drop into the Okanogan River, which they race across to reach the arena. The stampede events last for three days; ticket prices range from $5 to $10. ■ *Stampede Grounds, Omak, WA; (509)826-1002.*

Oregon State Fair It's everything a fair should be: food, games, rides, horse shows, and live entertainment. For 12 days the people of Salem go hog-wild. Ends on Labor Day. ■ *Salem, OR; (503)378-3247.*

Washington State International Kite Festival On the last day of this colorful, high-flying week, the Festival of Kites attempts to break its own record for number of kites in the air. Every day there's a different event, from lighted kites to handcrafted kites to stunt fun and games. The glorious spectacle is free to watch, but flying your own will cost you $20. The entire Long Beach peninsula is booked by January in anticipation, so plan (way) ahead. ■ *Long Beach, WA; (360)642-2400.*

Washington State Open Tennis Tournament The top players in Washington and the men's western pro circuit compete side by side during the first week in August at the exclusive Seattle Tennis Club. Tickets range from $1 to $5, and it's worth the admission just to stroll the idyllic grounds. Order tickets in advance. ■ *Seattle, WA; (206)324-3200.*

SEPTEMBER

Artquake Over Labor Day weekend, Portlanders let loose a grand celebration of the performing and fine arts. The Center for the Performing Arts is the hub of the festival, although there are events throughout the downtown area, especially in Pioneer Courthouse Square. There is no admission charge for many Artquake events; others ask a nominal entrance fee. ■ *Center for the Performing Arts and Park Blocks, Portland, OR; (503)227-2787.*

Bumbershoot The largest multi-arts festival north of San Francisco is a splendid and eclectic celebration. Select craftspeople, writers, and 500 performing artists on 15 stages throughout Seattle Center entertain the hordes over the long Labor Day weekend. A $10 daily pass ($9 if you buy in advance) is all you need to stay thoroughly entertained. ■ *Seattle Center, Seattle, WA; (206)682-4386.*

Ellensburg Rodeo The biggest rodeo in these parts brings riders in from far and wide for four days of Wild West events over Labor Day weekend. Admission to the big, colorful event is $9 to $18, depending on your seat. ■ *Ellensburg, WA; (509)962-7831.*

Fall Kite Festival Lincolnites love to fly kites of all shapes and colors, and last year so did over 20,000 people who attended the festivities; these include a lighted show at night and a Japanese-style kite battle, which entails teams of 5 to 25 people trying to knock each other's kites out of the sky. Prizes are awarded in various categories. ■ *Lincoln City, OR; (800)452-2151.*

Leavenworth Autumn Leaf Festival The last weekend of September is a grand time for a drive through the Cascade Mountains to Leavenworth, a mountain town gussied-up Tyrolean-style and home of this festival celebrating the glory of our deciduous trees. A parade, arts and crafts, and Bavarian music are all part of the festivities. Most events are free. ▪ *Leavenworth, WA; (509) 548-5807.*

Pendleton Round-Up and Happy Canyon This four-day rodeo, complete with cowboys, bucking broncos, bulls, and clowns, is said to be one of the biggest in the country. Over 500 contestants and 50,000 spectators make it so. Admission ranges from $7 to $15. A carnival downtown keeps things hopping while the rodeo riders are recovering. ▪ *Pendleton, OR; (800) 45-RODEO.*

Seattle Seahawks Football The Seahawks may play conservative ball (and may have seen better seasons than the next few promise to be), but the fans' loyalty is steadfast. Consequently, it's nearly impossible to get tickets ($19 to $38), and Kingdome-area parking is a crunch, so take a free bus from downtown. The season starts in September (preseason games in August) and runs through December; games are usually Sundays at 1pm. Avoid scalpers. ▪ *Kingdome, Seattle, WA; (206) 827-9766.*

Vancouver International Film Festival Similar to the film fest held in Seattle (see May), this event at the end of September/beginning of October features over 250 films from 40 countries. Prices are about $7 per movie. Order tickets by mid-September; (604) 685-8297. ▪ *Vancouver, BC; (604) 685-0260.*

Western Washington State Fair This 17-day extravaganza begins in early September. It's the rural fair you remember from your childhood, only bigger. Rodeo, music, barnyard animals, carnival rides, exhibits, and vast amounts of food (including the legendary scones and onion burgers) make for kid—and grown-up—heaven. ▪ *Puyallup, WA; (206) 841-5045.*

OCTOBER

Bibliomania The Northwest's first annual book festival, focusing on reading and literacy, had its debut in 1995 with a wide range of programs, including author appearances and signings, book publisher and seller exhibits, multimedia demonstrations, children's bookmaking activities, panel discussions, writing workshops, and more. ▪ *Pier 48, Seattle, WA; (206) 789-9868.*

Children's Show A plethora of activities, such as workshops, fashion shows, and entertainment, geared toward kids from toddlers to preteens. A three-day kids' event ($6). ▪ *Pacific National Exhibit, Showmart Building, Vancouver, BC; (604) 684-4616.*

International Writer's and Reader's Festival This five-day event during the third week of October brings together more than 50 Canadian and international authors, playwrights, and poets from diverse cultural backgrounds, life experiences, and places of origin, writing in every conceivable genre. Readings, interviews, and a poetry bash are informative, challenging, and entertaining. ▪ *Granville Island, BC; (604) 681-6330.*

Issaquah Salmon Days Issaquah celebrates the return of the salmon the first weekend of October with a parade, food, crafts, music, dancing, and displays. At the state fish hatchery you can get excellent views of the chinook and coho thrashing up the ladder. ▪ *Issaquah, WA; (206)392-0661.*

Portland Winterhawks Ice Hockey See tomorrow's NHL players today in the WHL (Western Hockey League). This developmental league grooms young hockey players for the big time (34 former Winterhawks have already made it). The 72-game season runs from October through March, with prices topping out at about $10.50. ▪ *Memorial Coliseum, Portland, OR, (503)238-6366.*

Salmon Festival When the salmon come home to spawn, the people of Gresham celebrate with an annual 8K run, a salmon bake, and arts and crafts. The name of the game here is environmental education. Old-growth and salmon-viewing walks (where you can see the fish spawning in the Sandy River Gorge) are conducted to teach the importance of our natural resources. ▪ *Oxbow Park, Gresham, OR; (503)248-5050.*

Vancouver Canucks Hockey A promising NHL team that made a name for itself in 1994, the Canucks host such teams as the Edmonton Oilers and the Calgary Flames. Season runs from October through April, and tickets are between $23 and $58. ▪ *Pacific Coliseum, Vancouver, BC; (604)254-5141.*

Vancouver Opera The season runs from October to June, with five different performances offering extraordinary melodies, captivating drama, and magnificent sets and costumes. Call for performance dates. ▪ *Queen Elizabeth Theatre, Vancouver, BC; (604)683-0222.*

West Coast Oyster Shucking Championship and Seafood Festival On the first full weekend in October, Shelton holds this very serious oyster shucking competition (the winner goes on to compete in nationals), along with a wine-tasting and a seafood cook-off. ▪ *Shelton, WA; (206)426-2021.*

NOVEMBER

Portland Trailblazers Basketball The Portland Trailblazers are not the most winning NBA team, but their home games are among the most exciting (and earsplitting). They've sold out every home game for the last 10 years! Tickets range from $10 to $50. ▪ *Memorial Coliseum, Portland, OR; (503)224-4400.*

Rainy Day Film Festival For eight years now, the folks at the museum have been showing films on the second Sunday of the month from November through April. Themes in the past have included nature and history, and featured artists have included Buster Keaton and Alfred Hitchcock. $3.50 per family. ▪ *Douglas County Museum, Roseburg, OR; (503)440-4507.*

Seattle SuperSonics Basketball From early November to late April, Seattle's home team tears up the court. In the past, the Sonics have played smart, competitive, and uneven basketball; they have a bright future, so grab tickets early ($7 to $65). Games are at 7pm. ▪ *Seattle Center Coliseum, Seattle, WA; (206)281-5850.*

Christmas Lighting Crafts, music, and food are part of the ceremony kicking off the Christmas season in Leavenworth. Around 4:45pm (usually on the first and second Saturdays of the month) the Bavarian village square is officially lit up for the season. Evening concerts and sleigh rides are the only things that require money. ■ *Leavenworth, WA; (509)548-5807.*

Community Hanukkah Celebration The arts and crafts, Hanukkah wares, games for children, and latke brunch are just the side attractions. The most significant thing about this event is the numbers—that is, the 1,000 or so people who come every year to the largest community Hanukkah celebration around. Everyone is welcome to take part in the *haimishe* (friendly) feeling the area's Jewish community creates when it gathers together for its Festival of Lights. You'll also find a vast selection of books on all aspects of Jewish life. The symbolic candle-lighting is quite moving. ■ *Stroum Jewish Community Center, Mercer Island, WA; (206)232-7115.*

Eagle Watching (Qualicum Beach) Bald eagles converge on these rivers from December through February. These scavengers are best seen before noon, when they're hunting spawning salmon. Bring binoculars and wear rain gear. ■ *Big and Little Qualicum rivers near Nanaimo, BC; (604)752-9532.*

Whale Watch Week For one week after Christmas (and then again in March), volunteers from the Science Center in Newport teach interested folks how to watch for gray whales and report their sightings from various stations along the coast. Volunteers assist approximately 11,000 people from all over the world. ■ *Newport, OR; (503)867-0100.*

Index

P

Pacific Beach, 326
Pacific Cafe, 231
Pacific City, 52
Pacific Palisades, 455
Pacific Sands, 54
Pacific Way Bakery and
   Cafe, 41
Pacioni's Pizzeria, 260
Packwood, 373
Packwood Hotel, 373
Paddler's Inn Bed and
   Breakfast, 495
Pagliacci's, 468
The Painted Table, 177
Painter's Lodge, 500
Palace Hotel, 312
Palmer House, 56
Palmers Restaurant and
   Pub, 256
Pan Pacific Hotel, 455
Pandasia, 186
Panorama Resort, 553
Papa Haydn, 11
Papandrea's Pizza, 136
Paradise Creek Quality
   Inn, 422
Paradise Grille, 152
Paradise Inn, 373
Paradise Ranch Inn, 106
Park Hill Hotel, 458
Park Royal Hotel, 458
Parkland, 282
Parksville, 490
Parma, 347
The Partridge Farm, 84
Pasco, 414
Passport, 261
Pastimes, 340
Pateros, 357
Patit Creek Restaurant, 419
Patsy Clark's, 390
Pazzo Ristorante, 11
Peerless Hotel, 118
Pendleton, 154
Penny Farthing Inn, 459
Penticton, 545
Pepper Sisters, 231
Pescatore, 141
The Pewter Pot, 363
Phnom Penh
   Restaurant, 435
Pho Hoang, 450
Phoenicia at Alki, 186
Phoenix Inn, 92
Piccolo's, 508
Piecora's, 192

Pilchuck School, 260
The Pillars, 285
Pine Meadow Inn, 107
Pine Room Cafe, 162
Pine Tavern
   Restaurant, 140
Pinehurst Inn at Jenny
   Creek, 119
The Pink Door, 187
The Pink Pearl, 444
Pinot Ganache, 332
Pirosmani, 177
Place Pigalle, 177
Plain, 358
Plainfield's Mayur, 25
Pleasant Beach Grill, 219
Pogacha, 215
Point No Point Resort, 481
Pon Proem, 217
Pond Motel, 319
The Ponderosa Guest
   Ranch, 153
Ponderosa Point
   Resort, 544
Ponti Seafood Grill, 178
Port Alberni, 490
Port Angeles, 316
Port Gamble, 301
Port Hadlock, 305
Port Hardy, 501
Port Ludlow, 304
Port Ludlow Golf and
   Meeting Retreat, 304
Port McNeill, 501
Port Orchard, 295
Port Orford, 73
Port Townsend, 306
Portland, 3; lodgings, 26;
   restaurants, 6
Portland Guest House, 29
Portland's White House, 29
Portofino, 21
Portside, 70
Poulsbo, 299
Pounder's, 472
Powell River, 522
Primavera, 115
Prince George, 534
Prince Rupert, 535
Princeton, 539
The Prior House, 476
Prosser, 412
Provinces Asian Restaurant
   & Bar, 203
The Public House, 309
Puget Sound, 225
Pullman, 420

The Purple House
   B&B, 420
Purple Rocks Art Bar and
   Cafe, 126
Puyallup, 274

Q

Quadra Island, 503
Qualicum, 496
Quality Inn on Clover
   Island, 416
The Quamichan Inn, 483
Quattro on Fourth, 435
Queen Ann Inn Bed and
   Breakfast, 160
Queen Charlotte
   City, 536
Queen Charlotte
   Islands, 535
Queen City Grill, 178
The Queen of Tarts and
   Confluence Gallery, 357
Quilcene, 303
Quilchena, 539
Quilchena Hotel, 539
Quimper Inn, 311

R

Radium Hot Springs, 553
Rainbow Inn, 257
Raincity Grill, 444
Raintree, 435
Raku Kushiyaki, 444
Ram's Head Inn, 562
Raphael's Restaurant and
   Lounge, 155
Ravenscroft Inn, 311
Ray's Boathouse, 179
Re-bar, 471
Red Hills Provincial
   Dining, 85
Red Lion at Lloyd
   Center, 30
Red Lion Hanford
   House, 414
Red Lion Inn, 415
Red Mountain Ski
   Area, 561
The Red Onion, 444
Redmond, OR, 152
Redmond, WA, 207
Reedsport, 67
Reflections Bed and
   Breakfast Inn, 296
Reflections
   Guesthouse, 544
Reiner's, 187
Reiner's Gasthaus, 360

X, Y, Z

We Stand by Our Reviews

Sasquatch Books is proud of *Northwest Best Places*. Our editors and contributors go to great pains and expense to see that all of the reviews are as accurate, up-to-date, and honest as possible. If we have misled you, please accept our apologies. However, if recommendations in the 11th edition of *Northwest Best Places* have seriously disappointed you, Sasquatch Books would like to refund your purchase price. To receive your refund:

1) Tell us where you purchased your book and return the book to: Satisfaction Guaranteed, Sasquatch Books, 1008 Western Avenue, Suite 300, Seattle, WA 98104.

2) Enclose the original receipt from the establishment in question, including date of visit.

3) Write a full explanation of your stay or meal and how *Northwest Best Places* misled you.

4) Include your name, address, and phone number.

Refund is valid only while the 11th edition of *Northwest Best Places* is in print. If the ownership, management, or chef has changed since publication, Sasquatch Books cannot be held responsible. Postage on the returned book is your responsibility. Please allow four weeks for processing.

Northwest Best Places
REPORT FORM

Based on my personal experience, I wish to nominate/confirm/disapprove for listing the following restaurant or place of lodging:

_____

_____

_____

_____

_____

(Please include address and telephone number of establishment, if convenient.)

REPORT:
(Please describe food, service, style, comfort, value, date of visit, and other aspects of your visit; continue on overleaf if necessary.)

_____

_____

_____

_____

_____

_____

_____

I am not concerned, directly or indirectly, with the management or ownership of this establishment.

Signed _____

Address _____

_____

_____

Phone Number _____

Date _____

Send to: *Northwest Best Places*
1008 Western Avenue, Suite 300
Seattle, WA 98104

Northwest Best Places
REPORT FORM

Based on my personal experience, I wish to nominate/confirm/disapprove for listing the following restaurant or place of lodging:

_____

_____

_____

_____

_____

(Please include address and telephone number of establishment, if convenient.)

REPORT:

(Please describe food, service, style, comfort, value, date of visit, and other aspects of your visit; continue on overleaf if necessary.)

_____

_____

_____

_____

_____

_____

_____

I am not concerned, directly or indirectly, with the management or ownership of this establishment.

Signed _____

Address _____

_____

_____

Phone Number _____

Date _____

Send to: *Northwest Best Places*
1008 Western Avenue, Suite 300
Seattle, WA 98104

Did you enjoy this book?

Sasquatch Books publishes high-quality books and guides related to the Pacific Northwest and California. Our books are available at bookstores and other retail outlets throughout the region. Here is a partial list of our current titles:

GUIDEBOOKS

Northern California Best Places
Restaurants, Lodgings, and Touring
*Edited by Rebecca Poole Forée and
Stephanie Irving*

Seattle Best Places
The Most Discriminating Guide to Seattle's
Restaurants, Lodgings, Shopping, Nightlife,
Arts, Sights, and Outings
*Edited by Nancy Leson and
Stephanie Irving*

Vancouver Best Places
The Most Discriminating Guide to
Vancouver's Restaurants, Lodgings, Shop-
ping, Nightlife, Arts, Sights, and Outings
*Edited by Kasey Wilson and
Stephanie Irving*

Portland Best Places
The Most Discriminating Guide to Portland's
Restaurants, Lodgings, Shopping, Nightlife,
Arts, Sights, and Outings
*Edited by Kim Carlson and
Stephanie Irving*

Northwest Cheap Sleeps
Recommended Lodgings for the Budget
Traveler in Oregon, Washington, and
British Columbia
*Edited by Stephanie Irving and
Nancy Leson*

Northern California Cheap Sleeps
Recommended Lodgings for the Budget
Traveler
Edited by Rebecca Poole Forée

Back Roads of Washington
74 Trips on Washington's Scenic Byways
Earl Thollander

Back Roads of Oregon
82 Trips on Oregon's Scenic Byways
Earl Thollander

Earl Thollander's Back Roads of California
65 Trips on California's Scenic Byways
Earl Thollander

FOOD AND WINE

Northwest Wines
A Pocket Guide to the Wines of
Washington, Oregon, and Idaho
Paul Gregutt and Jeff Prather

Pike Place Market Cookbook
Recipes, Anecdotes, and Personalities from
Seattle's Renowned Public Market
Braiden Rex-Johnson

The City Gardener's Cookbook
Totally Fresh, Mostly Vegetarian, Decidedly
Delicious Recipes from Seattle's P-Patches
Seattle P-Patches

REGIONAL INTEREST

Northwest Passages
A Literary Anthology of the Pacific Northwest
from Coyote Tales to Roadside Attractions
Edited by Bruce Barcott

West Coast Journeys, 1865-1879
The Travelogue of a Remarkable Woman
Caroline C. Leighton

FIELD GUIDES

Field Guide to the Bald Eagle

Field Guide to the Geoduck

Field Guide to the Gray Whale

Field Guide to the Grizzly Bear

Field Guide to the Humpback Whale

Field Guide to the Orca

Field Guide to the Pacific Salmon

Field Guide to the Slug

For a complete catalog of Sasquatch Books titles, or to inquire about ordering our books, please contact us at the address below.

SASQUATCH BOOKS

1008 Western Avenue, Suite 300 • Seattle, WA 98104
(206) 467-4300 or (800) 775-0817

A Book with a View

For the first time ever, you can visit a selection of establishments from *Northwest Best Places* before you make your reservation! *Northwest Best Places*, the video, shows you the wonderful diversity of outstanding Northwest destinations—from dude ranches to beach resorts, elegant urban hotels to island retreats—and includes a few fine places to eat along the way.

Experience the sights and sounds of more than thirty unique destinations in Oregon, Washington, and British Columbia, including:

- Youngberg Hill Farm: a stunning inn located on Oregon's bountiful Willamette Valley

- Sooke Harbour House: Vancouver Island's internationally acclaimed restaurant and inn

- The Herbfarm: the esteemed restaurant in the foothills of Washington's Cascade Range

- Kalaloch Lodge: a classic spot on the Olympic Peninsula

- A tugboat bunk and breakfast, teepees for the entire family, and much more, including little-known tips about this extraordinary region.

If you would like a copy of the *Northwest Best Places* video, ask your local bookseller or contact KCTS public television at:

KCTS Video
401 Mercer Street
Seattle, WA 98109
(800) 937-5387